VBA FOR MODELERS

DEVELOPING DECISION SUPPORT SYSTEMS WITH MICROSOFT® OFFICE EXCEL®

THIRD EDITION

S. Christian Albright
Kelley School of Business, Indiana University

SOUTH-WESTERN
CENGAGE Learning™

Australia • Brazil • Canada • Mexico • Singapore • Spain • United Kingdom • United States

SOUTH-WESTERN
CENGAGE Learning™

VBA for Modelers: Developing Decision Support Systems with Microsoft® Office Excel®
S. Christian Albright

Senior Acquisitions Editor:
Charles McCormick

Editorial Assistant: Bryn Lathrop

Technology Project Manager:
Chris Valentine

Senior Developmental Editor:
Laura Bofinger Ansara

Marketing Manager: Bryant Chrzan

Marketing Coordinator: Suellen Ruttkay

Marketing Communications Manager:
Libby Shipp

Senior Art Director: Stacy Jenkins Shirley

Print Buyer: Miranda Klapper

Production Service & Composition:
Pre-PressPMG

Cover Design: Lou Ann Thesing

Cover Image: ©Getty Images

Cover Printing, Printing & Binding:
Courier Stoughton

For product information and technology assistance, contact us at
Cengage Learning Customer & Sales Support, 1-800-354-9706

For permission to use material from this text or product, submit all requests online at **cengage.com/permissions**
Further permissions questions can be e-mailed to
permissionrequest@cengage.com

Library of Congress Control Number: 2009926655

ISBN-10: 1-439-07984-6
ISBN-13: 978-1-4390-7984-3

South-Western Cengage Learning
5191 Natorp Boulevard
Mason, OH 45040
USA

Cengage learning is a leading provider of customized learning solutions with office locations around the globe, including Singapore, the United Kingdom, Australia, Mexico, Brazil, and Japan. locate your local office at: **international.cengage.com/region**

Cengage Learning products are represented in Canada by Nelson Education, Ltd.

For your course and learning solutions, visit
academic.cengage.com

Purchase any of our products at your local college store or at our preferred online store **www.ichapters.com**

Printed in the United States of America
1 2 3 4 5 6 7 13 12 11 10

To my wonderful wife, Mary—she is my best friend and constant companion. To our talented son, Sam, and his equally talented wife, Lindsay, and to our dear Welsh corgi, Bryn, who absolutely *lives* to chase tennis balls, as many hours a day as possible!

About the Author

S. Christian Albright

Chris Albright got his B.S. degree in Mathematics from Stanford in 1968 and his Ph.D. in Operations Research from Stanford in 1972. Since then he has been teaching in the Operations & Decision Technologies Department in the Kelley School of Business at Indiana University (IU). He has taught courses in management science, computer simulation, statistics, and computer programming to all levels of business students: undergraduates, MBAs, and doctoral students. In addition, he has taught simulation modeling at General Motors and Whirlpool, and he has taught database analysis for the Army. He has published over 20 articles in leading operations research journals in the area of applied probability, and he has authored the books *Statistics for Business and Economics, Practical Management Science, Spreadsheet Modeling and Applications, Data Analysis for Managers, Data Analysis and Decision Making*, and *VBA for Modelers*. He also worked with the Palisade Corporation on the commercial version, *StatTools*, of his statistical StatPro add-in for Excel. His current interests are in spreadsheet modeling, the development of VBA applications in Excel, and programming in the .NET environment.

On the personal side, Chris has been married for 38 years to his wonderful wife, Mary, who retired several years ago after teaching 7th grade English for 30 years and is now working as a supervisor for student teachers at IU. They have one son, Sam, who currently lives in Philadelphia with his wife Lindsay and is about to become a lawyer after graduating from Penn Law School. Chris has many interests outside the academic area. They include activities with his family (especially traveling with Mary), going to cultural events at IU, power walking, and reading. And although he earns his livelihood from statistics and management science, his *real* passion is for playing classical piano music.

Brief Contents

Contents

Preface

I wrote *VBA for Modelers* for students and professionals who want to create decision support systems (DSSs) using Microsoft Excel-based spreadsheet models. The book assumes that readers are either familiar with spreadsheet modeling or are taking a concurrent course in management science or operations research. It does *not* assume any prior programming experience. The book contains two parts. Part I covers the essentials of VBA (Visual Basic for Applications) programming, and Part II provides many applications with their associated programming code.

There are many excellent books available for VBA programming, many others covering decision support systems, and still others for spreadsheet modeling. However, I have not found a book that attempts to unify these subjects in a practical way. *VBA for Modelers* is designed for this purpose, and I hope you will find it to be an important resource and reference in your own work.

Why This Book?

The original impetus for this book began about 13 years ago. Wayne Winston and I were experimenting with the spreadsheet approach to teaching management as we were writing the first edition of our *Practical Management Science* (*PMS*) book. Because I have always had an interest in computer programming, I decided to learn VBA, the relatively new macro language for Excel, and use it to a limited extent in my undergraduate management science modeling course. My intent was to teach the students how to wrap a given spreadsheet model, such as a product mix model, into an *application* with a "front end" and a "back end" by using VBA. The front end would enable a user to provide inputs to the model, usually through one or more dialog boxes, and the back end would present the user with a nontechnical report of the results. I found it to be an exciting addition to the usual modeling course, and my students overwhelmingly agreed.

The primary problem with teaching this type of course has been the lack of an appropriate VBA textbook. Although there are many good VBA trade books available, they usually go into much more technical VBA details than I have time to cover, and their objective is usually to teach VBA programming as an end in itself. I expect that many adopters of our *Practical Management Science* or *Spreadsheet Modeling and Applications* books will decide to uses parts of *VBA for Modelers* to supplement their management science courses, just as I have been doing. For readers who have taken a management science course, there is more than enough material in this book to fill an entire elective course or to be used for self-study.

However, even for readers who have no background or interest in management science, the first part of this book should have value. We are seeing an increasing number of our business students and graduates express interest in automating Excel with macros. In short, they want to become Excel "power users." Since the first edition of this book came out, I have been teaching a purely elective MBA course that covers the first part of the book. To my surprise and delight, it regularly attracts about 40 MBA students. Yes, that's *MBA students*, not computer science majors! They see real value in knowing how to program Excel. And it is amazing, and gratifying, to see how far these students can progress in a short 7-week course. Many find programming, especially for Excel, to be very addictive.

Objectives of the Book

VBA for Modelers shows how the power of spreadsheet modeling can be extended to the masses. Through VBA, complex management science models can be made accessible to nonexperts by providing them with simplified input screens and output reports. The book illustrates, in complete detail, how such applications can be developed for a wide variety of business problems. In writing the book, I have always concerned myself with the following questions: How much will readers be able to do on their own? Is it enough for readers to see the completed applications, marvel at how powerful they are, and possibly take a look at the code that runs in the background? Or should they be taken to the point where they can develop their *own* applications, code and all? I am still not sure what the correct answers are, and I suspect they vary according to the audience, but I know I *can* get students to the point where they can develop modest but useful applications on their own and, importantly, experience the thrill of programming success.

With these thoughts in mind, I have written this book so that it can be used at several levels. For the reader who wants to learn VBA from scratch and then apply it, I have provided a "VBA primer" in the first 17 chapters. It is admittedly not as complete as some of the thick Excel VBA books available, but I believe it covers the basics of VBA quite adequately. Importantly, it covers coding methods for working with Excel ranges in Chapter 6 and uses these methods extensively in later chapters, so that readers will not have to use trial and error or wade through online help, as I had to do when I was learning the language. Readers can then proceed to the applications chapters 18–34, and apply their skills. In contrast, there are probably many readers who do not have time to learn all of the details. They can still *use* the applications in the second part of the book for demonstration purposes. Indeed, the applications have been developed for generality. For example, the transportation model in Chapter 23 is perfectly general and can be used to solve *any* transportation model by supplying the appropriate input data.

Approach

I like to teach (and learn) through examples. I have found that I can learn a programming language only if I have a strong motivation to learn it. I doubt that you are any different. The applications in the latter chapters are based on many interesting management science models. They provide the motivation for you to learn the material. The examples illustrate that this book is not about programming for the sake of programming, but instead it is about developing useful applications for business. You probably already realize that Excel modeling skills make you more valuable in the workplace. This book will help you develop VBA skills that make you even *more* valuable.

Contents of the Book

The book is written in two parts. Part I, Chapters 1–17, is a VBA primer for students with little or no programming experience in VBA (or any other language). Although all of these chapters are geared to VBA, some are more about general programming concepts, whereas others deal with the unique aspects of programming for Excel. Specifically, Chapters 7, 9, and 10 discuss control logic (If–Then–Else constructions), loops, arrays, and subroutines, topics that are common to all programming languages. In contrast, Chapters 6 and 8 explain how to work with some of the most common Excel objects (ranges, workbooks, worksheets, and charts) in VBA. In addition, several chapters discuss aspects of VBA that can be used with Excel and any other applications (Access, Word, PowerPoint, and so on) that use VBA as their programming language. Specifically, Chapter 3 explains the Visual Basic Editor (VBE), Chapter 4 illustrates how to record macros, Chapter 17 explains how to run Excel's Solver add-in with VBA code, Chapter 11 explains how to build user forms (dialog boxes), and Chapter 12 discusses the important topic of error handling.

The material in Part I is reasonably complete, but it is available, in greater detail and with a somewhat different emphasis, in several other books. The unique aspect of *this* book is Part II, Chapters 18–34. Each chapter in this part discusses a specific application. Most of these are optimization and simulation applications, and many are quite general. For example, Chapter 20 discusses a general product mix application, Chapter 22 discusses a general production scheduling application, Chapter 23 discusses a general transportation application, Chapter 24 discusses a stock market-trading simulation, Chapter 28 discusses a multiple-server queue simulation, Chapter 29 discusses a general application for pricing European and American options, and Chapter 31 discusses a general portfolio optimization application. (Many of the underlying models for these applications are discussed in *Practical Management Science*, but I have attempted to make these applications stand-alone here.) The applications can be used as they stand to solve real problems, or they can be used as examples of VBA application development. All of the steps in the development of these applications are explained, and all of the VBA source code is included. Using an analogy to a car, you can simply get in and drive, or you can open the hood and see how everything works.

Chapter 18 gets the process started in a "gentle" way. It provides a general introduction to application development, with an important list of guidelines. It then illustrates these guidelines in a car loan application. This application should be within the grasp of most readers, even if they are not great programmers. By tackling this application first, readers get to develop a simple model, dialog boxes, reports, and charts, and then tie everything together. This car loan application illustrates an important concept that I stress throughout the book. Specifically, applications that really *do* something are often long and have a lot of details. But this does not mean that they are *difficult*. With perseverance—a word I use frequently—readers can fill in the details one step at a time and ultimately experience the thrill of getting a program to work correctly.

Virtually all management science applications require input data. An extremely important issue for VBA application development is how to get the required input data into the spreadsheet model. I illustrate a number of possibilities in Part II. If only a small amount of data is required, then dialog boxes work well. These are used for data input in many of the applications. However, there are many times when the data requirements are much too large for dialog boxes. In these cases, the data are usually stored in some type of database. I illustrate some common possibilities. In Chapter 20, the input data for a product mix model are stored in a separate worksheet. In Chapter 30, the stock price data for finding the betas of stocks are stored in a separate Excel workbook. In Chapter 32, the data for a DEA model are stored in a text (.txt) file. In Chapter 23, the data for a transportation model are stored in an Access database (.mdb) file. Finally, in Chapter 31, the stock price data required for a portfolio optimization model are located on a Web site and are imported into Excel, *at runtime*! In each case, I explain the VBA statements that are necessary to import the data into the Excel application.

New to the Third Edition

This edition does not contain as many changes as the second edition, but there are a few changes you should be aware of.

- Programmers can never let well enough alone. They are forever tinkering with their code, not just to make it work better, but often to make it more elegant and easier to understand. So users of the second edition will see minor changes to much of the code throughout the book, particularly in the use of object variables to refer to ranges, workbooks, worksheets, and so on. One benefit of using object variables is that you are assured of getting Intellisense to list their properties and methods as you write your code. This is not a trivial benefit, as you will soon realize.

- The second edition was written before the debut of Excel 2007. You are probably aware of the significant changes in the user interface between Excel 2003 and Excel 2007—Microsoft gave us a whole new look. We programmers wondered if a similar shift would occur in VBA and the VB Editor. For better or for worse, very little changed. We now need to use .xlsm extensions for files containing macros, we now need to refer to Solver.xlam (not Solver.xla) if we are programming for Solver, we can't change the menu/toolbar (now the *ribbon*) structure of Excel nearly as easily as before, and there are a few new objects, such as Excel tables, that we can now manipulate in code. But if you were expecting a complete rewrite of the book because of changes in Excel

2007, you won't see it. The vast majority of VBA code that worked in Excel 2003 still works, with no changes, in Excel 2007. Thank heavens! (One notable exception is the handy FileSearch object discussed in Chapter 13. It no longer exists in Office 2007, and any code that uses it no longer works.) Throughout this edition, if you see no mention of the version of Excel, this signifies that the code will work in either Excel 2003 or Excel 2007. (And when I mention Excel 2003, I generally mean Excel 2003 or earlier, back to Excel 97. Things didn't change much during those years, at least not with respect to VBA.)

- Have you heard of VSTO (Visual Studio Tools for Office), which is part of Microsoft's Visual Studio? There have been rumors for several years that VBA would go away, and that VSTO would take its place. The argument is that VBA applications in many corporate environments have been growing to a point that they can no longer be managed or maintained, and that a more powerful platform is needed. Maybe so, but VBA is still very much alive and will probably continue to thrive for many years to come. I don't discuss VSTO in this book, but if you are interested, I recommend the book *VSTO for Mere Mortals*, by Kathleen McGrath and Paul Stubbs.

How to Use the Book

I have already discussed several approaches to using this book, depending on how much you want to learn and how much time you have. For readers with very little or no computer programming background who want to learn the fundamentals of VBA, Chapters 1–12 should be covered first, in approximately that order. (I should point out that it is practically impossible to avoid "later" programming concepts while covering "early" ones. For example, I admit to using a few If statements and loops in early chapters, *before* discussing them formally in Chapter 7. I don't believe this should cause problems. I use plenty of comments, and you can always look ahead if you need to.) After covering VBA fundamentals in the first 12 chapters, the next 5 optional chapters can be covered in practically any order. Chapter 18 should be covered next. Beyond that, the applications in the remaining chapters can be covered in practically any order, depending on your interests. However, note that some of the details in certain applications will not make much sense without the appropriate training in the management science models. For example, Chapter 33 discusses an AHP (Analytical Hierarchy Process) application for choosing a job. The VBA code is fairly straightforward, but it will not make much sense without knowledge of AHP. I assume that the knowledge of the models comes from a separate source, such as *Practical Management Science*; I cover it only briefly here.

At the other extreme, readers can simply use the Excel application files to solve problems. Indeed, the applications have been written specifically for non-technical end users, so that readers at all levels should have no difficulty opening the application files and using them appropriately. In short, readers can decide how much of the material "under the hood" is worth their time.

Premium Web Site Content

A unique access code is provided with each new book. This code gives access to all of the Excel (.xlsx and .xlsm) and other files mentioned in the chapters, including those in the exercises. The Excel files require Excel 97 or a more recent version. Many of the files from Chapter 17 "reference" Excel's Solver. They will not work unless the Solver add-in is installed and loaded. Chapters 14 and 23 uses Microsoft's ActiveX Data Object (ADO) model to import the data from an Access database into Excel. This will work only in Excel 2000 or a more recent version. Finally, Chapter 13 uses the Office FileDialog object. This works only in Excel XP (2002) or a more recent version. Your new book's access code to premium Web site content also includes a link to download the student edition of Palisade's DecisionTools® Suite.

The book is also supported by a Web site at www.kelley.iu.edu/albright-books. The Web site contains errata and other useful information, including information about our other management science books.

Acknowledgments

I would like to thank all of my colleagues at Cengage Learning. Foremost among them are my current editor, Charles McCormick, and my former editor, Curt Hinrichs. The original idea was to develop a short VBA manual to accompany our *Practical Management Science* book, but Curt eventually persuaded me to write an entire book. Given the success of the first two editions, I appreciate Curt's insistence. I am also grateful to many of the professionals who worked behind the scenes to make this book a success: Laura Ansara, Senior Developmental Editor; Bryant Chrzan, Marketing Manager; Bryn Lathrop, Editorial Assistant; Stacy Shirley, Art Director; and Katy Gabel, Project Manager at Pre-PressPMG.

Next, I would like to thank the reviewers of past editions of the book. Thanks go to Gerald Aase, Northern Illinois University; Ravi Ahuja, University of Florida; Grant Costner, University of Oregon; R. Kim Craft, Rollins College; Lynette Molstad Gorder, Dakota State University; and Jim Hightower, California State University-Fullerton; Don Byrkett, Miami University; Kostis Christodoulou, London School of Economics; Charles Franz, University of Missouri; Larry LeBlanc, Vanderbilt University; Jerry May, University of Pittsburgh; Jim Morris, University of Wisconsin; and Tom Schriber, University of Michigan.

Finally, I want to thank my wife, Mary. She continues to support my book-writing activities, even when it requires me to work evenings and weekends in front of the PC. Fortunately, our energetic Welsh corgi, Bryn, keeps her sufficiently occupied while I work at the books.

S. Christian Albright
(e-mail at albright@indiana.edu,
Web site at www.kelley.iu.edu/albrightbooks)
Bloomington, Indiana
January 2009

Part I

VBA Fundamentals

This part of the book is for readers who need an introduction to programming in general and Visual Basic for Applications (VBA) for Excel in particular. It discusses programming topics that are common to practically all programming languages, including variable types and declarations, control logic, looping, arrays, subroutines, and error handling. It also discusses many topics that are specific to VBA and its use with Excel, including the Excel object model; recording macros; working with ranges, workbooks, worksheets, charts, and other Excel objects; developing user forms (dialog boxes); and automating Excel add-ins, including Excel's Solver add-in and Palisade's @RISK and StatTools add-ins, with VBA code.

Many of the chapters in Part I present a business-related exercise immediately after the introductory section. The objective of each such exercise is to motivate you to work through the details of the chapter, knowing that many of these details will be required to solve the exercise. The solutions are provided in "finished" files, but I urge you to try the exercises on your own, before looking at the solutions.

The chapters in this part should be read in approximately the order they are presented, at least up through Chapter 12. Programming is a skill that builds upon itself. Although it is not always possible to avoid referring to a concept from a later chapter in an earlier chapter, I have attempted to refrain from doing this as much as possible. The one small exception is in Chapters 6 (on ranges) and 7 (on control logic and loops). It is almost impossible to do any interesting in Excel without knowing about ranges, and it is almost impossible to do any interesting programming in general without knowing about control logic and loops. I compromised by putting the chapter on ranges first and using a few simple If statements and loops in it. I don't believe this should cause any problems.

1

Introduction to VBA Development in Excel

1.1 Introduction

My book *Practical Management Science* (co-authored with Wayne Winston) illustrates how to solve a wide variety of business problems by developing appropriate Excel models. If you are familiar with this modeling process, you probably do not need to be convinced of the power and applicability of Excel. You realize that Excel modeling skills will make you a valuable employee for virtually any company. This book takes the process one giant step farther. It teaches you how to develop applications in Excel by using Excel's programming language, Visual Basic for Applications (VBA).

In many Excel-modeling books, you learn how to model a particular business problem. You enter given inputs in a worksheet, you relate them with appropriate formulas, and you eventually calculate required outputs. You might also optimize a particular output with Solver, and you might create one or more charts to show outputs graphically. You do all of this through the Excel interface, using its menus and toolbars (and now ribbons in Excel 2007), entering formulas into its cells, using the chart tools, using the Solver dialog box, and so on. If you are conscientious, you document your work so that other people in your company can understand your completed model. For example, you clearly indicate the input cells so that other users will know which cells they should use for their own inputs and which cells they should leave alone.

Now suppose that your position in a company is to *develop* applications for other less-technical people in the organization to use. Part of your job is still to develop spreadsheet models, but the details of these models might be incomprehensible to many users. These users might realize that they have, say, a product mix problem, where they will have to supply certain inputs, and then some computer magic will eventually determine a mix of products that optimizes company profit. However, the part in-between is more than they can deal with. Your job, therefore, is to develop a user-friendly application with a model (possibly hidden from the user) surrounded by a "front end" and a "back end." The front end will present the user with dialog boxes or some other means for enabling them to define their problem. Here they will be asked to specify input parameters and possibly other information. Your application will take this data, build the appropriate model, optimize it if necessary, and eventually present the back end to the user—a nontechnical report of the results, possibly with accompanying charts.

This application development is possible with VBA, as I will demonstrate here. I make no claim that it is easy or that it can be done quickly, but I do claim that it is within the realm of possibility for people like yourself, not just for professional programmers. It requires a logical mind, a willingness to experiment and take full advantage of online help, plenty of practice, and, above all, perseverance. Even professional programmers seldom accomplish their tasks without difficulty and plenty of errors; this is the nature of programming. However, they learn from their errors, and they refuse to quit until they get their programs to work. Computer programming is essentially a process of getting by one small hurdle after another. This is where perseverance is so important. But if you are not easily discouraged, and if you love the feeling of accomplishment that comes from getting something to work, you will love the challenge of application development described in this book.

1.2 VBA in Excel 2007

As you are probably aware, Excel went through a major face lift in 2007. The look of Excel, especially its menus and toolbars, is now much different than in Excel 2003 and earlier. Unfortunately, a great many users have not converted to Excel 2007, so book authors, including myself, are in the uncomfortable position of having to write simultaneously for two audiences. Fortunately, not much about VBA changed in the transition. I will try to point out the differences as necessary throughout the book, hopefully without interrupting the flow too much.

Perhaps the main difference is in the file extensions you will see. In Excel 2003 and earlier, all Excel files (except for add-ins, not covered here) ended in .xls. It didn't matter whether they contained VBA code or not; they were still .xls files. In Excel 2007, you will see two new extensions. Files without VBA code now have .xlsx extensions, whereas files with VBA code *must* use .xlsm extensions. (If you try to save a file with VBA code as an .xlsx file, you won't be allowed to do so.) There is one exception: You can save your new files in the old Excel 2003 format, which is still an option (with Save As), in which case they will have .xls extensions. Why would you do this? The probable reason is that you want to share a file you created in Excel 2007 with a friend who still uses Excel 2003. Of course, if your file includes features new to Excel 2007, your friend won't be able to see them.

I have been using Excel 2007 for well over a year, and I personally think it is a great improvement, at least in most respects. So I will provide my example files in the new .xlsx and .xlsm formats. If you are using Excel 2003, you will be able to open these *if* you first install a free Office Compatibility Pack from Microsoft (just Google for it). Without this compatibility pack, Excel 2003 users cannot read files in the new .xlsx or .xlsm formats (although Excel 2007 users can always read files in the old .xls format).

Yes, it is a bit confusing, but the fortunate part is that VBA has changed very little. I will try *not* to include new features of Excel 2007 in my example files that Excel 2003 users (even those with the compatibility pack) could not see. And in the few cases where I need to do so, I will make it clear that these examples are for Excel 2007 users only. Let's just hope that this is the last major change we'll see in Excel, at least for a few years!

1.3 Example Applications

If you have used *Practical Management Science*, you probably have a good idea of what a spreadsheet model is. However, you might not understand what I mean by spreadsheet *applications* with front ends and back ends. In other words, you might not understand what this book intends to teach you. The best way to find out is to run some of the applications that will be explained later. At this point, *you* can become the nontechnical user by opening any of the following files that accompany this book: **Product Mix.xlsm**, **Scheduling.xlsm**, **Stock Options.xlsm**, **Transportation.xlsm**, **Stock Beta.xlsm**, or **Stock Query.xlsm**. (For the Stock Query file, you will need an open Internet connection.) Simply open any of these files and follow instructions. It should be easy. After all, the purpose of writing these applications is to make it easy for a nontechnical user to run them and get results they can understand. Now step back and imagine what must be happening in the background to enable these applications to do what they do. This is what you will be learning in this book. By running a few applications, you will become anxious to learn how to do it yourself. If nothing else, these sample applications illustrate just how powerful a tool VBA for Excel can be.

Enabling Macros

You might have encountered disturbing messages when you tried to open these applications. Microsoft realizes that many viruses are carried in VBA code, so it tries to protect users. First, it sets a macro security level to High by default. This level disallows *any* VBA macros to run. Obviously, this is not good when you are trying to learn VBA programming. The fix is easy.

For users of Excel 2003 or earlier, open Excel, select the **Tools → Macro → Security** menu item, and select Medium. For users of Excel 2007, open Excel, click on the Office button, then Excel Options, then the Trust Center tab, then Trust Center Settings, then the Macro Settings tab, and check the **Disable all macros with notification** option. You should need to do this only once. Second, even with this macro security setting, you are always asked whether you want to enable macros when you open a file that contains VBA code. You should typically enable macros. Otherwise, you will be safe from viruses, but none of the VBA code will run!

I'll make one final comment about enabling macros that pertains to Excel 2007 only. If you open a file that contains macros, that is, an .xlsm file, you sometimes see the message in Figure 1.1 and you sometimes instead see the button in Figure 1.2 (right above the formula bar). Thanks to John Walkenbach, a fellow VBA author, I finally discovered the pattern. If the VB editor (discussed in Chapter 3) is already open when you open the file, you'll see the message

Figure 1.1 Enable Macro Message

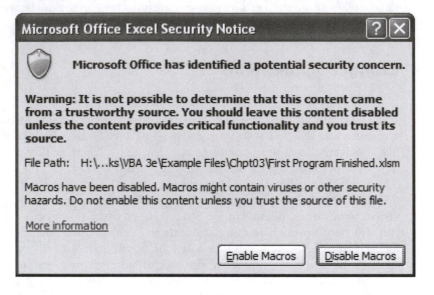

Figure 1.2 Enable Macro Button

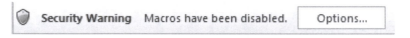

in Figure 1.1. If it isn't open, you'll see the button in Figure 1.2. Why did Microsoft do it this way? I have no idea.

1.4 Decision Support Systems

In many companies, programmers provide applications called **decision support systems (DSSs)**. These are applications, based on Excel or some other package, that help managers make better decisions. They can vary from very simple to very complex, but they usually provide some type of user-friendly interface so that a manager can experiment with various inputs or decision variables to see their effect on important output variables such as profit or cost. Much of what you will be learning, especially in the second part of this book, is how to create Excel-based DSSs. In fact, if you ran the applications in the previous section, you should have a good idea what decision support means. For example, the Transportation application helps a manager plan the optimal shipping of a product in a logistics network, and the Stock Options application helps a financial analyst price various types of financial options. The value that you, the programmer, provide by developing these applications is that other people in your company can then run them—easily—to make better decisions.

1.5 Required Background

Readers of this book probably vary widely in their programming experience. At one extreme, many of you have probably never programmed in VBA or any other language. At the other extreme, a few of you have probably programmed in Visual Basic, but have never used it to automate Excel and build Excel applications. In the middle, some of you have probably had some programming experience in another language such as C or Java but have never learned VBA. This book is intended to appeal to all of these audiences. Therefore, a simplified answer to the question, "What programming background do I need?" is "None." You need only a willingness to learn and experiment.

If you ran the applications discussed in Section 1.2, you are probably anxious to get started developing similar applications. If you already know the fundamentals of VBA for Excel, you can jump ahead to Part II of this book. But most of you will have to learn how to walk before you can run. Therefore, the chapters in Part I go through the basics of the VBA language, especially as it applies to Excel. The coverage of this basic material will provide you with enough explanations and examples of VBA's important features to enable you to understand the applications in Part II—and to do some Excel development on your own.

If you want more detailed guidance in VBA for Excel, you can learn from online help. Indeed, this is perhaps the best way to learn, especially in the middle of a development project. If you need to know one specific detail to get you past a hurdle in the program you are writing, you can look it up quickly in online help. A good way to do this will be demonstrated shortly.

This book does presume some modeling ability and general business back-ground. For example, if you ran the Product Mix application, you probably realize that it develops and optimizes a product mix model, one of the classic linear programming models. One (but not the only) step in developing this application is to develop a product mix model exactly as in Chapter 3 of *Practical Management Science*. As another example, if you ran the Stock Options application, you realize the need to understand option pricing (explained briefly in Chapter 12 of *Practical Management Science*). Many of the applications in this book are based on examples (product mix, scheduling, transportation, and so on) from *Practical Management Science*. You can refer to this book as necessary.

1.6 Visual Basic Versus VBA

Before going any further, I want to clear up one common misconception. Visual Basic (VB) is *not* the same as VBA. VB is a software development language that you can buy and run separately, without the need for Excel (or Office). Actually, there are several versions of VB available. The most recent is called VB.NET, which comes with Microsoft's Visual Studio .NET software development suite. (The .NET version of VB has many enhancements to the VB language.) Before VB.NET, there was VB6, still in use in thousands of applications. In contrast, VBA comes with Office. If you own Microsoft Office, you own VBA. The VB language is very similar to VBA, but it is not the same. The main difference is that VBA is the language you need to manipulate Excel, as you will do here. Think of it as follows. The VBA language consists of a "backbone" programming language with typical programming elements you find in all programming languages: looping, logical If–Then–Else constructions, arrays, subroutines, variable types, and others. In this respect, VBA and VB are essentially identical. However, the *for Applications* in Visual Basic for Applications means that any application software package, such as Excel, Access, Word, or even a non-Microsoft software package, can *expose* its object model and functionality to VBA, so that VBA can manipulate it programmatically. In short, VBA can be used to develop applications for any of these software packages. This book teaches you how to do so for Excel.

Excel's objects are discussed in depth in later chapters, but a few typical Excel objects you will recognize immediately are ranges, worksheets, workbooks, and charts. VBA for Excel knows about these Excel objects, and it is able to manipulate them with code. For example, it can change the font of a cell, it can name a range, it can add or delete a worksheet, it can open a workbook, and it can change the title of a chart. Part of learning VBA for Excel is learning the VB backbone language, the elements that have nothing to do with Excel specifically. But another part, and possibly the most challenging part, involves learning how to manipulate Excel's objects in code. That is, it involves learning how to write computer programs to do what you do every day through the familiar Excel interface. If you ever take a course in Visual Basic, you will learn the backbone elements of VBA, but you will not learn how to manipulate objects in Excel. This requires VBA, and you *will* learn it in this book.

By the way, there are also VBA for Access, VBA for Word, VBA for PowerPoint, and others. The only difference between them is that each has its own specific objects. To list just a few, Access has tables, queries, and forms; Word has paragraphs and footnotes; and PowerPoint has slides. Each version of VBA shares the same VB backbone language, but each requires you to learn how to manipulate the objects in the specific application. There is certainly a learning curve in moving, say, from VBA for Excel to VBA for Word, but it is not nearly as difficult as if they were totally separate languages. In fact, the power of VBA (and the relative ease of programming in it) has prompted many third-party software developers to license VBA from Microsoft so that they can use VBA as the programming language for their applications. In short, once you know VBA, you know a lot about what is happening in the programming world—and you can very possibly use this knowledge to obtain a valuable job in business.

1.7 Summary

VBA is the programming language of choice for an increasingly wide range of application developers. The main reason for this is that VBA used the familiar Visual Basic programming language and then adapts it to many Microsoft and even non-Microsoft application software packages, including Excel. In addition, VBA is a relatively easy programming language to master. This makes it accessible to a large number of nonprofessional programmers in the business world—including you! By learning how to program in VBA, you will definitely enhance your value in the workplace.

2

The Excel Object Model

2.1 Introduction

This chapter introduces the Excel object model—the concept behind it and how it is implemented. Even if you have programmed in another language, this will probably be new material, even a new way of thinking, for you. However, without understanding Excel objects, you will not be able to proceed very far with VBA for Excel. This chapter provides just enough information to get you started. Later chapters focus on many of the most important Excel objects and how they can be manipulated with VBA code.

2.2 Objects, Properties, Methods, and Events

Consider the many things you see in the everyday world. To name a few, there are cars, houses, computers, people, and so on. These are all examples of **objects**. For example, let's focus on a car. A car has attributes, and there are things you can do to (or with) a car. Some of its attributes are its weight, its horsepower, its color, and its number of doors. Some of the things you can do to (or with) a car are drive it, park it, accelerate it, crash it, and sell it. In VBA, the attributes of an object are called **properties**: the size property, the horsepower property, the color property, the number of doors property, and so on. In addition, each property has a **value** for any *particular* car. For example, a particular car might be white and it might have four doors. In contrast, the things you can do to (or with) an object are called **methods**: the drive method, the park method, the accelerate method, the crash method, the sell method, and so on. Methods can also have qualifiers, called **arguments**, that indicate *how* a method is performed. For example, an argument of the crash method might be speed—how fast the car was going when it crashed.

The following analogy to parts of speech is useful. Objects correspond to *nouns*, properties correspond to *adjectives*, methods correspond to *verbs*, and arguments of methods correspond to *adverbs*. You might want to keep this analogy in mind as the discussion proceeds.

Now let's move from cars to Excel. Imagine all of the things—objects— you work with in Excel. Some of the most common are ranges, worksheets, charts, and workbooks. (A workbook is really just an Excel file.) Each of these is an object in the Excel object model. For example, consider the single-cell range B5. This cell is a **Range** object.[1] Like a car, it has properties. It has a **Value** property: the value (either text or number) displayed in the cell. It has a **HorizontalAlignment** property: left, center, or right aligned. It has a **Formula** property: the formula (if any) in the cell. These are just a few of the many properties of a range.

A Range object also has methods. For example, you can copy a range, so **Copy** is a method of a Range object. You can probably guess the argument of the Copy method: the **Destination** argument (the paste range). Another range method is the **ClearContents** method, which is equivalent to highlighting the range and pressing the Delete key. It deletes the contents of the range, but it does not change the formatting. If you want to clear the formatting as well, there is also a **Clear** method. Neither the ClearContents method nor the Clear method has any arguments.

Learning the various objects in Excel, along with their properties and methods, is a lot like learning vocabulary in English—especially if English is not your native language. You learn a little at a time and generally broaden your vocabulary through practice and experience. Some objects, properties, and methods are naturally used most often, and you will pick them up quickly. Others you will never need, and you will probably remain unaware that they even exist. However, there are many times when you *will* need to use a particular object or one of its properties or methods that you have not yet learned. Fortunately, there is excellent online help available—a dictionary of sorts—for learning about objects, properties, and methods. It is called the **Object Browser** and is discussed in the next chapter.

There is one other feature of objects you should be aware of: **events**. Some Excel objects have events that they can respond to. A good example is the Workbook object and its **Open** event. This event happens—we say it **fires**—when the workbook is opened in Excel. In fact, you might not realize it, but the Windows world is full of events that fire constantly. Every time you click or double-click on a button, press a key, move your mouse over some region, or perform a number of other actions, various events fire. Programmers have the option of responding to events by writing **event handlers**. An event handler is a section of code that runs whenever the associated event fires. In later chapters, particularly Chapter 11, you will learn how to write your own event handlers. For example, it is often useful to write an event handler for the Open event of a workbook. Whenever the workbook is opened in Excel, the event handler then runs automatically. It could be used, for example, to ensure that the user sees a certain worksheet when the workbook opens.

---

[1]From here on, "proper" case, such as Range or HorizontalAlignment, will be used for objects, properties, and methods. This is the convention used in VBA.

2.3 Collections as Objects

Continuing the car analogy, imagine that you enter a used car lot. Each car in the lot is a particular car object, but it also makes sense to consider the *collection* of all cars in the lot as an object. This is called a **Collection** object. Clearly, the collection of cars is not conceptually the same as an individual car. Rather, it is an object that includes all of the individual car objects.

Collection objects also have properties and methods, but they are not the same as the properties and methods of the objects they contain. Generally, there are many *fewer* properties and methods for collections. The two most common are the **Count** property and the **Add** method. The Count property indicates the number of objects in the collection (the number of cars in the lot). The Add method adds a new object to a collection (a new car joins the lot).

It is easy to spot collections and the objects they contain in the Excel object model. Collection objects are plural, whereas a typical object contained in a collection is singular. A good example involves worksheets in a given workbook. The **Worksheets** collection (note the plural) is the collection of all worksheets in the workbook. Any one of these worksheets is a **Worksheet** object (note the singular). Again, these must be treated differently. You can count worksheets in the Worksheets collection, or you can add another worksheet to the collection. In contrast, typical properties of a Worksheet are its **Name** (the name on the sheet tab) and **Visible** (True or False) properties, and a typical method of a Worksheet is the **Delete** method. (Note that this Delete method reduces the Count of the Worksheets collection by one.)

The main exception to this plural/singular characterization is the **Range** object. There is no "Ranges" collection object. A Range object cannot really be considered singular *or* plural; it is essentially some of each. A Range object can be a single cell, a rectangular range, a union of several rectangular ranges, an entire column, or an entire row. Range objects are probably the most difficult to master in all of their varied forms. This is unfortunate because they are the most frequently used objects in Excel. Think of your own experience in Excel, and you will realize that you are almost always doing something with ranges. An entire chapter, Chapter 6, is devoted to Range objects so that you can master some of the techniques for manipulating these important objects.

2.4 The Hierarchy of Objects

Returning one last time to cars, what is the status of a car's hood, a car's trunk, or a car's set of wheels? These are also objects, with their own properties and methods. In fact, the set of wheels is a collection object that contains individual wheel objects. The point, however, is that there is a natural hierarchy, as illustrated in Figure 2.1. The Cars collection is at the top of the hierarchy. It contains a set of individual cars. The notation Cars (Car) indicates that the collection object is

Figure 2.1 Object Model for Cars

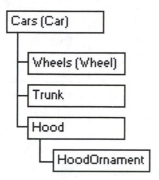

Part of the object model for cars

Cars (Car)
— Wheels (Wheel)
— Trunk
— Hood
— HoodOrnament

called Cars and that each member of this collection is a Car object. Each car "contains" a number of objects: a Wheels collection of individual Wheel objects, a Trunk object, a Hood object, and others not shown. Each of these can have its own properties and methods. Also, some can contain objects farther down the hierarchy. For example, the figure indicates that an object down the hierarchy from Hood is the HoodOrnament object. Note that each of the rectangles in this figure represents an *object*. Each object has properties and methods that could be shown emanating from its rectangle, but this would greatly complicate the figure.

The same situation occurs in Excel. The full diagram of the Excel object model appears in Figure 2.2. (This is the Excel 2003 version; the Excel 2007 version is only slightly different.) This figure shows how all objects, including collection objects, are arranged in a hierarchy. At the top of the hierarchy is the **Application** object. This refers to Excel itself. One object (of several) one step down from Application is the **Workbooks** collection, the collection of all open **Workbook** objects. This diagram, found in VBA's online help, is admittedly quite complex. All you need to realize at this point is that Excel has a very rich object model—a lot of objects; fortunately, you will need only a relatively small subset of this object model for most managerial applications. This relatively small subset is the topic of later chapters.

2.5 Object Models in General

Although the Excel object model is used in this book, you should now have some understanding of what it would take to use VBA for other applications such as Word, Access, or even non-Microsoft products. In short, you would need to learn *its* object model. You can think of each application "plugging in" its object model to the underlying Visual Basic language. Indeed, third-party software developers who want to license VBA from Microsoft need to *create* an object model

Figure 2.2 Excel Object Model

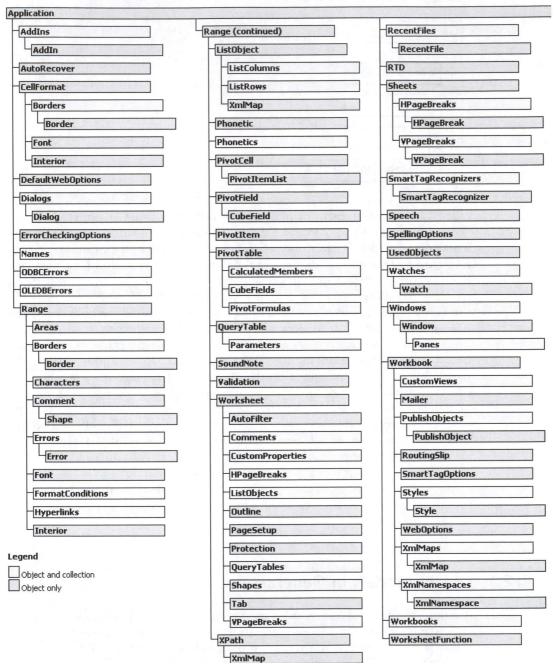

Microsoft Excel Object Model

Figure 2.3 Word Object Model

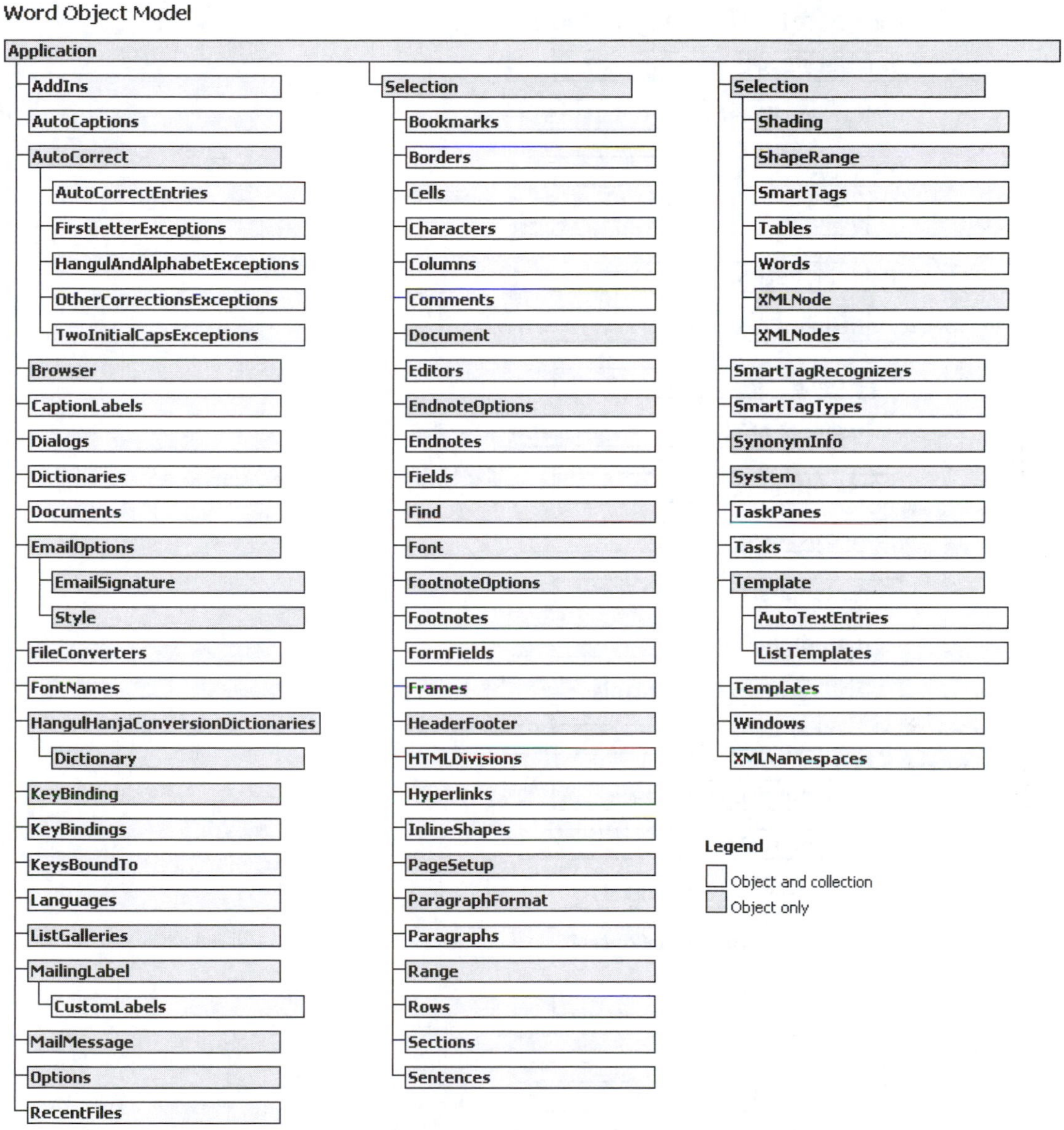

Word Object Model

Application		
AddIns	**Selection**	**Selection**
AutoCaptions	**Bookmarks**	**Shading**
AutoCorrect	**Borders**	**ShapeRange**
AutoCorrectEntries	**Cells**	**SmartTags**
FirstLetterExceptions	**Characters**	**Tables**
HangulAndAlphabetExceptions	**Columns**	**Words**
OtherCorrectionsExceptions	**Comments**	**XMLNode**
TwoInitialCapsExceptions	**Document**	**XMLNodes**
Browser	**Editors**	**SmartTagRecognizers**
CaptionLabels	**EndnoteOptions**	**SmartTagTypes**
Dialogs	**Endnotes**	**SynonymInfo**
Dictionaries	**Fields**	**System**
Documents	**Find**	**TaskPanes**
EmailOptions	**Font**	**Tasks**
EmailSignature	**FootnoteOptions**	**Template**
Style	**Footnotes**	**AutoTextEntries**
FileConverters	**FormFields**	**ListTemplates**
FontNames	**Frames**	**Templates**
HangulHanjaConversionDictionaries	**HeaderFooter**	**Windows**
Dictionary	**HTMLDivisions**	**XMLNamespaces**
KeyBinding	**Hyperlinks**	
KeyBindings	**InlineShapes**	
KeysBoundTo	**PageSetup**	**Legend**
Languages	**ParagraphFormat**	☐ Object and collection
ListGalleries	**Paragraphs**	☐ Object only
MailingLabel	**Range**	
CustomLabels	**Rows**	
MailMessage	**Sections**	
Options	**Sentences**	
RecentFiles		

appropriate for their application. Programmers can then use VBA to manipulate the objects in this model. This is a powerful idea, and it is the reason why VBA is the programming language of choice for so many developers—regardless of whether they are doing any work in Excel!

Figures 2.3 and 2.4 illustrate two other object models. (Again, these are the Office 2003 versions.) The object model in Figure 2.3 is for Word. A few of these objects are probably familiar, such as Sentence, Paragraph, and Footnote.

Figure 2.4 Part of Office Object Model

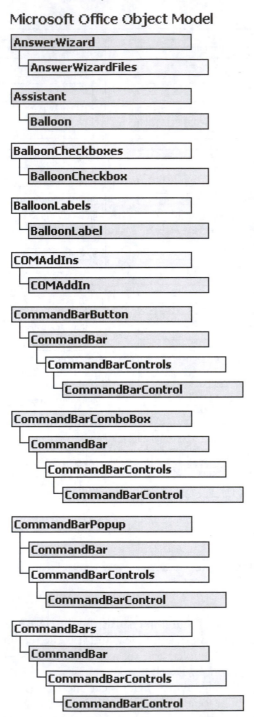

Microsoft Office Object Model

- **AnswerWizard**
  - AnswerWizardFiles
- **Assistant**
  - Balloon
- **BalloonCheckboxes**
  - BalloonCheckbox
- **BalloonLabels**
  - BalloonLabel
- **COMAddIns**
  - COMAddIn
- **CommandBarButton**
  - CommandBar
    - CommandBarControls
      - CommandBarControl
- **CommandBarComboBox**
  - CommandBar
    - CommandBarControls
      - CommandBarControl
- **CommandBarPopup**
  - CommandBar
  - CommandBarControls
    - CommandBarControl
- **CommandBars**
  - CommandBar
    - CommandBarControls
      - CommandBarControl

If you were taking a course in VBA for Word, you would need to learn the most common elements of this object model. Figure 2.4 shows part (about 40%) of the object model for Microsoft Office as a whole. You might wonder why Office has a separate object model from Excel or Word. The reason is that Office is an integrated suite, where all of its programs—Excel, Word, PowerPoint, and the rest—share a number of features. For example, they all have menus and toolbars, referred to collectively as CommandBars in the object model. Therefore, if you want to use VBA to manipulate toolbars or menus in Excel, as many programmers do, you have to learn part of the Office object model. But then this same knowledge would enable you to manipulate menus and toolbars in Word, PowerPoint, and so on. (Actually, menus and toolbars were replaced for the most part by ribbons in Excel 2007, but the CommandBar object is still around. This whole topic is discussed in Chapter 16.)

2.6 Summary

This chapter has introduced the concept of an object model, and it has briefly introduced the Excel object model that is the focus of the rest of this book. If you have never programmed in an object-oriented environment, you are in for a whole new experience. However, the more you do it, the more natural it becomes. It is certainly the direction today's programming world is headed, so if you want to be part of this world, you have to start thinking in terms of objects. You will get plenty of chances to do so throughout the book.

3

The Visual Basic Editor

3.1 Introduction

At this point, you might be asking where VBA lives. I claimed in Chapter 1 that if you own Excel, you also own VBA, but most of you have probably never seen it. You do your VBA work in the **Visual Basic Editor (VBE)**, which you can access easily from Excel by pressing the **Alt-F11** key combination. The VBE provides a very user-friendly environment for writing your VBA programs. This chapter walks you through the VBE and shows you its most important features. It also helps you write your first VBA program. By the way, you might also hear the term **Integrated Development Environment (IDE)**. This is a general term for an environment where you do your programming, regardless of the programming language. The VBE is the IDE for programming with VBA.

3.2 Important Features of the VBE

To understand this section most easily, you should follow along at your PC. Open Excel and press **Alt-F11** to get into the VBE.[1] It should look something like Figure 3.1, although the configuration you see might be somewhat different. By the time this discussion is completed, you will be able to make your screen look like that in Figure 3.1 or change it according to your own preferences. This is your programming workspace, and you have quite a lot of control over how it appears. This chapter provides some guidance, but the best way to learn is by experimenting.

The large blank pane on the right is the **Code** window. It is where you write your code. (If any of the windows discussed here are *not* visible on your screen, select the View menu from the VBE and click on the window you want to make visible.) The rest of the VBE consists of the top menu, one or more toolbars, and one or more optional windows. Let's start with the windows.

The **Project Explorer** window, repeated in Figure 3.2, shows an Explorer-type list of all open projects. (Your list will probably be different from the

---

[1] In Excel 2003 and earlier, the **Tools → Macro → Visual Basic Editor** menu item also gets you into the VBE, but Alt-F11 is quicker. In Excel 2007, you should first make the **Developer** ribbon visible. To do this, click on the Office button and then Excel Options. Under the Popular tab, select the third option at the top: Show Developer tab in the Ribbon. You need to do this only once. The Developer tab is a must for programmers. Among other things, you can get to the VBE by clicking on its Visual Basic button, but again, Alt-F11 is quicker.

Figure 3.1 Visual Basic Editor (VBE)

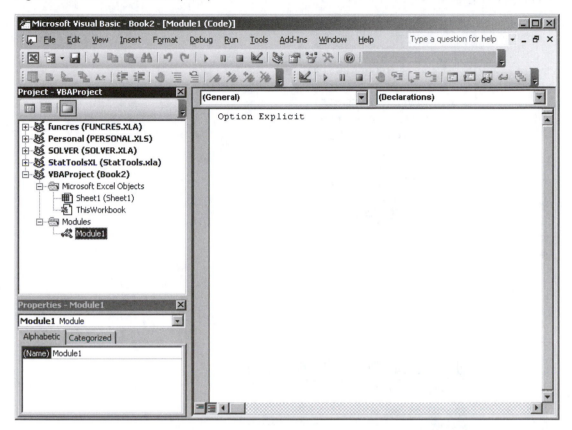

one shown here.) For example, the active project shown here has the generic name VBAProject and corresponds to the workbook Book2—that is, the file **Book2.xlsx**.[2] Below a given project, the Project Explorer window shows its "elements." In the Microsoft Excel Objects folder, these elements include any worksheets or chart sheets in the Excel file and an element called **ThisWorkbook**. There can also be folders for modules (for VBA code), user forms (for dialog boxes), and references (for links to other libraries of code you need), depending on whether you have any of these in your project. (Modules, user forms, and references are discussed in detail in later chapters.)

The **Properties** window, shown in Figure 3.3, lists a set of properties. This list depends on what is currently selected. For example, the property list in Figure 3.3 is relevant for the project itself. It indicates a single property only—the project's name. Therefore, if you want to change the name of the project from the generic

---

[2]For our purposes, there is no difference between a project and a workbook. However, VBA allows them to have separate names: **VBAProject** and **Book2**, for example. If you save Book2 as **Practice.xlsm**, say, the project name will still be **VBAProject**. Admittedly, it is somewhat confusing, but just think of projects as Excel files.

Figure 3.2 Project Explorer Window

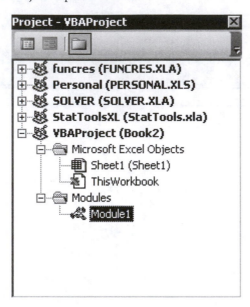

Figure 3.3 Properties Window

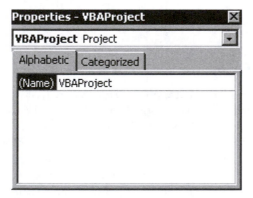

VBAProject to something more meaningful, such as **MyFirstVBA**, here is the place to do it. Chapter 11 discusses the use of the Properties window in more detail. At this point, you don't really need the Properties window, so you can close it by clicking on its close button (the upper right X).

The VBE also has at least three toolbars that are very useful: **Standard**, **Edit**, and **Debug**. They appear in Figures 3.4, 3.5, and 3.6, where some of the most useful buttons are pointed out. (If any of these toolbars are not visible on your PC, you can make them visible through the View menu.) From the Standard toolbar, you can run, pause, or stop a program you have written. You can also display the Project or Properties window (if it is hidden), and you can display the

Figure 3.4 Standard Toolbar

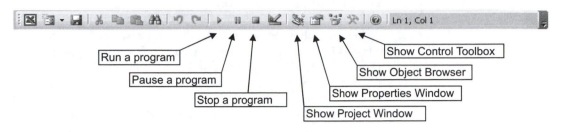

Figure 3.5 Edit Toolbar

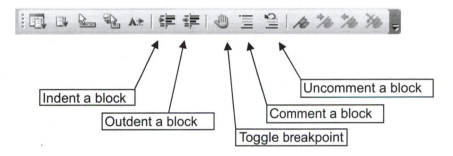

Figure 3.6 Debug Toolbar

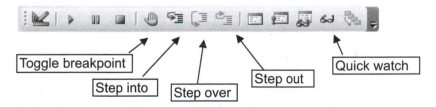

Object Browser or the Control Toolbox (more about these later). From the Edit toolbar, you can perform useful editing tasks, such as indenting or outdenting (the opposite of indenting), and you can comment or uncomment blocks of code, as is discussed later. Finally, although the Debug toolbar will probably not mean much at this point, it is invaluable when you need to debug your programs—as you will undoubtedly need to do! It is discussed in more detail in Chapter 5.

For future reference, here are a few menu items of particular importance.

- You usually need at least one module in a project where you will typically store your code. To insert a module, use the **Insert → Module** menu item. If you ever have a module you do not need, highlight the module in the Project window and use the **File → Remove Module** menu item. (Answer "no" to whether you want to export the module.)
- Chapter 11 explains how to build your own dialog boxes. VBA calls these **user forms**. To insert a new user form into a project, use the **Insert →**

UserForm menu item. You can delete an unwanted user form in the same way you delete a module.

- Under the Insert menu, there is also a **Class Module** item. You can ignore this. It is considerably more advanced and is not discussed in this book.

- The **Tools → Options** menu item is a lot like the Tools → Options menu item in Excel (or the Excel Options button in Excel 2007). It allows you to change the look and feel of the VBE in a variety of ways. You should probably leave the default settings alone—with one important exception. Try it now. Select **Tools → Options**, and make sure the **Require Variable Declarations** box under the Editor tab *is* checked. The effect of this is explained in Chapter 5. (You might also want to uncheck the **Auto Syntax Check** box, as I always do. If it is checked, the editor beeps at you each time you make a syntax error in a line and then press Enter. This can be annoying. Even if this box is unchecked, the editor still warns you about a syntax error by coloring the offending line red.)

- If you ever want to password-protect your project so that other people cannot see your code, use the **Tools → VBA Properties** menu item and click on the **Protection** tab. This gives you a chance to enter a password. (Just don't forget it, or you will not be able to see your *own* code!)

- If you click on the familiar **Save** button (or use the **File → Save** menu item), this saves the project currently highlighted in the Project window. It saves your code *and* anything in the underlying Excel spreadsheet. (It is all saved in the .xlsm file.) You can achieve the same objective by switching back to Excel and saving in the usual way from there. (Note, however, that in Excel 2007, if your file started as an .xlsx file without any VBA code, you will have to save it as an .xlsm file once it contains code.)

3.3 The Object Browser

VBA's **Object Browser** is a wonderful online help tool. To get to it, open the VBE and click on the Object Browser button on the **Standard** toolbar (see Figure 3.4). This opens the window shown in Figure 3.7. At the top left, there is a dropdown list of "libraries" that you can get help on. Our main interest is in the Excel library, the VBA library, and, to a lesser extent, the Office library. The Excel library provides help on all of the objects and their properties and methods in the Excel object model. The VBA library provides help on the VBA elements that are common to *all* applications that can use VBA: Excel, Access, Word, and others. The Office library provides help on objects common to all Office programs, such as CommandBars (menus and toolbars).

For now, select the Excel library. In the bottom left pane, you see a list of all objects in the Excel object model, and in the right pane, you see a list of all properties and methods for any object selected in the left pane. A property is designated by a hand icon, and a method is designated by a green rectangular icon. A few objects, such as the Workbook object, also have events they can respond to. An event is designated by a lightning icon.

Figure 3.7 Object Browser

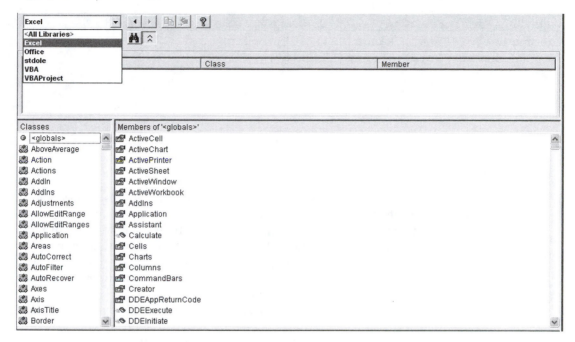

To get help on any of these items, simply select it and then click on the question mark button. It is too early in our VBA discussion to be asking for online help, but you should not forget about the Object Browser. It can be invaluable as you develop your projects. I use it constantly. You should too! (As I mentioned in the previous chapter, you can also visit the **MSDN Office Development Center** and then click on the Library tab to find similar online help about objects, properties, and methods.)

3.4 The Immediate and Watch Windows

There are two other windows in the VBE that you should be aware of: the **Immediate** and **Watch** windows. Each can be opened through the View menu or the Debug toolbar. (The Immediate window can also be opened quickly with the **Ctrl-g** key combination.) The Immediate window, shown in Figure 3.8, is useful for issuing one-line VBA commands. If you type a command and press Enter, the command takes effect immediately. For example, the first line in Figure 3.8 selects the range A1:B10 of the Data worksheet (assuming there is a Data worksheet in the active workbook). If you type this, press Enter, and switch back to Excel, you will see that the range A1:B10 has been highlighted. If you precede the command by a question mark, you can get an immediate answer to a question. For example, if you type the second line in the figure,

Figure 3.8 Immediate Window

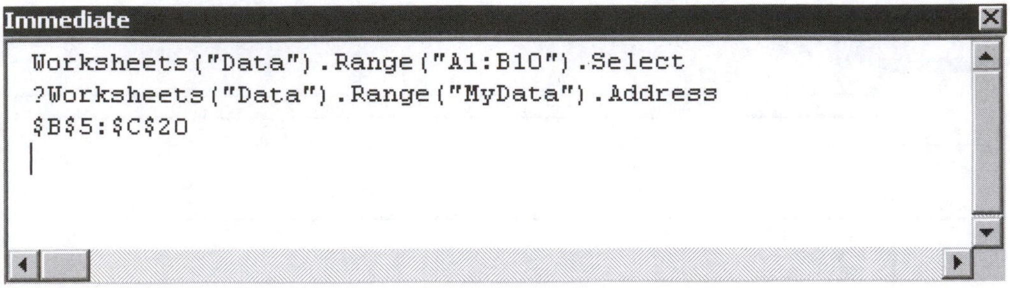

```
Immediate                                                    ×
 Worksheets("Data").Range("A1:B10").Select
 ?Worksheets("Data").Range("MyData").Address
 $B$5:$C$20
 |
```

which asks for the address of the range named MyData, and then press Enter, you immediately get the answer on the third line.

Many programmers send information to the Immediate window through their code. If you see the command Debug.Print, followed by something to be printed, the programmer is asking for this to be printed to the Immediate window. This is not a "permanent copy" of the printed information. It is usually a quick check to see whether a program is working properly.

The Watch window is used for debugging. Programs typically include several variables that change value as the program runs. If the program does not appear to be working as it should, you can put a "watch" on one or more key variables to see how they change as the program progresses. Debugging is discussed in some detail in Chapter 5.

3.5 A First Program

Although you do not yet know much about VBA programming, you know enough to write a simple program and run it. Besides, sooner or later you will have to stop reading and do some programming on your own. Now is a good time to get started. Although the example in this section is very simple, there are a few details you probably won't understand completely, at least not yet. Don't worry— later chapters will clarify the details. For now, just follow the directions and realize the thrill of getting a program to work!

This example is based on a simple data set in the file **First Program.xlsx**. It shows sales of a company by region and by month for a 3-year period. (See Figure 3.9, where some rows have been hidden. The range B2:G37 has the range name SalesRange.) Your boss wants you to write a program that scans the sales of each region and, for each, displays a message that indicates the number of months that sales in that region are above a user-selected value such as $150,000. To do this, go through the following steps. (In case you get stuck, the finished version is stored in the file **First Program Finished.xlsm**.)

1. **Open the file.** Get into Excel and open the **First Program.xlsx** file. Because it is going to contain VBA code, save it as **First Program.xlsm**.

Figure 3.9 Sales by Region and Month

	A	B	C	D	E	F	G
1	*Month*	*Region 1*	*Region 2*	*Region 3*	*Region 4*	*Region 5*	*Region 6*
2	Jan-98	144770	111200	163140	118110	105010	167350
3	Feb-98	155180	155100	129850	133940	140880	104110
4	Mar-98	86230	162310	142950	131490	150160	158720
5	Apr-98	148800	165160	123840	141050	175870	108100
6	May-98	157140	130300	114990	128220	147790	167470
7	Jun-98	126150	163240	149360	152240	167320	181070
8	Jul-98	174010	183360	122120	149730	134220	135530
9	Aug-98	171780	130050	124130	134510	175590	122230
10	Sep-98	126260	162690	123960	128260	172570	121300
11	Oct-98	150250	150070	97140	165670	111570	159440
12	Nov-98	180720	146370	122200	148150	106310	124800
13	Dec-98	130140	167210	179220	116150	193620	124550
14	Jan-99	145900	124890	97160	139640	156140	180100
15	Feb-99	123470	127730	159030	148450	158130	117560
16	Mar-99	120950	149830	127550	204700	161240	156710
35	Oct-00	124160	148560	120190	155600	132590	155510
36	Nov-00	109840	189790	127460	135160	149470	163330
37	Dec-00	127100	108640	145300	127920	151130	122900

2. **Get into the VBE.** Press Alt-F11 to open the VBE. Make sure the Project Explorer Window is visible. If it isn't, open it with the **View → Project Explorer** menu item.

3. **Add a module.** In the Project Explorer window, make sure the **First Program.xlsm** project is highlighted (click on it if necessary), and use the **Insert → Module** menu item to add a module, which will automatically be named Module1, to this project. This module will hold your VBA code.

4. **Start a sub.** Click anywhere in the Code window, type Sub CountHighSales, and press Enter. You should immediately see the contents in Figure 3.10. You have started a program called **CountHighSales**. (Any other descriptive name could be used instead of CountHighSales.) Including the keyword Sub informs VBA that you want to write a **subroutine** (also called a **procedure** or a **macro**), so it adds empty parentheses next to the name CountHighSales and adds the keywords End Sub at the bottom—two necessary elements of any subroutine. The rest of your code will be placed between the Sub and End Sub lines. Chapters 5 and 10 discuss subroutines in more detail, but for now, just think of a subroutine as a section of code that performs a particular task. For this simple example, there is only *one* subroutine.

5. **Type the code.** Type the code exactly as shown in Figure 3.11 between the Sub and End Sub lines. It is important to indent properly for readability. To indent as shown, press the Tab key. Also, note that there is no "word wrap" in the VBE. To finish a line and go to the next line, you need to press the Enter key. Other than this, the Code window is much like a word processor. Be sure to check your spelling carefully and fix any errors before proceeding. (Note that keywords such as Sub and End Sub are automatically colored blue by the VBE. This is a great feature for helping you program.)

Figure 3.10 Beginning Lines of a Subroutine

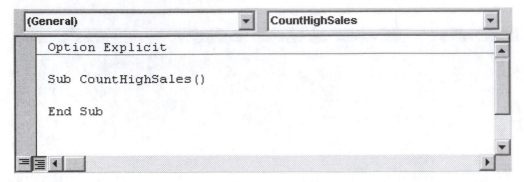

Figure 3.11 VBA Code

```
Sub CountHighSales()
    Dim i As Integer
    Dim j As Integer
    Dim numberHigh As Integer
    Dim salesCutoff As Currency

    salesCutoff = InputBox("What sales value do you want to check for?")
    For j = 1 To 6
        numberHigh = 0
        For i = 1 To 36
            If Range("SalesRange").Cells(i, j) >= salesCutoff Then _
                numberHigh = numberHigh + 1
        Next i
        MsgBox "For region " & j & ", sales were above " & Format(salesCutoff, "$0,000") _
            & " on " & numberHigh & " of the 36 months."
    Next j
End Sub
```

6. **Run the program from the VBE.** Your program is now finished. The next step is to run it. There are several ways to do so, two of which are demonstrated here. For the first method, make sure the cursor is *anywhere* within your subroutine and select the **Run → Run Sub/UserForm** menu item. (Alternatively, click on the "blue triangle" button on the Standard toolbar, or press the F5 key.) If all goes well, you should see the input box in Figure 3.12, where you can enter a value such as 150000. The program will then search for all values greater than or equal to $150,000 in the data set. Next, you will see a series of message boxes such as the one in Figure 3.13. Each message box tells you how many months the sales in some region are above the sales cutoff value you entered. This is exactly what you wanted the program to do!

7. **Run the program with a button.** The method of running the program in the previous step is fine for you, the programmer, but your boss won't want to get into the VBE to run the program. She probably doesn't even want to

Figure 3.12 InputBox for Sales Cutoff Value

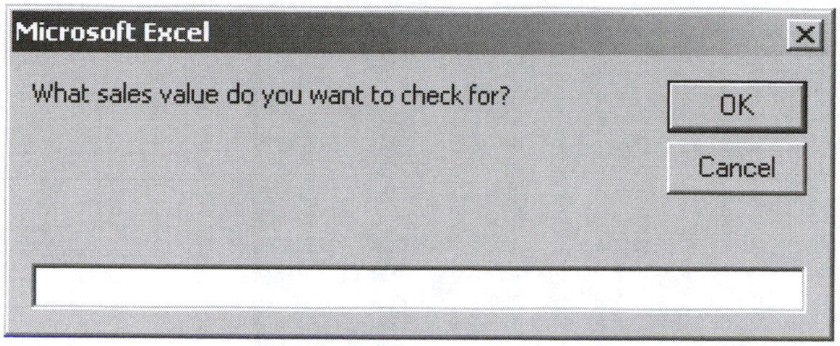

Figure 3.13 MessageBox for Region 2

see the VBE. She will instead want to run the program directly from the Excel worksheet that contains the data. You can make this easy for her. First, switch back to Excel (click on the Excel button on the bottom taskbar of your screen). Then click on the Insert dropdown on the Developer ribbon (see footnote 1 of this chapter for how to make the Developer tab visible), select the upper left "button" control, and drag a rectangular button somewhere on your worksheet, as shown in Figure 3.14. (In Excel 2003 and earlier, the button control is on the Forms toolbar, which you can make visible by right-clicking on any toolbar and checking the Forms option.) You will immediately be asked to assign a macro to this button. This is because the *only* purpose of a button is to run a macro. You should assign the CountHighSales macro you just wrote. Then you can type a more meaningful caption on the button itself. (Again, see Figure 3.14 for a possible caption.) At this point, the button is "selected" (there is a dotted border around it). To deselect it, click anywhere else on the worksheet. Now your button is ready to go. To run your program, just click on the button.

8. **Save the file.** In case you haven't done so already, save the file under the original (or a new) name. This will save your code and the button you created. Again, make sure you save it with the .xlsm extension.

A note on saving. You have undoubtedly been told to save frequently in all of your computer-related courses. Frequent saving is at least as important in a programming environment. After all the effort you expend to get a program working correctly, you don't want that sinking feeling when your unsaved work is wiped out by a sudden power outage or some other problem. So I will say it, too: **save, save, save!**

Figure 3.14 Button on the Worksheet

	A	B	C	D	E	F	G	H	I	J	K	L
1	Month	Region 1	Region 2	Region 3	Region 4	Region 5	Region 6					
2	Jan-98	144770	111200	163140	118110	105010	167350					
3	Feb-98	155180	155100	129850	133940	140880	104110					
4	Mar-98	86230	162310	142950	131490	150160	158720					
5	Apr-98	148800	165160	123840	141050	175870	108100					
6	May-98	157140	130300	114990	128220	147790	167470					
7	Jun-98	126150	163240	149360	152240	167320	181070					
8	Jul-98	174010	183360	122120	149730	134220	135530					
9	Aug-98	171780	130050	124130	134510	175590	122230					
10	Sep-98	126260	162690	123960	128260	172570	121300					
11	Oct-98	150250	150070	97140	165670	111570	159440					
12	Nov-98	180720	146370	122200	148150	106310	124800					
13	Dec-98	130140	167210	179220	116150	193620	124550					
14	Jan-99	145900	124890	97160	139640	156140	180100					
35	Oct-00	124160	148560	120190	155600	132590	155510					
36	Nov-00	109840	189790	127460	135160	149470	163330					
37	Dec-00	127100	108640	145300	127920	151130	122900					

Troubleshooting

What if you get an error message when you run your program? First, read your program carefully and make sure it is exactly like the one in Figure 3.11. In particular, the characters at the ends of the If and MsgBox lines are underscore (_) characters, and they must be preceded by a space. (Their purpose is to extend long lines of code to the next line.) Similarly, the ampersand (&) characters in the MsgBox line should have a space on each side of them. If you have any lines colored red, this is a sure sign you have typed something incorrectly. (This is another feature of the VBE that helps programmers. Red lines signify errors.) In any case, if you get some version of the dialog box in Figure 3.15, click on the End button. This stops a program with bugs and lets you fix any errors. Alternatively, click on the Debug button, and you will see a line code in yellow. This line is typically the offending line, or close to it. (Debugging is discussed in some detail in Chapter 5.)

Figure 3.15 A Typical Error Dialog Box

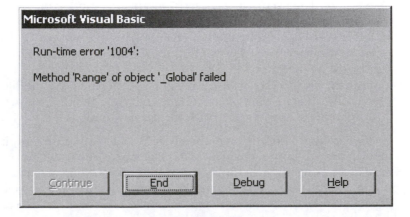

If your typing is correct and you still get an error, check steps 6 and 7. If you are using step 6 to run the program, make sure your cursor is somewhere *inside* the subroutine. If you are using the button method in step 7, make sure you have assigned the CountHighSales macro to the button. (Right-click on the button and select the Assign Macro menu item.) There are not too many things that can go wrong with this small program, so you should eventually get it to work. Remember, perseverance!

Brief Analysis of the Program

I could not expect you to write this program without my help at this point. But you can probably understand the gist of it. The four lines after the Sub line "declare" variables that are used later on. The next line displays an "InputBox" (see Figure 3.12) that asks for a user's input. The section starting with For j = 1 To 6 and ending with Next j is a "loop" that performs a similar task for each sales region. As you will learn in Chapter 7, loops are among the most powerful tools in a programmer's arsenal. For example, if there were 600 regions rather than 6, the only required change would be to change 6 to 600 in the For j = 1 To 6 line. Computers are excellent at performing repetitive tasks!

Within the loop on regions, there is another loop on months, starting with For i = 1 To 36 and ending with Next i. Within this loop there is an **If** statement that checks whether the sales value for the region in that month is at least as large as the sales cutoff value. If it is, the "counter" variable numberHigh is increased by 1. Once this inner loop has been completed, the results for the region are reported in a "MessageBox" (see Figure 3.13).

Again, the details are undoubtedly a bit unclear at this point, but you can probably understand the overall logic of the program. And if you typed everything correctly and ran the program as instructed, you now know the thrill of getting a program to work as planned. I hope you experience this feeling frequently as you work through the book.

3.6 Intellisense

A lot of things are advertised to be the best thing since sliced bread. Well, one of the features of the VBE really is. It is called **Intellisense**. As you were writing the program in the previous section, you undoubtedly noticed how the editor gave you hints and tried to complete certain words for you. You see Intellisense in the following situations:

- Every time you type the first line of a sub and then press Enter, Intellisense adds the **End Sub** line automatically for you.
- Whenever you start declaring a variable in a Dim statement, Intellisense helps you with the variable type. For example, if you type Dim numberHigh As In, it will guess that you want In to be Integer. All you have to do at this point is press the Tab key, and Integer will appear.
- Intellisense helps you with properties and methods of objects. For example, if you type Range("A1:C10"). (including the period), you will see all of the

properties and methods of a Range object. At this point you can scroll through the list and choose the one you want.

- Intellisense helps you with arguments of methods. For example, if you type Range("A1:C10").Copy and then type a space, you will see all of the arguments (actually, only one) of the Copy method. (Any arguments shown in square brackets are optional. All others are required.)
- Intellisense helps you with hard-to-remember constants. For example, if you type Range("A1").End(, you will see that there are four constants to choose from: xlDown, xlUp, xlToRight, and xlToLeft. (This corresponds to pressing the End key and then one of the arrow keys in Excel. You will learn more about it in Chapter 6.)

In short, Intellisense is instant online help. It doesn't necessarily help you with the *logic* of your program, but it helps you ensure that you get the syntax and spelling correct. After you get used to Intellisense, you will find that it is absolutely indispensable.

3.7 Color Coding and Case

Another feature of the VBE that enhances readability and helps you get your code correct is color coding.

- All keywords, such as Sub, End, For, and many others, are automatically colored blue.
- All comments (see Chapter 5) are colored green.
- All of the rest of your VBA is colored black.
- If you make a syntax error in a line of code and then press Enter, the offending line is colored red. This is a warning that you should fix the line before proceeding.

Besides coloring, the editor corrects case for you.

- All keywords start with a capital letter. Therefore, if you type sub and press Enter, the editor changes it to Sub.
- If you declare a variable with the spelling unitCost and then type it as UnitCost later on in the program, the editor automatically changes it to unitCost. (Whatever spelling you use when you declare the variable is the one used subsequently, even if it's something weird like uNItCost.) Actually, case doesn't matter at all to VBA—it treats unitCost the same as uNItCost or any other variation, but the editor at least promotes consistency.

3.8 Summary

This chapter has introduced the Visual Basic Editor (VBE)—its toolbars, some of its menu items, and its windows. It has also briefly discussed online VBA help and the Object Browser. You will be doing most of your development work in the

VBE, so you should become familiar with it right away. You will come to appreciate what a friendly and helpful programming environment it provides.

EXERCISES

1. Open Excel and open two new workbooks, which will probably be called Book1 and Book2 (or some such generic names). Get into the VBE and make sure the Project Explorer window is visible. Insert a module into Book1 and click on the plus sign next to Modules (for Book1) to see the module you just inserted. Now type the following sub in the Code window for this module and then run it. It should display the name of the workbook.

```
Sub ShowName()
    MsgBox "The name of this workbook is " & ThisWorkbook.Name
End Sub
```

Finally, go to the Project Explorer window and drag the module you inserted down to Book2. This should create a copy of the module in Book2. Run the sub in the copied module. It should display the name of the second workbook. The point of this exercise is that you can copy code from one workbook to another by copying the module containing the code, and copying a module is as simple as dragging in the Project Explorer window.

2. Open the **First Program.xlsm** file you created in Section 3.5, and get into the VBE so that you can look at the code. Select the **Debug** → **Add Watch** menu item, and type numberHigh in the text box. You are adding a "watch" for the variable numberHigh, so that you can see how it changes as the program runs. Next, place the cursor *anywhere* inside the code, and press the F8 key repeatedly. This "steps through" the program one line at a time. Every time the program sees a sales figure greater than the cutoff value you specify, numberHigh will increase by 1, which you should see in the Watch window. (You will probably get tired of pressing F8. You can stop the program prematurely at any time by clicking on the "blue square" Reset button on the Standard toolbar. Alternatively, you can click on the "blue triangle" Run button to run the rest of the program all at once.)

3. Get into the VBE and open the Immediate window. (The shortcut for doing so is **Ctrl-g**.) Then type the following lines, pressing the Enter key after each line. You should now understand why it is called the *Immediate* window.

```
?Application.Name
?Application.DefaultFilePath
?Application.Path
?Application.Version
?Application.UserName
?IsDate("February 29, 2005")
?IsDate("February 29, 2004")
?Workbooks.Count
?ActiveWorkbook.Name
```

4. Open a new workbook in Excel, get into the VBE, and insert a module into this new workbook. Type the following code in the Code window. Make sure there is *no* Option Explicit line at the top of the code window. (If there is one, delete it.)

```
Sub EnterUserNameSlowly()
    Range("A1") = "The user of this copy is Excel is listed below."
    yourName = Application.UserName
    nChars = Len(yourName)
    For i = 1 To nChars
            Range("A3") = Left(yourName, i)
            newHour = Hour(Now())
            newMinute = Minute(Now())
            newSecond = Second(Now()) + 1
            waitTime = TimeSerial(newHour, newMinute, newSecond)
            Application.Wait waitTime
    Next
End Sub
```

Next, return to Sheet1 of this workbook, add a button and assign the EnterUserNameSlowly sub to it, and then run the program by clicking on the button. Can you now explain what the code is doing? (If you like, look up the Wait method of the Application object in the Object Browser for online help.)

5. Open the **First Programs.xlsm** file you created in Section 3.5, and get into the VBE. Use the **Tools → VBAProject Properties** menu item, and click on the Protection tab. Check the **Lock project for viewing** box, enter a password in the other two boxes—don't forget it!—and click on OK. Get back to Excel, save the file, and close it. Now reopen the file and try to look at the code. You have just learned how to password-protect your code. Of course, you have to remember the password. Otherwise, not even you, the author, can look at the code! (If you ever want to remove the protection, just uncheck the Lock project for viewing box and delete the passwords from the boxes.)

Recording Macros

4.1 Introduction

This chapter illustrates a very quick way to start programming—by *recording* while you perform a task in Excel. Just as you can record yourself singing or playing the piano, you can record your keystrokes as you work in Excel. As the recorder records what you are doing, it generates VBA code in a module. If this sounds too good to be true, it is—at least to an extent. There are certain things you cannot record— loops and control logic, for example—and the recorded code, even though correct, is usually not very "stylish." Still, there are two reasons why recording can be useful. First, it is helpful for beginners. A beginning programmer can immediately generate code and then look at it and probably learn a few things. Second, it is useful even for experienced programmers who need to learn one particular detail of VBA code. For example, what is the VBA code for entering a comment in a cell? You could look it up in online help, but you could also record the process of entering a comment in a cell and then examine the resulting code. Recording often provides the clue you need to get past a particular coding hurdle.

4.2 How to Record a Macro

Recording is easy. In Excel 2007, select **Record Macro** from the Developer ribbon to display the dialog box in Figure 4.1. (In Excel 2003 and earlier, select the **Tools** → **Macro** → **Record New Macro** menu item. By the way, the "b" in .xlsb stands for binary. These files are stored in a different format than .xlsx files, which are stored in XML format.) This allows you to give the macro a descriptive name, provide an optional description of the macro, give it an optional shortcut key, and tell Excel where to store the recorded code.[1]

The storage location for the macro is particularly important. As Figure 4.1 indicates, you can store the macro in the current workbook, in a new workbook, or in a special workbook called **Personal.xlsb**. (This file was called **Personal.xls** in Excel 2003 and earlier.) If you store it in the current workbook, you can use

---

[1]A shortcut key is useful if you want to be able to run the macro with a Ctrl-key combination. For example, if you enter the letter k in the box, then the macro will run when you press the Ctrl-k key combination. Just be aware that if there is already a Ctrl-key combination, especially one that you use frequently, your new one will override it. For example, many people like to use Ctrl-s to save a file, so it is not wise to override this with your own use of Ctrl-s.

Figure 4.1 Record Macro Dialog Box

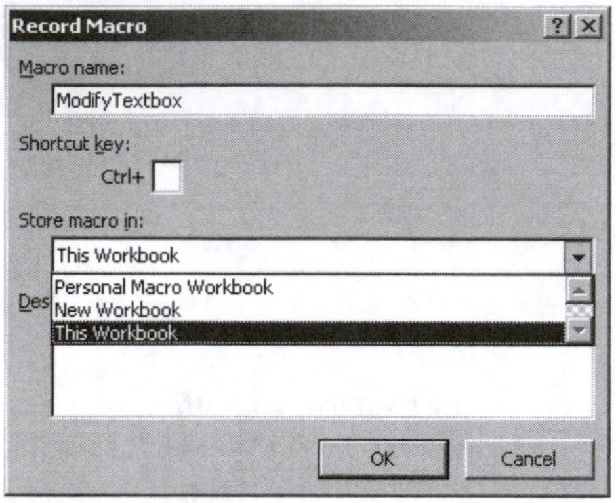

Figure 4.2 Stop Recording Button

the macro in that workbook but not in others (at least not without some extra work). This is sometimes acceptable, but suppose you want to record macros for tasks you do repeatedly. In fact, suppose your whole purpose in recording these macros is to have them available *at all times* when you are working in Excel. Then the **Personal.xlsb** file should be your choice. It is a special file that Excel stores in its **XLStart** folder so that it is opened every time Excel is opened.[2] It is actually opened as a hidden file so that you are not even aware of its presence—but its macros are always available.

Take a look at your own XLStart directory to see if you have a Personal.xlsb (or Personal.xls) file. (The easiest way is to search for Personal.xlsb in Windows Explorer. Provide the option to search in hidden or system folders.) If you do not, record a macro and specify the Personal Macro Workbook option in Figure 4.1 This will create a Personal.xlsb file on your computer, which you can then add to as often as you like. By the way, you can either *record* macros to the Personal.xlsb file, or you can type code directly into it in the VBE. That is, once you learn to program and not just record, you can add to your Personal.xlsb file anytime you like.

After you complete the dialog box in Figure 4.1 and click on OK, you should see the **Stop Recording** button on the Developer ribbon in Figure 4.2 (In Excel 2003 and earlier, this Stop Recording button is in its own toolbar.) So you can perform your task and then click on this button to stop the recording. Just remember that the recorder will record virtually *everything* you do until you click

---

[2]The XLStart folder is way down the directory structure on your hard drive. On my PC, the path to this folder is **C:\Documents and Settings\albright\Application Data\Microsoft\Excel\XLSTART.** Any Excel file in this folder is launched automatically when Excel is launched.

the Stop Recording button, so be careful—and don't forget to stop recording when you are finished.

Suppose you already have a module in your current workbook (or your Personal.xlsb file, if that is where you are saving the recorded macro). Then the chances are that Excel will create a *new* module and place the recorded macro in it. (Actually, the rules for whether it opens a new module or uses an existing module are somewhat obscure, but the point is that you might have to search through your modules to find the newly recorded code.)

4.3   Recorded Macro Examples

This chapter includes two files, **RecordingMacros.xlsm** and **RecordingMacros-Finished.xlsm**, to give you some practice in recording macros. The Recording-Macros.xlsm file includes six worksheets, each with a simple task to perform with the recorder on. The tasks selected are those that most spreadsheet users perform frequently. This section goes through these tasks and presents the recorded code. Although this recorded code gets the job done, it is not very elegant code. There-fore, the RecordingMacrosFinished.xlsm file contains the recorded code and modifications of it. This is a common practice when using the recorder. You usually record a macro to get one key detail. You then modify the recorded code to fit your specific purposes and discard any excess code you do not need.

For the rest of this section, it is best to open the RecordingMacros.xlsm file and work through each example with the recorder on. Your recorded code might be slightly different from the code in the file because you might do the exercises slightly differently. Don't worry about the details of the recorded code or the modified code at this point. Just recognize that recorded code often benefits from some modification, either to make it more general or to improve its readability.

Exercise 4.1   Entering a Formula

This exercise, shown in Figure 4.3, asks you to name a range and enter a formula to sum the values in this range.

The recorded code and modifications of it appear below in the **SumFormula** and **SumFormula1** subs. If you think about range operations in Excel, you will realize that you usually *select* a range—that is, highlight it—and then do something to it. Therefore, when you record a macro involving a range, you typically see the **Select** method in the recorded code. This is actually not necessary. When you want to do something to a range with VBA, you do *not* need to select it first. As you see in the modified version, the **Select** method is never used. However, there is a reference to the Exercise1 sheet, just to clarify that the ranges referred to are in the Exercise1 sheet.

Note how the recorded macro names a range. It uses the **Add** method of the **Names** collection of the **ActiveWorkbook**. This Add method requires two arguments: the name to be given and the range being named. The latter is done in **R1C1 notation**. For example, R7C2 refers to row 7, column 2—that is, cell B7. This is a typical example

Figure 4.3 Exercise 1 Worksheet

	A	B	C	D	E	F	G	H	I
1	Naming a range and entering a formula								
2									
3	Turn the recorder on, name the range with the numbers MonthlyCosts, then enter								
4	the formula =SUM(MonthlyCosts) at the bottom of the column, then turn the recorder off.								
5									
6	Month	Cost							
7	Jan-00	$10,897							
8	Feb-00	$11,164							
9	Mar-00	$10,062							
10	Apr-00	$12,039							
11	May-00	$11,111							
12	Jun-00	$10,223							
13	Jul-00	$11,558							
14	Aug-00	$12,553							
15	Total cost								

of recorded code being difficult to read. The modified code shown below uses a much easier way of naming a range (by setting the **Name** property of the range).

Recorded Code

```
Sub SumFormula()

' SumFormula Macro

    Range("B7:B14").Select
    ActiveWorkbook.Names.Add Name:= "MonthlyCosts", RefersToR1C1:= _
        "=Exercise1!R7C2:R14C2"
    Range("B15").Select
    ActiveCell.FormulaR1C1 = "=SUM(MonthlyCosts) "
    Range("B16").Select
End Sub
```

Modified Code

```
Sub SumFormula1()
    With Worksheets("Exercise1")
            .Range("B7:B14").Name = "MonthlyCosts"
            .Range("B15").Formula = "=SUM(MonthlyCosts) "
    End With
End Sub
```

Figure 4.4 Exercise 2 Worksheet

	A	B	C	D	E	F	G
1	Copying and pasting a formula						
2							
3	Column D is the sum of columns B and C. The typical formula is shown in cell D7.						
4	Turn on the recorder, copy this formula down column D, and turn the recorder off.						
5							
6	Month	Region 1 sales	Region 2 sales	Total sales			
7	Jan-00	$14,583	$10,531	$25,114			
8	Feb-00	$10,030	$12,861				
9	Mar-00	$14,369	$11,172				
10	Apr-00	$13,108	$14,957				
11	May-00	$14,410	$13,395				
12	Jun-00	$11,439	$12,306				
13	Jul-00	$12,753	$12,593				
14	Aug-00	$13,074	$11,631				
15	Sep-00	$10,957	$11,651				

Exercise 4.2   Copying and Pasting

This exercise, shown in Figure 4.4, asks you to copy a formula down a column.

The recorded code and modifications of it are shown below in the **CopyPaste** and **CopyPaste1** subs. Here again, you see Select and Selection several times in the recorded code. The recorded code also contains the strange line ActiveSheet.Paste. (Why does it paste to the ActiveSheet and not to a particular range? I still find this hard to understand.) The modified version is much simpler and easier to read.

Recorded Code

```
Sub CopyPaste()

' CopyPaste Macro

    Range("D7").Select
    Selection.Copy
    Range("D7:D15").Select
    ActiveSheet.Paste
    Application.CutCopyMode = False
End Sub
```

Modified Code

```
Sub CopyPaste1()
    With Worksheets("Exercise2")
        .Range("D7").Copy Destination:=.Range("D7:D15")
    End With
    ' The next line is equivalent to pressing the Esc key to get
    ' rid of the dotted line around the copy range.
    Application.CutCopyMode = False
End Sub
```

This exercise indicates how you can learn something fairly obscure by recording. Remember that when you copy and then paste in Excel, the copy range retains a dotted border around it. You can get rid of this dotted border in Excel by pressing the **Esc** key. How do you get rid of it in VBA? The answer appears in the recorded code—you finish with the line Application.CutCopyMode = False.

Exercise 4.3   Copying and Pasting Special as Values

This exercise, shown in Figure 4.5, asks you to copy a range of formulas and then use the Paste Values option to paste it onto itself.

The recorded code and its modifications are listed below in the **PasteValues** and **PasteValues1** subs. This time the recorded code is used as a guide to make a slightly more general version of the macro. Instead of copying a *specific* range (D8: D16), the modification copies the current *selection*, whatever it might be. Also, note that when recorded code contains a method, such as the **PasteSpecial** method of a **Range** object, it includes *all* of the arguments of that method. Typically, many of these use the default values of the arguments, so they do not really need to be included in the code. The modified code has dropped the Operation, SkipBlanks, and Transpose arguments because the actions performed in Excel did not change any of these. My point here is that recorded code is often *bloated* code.

Recorded Code

```
Sub PasteValues()
' PasteValues  Macro

    Range("D8:D16").Select
    Selection.Copy
    Selection.PasteSpecial Paste:=xlPasteValues, Operation:=xlNone, SkipBlanks:=False, Transpose:=False
    Application.CutCopyMode = False
End Sub
```

Modified Code

```
Sub PasteValues1()

' Note: This macro is somewhat more general. It copies and pastes to the current selection, whatever
' range it happens to be.

    With Selection
            .Copy
            .PasteSpecial Paste:=xlPasteValues
    End With
    Application.CutCopyMode = False
End Sub
```

Figure 4.5 Exercise 3 Worksheet

	A	B	C	D	E	F	G	H	I
1	Copying a range of formulas and pasting onto itself with the PasteSpecial Values option								
2									
3	Column D is the sum of columns B and C. Replace the formulas in column D with values.								
4									
5	Turn on the recorder, Copy column D, Paste Special (with the Values option), then turn off the recorder.								
6									
7	Month	Region 1 sales	Region 2 sales	Total sales					
8	Jan-00	$14,583	$10,531	$25,114					
9	Feb-00	$10,030	$12,861	$22,891					
10	Mar-00	$14,369	$11,172	$25,541					
11	Apr-00	$13,108	$14,957	$28,065					
12	May-00	$14,410	$13,395	$27,805					
13	Jun-00	$11,439	$12,306	$23,745					
14	Jul-00	$12,753	$12,593	$25,346					
15	Aug-00	$13,074	$11,631	$24,705					
16	Sep-00	$10,957	$11,651	$22,608					

Figure 4.6 Exercise 4 Worksheet

	A	B	C	D	E	F	G	H	I
1	Formatting the cells in a range								
2									
3	Format the following cells so that the font is Times New Roman, size 12, bold, and red.								
4									
5	Select the range *before* turning on the recorder.								
6									
7		Jan	Feb	Mar	Apr	May	Jun		

Exercise 4.4   Formatting Cells

This exercise, shown in Figure 4.6, asks you to format a range of labels in several ways.

The recorded code and its modifications appear below in the **Formatting** and **Formatting1** subs. This is a typical example of bloated code generated by the recorder. The exercise changes a few properties of the **Font** object, but the recorded code shows *all* of the Font's properties, whether changed or not. The modified code lists only the properties that are changed.

Recorded Code

```
Sub Formatting()
' Formatting Macro

    With Selection.Font
        .Name = "Roman"
        .Size = 10
        .Strikethrough = False
```

```
            .Superscript = False
            .Subscript = False
            .OutlineFont = False
            .Shadow = False
            .Underline = xlNone
            .ColorIndex = xlAutomatic
    End With
    With Selection.Font
            .Name = "Times New Roman"
            .Size = 12
            .Strikethrough = False
            .Superscript = False
            .Subscript = False
            .OutlineFont = False
            .Shadow = False
            .Underline = xlNone
            .ColorIndex = xlAutomatic
    End With
    Selection.Font.Bold = True
    Selection.Font.ColorIndex = 3
End Sub
```

Modified Code

```
Sub Formatting1()
    With Selection.Font
            .Name = "Times New Roman"
            .Size = 12
            .Bold = True
            .ColorIndex = 3
    End With
End Sub
```

Exercise 4.5   Creating a Chart

This exercise, shown in Figure 4.7, asks you to create a chart (as shown in Figure 4.8) on the same sheet as the data for the chart.

The recorded code and its modifications are listed in the **ChartOnSheet** and **ChartOnSheet1** subs. It is helpful to use the recorder when you want to use VBA to create or modify a chart. There are too many objects, properties, and methods associated with charts to remember, so you should let the recorder help you. Note that the modified version leaves most of the recorded code alone. It simply inserts some With constructions to avoid repetitive references to the same object. (The With construction is discussed in the next chapter.)

Figure 4.7 Exercise 5 Worksheet

	A	B	C	D	E	F	G
1	Creating a chart						
2							
3	Create a bar chart on this sheet for the following grade distribution.						
4							
5	Grade	Number					
6	A	25					
7	B	57					
8	C	43					
9	D	10					
10	F	4					

Figure 4.8 Exercise 5 Chart

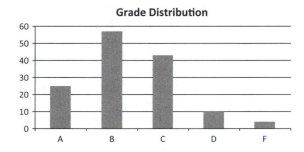

Recorded Code

```
Sub ChartOnSheet()
'
' ChartOnSheet Macro
'

'
    ActiveSheet.Shapes.AddChart.Select
    ActiveChart.SetSourceData Source:=Range("Exercise5!$A$5:$B$10")
    ActiveChart.ChartType = xlColumnClustered
    ActiveChart.Legend.Select
    Selection.Delete
    ActiveSheet.ChartObjects("Chart 1").Activate
    ActiveChart.ChartTitle.Select
    Range("A4").Select
End Sub
```

Modified Code

```
' Cleaned up macro. This one is problematic. First, with no help
' from the recorded macro about how to set the chart title, I had
' to search in online help for the right code. Luckily, I found it,
' as shown below. But there is still a problem. If I step through the
' code line by line (with the F8 key), it works fine. But if I run it
' all at once, it bombs, saying that there is no chart title! This is
' a Microsoft bug. Let's just say that their VBA for Excel charts is
' still a work in progress.

Sub ChartOnSheet1()
    Worksheets("Exercise5").Shapes.AddChart.Select
    With ActiveChart
        .SetSourceData Source:=Range("Exercise5!$A$6:$B$10")
        .ChartType = xlColumnClustered
        .HasLegend = False
        .HasTitle = True
        .ChartTitle.Text = "Grade Distribution"
    End With
    Range("A4").Select
End Sub
```

I claimed that you can often learn how to code a specific action in Excel by recording it. Well, that's not always true in Excel 2007. I've found this to be especially frustrating when dealing with charts. There are many times when the recorded code simply ignores what I did. For example, I changed the title of the chart to Grade Distribution, but this appears nowhere in the recorded code. The real problem is that the recorded code provides no clue on how to change the title of the chart. The only option is to search through online help (or the Web) and hope for the best. To make matters even worse, some code that worked in Excel 2003 does not work in Excel 2007. (The code for this exercise in my second edition is an example; it no longer works!) So the old code is broken, and there isn't much guidance on how to fix it. Many Excel programmers, including myself, are quite upset with Microsoft because of this, and we can only hope that things will improve in the next version of Excel.

Exercise 4.6 Sorting

This final exercise, in Figure 4.9, asks you to sort a range in descending order based on the Total column.

The recorded code and its modifications are listed in the **Sorting** and **Sorting1** subs. This again illustrates how you do not need to select a range before doing something to it. It also shows how the recorded code lists *all* arguments of the **Sort** method. The ones that have not been changed from their default values are omitted in the modified code.

Figure 4.9 Exercise 6 Worksheet

	A	B	C	D
1	Sorting a range			
2				
3	Sort on the Total column, from highest to lowest			
4				
5	Sales rep	January sales	February sales	Total
6	Adams	$3,843	$3,848	$7,691
7	Jones	$2,895	$3,223	$6,118
8	Miller	$3,707	$2,788	$6,495
9	Nixon	$3,544	$2,745	$6,289
10	Roberts	$3,672	$2,360	$6,032
11	Smith	$2,825	$2,369	$5,194
12	Thomas	$2,270	$2,035	$4,305
13	Wilson	$2,740	$2,625	$5,365

Recorded Code

```
Sub Sorting()

' Sorting Macro

    Range("D6").Select
    Selection.Sort Key1:=Range("D6"), Order1:=xlDescending, Header:=xlGuess, _
        OrderCustom:=1, MatchCase:=False, Orientation:=xlTopToBottom
End Sub
```

Modified Code

```
Sub Sorting1()
    Range("D6").Sort Key1:=Range("D6"), Order1:=xlDescending, Header:=xlYes
End Sub
```

As these exercises illustrate, you can learn a lot by recording Excel tasks and then examining the recorded code. However, you often need to modify the code to make it more readable and fit your specific needs. Also, be aware that there are many things you cannot record. Specifically, there is no way to record If logic and loops, two of the most important programming constructs available to a programmer. You have to program these manually—the recorder cannot do it for you. Finally, I repeat my frustration with recording in Excel 2007. It simply does not record all the actions, especially with charts, that it should record. We will just have to wait for the next version of Excel.

The following exercise allows you to try some recording on your own.

Exercise 4.7   Recording Print Settings

We all have our favorite print settings, and I can't count the number of times I've gone through the print settings dialog box to change the settings. It's always exactly the same steps and takes a number of mouse clicks. In short, it's a bother. This is a perfect situation for a recorded macro that does it once and saves it in the Personal.xlsb file for easy future use. Here are the steps.

1. Turn the recorder on, give the macro a name such as **PrintSettings**, and indicate that you want to store it in the Personal Macro Workbook.
2. Open the print settings dialog box, change the settings to the way you want them, and turn the recorder off.
3. Check the code. You'll see that every possible print setting has been recorded, not just those you changed. You can leave this as is, or you can streamline the code to change only settings you're interested in.
4. In Excel 2003 and earlier, you could now create a new toolbar with a new toolbar button to run your PrintSettings macro. (This process is explained in the second edition.) This is no longer possible in Excel 2007, but there is an alternative. At the top of the Excel screen, you see the **Quick Access Toolbar** (**QAT**). This is where you can create a button to run your favorite macros. The following steps explain the process.
5. Click on the dropdown next to the QAT and select **More Commands**.
6. In the top left dropdown, select **Macros**. You should see your PrintSettings macro in the list. Select it, and click on the **Add>>** button to add it to your QAT. By default, it will have a generic button icon. To change the icon, click on the **Modify** button and choose from the available icons. Then back your way out. (By the way, it would be nice to change the available icons or add to them, but I haven't found how to do so, at least not without writing some XML code. If you find an easy way, please send it to me!)

This process of recording a macro, saving it to your Personal.xlsb file, and creating a button on the QAT to run the macro makes you an instant programmer. You will be amazed at how useful simple little macros can be if you design them to automate tasks you perform frequently.

4.4 Summary

The macro recorder serves two basic purposes: (1) It allows beginning programmers to learn how common Excel operations translate into VBA code, and (2) it allows seasoned programmers to discover the one detail they need to get a program working. However, there are also two drawbacks to the recorder: (1) The recorded code is often far from elegant and bloated with unnecessary lines, and (2) it is incapable of capturing logic or loops, two of the most powerful aspects of VBA. In short, the recorder can be very useful, but it has its limits.

1. VBA can be used to format worksheet ranges in a variety of ways—the font, the interior (background of the cells), the alignment, and others. The recorder can be useful for learning the appropriate properties and syntax. Try the following. Open a new workbook and type some labels or numbers into various cells. Then turn on the recorder and format the cells in any ways you think are appropriate. Examine the recorded code. You will probably find that it sets many properties that you never intended to set. Delete the code that appears to be unnecessary and run your modified macro.

2. The **ColorIndex** property of the Font object (or the Interior object) determines the color of the font (or the background of a cell). For example, index 3 means red. Unfortunately, it is hard to remember which color goes with which index. Try the following. Open a new workbook and type a label in some cell. Highlight this cell, turn the recorder on, and change the color of the font (or the cell's background) repeatedly, choosing any colors you like from the color palettes. As you do so, keep track of the colors you've selected and then examine the recorded code. You should be able to match colors with indexes. (Actually, this has changed in Excel 2007. When you record these types of actions, you now see various properties, such as Color, ThemeColor, and TintAndShade. Still, recording is helpful.)

3. Using the recorder can be particularly useful for learning how to use VBA to modify charts. The file **Chart Practice.xlsx** contains a small database and a chart that is based on it. Open this file, turn the recorder on, and change any of the elements of the chart—the type of chart, the chart title, the axis labels, and so on. (You might be surprised at how many things you can change in a chart.) As you do this, write down the list of changes you make. Then examine the recorded code and try to match the sections of code with the changes you made. (If you want more information on any particular chart property you see in the code, place the cursor on it and press the F1 key. This provides immediate online help for the element you selected. Alternatively, look it up in the Object Browser.)

4. The previous exercise shows how to use the recorder to learn about properties of an *existing* chart. You can also use the recorder to learn how VBA can create a chart from scratch. Try the following. Open the **Chart Practice.xlsx** file, delete the chart, and then recreate it with the recorder on. Examine the recorded code to learn even more about how VBA deals with charts. (As with many recording sessions, you might want to practice building a chart *before* turning the recorder on. You don't want the recorder to record your mistakes!)

5. An operation I often perform is to highlight a range of cells that contain numbers and format them as integers, that is, as numbers with no decimals. Although this is

easy to do with Excel's **Format Cells** menu item, it takes a few steps. Record a general macro for performing this operation, store it in your Personal.xlsb file, and create a button on the QAT to run this macro. Once you are finished, you will always be a click away from formatting a range as integer. (*Hint:* Select a range of numbers *before* turning the recorder on. Your macro will then always work on the currently selected range, whatever it happens to be.)

6. (Note: This exercise and the next one are adapted from those in the second edition, which asked you to autoformat a range. Excel 2007 no longer supports autoformats, but similar functionality is still possible, as indicated here.) Many spreadsheets in the business world contain tables of various types. To dress them up, people often format them in various ways. To do this, highlight a table of data, including headers, and select an option of your choice from the **Format as Table** dropdown on the Home ribbon. Try it now with code, using the table in the **Table Data.xlsm** file. Then examine the code. You will see that it first creates a new **ListObject** object (that is, a table, discussed in Chapter 15), and it then sets the **TableStyle** property of the table to one of several built-in Excel constants, such as **TableStyleMedium1**. (If you ever need to learn the name of one of these constants, just repeat this exercise. It is a perfect example of how the recorder can be used to learn one critical detail of a program.)

7. Continuing the previous exercise, record a macro that formats a table with your favorite autoformatting option, and store the macro in your Personal.xlsb file. Then create a button on your QAT that runs this macro. When you are finished, you will be a click away from formatting any table with your favorite option.

8. I like to color-code certain cells in my spreadsheets. For example, I like to make the background of input cells blue, and I like to color cells with decision variables red. This is easy enough with the paint-can dropdown on the Home ribbon, but it is even easier if I create "color" buttons on my QAT. Try doing this with the recorder. Open a blank file, highlight any range, turn on the recorder, and color the background a color of your choice. Make sure you store the macro in your Personal.xlsb file. Then create a button with an appropriate icon on your QAT to run this macro. (Note: By highlighting the range before you turn the recorder on, your macro will be more general. It will color whatever range happens to be highlighted when you run it.)

5

Getting Started with VBA

5.1 Introduction

Now it is time to start doing some *real* programming in VBA—not just copying code in the book or recording, but writing your own code. This chapter gets you started with the most basic elements—how to create a sub, how to declare variables with a Dim statement, how to get information from a user with an input box, how to display information in a message box, and how to document your work with comments. It also briefly discusses strings, it explains how to specify objects, properties, and methods in VBA code, and it discusses VBA's extremely useful With construction and several other VBA tips. Finally, it discusses techniques for debugging, since programmers virtually never get their programs to work the first time through.

5.2 Subroutines

The logical section of code that performs a particular task is called a **subroutine**, or simply a **sub**. Subroutines are also called **macros**, and they are also called **procedures**. There is also a particular type of subroutine called a **function subroutine** that is discussed in Chapter 10. Subroutines, macros, and procedures are all essentially the same thing. I will call them all **subs**. A sub is any set of code that performs a particular task. It can contain one line of code or it can contain hundreds of lines. However, it is not good programming practice to let subs get too long. If the purpose of your application is to perform several related tasks, it is a good idea to break it up into several relatively short subs, each of which performs a specific task. In this case there is often a "main" sub that acts as the control center—it calls the other subs one at a time. The collection of subs that fit together is called a **program**. In other words, a program is a collection of subs that achieves an overall objective.

There are several places you can store your subs, but for now, you should store all of your subs in a **module**. When you look at a new project in the VBE, it will have no modules by default. However, you can add a module through the **Insert** menu, and then you can starting adding subs to it. It is also possible to double-click on a sheet or ThisWorkbook in the VBE Project Explorer to bring up a code window, but you should *not* enter your subs there, at least not yet. They are reserved for event handlers, which are discussed in Chapter 11. So again, for now, place all of your subs in modules.

Each sub has a name, which must be a single word. This word, which can be a concatenation of several words such as **GetUserInputs**, should indicate the purpose of the sub. You can use names such as **Sub1** or **MySub**, but this is a bad practice. You will have no idea in a week what **Sub1** or **MySub** is intended to do, whereas **GetUserInputs** clearly indicates the sub's purpose.

All subs must begin with the keyword **Sub** and then the name of the sub followed by parentheses, as in:

```
Sub GetUserInputs()
```

You can type this line directly into a module in the VBE, or you can use the **Insert → Procedure** menu item, which will prompt you for a name. (Again, if there is no module for the current project, you must insert one.) The editor will immediately insert the following line for you:

```
End Sub
```

Every sub must start with the Sub line, and it must end with the End Sub line. You will notice that the editor also colors the reserved words Sub and End Sub blue. In fact, it colors all reserved words blue as an aid to the programmer. Now that your sub is bracketed by the Sub and End Sub statements, you can start typing code in between.

Why are there parentheses next to the sub's name? As you will see in Chapter 10, a sub can take **arguments**, and these arguments must be placed inside the parentheses. If there are no arguments, which is often the case, then there is nothing inside the parentheses; but the parentheses still must be present. (This is similar to a few Excel worksheet functions that take no arguments, such as RAND( ), where the parentheses are also required.)

If a program contains several logically related subs, it is common to place all of them in a single module, although some programmers put some subs in one module and some in another, primarily for organizational purposes. The subs in a particular module can be arranged in any order. If there is a "main" sub that calls other subs to perform certain tasks, it is customary to place the main sub at the top of the module and then place the other subs below it, in the order they are called. But even this is not necessary; any order is accepted by VBA.

Later sections ask you to **run** a sub. There are several ways to do this, as explained in Chapter 3. For now, the easiest way is to place the cursor *anywhere* within the sub and click on the **Run** button (the blue triangle) on the VBE Standard toolbar. Alternatively, you can press the **F5** key, or you can use the **Run → Run Sub/UserForm** menu item.

5.3 Declaring Variables and Constants

Virtually all programs use variables. Variables contain values, much like the variables x and y you use in algebra. For example, the next three lines illustrate a simple use of variables. The first line sets the unitCost variable equal to 1.20, the second line sets the unitsSold variable to 20, and the third line calculates the variable totalCost as the product of unitCost and unitsSold. Of course, the value of totalCost here will be 24.0.

```
unitCost = 1.20
unitsSold = 20
totalCost = unitCost * unitsSold
```

Unlike algebra, you can also have a line such as the following:

```
totalCost = totalCost + 20
```

To understand this, you must understand that each variable has a location in memory, where its value is stored. If a variable appears to the left of an equals sign, then its new value in memory becomes whatever is on the right side of the equals sign. For example, if the previous value of totalCost was 260, then the new value will be 280, and it will replace the old value in memory. For this reason, you can think of the equals sign as "is replaced by."

Although it is not absolutely required (unless the line Option Explicit is at the top of the module), you should *always* declare all of your variables at the beginning of each sub with the keyword Dim.[1] (Dim is an abbreviation of dimension, a holdover from the old Basic language. It would make more sense to use the word Declare, but we are stuck with Dim.) Declaring variables has two advantages. First, it helps catch spelling mistakes. Suppose you use the variable unitCost several times in a sub, but in one case you misspell it as unitsCost. If you have already declared unitCost in a Dim statement, VBA will catch your spelling error, reasoning that unitsCost is not on the list of declared variables.

The second reason for declaring variables is that you can then specify the *types* of variables you have. Each type requires a certain amount of computer memory, and each is handled in a certain way by VBA. It is much better for you, the programmer, to tell VBA what types of variables you have than to let it try to figure this out from context. The variable types used most often are the following.

- **String** (for names like "Bob")
- **Integer** (for integer values in the range −32,768 to 32,767)
- **Long** (for really large integers beyond the Integer range)
- **Boolean** (for variables that can be True or False)
- **Single** (for numbers with decimals)
- **Double** (for numbers with decimals where you require more accuracy than with Single)
- **Currency** (for monetary values)
- **Variant** (a catch-all, where you let VBA decide how to deal with the variable)

---

[1] If you declare a variable inside a sub, it is called a *local* variable. It is also possible to declare a variable outside of subs, in which case it is a *module-level* variable. This issue is discussed in Chapter 10.

Variable declarations can be placed anywhere within a sub, but it is customary to include them right after the Sub line, as in the following:

```
Sub Test( )
    Dim i As Integer, unitCost As Currency, isFound As Boolean
    Other statements
End Sub
```

Some programmers prefer a separate Dim line for each variable. (I tend to favor this, but I'm not always consistent.) This can lead to a long list of Dim statements if there are a lot of variables. Others tend to prefer a single Dim, followed by a list of declarations separated by commas. You can use either convention or even mix them. However, you *must* follow each variable with the keyword As and then the variable type. Otherwise, the variable is declared as the default **Variant** type, which is considered poor programming practice. For example, variables i and j in the following line are (implicitly) declared as Variant, not as Integer. Only k is declared as Integer.

```
Dim i, j, k As Integer
```

If you want all of them to be Integer, the following declaration is necessary:

```
Dim i As Integer, j As Integer, k As Integer
```

Symbols for Data Types

It is also possible to declare (some) data types by the symbols in Table 1. For example, you could use Dim unitCost@ or Dim nUnits%, where the symbol follows the variable name. This practice is essentially a holdover from older versions of the BASIC language, and you might see it in legacy code (as I recently did). However, I don't recommend using this rather obscure "shorthand" way of declaring variables. After all, would *you* remember them?

Table 1 Symbols for variable types

Integer	%
Long	&
Single	!
Double	#
Currency	@
String	$

Figure 5.1 Error Message for Undeclared Variable

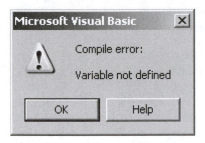

Using Option Explicit

You should *force* yourself to adopt the good habit of declaring all variables. You can do this by using the tip mentioned in Chapter 3. Specifically, select the **Tools → Options** menu item in the VBE and check the **Require Variable Declarations** box under the Editor tab. (By default, it is *not* checked.) From that point on, every time you open a new module, the line Option Explicit will be at the top. This simply means that VBA will force you to declare your variables. If you forget to declare a variable, it will remind you with an error message when you run the program. If you ever see the message in Figure 5.1—and you almost certainly will—you will know that you forgot to declare a variable (or misspelled one).

Object Variables

There is one other type of variable. This is an **object variable**, which "points" to an object. For example, suppose you have a Range object, specified by the range name Scores on a worksheet named Data, that you intend to reference several times in your program. To save yourself a lot of typing, you can **Set** a range object variable named scoreRange to this range with the lines

```
Dim scoreRange As Range
Set scoreRange = ActiveWorkbook.Worksheets("Data").Range("Scores")
```

From then on, you can simply refer to scoreRange. For example, you could change its font size with the line

```
scoreRange.Font.Size = 12
```

This is a lot easier than typing

```
ActiveWorkbook.Worksheets("Data").Range("Scores").Font.Size = 12
```

There are two fundamental things to remember about object variables.

- They must be declared just like any other variables in a Dim statement. The type can be the generic **Object** type, as in

```
Dim scoreRange as Object
```

or it can be more specific, as in

```
Dim scoreRange as Range
```

The latter is much preferred because VBA does not then have to figure out what *type* of object you want scoreRange to be. (It is *not* enough to include Range in the name of the variable.)

- When you define an object variable—that is, put it on the left of an equals sign—you must use the keyword Set. In fact, this is the only time you use the keyword Set. The following line will produce an error message because the keyword Set is missing:

```
scoreRange = ActiveWorkbook.Worksheets("Data").Range("Scores")
```

In contrast, assuming that totalCost is a variable of type Currency (or any non-object variable type), the following line will produce an error message because the keyword Set should *not* be included:

```
Set totalCost = 24.0
```

The moral is that you should always use the keyword Set when defining object variables, but you should never use it when defining other variables.

Intellisense with Variable Names

As I discussed in Chapter 3, you will soon get hooked on Intellisense, the instant online help the VB Editor offers as you are writing your code. One use of Intellisense that many programmers are not aware of concerns your own defined variables. (I didn't mention this in the previous edition because I wasn't aware of it myself until very recently!) Suppose you are well into a program and you want to use a variable that starts with un, but you forget how you spelled this variable name. You could scroll back to the top of the sub and see how you spelled it in your declarations section, but this takes time. A better way is to let Intellisense help you. Start typing the variable name, un, and then press the **Ctrl-Space** key combination. All declared variables that begin with un will be listed, and you can then "down arrow" to the correct variable (if there is more than one) and press the Tab key to insert it in your code. I know I will take frequent advantage of this trick, and I suspect you will too.

Variable Naming Conventions

Programmers have some surprisingly strong feelings about variable naming conventions. The one thing they all agree with is that variable names should indicate what the variables represent. So it is much better to use a name such as taxRate than to use a generic name like x. Your code becomes much easier to read, both for others and for yourself, if you use descriptive names.

Beyond this basic suggestion, however, there are at least three naming conventions used in the programming world, and each has its proponents. The **Pascal** convention uses names like TaxRate, where each "word" in the name is capitalized. The **camel** convention is similar, but it does not capitalize the *first* word. Therefore, it would use the name taxRate. (The term *camel* indicates that the hump is in the middle, just like a camel.) Finally, the **Hungarian** convention, named after a Hungarian programmer, prefixes variables with up to three characters to indicate their variables types. For example, it might use the name sngTaxRate to indicate that this variable is of type Single. Other commonly used prefixes are int (for Integer), bln (for Boolean), str (for String), and so on. The proponents of the Hungarian convention like it because it is self-documenting. If you see the variable sngTaxRate in the middle of a program, you immediately know that it is of type Single, without having to go back to the Dim statement that declares the variable.

Which convention should you use? This seems to depend on which convention is currently in style, and this changes over time. For a while, it seemed that the Hungarian convention was the "in thing," but it results in some rather long and ugly variable names. At the time of this writing, the camel convention appears to be the most popular, so I have adopted it throughout this book. But if you end up programming for your company, there will probably be a corporate style that you will be required to follow.

Constants

The term *variable* means that it can change. Specifically, the variables discussed above can change values as a program runs—and they usually do. There are times, however, when you want to define a **constant** that never changes during the program. The reason is usually the following. Suppose you have a parameter such as a tax rate that plays a role in your program. You know that its value is 28% and that it will never change (at least, not within your program). You could type the value 0.28 every place in your program where you need to use the tax rate. However, suppose a year from now the tax rate changes to 29%. To use your old program, you would need to search through all of the lines of code and change 0.28 to 0.29 whenever it appears. This is not only time-consuming, but it introduces the possibility of errors. (Maybe one of the 0.28 values you find is not a tax rate but is something else. You don't want to change it!)

A better approach is to define a constant with a line such as the following.

```
Const taxRate = 0.28
```

This line is typically placed toward the beginning of your sub, right below the variable declarations (the Dim statements). Then every place in your sub where you need a tax rate, you type taxRate rather than 0.28. If the tax rate does happen to change to 29% a year from now, all you have to change is the value in the Const line above.[2]

Another advantage to using constants is that your programs don't have "magic numbers." A magic number is a number found in the body of a program that seems to appear out of nowhere. A person reading your program sees a number such as 0.28 and has no idea what it could represent (unless you explain it with a comment or two). In contrast, if the person sees taxRate, there is no question what it means. So try your best to use constants and avoid magic numbers.[3]

5.4 Built-In Constants

There are many built-in constants that you will see frequently. They are either built into the VBA language, in which case they have the prefix **vb**, they are built into the Excel library, in which case they have the prefix **xl**, or they are built into the Microsoft Office library, in which case they have prefix **mso**. Actually, these constants all have integer values, and they are all members of **enumerations**. A simple example illustrates the concept of an enumeration. Consider the **Color** property of a Font. It can be one of 8 possible integer values, and no one on earth would possibly memorize these 8 values (they are *not* 1 through 8). Instead, you remember them by their constant names: vbBlack, vbBlue, vbCyan, vbGreen, vbMagenta, vbRed, vbWhite, and vbYellow. Using these constants, you can change the color of a font in a line such as

```
Range("A1").Font.Color = vbBlue
```

Similarly, Excel has a number of enumerations. One that is useful when dealing with ranges is the set of possible directions, corresponding to the four arrow keys: xlDown, xlUp, xlToRight, and xlToLeft. Again, these constants are really integer values that no one in the world remembers. You remember them instead by their more suggestive names.

To view many enumerations for VBA, Excel, and Office, open the Object Browser, open the VBA, Excel, or Office library, and search the class list for items

---

[2]Some programmers like to spell their constants with all uppercase letters, such as TAXRATE, to identify them as constants. However, I have not adopted this convention.

[3]The same idea applies to formulas in Excel. You should avoid embedding numbers in formulas. Instead, you should list these numbers in "input cells" and use cell references to the input cells in your formulas.

Figure 5.2 Typical Input Box

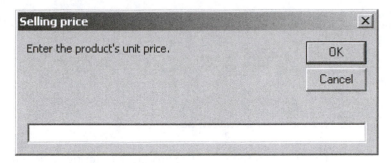

starting with Vb, Xl, or Mso. Each of them is an enumeration that holds a number of built-in constants. For example, the XlDirection enumeration holds the constants xlDown, xlUp, xlToRight, and xlToLeft, and the VbMsgBoxStyle enumeration holds all the constants that correspond to message box icons and buttons. You will see a few of these in the next section.

5.5 Input Boxes and Message Boxes

Two of the most common tasks in VBA programs are to get inputs from users and to display messages or results in some way. There are many ways to perform both tasks, and many of them are illustrated in later chapters. This section illustrates a very simple way to perform these tasks. It takes advantage of two built-in VBA functions: the **InputBox** and **MsgBox** functions. They are not complex or fancy, but they are very useful.

The **InputBox** function takes at least one argument: a prompt to the user.[4] A second argument that is often used is the title that appears at the top of the dialog box. An example is the following:

```
price = InputBox("Enter the product's unit price.", "Selling price")
```

If you type this line in a sub and run the sub, the dialog box in Figure 5.2 will appear.

This generic dialog box has OK and Cancel buttons, a title (which would be Microsoft Excel if you didn't supply one), a prompt, and a textbox for the user's input. When the user enters a value and clicks on OK, the user's input is assigned to the variable price.

The **MsgBox** function takes at least one argument: a message that you want to display. Two other optional arguments often used are a button indication and a title. A typical example is the following:

```
MsgBox "The product's unit price is $2.40.", vbInformation, "Selling price"
```

---

[4]If you look up InputBox in the VBA online help, you will see two items: the InputBox *method* and the InputBox *function*. Although they are similar, they are not quite the same. The discussion here is really about the *method*, the one most commonly used.

Figure 5.3 Typical Message Box

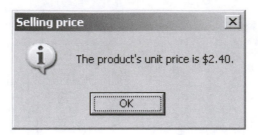

The first argument is the text "The product's unit price is $2.40." The second argument is vbInformation, a built-in VBA constant that inserts an "i" icon in the message box. The third argument is the title, "Selling price." If you type this line in a sub and run the sub, the message box in Figure 5.3 will appear.

I'll finish this section with some rather advanced code involving InputBox. You can ignore it at this point if you like, but my own students always ask about it. What if you prompt a user for a value with an InputBox, and the user either clicks on OK without entering anything in the text box or clicks on Cancel? Try it out, and you'll find that Excel produces an obscure error message. As a good programmer, you should anticipate this and handle it nicely.

It turns out that InputBox returns an empty string, `" "`, if the user does either of the above two actions. So you can check (by using an If construction) whether the response is an empty string. Furthermore, by using an undocumented VBA function, **StrPtr**, it is possible to check whether the user clicked on OK or Cancel. Finally (and this is optional), you can embed the check in a loop so that you allow the user to "get out of the game" by clicking on Cancel, but you keep asking for an input if the user clicks on OK with no input. The code in the file **OK vs Cancel in InputBox. xlsm** contains the required code. Open it, and try all the possibilities you can think of. I call this *bulletproof* code. It forces the user to do something correctly—and there are no obscure error messages. I will return to bulletproofing in Chapter 11.

5.6 Message Boxes with Yes and No Buttons

The previous section illustrates the most common use of a message box: to display a message. However, message boxes can be used for simple logic by including the appropriate buttons. For example, the following line not only displays the message with Yes and No buttons (see Figure 5.4), but it also captures the button pressed in the result variable. In this case, the second argument, vbYesNo, indicates that Yes and No buttons should be included. The value of result will be vbYes or vbNo, two built-in VBA constants. You could then use a logical If statement to proceed appropriately, depending on whether the result is vbYes or vbNo.

```
result = MsgBox("Do you want to continue?", vbYesNo, "Chance to quit")
```

Figure 5.4 Message Box with Yes and No Buttons

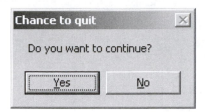

You can even use the InputBox and MsgBox functions in the same line, as in:

```
MsgBox InputBox("Type your name.", "User's name"), vbInformation, "User's Name"
```

The first argument of the MsgBox function is now the *result* of the InputBox function. When I ran this, I first saw the input box and typed my name, as in Figure 5.5. I then saw the message box in Figure 5.6, the "message" being my name.

Here are a couple of other points that apply to input boxes and message boxes, as well as to other VBA statements.

- **Continuing statements on more than one line.** Lines of code can often get long and run past the right side of the screen, particularly with messages. You

Figure 5.5 Input Box

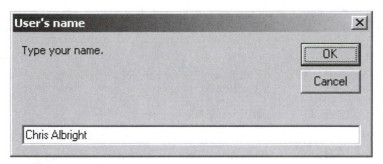

Figure 5.6 Message Box

can continue them on another line by using the **underscore** character, _, preceded by a space. (Don't forget the space!) For example, you can write

```
MsgBox InputBox("Type your full address, including city, state, and zip code.", "User's address"), _
    vbInformation, "User's Address"
```

This is treated as a *single* line of code. Actually, a line can be broken as many times as you like with the underscore character.

- **Whether to use parentheses.** If you have been paying close attention, you have noticed that the arguments of InputBox and MsgBox are sometimes included in parentheses, but sometimes they are not. For example, compare the line

```
MsgBox "Thank you for supplying your name.", vbExclamation, "Name accepted"
```

with the line

```
result = MsgBox("Do you want to continue?", vbYesNo, "Chance to quit")
```

The first simply displays a message. The second also captures the result of the message box (vbYes or vbNo) in the result variable. The rule for parentheses, for the InputBox function, the MsgBox function, and other VBA functions, is that parentheses are *required* when the result is captured in a variable or used in some way. In contrast, parentheses are *optional* (and are usually omitted) when no result is being captured or used in some way. This parentheses rule is difficult to understand until you become more proficient in VBA. However, if your program fails to work and you cannot find anything else wrong, check whether you have violated this rule. Then remove the parentheses or add them, and see whether the bug disappears.

Exercise 5.1   Displaying a Message

Before proceeding, try the following simple exercise. Open a new workbook and save it as **Input Output 1.xlsm**. Then create a sub called **RevenueCalc** that does the following: (1) It asks the user for the unit price of some product and stores it in the variable unitPrice, defined as Currency type; (2) it asks the user for the number of items sold and stores it in the variable quantitySold, defined as Integer type; (3) it calculates the **revenue** from this product and stores it in the variable revenue, defined as Currency type; and (4) it displays a message such as "The revenue from this product was $380."

Try to do as much of this as you can without help. Then consult the file **Input Output 1.xlsm** on the CD-ROM for a solution. You will probably have trouble with the MsgBox line. The message consists of two parts: a literal part ("The revenue from this product was ") and a variable part (the calculated revenue).[5]

---

[5]It also has a third part if you want to end the sentence with a period.

These two parts need to be **concatenated** with the ampersand symbol, &, a *very* common operation that is explained later in the chapter. The solution also contains a **Format** function to display the revenue as, say, $380 rather than 380. This is also explained in a later section.

5.7 Using Excel Functions in VBA

Excel has hundreds of functions you commonly use in Excel formulas: SUM, MIN, MAX, SQRT, VLOOKUP, SUMIF, and so on. It would be a shame if programmers had to reinvent this rich set of functions with their own VBA code. Fortunately, you do not have to. You can "borrow" Excel functions. You do so with a line such as

```
Application.WorksheetFunction.SUM(Range("A1:A10"))
```

When you type Application.WorksheetFunction and then a period, a list of most Excel functions appears. For example, if you choose SUM, as above, then you have to supply the same type of argument (a range or ranges) that you would in an Excel formula.

There is one peculiar "gotcha" that comes with borrowing Excel functions. It turns out that the VBA language has a few functions of its own. For example, open the Object Browser, choose the VBA library, and look at the Math class. Three notable VBA math functions you will see are log (natural logarithm), **sqr** (square root), and rnd (random number). You probably know that Excel also has these functions, except that they are spelled LN, SQRT, and RAND. The "gotcha" is that if VBA has a function, you are *not* allowed to borrow Excel's version of that function. Therefore, the statement Application.WorksheetFunction.SQRT(4) produces an error. If you want the square root of 4 in VBA, you must get it with sqr(4).

Fortunately, there are not many of these duplicated functions. You just have to be aware that a few, such as LN, SQRT, and RAND, will not work in VBA.

5.8 Comments

You might think that once you get your program to run correctly, your job is finished. This is not the case. Sometime in the future, you or someone else might have to modify your program as new situations arise. Therefore, it is extremely important that you *document* your work. There are several ways to document a program, including the use of meaningful names for subs and variables. However, the best means of documentation is the liberal use of **comments**. A comment is simply text that you type anywhere in your program to indicate to yourself or someone else what your code means or how it works. It is very easy to insert a comment anywhere in the program, inside a sub or outside a sub. You start the line with a single quote. That line is then colored green and is ignored by VBA. However, comments are *not* ignored by those who read your program. For them, the comments are often the most interesting part!

The following line is a typical comment:

```
' The purpose of the following section is to calculate revenue.
```

It is also possible to include a comment in the same line as a line of code. To do so, type the code, follow it with one or more spaces, then a single quote, and then the comment, as in

```
Range("A1").Value = "March Sales" ' This is the title cell for the sheet.
```

There is a tendency on the part of programmers to wait until the last minute, after the code has been written, to insert comments—if they insert them at all. Try instead to get into the good habit of inserting comments as you write your code. Admittedly, it takes time, but it also aids your logical thought process if you force yourself to explain what you are doing as you are doing it. Of course, comments can also be overdone. There is usually no point in documenting every single line of code. Use your discretion on what *really* needs to be documented. My best advice is that if you believe you or someone else might have trouble understanding what a block of code is supposed to do or how it works, add a comment. When you revisit your code in a few weeks or a few years, you will *really* appreciate the comments.

5.9　Strings

The InputBox function takes at least one argument, a prompt such as "Enter your name." Similarly, the MsgBox function takes at least one argument, a message such as "Thank you for the name." Technically, each of these is called a **string**. A string is simply text, surrounded by double quotes. Strings are nearly always arguments to InputBox, MsgBox, and other functions, and they are also used in many other ways in VBA. For example, because a string corresponds (loosely) to a label in Excel, if you want to use VBA to enter a label in a cell, you set the Value property of the Range object representing the cell to a string. You will see plenty more of this throughout the book. The point now is that strings are used in practically all VBA programs.

Often a string is a literal set of text, such as "The user's name is Chris Albright." (Again, remember that the double quotes are part of the string and cannot be omitted.) Many times, however, a string cannot be written literally and must be pieced together in sections. This is called **string concatenation**. As an example, suppose the following InputBox statement is used to get a product name:

```
product = InputBox("Enter the product's name.")
```

The user types the product's name into the text box, and it is stored as a string, "LaserJet 1100" for example, in the product variable. Now suppose you what to display a message in a message box such as "The product's name is Laser Jet 1100." What should the first argument of the MsgBox be? It cannot be the literal "The product's name is LaserJet 1100." This is because you, the programmer, do not know what product name will be entered in the input box. Therefore, you must "build" the message string by concatenating three strings: the literal "The product's name is ", the *variable* string product, and the literal period ".". To concatenate these, you use the concatenation character, the ampersand, &, surrounded on either side by a space. The resulting MsgBox statement is

```
MsgBox "The product's name is " & product & "."
```

Note how the ampersand is used twice to separate the *variable* information from the literal parts of the string. String concatenation—the alternation of literal and variable parts of a string—is extremely important and is used in practically all programs.

A completed sub that gets a product's name and then displays it in a message box appears below, along with the results from running it, in Figures 5.7 and 5.8.

```
Sub GetProductName()
    Dim product as String
    product = InputBox("Enter the product's name.")
    MsgBox "The product's name is " & product & ".", vbInformation
End Sub
```

One tricky aspect of string concatenation occurs when you use the underscore character to break a long string, even a totally literal one, into two lines. You might think that the following would work:

Figure 5.7 Input Box

Figure 5.8 Message Box

```
MsgBox "This is a long string, long enough to extend beyond _
    the screen, so it is broken up into two lines."
```

However, this produces an error message. If you break a string across two lines, you *must* concatenate it:

```
MsgBox "This is a long string, long enough to extend beyond " & _
    "the screen, so it is broken up into two lines."
```

(Note that there is a space after the word *beyond*, so that *beyond* and *the* will not run together in the message. There is also a space on each side of the ampersand, as required by VBA.) Alternatively, you could place the ampersand on the second line:

```
MsgBox "This is a long string, long enough to extend beyond " _
    & "the screen, so it is broken up into two lines."
```

Whether you put the ampersand at the end of the first line or the beginning of the second line is a matter of taste.

Exercise 5.2   Displaying a Message

Return to Exercise 5.1 from Section 5.4. There you obtained a unit price and a quantity sold from input boxes, calculated the revenue, and then displayed a message such as "The revenue from this product was $380." You should now understand that the last part of this message, the actual revenue, requires string concatenation. (See the **Input Output 1.xlsm** file.) Now try expanding your program slightly (and save your results in the file **Input Output 2.xlsm**). Start by using an input box to get the product's name. Then use input boxes to get the product's unit price and the quantity sold, and include the product's name in the prompts for these inputs. For example, a prompt might be "Enter the unit price for LaserJet 1100." Next, calculate the revenue. Finally, display a message that contains all of the information, something like "For the LaserJet 1100, the unit price is $500, the quantity sold is 25, and the revenue is $12,500." Do as much as you can on your own. If you need help, look at the file **Input Output 2.xlsm** on the CD-ROM.

Formatting Strings

If the revenue is 12500, how do you get it to appear as $12,500 in a message? This can be done with VBA's **Format** function. This function takes two arguments: the number to be formatted and a **format code** string that indicates how to format the number. To format 12500 in the usual currency format (with a dollar sign and comma separators), you can use Format(12500,"$#,##0"). If the variable revenue holds the actual revenue, then you would use Format(revenue,"$#,##0"). Using the Format function is tricky. Rather than memorizing a lot of formatting codes, it is best to select the Format option in Excel (right-click on any cell and choose Format Cells) and choose the Custom option. It will show you a number of formatting codes you can use in VBA.

Useful String Functions

String concatenation is useful when you need to "piece together" several small strings to create one long string. You might also need to get *part* of a string. There are three useful VBA string functions for doing this: **Right**, **Left**, and **Mid**. They are illustrated in the following lines.

```
shortString1 = Right("S. Christian Albright", 8)
shortString2 = Left("S. Christian Albright", 12)
shortString3 = Mid("S. Christian Albright", 4, 5)
```

The first line returns "Albright". In general, the **Right** function takes two arguments, a string and an integer n, and it returns the rightmost n characters of the string. The **Left** function is similar. It returns the leftmost n characters. In the second line, it returns "S. Christian". (The space after "S." is considered a character.) Finally, the **Mid** function takes a string and two integer arguments. The first integer specifies the starting character and the second specifies the number of characters to return. Therefore, the third line returns "Chris". Starting at the fourth character, "C", it returns the next five characters. Note that the third argument of Mid can be omitted, in which case Mid returns all characters till the end of the string. For example, Mid("Albright",3) returns "bright".

One other useful string function is the **Len** function. It takes a single argument, a string, and returns the number of characters in the string. For example, the following line

```
nCharacters = Len("S. Christian Albright")
```

returns 21. (Again, remember that spaces count!) One final string function that can come in handy is the **Instr** function. It checks whether a "substring is anywhere inside a given string, and if it is, where it begins within the string." I'll let you look up Instr in VBA help.

These functions can be used in many combinations. Suppose you want all but the last two characters of some string called thisString, but you don't know the number of characters in thisString. Then the following combination of Len and Left will do the job.

```
allBut2 = Left(thisString, Len(thisString) - 2)
```

For example, if thisString turns out to have 25 characters, allBut2 will be the leftmost 23 characters.

5.10   Specifying Objects, Properties, and Methods

Objects, properties, and methods were introduced in Chapter 2. Now it is time to see how they are implemented in VBA code. This is important material. Virtually nothing can be done in VBA for Excel without knowing how to manipulate its objects in code. The basic rules are as follows.

- **Specifying a member of a collection.** To specify a particular member of a collection, use the *plural* name of the collection, with the particular member specified in parentheses and enclosed inside quotes, as in Worksheets("Data"). In the special case of the Range object, where there is no plural, just write Range, followed by a specification of the range inside parentheses. (The next chapter is devoted entirely to Range objects because they are so important.) You can generally specify any particular member of a collection in one of two ways: by index (a number) or by name (a string). For example, you can specify Worksheets(2) or Worksheets("Data"). The name method is *much* preferred. After all, if someone inserts a new worksheet or moves an existing worksheet, then the worksheet in question might no longer be the *second* one. It is much easier to understand the reference to the worksheet's name. (The "2" actually refers to the second sheet from the left, not necessarily the second sheet created.)
- **Specifying objects down a hierarchy.** To specify objects down a hierarchy, separate them with a period, with objects farther down the hierarchy to the right, as in

```
Workbooks("Sales").Worksheets("March").Range("Midwest")
```

You essentially read this line backward. It specifies the range named Midwest from the March worksheet of the Sales workbook. We say that an object to the right is **qualified** by any objects listed to its left. It is possible that in all of your open workbooks there are multiple ranges named Midwest. The above line specifies the one you want: the Midwest range in the March worksheet of the Sales workbook.

This rule has a number of variations. For example, if you refer simply to Range ("Midwest"), do you need to qualify it with a particular workbook and worksheet? The answer is sometimes "yes" and sometimes "no." It depends on the context. Specifically, there are built-in VBA objects called **ActiveWorkbook** and **ActiveSheet** (but no ActiveWorksheet). They refer to the workbook and sheet currently selected. If you refer simply to Range("Midwest"), this is equivalent to

```
ActiveWorkbook.ActiveSheet.Range("Midwest")
```

Because this is probably what you want, the shorter Range("Midwest") is perfectly acceptable. However, if you specify Range("A1"), be sure that the *active* worksheet contains the cell A1 you are interested in. That is, if you do not qualify Range("A1"), VBA will guess which A1 cell you mean, and it might not guess correctly. It is safer to qualify it, as in Worksheets("Data").Range("A1"), for example.

- **Specifying a property.** To specify a property of an object, list the property name to the right of the object, separated by a period, as in

```
Range("A1").Value
```

This refers to the Value property of the range A1—that is, the contents of cell A1. A property can be set or returned. For example, the following line enters the string "Sales for March" in cell A1:

```
Range("A1").Value = "Sales for March"
```

In contrast, the following line gets the label in range A1 and stores it as a string in the variable title:

```
title = Range("A1").Value
```

- **Specifying a method.** To specify a method for an object, list the method name to the right of the object, separated by a period, as in

```
Range("Midwest").ClearContents
```

- **Specifying arguments of a method.** If a method has arguments, list them, separated by commas, next to the method's name. Each argument should have the name of the argument (which can be found from online help), followed by :=, followed by the value of the argument. For example, the following copies the range A1:B10 to the range D1:E10. Here, Destination is the name of the argument of the Copy method.

```
Range("A1:B10").Copy Destination:=Range("D1:E10")
```

It is possible to omit the argument name and the := and to write

```
Range("A1:B10").Copy Range("D1:E10")
```

However, this can be dangerous and can lead to errors unless you know the rules well. It is better to supply the argument name and :=. Even if you are an experienced programmer, this practice makes your code more readable for others.

By the way, when methods have arguments, Intellisense helps a great deal. In the above line, as soon as you type .Copy and then a space, Intellisense shows you a list of the arguments, both required and optional, of the Copy method. In this case, there is only one argument, Destination, and Intellisense shows it in square brackets, indicating that is optional.

These are the rules, and you can return to this section as often as you like to refresh your memory. They are reinforced with many examples in later chapters.

Exercise 5.3 Calculating Ordering Costs

The file **Input Output 3_1.xlsx** is a template for calculating the total order cost for ordering a product with quantity discounts. The table (range-named LTable) in the range A4:C8 contains unit costs for various order quantity intervals. The range B11:B13 contains a typical order cost calculation, where the input is the order quantity in cell B11 and the ultimate output is the total cost in cell B13. Take a look at this file to see how a VLOOKUP function is used to calculate the appropriate unit cost in cell B12.

The file **Input Output 3_2.xlsm** indicates what the exercise is supposed to accomplish. Open it now and click on the "Create table" button. It asks for three possible order quantities, and then it fills in the table in the range D12:E14 with these order quantities and the corresponding total costs. Basically, it plugs each potential order quantity into cell B11 and transfers the corresponding total cost from cell B13 to column E of the table. If you then click on the "Clear table" button, the information in this table is deleted.

Now that you see what the finished application should do, go back to the **Input Output 3_1.xlsx** file, save it as an .xlsm file, and attempt to write two subs, **CreateTable** and **ClearTable**, which will eventually be attached to buttons. Go as far as you can on your own. If you need help, look at the code in the **Input Output 3_2.xlsm** file on the CD-ROM.

This exercise will undoubtedly leave you wishing for more. First, even with only three order quantities, there is a lot of repetitive code. Copying and pasting your code (and then making suitable modifications) can minimize the amount of typing required. Second, the program ought to allow *any* number of entries in the table, not just three. To see how these issues can be addressed, open the file **Input Output 3_3.xlsm**, click on its buttons, and look at its code. There are probably a few lines you will not understand yet, but at least this gives you something to strive for. You will eventually understand all of the code in this file.

5.11 With Construction

There is an extremely useful shortcut you can take when working with objects and their properties and methods. It is the **With** construction. Unless you have programmed in VBA, you have probably never seen it. The easiest way to explain the **With** construction is by using an example. Suppose you want to set a number of properties for the range A1 in the March worksheet of the Sales workbook. You could use the following code.

```
Workbooks("Sales").Worksheets("March").Range("A1").Value = "Sales for March"
Workbooks("Sales").Worksheets("March").Range("A1").HorizontalAlignment = xlLeft
```

```
Workbooks("Sales").Worksheets("March").Range("A1").Font.Name = "Times New Roman"
Workbooks("Sales").Worksheets("March").Range("A1").Font.Bold = True
Workbooks("Sales").Worksheets("March").Range("A1").Font.Size = 14
```

As you can see, there is a lot of repetition in these five lines, which means a lot of typing (or copying and pasting). The **With** construction enables you to do it much more easily:

```
With Workbooks("Sales").Worksheets("March").Range("A1")
    .Value = "Sales for March"
    .HorizontalAlignment = xlLeft
    With .Font
        .Name = "Times New Roman"
        .Bold = True
        .Size = 14
    End With
End With
```

The first line has the keyword **With**, followed by an object reference. The last line brackets it with the keywords **End With**. In between, any object, property, or method that starts with a period "tacks on" the object following the With. For example, .Value in the second line is equivalent to

```
Workbooks("Sales").Worksheets("March").Range("A1").Value
```

This example also illustrates how With constructions can be *nested*. The line With .Font is equivalent to

```
With Workbooks("Sales").Worksheets("March").Range("A1").Font
```

Then, for example, the .Name reference inside this second With is equivalent to

```
Workbooks("Sales").Worksheets("March").Range("A1").Font.Name
```

The use of With (and nested With) constructions can save a lot of typing. (It also speeds up the execution of your programs slightly.) However, make sure you do the following two things:

- **Remember End With.** The End With line must accompany each With. A good habit is to write the End With line immediately after typing the With line. That way, you don't forget.
- **Indent appropriately.** Indenting is not required—your programs will run perfectly well without it—but errors are much easier to catch (and avoid) if you indent, and your programs are *much* easier to read. Compare the above code to the following version:

```
With Workbooks("Sales").Worksheets("March").Range("A1")
.Value = "Sales for March"
.HorizontalAlignment = xlLeft
With .Font
.Name = "Times New Roman"
.Bold = True
.Size = 14
End With
End With
```

This version without indenting is certainly harder to read, and if you forgot the next-to-last line, it could be difficult to find the error. By the way, do *not* indent by pressing the Space key repeatedly. This usually does not line things up properly. Instead, use the **Tab** key (or the **Shift-Tab** key combination for outdenting, the opposite of indenting). To indent or outdent an entire block of code, use the VBE toolbar buttons on the Edit toolbar for this purpose.

Exercise 5.4   Using With Constructions

Open the file **Input Output 3_2.xlsm** (or your own finished version in **Input Output 3_1.xlsm**) from the previous exercise and save it as **Input Output 3_4.xlsm**. Then use the With construction wherever possible. For one possible solution, see the file **Input Output 3_4.xlsm** on the CD-ROM.

5.12 Other Useful VBA Tips

This section illustrates a few miscellaneous features of VBA that are frequently useful.

Screen Updating

A VBA program for Excel sometimes makes many changes in one or more worksheets before eventually showing results. During this time the screen can flicker, which wastes time and is certainly annoying. The following line "turns off" screen updating. It essentially says, "Do the work and just show me the results at the end."

```
Application.ScreenUpdating = False
```

To appreciate how this works, open the file **Screen Updating.xlsm**. It has two buttons, each attached to a sub. Each sub performs the same operations, but one turns off screen updating and the other leaves it on. You will notice the difference! If you do decide to turn off screen updating (typically at the beginning of a sub), then it is good programming practice to turn it back on just before the end of the sub. You do this with the line

```
Application.ScreenUpdating = True
```

Figure 5.9 Excel Warning Message

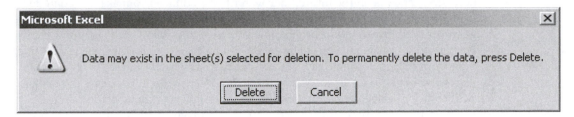

Display Alerts

If you use the Excel interface to delete a worksheet, you get a warning, as shown in Figure 5.9. In some applications you don't want this warning; you just want the worksheet to be deleted. In this case (and other cases where you don't want an Excel warning), you can use the following line:

```
Application.DisplayAlerts = False
```

This can actually be a bit dangerous—you might *want* a warning later on—so it is a good idea to turn display alerts back on immediately, as in the following lines:

```
Application.DisplayAlerts = False
Worksheets("Report").Delete
Application.DisplayAlerts = True
```

Timer Function

Programmers often like to see how long their programs (or parts of their programs) take to run. This is easy to do with the VBA **Timer** function. It returns the current clock time. If it is used twice, once at the beginning of some code and once later on, then the difference in the two times is the elapsed run time. The following lines illustrate how it can be used. The start time is captured in the variable startTime. This is followed by any number of programming lines. Finally, the variable elapsedTime captures the current time (from Timer) minus the start time. Note that these times are measured in *seconds*.

```
startTime = Timer
' Enter any code in here.
elapsedTime = Timer - startTime
MsgBox "This section took " & elapsedTime & " seconds to run."
```

5.13 Good Programming Practices

As a programmer, your primary goal is to write code that works correctly to accomplish a specified task. However, really good programmers strive for more than just accuracy.

They want their programs to be readable and easy to maintain, so that if changes are necessary sometime in the future, they won't be too difficult to make. (Keep in mind that the person responsible for making these changes is often *not* the original programmer.) Therefore, good programmers consistently follow a set of good habits. Even if you are a beginning programmer, you should strive to follow these good habits right from the start. Admittedly, you can practice poor habits and still write programs that work, but your programs will probably not be very readable or easy to maintain. Besides, poor habits typically increase the chance of programming errors.

Not all programmers agree completely on a programming "style" that should be followed, but they would almost certainly agree on the following list.

- **Provide sufficient comments.** As discussed earlier in this chapter, providing a liberal number of comments is the best way to make your programs understandable, both to others and to yourself (at a later date). It is always better to include too many comments than too few.

- **Indent consistently.** Some programmers write code with no indenting—all lines are left-aligned on the page. Unless the program is short and simple, this type of code is practically impossible to read, and the potential for errors increases dramatically. Indenting provides a logical structure to your program, and it indicates that you are *aware* of this logical structure. You will have plenty of chances to see the proper use of indenting as you read through the examples in this book.[6]

- **Use white space liberally.** Don't be afraid to insert blank lines in your subs. Like indenting, this tends to give a more logical structure to your code, and it is greatly appreciated by those who try to read your code.

- **Break long lines into multiple lines.** It is no fun to read a line of code that scrolls off to the right of the screen. Therefore, keep your lines short enough that they fit inside the Code window. When necessary, use the underscore character, _, to break long lines.

- **Name your variables appropriately.** I already harped on this earlier in the chapter, but it bears repeating. The days when programmers could get away with meaningless variable names like KK, X, and PR, are gone. Variable names like fixedCost and lastName produce much more readable code.

- **Declare all of your variables, usually at the beginnings of subs.** I have already stated that Option Explicit should be at the top of each of your modules. This *forces* you to declare your variables with Dim statements. Actually, these Dim statements can be placed just about anywhere within a sub (before the variable is used), but it is a good programming practice to place them right after the Sub statement. This makes it easy to find a list of all your variables. (This doesn't count **module-level** variables, which must be declared *before* any subs. They are discussed in Chapter 10.)

- **Use the Variant type as little as possible.** Remember that a Variant type is a catch-all; it can hold any type of variable. The way a Variant variable is stored

---

[6]Microsoft's Visual Studio .NET, its most recent integrated development environment, automatically indents for you. Unfortunately, the VBE for Excel is not quite up to this level yet, so you have to indent manually.

and manipulated depends on the context of the program. Essentially, you are making the computer determine the type of variable you really have, and this is not efficient. If you know that your variable is really an integer, say, then declare it as Integer, not as Variant. The use of Variant types is usually a sign of sloppy programming.

- **Break a complex program into small subs.** This is the topic of Chapter 10, but even at this point it should make sense. It is much more difficult to read and debug a long complex sub than to work with a series of shorter subs, each devoted to performing a single task. Think of this as the "divide and conquer" rule.

As you start writing your own programs, refer back to this list from time to time. If you find that you are consistently violating one or more of these rules, you know that you have room to improve—and you should strive to do so.

5.14 Debugging

Some programmers are more skillful and careful than others, but the sad fact is that we *all* make errors, known in the programming world as **bugs**. The art of finding and getting rid of bugs, **debugging**, is almost as important as programming itself. Debugging is basically detective work, and, like programming, it takes practice. This section gets you started.

There are really three types of errors: **syntax** errors, **runtime** errors, and **logic** errors.

Syntax Errors

Syntax errors are usually the easiest to spot and fix. They occur when you spell something wrong, omit a keyword, or commit various other "grammatical" errors. They are easy to spot because the VBE typically detects them immediately, colors the offending line red, and displays a warning in a message box.[7] You have probably experienced this behavior several times already, but in case you haven't, type the following line of code and press the Enter key:

```
If FirstNumber > SecondNumber
```

You will be reminded immediately that this line contains a syntax error: the keyword **Then** is missing. Sometimes the resulting error message tells you in clear terms what the error is, and other times it is more mysterious. But at least you know that there is something wrong with your syntax, you know approximately where the error is, and you have a chance to fix it right away. There is no excuse for not doing so. If you are not sure of the correct syntax, you can look it up in online help.

---

[7]This is the default behavior of the VBE, and you should probably leave it in place. However, if you get tired of the warnings, you can select VBE's **Tools → Options** menu item and uncheck the Auto Syntax Check under the Editor tab.

Runtime Errors

Runtime errors are more difficult to spot and fix. They occur when there is something wrong with your code, but the error is not discovered until you *run* your program. The following lines illustrate a typical example.

```
Option Explicit
Option Base 1

Sub Test()
    Dim mArray(10) As Integer, i As Integer, nReps As Integer
    nReps = InputBox("Enter the number of replications.")
    For i = 1 To nReps
        myArray(i) = 20 * i
    Next
End Sub
```

This code has no syntax errors, but it is likely to produce a runtime error. The user is asked to enter a number of replications, which is stored in the variable nReps. If the user enters a value less than or equal to 10, the program will run fine. However, if the user enters a number greater than 10, the program will try to fill an array with more values than it is dimensioned for. (Arrays are covered in Chapter 9.) If you run this program and enter 15 in the input box, you will get the error message shown in Figure 5.10. It is one of Microsoft's cryptic error messages that you will come to despise, both because it means that *you* made an error and because you can't make any sense out of the message.

At this point, you have the three options indicated by the enabled buttons: (1) you can ask for help, which is often not very helpful; (2) you can end the program, which doesn't do anything to help you locate the problem; or (3) you can click on Debug. This latter option displays the offending line of code colored in yellow. If you then move the cursor over variables, you can see their current values, which often

Figure 5.10 Error Dialog Box

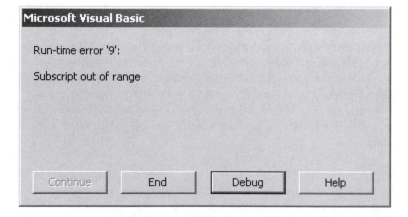

Figure 5.11 Code after Clicking on Debug

```
(General)                                          ▼    Test                                    ▼

    Option Explicit
    Option Base 1
    Sub Test()
        Dim myArray(10) As Integer, i As Integer, nReps As Integer
        nReps = InputBox("Enter the number of replications.")
        For i = 1 To nReps
⇨ |            myArray(i) = 20 * i
        Next              i = 11
    End Sub
```

provides just the clue you need. Figure 5.11 shows what happens if you click on Debug and then put the cursor over the variable i in the offending line. Its current value is 11, and the array is dimensioned for only 10 elements.

This is the clue you need to fix the program, as shown below. The trick is to redimension the array *after* discovering the value of nReps. The details of the fix are not important at this point. The important thing is that you found the location of the bug, and that is often all you need to fix the problem.

```
Sub Test()
    Dim myArray() As Integer, i As Integer, nReps As Integer
    nReps = InputBox("Enter the number of replications.")
    ReDim myArray(nReps)
    For i = 1 To nReps
            myArray(i) = 20 * i
    Next
End Sub
```

The problem with runtime errors is that there is an infinite variety of them, and the error messages provided by Microsoft can be quite misleading. Consider the following sub, which purposely violates the cardinal rule of indenting to mask the error in the program. Can you spot it?

```
Sub Test()
Dim cell As Range
For Each cell In Range("A1:D10")
If cell.Value > 10 Then
With cell.Font
.Bold = True
.Italic = True
End If
Next
End Sub
```

The properly indented version listed below clearly indicates the problem—the With construction is missing an End With.

```
Sub Test()
    Dim cell As Range
    For Each cell In Range("A1:D10")
        If cell.Value > 10 Then
            With cell.Font
                .Bold = True
                .Italic = True
        End If
    Next
End Sub
```

However, if you run this program (either version), you will get the error message in Figure 5.12, and the End If line of the sub will be highlighted in yellow! As you can imagine, this type of misleading information can drive a programmer crazy. Of course, some snooping around indicates that the problem is *not* with the If–End If construction but is instead with the With–End With. However, an unsuspecting programmer could be led down a time-consuming blind alley searching for the bug. Therefore, it is best to interpret runtime error messages with caution. They typically point you in the general *neighborhood* of the offending code, but they do not always pinpoint the problem. And, as you can probably guess, the Help button in this case would not be of any help at all.

When you get any of these runtime error messages, your program goes into **break mode**, which essentially means that it is "on hold." You always know a program is in break mode when a line of code is highlighted in yellow. Sometimes you can fix a line of code while in break mode and then click on the **Run Sub/ Userform** button on the VBE Standard toolbar to let the program finish. (See Figure 5.13) Other times, it is impossible to continue. You need to click on the **Reset** button, fix the error, and then rerun the program. It is usually best to do the latter. If you ever get a message to the effect that something can't be done because the program is in break mode, get back into the VBE and click on the Reset button. In this case, the reason you can't run your program is that it is already running!

Figure 5.12 Misleading Error Message

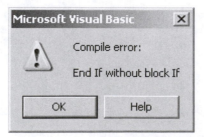

Figure 5.13 VBE Standard Toolbar

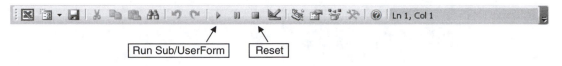

Run Sub/UserForm   Reset

Logic Errors

The third general type of error, a logic error, is the most insidious of the three because you frequently don't even know that you *have* an error. You run the program, it produces some results, and you congratulate yourself that your work is finished. However, if your program contains any logic errors, even a single tiny error, the results can be totally wrong! You might or might not get an error message to alert you to the problem.

Here is a typical example. (This file is not included on the CD, but you might want to create it for practice.) You want to average the numbers in column A (through row 10) in Figure 5.14 and display the average in a message box. The correct average, calculated with Excel's AVERAGE function, appears in cell A12.

The AverageScores sub listed below contains no syntax errors and no runtime errors.[8] If you run it, it will display the message box in Figure 5.15—with the *wrong* average! Unless you have read ahead to the next chapter, you probably don't know enough about Range objects to spot the problem, but there is a bug, and it is quite subtle.

Figure 5.14 Scores to Average

	A	B
1	Scores	
2	87	
3	78	
4	98	
5	82	
6	77	
7	99	
8	80	
9	85	
10	76	
11		
12	84.67	

---

[8]Of course, you would never write such complex code to perform such a simple task. It is done here only to illustrate a point.

Figure 5.15 Display of Incorrect Average

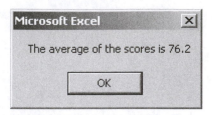

```
Sub AverageScores()
    Dim scoreRange As Range, cell As Range, sum As Single

    With Range("A1")
            Set scoreRange = Range(.Offset(0, 0), .End(xlDown))
    End With

    For Each cell In ScoreRange
            If IsNumeric(cell.Value) Then sum = sum + cell.Value
    Next

    MsgBox "The average of the scores is " & sum / scoreRange.Cells.Count
End Sub
```

There are actually two problems. The first problem, and probably the more important one, is that if the correct average had not been calculated separately in cell A12, you would probably have accepted the answer in the message box as being correct. (How many programs in the real world have errors that no one is even aware of? I suspect the number is huge. Is it possible, for example, that there are errors in the gigantic programs used by the IRS to check your tax returns? It's a scary thought!)

However, assuming that you are suspicious of the answer in the message box, the second problem is to find the error and fix it. Fortunately, the VBE has some powerful tools for debugging your programs. One of the most useful methods is to **step through** a program one line at a time, possibly keeping a **watch** on one or more key variables. VBE's **Debug** toolbar is very handy for doing this. (See Figure 5.16.) Equivalently, you can use menu items and shortcut keys to perform the same tasks.

Let's use this method to find the faulty logic in the average example. To do this—and you should follow along at your own PC—get into the VBE and put a

Figure 5.16 VBE Debug Toolbar

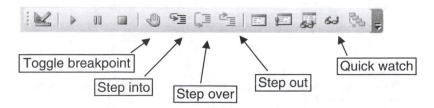

Figure 5.17 Watch Window

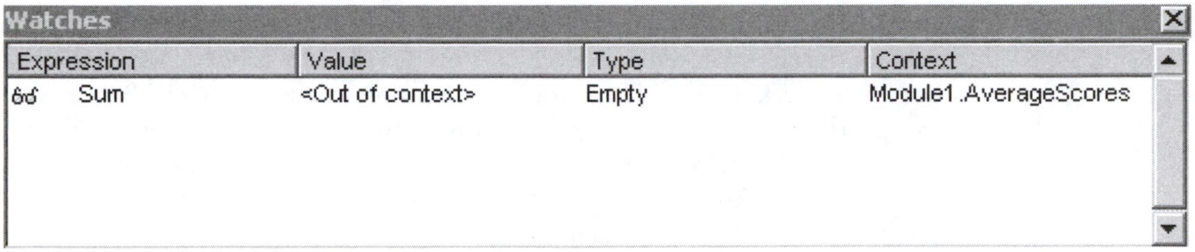

Figure 5.18 Watch Window After For Each Loop

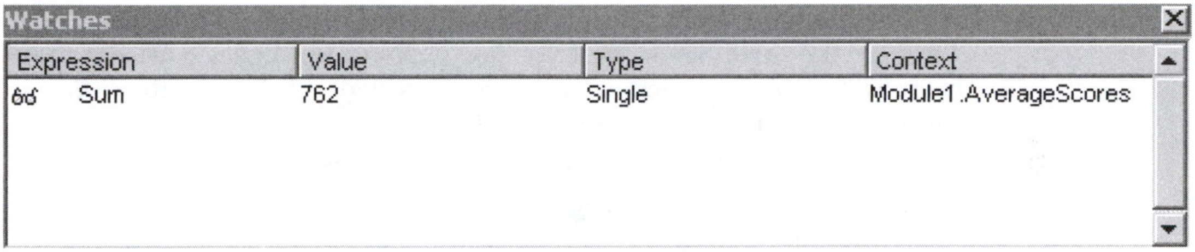

watch on the key variable sum. The easiest way to do this is to put the cursor anywhere on the sum variable (any place it appears in the code) and click on the **Quick watch** button. The **Watch window** then opens, as shown in Figure 5.17. It allows you to watch the contents of sum as the program executes. In general, you can put watches on as many variables as you like.

At this point, sum has not yet been defined, so its value is listed as "out of context." But it changes as you step through the program. To do this, put the cursor anywhere inside the **AverageScores** sub and repeatedly click on the **Step into** button. (Alternatively, press the **F8** key repeatedly.) This executes a line of code at a time. If the line changes the value of sum, the updated value will appear in the Watch window. By the time the For Each loop is finished, the Watch window appears as in Figure 5.18.

If you sum the numbers in the range A2:A10 of Figure 5.14, you will find that the sum is indeed 762. This means that the problem is *not* with the logic for calculating sum. The only other possible problem is with the number that sum is divided by to obtain the average. (Now do you see the error?) A careful look at the code shows that scoreRange includes the label in cell A1. Therefore, scoreRange.Cells.Count returns 10, not 9. The correct average is 762/9, not 762/10. (You might recall that Excel's COUNT worksheet function counts only cells with numbers. In contrast, VBA's Count property, as used here, counts all cells, even empty cells or cells with labels.)

The general point made by this example is that stepping through a program, together with a careful use of the Watch window, can localize a problem and enable you to fix it. You can also employ some other debugging tools to fine-tune your search for bugs. This is particularly important if you have a large program with several subs and you are confident that most of them are bug-free. You then can use the following tools.

- **Set breakpoints.** Put the cursor on any line of code and click on the **Toggle breakpoint** button. This puts a red dot in the left-hand margin of the Code window (or it removes the red dot if one was already there). If you now run the program, it will execute until it encounters this line of code, at which time it goes into break mode. Then you can examine values of variables or step through the program from this point on. In general, whenever you click on the **Run Sub/Userform** button, the program advances to the *next* breakpoint. (If there isn't another breakpoint, the program runs to completion.)
- **Step over subs.** As you are stepping through a program, you might get to a line that **calls** another sub. (Calling other subs is discussed in Chapter 10.) If you do not want to step through that sub line by line (because you are confident it is bug-free), click on the **Step over** button. This executes the sub all at once, without stepping through it line by line.
- **Step out of subs.** Similarly, if you are stepping through a sub and decide there is no point in stepping through the rest of it, click on the **Step out** button. The rest of the sub is executed all at once and control passes back to the calling sub, which you can then continue to step through.

These tools are great for debugging, but they are not magic bullets. Incorrect logic creeps into almost all programs of any reasonable size, and it is the programmer's task to find them. This requires a thorough knowledge of the program, a lot of detective work, and perseverance. The easy way out is to seek immediate help from someone else (your instructor?) as soon as something goes wrong. However, you should try to find the bugs yourself, using the tools described here. It is probably the most effective way to become a good programmer. You will learn at least as much from your errors as from any programming manuals.

5.15 Summary

This chapter has covered a lot of VBA programming fundamentals, including sub-routines (subs); variables; input boxes and message boxes; comments; strings and string operations; specification of objects, properties, and methods; With constructions; a few other VBA elements; and debugging. All of these fundamentals are used repeatedly in later chapters. Don't worry if they are not yet completely clear. It takes plenty of practice to master these VBA fundamentals.

EXERCISES

1. Open a new workbook, get into the VBE, insert a module, and type the following code in the code window.

```
Sub Variables()
    Dim nPounds As Integer, dayOfWeek As Integer
    nPounds = 17.5
```

```
    dayOfWeek = "Monday"
    MsgBox nPounds & " pounds were ordered on " & dayOfWeek
End Sub
```

There are two problems here. One causes the program to fail, and the other causes an incorrect result. Explain what they are and then fix them.

2. Open a new workbook, get into the VBE, insert a module, and type the following code in the code window.

```
Sub CalculateExpenses()
    customerName = InputBox("Enter the name of a customer.")
    nPurchases = InputBox("Enter the number of purchases made by " & customerName _
        & " during the month.")
    totalSpent = 0
    For counter = 1 To nPurchases
        amountSpent = InputBox("Enter the amount spent by " & customerName _
            & " on purchase " & counter)
        totalSpent = totalSpent + amountSpent
    Next
    MsgBox customerName & " spent a total of " & Format(totalSpent, "$#,##0.00") & _
        " during the month.", vbInformation
End Sub
```

   a. Make sure there is no Option Explicit line at the top of the module. (If there is, delete it.) Then run the program. It should work fine. (If it doesn't, check your spelling.)

   b. Enter an Option Explicit line at the top of the module. Now run the program. It should produce an error message. The problem is that the Option Explicit statement forces you to declare variables, and none of the variables in this sub have been declared. Declare them appropriately with a Dim statement (or several Dim statements) and rerun the program. Now it should work.

3. Write a program, and store it in a file called **TravelExpenses.xlsm**, that does the following: (a) It asks for a person's first name and stores is it in firstName; (b) it asks for a person's last name and stores it in lastName; (c) it asks for the number of miles the person traveled on a recent trip and stores it in nMiles; (d) it asks for the average miles per gallon the person got on the trip and stores it in milesPerGallon; (e) it asks for the average price per gallon paid for gas on the trip and stores it in avgPrice; (f) it calculates the cost of the trip and stores it in tripCost; and (g) it displays a message such as "Bob Jones traveled 800 miles, got 31.3 miles per gallon on average, paid $2.49 per gallon on average, and paid a total of $63.64 for gas." Make sure there is an Option Explicit line at the top of the module and that you declare all of your variables appropriately.

4. Write a program, and store it in a file called **String Funtions.xlsm**, that does the following: (a) It asks the user for a word with at least 10 characters and stores it in myWord; (b) it displays a message indicating the number of characters in the word;

(c) it displays a message showing the first four characters of the word; (d) it displays a message showing the last six characters of the word; (e) it displays a message showing the fifth character in the word; (f) it displays a message showing all but the first two and last two characters in the word; and (g) it displays the word in reversed order. (*Hint*: For the last part, look up Strings in the VBA library of the Object Browser.)

5. The file **Formatting 1.xlsm** contains the following code for formatting some data. It is all correct. Rewrite the code so that there are no With constructions, and then run the modified program to make sure it still works. Can you see how With constructions reduce repetitive code?

```
Sub Formatting()
    With ActiveWorkbook.Worksheets("Sheet1")
        With .Range("A1")
            .Value = "Expenses for March"
            With .Font
                .Name = "Arial"
                .Bold = True
                .ColorIndex = 5
                .Size = 14
            End With
            .HorizontalAlignment = xlLeft
        End With
        With Range("A3:A6")
            .InsertIndent 1
            With .Font
                .Italic = True
                .Bold = True
            End With
        End With
        With .Range("B3:B6")
            .Interior.ColorIndex = 37
            .NumberFormat = "$#,##0"
        End With
    End With
End Sub
```

6. The file **Formatting 2.xlsm** contains the following code for formatting some data. This code works perfectly well, but it is a bit repetitive, to say the least. Rewrite it by using as many With constructions as make sense, using appropriate indentation, and then run your modified code to make sure it still works.

```
Sub Formatting()
    ActiveWorkbook.Worksheets("Sheet1").Range("A1").Font.Bold = True
    ActiveWorkbook.Worksheets("Sheet1").Range("A1").Font.Size = 14
    ActiveWorkbook.Worksheets("Sheet1").Range("A1").HorizontalAlignment = xlLeft
    ActiveWorkbook.Worksheets("Sheet1").Range("A3:A6").Font.Bold = True
    ActiveWorkbook.Worksheets("Sheet1").Range("A3:A6").Font.Italic = True
    ActiveWorkbook.Worksheets("Sheet1").Range("A3:A6").Font.ColorIndex = 5
    ActiveWorkbook.Worksheets("Sheet1").Range("A3:A6").InsertIndent 1
    ActiveWorkbook.Worksheets("Sheet1").Range("B2:D2").Font.Bold = True
    ActiveWorkbook.Worksheets("Sheet1").Range("B2:D2").Font.Italic = True
```

```
    ActiveWorkbook.Worksheets("Sheet1").Range("B2:D2").Font.ColorIndex = 5
    ActiveWorkbook.Worksheets("Sheet1").Range("B2:D2").HorizontalAlignment = xlRight
    ActiveWorkbook.Worksheets("Sheet1").Range("B3:D6").Font.ColorIndex = 3
    ActiveWorkbook.Worksheets("Sheet1").Range("B3:D6").NumberFormat = "$#,##0"
End Sub
```

7. The file **Formatting 3.xlsm** contains code that is very difficult to read. Besides that, it contains an error. Reformat it with indenting, white space, and comments, and fix the error so that it runs correctly.

8. The **Count Large.xlsm** file has quantities sold for 1000 products for each of 60 months, for a total of 60,000 values. The following code counts the number of these that are greater than 100. Check how long it takes to do this by inserting the Timer function appropriately in the code and displaying the elapsed time in a message box.

```
Sub CountLarge()
    Dim cell As Range, nLarge As Long
    For Each cell In Range("Sales")
        If cell.Value > 100 Then nLarge = nLarge + 1
    Next
    MsgBox nLarge & " cells in the Sales range have a quantity larger than 100.", _
        vbInformation
End Sub
```

9. Write single lines of code for each of the following.
   a. Set the value of cell A17 in the Sales sheet of the active workbook to 1325.
   b. Capture the value of cell B25 in the Quantities sheet of the workbook **Sales.xlsx** in the variable marchSales.
   c. Clear the contents of the range named Sales.
   d. Copy the range A1:A10 on the Sheet1 worksheet of the active workbook to the range A1:A10 of the MarchSales sheet in the **Sales.xlsx** workbook. (You can assume that **Sales.xlsx** is *not* the active workbook.)

10. The file **Exam Scores.xlsx** has scores for an exam in the range A1:A200. Write a sub that reports the average, standard deviation, minimum, and maximum of the scores in a message box. Use Excel's functions (with Application.WorksheetFunction) to do the arithmetic.

11. Open a new workbook, name it **Random Number.xlsm**, and delete all but the first sheet if necessary. Write a sub that enters a random number in cell A1. Try this two ways. First, use Excel's RAND() function (with Application. WorksheetFunction) to set the Value property of this cell. Does this work? It shouldn't. Second, set the Value property of the cell to VBA's **rnd** function. Does this work? It should. The moral is that if VBA has a function that does something, you have to use it; you can't "borrow" Excel's function that does the same thing.

6

Working with Ranges

6.1 Introduction

This chapter focuses on ways to work with ranges in VBA. This is a particularly important topic because the majority of operations in Excel are *range* operations. You select ranges, you enter values and formulas in ranges, you format ranges in various ways, you copy ranges, and so on. Therefore, it is important to be able to automate these common tasks with VBA code. Unfortunately, it can be difficult to do even the simplest tasks unless you know the correct techniques, and online help is sometimes more confusing than helpful. This chapter presents sample VBA code that accomplishes many common tasks. You can then adapt this code to your own programs.

6.2 Exercise

The following exercise illustrates the type of problem you will be able to solve once you master the techniques in this chapter. You should probably not try this exercise yet, but you should keep it in mind as you read through the rest of the chapter. By the end, you should have more than enough tools to solve it—one way or another.

Exercise 6.1

The file **Calculate NPV.xlsx** contains a model for calculating the net present value (NPV) from an investment. (See Figure 6.1.) Five inputs are listed in the range B4:B8. These are used to implement the calculations for cash inflows in row 12, and the net present value (NPV) is then calculated with the formula **=NPV(B8,B12:K12)-B4** in cell B14. All of the logic to this point is incorporated in the worksheet and does not need to be changed at all. When you enter different inputs in the B4:B8 range, the NPV in cell B14 automatically recalculates.

Rows 18–22 contain possible values of the inputs, where each row is sorted in increasing order. The values shown are for illustration only—you can change them if you like. The goal of the exercise is to ask the user for any *two* of the five inputs. Then the application should find the minimum and maximum values for these two inputs from the corresponding 18–22 rows, substitute each combination (min of first and min of second, min of first and max of second, max of first and min of second, and max of first and max of

Figure 6.1 Setup for Exercise

	A	B	C	D	E	F	G	H	I	J	K	L
1	Calculating the net present value of a stream of cash flows											
2												
3	Inputs											
4	1. Cash outflow, beginning of year 1	$40,000										
5	2. Cash inflow, end of year 1	$12,000										
6	3. Pct increase in cash inflow per year	12%										
7	4. Number of years of cash inflows	10										
8	5. Discount rate	16%										
9												
10	Model of cash inflows (all occur at the ends of years)											
11	Year	1	2	3	4	5	6	7	8	9	10	
12	Cash inflow	$12,000	$13,440	$15,053	$16,859	$18,882	$21,148	$23,686	$26,528	$29,712	$33,277	
13												
14	Net present value (NPV)	$48,787		Note that the values in each of rows 18-22 are in increasing order, so that the minimum value is at the left and the maximum value is at the right. Even if more values are added, you can assume that they will always be placed in increasing order.								
15												
16	Possible values of the inputs to test											
17												
18	1. Cash outflow, beginning of year 1	$10,000	$15,000	$20,000	$25,000	$30,000	$35,000	$40,000				
19	2. Cash inflow, end of year 1	$4,000	$5,000	$6,000	$7,000	$8,000	$9,000	$10,000	$11,000	$12,000		
20	3. Pct increase in cash inflow per year	2%	3%	4%	5%	6%	7%	8%	9%	10%	11%	12%
21	4. Number of years of cash inflows	5	6	7	8	9	10					
22	5. Discount rate	8%	9%	10%	11%	12%	13%	14%	15%	16%		
23												
24	Sensitivity table (NPV for combinations of min and max of two selected inputs)											
25			NPV									

Figure 6.2 Completed Solution

	A	B	C	D	E	F	G	H	I	J	K	L
1	Calculating the net present value of a stream of cash flows											
2												
3	Inputs											
4	1. Cash outflow, beginning of year 1	$40,000										
5	2. Cash inflow, end of year 1	$12,000										
6	3. Pct increase in cash inflow per year	12%										
7	4. Number of years of cash inflows	10										
8	5. Discount rate	16%										
9												
10	Model of cash inflows (all occur at the ends of years)											
11	Year	1	2	3	4	5	6	7	8	9	10	
12	Cash inflow	$12,000	$13,440	$15,053	$16,859	$18,882	$21,148	$23,686	$26,528	$29,712	$33,277	
13												
14	Net present value (NPV)	$48,787		Note that the values in each of rows 18-22 are in increasing order, so that the minimum value is at the left and the maximum value is at the right. Even if more values are added, you can assume that they will always be placed in increasing order.								
15												
16	Possible values of the inputs to test											
17												
18	1. Cash outflow, beginning of year 1	$10,000	$15,000	$20,000	$25,000	$30,000	$35,000	$40,000				
19	2. Cash inflow, end of year 1	$4,000	$5,000	$6,000	$7,000	$8,000	$9,000	$10,000	$11,000	$12,000		
20	3. Pct increase in cash inflow per year	2%	3%	4%	5%	6%	7%	8%	9%	10%	11%	12%
21	4. Number of years of cash inflows	5	6	7	8	9	10					
22	5. Discount rate	8%	9%	10%	11%	12%	13%	14%	15%	16%		
23												
24	Sensitivity table (NPV for combinations of min and max of two selected inputs)											
25		Input 3	Input 5	NPV								
26		0.02	0.08	$47,074								
27		0.02	0.16	$22,029								
28		0.12	0.08	$91,583								
29		0.12	0.16	$48,787								

second) in the appropriate cells in the B4:B8 range and report the input values and corresponding NPVs in a table, starting in row 25. As an example, if the user selects inputs 3 and 5, the final result should appear as in Figure 6.2. Note that the values for the third input go from 2% to 12%, whereas the values for the fifth input go from 8% to 16%. Of course, these limits could change if the values in rows 18–22 are changed. The VBA should be written to respond correctly, regardless of the values in rows 18–22 (assuming they are always listed in increasing order from left to right).

Figure 6.2 is taken from the file **Calculate NPV Finished.xlsm**. You can open this file and click on the Run Sensitivity Analysis button to see in more detail how the application should work. (Don't forget to *enable* the macros when you open the file!) However, try not to look at the code in this file until you have tried to develop the application on your own, starting with the file **Calculate NPV.xlsx**. (For a more ambitious version, take a look at the file **Calculate NPV Finished with Loops.xlsm.**)

6.3 Important Properties and Methods of Ranges

This section lists several of the more important and frequently used properties and methods of **Range** objects. You can skim over it as a first reading, because it is primarily for reference. However, you should find this section useful as you work through the exercises and examples in this chapter and later chapters. Of course, you can find all of this information (and much more) online in the Object Browser.

Properties

The following properties of a Range object are listed alphabeticaly, not necessarily in order of their importance (or usefulness).

- **Address.** This property returns the address of a range as a string, such as "B2:C6".
- **Cells.** This returns a reference to a Range object and is often used to refer to a particular cell. For example, Range("A1:A10").Cells(3) refers to the third cell in the range, A3, whereas Range("A1:C10").Cells(3,2) refers to the cell in the third row and second column of the range, cell B3. If the range has multiple rows and columns, then it is customary to use two arguments in Cells, where the first is the row and the second is the column. However, if the range is only part of a single column or a single row, then a single argument of Cells suffices.

A technical note. There is one technical aspect of the Excel object model that should be discussed, at least once. Many objects, including the Range object, have *properties* that are in fact references to *objects* down the hierarchy. The Cells property is an example. If you look up the **Range** object in the Object Browser, you will indeed see that **Cells** is classified as a *property*. However, the purpose of this property is to return an *object*. For example, consider the code Range("A1:G10").Cells(3,5).Value. Cells(3,5) is a property of the Range("A1:G10") object, but it returns an *object*, the range (cell) E3. The Value property then returns the contents of cell E3. This distinction between objects and properties can be confusing, especially for beginners. Fortunately, it has little impact on you as you do your actual programming.

- **Column.** This returns the number of the first column in the range, where column A has number 1, column B has number 2, and so on.
- **CurrentRegion.** This returns a reference to a range bounded by any combination of blank rows and blank columns. For example, the CurrentRegion of cell A3 in Figure 6.2 is the range A3:B8. As another example, if the range consists of A1:B10 and C5:D8, then the current region is the smallest rectangular region enclosing all of this, A1:D10.[1]
- **EntireColumn.** This returns a reference to the range consisting of the entire column(s) in the range. For example, Range("A1:C3").EntireColumn returns the entire columns A, B, and C.
- **Font.** This returns a reference to the font of the range, and then the properties (such as Size, Name, Bold, Italic, and so on) of this font can be changed, as in Range("A1:D1").Font.Bold = True.
- **Formula.** This returns or sets the formula in the range as a string, such as "=SUM(A1:A10)". Note that it includes the equals sign.
- **FormulaR1C1.** This returns the formula in a range as a string in R1C1 (row-column) notation. This is particularly useful for formulas that are copied down or across. For example, suppose each cell in the range C3:C10 is the sum of the corresponding cells in columns A and B. For example, cell C3 is the sum of cells A3 and B3. Then the FormulaR1C1 property of the range C3:C10 is "=RC[-2]+RC[-1]". The R by itself means to stay in the *same* row. The [-2] and [-1] next to C reference two cells to the left and one cell to the left, respectively. To gain some experience with R1C1 notation, try the following. Enter some numbers in the range A1:D10 and calculate row sums and column sums with the SUM function in column E and row 11, respectively. Now click on the Office button, then Excel Options, and under the Formulas tab, check the **R1C1 reference** style option. (To get there in Excel 2003, use the **Tools → Options** menu item, and click on the General tab.) You might be surprised at how your formulas now appear.
- **HorizontalAlignment.** This returns the horizontal alignment of the cells in the range. The three possible values are **xlRight**, **xlLeft**, and **xlCenter**.
- **Interior.** This returns a reference to the interior of the cells in a range. It is often used to color the background of the cells, as in Range("A1").Interior.Color = vbRed. (This colors cell A1 red, because vbRed is a built-in constant that refers to red.)
- **Name.** This returns the name of the range (if any has been specified). If it is used in a line such as Range("B3:E20").Name = "Sales", it creates a range name for the specified range.
- **NumberFormat.** This returns the format code (as a string) for the range. This is usually used to specify the number format for a range, as in Range("C3:C10").NumberFormat = "#,##0.00". However, it is difficult to learn (or remember) these format codes, so you might try the following. Format a

---

[1]If you have ever used Excel's pivot tables, the CurrentRegion is how Excel guesses where your data set lives, assuming the cursor is somewhere within the data set. It returns the CurrentRegion of the cursor location. The same goes for the new Excel Tables in Excel 2007.

cell such as A1 manually in some way and then use the line Debug. Print Range ("A1").NumberFormat. This will print the number format of cell A1 to the Immediate Window of the VBE (which you can open, if it isn't already open, with Ctrl-g). You can then see the appropriate format code.

- **Offset.** This returns a reference relative to a range, where the range is usually a single cell. This property is *very* useful and is used constantly in the applications in later chapters. It is explained in more detail in the next section.
- **Row, EntireRow.** These are similar to the Column and EntireColumn properties.
- **Value.** This is usually used for a single-cell range, in which case it returns the value in the cell (which could be a label, a number, or the result of a formula). Note that the syntax Range("A1").Value can be shortened to Range("A1"). That is, if .Value is omitted, it is taken for granted. This is because the Value property is the **default property** of a Range object. I used to take frequent advantage of this shortcut. Now I try to remember to include .Value, even though it isn't necessary, because it makes the code more readable.

Methods

The following list, again shown in alphabetical order, indicates some of the more important methods of a Range object.

- **Clear.** This deletes everything from the range—the values *and* the formatting.
- **ClearContents.** This can be used instead of **Clear** to delete only the values (and formulas) and leave the formatting in place.
- **Copy.** This copies a range. It has a single (optional) argument named **Destination**, which is the paste range. For example, the line Range("A1:B10").Copy Destination:=Range("E1:F10") copies the range A1:B10 to the range E1:F10.
- **PasteSpecial.** This pastes the contents of the clipboard to the range according to various specifications spelled out by its arguments. A frequently used option is the following. Suppose you want to copy the range C3:D10, which contains formulas, to the range F3:G10 as *values*. The required code is as follows.

```
Range("C3:D10").Copy
Range("F3:G10").PasteSpecial Paste:=xlPasteValues
```

The Paste argument, which can be one of several built-in Excel constants, indicates *how* you want to paste the copy. (To appreciate how many ways you can "paste special," copy a range in Excel and then click on the Paste dropdown on the Home ribbon You'll see quite a few possibilities.)

- **Select.** This selects the range, which is equivalent to highlighting the range in Excel.
- **Sort.** This sorts the range. The specific way it sorts depends on the arguments used. For a typical example, suppose you want to sort the data set in Figure 6.3 (see Section 6.5) in ascending order on Score 2 (column C). The following line does the job. The **Key1** argument specifies which column to sort on, and

the **Header** argument specifies that there are column headings at the top of the range that should *not* be part of the sort.

```
Range("A1:F19").Sort Key1:=Range("C2"), Order1:=xlAscending, Header:=xlYes
```

The lists shown here indicate only a fraction of the properties and methods of the Range object, but they should suffice for most of your programming needs. If you want to learn more, or if you want to look up any specific property or method, the best way is to open the Object Browser in the VBE, select the Excel library, scroll down the left pane for the Range object, select any property or method in the right pane, and click on the question mark button for help.

6.4 Specifying Ranges with VBA

Once a range is referenced properly in VBA code, it is relatively easy to set (or return) properties of the range or use methods of the range. In my experience, the hard part is usually referencing the range in the first place. Part of the reason is that there are so many ways to do it. This section describes the basic syntax for several of these methods, and the next section presents a number of small subs that implement the methods. Like the previous section, the material here is mostly for reference. However, keep the exercise in Section 6.2 in mind as you read this section and the next. You will need to implement some of these ideas to do the exercise.

The most common ways to reference a range are as follows:

- **Use an address.** Follow Range with an address in double quotes, such as Range("A1") or Range("A1:B10").
- **Use a range name.** Follow Range with the name of a range in double quotes, such as Range("Sales"). This assumes there is a range with the name Sales in the active workbook.
- **Use a variable for a range name.** Declare a string variable, such as salesName, and set it equal to the name of the range. This would be done with a line such as

```
salesName = Range("Sales").Name
```

Then follow Range with this variable, as in Range(salesName). Note that there are now no double quotes. They are essentially included in the variable salesName (because it is a string variable).

- **Use a Range object variable.** Declare a variable, such as salesRange, as a Range *object* and define it with the keyword **Set**. This can be done with the following two lines:

```
Dim salesRange as Range
Set salesRange = Range("Sales")
```

Then simply refer to salesRange from then on. For example, to change the font size of the range, you could write salesRange.Font = 12. This use of a Range object variable is the favorite of most experienced programmers. It also has a big advantage: When you type an object variable and then follow it with a period, you are assured of getting help with Intellisense. Once you get used to Intellisense, you will really miss it when it doesn't appear–which *does* happen in some cases. So in this edition, I use object variables even more than in the previous editions.

- **Use the Cells property.** Follow Range with the **Cells** property, which takes one or two arguments. For example,

```
Range("B5:B14").Cells(3)
```

refers to the third cell in the range B5:B14—that is, cell B7. In contrast,

```
Range("C5:E15").Cells(4,2)
```

refers to the cell in the fourth row and second column of the range C5:E15—that is, cell D8. In the first case, B5:B14 is a single-column range, so it suffices to use a single argument for the Cells property. (The same is true for a single-row range.) However, in the second case, where C5:E15 spans multiple rows and columns, it is more natural to use two arguments for the Cells property. The first argument refers to the row, the second to the column.

- **Use the Offset property.** Follow Range with the **Offset** property, which takes two arguments. For example, the reference

```
Range("A5").Offset(2,3)
```

says to start in cell A5, then go 2 rows down and 3 columns to the right. This takes you to cell D7. The first argument of Offset indicates the *row* offset. Use a positive offset to go down and a negative offset to go up. The second argument indicates the *column* offset. Use a positive offset to go to the right and a negative offset to go to the left. Either argument can be 0, as in

```
Range("A5").Offset(0,3)
```

This refers to cell D5. As you'll see in later chapters, the Offset property is my favorite. I use it all the time.

- **Use top left and bottom right arguments.** Follow Range with two arguments, a top left cell and a bottom right cell, separated by commas. This corresponds to the way you often select a range in Excel. You click on the top left cell, hold down the Shift key, and click on the bottom right cell. For example,

```
Range(Range("C1"),Range("D10"))
```

returns the range C1:D10. Another example, which uses a With construction to save typing, is as follows:

```
With Range("A1")
  Range(.Offset(1, 1), .Offset(3, 3)).Select
End With
```

This code selects the range B2:D4. The top left cell is the cell offset by 1 row and 1 column from A1, namely, B2. Similarly, the bottom right cell is the cell offset by 3 rows and 3 columns from A1, namely, D4. Note, for example, that Offset(1,1). is equivalent to Range("A1").Offset(1,1) because it is inside the With construction.

- **Use the End property.** You have probably used the **End-Arrow** key combination to select ranges in Excel, particularly if they are large ranges. For example, if the range A1:M100 is filled with values and you want to select it, click on cell A1, hold down the Shift key, then press the End and down arrow keys in succession, and finally press the End and right arrow keys in succession. It beats scrolling! The question is how to do this in VBA. It is easy once you know the **End** property. This takes one argument to determine the direction. It can be any of the built-in constants **xlDown**, **xlUp**, **xlToRight**, or **xlToLeft**. The following example is typical, where we assume there is a data set starting in cell A1 that we want to select:

```
With Range("A1")
  Range(.Offset(0,0), .End(xlDown).End(xlToRight)).Select
End With
```

The middle line selects a range that is specified by a top left cell and a bottom right cell. The first argument, .Offset(0,0), which is equivalent to Range("A1"). Offset (0,0) because it is inside a With, is simply cell A1. The second argument, .End(xlDown).End(xlToRight), which is equivalent to Range("A1").End(xlDown).End (xlToRight) because it is inside a With, is at the bottom right of the rectangular range that begins up in cell A1. The advantage of using the End property is that you do not need to know the *size* of the range. The above code specifies the correct range regardless of whether the data set range is A1:B10 or A1:M500.

To use the End property correctly in VBA, you have to understand exactly how the End-Arrow key combinations work in Excel. Depending on the position of blank cells in your worksheet, it is easy to make mistakes. See the file **Using End-Down Correctly.xlsm** for an illustration of the pitfalls you might experience. They are fairly easy to avoid if you know how to recognize them.

Figure 6.3 Employee Performance Scores

	A	B	C	D	E	F	G	H	I	J	K
1	Employee	Score1	Score2	Score3	Score4	Score5		Some extra junk might be over here.			
2	1	90	87	76	95	86					
3	2	78	90	99	84	84					
4	3	72	60	84	58	69					
5	4	82	66	81	69	72					
6	5	95	85	82	77	93					
7	6	90	93	66	88	93					
8	7	90	100	57	70	89					
9	8	90	98	61	56	83					
10	9	96	67	85	56	97					
11	10	87	69	77	78	76					
12	11	81	68	61	66	93					
13	12	58	57	72	75	77					
14	13	70	92	59	99	85					
15	14	69	71	89	68	72					
16	15	85	94	66	78	67					
17	16	55	79	99	98	76					
18	17	60	75	63	67	90					
19	18	83	93	88	58	56					
20											
21	Some extra junk might be down here.										

6.5 Examples of Ranges with VBA

It is one thing to know the information in the previous two sections in an abstract sense. It is another to use this information correctly to perform useful tasks. This section presents a number of small subs for illustration. (All of these subs are listed in Module1 of the file **Ranges.xlsm**.) When presenting example subs that actually *do* something, it is always difficult to avoid aspects of VBA that have not yet been covered. Whenever this occurs, there is a brief explanation of anything new.

Watching Your Subs Run

It is very informative to run these subs and watch what they do. Here is a useful strategy. First, make sure that only Excel and the VBE are open. (No other program icons should appear on your taskbar at the bottom of the screen.) Then right-click on any blank gray part of this taskbar to bring up a menu, and select **Tile Windows Vertically**. You should see the VBE code on one side and the Excel worksheet on the other. Next, put your cursor anywhere within a sub you want to run, and press the **F8** key repeatedly. This steps through your sub one line at a time. By having the Excel window visible, you can immediately see the effect of each line of code.

The Data Set

Most of the examples in this section are based on a small database of performance scores on various activities for a company's employees. These data are in the **Ranges.xlsm** file and are listed in Figure 6.3. The subs in this section all do something with this data set—perhaps nothing earthshaking, but illustrative of the methods you can use to work with ranges.[2] (The labels in cells A21 and H1 are used only to indicate that the data set is separated by a blank row and a blank column from other data that might be on the worksheet.)

EXAMPLE 6.1 Using Addresses

The **Range1** sub refers to ranges by their literal addresses. This is the easiest way to go if you know that the location and size of a data range are not going to change. For several ranges, this sub displays the address of the range in a message box by using the **Address** property of a **Range** object. For example, the line

```
MsgBox Range("A2:A19").Address
```

displays the address of the range "A2:F19" in a message box.

```
Sub Range1()
    ' This sub refers to ranges literally. It would be used if you
    ' know the size of a data range is not going to change.
    MsgBox Range("A1").Address
    MsgBox Range("B1:F1").Address
    MsgBox Range("A2:A19").Address
    MsgBox Range("B2:F19").Address

    ' The following two lines are equivalent because the Value property is the default
    ' property of a Range object. Note how string concatenation is used in the message.
    MsgBox "The first score for the first employee is " & Range("B2").Value
    MsgBox "The first score for the first employee is " & Range("B2")
End Sub
```

Toward the end of this sub, note how .Value can be used but is not necessary. Many programmers tend to take advantage of this shortcut. I try to avoid it for two reasons. First, your code is more self-explanatory if you include all properties explicitly, including default properties. Second, if you move from VBA to Microsoft's newer programming language, VB.NET, you will find that there are no default properties; you are *required* to include all properties explicitly.

EXAMPLE 6.2 Creating and Deleting Range Names

The **Range2** sub first uses the **Name** property of a **Range** object to create several range names. Then to restore the workbook to its original condition, which is done for illustration purposes only, these range names are deleted. To delete a

---

[2]Many of my former students e-mail me about tasks they would like to automate with VBA in their jobs. I find that most of these tasks are rather mundane, but if VBA can help them do their jobs more efficiently, it is certainly worth the effort to write the programs.

range name, you first set a reference to a particular name in the **Names** collection of the ActiveWorkbook. Then you use the **Delete** method.

```
Sub Range2()
    ' This sub creates range names for various ranges, again assuming the data
    ' range is not going to change.
    Range("B1:F1").Name = "ScoreNames"
    Range("A2:A19").Name = "EmployeeNumbers"
    Range("B2:F19").Name = "ScoreData"
    MsgBox "Names have been created.", vbInformation

    ' Delete these range names if you don't really want them.
    ActiveWorkbook.Names("ScoreNames").Delete
    ActiveWorkbook.Names("EmployeeNumbers").Delete
    ActiveWorkbook.Names("ScoreData").Delete
    MsgBox "Names have been deleted.", vbInformation

    ' Alternatively, delete them all at once with the following lines.
    Dim nm As Object
    For Each nm In ActiveWorkbook.Names
        nm.Delete
    Next
End Sub
```

If there were, say, 50 names in the Names collection, it would be tedious to write 50 similar lines of code to delete each one. The **For Each** construction at the bottom of the sub illustrates a much quicker way. For Each loops are not discussed formally until the next chapter, but you can probably see what this one is doing. It goes through each member of the Names collection, using a generic variable name nm for a typical member. Then nm.Delete deletes this range name from the collection.

EXAMPLE 6.3 Formatting Ranges

The **Range3** sub first names a range, then it uses the range name to turn the **Bold** property of the font of this range to True. For illustration (and to restore the sheet to its original condition), it then sets the Bold property to False. Note that the Bold property of a Font object is one of many **Boolean** properties in Excel. A Boolean property has only two possible values: True and False.

```
Sub Range3()
    ' If a range has a range name, you can refer to it by its name.
    Range("B2:F19").Name = "ScoreData"
    Range("ScoreData").Font.Bold = True
    MsgBox "The ScoreData range has been boldfaced."

    ' Now turn bold off, and delete the range name.
    Range("ScoreData").Font.Bold = False
    ActiveWorkbook.Names("ScoreData").Delete
End Sub
```

Note the object hierarchy in the line

```
Range("ScoreData").Font.Bold = True
```

Each **Range** object has a **Font** object down the hierarchy from it, and the **Font** object then has a **Bold** property. This line shows the proper syntax for referring to this property.

EXAMPLE 6.4   Using a String Variable for a Range Name

The **Range4** sub is almost identical to the **Range3** sub, except that it uses the string variable rngName to capture and then use the name of a range.

```
Sub Range4()
' This is the same as the previous sub except that the range name has been
' stored in the string variable rngName. Note the lack of double quotes except in
' the line defining rngName. Being a string variable, rngName essentially includes
' the double quotes, so they aren't needed later on.
Dim rngName As String
rngName = "ScoreData"
Range("B2:F19").Name = rngName
Range(rngName).Font.Bold = True
MsgBox "The ScoreData range has been boldfaced."

' Now turn bold off, and delete the range name.
Range(rngName).Font.Bold = False
ActiveWorkbook.Names(rngName).Delete
End Sub
```

Note the lack of double quotes around rngName in the line

```
Range(rngName).Font.Bold = True
```

Because rngName is a string variable, it essentially includes the double quotes, so they shouldn't entered in the code.

EXAMPLE 6.5   Using the Cells Property and the Top Left, Bottom Right Combination

The **Range5** sub refers to ranges with the **Cells** property. Remember that if the Cells property uses two arguments, the first refers to the row and the second to the column. This sub also shows how to refer to a range by its top left and bottom right cells. As explained in the comments, a With construction can be used to save typing.

```
Sub Range5()
    ' This sub illustrates another way to refer to a range: with the Cells property.
    Range("B2:F19").Name = "ScoreData"

    ' The following displays the address of the 2nd row, 3rd column cell of the
    ' ScoreData range. (This is cell D3.)
    MsgBox Range("ScoreData").Cells(2, 3).Address

    ' The following shows how to specify a range in the format
    ' Range(TopLeft,BottomRight)
    ' where TopLeft refers to the top left cell in the range, BottomRight refers to
    ' the bottom right cell in the range. The top left in the following is cell C3,
    ' the bottom right is cell E4.
    MsgBox Range(Range("ScoreData").Cells(2, 2), Range("ScoreData").Cells(3, 4)).Address

    ' This is cumbersome (having to spell out Range("ScoreData") twice).
    ' The following With construction is equivalent but simpler.
    With Range("ScoreData")
        MsgBox Range(.Cells(2, 2), .Cells(3, 4)).Address
    End With

    ' An alternative (the preferred method of professional programmers) is to Set a
    ' range object variable first, then refer to it, as follows.
    Dim scoreRange As Range
    Set scoreRange = Range("ScoreData")
    With scoreRange
        MsgBox Range(.Cells(2, 2), .Cells(3, 4)).Address
    End With
End Sub
```

EXAMPLE 6.6   Using the End Property and the Offset Property

The **Range6** sub uses the **End** property to specify the bottom right cell of a range that might expand or contract as data are added to, or deleted from, a worksheet. It also uses the **Offset** property as a convenient way to specify other ranges relative to some "anchor" cell. In the middle of the sub, the **Count** property of the **Columns** collection is used to count the columns in a range. Similarly, .Rows.Count counts the rows. Finally, note how string concatenation is used in the MsgBox statements.

```
Sub Range6()
    ' Up to now, we have made the implicit assumption that the range of the data will
    ' not change, so that we can refer to it literally (e.g., B2:F19). But a more general
    ' approach is to assume the number of rows and/or columns could change. This sub
    ' shows how to find the range. Think of the With Range("A1") statement as setting
    ' an "anchor" that everything else is offset relative to.
    With Range("A1")
        Range(.Offset(0, 1), .End(xlToRight)).Name = "ScoreNames"
        Range(.Offset(1, 0), .End(xlDown)).Name = "EmployeeNumbers"
        Range(.Offset(1, 1), .End(xlDown).End(xlToRight)).Name = "ScoreData"
    End With

    ' Alternatively, we could first find the number of columns and the number of rows
    ' in the data set, then use these.
```

```
        Dim nScores As Integer, nEmployees As Integer
        With Range("A1")
            nScores = Range(.Offset(0, 1), .End(xlToRight)).Columns.Count
            MsgBox "There are " & nScores & " scores for each employee.", vbInformation, _
                "Number of scores"
            nEmployees = Range(.Offset(1, 0), .End(xlDown)).Rows.Count
            MsgBox "There are " & nEmployees & " employees in the data set.", _
                vbInformation, "Number of employees"

            ' Now (just for variety) include row 1, column A in the range.
            Range(.Offset(0, 0), .Offset(nEmployees, nScores)).Name = "EntireDataSet"
            MsgBox "The entire data set is in the range " & Range("EntireDataSet").Address, _
                vbInformation, "Data set address"
        End With

        ' Delete all range names.
        Dim nm As Object
        For Each nm In ActiveWorkbook.Names
            nm.Delete
        Next
    End Sub
```

EXAMPLE 6.7 Referring to Rows and Columns

It is often necessary to refer to a row or column of a range. It might also be necessary to refer to an *entire* row or column, as you do when you click on a row number of a column label in the margin of a worksheet. The **Range7** sub shows how to do either. For example, .Rows(12) refers to the 12th row of a range, whereas .Columns(4).EntireColumn refers to the entire column corresponding to the 4th column in the range (in this case, column D). The end of this sub indicates that you cannot refer to multiple columns with numbers, such as Columns("4:5"). However, it is possible to refer to a *single* column with a number, such as Columns(4).

```
Sub Range7()
    ' This sub shows how to select rows or columns
    With Range("A1:F19")
        .Rows(12).Select
        MsgBox "12th row of data range has been selected."
        .Rows(12).EntireRow.Select
        MsgBox "Entire 12th row has been selected."
        .Columns(4).Select
        MsgBox "4th column of data range has been selected."
        .Columns(4).EntireColumn.Select
        MsgBox "Entire 4th column has been selected."
    End With
    Rows("4:5").Select
    MsgBox "Another way to select rows."
    Columns("D:E").Select
    MsgBox "Another way to select columns."

    ' The following line does NOT work – it produces an error.
    ' Columns("4:5").Select
End Sub
```

EXAMPLE 6.8   Formatting Cells in a Range

One of the most useful things you can do with VBA is format cells in a range. The **Range8** sub illustrates how to apply various formats to a range. Note in particular the **ColorIndex** property of the **Font** or the **Interior** of a Range. The integer value of ColorIndex indicates the color. For example, 1 is black, 3 is red, and 5 is blue. (To learn more about these obscure numbers open my file **ColorIndex, Color Lists. xlsm** on the CD-ROM.) By the way, to confuse the coloring issue a bit more, there is also a **Color** property. Its possible values are a set of eight built-in VB constants vbRed, vbBlue, vbYellow, vbBlack, vbGreen, vbMagenta, vbWhite, and vbCyan. Thus, you can set the ColorIndex property to 3 or the Color property to vbRed; each has exactly the same effect. The advantage of ColorIndex is that there are many more than eight color choices. (Excel 2007 provides still one more way of coloring, with its **TintAndShade** property. You typically see it when you record code.)

This is a particularly good example for tiling the Excel and VBE windows vertically and then stepping through the code one line at a time (with the F8 key). You can then see the code in one window and the effect of the formatting in the other window.

```
Sub Range8()
    ' Here are some common ways to format data in ranges.
    With Range("A1")
        Range(.Offset(0, 1), .End(xlToRight)).Name = "ScoreNames"
        Range(.Offset(1, 0), .End(xlDown)).Name = "EmployeeNumbers"
        Range(.Offset(1, 1), .End(xlDown).End(xlToRight)).Name = "ScoreData"
    End With

    ' Do some formatting.
    With Range("ScoreNames")
        .HorizontalAlignment = xlRight
        With .Font
            .Bold = True
            .ColorIndex = 3 ' 3 is red.
            .Size = 16
        End With
        .EntireColumn.AutoFit
    End With
    With Range("EmployeeNumbers").Font
        .Italic = True
        .ColorIndex = 5 ' 5 is blue.
        .Size = 12
    End With
    With Range("ScoreData")
        .Interior.ColorIndex = 15 ' 15 is light gray.
        .Font.Name = "Times Roman"
        .NumberFormat = "0.0"
    End With
    MsgBox "Formatting has been applied"

    ' Restore the original style. ("Normal" is a name for the default style.)
    Range("ScoreNames").Style = "Normal"
    Range("EmployeeNumbers").Style = "Normal"
    Range("ScoreData").Style = "Normal"
```

```
    MsgBox "Original formatting restored"
    ' Apply an autoformat (you can pick from many choices).
    With Range("A1")
        Range(.Offset(0, 0), .End(xlDown).End(xlToRight)) _
            .AutoFormat xlRangeAutoFormatClassic3
    End With
    MsgBox "Classic 3 autoformatting has been applied."
    ' Restore the original style.
    Range("A1").Style = "Normal"
    Range("ScoreNames").Style = "Normal"
    Range("EmployeeNumbers").Style = "Normal"
    Range("ScoreData").Style = "Normal"
    MsgBox "Original formatting restored"
End Sub
```

EXAMPLE 6.9   Entering Formulas

The **Range9** sub illustrates how to enter formulas in cells with VBA. There are two properties you can use: the **Formula** property and the **FormulaR1C1** property. The **Formula** property requires a string that matches what you would type if you were entering the formula directly into Excel. For example, to enter the formula **=Average(Score1)**, you set the Formula property equal to the string "=Average(Score1)".

The **FormulaR1C1** property is harder to learn, but it is sometimes more natural given how relative addresses work in Excel. For example, suppose you have two columns of numbers and you want to form a third column to their right where each cell in this third column is the sum of the two numbers to its left. You would then set the FormulaR1C1 property of this range equal to "=Sum(RC[-2]:RC[-1])". The R with no brackets next to it means to stay in the *same* row. The C with brackets next to it means, in this case, to go from 2 columns to the left to 1 column to the left. That is, using square brackets is equivalent to relative addressing in Excel. (Remember that for rows, plus means down, minus means up. For columns, plus means to the right, minus means to the left.) If you want absolute address in R1C1 notation, you omit the square brackets and use numbers to refer to rows and columns. For example, R2C4 is equivalent to $D$2.

Note that this sub uses a couple of **For** loops in the middle. For loops are discussed in detail in the next chapter. All you need to know here is that the variable i goes from 1 to the number of scores. First, it is 1, then 2, then 3, and so on. You should study this sub carefully. It is probably the most difficult example so far. Also, it is another excellent candidate for tiling the Excel and VBE windows vertically and then using the F8 key to step through the code one line at a time.

```
Sub Range9()
    ' This sub shows how to enter formulas in cells. You do this with the Formula
    ' property or the FormulaR1C1 property of a range. Either property takes a
    ' string value that must start with an equals sign, just as you enter a formula
```

```
' in Excel. First, I'll name a range for each column of scores, then use the
' Formula property to get the average of each column right below the scores in
' that column.
Dim nScores As Integer, nEmployees As Integer, i As Integer

' Determine the number of score columns and the number of employees. Then name
' the score ranges Score1, Score2, etc.
With Range("A1")
    nScores = Range(.Offset(0, 1), .End(xlToRight)).Columns.Count
    nEmployees = Range(.Offset(1, 0), .End(xlDown)).Rows.Count
    For i = 1 To nScores
        Range(.Offset(1, i), .Offset(1, i).End(xlDown)).Name = "Score" & i
    Next
End With

' For each score column, enter the average formula just below the last score.
' Note how string concatenation is used. For i = 1, for example, the string on
' the right will be "=Average(Score1)".
For i = 1 To nScores
    Range("A1").Offset(nEmployees + 1, i).Formula = "=Average(Score" & i & ")"
Next

' Now use the FormulaR1C1 property to find the average score for each employee.
' Note how each cell in the column of averages has the SAME formula in R1C1
' notation. It is the average of the range from nScores cells to the left to 1
' cell to the left. For example, if nScores is 4, this is RC[-4]:RC[-1]. The
' lack of brackets next to R mean that these scores all come from the same row
' as the cell where the formula is being placed.
With Range("A1").Offset(0, nScores + 1)
    Range(.Offset(1, 0), .Offset(nEmployees, 0)).FormulaR1C1 = _
        "=Average(RC[-" & nScores & "]:RC[-1])"
End With
End Sub
```

If you want to enter a formula in a cell through VBA, it seems natural to use the Formula (or FormulaR1C1) property. However, the following two lines have exactly the same effect—they both enter a formula into a cell:

```
Range("C1").Formula = "=SUM(A1:B1)"
Range("C2").Value = "=SUM(A1:B1)"
```

Given that this is true (and you can check it yourself), why bother with the Formula property at all? The only time it makes a difference is if you *read* the property in VBA. In the above lines, I've *written* the Formula or Value properties, that is, I have specified the values for these properties. But suppose I enter the following two lines after the above two lines:

```
MsgBox Range("C1").Formula
MsgBox Range("C2").Value
```

The first will return =SUM(A1:B1), and the second will return 10 (assuming A1 and B1 each contain 5). Here, I am *reading* the properties, and here it makes a difference.

Another related property of a range is the Text property. It is very similar to the Value property. Let's say cell D1 is the average of several values, and this average turns out to be 38.33333... However, you format cell D1 to have only two decimals. Then the following two lines will return 38.33333... and 38.33, respectively. In words, the Text property returns what you see in the cell after formatting.

```
MsgBox Range("D1").Value
MsgBox Range("D2").Text
```

By the way, Text is a *read only* property. If you try to use it to *write* a value to a range, you'll get an error. For example, the following line will *not* work. You would have to use the Value property instead.

```
Range("A1").Text = "Sales"
```

EXAMPLE 6.10 Referring to Other Range Objects

The **Range10** sub introduces the **CurrentRegion** and **UsedRange** properties, as explained in the comments. It also demonstrates how to refer to a **Union** of possibly noncontiguous ranges. Finally, it illustrates the **Areas** property of a range. Of all these properties, CurrentRegion is probably the one you're most likely to use in your own programs.

```
Sub Range10()
    ' Here are some other useful range properties. The CurrentRegion and UsedRange
    ' properties are rectangular ranges. The former is the range "surrounding" a
    ' given range. The latter is a property of a worksheet. It indicates the smallest
    ' rectangular range containing all nonempty cells.
    MsgBox "The range holding the dataset is " & Range("A1").CurrentRegion.Address, _
        vbInformation, "Current region"
    MsgBox "The range holding everything is " & ActiveSheet.UsedRange.Address, _
        vbInformation, "Used range"

    ' It is sometimes useful to take the union of ranges that are not necessarily
    ' contiguous.
    Dim UnionRange As Range
    Set UnionRange = Union(Range("A1").CurrentRegion, Range("A21"), Range("H1"))
    With UnionRange
        .Name = "UnionOfRanges"
        MsgBox "The address of the union is " & .Address, vbInformation, _
            "Address of union"
        ' The Areas property returns the "pieces" in the union.
        MsgBox "The union is composed of " & .Areas.Count & " distinct areas.", _
            vbInformation, "Number of areas"
    End With
End Sub
```

6.6 Summary

The examples in this chapter present a lot of material, more than you can probably digest on first reading. However, they give you the clues you need to complete Exercise 6.1 and to understand the applications in later chapters. Indeed, you can feel free to borrow any parts of these examples for your own work, either for the exercise or for later development projects. As stated in the introduction, most of the operations you perform in Excel are done with ranges, and my primary objective in this book is to show you how to perform these operations with VBA. Therefore, I expect that you will frequently revisit the examples in this chapter as you attempt to manipulate ranges in your own VBA programs.

EXERCISES

1. The file **Employee Scores.xlsx** contains the same data set as in the **Ranges.xlsm** file (the file that was used for the examples in Section 6.5). However, the VBA code has been deleted. Also, there is now a heading in cell A1, and the data set begins in row 3. Save a copy of this file as **Employee Scores 1.xlsx** and work with the copy to do the following with VBA. (Place the code for all of the parts in a single sub.)
   a. Boldface the font of the label in cell A1, and change its font size to 14.
   b. Boldface and italicize the headings in row 3, and change their horizontal alignment to the right.
   c. Change the color of the font for the employee numbers in column A to blue.
   d. Change the background (the Interior property) of the range with scores to light gray.
   e. Enter the label Averages in cell A22 and boldface it.
   f. Enter a formula in cell B22 that averages the scores above it. Copy this formula to the range C22:F22.
2. Repeat the previous exercise, starting with a fresh copy, **Employee Scores 2.xlsx**, of the original **Employee Scores.xlsx** file. Now, however, begin by using VBA to name the following ranges with the range names specified: cell A1 as title, the headings in row 3 as headings, the employee numbers in column A as empNumbers, and the range of scores as scores. Refer to these range names as you do parts **a–f**.
3. Repeat Exercise 1 once more, starting with a fresh copy, **Employee Scores 3.xlsx**, of the original **Employee Scores.xlsx** file. Instead of naming ranges as in Exercise 2, declare Range object variables called titleCell, headingRange, empNumbersRange, and scoresRange, and "Set" them to the ranges described in Exercise 2. Refer to these object variables as you do parts **a–f**.
4. Repeat the previous three exercises. However, write your code so that it will work even if more data are added to the data set—new scores, new employees, or both. Try your programs on the original data. Add an extra column of scores and some extra employees, and see if it still works properly.

5. Write a reference (in VBA code) to each of the following ranges. (You can assume that each of these ranges is in the active worksheet of the active workbook, so that you don't have to qualify the references by worksheet or workbook.)
   a. The third cell of the range A1:A10.
   b. The cell at the intersection of the 24th row and 10th column of the range A1: Z500.
   c. The cell at the intersection of the 24th row and 10th column of a range that has the range name Sales.
   d. The cell at the intersection of the 24th row and 10th column of a range that has been "set" to the Range object variable salesRange.
   e. The entire column corresponding to cell D7.
   f. The set of entire columns from column D through column K.
   g. A range of employee names, assuming the first is in cell A3 and they extend down column A (although you don't know how many there are).
   h. A range of sales figures in a rectangular block, assuming that Region labels are to their left in column A (starting in cell A4) and Month labels are above them in row 3 (starting in cell B3). You don't know how many regions or months there are, and you want the range to include only the sales figures, not the labels.
   i. The cell that is 2 rows down from and 5 columns to the right of the active cell. (The active cell is where the cursor is. It can always be referred to in VBA as ActiveCell.)

6. The file **Product Sales.xlsx** has sales totals for 12 months and 10 different products in the range B4:M13. Write a VBA sub to enter formulas for the totals in column N and row 14. Use the **FormulaR1C1** property to do so. (You should set this property for two ranges: the one in column N and the one in row 14.)

7. Repeat the previous exercise, but now assume the data set could change, either by adding more months, more products, or both. Using the **FormulaR1C1** property, fill the row below the data and the column to the right of the data with formulas for totals. (*Hint*: First find the number of months and the number of products, and store these numbers in variables. Then use string concatenation to build a string for each FormulaR1C1 property. Refer to the **Range9** sub in the **Ranges.xlsm** file for a similar formula.)

8. Do the previous two exercises by using the **Formula** property rather than the **FormulaR1C1** property. (*Hint*: Enter a formula in cell N4 and then use the Copy method to copy down. Proceed similarly in row 14. Do *not* use any loops.)

9. The file **Exam Scores.xlsx** has four exam scores, in columns B through E, for each of the students listed in column A.
   a. Write a VBA sub that sorts the scores in increasing order on exam 3.
   b. (More difficult, requires an If statement, can be postponed until after reading Chapter 7.) Repeat part **a**, but now give the user some choices. Specifically, write a VBA sub that (1) uses an input box to ask for an exam from 1 to 4, (2) uses an input box to ask whether the user wants to sort scores in ascending or descending order (you can ask the user to enter A or D), and (3) sorts the data on the exam requested and the order requested. Make sure the headings in row 3 are *not* sorted.

7

Control Logic and Loops

7.1 Introduction

All programming languages contain logical constructions for controlling the sequence of statements through a program, and VBA is no exception. This chapter describes the two constructions used most often: the **If** and **Case** constructions. The If construction has already been used informally in previous chapters—it is practically impossible to avoid in any but the most trivial programs—but this chapter discusses it in more detail. The Case construction is an attractive alternative to a complex If construction when each of several cases requires its own code.

This chapter also discusses the extremely important concept of loops. Have you ever had to stuff hundreds of envelopes? If you have ever had to perform this or any similar mind-numbing task over and over, you will appreciate loops. Perhaps the single most useful feature of computer programs is their ability to loop, that is, to repeat the same type of task any number of times—10 times, 100 times, even 10,000 or more times. All programming languages have this looping ability, the only difference among them being the way they implement looping. VBA does it with **For** loops, **For Each** loops, and **Do** loops, as this chapter illustrates. Fortunately, it is quite easy. It is amazing how much work you can make the computer perform by writing just a few lines of code.

The material in this chapter represents essential elements of almost all programming languages, including VBA. Without control logic and loops, computer programs would lose much of their power. Therefore, it is extremely important that you master the material in this chapter. You will get a chance to do this with the exercise in the next section and the programming exercises at the end of the chapter. Beyond this, you will continue to see control logic and loops in virtually all later chapters.

7.2 Exercise

The following exercise is typical in its need for control logic and loops. You can keep it in mind as you read through this chapter. It is not too difficult, but it will keep you busy for a while. Even more important, it will give you that wonderful feeling of accomplishment once you solve it. It is a great example of the power of the tools in this chapter.

Figure 7.1 Template for Record Highs and Lows for Wal-Mart

	A	B	C	D	E	F	G	H	I
1	Adjusted closing prices			Record values from 1998 on, based on data back through 1992					
2	Date	WMT		Date	Price	High or Low			
3	Oct-92	13.28							
4	Nov-92	14.04							
5	Dec-92	13.98							
6	Jan-93	14.22							
189	Apr-08	57.50							
190	May-08	57.51							
191	Jun-08	55.97							
192	Jul-08	58.38							
193	Aug-08	59.07							
194	Sep-08	59.89							

Exercise 7.1 Finding Record Highs and Lows for Stock Prices

The file **Records.xlsx** contains two worksheets. The Prices sheet contains monthly adjusted closing prices (adjusted for dividends and stock splits) for several large companies from October 1992 until the September 2008. The Records sheet is a template for calculating the record highs and lows for any one of these companies. It is shown in Figure 7.1 (with a number of hidden rows). The Wal-Mart prices in column B have been copied from the WMT column of the Prices sheet.

The purpose of the exercise is to scan column B from top to bottom. If you see a price that is higher than any price so far, then it is called a "record high." Similarly, if a price is lower than any price so far, then it is called a "record low." The objective is to find each record high and record low that occurs from January 1998 on and record these record highs and lows in columns D, E, and F. Column D records the date, column E records the price, and column F records whether it is a record high or low. Note that the record highs and lows are based on the data from October 1992 through December 1997, as well as more recent dates. For example, for a price in March 2001 to be a record high, it must beat all prices from October 1992 through February 2001. You simply do not tabulate record highs and lows before 1998.

The file **Records Finished 1.xlsm** contains the finished application. You can open it, copy (manually) any stock's price data from the Prices sheet to the Records sheet, and then click on the button. Figures 7.2 and 7.3 indicate the results you should obtain for Wal-Mart. The message box in Figure 7.2 summarizes the results, whereas columns D, E, and F show the details of the record prices. Feel free to run the program on other stocks' prices, but do *not* look at the VBA code in the file until you have given it your best effort.

If you like, you can extend this exercise in a natural direction. Modify your code so that there is now a loop over all stocks in the Prices sheet. For each stock, your modified program should copy the prices from the Prices sheet to the Records sheet and *then* continue as in the first part of the exercise. Essentially, the code from the first part of the exercise should be placed inside a loop on the stocks. The finished version of this part of the exercise is in the file **Records Finished 2.xlsm**. Again, feel free to open the file and click on the button to see the results you should

Figure 7.2 Summary of Results

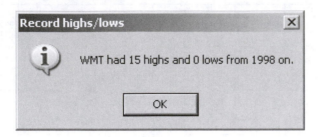

Figure 7.3 Detailed Results

	A	B	C	D	E	F	G	H	I	J	K	L
1	Adjusted closing prices			Record values from 1998 on, based on data back through 1992								
2	Date	WMT		Date	Price	High or Low						
3	Oct-92	13.28		Feb-98	20.950	High						
4	Nov-92	14.04		Mar-98	23.020	High						
5	Dec-92	13.98		May-98	24.980	High						
6	Jan-93	14.22		Jun-98	27.570	High						
7	Feb-93	14.19		Jul-98	28.650	High						
8	Mar-93	13.88		Oct-98	31.380	High						
9	Apr-93	11.69		Nov-98	34.220	High						
10	May-93	12.18		Dec-98	37.040	High						
11	Jun-93	11.49		Jan-99	39.110	High						
12	Jul-93	11.10		Feb-99	39.170	High						
13	Aug-93	11.28		Mar-99	41.970	High						
14	Sep-93	10.79		Jun-99	43.980	High						
15	Oct-93	11.56		Oct-99	51.390	High						
16	Nov-93	12.56		Nov-99	52.590	High						
17	Dec-93	10.97		Dec-99	63.120	High						
18	Jan-94	11.63										
19	Feb-94	12.45										

obtain, but do not look at the code until you have attempted it yourself. (And, at least as of October 2008, don't buy GM stock!)

7.3 If Constructions

An If construction is useful when there are one or more possible conditions, each of which requires its own code. Here, a **condition** is any expression that is either true or false. Typical conditions are Total <= 200, SheetName = "Data", and isFound (where isFound is a Boolean variable that evaluates to True or False). You often need to check whether a condition is true or false and then proceed accordingly. This is the typical situation where an If construction is useful.

There are several versions of the If construction, in increasing order of complexity.

- **Single-line If.** The simplest version can be written on a single line. It has the form

If *condition* Then *statement1* [**Else** *statement2*]

Here, *condition* is any condition and *statement1* and *statement2* are any statements. (The convention in writing generic code like this is that any parts in square brackets are *optional*. In other words, the Else part of this statement is optional. Note that you do *not* actually type the square brackets.) This simple form requires only a single line of code (and there is no End If). An example is

```
If numberOrdered <= 200 Then unitCost = 1.30
```

Another example is

```
If numberOrdered <= 200 Then unitCost = 1.30 Else unitCost = 1.20
```

- **If-Then-Else-End If.** A more common version of the If construction requires several lines and has the form:

```
If condition Then
    Statements1
[Else
    Statements2]
End If
```

(Again, the square brackets denote that the lines within them are optional.) In this form, the condition is first tested. If it is true, then the statements denoted by *Statements1* are executed. You might also want to execute another set of statements, denoted by *Statements2*, in case the condition does not hold. If so, you must insert these after the keyword **Else**. In fact, there are four keywords in this form: **If**, **Then**, **Else**, and **End If**. (Note the required space between "End" and "If". However, the editor will fill in the space for you if you omit it.) An example of this construction is the following:

```
If numberOrdered <= 200 Then
    unitCost = 1.30
    MsgBox "The unit cost is " & unitCost
Else
    unitCost = 1.25
    MsgBox "The unit cost is " & unitCost
End If
```

- **If-Then-ElseIf-Else-End If.** The most general version of the If construction allows more than a single condition to be tested by using one or more **ElseIf** keywords. (Note that there is *no* space between "Else" and "If". It is all one word.) The general form is

```
If condition1 Then
    Statements1
[ElseIf condition2 Then
    Statements2
ElseIf condition3 Then
    Statements3
...
Else
    OtherStatements]
End If
```

This construction performs exactly as it reads. There can be as many ElseIf lines as needed (denoted by the . . .), and the Else part is not required. It is used only if you want to execute some statements in case all of the above conditions are false. An example of this version is the following:

```
If numberOrdered <= 200 Then
    unitCost = 1.30
ElseIf numberOrdered <= 300 Then
    unitCost = 1.25
ElseIf numberOrdered <= 400 Then
    unitCost = 1.20
Else
    unitCost = 1.15
End If
```

In this construction, the program goes through the conditions until it finds one that is true. Then it executes the corresponding statement(s) and jumps down to the End If line. If none of the conditions holds and there is an Else line, the statement(s) following it are executed.

- **Nested If statements.** It is also possible to *nest* If constructions, in which case proper indentation is *strongly* recommended for ease of reading. Here is an example:

```
If product = "Widgets" Then
    If numberOrdered <= 200 Then
        unitCost = 1.30
    Else
        unitCost = 1.20
    End If
ElseIf product = "Gadgets" Then
    If numberOrdered <= 500 Then
        unitCost = 2.70
    ElseIf numberOrdered <= 600 Then
        unitCost = 2.60
    Else
        unitCost = 2.50
    End If
Else
    unitCost = 2.00
End If
```

The meaning of this code should be self-evident, but only because the lines are indented properly. Try to imagine these lines without any indentation, and you will understand why the indentation is so important! Besides indentation, make sure you follow every If with an eventual End If (unless the If construction is of the simple one-line version). In fact, it is a good practice to type the End If line right after you type the If line, just so you don't forget. Also, every condition must be followed by the keyword Then. If you mistakenly type something like If numberOrdered <= 200 and press Enter, you will immediately see your mistake: the offending line will be colored red. You can fix it by adding Then.

The file **If Examples.xlsm** contains several examples to illustrate If constructions. They are all based on the small data set shown in Figure 7.4. Each example changes the formatting of the data in some way. The Restore button is attached to a sub that restores the data to its original "plain vanilla" formatting. In each example there is a

Figure 7.4 Data Set for If Examples

	A	B	C	D
1	Sample database to use for If examples			
2		Restore		
3	Employee	Score1	Score2	Score3
4	1	90	87	76
5	2	78	90	99
6	3	72	60	84
7	4	82	66	81
8	5	95	85	82
9	6	90	93	66
10	7	90	100	57
11	8	90	98	61
12	9	96	67	85
13	10	87	69	77
14	11	81	68	61
15	12	58	57	72
16	13	70	92	59
17	14	69	71	89
18	15	85	94	66
19	16	55	79	99
20	17	60	75	63
21	18	83	93	88

For Each loop that goes through all of the cells in some range. (**For Each** loops are discussed in detail in Section 7.6.) There is then at least one If construction that decides how to format cells in the range. (Note: In all of these If subs, I use the variable cell. This is *not* a keyword in VBA. I could just as well have used cel or cl or cll, etc.)

EXAMPLE 7.1   Single-Line If Construction

The **If1** sub illustrates a one-line If construction. If an employee's first score (in column B) is greater than 80, the corresponding employee number is boldfaced. Note that the range A4:A21 has been range-named Employee.

```
Sub If( )
    ' Example of a one-line If (note there is no End If).
    Dim cell As Range
    Const cutoff = 80

    ' Go down the Employee column. If the Employee's first score is greater than
    ' the cutoff, boldface the font of the Employee number.
    For Each cell In Range("Employee")
        If cell.Offset(0, 1).Value > cutoff Then cell.Font.Bold = True
    Next
End Sub
```

EXAMPLE 7.2   If-ElseIf-End If Construction

The **If2** sub illustrates an If with a single ElseIf (and no Else). If an employee's first score is less than 70, the sub colors the corresponding employee number red (color index 3). Otherwise, if it is greater than 85, the sub colors the employee number blue (color index 5). If the score is from 70 to 85, no action is taken. Hence, there is no need for an Else.

```
Sub If( )
    ' Example of a typical If-ElseIf-End If construction. Note that ElseIf is one
    ' word, but End If is two words.
    Dim cell As Range
    Const cutoff1 = 70, cutoff2 = 85
    Const color1 = 3, color2 = 5

    ' Go down the Employee column. If the Employee's first score is less than
    ' cutoff1, color the Employee number red; if greater than cutoff2, color it blue.
    ' Because there is no Else condition, nothing happens for scores between
    ' cutoff1 and cutoff2.
    For Each cell In Range("Employee")
        If cell.Offset(0, 1).Value < cutoff1 Then
            cell.Font.ColorIndex = color1
        ElseIf cell.Offset(0, 1).Value > cutoff2 Then
            cell.Font.ColorIndex = color2
        End If
    Next
End Sub
```

EXAMPLE 7.3 If-Elself-Else-End If Construction

The **If3** sub extends the **If2** sub. Now there is an Else part to handle scores from 70 to 85. All such scores are colored green (color index 4).

```
Sub If()
    ' Example of a typical If-Elself-Else-End If construction.
    Dim cell As Range
    Const cutoff1 = 70, cutoff2 = 85
    Const color1 = 3, color2 = 5, color3 = 4

    ' Go down the Employee column. If the Employee's first score is less than
    ' cutoff1, color the Employee number red; if greater than cutoff2, color it blue.
    ' Otherwise, color it green.
    For Each cell In Range("Employee")
        If cell.Offset(0, 1).Value < cutoff1 Then
            cell.Font.ColorIndex = color1
        Elself cell.Offset(0, 1).Value > cutoff2 Then
            cell.Font.ColorIndex = color2
        Else
            cell.Font.ColorIndex = color3
        End If
    Next
End Sub
```

EXAMPLE 7.4 Nested If Constructions

The **If4** sub illustrates how a nested If construction allows you to test whether all three of an employee's scores are greater than 80 (in which case the employee's number is boldfaced). Note that the statement setting Bold to True is executed only if *each* of the three If conditions is true.

```
Sub If()
    ' Example of nested If's.
    Dim cell As Range
    Const cutoff = 80

    ' Go down Employee column. If all scores for a Employee are greater than cutoff,
    ' boldface the Employee number. Note the indenting – important for readability!
    For Each cell In Range("Employee")
        If cell.Offset(0, 1).Value > cutoff Then
            If cell.Offset(0, 2).Value > cutoff Then
                If cell.Offset(0, 3).Value > cutoff Then
                    cell.Font.Bold = True
                End If
            End If
        End If
    Next
End Sub
```

EXAMPLE 7.5 Compound (And, Or) Conditions

Conditions can be of the *compound* variety, using the keywords **And** and **Or**. It is often useful to group the conditions in parentheses to eliminate any ambiguity. For example, the compound condition in the line

```
If condition1 And (condition2 Or condition3) Then
```

is true if *condition1* is true and at least one of *condition2* and *condition3* is true. Note that the individual conditions must be spelled out completely. For example, it is tempting to write

```
If color = "red" Or "blue" Then
```

However, this will generate an error message. The corrected line is

```
If color = "red" Or color = "blue" Then
```

The **If5** sub illustrates a typical compound condition. It first checks whether an employee's first score is greater than 80 *and* at least one of the employee's last two scores is greater than 85. If this compound condition is true, then it boldfaces the employee's number, it colors the first score red, and it colors blue any second or third score that is greater than 85.

```
Sub If( )
    ' Example of compound conditions (with And/Or).
    Dim cell As Range
    Const cutoff1 = 80, cutoff2 = 85
    Const color1 = 3, color2 = 5

    ' Boldface Employee numbers who did well on the first score and even better on
    ' at least one of the last two scores. Note the indenting for clear readability.
    For Each cell In Range("Employee")
        If cell.Offset(0, 1).Value > cutoff1 And _
            (cell.Offset(0, 2).Value > cutoff2 Or
                cell.Offset(0, 3).Value > cutoff2) Then
            cell.Font.Bold = True
            cell.Offset(0, 1).Font.ColorIndex = color1
            If cell.Offset(0, 2).Value > cutoff2 Then
                cell.Offset(0, 2).Font.ColorIndex = color2
            If cell.Offset(0, 3).Value > cutoff2 Then
                cell.Offset(0, 3).Font.ColorIndex = color2
        End If
    Next
End Sub
```

7.4 Case Constructions

If constructions can become fairly complex, especially when there are multiple ElseIf parts. The **Case** construction discussed here is often used by programmers as a less complex alternative. Suppose the action you take depends on the value of some variable. For example, you might have a product index that can have values from 1 to 10, and for each product index you need to take a different action. This could be accomplished with an If construction with multiple ElseIf lines. However, the Case construction provides an alternative. The general form of this construction is

```
Select Case someVariable
    Case value1
        Statements1
    Case value2
        Statements2
    ...
    [Case Else
        Other Statements]
End Select
```

(As usual, the square brackets are not typed. They indicate only that the Else part is optional.) Here, the keywords are **Select Case**, **Case**, and **End Select**, and *someVariable* is any variable on which the various cases are based. Then *value1*, *value2*, and so on, are mutually exclusive values of *someVariable* that require different actions, as specified by *Statements1*, *Statements2*, and so on. Actually, these values can be single values or ranges of values. For example, if *someVariable* is named productIndex, then you might need to do one thing if productIndex is from 1 to 5, another thing if productIndex is 6, and still another if productIndex is from 7 to 10. You can also include the Case Else, although it is not required. It specifies the action(s) to take if none of the other cases hold.

The following is a typical example of how the cases can be specified.

```
Select Case productIndex
    Case Is <= 3
        unitPrice = 1.2 * unitCost
    Case 4 To 6
        unitPrice = 1.3 * unitCost
    Case 7
        unitPrice = 1.4 * unitCost
    Case Else
        unitPrice = 1.1 * unitCost
End Select
```

Note the three ways the values are specified after the keyword Case: Is <= 3, 4 To 6, and 7 (where **Is** and **To** are keywords). What are the rules? VBA's online help tells us that the following can come after the keyword Case:

Delimited list of one or more of the following forms: *expression*, *expression* **To** *expression*, **Is** *comparisonoperator expression*. The **To** keyword specifies a range of values. If you use the **To** keyword, the smaller value must appear before **To**. Use the **Is** keyword with comparison operators (except **Is** and **Like**) to specify a range of values. If not supplied, the **Is** keyword is automatically inserted.

As is often the case with VBA's online help, this gives the *precise* rules, but it is not easy to read. Your alternative is to mimic the examples you see here or in other sources. Alternatively, there is nothing you can accomplish with Case constructions that you cannot also accomplish with (somewhat complex) If constructions. The construction that is used is often a matter of programming taste more than anything else.

The file **Case Examples.xlsm** illustrates Case constructions. It is based on the small data set in Figure 7.5. As with the If examples, the examples here change the formatting of the data, so the Restore button is attached to a macro that restores the formatting to its original form. Note that the range A4:A21 has been named Family.

Figure 7.5 Data set for Case examples

	A	B	C	D	E
1	Sample database to illustrate Case constructions				
2	Restore				
3	Family	Income			
4	1	$43,800			
5	2	$40,200			
6	3	$23,100			
7	4	$47,400			
8	5	$39,700			
9	6	$27,700			
10	7	$43,600			
11	8	$51,300			
12	9	$37,600			
13	10	$37,200			
14	11	$74,800			
15	12	$57,400			
16	13	$38,000			
17	14	$55,400			
18	15	$44,800			
19	16	$55,400			
20	17	$41,400			
21	18	$54,500			

EXAMPLE 7.6   Single Statement After Each Case

The **Case1** sub uses a For Each loop to go through each cell in the Family range. The Case construction is then based on the family's income, that is, the value in cell.Offset(0,1). Depending on which of four income ranges the family's income is in, the income is colored red, green, blue, or magenta. (I assume that all values are listed to the nearest dollar; there are no values such as $50,000.50.) The data are then sorted according to Income, so that all of the incomes of a particular color are adjacent to one another.

```
Sub Case1()
    Dim cell As Range
    Const cutoff1 = 35000, cutoff2 = 50000, cutoff3 = 65000
    Const color1 = 3, color2 = 4, color3 = 5, color4 = 7

    ' Go through families, color the income a different color for different
    ' income ranges, then sort on income.
    For Each cell In Range("Family")
        With cell
            Select Case .Offset(0, 1).Value
                Case Is < = cutoff1
                    .Offset(0, 1).Font.ColorIndex = color1
                Case cutoff1 + 1 To cutoff2
                    .Offset(0, 1).Font.ColorIndex = color2
                Case cutoff2 + 1 To cutoff3
                    .Offset(0, 1).Font.ColorIndex = color3
                Case Else ' above cutoff3
                    .Offset(0, 1).Font.ColorIndex = color4
            End Select
        End With
    Next
    Range("B3").Sort Key1:=Range("B4"), Order1:=xlAscending, Header:=xlYes
End Sub
```

EXAMPLE 7.7   Multiple Statements After Cases

The **Case2** sub is very similar to the **Case1** sub. The main difference is that it shows how multiple statements can follow any particular case. Here, the incomes less than or equal to 35,000 are colored red. In addition, if they are less than 30,000, they are also italicized. Similarly, incomes greater than 65,000 are colored magenta, and if they are greater than 70,000, they are boldfaced.

```
Sub Case2()
    ' This is the same as Case1, but if shows how multiple statements can be used
    ' in any particular case.
    Dim cell As Range
    Const cutoff1 = 35000, cutoff2 = 50000, cutoff3 = 65000
    Const cutoff0 = 30000, cutoff4 = 70000
    Const color1 = 3, color2 = 4, color3 = 5, color4 = 7

    For Each cell In Range("Family")
        With cell
```

```
            Select Case .Offset(0, 1).Value
                Case Is < = cutoff1
                    .Offset(0, 1).Font.ColorIndex = color1
                    If .Offset(0, 1) < cutoff0 Then .Offset(0, 1).Font.Italic = True
                Case cutoff1 + 1 To cutoff2
                    .Offset(0, 1).Font.ColorIndex = color2
                Case cutoff2 + 1 To cutoff3
                    .Offset(0, 1).Font.ColorIndex = color3
                Case Else ' above cutoff3
                    .Offset(0, 1).Font.ColorIndex = color4
                    If .Offset(0, 1) > cutoff4 Then .Offset(0, 1).Font.Bold = True
            End Select
        End With
    Next
    Range("B3").Sort Key1:=Range("B4"), Order1:=xlAscending, Header:=xlYes
End Sub
```

If you find that you favor Case constructions to If constructions in situations like these, just remember the following: The construction must begin with Select Case, it must end with End Select, and every "case" line in the middle must start with Case.

7.5 For Loops

Loops allow computers to do what they do best: repetitive tasks. There are actually two basic types of loops in VBA: **For** loops and **Do** loops. Of these two types, For loops are usually the easier to write, so I will discuss them first.

For loops take the following general form, where the keywords are **For**, **To**, **Step**, and **Next**.

```
For counter = first To last [Step increment]
    statements
Next [counter]
```

(As usual, square brackets indicate optional elements. You should not type the brackets.) There is always a "counter" variable. Many programmers name their counters i, j, k, m, or n, although any variable names can be used. The first line states that the counter goes from *first* to *last* in steps of *increment*. For each of these values, the *statements* in the body of the loop are executed. The default value of the Step parameter is 1, in which case the Step part can be omitted (as it usually is). The loop always ends with the keyword Next. It is possible, but not required, to write the counter variable in the Next line. This is sometimes useful when there are multiple For loops and there could be some ambiguity about which Next goes with which For.

The following is a simple example of a For loop that sums the first 1000 positive integers and reports their sum. This is actually a very common operation, where you accumulate some type of total within a loop. It is always a good idea to *initialize* the total to 0 just before starting the loop, as is done here.

```
sum = 0
For i = 1 to 1000
    sum = sum + i
Next
MsgBox "The sum of the first 1000 positive integers is " & sum
```

Virtually any types of statements can be used in the body of the loop. The following example illustrates how If logic can be used inside a loop. Here, you can assume that the worksheet Salaries has 500 employee names in column A (starting in row 2) and that their corresponding salaries are in column B. This code counts the number of employees with salaries greater than $50,000. The loop finds this number, totalHigh, by adding 1 to the current value of totalHigh each time it finds a salary greater than $50,000. Note how the counter variable i is used in the Offset to find the salary for employee i.

```
totalHigh = 0
With Worksheets("Salaries").Range("A1")
    For i = 1 to 500
        If .Offset(i,1) > 50000 Then totalHigh = totalHigh + 1
    Next
End With
MsgBox "The number of employees with salaries greater than $50,000 is " & totalHigh
```

Exiting a For Loop Prematurely

Sometimes you need to exit a For loop prematurely. This is possible with the Exit For statement. It immediately takes you out of the loop. For example, suppose again that 500 employee names are in column A, starting in row 2, and you want to know whether there is an employee named James Snyder. The following code illustrates one way to do this. It uses a Boolean variable isFound that is initially set to False. The program then loops through all employees. If it finds James Snyder, it sets isFound to True, exits the loop, and reports that James Snyder has been found. However, if it gets through the loop *without* finding James Snyder, then isFound is still False, so it then displays a message to this effect.

```
Dim isFound as Boolean
isFound = False
With Worksheets("Salaries").Range("A1")
    For i = 1 to 500
        If .Offset(i,0).Value = "James Snyder" Then
            isFound = True
            Exit For
        End If
    Next
End With
If isFound Then
    MsgBox "James Snyder is in the employee list."
Else
    MsgBox "James Snyder is not in the employee list."
End If
```

By the way, most beginning programmers (and even some experienced programmers) would write the fourth from last line as

```
If isFound = True then
```

This is technically correct, but the = True part is not necessary. Remember that a condition in an If statement is any expression that evaluates to True or False. Therefore, the "condition" isFound, all by itself, works just fine. It is Boolean, so its value is True or False. Similarly, the line

```
If Not isFound then
```

could be used for the opposite condition. The keyword **Not** turns True into False, and vice versa. Therefore, an equivalent way to end this example is as follows:

```
If Not isFound Then
    MsgBox "James Snyder is not in the employee list."
Else
    MsgBox "James Snyder is in the employee list."
End If
```

Again, the point of this discussion is that if you use a Boolean variable as the condition in an If statement, you do *not* have to include = True or = False in the condition.

Nested For Loops

It is also common to **nest** For loops. This is particularly useful in Excel if you want to loop through all of the cells in a *rectangular* range. Then there is one counter such as i for the rows and another counter such as j for the columns.[1] The following example illustrates nested loops.

EXAMPLE 7.8   Nested For Loops

Consider the worksheet named Sales with the data in Figure 7.6. (This data set and accompanying code are in the file **For Examples.xlsm**.) Each row corresponds to a sales region, and each column corresponds to a month. The numbers in the body of the table are sales figures for various regions and months, and we want the total sales over all regions and months. Then the nested For loops in the

---

[1] I sometimes use more meaningful counter names, such as iRow and iCol. However, the generic names i and j are used by many programmers in such situations.

following **GetGrandTotal** sub do the job. Note how the sales figure for region i and month j is captured by the offset relative to cell A3. Note also how the counter variables are included in the Next lines (Next i and Next j) for clarity. Actually, the indentation achieves the same effect—easy readability.

```
Sub GetGrandTotal( )
    ' Calculate and display the total of all sales.
    Dim total As Single
    Dim iRow As Integer
    Dim iCol As Integer

    ' The following line is not absolutely necessary because numeric variables
    ' are initialized to 0. But it never hurts to play it safe.
    total = 0

    ' Loop through all rows and all columns within each row.
    With Worksheets("Sales").Range("A3")
        For iRow = 1 To 13
            For iCol = 1 To 9
                total = total + .Offset(iRow, iCol)
            Next iCol
        Next iRow
    End With

    MsgBox "Total sales for the 13 regions during this 9-month period is " & total
End Sub
```

Continuing this example, suppose you want to append a "Totals" row to the bottom, where you sum sales across regions for each month, and a "Totals" column to the right, where you sum sales across months for each region. The following **GetTotals** sub accomplishes this. It is actually quite general. It first finds the number of months and number of regions in the data set so that it will work for any numbers of months and regions, not just those in Figure 7.6. For

Figure 7.6 Monthly Sales by Region

	A	B	C	D	E	F	G	H	I	J
1	Sales by region and month									
2										
3		Jan-08	Feb-08	Mar-08	Apr-08	May-08	Jun-08	Jul-08	Aug-08	Sep-08
4	Region 1	2270	1290	1600	2100	1170	1920	1110	2060	3130
5	Region 2	1730	3150	1180	740	1650	900	1830	1220	1620
6	Region 3	1840	1700	2170	3300	1390	1660	1720	2090	880
7	Region 4	3280	1920	2000	1270	1510	2280	2730	2160	1380
8	Region 5	2090	2110	2040	2270	1650	1910	2220	3380	1850
9	Region 6	1820	2570	2060	2190	1840	3310	1920	1080	940
10	Region 7	2400	1880	2980	2370	1910	2580	3470	2220	2200
11	Region 8	1680	1680	3120	1010	1550	2880	1410	2800	1520
12	Region 9	2230	2960	2240	2120	1870	2790	1390	2290	1620
13	Region 10	2040	2310	2120	2750	1220	1270	2080	2150	2650
14	Region 11	1430	2970	1800	2510	1660	1900	2910	770	2740
15	Region 12	1760	1590	1610	1550	1730	1150	3660	1670	3440
16	Region 13	1870	1330	1930	2080	2210	1850	3360	1930	1100

example, the following line, inside With Range("A3"), shows how to count the number of month labels to the right of cell A3.

```
nMonths = Range(.Offset(0, 1), .Offset(0, 1).End(xlToRight)).Columns.Count
```

This is a very common operation for counting columns (or rows), so you should get used to it.

```
Sub GetTotals( )
    Dim nMonths As Integer, nRegions As Integer
    Dim iRow As Integer, iCol As Integer
    Dim regionTotal As Single, monthTotal As Single

    With Worksheets("Sales").Range("A3")
        ' Capture the number of months and number of regions.
        With Range("A3")
            nMonths = Range(.Offset(0, 1), .Offset(0, 1).End(xlToRight)).Columns.Count
            nRegions = Range(.Offset(1, 0), .Offset(1, 0).End(xlDown)).Rows.Count
        End With

        ' Insert labels.
        .Offset(0, nMonths + 1).Value = "Totals"
        .Offset(nRegions + 1, 0).Value = "Totals"

        ' Get totals in right column.
        For iRow = 1 To nRegions
            regionTotal = 0   ' This is absolutely necessary!
            For iCol = 1 To nMonths
                regionTotal = regionTotal + .Offset(iRow, iCol).Value
            Next iCol
            ' Display total.
            .Offset(iRow, nMonths + 1).Value = regionTotal
        Next iRow

        ' Get totals in bottom row.
        For iCol = 1 To nMonths
            monthTotal = 0   ' This is also absolutely necessary.
            For iRow = 1 To nRegions
                monthTotal = monthTotal + .Offset(iRow, iCol).Value
            Next iRow
            ' Display total.
            .Offset(nRegions + 1, iCol).Value = monthTotal
        Next iCol
    End With
End Sub
```

Pay particular attention in this sub to the initialization statements for region-Total and monthTotal. For example, in the first pair of loops (where the totals in the right column are calculated), the outer loop goes through all of the rows for the regions. For a particular region, you *must* first reinitialize regionTotal to 0, and *then* loop through all of the months, adding each month's sales value to the current regionTotal value. Make sure you understand why the regionTotal = 0 and month-Total = 0 statements are not only necessary, but must be placed exactly where they have been placed for the program to work properly.

In fact, a good way to learn how this works is to purposely do it wrong and see what happens. For example, delete (or comment out) the regionTotal = 0 and monthTotal = 0 lines in the **For Examples.xlsm** file, run the program, and step through the code, periodically checking the value of regionTotal. You really *can* learn from your mistakes. (I have been programming for years, but I still have to think through this type of initialization logic each time I do it!)

The For loop examples to this point have had the counter variable going from 1 to some fixed number, in steps of 1. Other variations are possible, including the following:

- **Variable upper limit.** It is possible for the upper limit to be a variable that has been defined earlier. In the following lines, the number of customers is first captured in the variable nCustomers (as the number of rows in the Data range). Then nCustomers is used as the upper limit of the loop.

```
nCustomers = Range("Data").Rows.Count
For i = 1 to nCustomers
     Statements
Next
```

- **Lower limit other than 1.** It is possible for the lower limit to be an integer other than 1, or even a variable that has been defined earlier, as in the following lines. Here, the minimum and maximum scores in the Scores range are first captured in the minScore and maxScore variables. Then a loop uses these as the lower and upper limits for its counter.

```
minScore = Application.WorksheetFunction.Min(Range("Scores"))
maxScore = Application.WorksheetFunction.Max(Range("Scores"))
For i = minScore to maxScore
     Statements
Next
```

- **Counting backward.** It is possible to let the counter go backward by using a negative value for the Step parameter, as in the following lines. Admittedly, this is not common, but there are times when it is very useful.

```
For i = 500 to 1 Step -1
     Statements
Next
```

- **Lower limit greater than upper limit.** Another relatively uncommon situation, but one that *can* occur, is when the lower limit of the counter is greater than the upper limit (and the Step parameter is positive). This occurs in the following lines. What does the program do? It never enters the body of the loop at all; it just skips over the loop entirely. And, unlike what you might expect, there is no error message! (It is instructive to understand why this is the case. When VBA encounters a For loop, it sets the counter equal to the lower limit. Then it checks whether the counter is less than or equal to the upper limit. If it is, the body of the loop is executed, the counter is incremented by the step size, and the same check is made again. As soon as this check is *not* satisfied, execution passes to the next line after the loop.)

```
lowLimit = 10
highLimit = 5
For i = lowLimit to highLimit
    Statements
Next
```

7.6   For Each Loops

There is another type of For loop in VBA that is not present in all other programming languages: the **For Each** loop. Actually, this type of loop has been used a few times in this and previous chapters, so you are probably somewhat familiar with it by now. It is used whenever you want to loop through all objects in a collection, such as all cells in a Range or all worksheets in a workbook's Worksheets collection. Unlike the For loops in the previous section, you (the programmer) probably have no idea how many objects are in the collection, so you don't know how many times to go through the loop. Fortunately, you don't need to know. The For Each loop figures it out for you. If there are three worksheets, say, then it goes through the loop three times. If there are 15 worksheets, then it goes through the loop 15 times. The burden is not on you, the programmer, to figure out the number of objects in the collection.

The typical form of a For Each loop is the following.

```
Dim item as Object
For Each item in Collection
    Statements
Next
```

Here, the declaration of the object variable *item* is shown explicitly. Also, *item*, *Object*, and *Collection* have been italicized to indicate that they will vary depending on the type of collection. In any case, *item* is a generic name for a particular item in the collection. Programmers generally use a short variable name, depending on the type of item. For example, if you are looping through all worksheets, you might use the variable name wsht, or even ws. Actually, any name will do. In this case, *Object* should be replaced by Worksheet, and *Collection* should be replaced by Worksheets (or ActiveWorkbook.Worksheets). The following code illustrates how you could search through all worksheets of the active workbook for a sheet named Data. If you find one, you can exit the loop immediately. Note that you must declare the generic ws variable as an object—specifically, a Worksheet object.

```
Dim ws as Worksheet
Dim isFound as Boolean
isFound = False
For Each ws in ActiveWorkbook.Worksheets
    If ws.Name = "Data" Then
        isFound = True
        Exit For
    End If
Next
If isFound Then
    MsgBox "There is a worksheet named Data."
Else
    MsgBox "There is no worksheet named Data."
End If
```

The important thing to remember about For Each loops is that the generic item, such as ws in the above code, is an *object* in a collection. Therefore, it has the same properties and methods as any object in that collection, and they can be referred to in the usual way, such as ws.Name. Also, there is no built-in loop counter unless you want to create one—and there *are* situations where you will want to do so. As an example, the code below generalizes the previous code slightly. It counts the number of worksheets with a name that starts with "Sheet". (To do this, it uses the string function **Left**. For example, Left("Sheet17",5) returns the leftmost 5 characters in "Sheet17", namely, "Sheet".)

```
Dim ws as Worksheet
Dim counter as Integer
counter = 0
For Each ws in ActiveWorkbook.Worksheets
    If Left(ws.Name, 5) = "Sheet" Then
        counter = counter + 1
    End If
Next
MsgBox "There are " & counter & " sheets with a name starting with Sheet."
```

For Each with Ranges

One particular type of "collection" is a Range object. Remember that there is no "Ranges" collection, but the singular Range acts like a collection, and you can use it in a For Each loop. Then the individual items in the collection are the cells in the range. The following is a typical example. It counts the number of cells in a range that contain formulas. (To do so, it uses the built-in **HasFormula** property, which returns True or False.) Note again that cell is *not* a keyword in VBA. It is used here to denote a typical member of the Range collection—that is, a typical cell. Instead of cell, any other name (such as cl) could have been used for this generic object. In any case, this generic member must first be declared as a Range object.

```
Dim cell as Range
Dim counter as Integer
counter = 0
```

```
For Each cell in Range("Data")
    If cell.HasFormula Then counter = counter + 1
Next
MsgBox "There are " & counter & " cells in the Data range that contain formulas."
```

If you have programmed in another language, but not in VBA, it might take you a while to get comfortable with For Each loops. They simply do not exist in programming languages that do not have objects and collections. However, they can be extremely useful. For examples, refer back to any of Examples 7.4–7.7 in this chapter. They all use a For Each loop to loop through all cells in a range.

To see a few more For Each examples, examine the code in the file **For Each Examples.xlsm**. This code illustrates how you can loop through the Worksheets collection, the Charts collection (that includes chart sheets), the Sheets collection (that includes worksheets and chart sheets), and the Names collection (that includes range names). Of course, there are many more collections in Excel that you can loop through with For Each loops.

7.7 Do Loops

The For loops in Section 7.5 are perfect for looping a fixed number of times. However, there are many times when you need to loop *while* some condition holds or *until* some condition holds. You then can use a **Do** loop. Do loops are somewhat more difficult to master than For loops, partly because you have to think through the logic more carefully, and partly because there are four variations of Do loops available. Usually, *any* of these variations can be used, but you have to decide which one is most natural and easy to read.

The four variations are as follows. In each variation, the keyword **Do** appears in the first line of the loop, and the keyword **Loop** begins the last line of the loop. The first two variations check a condition at the top of the loop, whereas the last two variations check a condition at the bottom of the loop.

Variation 1: Do Until ... Loop

```
Do Until condition
    Statements
Loop
```

Variation 2: Do While ... Loop

```
Do While condition
    Statements
Loop
```

Variation 3: Do ... Loop Until

```
Do
    Statements
Loop Until condition
```

Variation 4: Do ... Loop While

```
Do
    Statements
Loop While condition
```

Here are some general comments that should help your understanding of Do loops.

- **Conditions at the top.** In the first two variations, the program checks the condition just before going through the body of the loop. In an Until loop, the statements in the body of the loop are executed only if the condition is *false*; in a While loop, the statements are executed only if the condition is *true*. If you stop and think about it, this is not something you need to memorize; it just makes sense, given the meaning of the words "until" and "while."

- **Conditions at the bottom.** The same holds in variations 3 and 4. The difference here is that the program decides whether to go through the loop *again*. The effect is that the statements in the loop might *never* be executed in the first two variations, but they will certainly be executed *at least once* in the last two variations.

- **Exit Do statement.** As with a For loop, you can exit a Do loop prematurely. To do so, you use an Exit Do statement inside the loop.

- **Possibility of infinite loops.** A Do loop has no built-in counter as in a For loop. Therefore, you as a programmer *must* change something within the loop to give it a chance of eventually exiting. Otherwise, it is easy to be caught in an **infinite loop** from which the program can never exit. The following is a simple example. It shows that it is easy to get into an infinite loop. It happens to all of us. You can assume that isValid has been declared as a Boolean variable—it is either True or False.

```
isValid = False
Do Until isValid
    password = InputBox("Enter a valid password.")
Loop
```

Go through the logic in these statements to see if you can locate the problem. Here it is. The Boolean variable isValid is never changed inside the loop. It is initialized to False, and it never changes. But the loop continues until isValid is True, which will never occur. If you type this code into a sub and then run it, the sub will never stop!

Breaking Out of an Infinite Loop: A Lifesaver

This might not sound too bad, but suppose you have spent the last hour writing a program, you have not saved your work (shame on you!), and you decide to test your program by running it. All of a sudden, you realize that you are in an infinite loop that you cannot get out of, and panic sets in. How can you save your work? Fortunately, there is a way to break out of an infinite loop (or terminate a program that has been running too long)—use the **Ctrl-Break** key combination. (The **Break** key is at the top of most keyboards.) This allows you to exit the program and save your work. This brush with disaster also reminds you to save more often!

How do you avoid the infinite loop in the above example? Let's suppose that any password of the form "VBAPass" followed by an integer from 1 to 9 will be accepted. In this case the following code will do the job. It checks whether the user enters one of the valid passwords, and if so, it sets isValid to True, allowing an exit from the loop. But there is still a problem. What if the poor user just doesn't know the password? She might try several invalid passwords and eventually give up, either by entering nothing in the input box or by clicking on the Cancel button. The program checks for this by seeing whether password, the string returned from the InputBox statement, is an empty string, "". (Clicking on the **Cancel** button of an input box returns an empty string.) In this case, the program not only exits the loop, but it ends abruptly because of the keyword End. After all, you don't want the user to be able to continue if she doesn't know the password.

```
isValid = False
Do Until isValid
    password = InputBox("Enter a valid password.")
    If password = "" Then
        MsgBox "Sorry, but you cannot continue."
        End
    Else
        For i = 1 to 9
            If password = "VBAPass" & i Then
                isValid = True
                Exit For
            End If
        Next
    End If
Loop
```

Study this code carefully. Note that the **Exit For** statement provides an exit from the For loop, because the program has found that the user entered a valid password such as VBAPass3. In this case there is no need to check whether she entered VBAPass4, VBAPass5, and so on. In addition, by this time, isValid has just been set to True. Therefore, when control passes back to the top of the Do loop, the condition will be true, and the Do loop will be exited.

There is an important lesson in this example. It is easy to get into an infinite loop—we all do it from time to time. If you run your program and it just seems to "hang," the chances are good that you are in an infinite loop. In that case, press **Ctrl-Break** to stop the program, save your file, and check your loops carefully.

EXAMPLE 7.9   Locating a Name in a List

The file **Do Loop Examples.xlsm** illustrates a typical use of Do loops. It starts with a database of customers in a Data worksheet, as shown in Figure 7.7 (with several hidden rows). Column A contains a company's customers for 2007, and column B contains the customers for 2008. The year 2009 has not yet occurred, so the company doesn't know its customers for 2009—hence the empty list in column C. The user first selects a column from 1 to the number of columns (here **3**, but the program is written more generally for any number of columns). The goal of the program is to check whether a customer with name Kreuger is in the selected column. (The blank Customer 2009 column is included here for illustration. It shows what happens if you try to locate a particular name in a *blank* list.)

Figure 7.7 Customer Lists

	A	B	C
1	**Customer 2007**	**Customer 2008**	**Customer 2009**
2	Barlog	Aghimien	
3	BarnettBang		
4	Bedrick	Barnett	
5	Brulez	Bedrick	
6	Cadigan	Brulez	
7	Castleman	Cadigan	
8	Chandler	Castleman	
9	Chen	Chandler	
10	Cheung	Cheung	
11	Chong	Chong	
12	Chou	Cochran	
92	Yablonka	Tracy	
93	Zick	Ubelhor	
94	Ziegler	Usman	
95		Vicars	
96		Villard	
97		Wendel	
98		Wier	
99		Wise	
100		Yablonka	
101		Yeiter	
102		Zakrzacki	
103		Zhou	

The **DoLoop1** sub shows how to perform the search with a **Do Until** loop. It searches down the selected column for a user-supplied name until it finds the name or it runs into a blank cell, the latter signifying that it has checked the entire customer list for that column. If it finds the name along the way, it exits the loop prematurely with an Exit Do statement. Note that the program works even if column C is chosen. You should reason for yourself exactly what the program does in this case—and why it works properly.

```vba
Sub DoLoop1()
    Dim selectedColumn As Integer
    Dim nColumns As Integer
    Dim rowCount As Integer
    Dim foundName As Boolean
    Dim requestedName As String

    ' Count the columns.
    With Range("A1")
        nColumns = Range(.Offset(0, 0), .End(xlToRight)).Columns.Count
    End With

    ' Ask for a name to be searched for.
    requestedName = InputBox("What last name do you want to search for?")

    ' No error checking – assumes user will enter an appropriate value!
    selectedColumn = InputBox("Enter a column number from 1 to " & nColumns)

    ' Go to the top of the selected column.
    With Range("A1").Offset(0, selectedColumn - 1)
        rowCount = 1
        foundName = False

        ' Keep going until a blank cell is encountered. Note that if there are no names
        ' at all in the selected column, the body of this loop will never be executed.
        Do Until .Offset(rowCount, 0).Value = ""
            If UCase(.Offset(rowCount, 0).Value) = UCase(requestedName) Then
                foundName = True
                MsgBox requestedName & " was found as name " & rowCount_
                    & " in column " & selectedColumn & ".", vbInformation, "Match found"
                ' Exit the loop prematurely as soon as a match is found.
                Exit Do
            Else
                ' Unlike a For loop, any counter must be updated manually in a Do loop.
                rowCount = rowCount + 1
            End If
        Loop
    End With

    ' Display appropriate message if no match is found.
    If Not foundName Then
        MsgBox "No match for " & requestedName & " was found.", vbInformation, "No match"
    End If
End Sub
```

Probably the most important parts of this loop are the row counter variable, rowCount, and the "updating" statement, rowCount = rowCount + 1. Without these, there would be an infinite loop. But because rowCount increases by 1 every time through the loop, the condition following Do Until is always based on a *new* cell. Eventually, the program will find the requested name or it will run out of customers in the selected column. That is, it will eventually end.

A note on VBA's UCase and LCase functions. The condition that checks for the requested name uses VBA's built-in **UCase** (uppercase) function. This function transforms any string into one with all uppercase characters. This is often useful when you are not sure whether names are capitalized fully, partially, or not at all. By checking for uppercase only, you take all guesswork out of the search. Similarly, VBA has an **LCase** (lowercase) function that transforms all characters to lowercase.

Changing Do Until to Do While

It is easy to change a Do Until loop to a Do While loop or vice versa. You just change the condition to its opposite. The **Do Loop Examples.xlsm** file contains a **DoLoop2** sub that uses Do While instead of Do Until. The only change is that the Do Until line becomes the following. (Note that <> means "not equal to.")

```
Do While .Offset(rowCount, 0).Value <> ""
```

Putting conditions at the bottom of the loop

It is also possible to perform the search for the requested name using variation 3 or 4 of a Do loop—that is, to put the conditions at the *bottom* of the loop. The **DoLoop3** and **DoLoop4** subs of the **Do Loop Examples.xlsm** file illustrate these possibilities. However, for this particular task (of finding a particular name), it is probably more natural to place the condition at the top of the loop. This way, if the first element of the selected column's list is blank, as for the year 2009, the body of the loop is never executed at all.

7.8 Summary

The programming tools discussed in this chapter are arguably the most important tools in VBA or any other programming language. It is hard to imagine many interesting, large-scale applications that do not require some control logic and loops. They appear everywhere. Fortunately, they are not difficult to master, and your knowledge of them will be reinforced by numerous examples in later chapters.

EXERCISES

1. Write a sub that requests a positive integer with an input box. Then it uses a For loop to sum all of the odd integers up to the input number, and it displays the result in a message box.

2. Change your sub from the previous exercise so that it enters all of the odd integers in consecutive cells in column A, starting with cell A1, and it shows the sum in the cell just below the last odd integer.

3. The file **Sales Data.xlsx** contains monthly sales amounts for 40 sales regions. Write a sub that uses a For loop to color the interior of every other row (rows 3, 5, etc.) gray. Use ColorIndex 15 for gray, and color only the data area, columns A–M.

4. Starting with the original **Sales Data.xlsx** file from the previous exercise, write a sub that italicizes each monthly sales amount that is greater than $12,000 and changes the font color to red for each label in column A where the yearly sales total for the region is greater than $130,000.

5. Starting with the original **Sales Data.xlsx** file from the previous exercise, write a sub that examines each row for upward or downward movements in quarterly totals. Specifically, for each row, check whether the quarterly totals increase each quarter and whether they decrease each quarter. If the former, color the region's label in column A red; if the latter, color it blue.

6. An InputBox returns a string—whatever the user enters in the box. However, it returns a blank string if the user enters nothing and clicks on OK or clicks on Cancel. Write a sub that uses an InputBox to ask the user for a product code. Embed this in a Do loop so that the user has to keep trying until the result is *not* a blank string.

7. Continuing the previous exercise, suppose all valid product codes start with the letter P and are followed by 4 digits. Expand the sub from the previous exercise so that the user has to keep trying until a *valid* code has been entered.

8. Continuing exercise 6, rewrite your sub in three different ways. In Exercise 6, you chose one of the four possible versions of Do loops in your code: using a While or Until condition, and placing the condition at the top of the loop or the bottom of the loop. Rewrite your sub in each of the three other possible ways.

9. Write a sub that displays a message box. The message should ask whether the total receipt for a sale is greater than $100, and it should display Yes and No buttons. If the result of the message box is **vbYes** (the built-in VBA constant that results from clicking on the Yes button), a second message box should inform the user that she gets a 10% discount.

10. Write a sub that asks for the unit cost of a product with an input box. Embed this within a Do loop so that the user keeps being asked until she enters a positive numeric value. (*Hint*: Use VBA's **IsNumeric** function. Also, remember that if the user clicks on the **Cancel** button, an empty string is returned.)

11. Write a sub that asks for a product index from 1 to 100. Embed this within a Do loop so that the user keeps being asked until he enters an integer from 1 to 100. (*Hint*: Use a For loop for checking.)

12. All passwords in your company's system must be eight characters long, must start with an uppercase letter, and must consist only of uppercase letters and digits—no spaces. Employees are issued a password, but then they are allowed to change it to one of their own choice.

    a. Write a sub to get a user's new password. It should use an input box, embedded within a Do loop, to get the password. The purpose of the loop is to check that they indeed enter a *valid* password.

b. Expand your sub in part **a** to include a second input box that asks the user to verify the password in the first input box (which by then is known to be valid). Embed the whole procedure within an "outer" Do loop. This outer loop keeps repeating until the user provides a valid password in the first input box and enters the *same* password in the second input box.

13. Repeat the previous exercise, but now assume that, in addition to the other restrictions on valid passwords, passwords can have at most two digits—the rest must be uppercase letters.

14. Repeat Exercise 12, but now perform a second check. Use the file **Passwords.xlsx**, which has a single sheet called Passwords. This sheet has a list of all passwords currently being used by employees in column A, starting in cell A1. If the new employee selects one of these passwords, an appropriate message is displayed, and the user has to choose another password. When the user finally chooses a valid password that is not being used, a "Congratulations" message should be displayed, and the new password should be added to the list.

15. Write a sub that asks the user for three things in three successive input boxes: (1) a last name, (2) a "first" name (which can actually be their middle name if they go by their middle name), and (3) an initial. Use Do loops to ensure that the first name and last name are all letters—no digits, spaces, or other characters. Also, check that the initial is a single letter or is blank (since some people don't like to use an initial). If an initial is given, ask the user in a message box with Yes and No buttons whether the initial is a *middle* initial. (The alternative is that it is a *first* initial.) Then display a message box listing the user's full name, such as "Your full name is F. Robert Jacobs", "Your name is Wayne L. Winston", or "Your name is Seb Heese".

16. Assume you have a mailing list file. This file is currently the active workbook, and the active sheet of this workbook has full names in column A, starting in cell A1, with last name last and everything in uppercase letters (such as STEPHEN E. LEE). Write a sub that counts the number of names in the list with last name LEE and then displays this count in a message box. Note that there might be last names such as KLEE, which should not be counted.

17. The file **Price Data.xlsx** has a single sheet that lists your products (by product code). For each product, it lists the unit price and a discount percentage that customers get if they purchase at least a minimum quantity of the product. For example, the discount for the first product is 7%, and it is obtained if the customer purchases at least 20 units of the product. Write a sub that asks for a product code with an input box. This should be placed inside a Do loop that checks whether the code is one in the list. It should then ask for the number of units purchased, which must be a positive number. (You don't have to check that the input is an *integer*. We'll assume the user doesn't enter something like 2.73.) Finally, it should display a message something like the following: "You purchased _ units of product _. The total cost is _. Because you purchased at least _ units, you got a discount of _ on each unit." Of course, your code will fill in the blanks. Also, the last sentence will not be displayed if the user didn't purchase enough units to get a discount. (*Note*: You should write this sub, and the subs in the next two exercises, so that they are valid even if the list of products expands in the future.)

18. Continuing the previous exercise, write a sub that first asks the user for the number of different products purchased. Then use a For loop that goes from 1

to this number, and place the code from the previous exercise (modified if necessary) inside this loop. That is, each time through the loop you should get and display information about a particular product purchased. At the end of the sub, display a message that shows the total amount spent on all purchases.

19. Again, use the **Price Data.xlsx** file described in Exercise 17. Write a sub that asks the user for a purchase quantity that can be any multiple of 5 units, up to 50 units. Then enter a label in cell E3 something like "Cost of _ units", where the blank is filled in by the user's input. Below this, enter the total cost of this many units for each product. For example, cell E4 will contain the purchase cost of this many units of the first product in the list. Enter these as values, not formulas.

20. The file **Customer Accounts.xlsx** has account information on a company's customers. For each customer listed by customer ID, Sheet1 has the amount the customer has purchased during the current year and the amount the customer has paid on these purchases so far. For example, the first customer purchased an amount worth $2466 and has paid up in full. In contrast, the second customer purchased an amount worth $1494 and has paid only $598 of this. Write a sub to create a list on Sheet2 of all customers who still owe more than $1000. (It should first clear the contents of any previous list on this sheet.) The list should show customer IDs and the amounts owed. This sub should work even if the data change, including the possibility of more or fewer customer accounts.

21. (More difficult) The file **Customer Orders.xlsx** shows orders by date for a company's customers on Sheet1. Many customers have ordered more than once, so they have multiple entries in the list. Write a sub that finds the total amount spent by each customer on the list and reports those whose total is more than $2000 on Sheet2. As part of your sub, sort the list on Sheet2 in descending order by total amount spent. (*Hint*: The data on Sheet1 are currently sorted by date. It might be helpful to use VBA to sort them by Customer ID. Then at the end of the sub, restore the list to its original condition by sorting on date.)

22. You are a rather paranoid business executive, always afraid that a competitor might be snooping on your sensitive e-mail messages. Therefore, you decide to use a very simple form of encryption. The table in the file **Scramble.xlsx** shows your scheme. For example, all instances of the letter "a" are changed to the letter "e", all instances of "b" are changed to "v". Note at the bottom of the table that uppercase letters are scrambled differently than lowercase letters. For example, all instances of "A" are changed to "D". (Spaces, periods, and other nonalphabetic characters are not changed.) Write two subs, **Scramble** and **Unscramble**. In each, ask the user for a message in an input box. In the **Scramble** sub, this will be an original message; in the **Unscramble** sub, it will be a scrambled message. Then in the **Scramble** sub, scramble the message and display it. Similarly, in the **Unscramble** sub, unscramble the message and display it. (Of course, in a real situation we would assume that you and the person you are e-mailing each have the **Scramble.xlsm** file. You would use the **Scramble** sub, and the person you are e-mailing would use the **Unscramble** sub.)

23. (More difficult) A prime number is one that is divisible only by itself and 1. The first few prime numbers are 2, 3, 5, 7, 11, and 13. Note that 2 is the only *even* prime number.

a. Write a sub that finds the first *n* prime numbers, where you can choose *n*, and lists them in column B of Sheet1 of the **Primes.xlsm** file. The first few are already listed for illustration. (*Hint*: You should use VBA's **Mod** function. It returns the remainder when one number is divided by another. For example, **45 Mod 7** returns 3. A number *n* is *not* prime if *n* Mod *k* = 0 for some integer *k* between 1 and *n*. For example, 39 is not prime because 39 Mod 3 = 0.)

b. Change the sub in part **a** slightly so that it now finds all prime numbers less than or equal to some number *m*, where you can choose *m*, and lists them in Sheet2 of the **Primes.xlsm** file.

24. (More difficult) The cipher in problem 22 is a really simple one that hackers would break in no time. The file **Cipher.xlsx** explains a much more sophisticated cipher. (It has been around for centuries, and it too can be broken fairly easily by experts, but it is safe from most onlookers.) Write a sub that first asks the user for a *key*, a word with all uppercase letters. Then it asks the user for a message that contains only lowercase words and spaces. The sub should delete all of the spaces from this message and then encode what remains, using the explanation in the file and the given key. It should report the encoded message, without any spaces, in a message box. (You can test it on the following. If the key is VBAMODELERS and the message is "the treasure is buried in the garden", the encoded message, with spaces included, is "OIE FFHEDYIW DT BGFLIO ME LCF GMFGIY". In the same sub, and using the same encoded message and key, decode the message and report it in a message box. Of course, it should be the same as the original message.

25. Consider the following model of product preferences. Assume that a retailer can stock any of products 1 through *n*. Each customer is of one of several types, defined by the customer's ranked preferences for the products. You can think of these types as customer segments. Each customer in a segment has the same preferences for the various products and will purchase accordingly. For example, if *n*=5 and a customer is of type {2, 1, 4}, this customer would purchase any of products 1, 2, and 4, but not products 3 or 5. Furthermore, this customer prefers product 2 to product 1 and product 1 to product 4. So if the retailer stocks products 1, 3, 4, and 5, this customer will purchase her highest ranked stocked product, product 1. (She would prefer product 2, but it isn't stocked.) But if the retailer stocks only products 3 and 5, this customer won't purchase anything. The file **Preferences.xlsx** has instructions, where your task is to write a macro that takes (1) a customer population size, (2) any given set of customer types, (3) the proportions of all customers in the customer types, (4) the profit margin for each product, and (5) the products offered by the retailer, and it then finds (1) which product each customer type purchases, if any, (2) the number of customers who purchase each offered product, and (3) the retailer's total profit. (**Note:** You might think that with all profit margins being positive, it would certainly make sense for the retailer to offer all *n* products. However, this is not necessarily the case. For example, imagine that product 1 has a relatively small profit margin, product 2 has a relatively large profit margin, and a lot of customers' first and second preferences, in that order, are products 1 and 2. Then by *not* offering product 1, a lot of customers would go to their second preference, product 2, and the retailer would possibly make more profit.)

8 Working with Other Excel Objects

8.1 Introduction

This chapter extends the information given in Chapters 6 and 7. Chapter 6 focused on Range objects. This chapter illustrates how to work with three other common objects in Excel: workbooks, worksheets, and charts. In doing so, it naturally illustrates further uses of control logic and loops, which were discussed in Chapter 7. Workbooks, worksheets, and charts are certainly not the only objects you will encounter in Excel, but if you know how to work with these objects and ranges, you will be well along the way. All of the objects in this chapter have many properties and methods, and only a small fraction of them are illustrated. As usual, you can learn much more from online help, particularly the Object Browser.

8.2 Exercise

The exercise in this section illustrates the manipulation of multiple workbooks, worksheets, and ranges. It is fairly straightforward, although you have to be careful to keep your bearings as you move from one workbook or worksheet to another. You should work on this exercise, or at least keep it in mind, as you read through the rest of this chapter. All of the tools required to solve it are explained in the chapter (or were already explained in a previous chapter). When you finally get it working, you can consider yourself a legitimate Excel programmer.

Exercise 8.1 Consolidating Data from Multiple Sheets

Consider a company that sells several of its products to five large customers. The company currently has a file with two sheets, Revenues and Costs, for each customer. These files are named **Customer1.xlsx** through **Customer5.xlsx**. Each sheet shows the revenues or costs by day for all products sold to that customer. For example, a sample of the revenue data for customer 1 appears in Figure 8.1. Each of the customer files has data for the *same* dates (currently, from January 2009 through June 2009, although new data could be added in the future). In contrast, different customers have data for *different* numbers of products. For example, customer 1 purchases products 1 to 4, customer 2 purchases products 1 to 6, and so on.

Figure 8.1 Sample Revenue Data for Customer 1

	A	B	C	D	E
1	Date	Product 1	Product 2	Product 3	Product 4
2	25-Jan-09	1890	2010	1150	2480
3	26-Jan-09	2880	2670	2280	3520
4	27-Jan-09	1520	2400	3430	1710
5	28-Jan-09	2270	2530	3220	2050
6	31-Jan-09	3280	2730	2080	2670
7	01-Feb-09	2630	1970	2900	1930
8	02-Feb-09	3030	3250	2410	3260
9	03-Feb-09	1990	1600	2360	2220
10	04-Feb-09	2800	1970	2650	2450
11	07-Feb-09	2360	2640	3280	2120
12	08-Feb-09	2680	2370	2600	1600
13	09-Feb-09	3260	2500	2550	2010
14	10-Feb-09	3130	1920	2440	2460
15	11-Feb-09	3090	3160	1830	2560

Figure 8.2 Template for Consolidated File

	A	B	C	D	E	F	G	H	I	J	K	L	M
1		Customer 1		Customer 2		Customer 3		Customer 4		Customer 5		Total all customers	
2	Date	Revenues	Costs	Revenues	Costs	Revenues	Costs	Revenues	Costs	Revenues	Costs	Revenues	Costs
3													

The purpose of the exercise is to consolidate the data from these five workbooks into a single Summary sheet in a workbook named **Consolidating.xlsm**. This file already exists, but it includes only headings, as shown in Figure 8.2. When it is finished, the dates will go down column A, the revenues and costs for customer 1 will go down columns B and C, those for customer 2 will go down columns D and E, and so on. The revenues and costs for all customers combined will go down columns L and M. Note that the revenues and costs in columns B and C, for example, are totals over all products purchased by customer 1.

Figure 8.3 shows part of the results for the finished application. The button on the right runs the program. The program should have a loop over the customers that successively opens each customer's file, sums the revenues and costs for that customer, places the totals in the consolidated file, and then closes the customer's file. Finally, after entering all of the information in Figure 8.3 through column K, the program should enter *formulas* in columns L and M to obtain the totals.

Figure 8.3 Results from Finished Application

	A	B	C	D	E	F	G	H	I	J	K	L	M	N	O	P
1		Customer 1		Customer 2		Customer 3		Customer 4		Customer 5		Total all customers				
2	Date	Revenues	Costs	Revenues	Costs	Revenues	Costs	Revenues	Costs	Revenues	Costs	Revenues	Costs			
3	25-Jan-09	7530	5730	13810	8740	5290	2960	6520	5400	13310	7470	46460	30300			
4	26-Jan-09	11350	5500	15860	9080	5510	3100	7100	4290	12610	7380	52430	29350		Consolidate	
5	27-Jan-09	9060	5770	14840	9190	5000	3410	7250	4990	12570	7570	48720	30930			
6	28-Jan-09	10070	5750	14910	9270	4800	2770	8500	4650	12900	7900	51180	30340			
7	31-Jan-09	10760	6180	13540	9180	4050	2700	7650	3550	12880	7050	48880	28660			
8	1-Feb-09	9430	5750	18810	9410	4770	2510	8830	3960	12000	7890	53840	29520			
9	2-Feb-09	11950	6010	16550	9760	4150	2690	8540	4720	11390	7010	52580	30190			
10	3-Feb-09	8170	5830	15040	8960	4300	2830	7610	5180	11900	8490	47020	31290			
11	4-Feb-09	9870	6240	17660	9120	5750	2720	7220	4070	12460	6800	52960	28950			
12	7-Feb-09	10400	5630	14560	9390	3990	2730	6560	4780	12560	7900	48070	30430			
13	8-Feb-09	9250	5820	13690	8960	4300	2820	7330	4320	10920	7620	45490	29540			
14	9-Feb-09	10320	7030	17180	9070	3470	2800	6640	4410	11230	8350	48840	31660			
15	10-Feb-09	9950	5950	14940	9240	4350	3330	6120	4120	12870	7520	48230	30160			
16	11-Feb-09	10640	5700	12850	9170	5340	2860	7150	4260	12740	6880	48720	28870			
17	14-Feb-09	9250	6010	13320	8650	5090	2990	7040	4700	12420	7590	47120	29940			
18	15-Feb-09	9100	6190	13560	8340	4430	3690	7670	4980	13310	7060	48070	30260			

To see how this application works, make sure none of the individual customer's files is open, open the **ConsolidatingFinished.xlsm** file, and click on the button. Although you will have to watch closely to notice that anything is happening, each of the customer's files will be opened for a fraction of a second before being closed, and the results in Figure 8.3 will appear. As usual, you can cheat by looking at the VBA code in the finished file, but you should resist doing so until you have given it your best effort.

8.3 Collections and Members of Collections

Collections and members of collections (remember, plural and singular?) were already discussed in Chapter 5, but these ideas bear repeating here as I discuss workbooks, worksheets, and charts. There are actually two ideas you need to master: (1) specifying a member of a collection, and (2) specifying a hierarchy in the object model.

The three collections required for this chapter are the **Workbooks**, **Worksheets**, and **Charts** collections.[1] The Workbooks collection is the collection of all open workbooks. (It does *not* include Excel files on your hard drive that are not currently open.) Any member of this collection—a particular workbook—can be specified with its name, such as Workbooks("Customers.xlsx"). This refers to the Customers.xlsx file (assumed to be open in Excel). Similarly, a particular worksheet such as the Data worksheet can be referenced as Worksheets("Data"), and a particular chart sheet such as the Sales chart sheet can be referenced as Charts ("Sales"). The point is that if you want to reference any particular member of a collection, you must spell out the plural collection name and then follow it in parentheses with the name of the member in double quotes.[2]

---

[1]The **ChartObjects** collection is also mentioned in Section 8.6.

[2]It is also possible to refer to a member with a numeric index, such as Worksheets(3), but this method is typically not be used. (It is difficult to remember what the *third* worksheet is, for example. By the way, *third* refers to the third sheet from the left.)

As for hierarchy, it works as follows. The Workbooks collection consists of individual workbooks. Any particular workbook *contains* a Worksheets collection and a Charts collection. If a particular worksheet, such as the Data worksheet, belongs to the *active* workbook, you can refer to it simply as Worksheets("Data"). You could also refer to it as ActiveWorkbook.Worksheets("Data"). However, there are times when you need to spell out the workbook, as in Workbooks("Customers. xls").Worksheets("Data"). This indicates explicitly that you want the Data worksheet from the Customers workbook.

In a similar way, you can specify the Sales chart sheet as Charts("Sales") or, if the Sales sheet is in the active workbook, as ActiveWorkbook.Charts("Sales"). Alternatively, to designate the Sales chart sheet in the Customers workbook, you can write Workbooks("Customers.xlsx").Charts("Sales").

The Worksheets collection is one step down the hierarchy from the Workbooks collection. Range objects are one step farther down the hierarchy. Suppose you want to refer to the range A3:C10. If this is in the active worksheet, you can refer to it as Range("A3:C10") or as ActiveSheet.Range("A3:C10"). If you want to indicate explicitly that this range is in the Data sheet, then you should write Worksheets("Data").Range("A3:C10"). But even this assumes that the Data sheet is in the active workbook. If you want to indicate explicitly that this sheet is in the Customers file, then you should write Workbooks("Customers.xlsx").Worksheets("Data").Range("A3:C10"). You always read this type of reference from right to left—the range A3:C10 of the Data sheet in the Customers file.

Once you know how to refer to these objects, you can easily refer to their properties by adding a dot and then a property or method after the reference. Some examples are:

```
ActiveWorkbook.Worksheets("Data").Range("C4").Value = "Sales for 1999"
```

and

```
Charts("Sales").Delete
```

Many other examples appear throughout this chapter.

One final concept mentioned briefly in Chapter 2 is that the Workbooks, Worksheets, and Charts *collections* are also objects and therefore have properties and methods. Probably the most commonly used property of each of these collections is the **Count** property. For example, ActiveWorkbook.Worksheets.Count returns the number of worksheets in the active workbook. Probably the most commonly used method of each of these collections is the **Add** method. This adds a new member to the collection (which then becomes the *active* member). For example, consider the following lines:

```
ActiveWorkbook.Worksheets.Add
ActiveSheet.Name = "NewData"
```

The first line adds a new worksheet to the active workbook, and the second line names this new sheet NewData.

Before proceeding to examples, I want to make some comments about reference to objects and Intellisense. Once you type an object and then a period, if VBA recognizes the *type* of object (range, worksheet, or whatever), then Intellisense *should* provide a list of its properties and methods. It is very disconcerting when this list doesn't appear. In fact, I usually assume I've made a mistake. But VBA doesn't seem to be totally consistent about providing Intellisense for objects. For example, I opened a new workbook and entered the code Worksheets ("Sheet1"). (including the period), but no Intellisense appeared. Why not? I have no idea. There shouldn't be any doubt that this refers to a worksheet object, but Intellisense acts as if it's not sure.

There are two remedies for this. The first is to Set object variables and then refer to them. If I declare ws as a Worksheet object, then type the line Set ws = Worksheets("Sheet1"), and finally type ws. (including the period), I get Intellisense. Maybe this is why professional programmers declare and use so many object variables. I am certainly using them more than I used to.

The second remedy is much less well known. Suppose you open a new workbook, and you change the name of the Sheet1 worksheet to DataSheet (or any other name). If you look in the Project Explorer in the VBE, you'll see (under the Microsoft Excel Objects folder) the strange notation **Sheet1 (DataSheet)**. The name in parentheses is the (new) *name* of the worksheet, so you can refer to it with the usual Worksheets("DataSheet")–and probably not get Intellisense. But you can also refer to Sheet1 (not Worksheets("Sheet1"), just Sheet1). This is called the **codename** of the sheet, and it never changes, not even when you change the name of the sheet. Admittedly, it's confusing, and I'm not sure why Excel provides a name and a codename for each sheet. However, the good news is that when you type Sheet1. (including the period), you *do* get Intellisense!

8.4 Examples of Workbooks in VBA

The file **Workbooks.xlsm** illustrates how to open and close workbooks, how to save them, how to specify the paths where they are stored, and how to display several of their properties, all with VBA. It is the basis for the following examples.

EXAMPLE 8.1   Opening and Closing Workbooks

The **Workbooks1** sub shows how to open and close a workbook. It also uses the **Count** property of the Worksheets collection to return the number of worksheets in a workbook, and it uses the **Name** property of a Workbook to return the name of the workbook. As illustrated in the sub, the opening and closing operations are done slightly differently. To open a workbook, you use the **Open** method of the Workbooks collection, followed by the **Filename** argument. This argument specifies the

Figure 8.4 Information About Opened File

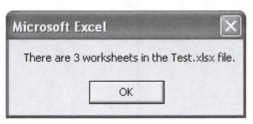

name (including the path) of the workbook file. To close a workbook, you use the **Close** method of that workbook without any arguments.[3] Note that the file you are trying to open must exist in the location you specify. Otherwise, you will obtain an error message. Similarly, the file you are trying to close must currently be open.

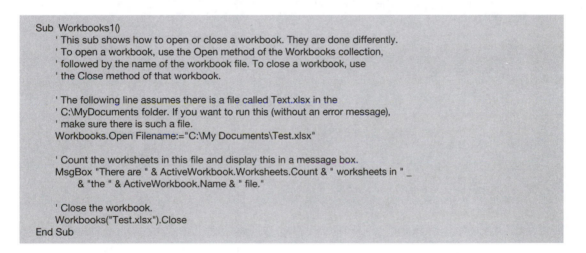

```
Sub Workbooks1()
    ' This sub shows how to open or close a workbook. They are done differently.
    ' To open a workbook, use the Open method of the Workbooks collection,
    ' followed by the name of the workbook file. To close a workbook, use
    ' the Close method of that workbook.

    ' The following line assumes there is a file called Text.xlsx in the
    ' C:\MyDocuments folder. If you want to run this (without an error message),
    ' make sure there is such a file.
    Workbooks.Open Filename:="C:\My Documents\Test.xlsx"

    ' Count the worksheets in this file and display this in a message box.
    MsgBox "There are " & ActiveWorkbook.Worksheets.Count & " worksheets in " _
        & "the " & ActiveWorkbook.Name & " file."

    ' Close the workbook.
    Workbooks("Test.xlsx").Close
End Sub
```

If you run this sub, then assuming the Test.xlsx file exists in the C:\My Documents folder and has three worksheets, the message in Figure 8.4 will be displayed.

EXAMPLE 8.2 Saving a Workbook

The **Workbooks2** sub illustrates how to save an open workbook. This requires either the **Save** method or the **SaveAs** method, both of which mimic the similar operations in Excel. The Save method requires no arguments—it simply saves the file under its current name—whereas the SaveAs method typically has arguments that specify how to perform the save. There are quite a few optional arguments for the SaveAs method. The code below illustrates

---

[3]This is not precisely true. The Open and Close methods both have optional arguments I have not mentioned here. You can find full details in online help.

Figure 8.5 Confirmation of Saved Name

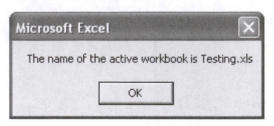

two of the more common arguments: **Filename** (the name and path of the file) and **FileFormat** (the type of format, such as the .xls or .xlsx format, to save the file as). The type for .xls format is xlWorkbookNormal; for .xlsx format, it is xlOpenXML-Workbook; and for .xlsm, it is xlOpenXMLWorkbookMacroEnabled. You can look up other arguments in online help.

```
Sub Workbooks2()
    ' This sub shows how to save an open workbook. It mimics the familiar Save
    ' and SaveAs menu items.
    With ActiveWorkbook
        ' This saves the active workbook under the same name - no questions asked.
        .Save

        ' The SaveAs method requires as arguments information you would normally fill
        ' out in the SaveAs dialog box.
        .SaveAs Filename:="C:\My Documents\Testing", _
            FileFormat:=xlOpenXMLWorkbook

        ' Check the name of the active workbook now.
        MsgBox "The name of the active workbook is " & .Name
    End With
End Sub
```

If you run this sub from the **Workbooks.xlsm** file, the SaveAs method will save a copy of this file in the C:\My Documents folder as **Testing.xlsx** and the message in Figure 8.5 will be displayed.

EXAMPLE 8.3   Locating the Path of a Workbook

When you open a workbook in Excel through the usual menu interface, you often need to search through folders to find the file you want to open. This example illustrates how the path to a file can be specified in VBA. Suppose, as in Exercise 8.1, that you are writing a sub in one workbook that opens another workbook. Also, suppose that both of these workbooks are in the *same* folder on your hard drive. Then you can use ThisWorkbook.Path to specify the path of the workbook to be opened. VBA always uses the **ThisWorkbook** object to refer to the workbook containing the VBA code. It then uses the **Path** property to specify the path to this workbook. For example, if the workbook containing the code is in the folder C:\VBA Examples\Chapter 8, then ThisWorkbook.Path returns the string

"C:\VBA Examples\Chapter 8". If another file in this same folder has file name Test.xlsx, then you can refer to it with the concatenated string

```
ThisWorkbook.Path & "\Test.xlsx"
```

Note that the second part of this string starts with a backslash. The Path property does not end with a backslash, so the backslash required for separating the folder from the filename must begin the literal part of the string.

The **Workbooks3** sub illustrates the entire procedure. It assumes that another file named Customer.xlsx exists in the same folder as the one in which the workbook containing the VBA resides.

```
Sub Workbooks3()
    ' This sub assumes a file named Customer.xlsx exists in the same folder as
    ' the file containing this code. Otherwise, an error message will be displayed.
    Workbooks.Open ThisWorkbook.Path & "\Customer.xlsx"
    MsgBox "The Customer.xlsx file is now open.", vbInformation

    Workbooks("Customer.xlsx").Close
    MsgBox "The Customer.xlsx file is now closed.", vbInformation
End Sub
```

EXAMPLE 8.4 Checking Properties of a Workbook

The **Workbooks4** sub illustrates a few properties you can check for an open workbook. These include its name, its file format, whether it is password-protected, whether it is an add-in, its path, whether it is read only, and whether it has been changed since the last time it was saved. Most of these properties would be used only in more advanced applications, but it nice to know that they are available.

```
Sub Workbooks4()
    ' This sub shows some properties you can obtain from an open workbook.
    With ActiveWorkbook
        ' Display the file's name.
        MsgBox "The active workbook is named " & .Name

        ' Check the file format (.xls, .xlsm, .csv, .xla, and many others). Actually, this
        ' will display an obscure number, such as 52 for .xlsm. You have to search
        ' online help to decipher the number!
        MsgBox "The file format is " & .FileFormat

        ' Check whether the file is password protected (True or False).
        MsgBox "Is the file password protected? " & .HasPassword

        ' Check whether the file is an add-in, with an .xla or .xlam extension (True or False).
        MsgBox "Is the file an add-in? " & .IsAddin
```

```
        ' Check the file's path.
        MsgBox "The path to the file is " & .Path

        ' Check whether the file is ReadOnly (True or False).
        MsgBox "Is the file read only? " & .ReadOnly

        ' Check whether the file has been saved since the last changed (True or False).
        MsgBox "Has the file been changed since the last save? " & .Saved
    End With
End Sub
```

8.5   Examples of Worksheets in VBA

This section presents several examples to illustrate typical operations with worksheets. Each example is based on the file **Worksheets.xlsm**. It contains an AllStates sheet that lists states in column A where a company has offices, as shown in Figure 8.6. Then for each state in the list, there is a sheet for that state that shows where the company's headquarters are located, how many branch offices it has, and what its 2008 sales were. For example, there is a sheet named Texas, and it contains the information in Figure 8.7.

Figure 8.6 State List

	A	B	C
1	**States where the company has offices**		
2	Michigan		
3	Illinois		
4	Ohio		
5	Massachusetts		
6	California		
7	Minnesota		
8	New York		
9	Indiana		
10	Pennsylvania		
11	Texas		

Figure 8.7 Information for a Typical State

	A	B
1	Headquarters	Dallas
2	Branch offices	4
3	Sales in 2008	$17,500

EXAMPLE 8.5 Displaying Information on All States

The **Worksheets1** sub loops through all sheets other than the AllStates sheet and displays information about each state in a separate message box. A typical state's sheet is referred to as ws (any other generic variable name could be used). The loop excludes the AllStates sheet by using an If statement to check whether the sheet's name is not AllStates. If this condition is true—the sheet's name is not AllStates—then the message is displayed. (Again, remember that <> means "not equal to.")

```vba
Sub Worksheets1()
    Dim ws As Worksheet

    ' Go through each state (however many there are) and display info for that state.
    For Each ws In ActiveWorkbook.Worksheets
        With ws
            If .Name <> "AllStates" Then
                MsgBox "The headquarters of " & .Name & " is " _
                    & .Range("B1").Value & ", there are " & .Range("B2").Value _
                    & " branch " & "offices, and sales in " & Year(Date) & " were " & _
                    Format(.Range("B3").Value, "$#,##0") & ".", _
                    vbInformation, .Name & " info"
            End If
        End With
    Next
End Sub
```

If you run this sub, you will see a message such as the one in Figure 8.8 for each state.

EXAMPLE 8.6 Displaying States and Headquarters

The **Worksheets2** sub is similar to the **Worksheets1** sub. It lists all states in the workbook and their headquarters in a *single* message box, with each state on a different line. The new line is accomplished with the built-in constant vbCrLf (short for carriage return and line feed). Another built-in constant vbTab is used to indent. Note how string concatenation is used to "build" the long message variable.

Figure 8.8 Information about a Typical State

Texas info

The headquarters of Texas is Dallas, there are 4 branch offices, and sales in 2008 were $17,500.

OK

Figure 8.9 State and headquarters information

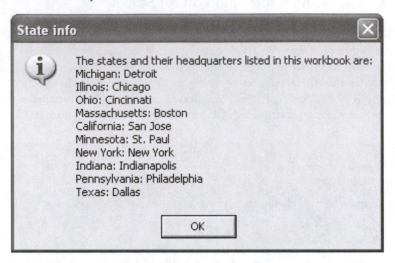

```
Sub Worksheets2()
    ' This sub just lists all of the states and their headquarters from the state sheets.
    Dim ws As Worksheet
    Dim message As String
    message = "The states and their headquarters listed in this workbook are:"
    ' Note the built-in vbCrLf constant. It codes in a line break.
    For Each ws In ActiveWorkbook.Worksheets
        If ws.Name <> "AllStates" Then _
            message = message & vbCrLf & ws.Name & ": " & ws.Range("B1").Value
    Next
    MsgBox message, vbInformation, "State info"
End Sub
```

When you run this sub, the message box in Figure 8.9 is displayed.

EXAMPLE 8.7   Adding a New State

The **Worksheets3** sub allows a new state to be added. It first asks the user to specify a new state not already in the list and then asks the user for information about this new state. The sub then copies an existing state's sheet to create a new sheet (essentially a template), it names the new sheet appropriately, and puts its information in cells B2, B3, and B4. Note how the Do loop is used to keep asking the user for a new state until one not already on the current list is provided.

```
Sub Worksheets3()
    ' This sub asks the user for a new state and its information,
    ' then creates a new sheet for the new state.
```

```
    Dim isNew As Boolean
    Dim newState As String
    Dim headQuarters As String
    Dim nBranches As Integer
    Dim Sales As Currency
    Dim ws As Worksheet

    ' Keep asking for a new state until the user provides one that is new.
    Do
        newState = InputBox("Enter a new state.", "New state")
        isNew = True
        For Each ws In ActiveWorkbook.Worksheets
            If newState = ws.Name Then
                MsgBox "This state already has a worksheet. Enter another state.", _
                    vbExclamation, "Duplicate state"
                isNew = False
                Exit For
            End If
        Next
    Loop Until isNew

    ' Get the required information for the new state. There's no error checking
    ' here. It probably should be added, just in case...
    headQuarters = InputBox("Enter the headquarters of " & newState, "Headquarters")
    nBranches = InputBox("Enter the number branch offices in " & newState, _
        "Branch offices")
    sales = InputBox("Enter sales in " & Year(Date) & " in " & newState, "Sales")

    ' Add the name of the new state to the list in the AllStates sheet.
    Worksheets("AllStates").Range("A1").End(xlDown).Offset(1, 0).Value = newState

    ' Copy the second sheet (or it could be any other state's sheet) to obtain a new
    ' sheet, which becomes the active sheet. Then change its name and information.
    Worksheets(2).Copy after:=Worksheets(Worksheets.Count)
    With ActiveSheet
        .Name = newState
        .Range("B1").Value = headQuarters
        .Range("B2").Value = nBranches
        .Range("B3").Value = Sales
    End With
End Sub
```

Examine the line

```
Worksheets("AllStates").Range("A1").End(xlDown).Offset(1,0).Value = newState
```

Starting in cell A1, this line uses .End(xlDown) to go to the bottom of the current list. Then it uses .Offset(1,0) to go one more row down. This is the first blank cell, where the name of the new state is placed.

Note also the line

```
Worksheets(2).Copy after:=Worksheets(Worksheets.Count)
```

This line makes a copy of the second sheet, and it places the copy after the worksheet referred to as Worksheets(Worksheets.Count). To see the effect of this, assume there are currently 8 worksheets. Then Worksheets.Count is 8, so the copy is placed after Worksheets(8). This means it is placed just after (to right of) all existing worksheets. This provides an example where it *is* useful to refer to a worksheet by number rather than by name.

EXAMPLE 8.8   Sorting Worksheets

The **Worksheets4** sub illustrates how to sort the worksheets for the individual states in alphabetical order. The trick is to use VBA's **Sort** method to sort the states in column A of the AllStates sheet. It then uses the **Move** method of a worksheet, with the **After** argument, to move the sheets around according to the sorted list in the AllStates sheet.

```vba
Sub Worksheets4()
    ' This sub puts the state sheets (not including the AllStates sheet) in alphabetical
    ' order. It first sorts the states in the AllStates sheet, then uses this order.

    Dim sheet1 As String
    Dim sheet2 As String
    Dim cell As Range

    ' Sort the states in the AllStates sheet.
    With Worksheets("AllStates")
        .Range("A1").Sort Key1:=.Range("A1"), Order1:=xlAscending, Header:=xlYes
        With .Range("A1")
            Range(.Offset(1, 0), .End(xlDown)).Name = "States"
        End With
    End With

    ' Rearrange the order of the other sheets according to the sorted list
    ' in the AllStates sheet. Sheet1 is always the name of the "current" sheet,
    ' whereas Sheet2 is always the name of the next sheet in alphabetical order.
    sheet1 = "AllStates"
    For Each cell In Range("States")
        sheet2 = cell.Value
        Worksheets(sheet2).Move after:=Worksheets(sheet1)
        sheet1 = sheet2
    Next

    Worksheets("AllStates").Activate
    Range("A1").Select
    MsgBox "State sheets are now in alphabetical order."
End Sub
```

Pay very close attention to how the For Each loop works. The worksheet that sheet1 refers to is initially the AllStates sheet. After that, sheet1 always refers to the current sheet in alphabetical order, and sheet2 refers to the *next* sheet in alphabetical order, which is moved to the right of sheet1. After the move, the value of the variable sheet1 is replaced by the value of sheet2 to get ready for the *next* move. This logic is a bit tricky, especially if you are new to programming. To understand it better, try the following. Open the

Worksheets.xlsm file, get into the VBE, and create watches for the sheet1 and sheet2 variables. (You do this with the **Debug→Add Watch** menu item.) Then put your cursor anywhere inside the **Worksheets4** sub and step through the program one line at a time by repeatedly pressing the F8 key. Once you get toward the bottom of the sub, you can see in the Watch window how the values of sheet1 and sheet2 keep changing.

8.6 Examples of Charts in VBA

A Chart object is one of the trickiest Excel objects to manipulate with VBA. The reason is that a chart has so many objects associated with it, and each has a large number of properties and methods. If you need to create charts in VBA, it is probably best to record most of the code and then modify the recorded code as necessary, making frequent visits to online help. Alternatively, you can use the Excel's chart tools to create the chart, and then use VBA only to modify the existing chart in some way.[4]

The following subs indicate some of the possibilities. They are listed in the file **Charts.xlsm**. This file has monthly sales for several products; a portion is shown in Figure 8.10. I first used Excel's chart tools manually (no VBA) to create a line chart on the same sheet as the data. This chart shows the monthly time series movement of two of the products, as illustrated in Figure 8.11. Although VBA could be used to build the chart from scratch, it is much easier to build a chart first with Excel's tools and then use VBA to fine-tune it.

Location of a Chart

The first issue is the location of the chart. As you probably know, a chart can be placed on a separate chart sheet (a special type of sheet reserved only for charts, with no rows and columns), or it can be embedded in a worksheet, as in Figure 8.11. The choice is usually a matter of taste. (If you are using Excel's tools you make this choice in the Design ribbon under the Chart Tools group.) In the first case, assuming the name of the chart sheet is SalesChart, you would refer to it in VBA as Charts("SalesChart"). Here, Charts is the collection of all chart sheets, and it is followed by the name of the particular chart sheet.

In the second case, assuming this chart is the *only* embedded chart on a worksheet called Sales, you must first refer to the object "containing" the chart as Worksheets("Sales").ChartObjects(1). Then the **Chart** object itself is one step down the hierarchy from the **ChartObject** object. Admittedly, it is confusing

---

[4]As in Chapter 4, I will remind you that recording takes you only so far in Excel 2007. If the recorder is on and you make changes to a chart, a surprising number of these changes are not recorded at all. I find it hard to believe that this was intentional on Microsoft's part. The more likely explanation is that they ran out of time. Still, these actions *can* be coded, or at least most of them can; you just have to search in online help and perform some trial and error. Hopefully, this problem will be fixed in the next version of Excel.

Figure 8.10 Monthly Product Sales Data

	A	B	C	D	E	F	G	H
1	Month	Product1	Product2	Product3	Product4	Product5	Product6	Product7
2	Jan-07	791	613	450	434	488	400	559
3	Feb-07	781	649	646	548	442	652	423
4	Mar-07	520	631	488	622	513	545	726
5	Apr-07	635	615	568	709	686	461	629
6	May-07	418	463	433	523	548	655	420
7	Jun-07	431	504	580	540	767	487	631
8	Jul-07	786	534	490	408	653	704	708
9	Aug-07	695	734	618	564	620	453	553
10	Sep-07	547	671	699	721	657	448	760
11	Oct-07	703	580	441	459	617	436	472
12	Nov-07	579	658	419	523	424	720	529
13	Dec-07	601	592	408	666	800	691	723
14	Jan-08	522	724	410	764	504	481	657
15	Feb-08	425	614	553	799	488	619	733

Figure 8.11 Sales Chart of Two Selected Products

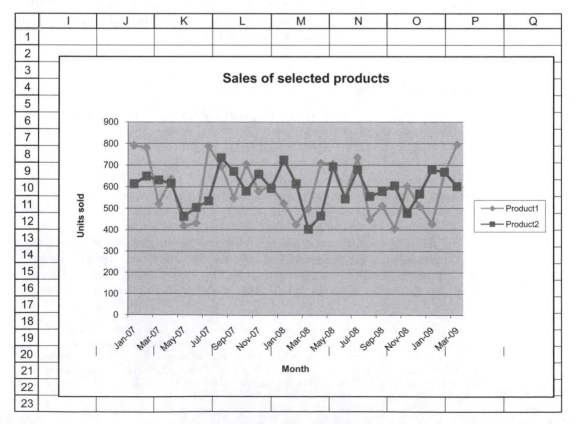

and probably sounds like double-talk, but just think of **ChartObject** objects as floating above a worksheet's cells. These objects have no other purpose than to "hold" **Chart** objects. You can resize and move the ChartObject containers, and then you can manipulate the properties of the underlying chart, such as its axes and its legend. Finally, just to make sure the point is clear, remember that the ChartObject object is relevant only for charts placed on a worksheet. It is not relevant for chart sheets. (If Microsoft changed this system in a future release, many of us would be very happy. Working with ChartObject objects and Chart objects can be very confusing!)

EXAMPLE 8.9   Displaying Properties of a Chart

The **Charts1** sub works with the chart contained in the first (only) ChartObject container of the Sales sheet of the **Charts.xlsm** file. Remember that the chart itself was *not* created with VBA. The VBA below simply displays properties of the chart that already exists. It first refers to the **ChartObject** container and displays its **Left**, **Top**, **Height**, and **Width** properties. These are properties of many objects in Excel that can be moved and resized, and they are always measured in **points**, where a point is 1/72 of an inch. **Top** is the distance from the top of the container to the top of row 1, **Left** is the distance from the left of the container to the left of column A, and **Height** and **Width** are the height and width of the container.

The sub then uses the With .Chart statement to refer to the **Chart** object contained in the ChartObject container and proceeds to examine a number of its properties. Note that some properties can return obscure numbers. For example, the **ChartType** property in this example returns 65, evidently the index for a line chart of the type shown. The other properties should be fairly self-explanatory. You should run this sub to see what the message boxes display.

```
Sub Charts1()
    ' This sub illustrates some of the properties of a chart. The chart already
    ' exists (was built with the Chart Wizard) on the Sales sheet.

    With Worksheets("Sales").ChartObjects(1)
        MsgBox "The next four messages indicate the position of the chart."
        MsgBox "Left property: " & .Left
        MsgBox "Top property: " & .Top
        MsgBox "Height property: " & .Height
        MsgBox "Width property: " & .Width
        MsgBox "The next few messages indicate some properties of the chart."
        With .Chart
            MsgBox "Chart name: " & .Name
            MsgBox "Chart type: " & .ChartType
            MsgBox "HasLegend property: " & .HasLegend
            MsgBox "HasTitle property: " & .HasTitle
            MsgBox "Title: " & .ChartTitle.Text
            MsgBox "Number of series plotted: " & .SeriesCollection.Count
            MsgBox "Some properties of the horizontal axis (there are many!):"
            With .Axes(xlCategory)
```

```
                  MsgBox "Format of tick labels: " & .TickLabels.NumberFormat
                  MsgBox "Title: " & .AxisTitle.Caption
                  MsgBox "Font size of title: " & .AxisTitle.Font.Size
             End With
             MsgBox "Some properties of the vertical axis:"
             With .Axes(xlValue)
                  MsgBox "Title: " & .AxisTitle.Caption
                  MsgBox "Font size of title: " & .AxisTitle.Font.Size
                  MsgBox "Minimum scale: " & .MinimumScale
                  MsgBox "Maximum scale: " & .MaximumScale
             End With
        End With
    End With
End Sub
```

EXAMPLE 8.10   Changing Properties of a Chart

The previous sub simply *displays* the current values of various chart properties. The **Charts2** sub *modifies* the chart. Specifically, it allows the user to choose which two products (out of the seven available) to plot. It uses the **SeriesCollection** object, which is one step down the hierarchy from the **Chart** object. In general, a chart plots a number of **Series** objects, labeled **SeriesCollection(1)**, **SeriesCollection(2)**, and so on. The properties of each series can be changed, as described in the comments in the sub, to plot different data. Specifically, the **Values** property designates the data range for the series, the **XValues** property designates the range for the values on the horizontal axis, and the **Name** property is a descriptive name for the series that is used in the legend. Note that the data ranges in the Sales sheet have already been range-named Product1 through Product7. These range names are used in the sub. Also, note how the line

```
.Name = Range("Product" & index1).Cells(1).Offset(-1, 0).Value
```

uses .Cells(1) to go to the first sales figure in a product range and then uses .Offset (-1,0) to go one row above to find the product's name (such as Product1).

```
Sub Charts2()
    ' This sub allows you to change the product columns (two of them) that are charted.
    ' It assumes the chart currently has two series plotted.

    Dim productIndex1 As Integer
    Dim productIndex2 As Integer

    MsgBox "You can choose any two of the products to plot versus time."
    productIndex1 = InputBox("Enter the index of the first product to plot (1 to 7)")
    productIndex2 = InputBox("Enter the index of the second product to plot (1 to 7, not " _
        & productIndex1 & ")")

    ' Note that the columns of data already have range names Product1, Product2, etc.
    With Worksheets("Sales").ChartObjects(1).Chart
        With .SeriesCollection(1)
```

```
                    ' The Values property indicates the range of the data being plotted.
                    ' The XValues property indicates the values on the X-axis (in this case,
                    ' the months). The Name property is the name of the series (which is
                    ' shown in the legend). This name is found in row 1, right above the
                    ' first cell in the corresponding Product range.
                    .Values = Range("Product" & productIndex1)
                    .XValues = Range("Month")
                    .Name = Range("Product" & productIndex1).Cells(1).Offset(-1, 0).Value
                End With

                ' The XValues property doesn't have to be set again, since both series
                ' use the same values on the horizontal axis.
                With .SeriesCollection(2)
                    .Values = Range("Product" & productIndex2)
                    .Name = Range("Product" & productIndex2).Cells(1).Offset(-1, 0).Value
                End With
            End With
        End Sub
```

EXAMPLE 8.11 More Properties and Methods of Charts

The **Charts3** sub indicates some further possibilities when working with charts. Try running it to see the effects on the chart. (Does anyone memorize all of these properties and methods? I doubt it, but some experimentation with the recorder on and a few visits to online help will enable you to create this same level of code—when you really need it.)

```
Sub Charts3()
    ' This sub shows some other things you can do to fine tune charts. In general,
    ' you learn some of the coding from recording, some from the Object Browser,
    ' and the rest from trial and error.

    Dim cht As Chart
    Dim color1 As Integer
    Dim color2 As Integer

    ' Use this next statement so that the random colors chosen later on will be
    ' different from run to run.
    Randomize

    Set cht = Worksheets("Sales").ChartObjects(1).Chart
    With cht

        ' Change properties of background (PlotArea).
        With .PlotArea
            MsgBox "The plot area will be changed from gray to blank."
            .ClearFormats
            MsgBox "It will now be restored to light gray."
            .Interior.ColorIndex = 15
        End With

        ' Remove and restore grid lines.
        With .Axes(xlValue)
```

```
        MsgBox "The horizontal grid lines will be deleted."
        .HasMajorGridlines = False
        MsgBox "They will now be restored."
        .HasMajorGridlines = True
    End With

    ' Generate two random colors (making sure they aren't the same).
    MsgBox "The two series will now to some random change colors."
    color1 = Int(Rnd * 40) + 1
    Do

        color2 = Int(Rnd * 40) + 1
    Loop Until color2 <> color1

    ' Change some colors in the chart.
    With .SeriesCollection(1)
        .Border.ColorIndex = color1
        .MarkerBackgroundColorIndex = color1
        .MarkerForegroundColorIndex = color1
    End With
    With .SeriesCollection(2)
        .Border.ColorIndex = color2
        .MarkerBackgroundColorIndex = color2
        .MarkerForegroundColorIndex = color2
    End With
    End With
End Sub
```

8.7 Summary

This chapter has built upon your knowledge of Range objects from Chapter 6. It is necessary to be able to manipulate workbooks, worksheets, and charts with VBA code in many applications, and this chapter has illustrated some of the most useful techniques for doing so. At this point, it is not important that you memorize all the properties and methods of these objects. It is more important that you have some feeling for what is *possible* and that you know how to find help when you need it. You can always revisit the examples in this chapter to search for key details, and you can always visit the Object Browser for excellent online help.

EXERCISES

1. Suppose you have a lot of Excel files currently open. You would like to count the number of these files that contain a worksheet with the name Revenues. Write a sub that reports the result in a message box.

2. Repeat the previous exercise, but now count the number of files that contain a worksheet with Revenue somewhere in the name. For example, this would include sheets with names "2005 Revenues" and "Revenues for Quarter 1".

3. Write a general purpose sub that opens a particular workbook, such as **C:\My Files\Company Data.xlsx,** adds a new worksheet named FormulaList after the original worksheets, and then goes through all of the original worksheets hunting for cells with formulas. Each time it finds a formula, it records information about

it in a new row of the FormulaList worksheet. Specifically, it records the worksheet's name in column A, it records the formula as a string in column B, and it records the formula's value in column C. (*Hint*: To check whether a cell contains a formula, use VBA's **HasFormula** property of a range.)

4. Write a sub that counts the number of worksheets in a particular (open) workbook and also counts the number of sheets. Note that the **Worksheets** collection includes only worksheets (those with rows and columns), whereas the **Sheets** collection contains worksheets and chart sheets. Then test your sub by creating a workbook with some worksheets and at least one chart sheet and running your sub on it.

5. The file **Chart Example.xlsx** contains two sheets. The first sheet contains some data and four column charts based on the data. The second sheet is a chart sheet that is also based on the data. Write a sub that counts the number of ChartObject objects in the workbook and also counts the number of charts in the workbook. The counts should be 4 and 5, respectively.

6. Open a new workbook and insert a module in this workbook. Then write a sub that does the following: (1) It opens some workbook that you know exists on your hard drive (you can choose which one); (2) it displays a message indicating the number of worksheets in this workbook; (3) it closes the workbook; and (4) it tries to open a workbook that you know does not exist on your hard drive. What happens when it tries to open this latter workbook?

7. Open a new workbook and save it under any name you like. Then write a sub that displays a message like: "The name of this workbook is _, and it was created by _." The blanks should be filled in by appropriate properties of the ActiveWorkbook (or the Application) object.

8. Suppose you have a folder on your hard drive that contains a number of Excel files with the names **Customer1.xlsx**, **Customer2.xlsx**, and so on. You're not sure how many such files there are, but they are named this way, with consecutive integers. Write a sub to open each file, one at a time, save it under a new name, and then close it. The new names should be **CustomerOrders1.xlsx**, **CustomerOrders2.xlsx**, and so on.

9. Continuing the previous exercise, suppose you want to check whether the Customer files are "read only." Write a sub that (1) counts the number of Customer files in the folder and the number of them that are read only and (2) displays this information in a message box.

10. The file **Cities.xlsx** contains an AllCities sheet that lists all cities where a company has offices. Write a sub that does the following: (1) for each city in the list, it checks whether there is a sheet with the name of that city in the workbook, and if there isn't one, it adds one, and (2) it deletes any city sheet if the sheet's name is not in the current AllCities list. The sub should be written so that it can be run at any time and will always respond with the current list of cities in the AllCities sheet. (Note: Your sub should work if the AllCities list has exactly one city or if it has no cities.)

11. The AllProducts sheet in the file **Product Info.xlsx** lists information on various software packages a company sells. Each product has an associated category listed in column B. Write a sub that creates a sheet for each category represented in the list, with the name of the sheet being the category (such as Business). For each category sheet, it should enter the product names and their prices in columns A and B, starting in row 4. Each category sheet should have an appropriate label,

such as "Products in the Business category", in cell A1; it should have labels "Product" and "Price" in cells A3 and B3; and the column width for its column A should be the same as the column width of column A in the AllProducts sheet. (Note that there are only three categories represented in the current data. However, the program should be written so that it works for any number of categories—and any number of products—that might be present.)

12. The AllProducts sheet in the file **Product Purchases.xlsx** has unit prices for all software packages a mail-order company sells. It also has an Invoice sheet. Whenever the company takes an order from a customer, the order taker gets the customer's name, the date, and the quantity of each product the customer wants to purchase. These quantities are written in column C of the AllProducts sheet. The information on this sheet is then used to create an invoice for the customer on the Invoice sheet. The current Invoice sheet is a "template" for a general invoice. The manager wants you to write two subs, **ClearOld** and **CreateInvoice**, and attach them to the buttons at the top of the AllProducts sheet. They should do the following.

   a. The **ClearOld** sub should clear any quantities from a previous order from column C of the AllProducts sheet. It should also clear any old data from the Invoice sheet from row 5 down.

   b. The **CreateInvoice** sub should be run right after the order taker has gotten the information from the customer and has entered quantities in column C of the AllProducts sheet. (When you test your macro, you should first enter some quantities in column C.) The sub should use input boxes to ask for the customer's name and the date, and it should use these to complete the labels in cells A1 and A2 of the Invoice sheet. It should then transfer the relevant data about products (only those ordered) to the Invoice sheet, it should calculate the prices for each product ordered (unit price times quantity ordered), and it should calculate the tax on the order (5% sales tax) and the total cost of the order, including tax, in column D, right below the prices of individual products, with appropriate labels in column C (such as "5% sales tax" and "Total Cost").

   c. As a finishing touch, add some code to the **CreateInvoice** sub to print the finished invoice. (Although the chapter didn't discuss printing, you should be able to discover how to do it, either by using the recorder or by looking up online help.)

13. The file **Sales Chart Finished.xlsm** has monthly data on two products, a corresponding chart and four buttons. The ranges of the product data in columns B and C are range-named Product1 and Product2. To understand what you are supposed to do, open this file and click on the buttons. It should be clear what's going on. Unfortunately (for you), the code behind the buttons is password protected. Your job is to create similar code yourself in the file **Sales Chart.xlsx**. This file has the same chart and same buttons, but there is no code yet (which means that the buttons aren't attached to any macros). This code is tricky, and you'll probably have to look through the code in the examples a few times, as well as online help, to get everything working correctly. (I did!)

Arrays

9.1 Introduction

Chapter 7 emphasized the benefits of loops for performing repeated tasks. Loops are often accompanied by the topic of this chapter, arrays. Arrays are lists, where each element of the list is an indexed element of the array. For example, suppose you need to capture the names and salaries of your employees, which are currently listed in columns A and B of a worksheet. Later on in the program, you plan to analyze them in some way. You might use a loop (either a For loop or a Do loop) to go through each employee in the worksheet, but how do you store the employee information in memory for later processing? The answer is that you store it in employee and salary arrays. The name and salary of employee 1 are stored in employee(1) and salary(1), those for employee 2 are stored in employee(2) and salary(2), and so on.

A useful analogy is to the small mailboxes you see at a post office. An array is analogous to a group of mailboxes, numbered 1, 2, and so on. You can put something into a particular mailbox—that is, into an array element—in a statement such as employee(5) = "Bob Jones". Similarly, you can read the contents of a particular mailbox with a statement such as MsgBox "The fifth employee is" & employee(5). In other words, array elements work just like normal variables, except that you have an indexed list of them. This indexing makes them particularly amenable to looping, as this chapter illustrates.

9.2 Excercise

The following exercise is typical in its use of arrays. Although there are certainly ways to do the exercise *without* arrays, they make the job much easier. Actually, this exercise is simpler than the examples discussed later in this chapter, but you should study the examples before attempting this exercise.

Exercise 9.1 Aggregating Sales Data

Consider a large appliance/electronics store with a number of salespeople. The company keeps a spreadsheet listing the names of the salespeople and the dollar amounts of individual sales transactions. This information is in the file **Transactions.xlsx**, as illustrated in Figure 9.1 (Note the many hidden rows.) Periodically, salespeople are hired and fired. The list in column A is always the most current list, and it is always shown in alphabetical order. Column B lists the corresponding Social

Figure 9.1 Salespeople and Transaction Data

	A	B	C	D	E	F	G	H	I
1	Data on sales people			Individual sales				Aggregated sales	
2	Name	SS#		Salesperson SS#	Date	Dollar amount		Salesperson	Dollar amount
3	Adams	776-61-4492		640-34-5749	1-Mar-08	$323			
4	Barnes	640-34-5749		365-99-1247	1-Mar-08	$260			
5	Cummings	115-12-5882		365-99-1247	1-Mar-08	$305			
6	Davis	736-95-5401		932-62-4204	1-Mar-08	$366			
7	Edwards	880-52-9379		986-38-6372	1-Mar-08	$217			
8	Falks	348-79-3515		449-44-7141	1-Mar-08	$294			
9	Gregory	546-44-7576		640-34-5749	1-Mar-08	$289			
10	Highsmith	467-86-5786		769-79-9580	1-Mar-08	$460			
11	Invery	765-85-7850		932-62-4204	1-Mar-08	$567			
12	Jacobs	986-38-6372		449-44-7141	1-Mar-08	$970			
13	Ketchings	769-79-9580		919-58-6925	1-Mar-08	$426			
14	Leonard	468-38-8871		115-12-5882	1-Mar-08	$214			
15	Moore	919-58-6925		546-44-7576	1-Mar-08	$306			
16	Nixon	126-27-9832		467-86-5786	1-Mar-08	$258			
17	Price	631-55-5579		546-44-7576	1-Mar-08	$287			
18	Reynolds	529-61-3561		765-85-7850	2-Mar-08	$183			
19	Stimson	474-60-8847		640-34-5749	2-Mar-08	$196			
20	Travis	449-44-7141		365-99-1247	2-Mar-08	$322			
21	Vexley	539-55-4012		640-34-5749	3-Mar-08	$180			
22	Wheaton	833-44-9683		474-60-8847	3-Mar-08	$205			
23	Zimmerman	932-62-4204		126-96-8510	3-Mar-08	$286			
24				126-96-8510	3-Mar-08	$264			
781				348-79-3515	23-Jul-08	$333			
782				932-62-4204	23-Jul-08	$167			
783				952-12-3694	24-Jul-08	$253			
784				776-61-4492	24-Jul-08	$211			
785				952-12-3694	24-Jul-08	$56			

Security numbers. The sales data in columns D to F are sorted by date. Also, some of these sales are for salespeople no longer with the company. That is, some of the Social Security numbers in column D have no corresponding values in column B.

The purpose of the exercise is to write a program to fill columns H and I with aggregate dollar amounts for each salesperson currently employed. You can open the file **Transactions Finished.xlsm** and click on its button to see the results, which should appear as in Figure 9.2. However, do not look at the VBA code until you have tried writing the program yourself. Make sure you think through a solution method before you begin programming. Most important, think about what arrays you will need and how they will be used.

9.3 The Need for Arrays

Many beginning programmers think that arrays are difficult to master, and they react by arguing that arrays are not worth the trouble. They are wrong on both counts. First, arrays are not that difficult. If you understand the mailbox analogy and keep it in mind, you should catch on to arrays quite easily. Second, arrays are definitely not just a "luxury" for computer programmers. They are absolutely necessary for dealing with lists. Consider a slightly different version of the employee salary example from

Figure 9.2 Results

	H	I	J	K	L	M	N	O
1	Aggregated sales							
2	Salesperson	Dollar amount	First sale	Last sale				
3	Adams	$12,429	3/4/2005	7/24/2005				
4	Barnes	$11,308	3/1/2005	7/1/2005				
5	Cummings	$8,117	3/1/2005	7/20/2005				
6	Davis	$9,831	3/7/2005	7/22/2005			Aggregate	
7	Edwards	$7,602	3/6/2005	7/16/2005				
8	Falks	$9,223	3/4/2005	7/23/2005				
9	Gregory	$7,112	3/1/2005	7/18/2005				
10	Highsmith	$7,234	3/1/2005	7/14/2005				
11	Invery	$9,436	3/2/2005	7/17/2005				
12	Jacobs	$12,012	3/1/2005	7/21/2005				
13	Ketchings	$10,935	3/1/2005	7/23/2005				
14	Leonard	$8,765	3/7/2005	7/17/2005				
15	Moore	$8,551	3/1/2005	7/22/2005				
16	Nixon	$11,374	3/4/2005	7/20/2005				
17	Price	$8,055	3/5/2005	7/6/2005				
18	Reynolds	$9,246	3/10/2005	7/19/2005				
19	Stimson	$10,161	3/3/2005	7/15/2005				
20	Travis	$8,202	3/1/2005	7/6/2005				
21	Vexley	$8,594	3/7/2005	7/22/2005				
22	Wheaton	$9,030	3/14/2005	7/17/2005				
23	Zimmerman	$10,224	3/1/2005	7/23/2005				

the introduction. Now suppose you would like to go through the list of employees in columns A and B (again inside a loop) and keep track of the names and salaries of all employees who make a salary greater than $50,000. Later on, you might want to analyze these employees in some way, such as finding their average salary.

The easiest way to proceed is to go through the employee list with a counter initially equal to 0. Each time you encounter a salary greater than $50,000, you add 1 to the counter and store the employee's name and salary in hiPaidEmp and hiSalary arrays. Here is how the code might look (assuming the employees start in row 2 and the number of employees in the data set is known to be nEmployees).

```
counter = 0
With Range("A1")
    For i = 1 to nEmployees
        If .Offset(i,1).Value > 50000 Then
            counter = counter + 1
            hiPaidEmp(counter) = .Offset(i,0).Value
            hiSalary(counter) = .Offset(i,1).Value
        End If
    Next
End If
```

After this loop is completed, you will know the number of highly paid employees—it is the final value of counter. More important, you will know the identities and salaries of these employees. The information for the first highly paid employee is stored in hiPaidEmp(1) and hiSalary(1), the information for the second is stored in hiPaidEmp(2) and hiSalary(2), and so on. You are now free to analyze the data in these newly created lists in any way you like.

Admittedly, there is a nonarray solution to this example. Each time you find a highly paid employee, you could immediately transfer the information on this employee to another section of the worksheet (columns D and E, say) rather than storing it in arrays.[1] Then you could analyze the data in columns D and E later. In other words, there is usually a way around using arrays—especially if you are working in Excel where you can store information easily. However, most programmers agree that arrays represent the best method for working with lists, not only in VBA but in all other programming languages. They offer power and flexibility that simply cannot be achieved without them.

9.4 Rules for Working with Arrays

When you declare a variable with a Dim statement, VBA knows from the variable's type how much memory to set aside for it. The situation is slightly different for arrays. Now, VBA must know how *many* elements are in the array, as well as their variable type, so that it can set aside the right amount of memory for the entire array. Therefore, when you declare an array, you must indicate to VBA that you are declaring an *array* of a certain type, not just a single variable. You must also tell VBA how many elements are in the array. You can do this in the declaration line or later in the program. Finally, you must indicate what index you want the array to begin with. Unlike what you might expect, the default first index is *not* 1; it is 0. However, you can override this if you like.

Here is a typical declaration of two arrays named employee and salary:

```
Dim employee(100) As String, salary(100) As Currency
```

This line indicates that (1) each element of the employee array is a string variable, (2) each element of the salary array is a currency variable, and (3) each array has 100 elements. (This assumes an option base of 1. See below.)

The Option Base Statement

Surprisingly, unless you add a certain line to your code, the first employee will *not* be employee(1) and the last employee will not be employee(100); they will be employee(0) and ezmployee(99). This is because the default in VBA is called **0-based indexing**.

---

[1]This same type of comment is true for the the other examples in this chapter. However, if the lists are really long, the array solutions will be considerably faster. Besides, in situations where the lists are *extremely* long, the contents might not even fit in a worksheet.

This means that the indexes of an array are 0, 1, 2, and so on. There is a technical reason for having 0-based indexing as the default; however, most of us do not think this way. Most of us prefer **1-based indexing**, where the indexes are 1, 2, 3, and so on. The simple reason is that when we count, we typically begin with 1. If you want your arrays to be 1-based, you can use the following **Option Base** line:

```
Option Base 1
```

This line should be placed at the top of each of your modules, right below the **Option Explicit** line (which, if you remember, forces you to declare your variables).

Even if 0-based indexing is in effect, you can override it by indicating explicitly how you want a particular array to be indexed. The following line shows how you can do this for the employee and salary arrays.

```
Dim employee(1 To 100) As String, salary(1 To 100) As Currency
```

Now the first employee will be employee(1) and the last will be employee(100), regardless of any Option Base line at the top of the module.[2] By the way, if you do *not* use an Option Base 1 line and declare an array, say, as salary(100), then the array will have 101 elements, indexed 0 to 100.

Dynamic Indexing and Redim

There are many times where you know you need an array. However, when you are writing the code, you have no way of knowing how many elements it will contain. For example, you might have an InputBox statement near the top of your sub asking the user for the number of employees at her company. Once she tells you that there are 150 employees, then (but not until then) you will know you need an array of size 150. So how should you declare the array in this case? You do it in two steps. First, you declare that you need an *array*, as opposed to a single variable, in the Dim statement by putting empty parentheses next to the variable name, as in

```
Dim employee() as String
```

Then in the body of the sub, once you learn how many elements the array should have, you use the **Redim** statement to set aside the appropriate amount of memory for the array. The following two lines illustrate a typical example.

```
nEmployees = InputBox("How many employees are in your company?")
Redim employee(1 to nEmployees)
```

---

[2]Interestingly, Microsoft's newest technology, .NET, *requires* programmers to use 0-based indexing—it cannot be overridden. Don't be surprised if this happens to VBA sometime in the future. If it does, we will all have to get used to counting starting at 0.

If the user enters 10, then the employee array will be of size 10. If she enters 1000, it will be of size 1000. The Redim statement enables the array to adjust to the precise size you need.

You can actually use the Redim statement as many times as you like in a sub to readjust the size of the array. (The examples later in the chapter illustrates why you might want to do this. It is actually not at all uncommon.) The only problem is that when you use the Redim statement to change the size of an array, all of the previous *contents* of the array are deleted. This is often not what you want. Fortunately, you can override this default behavior with the keyword **Preserve**, as in the following lines.

```
nEmployees = nEmployees + 1
Redim Preserve employee(1 to nEmployees)
```

These lines would be appropriate if you just discovered that you have one extra employee, so that you need one extra element in the employee array. To keep from deleting the names of the previous employees when you redimension the array, you insert the keyword Preserve in the Redim line. This gives you an extra array element, but the previous elements retain their current values.

Multiple Dimensions

Arrays can have more than one dimension. (The arrays so far have been one-dimensional.) For example, a two-dimensional array has two indexes, as in employee(2,18). This might be appropriate if you want to index your employees by location and by number, so that this refers to employee 18 at location 2. The main difference in working with multidimensional arrays is that you must indicate the number of elements for *each* dimension. As an example, the following line indicates that the employee array requires 10 elements for the first dimension and 100 for the second dimension.

```
Dim employee(1 to 10,1 to 100) As String
```

Therefore, VBA will set aside 10*100 = 1000 locations in memory for this array.

Note that this *could* be quite wasteful. If the first dimension is the employee location and the second is the employee number at a location, suppose there are 100 employees at location 1 but only 5 at location 2. Then the array elements employee(2,6) through employee(2,100) are essentially wasted. Even though today's computer memory is cheap and abundant, computer programmers worry about this sort of thing. Therefore, they warn against using multidimensional arrays unless it is really necessary. You will sometimes see code with two-dimensional arrays, but you will rarely see arrays with three or more dimensions.

9.5 Examples of Arrays in VBA

The best way to understand arrays—and to appreciate the need for them—is to look at some examples. The first example is a fairly simple one. The next three are more challenging and interesting. They are typical of the examples that really *require* arrays.

EXAMPLE 9.1 Looking Up a Price

The VLookup and HLookup functions in Excel are very useful for looking up information in a table. This example illustrates how you can accomplish the same thing with VBA and arrays. The file **Unit Prices.xlsm** contains a table of product codes and unit prices, as shown in Figure 9.3 (with many hidden rows). We want to write a program that asks the user for a product code. It then searches the list of product codes for a matching product code. If it finds one, it displays an appropriate message, such as in Figure 9.4. If it does not find a match, it displays a message to this effect.

Although there are many ways to write the required program, the **Lookup-Price** sub listed below illustrates how to do it with arrays. The number of products is found first, then the productCode and unitPrice arrays are redimensioned appropriately and a For loop is used to populate these arrays with the data in columns

Figure 9.3 Table of Product Information

	A	B	C
1	**Table of unit prices for products**		
2			
3	Product code	Unit price	
4	L2201	50.99	
5	N1351	34.99	
6	N7622	10.95	
7	B7118	99.95	
8	R1314	105.99	
9	W6734	42.95	
10	T4463	72.99	
11	G9196	62.95	
12	B3850	101.99	
1211	F5012	80.95	
1212	D8665	51.95	
1213	R7932	93.95	
1214	R8509	14.95	
1215	L4701	3.95	

Figure 9.4 Unit Price of Requested Product

A and B of the worksheet. Next, after a user specifies a product code, another For loop searches the productCode array for a match to the requested code. If one is found, the corresponding element of the unitPrice array is stored in the requestedPrice variable. In either case an appropriate message is displayed at the end. Note the Option Base 1 line at the top of the module. As in most examples, it is more natural to index the products starting with 1 than with 0.

```
Option Explicit
Option Base 1

Sub LookupPrice()
    Dim productCode() As String
    Dim unitPrice() As Currency
    Dim i As Integer
    Dim found As Boolean
    Dim requestedCode As String
    Dim requestedPrice As Currency
    Dim nProducts As Integer

    ' Find the number of products, redimension the arrays, and fill them
    ' with the data in the lists.
    With Range("A3")
        nProducts = Range(.Offset(1, 0), .End(xlDown)).Rows.Count
        ReDim productCode(nProducts)
        ReDim unitPrice(nProducts)
        For i = 1 To nProducts
            productCode(i) = .Offset(i, 0).Value
            unitPrice(i) = .Offset(i, 1).Value
        Next
    End With

    ' Get a product code from the user (no error checking).
    requestedCode = InputBox("Enter a product code (an uppercase letter" _
        & "followed by four digits).")

    ' Look for the code in the list. Record its unit price if it is found.
    found = False
    For i = 1 To nProducts
        If productCode(i) = requestedCode Then
            found = True
            requestedPrice = unitPrice(i)
            Exit For
        End If
    Next
```

```
' Display an appropriate message.
If found Then
    MsgBox "The unit price of product code " & requestedCode & " is " & _
        Format(requestedPrice, "$0.00"), vbInformation, "Product found"
Else
    MsgBox "The product code " & requestedCode & " is not on the list.", _
        vbInformation, "Product not found"
End If
End Sub
```

EXAMPLE 9.2 Keeping Track of Products Sold

A company keeps a spreadsheet of each sales transaction it makes. These transaction data, sorted by date, are listed in columns A to C of the **Product Sales.xlsm** file. (See Figure 9.5, which has many hidden rows.) Each row shows the four-digit code of the product sold, plus the date and dollar amount of the transaction. Periodically, the company wants to know how many separate products have been sold, and it wants a

Figure 9.5 Transaction Data

	A	B	C
1	**Individual sales data**		
2	Product Code	Date	Amount ($)
3	2508	1/2/2008	469
4	1111	1/5/2008	481
5	1107	1/6/2008	434
6	1119	1/6/2008	596
7	2502	1/10/2008	552
8	2523	1/11/2008	401
9	2515	1/13/2008	533
10	1107	1/15/2008	375
11	1108	1/15/2008	528
12	1118	1/15/2008	628
13	2513	1/23/2008	465
188	2515	12/21/2008	454
189	1111	12/23/2008	463
190	2515	12/23/2008	532
191	1104	12/25/2008	524
192	1111	12/26/2008	535
193	2510	12/30/2008	512

list of all products sold, the number of transactions for each product sold, and the total dollar amount for each product sold. It wants this list to be placed in columns E to G, and it wants the list to be sorted in descending order by dollar amount.

The **ProductSales** sub listed below does the job. When a button is clicked to run this sub, the message box in Figure 9.6 appears, and the list in Figure 9.7 is created. (This figure does not show all 49 products sold. Some rows have been hidden.)

The idea behind the program is to loop through the product codes in column A, which are stored in an array called productCodesData, one at a time. We use these to build an array called productCodesFound. It eventually contains the *distinct* product codes in column A. At each step of the loop, we compare a product code in column A to all product codes already found. If this product code has already been found, we

Figure 9.6 Number of Products Sold

Figure 9.7 Results

	E	F	G
1	**Summary data**		
2	Product Code	Quantity	Amount ($)
3	1118	7	3818
4	1106	8	3764
5	2520	7	3696
6	1120	6	3415
7	2505	6	3306
8	2516	6	3296
9	2501	6	3270
10	1101	7	3129
11	2525	5	2979
12	1104	6	2919
13	2508	5	2878
14	2519	6	2830
49	2510	1	512
50	1109	1	451
51	2514	1	342

add 1 to its number of transactions and we add the dollar amount of the current transaction to the total dollar amount for this product. Otherwise, if the product code is one we have not already found, we add an item to the productCodesFound array, and we set the number of transactions for this new product to 1 and its total dollar amount to the dollar amount of the current transaction. Three other arrays facilitate the bookkeeping. The dollarsData array stores the data in column C, and the transactionsCount and dollarsTotal arrays store the numbers of transactions and total dollar amounts for all product codes found.

Once all product codes in column A have been examined, we enter the data from the productCodesFound, transactionsCount, and dollarsTotal arrays in columns E to G, and we sort them on column G in descending order.

```vb
Option Explicit
Option Base 1

Sub ProductSales()
    ' These are inputs: the number of transactions, the product code for each
    ' sale, and the dollar amount of each sale.
    Dim nSales As Integer
    Dim productCodesData() As Integer
    Dim dollarsData() As Single

    ' The following are outputs: the product codes found, the number of transactions
    ' for each product code found, and total dollar amount for each of them.
    Dim productCodesFound() As Integer
    Dim transactionsCount() As Integer
    Dim dollarsTotal() As Single
    ' Variables used in finding unique product codes.
    Dim isNewProduct As Boolean
    Dim nFound As Integer

    ' Counters.
    Dim i As Integer
    Dim j As Integer

    ' Clear any old results in columns E to G.
    With Range("E2")
        Range(.Offset(1, 0), .Offset(0, 2).End(xlDown)).ClearContents
    End With

    ' Find number of sales in the data set, redimension the productCodesData and
    ' dollarsData arrays, and fill them with the data in columns A and C.
    With Range("A2")
        nSales = Range(.Offset(1, 0), .End(xlDown)).Rows.Count
        ReDim productCodesData(nSales)
        ReDim dollarsData(nSales)
        For i = 1 To nSales
            productCodesData(i) = .Offset(i, 0).Value
            dollarsData(i) = .Offset(i, 2).Value
        Next
    End With

    ' Initialize the number of product codes found to 0.
    nFound = 0

    ' Loop through all transactions.
```

```
For i = 1 To nSales

    ' Set the Boolean isNewProduct to True, and change it to False only
    ' if the current product code is one already found.
    isNewProduct = True
    If nFound > 0 Then
        ' Loop through all product codes already found and compare them
        ' to the current product code.
        For j = 1 To nFound
            If productCodesData(i) = productCodesFound(j) Then
                ' The current product code is not a new one, so update
                ' its transactionsCount and dollarsTotal values appropriately, and
                ' exit this inner loop.
                isNewProduct = False
                transactionsCount(j) = transactionsCount(j) + 1
                dollarsTotal(j) = dollarsTotal(j) + dollarsData(i)
                Exit For
            End If
        Next
    End If

    If isNewProduct Then
        ' The current product code is a new one, so update the list of
        ' codes found so far, and initialize the transactionsCount and dollarsTotal
        ' values for this new product.
        nFound = nFound + 1
        ReDim Preserve productCodesFound(nFound)
        ReDim Preserve transactionsCount(nFound)
        ReDim Preserve dollarsTotal(nFound)
        productCodesFound(nFound) = productCodesData(i)
        transactionsCount(nFound) = 1
        dollarsTotal(nFound) = dollarsData(i)
    End If
Next

' Place the results in columns E to G.
For j = 1 To nFound
    With Range("E2")
        .Offset(j, 0).Value = productCodesFound(j)
        .Offset(j, 1).Value = transactionsCount(j)
        .Offset(j, 2).Value = dollarsTotal(j)
    End With
Next

' Sort on column G in descending order, and display an appropriate message.
Range("E3").Sort Key1:=Range("G3"), Order1:=xlDescending, Header:=xlYes
MsgBox "There are " & nFound & " different products that have been sold."
End Sub
```

Although there are plenty of comments in the above code, some further explanation might be useful.

- The productCodesData and dollarsData arrays are redimensioned *without* the keyword **Preserve**, whereas the CodesFound, transactionsCount, and dollarsTotal arrays are redimensioned with it. The reason is that the former two arrays are redimensioned only once, so there is no need to worry about deleting previous contents—there aren't any. However, the latter three arrays are redimensioned every time a new product code is found, and when this happens, we do *not* want to delete previous contents.

- When we find a new product code, we increase nDistinctCodes by 1 and redimension the productCodesFound, transactionsCount, and dollarsTotal arrays by adding an extra element to each. After doing this, we place the appropriate values in the newly created elements of these arrays. For example, if nDistinctCodes goes from 34 to 35, we must specify element number 35 of these arrays.
- To specify a range that is to be sorted, it suffices to specify any cell within this range. Similarly, to specify the column to sort on (in the Key1 argument), it suffices to specify any cell within this column.

EXAMPLE 9.3 Traveling Salesperson Heuristic

This example deals with a famous problem in management science: the traveling salesperson problem. A salesperson starts in a certain city, visits a number of other cities exactly once, and returns to the original city. The problem is to find the route with the minimum total distance. Although this problem is easy to state, it is extremely difficult to solve optimally, even for a moderately small number of cities such as 25. Therefore, management scientists have developed **heuristics** that usually give good, but not necessarily optimal, solutions. The advantage of the heuristics is that they are quick and easy to implement. This example illustrates the **nearest-neighbor** heuristic. It is very easy to state: The salesperson always goes next to the closest city not yet visited. Finally, he must return to the original city (labeled here as city 1) at the end.

The **Traveling Salesperson.xlsm** file implements this heuristic for any number of cities. There are actually two subs in this file. The first, **GenerateDistances**, generates random distances between the cities. It doesn't use any arrays, but it provides a good illustration of For loops. By running this sub repeatedly, you can generate many problems, each with a *different* set of distances. Figure 9.8 shows a matrix of distances generated by the **GenerateDistances** sub. Note that the distances are symmetric. For example, the distance from city 5 to city 10 is the

Figure 9.8 Distances for Traveling Salesperson Problem

	A	B	C	D	E	F	G	H	I	J	K	L	M	N	O	P
11	Distance matrix (symmetric, so values above the diagonal are the same as values below)															
12		City 1	City 2	City 3	City 4	City 5	City 6	City 7	City 8	City 9	City 10	City 11	City 12	City 13	City 14	City 15
13	City 1		100	60	20	68	32	14	33	4	54	59	21	92	97	7
14	City 2	100		97	5	59	84	21	18	87	11	95	42	13	32	4
15	City 3	60	97		91	69	8	40	25	49	25	67	10	46	9	48
16	City 4	20	5	91		91	11	44	24	71	69	24	54	43	20	72
17	City 5	68	59	69	91		15	86	49	38	45	89	73	70	84	9
18	City 6	32	84	8	11	15		45	28	28	14	68	91	42	84	87
19	City 7	14	21	40	44	86	45		47	28	13	76	50	76	98	86
20	City 8	33	18	25	24	49	28	47		48	96	35	69	37	14	100
21	City 9	4	87	49	71	38	28	28	48		66	24	90	48	74	75
22	City 10	54	11	25	69	45	14	13	96	66		74	4	60	71	49
23	City 11	59	95	67	24	89	68	76	35	24	74		60	68	46	6
24	City 12	21	42	10	54	73	91	50	69	90	4	60		52	44	44
25	City 13	92	13	46	43	70	42	76	37	48	60	68	52		18	86
26	City 14	97	32	9	20	84	84	98	14	74	71	46	44	18		54
27	City 15	7	4	48	72	9	87	86	100	75	49	6	44	86	54	

same as the distance from city 10 to city 5. This is guaranteed by the way GenerateDistances is written.

The GenerateDistances sub appears below.

```vba
Sub GenerateDistances()
    ' This sub enters random integers from 1 to 100 above the diagonal and
    ' then enters values below the diagonal to make the matrix symmetric.

    Dim i As Integer ' row counter
    Dim j As Integer ' column counter
    Dim nCities As Integer
    Dim response As String
    Dim isValid As Boolean

    ' Clear everything from previous run (if any).
    ActiveSheet.UsedRange.ClearContents

    ' Turn off screen updating.
    Application.ScreenUpdating = False

    ' Restore labels.
    Range("A1").Value = "Traveling salesperson model"
    Range("A11").Value = "Distance matrix (symmetric, so values above " _
        & "the diagonal are the same as values below)"

    ' Find size of problem.  Keep asking until an integer >= 2 is entered.

    Do
        isValid = True
        response = InputBox("Enter the number of cities, an integer >= 2.")
        If Not IsNumeric(response) Then
            isValid = False
        Else
            If Int(response) < > response Or response < 2 Then
                isValid = False
            End If
        End If
    Loop Until isValid
    nCities = response

    ' Fill up the distance matrix with random numbers.
    With Range("A12")
        ' Enter labels.
        For i = 1 To nCities
            .Offset(i, 0).Value = "City " & i
            .Offset(i, 0).HorizontalAlignment = xlLeft
            .Offset(0, i).Value = "City " & i
        Next

        ' First fill up above the diagonal.
        For i = 1 To nCities - 1

            ' Generate random distances from 1 to 100. (Note: This uses Excel's
            ' RandBetween function, which is new to Excel 2007.)
            For j = i + 1 To nCities
                .Offset(i, j).Value = WorksheetFunction.RandBetween(1, 100)
            Next
        Next
```

```
       ' Now fill up below the diagonal to make the matrix symmetric.
       For i = 2 To nCities
           For j = 1 To i - 1
               .Offset(i, j).Value = .Offset(j, i).Value
           Next
       Next
   End With

   Application.ScreenUpdating = True
End Sub
```

Here are a couple of notes about the GenerateDistances sub.

- In the previous edition, I used the VBA function Rnd to generate random distances. Now I've taken advantage of Excel 2007's new RandBetween function.
- The first set of nested For loops fills up the matrix *above* the diagonal, and the second set creates a mirror image *below* the diagonal.

The second sub, **NearestNeighbor**, uses arrays to implement the nearest-neighbor heuristic. Once the distances are known, the NearestNeighbor sub can be run (by clicking on the second button in Figure 9.8) to generate the nearest-neighbor route. When it is run (for the distances in Figure 9.8), the route and total distance are specified in the worksheet, as shown in Figure 9.9. For this solution, the traveler first goes from city 1 to city 9, then to city 11, and so on. (For this small problem, you can check manually, using Figure 9.8 as a guide, that this is indeed the solution to the nearest-neighbor heuristic.)

The NearestNeighbor code is listed below. Although there are plenty of comments, a few explanations should be helpful.

- This is the probably the most complex program so far, so I've added comments at the top of the sub to explain the variables. This is always a good idea, especially when the variable names might not be totally self-explanatory. The more documentation, the better!
- The Option Base 1 statement is placed at the top of the module, so that all arrays begin with index 1.
- There are two arrays, the Boolean array wasVisited and the integer array route. If wasVisited(6) is True, for example, this means that city 6 has been visited, so it cannot be visited again. Otherwise, if wasVisited(6) is False, then city 6 is a candidate for the next visit. The route array identifies the cities on the different

Figure 9.9 Route Information

stops of the route. For example, if route(8) equals 3, this means that city 3 is the 8th city to be visited.

- wasVisited and route are dimensioned initially with empty parentheses, just to make the sub more general. Once the number of cities is known, the arrays are redimensioned appropriately. Note that the **Preserve** keyword is not necessary because the arrays are empty anyway at the time they are redimensioned.

- Several variables need to be initialized appropriately before the real work can be done. They include route(1), route(nCities+1), nowAt, totalDistance, and the wasVisited array.

- The heuristic is performed with two nested For loops. The outer loop goes over the "steps" of the route. Its purpose is to discover which city will be the second visited, which will be third, and so on. The inner loop finds the nearest neighbor city for that step. It does this with a "running minimum," where it finds the smallest distance to all cities from the current city (nowAt) among all those not yet visited. The best of these is stored in the variable nextAt. After this inner loop is completed, nowAt becomes nextAt in preparation for the next pass through the outer loop.

- After the loops are completed, the distance back to city 1 is added to the totalDistance variable, and the contents of the route array and the total distance are placed in the worksheet.

```
Sub NearestNeighbor()
    ' This sub runs the nearest neighbor heuristic.

    ' Definition of variables:
    '    nCities - number of cities in the problem
    '    distance - array of distances between pairs of cities
    '    wasVisited - a Boolean array: True only if a city has been visited so far
    '    step - a counter for the number of cities visited so far
    '    route - an array where element i is the i-th city visited
    '         Note that Route(1) and Route(NCities+1) must both be 1.
    '    nowAt - city current at
    '    nextAt - city to visit next
    '    totalDistance - total distance traveled
    '    minDistanceance - the minimum distance to the nearest (yet unvisited) neighbor
    '    i, j - city counters

    Dim nCities As Integer
    Dim distance() As Integer
    Dim wasVisited() As Boolean
    Dim step As Integer
    Dim route() As Integer
    Dim nowAt As Integer
    Dim nextAt As Integer
    Dim totalDistance As Integer
    Dim minDistance As Integer
    Dim i As Integer
    Dim j As Integer

    ' Get the size of the problem (number of nodes) and redimension the various
    ' arrays appropriately.
    With Range("A12")
        nCities = Range(.Offset(1, 0), .Offset(1, 0).End(xlDown)).Rows.Count
    End With
```

```
ReDim distance(nCities, nCities)
ReDim wasVisited(nCities)
ReDim route(nCities + 1)

' Enter the distances into the Distance matrix.
With Range("A12")
    For i = 1 To nCities
        For j = 1 To nCities
            If i <> j Then distance(i, j) = .Offset(i, j).Value
        Next
    Next
End With

' Start and end at city 1.
route(1) = 1
route(nCities + 1) = 1

' Only city 1 has been visited so far.
wasVisited(1) = True
For i = 2 To nCities
    wasVisited(i) = False
Next

' Initialize other variables.
nowAt = 1
totalDistance = 0

' Go through the steps on the route, one at a time, to see which cities
' should be visited in which order.
For step = 2 To nCities

    ' Find which city should be visited next by finding a 'running minimum'
    ' of distances from the current city to all other cities.  The next
    ' city is a candidate only if it is not the current city and it has
    ' not yet been visited.  Start the running minimum (minDistance) at a
    ' LARGE value, so that anything will beat its initial value.
    minDistance = 10000
    For j = 2 To nCities
        If j <> nowAt And Not wasVisited(j) Then
            If distance(nowAt, j) < minDistance Then
                ' Capture the best candidate so far and its associated
                ' distance from the current city.
                nextAt = j
                minDistance = distance(nowAt, nextAt)
            End If
        End If
    Next

    ' Store the city to go to next in Route, record that this city has
    ' been visited, and update the total distance.
    route(step) = nextAt
    wasVisited(nextAt) = True
    totalDistance = totalDistance + minDistance

    ' Get ready for the next time through the loop.
    nowAt = nextAt
Next step

' Update the total distance to include the return to city 1
totalDistance = totalDistance + distance(nowAt, 1)
```

```
         ' Start entering output two rows down from distance matrix.
         With Range("B12").Offset(nCities + 2, 0)

             ' Enter labels.
             .Offset(0, -1).Value = "Nearest neighbor route"
             .Offset(1, 0).Value = "Stop #"
             .Offset(1, 1).Value = "City"

             ' Record the route from city 1 back to city 1 in the spreadsheet.
             For step = 1 To nCities + 1
                 .Offset(step + 1, 0).Value = step
                 .Offset(step + 1, 1).Value = route(step)
             Next step

             ' Record the total distance.
             .Offset(nCities + 4, -1).Value = "Total distance is " & totalDistance
         End With
     End Sub
```

You should go through this code line by line until you understand how it works. It is structured to do exactly what you would do if you had to perform the nearest-neighbor heuristic manually. Of course, its advantage is that it is extremely fast—and it doesn't make mistakes.

EXAMPLE 9.4 Merging Lists

Like the previous example, this example is easy to describe but no less challenging to implement. It is an example of merging two lists and is contained in the file **Merging Lists.xlsm**. As in all applications in Part II of the book, there is an Explanation sheet (see Figure 9.10) that users see when they open the file. It

Figure 9.10 Explanation of Merging Example

Merging Customer Lists

You have two lists of customers: those who bought last year and those who bought this year. Each of these lists is in alphabetical order (by last name of customer). To simplify the application, we'll assume that no two last names in the database are identical. For example, if you see Smith on last year's list and this year's list, you can assume that it is the same Smith in both cases. You want to create a new list that merges the names from these two lists into a common customer list.

Go to Lists Sheet

explains the purpose of the application, and it has a button that runs a simple macro to take them to the Lists worksheet (the one with the data). The code attached to this button is very simple:

```
Sub GoToLists()
    Worksheets("Lists").Activate
    Range("A2").Select
End Sub
```

The lists (with some hidden rows) in the Lists sheet are already sorted in alphabetical order and appear in Figure 9.11. Note that some customers are in last year's list only, some are in this year's list only, and some are in both. The merged list in column D should include each customer in either list exactly once.

Figure 9.11 Lists To Be Merged

	A	B	C	D
1	**Existing lists**	Merge Lists		**Merged list**
2				
3	Customers last year	Customers this year		Customers
4	Barlog	Aghimien		
5	Barnett	Bang		
6	Bedrick	Barnett		
7	Brulez	Bedrick		
8	Cadigan	Brulez		
9	Castleman	Cadigan		
93	Wyatt	Theodas		
94	Yablonka	Tracy		
95	Zick	Ubelhor		
96	Ziegler	Usman		
97		Vicars		
98		Villard		
99		Wendel		
100		Wier		
101		Wise		
102		Yablonka		
103		Yeiter		
104		Zakrzacki		
105		Zhou		

A Conceptual Method

Before discussing any VBA code, you must have a mental picture of how you would do the merging manually. After all, it is pointless to try to write code for a procedure unless you thoroughly understand the steps you would take to perform it manually. Here is one reasonable approach.

1. Start at the top of each of the existing lists and compare the names.
    - If they are the same, transfer this common name to column D and move down one row in both column A and column B for the next comparison.
    - If the name in column A comes before the name in column B in alphabetical order, transfer the name in column A to column D and move down one row in column A (but *not* in column B) for the next comparison. Proceed similarly if the name in column B comes before the name in column A in alphabetical order. For example, the second comparison in the above lists will be between Barlog and Bang.
2. Continue as in step 1, always making a comparison between a name in column A and a name in column B, until you have transferred all of the names from at least one of the column A and column B lists. Then if there are names left in one of the lists, transfer all of them to column D.

Try this procedure on the lists in Figure 9.11, and you will see that it works perfectly. Even though the list in column B is longer, you will finish transferring the names from column B first, with Zick and Ziegler left in the column A list. The last step of the procedure is to move these two names to the bottom of the merged list in column D.

Coding the Method

Now it is a matter of coding this procedure. The **MergeLists** sub listed below contains the relevant code. It is written to work for *any* two lists in columns A and B, not just the ones shown in Figure 9.11. (The only restriction is that the names should be unique, in the sense that there should be only one Smith, say, in either list, and if Smith appears in both lists, it should be the same Smith. Duplicated names raise other issues that are not addressed here.) Again, there are plenty of comments, but a few explanations should help.

- There are three arrays, list1, list2, and list3, with sizes listSize1, listSize2, and listSize3. The first two are filled with the two known customer lists. The third is filled by the merging procedure.
- The array sizes listSize1 and listSize2 can be obtained immediately by looking at the existing customer lists. The array size listSize3 will be known only at the end of the procedure. We could redimension list3 right away with size listSize1+listSize2 (that will certainly be large enough—do you see why?), but instead we redimension list3 with one extra element every time we add a new customer to the merged list. This means that the final list3 will be dimensioned exactly as large as it needs to be. To keep from deleting previous customers from the merged list, the **Preserve** keyword is necessary.

- The "flow" of the sub is that any previous merged list is first deleted from column D with the **ClearContents** method. Next, the list sizes of the existing lists are found, and the list1 and list2 arrays are filled with existing customer names. Finally, the merging procedure is used to fill the list3 array, which is eventually written to column D.

- Note how the conceptual method described earlier is implemented in VBA. The sub uses the index1 and index2 integer variables to indicate how far down the existing customer lists the procedure is. The corresponding customer names are name1 and name2. A comparison between them indicates which to add to the merged list, as well as which of index1 and index2 to increment by 1. A **Do While** loop is arguably the more natural approach here. It says to keep going through the lists while there is at least one name remaining in each list.

- After the Do loop is completed, the contents of the list not yet completed (if either) are transferred to the merged list. Then the contents of list3 are written to column D of the worksheet.

```
Sub MergeLists()
    ' The listSizex variables are list sizes for the various lists (x from 1 to 3).  The
    ' listx arrays contains the members of the lists (again, x from 1 to 3). The lists
    ' are indexed from 1 to 3 as follows:
    '    list1 - customers from last year (given data)
    '    list2 - customers from this year (given data)
    '    list3 - customers who bought in either or both years (to be found)

    Dim i1 As Integer, i2 As Integer, i3 As Integer ' counters
    Dim listSize1 As Integer, listSize2 As Integer, listSize3 As Integer
    Dim list1() As String, list2() As String, list3() As String
    Dim index1 As Integer, index2 As Integer
    Dim name1 As String, name2 As String

    ' Delete the old merged list (if any) in column D.
    With Range("D3")
        Range(.Offset(1, 0), .Offset(1, 0).End(xlDown)).ClearContents
    End With

    ' Get the list sizes and the names for the given data in columns A, B.
    With Range("A3")
        listSize1 = Range(.Offset(1, 0), .End(xlDown)).Rows.Count
        ReDim list1(listSize1)
        For i1 = 1 To listSize1
            list1(i1) = .Offset(i1, 0).Value
        Next
        listSize2 = Range(.Offset(1, 1), .Offset(0, 1).End(xlDown)).Rows.Count
        ReDim list2(listSize2)
        For i2 = 1 To listSize2
            list2(i2) = .Offset(i2, 1).Value
        Next
    End With

    ' Create the merged list. First, initialize new list size to be 0.
    listSize3 = 0

    ' Go through list1 and list2 simultaneously. The counters index1 and index2
    ' indicate how far down each list we currently are, and name1 and name2 are
```

```
    ' the corresponding customer names. First, initialize index1 and index2.
    index1 = 1
    index2 = 1

    ' Keep going until we get past at least one of the lists.
    Do While index1 < = listSize1 And index2 < = listSize2
        name1 = list1(index1)
        name2 = list2(index2)

        ' Each step through the loop, add one customer name to the merged list, so
        ' update the list size and redim list3 right now.
        listSize3 = listSize3 + 1
        ReDim Preserve list3(listSize3)

        ' See which of the two names being compared is first in alphabetical order.
        ' It becomes the new member of the merged list. Once it's added, go to the
        ' next name (by updating the index) in the appropriate list. In case of a tie,
        ' update both indexes.
        If name1 < name2 Then
            list3(listSize3) = name1
            index1 = index1 + 1
        Elself name1 > name2 Then
            list3(listSize3) = name2
            index2 = index2 + 1
        Elself name1 = name2 Then
            list3(listSize3) = name2
            index1 = index1 + 1
            index2 = index2 + 1
        End If
    Loop

    ' By this time, we're through at least one of the lists (list1 or list2).
    ' Therefore, add all leftover names from the OTHER list to the merged list.
    If index1 > listSize1 And index2 <= listSize2 Then
        ' Some names remain in list2.
        For i2 = index2 To listSize2
            listSize3 = listSize3 + 1
            ReDim Preserve list3(listSize3)
            list3(listSize3) = list2(i2)
        Next
    Elself index1 <= listSize1 And index2 > listSize2 Then
        ' Some names remain in list1.
        For i1 = index1 To listSize1
            listSize3 = listSize3 + 1
            ReDim Preserve list3(listSize3)
            list3(listSize3) = list1(i1)
        Next
    End If

    ' Record the merged list in column D of the worksheet.
    With Range("D3")
        For i3 = 1 To listSize3
            .Offset(i3, 0).Value = list3(i3)
        Next
    End With

    ' End with the cursor in cell A2.
    Range("A2").Select
End Sub
```

The introduction to this chapter claimed that arrays are useful for working with lists. This merging example is a perfect example of this claim. The merging could certainly be done without arrays, but arrays provide the perfect means for accomplishing the job.

9.6 Array Functions

This chapter concludes with a brief description of a rather curious construct in VBA: the Array function. The following code illustrates how Array functions work.

```
Option Base 1

Sub ArrayFunctionExample()
    Dim days as Variant
    days = Array("Mon","Tues","Wed","Thurs","Fri","Sat","Sun")
    MsgBox "The first day in the array is " & days(1)
End Sub
```

The keyword **Array**, followed by a list inside parentheses, is used to "populate" the variable days. Then days acts like a typical array. For example, days(1) in the message box statement will be "Mon". (It would be "Tues" if the **Option Base 1** statement were not included. Remember, the default is **0-based indexing**.) However, days is not *declared* like a typical array. It must be declared as a Variant, with no empty parentheses in the Dim statement. VBA figures out that you want days to be an array only after you set days equal to the Array function in the third line of the sub.

You might not use Array functions very often, but as this example code shows, they provide a convenient way to populate an array.

9.7 Summary

You already know from previous chapters how powerful looping can be in computer programs. Arrays increase this power tremendously, especially when processing lists in some way. This power has been illustrated by a variety of examples, and I will continue to illustrate the power of arrays in later chapters. Arrays are well worth the effort required to master them.

EXERCISES

1. Write a sub that creates an array day of size 7 and then populates it with the days of the week: Monday, Tuesday, and so on. It then loops through this array and writes its elements to the range A1:G1 of the first worksheet.
2. Write a sub that creates two arrays month and daysInMonth of size 12 each. It then populates the first array with the months January, February, etc., and it populates

the second with the number of days in these months: 31, 28 (assume it is not a leap year), etc. Then it loops through these arrays and writes their elements to the range A1:L2. For example, cells A1 and A2 will have January and 31.

3. Do the previous exercise in a slightly different way. Insteady of two one-dimensional arrays, create one two-dimensional array monthInfo of size 12 by 2. The first dimension should contain the month and the second should contain the number of days in the month. For example, monthInfo(6,1) should be June and monthInfo(6,2) should be 30. Use nested loops to fill the range A1:L2 as in the previous exercise. (Note: You will need to declare this array as Variant because it contains two different types of data, strings and integers.)

4. Write a sub that asks the user for an integer such as 100 and stores it in the variable upperLimit. It then asks the user for another integer such as 3 and stores it in the variable factor. It then creates an array called multiple, of the appropriate size, that contains all the multiples of factor no greater than upperLimit. Finally, it uses a loop to sum all of the elements in the array and reports this sum with an appropriate message in a message box. For example, if the two inputs are 100 and 3, it should report "The sum of all multiples of 3 no greater than 100 is 1683."

5. Write a sub that creates an array card of size 52. Its first 4 elements should be 1, its next 4 elements should be 2, its next 4 elements should be 3, and so on. You should be able to do this with a pair of nested For loops. You should *not* do it by "brute force" with 52 statements or 13 For loops. (This type of array is used in the final chapter to simulate poker hands. You are essentially setting up the deck here.)

6. The file **RandomNumbers.xlsx** contains 50,000 random numbers in column A. (To generate these, I used Excel's RAND function and then "froze" them by copying values over the formulas.) Write a sub that creates an array called frequency of size 10. It then populates the array by looping over the random numbers and putting them into "bins." Specifically, frequency(1) should contain the count of all random numbers from 0 to 0.1, frequency(2) should contain the count of all random numbers from 0.1 to 0.2, and so on. Because every random number has to be in one of these bins, the counts should add to 50,000, which you should check. Report the final contents of the array in a message box. (How should you deal with the endpoints such as 0.1? It doesn't really matter, because there is virtually no chance that a random number will fall *exactly* on one of the breakpoints.)

7. Write a sub that does the following: (1) It declares an array called practiceArray of size 100; (2) it stores the value i in element i (for i from 1 to 100); and (3) it uses a For loop to switch the contents of the elements i and i+1 for each i from 1 to 99. At the end, transfer the contents of practiceArray to column A of a worksheet. The effect of all the switching should be to push the 1 down to the bottom of the list. Is that what you got? (*Hint*: When you switch two array elements, you need a third "temporary" variable.)

8. The file **High Spenders.xlsx** contains a list of customers and the amounts they spent during the past month. Write a sub that captures the existing lists in two arrays and then creates two new arrays of customer names and amounts spent for customers who spent at least $500. After these new arrays have been filled, transfer their contents to columns D and E of the worksheet.

9. The file **Customer Lists.xlsx** contains two lists of customers: those who purchased from our company last year and those who purchased this year. Write a sub that captures the existing lists in two arrays and then creates three new arrays of customers who purchased only last year, customers who purchased only this year, and customers who purchased in both years. After these new arrays have been filled, transfer their contents to columns D, E, and F of the worksheet.

10. The file **Flights.xlsx** has a list of flights in columns A, B, and C flown by EastWest Airlines. The list includes the flight number, the origin, and the destination of each flight. You are interested in flights that leave from any city in column E and end up at any city in column F. You need to list such flights in columns H, I, and J. Write a VBA program to do so, using arrays. Your program should work even if the lists in columns A to C and in E to F change. To see how it should work, look at the **Flights Finished.xlsm** file. Its code is password-protected.

11. Suppose you have a list of customers, labeled from 1 to n, and you want to choose a random subset of them of size m (where m < n). Write a sub to do this. It should first ask the user for n and m, using two input boxes. It should then fill an array of size m called chosen, where chosen(1) is the index of the first person chosen, chosen(2) is the index of the second person chosen, and so on. No person can be chosen more than once, so no two elements of the chosen array should have the same value. Finally, the sub should list the values of the chosen array in column A of a worksheet. Note that you can use Excel's RandBetween function to generate a random integer from 1 to n.

12. The file **Incomes.xlsx** has annual incomes for many households in a particular town. As in the previous exercise, choose a random subset of m households. Then report the average of *all* incomes in the file and the average of the incomes in the subset in a message box. Unlike the previous exercise, the user cannot select n; it is the number of households listed in the file. However, the user should be allowed to choose the sample size m.

13. Consider the following state lottery. Five random digits are selected. This is the "winning number." You can buy as many lottery cards as you like at $1 per card. Each card contains five random digits. If you get a card that matches the winning number, you win $100,000. (Assume that order matters. If the winning number is 21345, then 12345 doesn't win.) Write a sub that does the following. It first generates a random winning number and stores it in a string variable (so that you can use string concatenation), and it asks the user how many cards he wants to buy. It then uses a For loop to generate this many cards and store their numbers in a card array (which should be a *string* array). Next, it uses a Do loop to keep checking cards until a winner has been found or no more cards remain. Finally, it displays a message stating whether you are a winner and your net gain or loss. Note that you can generate a single random digit from 0 to 9 with Excel's RandBetween function.

14. The previous exercise is realistic because a lottery player must commit to the number of cards purchased *before* learning the winning number. However, suppose you want to see how many cards you would have to buy, on average, before getting a card with the winning number. Write a sub that does the following. It has an "outer" For loop that goes from 1 to 100, so that you can

repeat the whole process 100 times, each with a different winning number. Each time you go through this loop, you generate a winning card, you use a Do loop to keep generating cards until you get a winner, and you keep track of the number of cards required in an element of the requiredCards array (of size 100). At the end of the program, you should display summary measures of requiredCards in a message box: the average of its elements, the smallest of its elements, and the largest of its elements. For example, the latter is the most cards you ever had to buy in any of the 100 lotteries. (*Note*: Although you will be working with integers, they will likely be very *large* integers. Therefore, declare them as **Long**, not Integer, types. Also, don't be surprised if this program takes a while to run. It took mine about a minute.)

15. If you have ever studied relational databases, you have heard of **joins**. This exercise illustrates what a join is. The file **Music CDs 1.xlsx** contains data on a person's classical music CD collection. There are three sheets. The Labels sheet lists all music labels (such as Philips), where they are indexed with consecutive integers. The CDs sheet lists the person's CDs. Specifically, it shows for each CD the index of the music label, the composer, and the piece(s) on the CD. We say that the tables on these two sheets are "related" through the label indexes. Write a sub, using arrays, to join the information on these two sheets. The joined information should be placed on the Join sheet. As the headings indicate, it should show, for each CD, the music label (its name, not its index), the composer, and the piece(s).

16. The previous exercise demonstrated a **one-to-many** relationship. This means that each CD has only one music label, but many CDs can have the same label. Relationships can also be **many-to-many**, as this exercise illustrates. The file **Music CDs 2.xlsx** contains four sheets. The Works sheet lists works of music, along with the composers, and they are indexed by consecutive integers. The Conductors sheet lists conductors, which are also indexed by consecutive integers. The CDs sheet has an entry for each CD owned. For each entry, it shows the index of the work and the index of the conductor. The relationship is now many-to-many because it is possible to have more than one CD of a given work, each conducted by a different conductor, and it is possible to have more than one CD with a given conductor, each conducting a different work. Write a sub, using arrays, to fill the Join sheet, which currently has only headings. As these headings indicate, each row should list the composer, the work, and the conductor for a particular CD. (This sheet should end up with as many rows as the CDs sheet.) Finally, the sub should keep track of any works on the Works sheet that you do not own, and it should display these in some way (you can decide how).

17. (More difficult) Your company makes steel rods of a fixed diameter and length 50 inches. Your customers request rods of the following lengths (all in inches): 5, 8, 12, 15, 20, and 25. Write a sub to find all ways to cut the rods so that any leftovers are unusable. For example, one way to do it is with one 5-inch rod, one 8-inch rod, and three 12-inch rods. This uses 49 inches of the rod, and the other inch is unusable. As you find usable patterns, list them in the **Patterns.xlsx** file. (One possible pattern is already shown in row 5 for illustration.)

18. Practically all computer science majors are required at some time in their college careers to write a **sort routine**. You start with an array of numbers (or even strings),

and you need to write a sub that ends with this same array but in increasing order. For example, if the array elements are A(1)=17, A(2)=12, A(3)=19, and A(4)=7, then the end result will have A(1)=7, A(2)=12, A(3)=17, and A(4)=19.

   a. Given access to Excel, there is a very easy way to do this. Write a sub that does the following. It first populates an array of any size with any set of numbers. (You can choose these.) It then stores the first number in cell A1 of a work-sheet, the second in cell A2, and so on. Next, it uses the Sort method of a Range object to sort this range. Finally, it uses a loop to store the contents of the range into the array, overwriting the previous contents. In essence, you get Excel to do the hard part of sorting.

   b. (More difficult) Repeat part a, but do it without the help of Excel's Sort method. To do this, you need a strategy. Here is a fairly simple one (although not very efficient for large arrays). Loop through the array to find the smallest number. Let's say A(15) is the smallest. Then exchange the contents of A(1) and A(15). (This exchange requires a variable I'll call temp. Put A(15) into temp, put A(1) into A(15), and put temp into A(1).) Next, find the smallest of the elements from A(2) on. Let's say this is A(7). Then exchange elements A(2) and A(7). See the pattern? It is called a **bubble sort** because the small numbers "bubble up" to the front of the array. Now it's "just" a matter of programming this algorithm with a set of nested loops.

19. (More difficult) The Data sheet in the Variable Number of Lists.xlsx file contains three lists of varying lengths. The Combinations sheet shows all combinations of these lists. Write a sub, using arrays, to generate the data on the Combinations sheet. It should work for *any* number of lists of any lengths.

20. (Very useful for dumping data to a worksheet). Suppose your program fills a large two-dimensional array called results with values, and you would like it to "dump" these values into an Excel range. For example, if results is m by n, you would like the program to dump the values into a range with m rows and n columns. One way is use two nested loops to dump the data one element at a time into an appropriate cell. This approach turns out to be *very* slow. A much better approach is to set the Value property of an m-row, n-column range to results, that is, one statement with no loops. Compare these two methods. First, initialize the i, j element of an m by n array to i+j. (Any values would do.) Now try the two methods just described to dump the results to an m-row, n-column Excel range. You should find a *big* difference. (On my PC, with m=2500, n=500, the looping method took several *minutes*, whereas the single-statement method took less than a *second*!)

10 More on Variables and Subroutines

10.1 Introduction

To this point, all programs have been single, self-contained subs. This chapter illustrates how individual subs can be part of an overall program, which is very important for the applications discussed in the second part of the book. A typical program can have many subs in one or more modules, and they can be related. First, they can share the same variables. For example, one sub might use an input box to capture an employee's salary in the variable salary. Then another sub might use this same variable in some way. Both subs need to know the value of this salary variable. In technical terms, the salary variable must have the appropriate **scope**.

Subs can also **call** one another, and they can **pass arguments** (share information) when they make the call. As programs become longer and more complex, it is common to break them down into smaller subs, where each sub performs a specific task. There is often a "main" sub that calls the other subs. In effect, the main sub acts as a control center. Making programs **modular** in this way makes them easier to read. Perhaps even more important, it makes them easier to debug. In addition, there is a better chance that the smaller subs will be **reusable** in other programs. In fact, one of the most important ideas in computer programming is the idea of reusable code. Professional programmers attempt to make their subs as general and self-contained as possible so that other programmers will not have to reinvent the wheel every time they write a program.

Finally, this chapter introduces a particular type of subroutine called a **function subroutine**. Unlike the subroutines discussed so far, the purpose of a function subroutine is to return a value. Actually, all of the Excel functions you use in formulas, such as Sum, Max, and so on, are really function subroutines. This chapter illustrates how you can develop your *own* custom functions and then use them in VBA programs or in Excel worksheets.

10.2 Exercise

The emphasis in this chapter is on dividing an overall program into several subroutines, each of which performs a particular task. The following exercise is typical. It could be written in one fairly long sub, but a much better way is to modularize it. By the time you have finished reading this chapter, you should be able to solve this exercise according to the specific instructions without much difficulty.

Exercise 10.1 Updating Customer Accounts

Consider a company that services air conditioners and heaters. It currently has 30 residential customers in a certain region, and it keeps track of service charges for these customers in the file **Customer Accounts.xlsx**. This file contains a sheet called NewCharges. Each month the company deletes the charges from the previous month and adds charges for the current month to this sheet. Figure 10.1 shows the charges for the most recent month.

The file also contains a separate sheet for each customer, where the sheet name is the customer's account number. For example, the sheet for customer Stevens (account number S3211) appears in Figure 10.2 (with several rows hidden). Columns A and B list all of Stevens's charges since the account was opened, and columns D to G summarize the yearly totals. The totals in column E are sums of charges for the various years. The discounts in column F are based on the company's discount policy: no discount on the first $100 (for any year), 5% discount on the next $100, and 7.5% discount on all charges over $200. The net in column G is the total minus the discount.

The purpose of the exercise is to update the customer account sheets with the charges on the NewCharges sheet. This includes new entries in columns A and B, plus updates of the total and discount for the current year (2008) in columns E and F. As an example, after running the program, the Stevens account sheet should appear as in Figure 10.3. Of course, if a customer has no charge in the NewCharges sheet, this customer's account sheet does not need to be updated.

This exercise can be done in many ways, but to get the most benefit from it, it should be done as follows. There should be a **Main** sub that loops through all of the charges in the NewCharges sheet. For each charge, an **Update** sub should be called that takes three arguments: the customer's account number, the date of the charge, and the amount of the charge. This Update sub should add the new charge to the end

Figure 10.1 New Charges

	A	B	C	D
1	Information on new charges			
2				
3	Date	Customer	Account #	Charge
4	2-Jul-08	Astrid	A1865	$89.42
5	6-Jul-08	Bricker	B1808	$70.94
6	10-Jul-08	Allenby	A1151	$87.11
7	13-Jul-08	Argos	A1225	$71.15
8	14-Jul-08	Exley	E3597	$96.15
9	18-Jul-08	Owens	O2752	$77.94
10	19-Jul-08	Stevens	S3211	$133.12
11	20-Jul-08	Spinaker	S2378	$81.17
12	22-Jul-08	West	W3697	$152.77

Figure 10.2 Typical Customer Account Sheet

	A	B	C	D	E	F	G
1	**Stevens account**						
2							
3	**All charges**			**Summary by year**			
4	Date	Charge		Year	Total	Discount	Net
5	28-Apr-00	$140.20		2000	$296.41	$12.23	$284.18
6	24-Aug-00	$156.21		2001	$523.50	$29.26	$494.24
7	9-Jan-01	$130.51		2002	$459.42	$24.46	$434.97
8	2-May-01	$160.87		2003	$519.48	$28.96	$490.52
9	8-Sep-01	$109.23		2004	$531.14	$29.84	$501.31
10	25-Dec-01	$122.88		2005	$528.74	$29.66	$499.09
11	19-May-02	$112.77		2006	$652.02	$38.90	$613.11
12	8-Sep-02	$126.00		2007	$450.48	$23.79	$426.70
13	21-Oct-02	$110.60		2008	$143.19	$2.16	$141.03
14	23-Nov-02	$110.05					
35	31-May-07	$161.20					
36	28-Sep-07	$121.42					
37	25-Feb-08	$143.19					

Figure 10.3 Updated Account Sheet

	A	B	C	D	E	F	G
1	**Stevens account**						
2							
3	**All charges**			**Summary by year**			
4	Date	Charge		Year	Total	Discount	Net
5	28-Apr-00	$140.20		2000	$296.41	$12.23	$284.18
6	24-Aug-00	$156.21		2001	$523.50	$29.26	$494.24
7	9-Jan-01	$130.51		2002	$459.42	$24.46	$434.97
8	2-May-01	$160.87		2003	$519.48	$28.96	$490.52
9	8-Sep-01	$109.23		2004	$531.14	$29.84	$501.31
10	25-Dec-01	$122.88		2005	$528.74	$29.66	$499.09
11	19-May-02	$112.77		2006	$652.02	$38.90	$613.11
12	8-Sep-02	$126.00		2007	$450.48	$23.79	$426.70
13	21-Oct-02	$110.60		2008	$276.31	$10.72	$141.03
14	23-Nov-02	$110.05					
35	31-May-07	$161.20					
36	28-Sep-07	$121.42					
37	25-Feb-08	$143.19					
38	19-Jul-08	$133.12					

of the customer's charges (as in cells A38 and B38 in Figure 10.3 for Stevens), and it should update the Total and Discount cells for the current year. To find the discount, it should call a function subroutine that calculates the discount for any yearly total passed to it. (When writing this program, you can assume that all new charges are indeed for the year 2008.)

As usual, you can try running the program in the completed file Customer Accounts Finished.xlsm, but you should not look at the code until you have tried writing the VBA code yourself. Also, if you're interested in a more challenging version of this problem, see the code in the file Customer Accounts Extra.xlsm, which allows the new charges to go into the next year.

10.3 Scope of Variables and Subroutines

This section discusses the important concept of **scope**, or "Which parts of a program have access to which other parts?" Variables and subroutines both have scope. I will discuss each.

Scope of Variables

You already know how to declare a variable with a **Dim** statement. Here is a typical example:

```
Sub Test1()
    Dim salary As Currency
    salary = 50000
    ' Other lines of code would go here.
End Sub
```

When a variable such as salary is declared *inside* a sub in this way, it is called a **procedure-level** variable, or a **local** variable. The only sub that recognizes this variable is the sub that contains it. Suppose there is another sub with the following lines:

```
Sub Test2()
    MsgBox "The value of salary is " & salary
    ' Other lines of code would go here.
End Sub
```

If you run Test1 and then Test2, the message box in Test2 will *not* display "The value of salary is 50000". This is because Test2 does not know the value of the salary variable; only Test1 knows it. In fact, Test2 can have its own salary variable, as in

```
Sub Test2()
    Dim salary As Currency
    salary = 40000
    MsgBox "The value of salary is " & salary
    ' Other lines of code would go here.
End Sub
```

If you run Test1 and then Test2, Test2 will have no memory that salary was 50000 in Test1. It knows only about *its* version of salary, defined as 40000. In other words, local variables in different subs can have the same names, but they lead independent existences. Technically, they have different memory locations.

What if you want different subs to have access to common variables? Then you can declare these variables at the *top* of a module, before any subs. Actually, you have two options. First, you can declare a variable at the top of a module with the usual **Dim** keyword, as in

```
Dim salary As Currency
```

This variable is then a **module-level** variable, which means that every sub in the module has access to salary. (An alternative to the keyword Dim is the keyword **Private**. A Private variable also has module-level scope.) The second possibility is to declare a variable at the top of a module with the keyword **Public**, as in

```
Public salary As Currency
```

Then salary has **project-level** scope, which means that *all* modules in the entire project have access to it.[1] This is often useful when you have two or more modules in your project. (It is also useful when you have "event handlers" for **user forms**, as explained in Chapter 11. Then Public variables are also recognized by the event handlers.)

If you declare a variable to have module-level or project-level scope, then you almost surely do *not* want to declare the same variable inside a sub with a Dim statement. For example, consider the following code:

```
Public salary As Currency

Sub Test1()
    salary = 50000
End Sub

Sub Test2()
    Dim salary As Currency
    MsgBox "Salary is " & salary
End Sub
```

If you run Test1 and then Test2, then the message box in Test2 will *not* display "Salary is 50000" as you might expect—it will display "salary is 0". The reason is that the Dim statement in Test2 creates a local version of salary that

---

[1]Some programmers use the term **global variable** rather than **public variable**. This is the term used in some other programming languages.

overrides the public version. This local version is initialized to 0 by default. Hence the message says that salary is 0, which is probably not what you want.

Scope of Subroutines

Subroutines also have scope. As discussed in the next section, one sub can **call** another inside a program. Scope then determines which subs can call which others. The default is that all subs have **public** scope unless specified otherwise. This means that when you define a sub as in

```
Sub Test()
```

any other sub in the entire project can call this Test sub. To make this more explicit, you can precede Sub with the keyword **Public**, as in

```
Public Sub Test()
```

However, this is not really necessary because a sub's scope is public by default.

Now suppose that you want Test to be callable only by subs within its module. Then you *must* precede Sub with the keyword **Private**, as in

```
Private Sub Test()
```

Then any sub in the same module as Test can call Test, but subs outside of the module containing Test have no access to Test. By the way, the scoping rules for subs are exactly the same for function subroutines, the topic of Section 10.6.

10.4 Modularizing Programs

There is a tendency for beginning programmers to write one long sub in a program—a sub that does it all. This is a bad habit for at least three reasons:

- **Hard to read.** Long subs are hard to read. Would you like to read a book with a single long chapter or a chapter with a single long paragraph? (If you've read much William Faulkner, you know what I mean.)
- **Hard to debug.** Long subs are hard to debug. There are too many lines with possible bugs.
- **Hard to reuse.** It is difficult to reuse the code from long subs in other programs.

A preferred approach is to modularize programs so that they become a sequence of relatively short subs, each with a very specific task to perform. These short subs then overcome the three criticisms above: (1) their brevity and focus make them easier to read; (2) they can be tested independently, or at least in sequence, so that bugs are easier to detect and fix; and (3) there is a much greater chance that they can be reused in other programs.

The question, then, is how to tie the subs together into an overall program. Fortunately, this is quite easy. You have one sub **call** another sub. Here is a typical setup:

```
Sub Main()
    Call Task1
    Call Task2
End Sub

Sub Task1()
    Call Task3
    ' Other lines of code would go here.
End Sub

Sub Task2()
    ' Lines of code would go here.
End Sub

Sub Task3()
    ' Lines of code would go here.
End Sub
```

The Main sub does nothing but call the Task1 sub and then the Task2 sub. The Task1 sub in turn calls the Task3 sub, and it then executes some other statements. We say that Main **passes control** to Task1, which then passes control to Task3. When Task3 is completed, it passes control back to Task1. When Task1 is completed, it passes control back to Main, which immediately passes control to Task2. Finally, when Task2 is completed, it passes control back to Main. At this point, the program ends. This code also indicates how easy it is to call another sub. You simply type the keyword **Call**, followed by the name of the sub being called.

It is also possible to omit the keyword **Call**, and many programmers do so. Instead of writing, say, Call Test1, they simply write Test1. However, I prefer to use the keyword Call, mostly to remind myself that a sub is being called. Here is my reasoning. Suppose you see the following line in the middle of a sub:

```
TaxCalc
```

You might think that this is some variable name you had forgotten about, rather than a call to a sub called **TaxCalc**. But if the line uses Call, as in

```
Call TaxCalc
```

there is no doubt that a subroutine named TaxCalc is being called. Still, you can choose: include Call or omit it.

There is a trade-off when modularizing a program. At one extreme, you can have a single long sub. At the other extreme, you can create a separate sub for every small task your program performs. You typically need to find a middle ground that breaks an overall program into reasonable chunks. Different programmers argue about the term "reasonable." For example, I have heard one programmer say he doesn't like subs with more than 10 lines, which I believe is a bit restrictive. However, all programmers agree that some modularizing is appropriate in long programs.

EXAMPLE 10.1 Traveling Salesperson Model Revisited

To see how modularizing works, I rewrote the code for the traveling salesperson nearest-neighbor heuristic from the previous chapter. The modified code is the file **Traveling Salesperson Modified.xlsm**. Now instead of one long **Nearest-Neighbor** sub, there is a short **NearestNeighbor** "main" sub that calls four other subs, **GetProblemData**, **Initialize**, **PerformHeuristic**, and **DisplayResults**, to do the work. The code appears below. (The comments have been omitted to emphasize the overall structure.) Note how the names of the subs indicate the basic tasks to be performed. This is always good programming practice.

Compare the code below with the one-sub code in the original **Traveling Salesperson.xlsm** file. You will probably agree that the "divide-and-conquer" strategy used here makes the program easier to understand. It not only helps you see the big picture, but it also helps you to understand the details by presenting them in bite-sized chunks.

```
Option Explicit
Option Base 1

Dim nCities As Integer
Dim distance() As Integer
Dim wasVisited() As Boolean
Dim route() As Integer
Dim totalDistance As Integer

Sub NearestNeighbor()
    Call GetProblemData
    Call Initialize
    Call PerformHeuristic
    Call DisplayResults
End Sub

Sub GetProblemData()
    Dim i As Integer, j As Integer
    With Range("A12")
        nCities = Range(.Offset(1, 0), .Offset(1, 0).End(xlDown)).Rows.Count
        ReDim distance(nCities, nCities)
        For i = 1 To nCities
            For j = 1 To nCities
                If i <> j Then distance(i, j) = .Offset(i, j).Value
            Next
        Next
    End With

    ReDim wasVisited(nCities)
    ReDim route(nCities + 1)
End sub
```

```
Sub Initialize()
    Dim i As Integer
    route(1) = 1
    route(nCities + 1) = 1
    wasVisited(1) = True
    For i = 2 To nCities
        wasVisited(i) = False
    Next
    totalDistance = 0
End Sub

Sub PerformHeuristic()
    Dim step As Integer
    Dim i As Integer
    Dim nowAt As Integer
    Dim nextAt As Integer
    Dim minDistance As Integer

    nowAt = 1
    For step = 2 To nCities
        minDistance = 10000
        For i = 2 To nCities
            If i <> nowAt And Not wasVisited(i) Then
                If distance(nowAt, i) < minDistance Then
                    nextAt = i
                    minDistance = distance(nowAt, nextAt)
                End If
            End If
        Next i
        route(step) = nextAt
        wasVisited(nextAt) = True
        totalDistance = totalDistance + minDistance
        nowAt = nextAt
    Next step

    totalDistance = totalDistance + distance(nowAt, 1)
End Sub

Sub DisplayResults()
    Dim step As Integer
    With Range("B12").Offset(nCities + 2, 0)
        .Offset(0, -1).Value = "Nearest neighbor route"
        .Offset(1, 0).Value = "Stop #"
        .Offset(1, 1).Value = "City"

        For step = 1 To nCities + 1
            .Offset(step + 1, 0).Value = step
            .Offset(step + 1, 1).Value = route(step)
        Next step

        .Offset(nCities + 4, -1).Value = "Total distance is " & totalDistance
    End With
End Sub
```

When you divide a program into multiple subs, you have to be careful with variable declarations. If a particular variable is required by more than one of the subs, it should be declared at the top of the module. The **module-level** variables above are nCities, totalDistance, and the distance, wasVisited, and route arrays. Other variables that are needed only in a specific sub, such as the step variable in the DisplayResults sub, should be declared locally. In general, this forces you to examine your variables (and the logical structure of your program) carefully to see what belongs where. You *could* take the easy way out by declaring *all* variables at the top as module-level variables, but this is considered very poor programming practice. It signals that you haven't thought very carefully about the overall structure of your program.

10.5 Passing Arguments

In a typical modular program, a particular sub can be called several times. Each time it is called, the sub performs the same basic task, but possibly with different inputs (and different outputs). As a very simple example, suppose a main sub calls a display sub to display a customer's name in a message box. You want the display sub to be very general, so that it will display any name given to it. The question is how you get the customer's name from the main sub to the display sub. There are two ways: (1) by using module-level variables and (2) by **passing arguments**. These two methods are compared below.

Module-Level Variables Method

The following program illustrates the use of module-level variables. It assumes there is a range called Names that contains the last names and first names of 10 customers. I want to display each customer's full name in a message box. To do so, I declare module-level variables lastName and firstName in the first line. Then the **Main** sub loops through the rows of the Names range, stores the last and first names of the current customer in the lastName and firstName variables, and calls the **DisplayName** sub to display the customer's full name. The DisplayName sub knows the current values of lastName and firstName because they are module-level variables.

```
Dim lastName As String, firstName As String

Sub Main()
    Dim i as Integer
    For i = 1 to 10
        lastName = Range("Names").Cells(i,1)
        firstName = Range("Names").Cells(i,2)
        Call DisplayName
    Next
End Sub

Sub DisplayName()
    Dim customerName As String
    customerName = firstName & " " & lastName
    MsgBox "The customer's full name is " & customerName
End Sub
```

Passing Arguments Method

Alternatively, you can **pass arguments** (in this case, names) from the Main sub to the DisplayNames sub. In this context, you refer to the Main sub as the **calling** sub and the DisplayNames sub as the **called** sub. To implement the method, the variables lastName and firstName are no longer declared as module-level variables. They are now declared locally in the Main sub, and they are passed to the DisplayName sub as arguments in the second-to-last line of Main. Specifically, to pass arguments you type the name of the called sub (Display-Name) and then list the variables being passed, separated by commas and included within parentheses. The first line of the called sub then indicates the arguments it expects to receive.

```
Sub Main()
    Dim i as Integer, firstName as String, lastName as String
    For i = 1 to 10
        lastName = Range("Names").Cells(i,1)
        firstName = Range("Names").Cells(i,2)
        Call DisplayName(lastName, firstName)
    Next
End Sub

Sub DisplayName(lName As String, fName As String)
    Dim customerName As String
    customerName = fName & " " & lName
    MsgBox "The customer's full name is " & customerName
End Sub
```

Note that the arguments in the first line of the DisplayName sub are lName and fName. They are *not* the same as the names passed to it, lastName and firstName. This is perfectly legal. The variables being passed from the calling sub and the arguments in the called sub do not need to have the same names, although they often do. The only requirements are that *they must match in number, type, and order*. If Main passes two string variables to DisplayName, then DisplayName must have two arguments declared as string type. Otherwise, VBA will display an error message. Also, if the last name is the first variable in the passing statement, it must be the first argument in the argument list of the called sub.[2]

Summarizing, here are the rules for passing arguments:

- To call a sub with arguments, type its name and follow it with arguments separated by commas and included within parentheses. The arguments should be declared locally within the calling sub, as in:

```
Dim lastName as String, firstName as String
Call DisplayName(lastName, firstName)
```

---

[2]Actually, this is not quite true. It is possible to include the *names* of the arguments when calling the sub, in which case the arguments can come in a different order, but I will not use this variation here.

- The called sub should declare its arguments inside parentheses next to the name of the sub, as in:

```
Sub DisplayName(lName As String, fName As String)
```

- The names of the variables in the calling sub do not need to be the same as the names of the arguments in the called sub, but they must match in number, type, and order.

Now you have two ways to deal with shared variables. You can declare them as module-level (or project-level with the keyword Public) variables at the top of a module, or you can pass them as arguments from one sub to another. Which method is better? Most professional programmers favor passing arguments whenever possible. The reason is that this makes a sub such as DisplayName totally self-contained. It can be reused exactly as it stands in a different program, because it is not dependent on a list of module-level variables that might or might not exist. However, passing variables is a somewhat more difficult concept, and it is sometimes more awkward to implement than the "global variable" approach. Therefore, both methods can be used, and you will see both in the applications in the second part of the book.

EXAMPLE 10.2   Formatting Extremes

The file **Format Extremes.xlsm** contains monthly sales values for a company's sales regions. (See Figure 10.4.) The company wants to highlight the extreme sales in each month. Specifically, it wants to color the minimum sale in each month red and italicize it, and it wants to color the maximum sale in each month blue and boldface it.

This task is accomplished with the **FormatExtremes** and **ChangeFont** subs listed below. The FormatExtremes sub is the main sub. (It is attached to the button on the sheet.) It loops through all of the cells in the sales range with a pair of nested For loops. For each cell, it calls the ChangeFont sub to change the font of the cell appropriately if the sales value in this cell is an extreme for the month. Four arguments are passed to ChangeFont sub: the cell (a range object), the sales value in the cell, the minimum sales value for the month, and the maximum sales value for the month. All of these arguments have the same names in the called sub as in the calling sub, but they could be different and the program would still work correctly.

Figure 10.4 Sales Data

	A	B	C	D	E	F	G	H	I	J	K	L	M
1	Sales by region and month												
2													
3		Jan	Feb	Mar	Apr	May	Jun	Jul	Aug	Sep	Oct	Nov	Dec
4	Region 1	25630	19660	15270	33810	19360	15770	22490	8350	18310	18160	14040	10680
5	Region 2	18490	10060	13150	17350	12120	16940	24120	4550	13920	11020	10370	8590
6	Region 3	13360	12630	20350	10850	17650	20570	18500	36460	7530	11880	18110	18760
7	Region 4	17280	22930	19310	12230	16490	6760	12850	18930	16640	13590	8180	10830
8	Region 5	10970	10550	11780	7210	23280	7320	15840	19690	19280	8690	9810	10540
9	Region 6	7990	14690	20680	17130	12620	7400	8420	13810	7090	8990	12570	15260
10	Region 7	40310	10820	18310	13900	6390	13290	12980	28440	15530	25940	16600	18160
11	Region 8	10770	18250	29580	21020	10200	9380	15210	5750	13710	11770	10820	23160
12	Region 9	10530	14170	24630	16910	21670	11750	10470	19150	20170	13370	20600	26180
13	Region 10	8600	22950	14080	16760	17270	16670	18650	10370	12040	13810	8000	11690
14	Region 11	11510	15660	16870	17930	15110	7760	12090	10260	23240	14760	15430	16540
15	Region 12	10360	11490	15000	14060	9770	13110	24320	24500	13300	15610	21040	12620
16	Region 13	18670	12350	20450	9860	16730	10100	12870	11390	16220	11760	18480	13330
17	Region 14	16360	18640	17050	25080	10760	14420	16730	17260	22470	11980	10710	19640
18	Region 15	20760	13610	6340	12510	14570	11930	26490	21130	21530	20390	24960	16100
19	Region 16	18690	23710	10530	18050	17730	7230	20750	23370	18070	10490	18980	12390

```
Sub FormatExtremes()
    Dim nMonths As Integer, nRegions As Integer
    Dim i As Integer, j As Integer
    Dim minVal As Single, maxVal As Single, salesVal As Single
    Dim cell As Range

    With Range("A3")
        nMonths = Range(.Offset(0, 1), .Offset(0, 1).End(xlToRight)).Columns.Count
        nRegions = Range(.Offset(1, 0), .Offset(1, 0).End(xlDown)).Rows.Count
        ' Restore to normal.
        With Range(.Offset(1, 1), .Offset(nRegions, nMonths)).Font
            .ColorIndex = 1
            .Bold = False
            .iItalic = False
        End With
        ' Look for extremes (those the match the min or max in any column).
        For j = 1 To nMonths
            minVal = WorksheetFunction.Min(Range(.Offset(1, j), .Offset(nRegions, j)))
            maxVal = WorksheetFunction.Max(Range(.Offset(1, j), .Offset(nRegions, j)))
            For i = 1 To nRegions
                Set cell = .Offset(i, j)
                salesVal = cell.Value
                Call ChangeFont(cell, salesVal, minVal, maxVal)
            Next
        Next
    End With
End Sub

Sub ChangeFont(cell As Range, sales As Single, minVal As Single, maxVal As Single)
    With cell
        If sales = minVal Then
            .Font.ColorIndex = 3
            .Font.Italic = True
        ElseIf sales = maxVal Then
            .Font.ColorIndex = 5
```

```
            .Font.Bold = True
        End If
    End With
End Sub
```

Note how general the ChangeFont sub is. You could easily use it in any other program that needs to change the font of particular cells. All you need to pass to it are the cell (again, as an object), a sales value, and minimum and maximum sales values to compare to.

Passing by Reference and by Value (Optional)

When you pass a variable such as lastName from one sub to another, the default method is **by reference**. This means that the variables in the calling and the called subs share the same memory location, so that any changes to lastName in the called sub will be reflected in the calling sub. For example, suppose last-Name has value "Jones" when it is passed, and then the called sub changes it in a line such as

```
lastName = "Smith"
```

Then the value of lastName will be "Smith" when control passes back to the calling sub.

If this is *not* the behavior you want, you can pass the variable **by value**. This sends a *copy* of lastName to the called sub, so that any changes made there to lastName are *not* reflected in the calling sub. In the above example, lastName would remain "Jones" in the calling sub. If you want to pass by value, the called sub must have the keyword **ByVal** (all one word) next to the argument, as in

```
Sub DisplayName(ByVal lastName As String, ByVal firstName As String)
```

On the other hand, if you want to emphasize that you are passing by reference, you can write

```
Sub DisplayName(ByRef lastName As String, ByRef firstName As String)
```

However, the keyword **ByRef** is never really necessary because passing by reference is the default method. Because it is the method I use in all later examples, you will never see either keyword, **ByRef** or **ByVal**.[3]

---

[3]Interestingly, in its newest technology, .NET, Microsoft passes "by value" by default. This means you have to specify ByRef explicitly if you want to pass "by reference."

Passing Arrays (Optional)

Consider the following scenario. You have written a general-purpose sub called **SortNames** that takes any array of last names and sorts them in alphabetical order. (The details of how it does this are irrelevant for now.) You would like to be able to call SortNames from any sub by passing any array of last names to it. In particular, you want this to work regardless of the *size* of the array being passed. That is, it should work for a 10-element array, a 1000-element array, or an array of any other size. What is the appropriate way to proceed?[4]

The following code does the job. (The next-to-last line indicates the detailed code for sorting. It is not relevant for this discussion.)

```
Sub CallingSub()
    Dim names(100) As String
    For i = 1 To 100
        names(i) = Range("Names").Cells(i).Value
    Next
    Call SortNames(names)
End Sub

Sub SortNames(names() As String)
    Dim nNames As Integer
    nNames = UBound(names)
    ' Other lines of code would go here.
End Sub
```

The calling sub stores 100 names in an array of size 100. (It populates this array by pulling the names from a worksheet range, which is assumed to be filled with 100 last names.) It then passes the names array to the SortNames sub with the line

```
Call SortNames(names)
```

Note that there are no parentheses next to the names argument in this line. VBA know that names is an array only because it was declared earlier to be an array. On the other end, the first line of the SortNames sub uses empty parentheses next to the names argument to indicate that it is expecting an array. It will know how large an array to work with only when an array of a specific size is passed to it.

Note that you can determine the size of the array that has been passed to SortNames by writing with the line

```
nNames = UBound(names)
```

somewhere inside the SortNames sub, as was done above. The VBA **UBound** function returns the largest index in the array.[5] Therefore, when an array of size

---

[4]I have included this section because passing arrays is a common operation and many VBA books don't tell you how to do it!

[5]If the default 0-based indexing is in effect, **UBound** returns 1 less than the number of array elements.

100 is passed to SortNames, nNames becomes 100. If an array of size 1000 were passed instead, nNames would be 1000. The point is that this procedure works regardless of the size of the array that is passed.

10.6 Function Subroutines

The subroutines to this point—the things called subs—can perform virtually any task. They can sort numbers in a worksheet, they can create and manipulate charts, they can add or delete worksheets, and so on. This section discusses a special type of subroutine called a **function subroutine** that has a much more specific objective: It returns a value. The following simple example illustrates one possibility. It returns the larger of two numbers passed to it (number1 and number2) in the variable Larger.

```
Function Larger(number1 As Single, number2 as Single) As Single
    If number1 >= number2 Then
        Larger = number1
    Else
        Larger = number2
    End If
End Function
```

This function subroutine looks a lot like a typical sub. For example, it can take arguments, in this case number1 and number2, both of Single type. However, it has some important differences:

- Instead of beginning with Sub and ending with End Sub, it begins with **Function** and ends with End Function.
- It returns a certain *type* of variable, in this case Single. This type is specified in the first line, after the argument list.
- It returns the value assigned to its name. In the example, the return value will come from one of the two lines that begin Larger =. For example, if the numbers 3 and 5 are passed to this function, it returns 5.

A function subroutine can be used in one of two ways. It can be called by another sub (or even another function subroutine), or it can be used as a new function in an Excel formula. Here is an example of the first method, where the calling sub calls Larger in the next-to-last line.

```
Sub CallingSub()
    Dim firstNumber As Single, secondNumber As Single
    firstNumber = 3
    secondNumber = 5
    MsgBox "The larger of the two numbers is " & Larger(firstNumber, secondNumber)
End Sub
```

The message box will report that the larger number is 5. Note once again that the variables being passed can have different names from the arguments of the function, but they should agree in number, type, and order. In this case, Larger is expecting two arguments of type Single.

To illustrate the second method , open a new workbook in Excel, get into the VBE, insert a new module, and type the code for the Larger function exactly as above. Now enter the formula =**Larger(5,3)** in any cell. It will recognize your new function, and it will correctly enter 5 in the cell. In fact, as you start typing the formula in Excel, you will even get some help from Intellisense. Unfortunately, it doesn't list the arguments it expects, as it does with built-in Excel functions.

This creates a whole new realm of possibilities for you as a programmer. You can define your own functions and then use them in Excel formulas! You might not need to do this very often because Excel already includes so many of its own functions. However, there might be a *few* times when you want to create your own functions. Here are some things you should know.

- If you write the code for a function in Workbook1 and then try to use this function in a formula in Workbook2, it won't be recognized. The problem is that Workbook2 recognizes only the functions written in *its* modules. There are at least two solutions to this problem. First, you can set a **reference** to Workbook1 in Workbook2. To do so, make sure Workbook1 is open. Then activate Workbook2, get into the VBE, select the **Tools** → **References** menu item, and check the Workbook1 box. The problem with this method is that Workbook1 must be open. A better method is to put all of your favorite functions in your **Personal.xlsb** file (recall Chapter 4), and then set a reference to it, again through **Tools** → **References**, in any workbook where you want to use these functions. The advantage of this method is that the **Personal.xlsb** file is always open (unless you deliberately close it).
- Suppose you want to write a function that accepts one or more *lists* as arguments. In particular, these lists might come from worksheet ranges. For example, suppose you want to emulate Excel's Sum function. Then the following code will work (you can find it in the **Functions.xlsm file**):

```
Public Function MySum(values As Variant) As Single
    Dim v As Variant, total As Single
    For Each v In values
        total = total + v
    Next
    MySum = total
End Function
```

The point here is that the values argument, which contains the list of values to be summed, must be declared as a Variant, even though it acts like a collection. This enables you to use the For Each loop inside the function. Importantly, this list could come from a worksheet range, as illustrated in Figure 10.5. The gray cells contain row and column sums, indicated by the typical formula in the text box. It is even possible to copy this formula across and down, just like any other Excel formula.

Figure 10.5 Using the MySum Function in a Worksheet

	A	B	C	D
1	Illustration of MySum function			
2				
3	98	35	68	201
4	12	87	77	176
5	59	23	39	121
6	40	37	46	123
7	19	98	20	137
8	73	95	94	262
9	31	38	43	112
10	332	413	387	
11				
12				
13		Formula in cell B10 is:		
14		=MySum(B3:B9)		
15				

EXAMPLE 10.3 Concatenating Names

This example illustrates a useful string function I developed called **FullName**. It is *not* a built-in Excel function. It is defined by the code listed below. (You can find this code in the **Functions.xlsm** file.) The function takes four arguments: a person's first name, last name, initial (if any), and a Boolean variable. The Boolean variable is True if the initial is the person's *middle* initial, and it is False if the initial is really the initial of the person's first name (in which case, the "first name" argument is really the person's middle name). The "initial" argument can have a period after it, or it can have no period. (The code uses VBA's **Left** function, with last argument 1, to chop off the period in case there is one. Then the code adds a period, just to ensure that there is one after the initial.) Also, the "initial" argument can be an empty string (no initial in the name), in which case the Boolean value is irrelevant. (Those of us who go by our middle names wish everyone would use this type of function to ensure that they get our names correct!)

```
Function FullName(firstName As String, lastName As String, initial As String, _
        isMiddleInitial As Boolean) As String
    If initial = "" Then
        FullName = firstName & " " & lastName
    ElseIf isMiddleInitial Then
        FullName = firstName & " " & Left(initial, 1) & ". " & lastName
    Else
        FullName = Left(initial, 1) & ". " & firstName & " " & lastName
    End If
End Function
```

Figure 10.6 FullName Examples

	A	B	C
1	**Concatenating names**		
2			
3	S.	Wayne	Abraham
4	Christian	L	
5	Albright	Winston	Lincoln
6			
7	S. Christian Albright	Wayne L. Winston	Abraham Lincoln

Figure 10.6 illustrates the use of this function. The "inputs" to the function are in rows 3–5. The formulas in cells A7 to C7 are

=FullName(A4,A5,A3,FALSE)

=FullName(B3,B5,B4,TRUE)

and

=FullName(C3,C5,C4,TRUE)

Note that the arguments after FullName must be in the correct order: first name, last name, initial, and Boolean; however, they could come from any cells in the spreadsheet. Also, note that Abraham Lincoln has no middle initial. Therefore, the Boolean value in the cell C7 formula is irrelevant—it could be TRUE or FALSE.

EXAMPLE 10.4 Generating Random Numbers

If you have done any spreadsheet simulation, you know the need for random numbers from various probability distributions. Some simulation add-ins such as @RISK have their own collections of random number functions. This example illustrates a simple function you can write and use in your own simulations, *without* the need for an add-in such as @RISK. It generates random values from *any* discrete distribution, where you supply the possible values and their corresponding probabilities. Its code is listed below. (It is stored in the file **Functions.xlsm**.)

```
Public Function Discrete(value As Variant, prob As Variant)
    ' We assume that the value array contains integers in ascending order.
    Dim i As Integer
    Dim cumProb As Single
    Dim uniform As Single

    ' The following line ensures that we'll get different random numbers
    ' each time we run this procedure.
    Randomize

    ' The following line ensures that the function recalcs (with new random
    ' numbers) if it's entered as a formula in a worksheet.
```

```
        Application.Volatile

        ' Generate a uniform random number.
        uniform = Rnd

        ' Find the first cumulative probability that's greater than uniform,
        ' and return the corresponding value.
        cumProb = prob(1)
        i = 1
        Do Until cumProb > uniform
             i = i + 1
             cumProb = cumProb + prob(i)
        Loop
        Discrete = value(i)
End Function
```

Several points might require some explanation.

- The **Application.Volatile** line ensures that if this function is entered in a worksheet, it will recalculate (and thereby generate a *different* random number) each time the worksheet recalculates.
- The Randomize line ensures that you won't get the *same* random number each time this function is called. (This would certainly destroy the function's usefulness in simulation.)
- The Rnd function is a built-in VBA function similar to Excel's Rand function. It generates random numbers uniformly distributed between 0 and 1.
- The loop finds the place where the uniform random number "fits" in the probability distribution. For example, with the probabilities given in Figure 10.7, the cumulative probabilities are 0.1, 0.4, 0.9, and 1.0, so if the uniform random number is 0.532, then the function returns the third value (3) because 0.532 fits between 0.4 and 0.9.
- The arrays, value and prob, must be declared as Variant types with no parentheses. This is a rather obscure rule, but it's the only way that allows us to use such a function in an Excel formula.
- The following code indicates how we could call such a function in a VBA module (as opposed to using it in an Excel formula):

```
Sub TestDiscrete()
      ' This sub tests the Discrete random number generator.
      Dim value As Variant, prob As Variant, i As Integer
      value = Array(1, 2, 3, 4)
      prob = Array(0.1, 0.3, 0.5, 0.1)
      For i = 1 To 30
           MsgBox Discrete(value, prob)
      Next
End Sub
```

This function is illustrated in Figure 10.7, where several random numbers are generated. (See the Discrete sheet in the **Functions.xlsm** file.) The formula in cell B10, which is then copied down, is

```
= Discrete($A$4:$A$7,$B$4:$B$7)
```

Figure 10.7 Random Numbers from a Discrete Distribution

	A	B	C	D	E	F
1	Generating random numbers from a discrete distribution					
2						
3	Value	Probability				
4	1	0.1				
5	2	0.3				
6	3	0.5				
7	4	0.1				
8						
9	Random numbers					
10		2				
11		3				
12		1				
13		3				
14		3				
15		3				
16		3				
17		2				
18		3				
19		3				

If you open this file and recalculate (by pressing the F9 key, for example), you will see that all of the random numbers change.

If you want to use this function or develop your own random number functions, you will probably want it to be available regardless of which files are open. As discussed earlier, a good option is to place the code in your **Personal.xlsb** file, and then set a reference to the **Personal.xlsb** file in any file where you want to use the function. (Remember, you set a reference in the VBE from the **Tools** → **References** menu item.)

The file Functions.xlsm contains the function subroutines discussed above, plus others. It also asks you to develop a couple of your own.

10.7 The Workbook_Open Event Handler

In Chapter 2, I briefly discussed **events** and **event handlers**. An event handler is a sub that runs whenever a certain event occurs (or **fires**). Event handlers are discussed in much more detail in the next chapter when you learn about user forms. However, there is one simple event handler that you can use right away. It responds to the event where a workbook is opened. In short, if you want anything to occur when you open an Excel workbook, you can write the appropriate code in this event handler.

Event handlers have built-in names—you have no control over the names given to these subroutines. The particular event handler discussed here has the name **Workbook_Open**. Also, it is a **Private** sub by default. Therefore, its first line is always the following:

```
Private  Sub  Workbook_Open()
```

Another distinguishing feature of this subroutine is that you do *not* place it in a module. Instead, you store it in the **ThisWorkbook** code window. To get to this window, double-click on the ThisWorkbook item in the VBE Project Explorer (see Figure 10.8). This opens a code window that looks just like a module code window, except that it is reserved for event handlers having to do with workbook events.

The code in a Workbook_Open sub is usually not very elaborate. A typical use of this sub is to ensure that a worksheet named Explanation is activated when a user opens a workbook. (I use it for this purpose in all of the applications in the second half of the book.) The following sub is all that is required:

```
Private  Sub  Workbook_Open()
    Worksheets("Explanation").Activate
End  Sub
```

Of course, you could place other statements in this sub—to hide certain worksheets, for example. Again, if there are any actions you want to occur when a workbook opens, the Workbook_Open sub is the place to put them.

As you might guess, there is also an event handler for the event where a workbook is *closed*. It is named **Workbook_BeforeClose**. Because this subroutine is somewhat more complex (it takes a rather obscure argument, for example) and is not used in later applications, I will not discuss it here. However, if you are interested, you can find online help for it in the Object Browser.

Figure 10.8 ThisWorkbook Item in Project Explorer

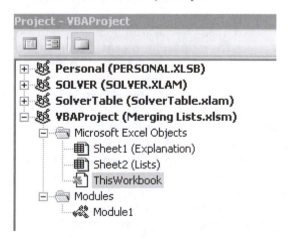

10.8 Summary

Long programs should not be written in a single long sub; this is considered poor style. In this chapter I illustrated how to organize long programs into a sequence of shorter subs, each of which performs a specific task. The resulting code is easier to read and debug, and pieces of it are more likely to be reusable in other programs. I discussed how it is a good programming practice to pass arguments from one sub to another whenever possible. When this is done, the called subs can often be written in a totally self-contained manner, which allows them to be reused in other programs. I also introduced function subroutines. Their purpose is to return a value, and they can be called by other subs (even other function subroutines), or they can be used as new spreadsheet functions. Finally, I briefly discussed event handlers. Specifically, I illustrated how the Workbook_Open sub can be used to perform any desired actions when a workbook is opened.

EXERCISES

1. Write a sub called **Main** that asks the user to type a first name and last name in an input box, which is captured in a string variable fullName. It then calls a sub called **ProperCase** that takes a single argument, a string, and converts this argument to proper case. For example, if the user enters the name gEORge buSH, the sub should return George Bush. The main sub should then display the result, such as George Bush, in a message box.

2. Repeat the previous exercise, but now ask for two separate names, firstName and lastName, in two separate input boxes, and pass these *two* arguments to the **ProperCase** sub (which will need to be modified).

3. Write a Function subroutine called **Tax** that takes a single argument grossIncome of type Currency. It should calculate the tax on any income using the following tax schedule: (1) if income is less than or equal to $15,000, there is no tax; (2) if income is greater than $15,000 and less than or equal to $75,000, the tax is 15% of all income greater than $15,000; and (3) if income is greater than $75,000, the tax is 15% of all income between $15,000 and $75,000 plus 20% of all income greater than $75,000. (Don't you wish taxes were this easy!) Then write a **Main** sub that asks a user for his income, gets the function subroutine to calculate the tax on this income, and reports the tax in a message box.

4. Expanding on the previous exercise, the file **Tax Schedule.xlsx** has a tax schedule. Write a **Main** sub, just as in the previous exercise, that asks for an income and passes it to a **Tax** function. However, the Tax function now finds the tax by using the tax schedule in the sheet. (This tax schedule is similar to the one in the previous exercise and is illustrated with the sample tax calculation on the sheet.) The Tax function should be flexible enough to work even if more rows (breakpoints) or different breakpoints or percentages are added to the tax schedule.

5. Write a function subroutine called **Add** that mimics Excel's SUM function. It should accept an array of type Single, and it should return the sum of the elements

of the array. Then write a short **Main** sub that sets up an array, passes it to your function, and reports the result.

6. Write a function subroutine called **AddProduct** that mimics Excel's SUMPRODUCT function. It should accept two arrays of type Single, both of the same size, and it should return the sum of the products of the two arrays. For example, if you pass it the arrays (3,5,1) and (4,3,6), it should return $3*4 + 5*3 + 1*6 = 33$.

7. Write a function subroutine called **NextCell** that takes a string argument Address, which should look like the address of a cell, such as C43. The function returns True or False depending on whether the cell to the right of this one contains a formula. For example, if you pass it C43, it checks whether cell D43 contains a formula.

8. Write a function subroutine called **NameExists** of type Boolean that takes two arguments of type Range and String, respectively. It searches all of the cells in the given range and checks whether any of them have their Value property equal to the given string. For example, if the string is "Davis", it checks whether "Davis" is in any of the cells. (A cell containing "Sam Davis" wouldn't count. The contents have to be "Davis" exactly.) If so, it returns True. Otherwise, it returns False.

9. Open a new workbook and add several worksheets. Each worksheet should be named as some state, such as Pennsylvania. Write a **Main** sub that creates an array called capitol. It should have as many elements as the number of sheets, and you should populate it with the capitols of your states. For example, if Pennsylvania is the third sheet, you should set capitol(3) equal to Harrisburg. Now write a sub called **EnterLabel** that takes two string arguments, a state and a capitol, and enters a label, such as "The capitol of Pennsylvania is Harrisburg", in that state's cell A1. Finally, use a loop in the Main sub to go through the sheets and send the sheet name and the appropriate element of the array to the EnterLabel sub. After the Main sub runs, there should be an appropriate label in cell A1 of each sheet.

10. Open a new workbook with a single worksheet, and enter some integers in the range A1:B10. (Any integers will do.) Write a **Main** sub that has a For loop from i=1 to i=10. Each time through this loop, a sub **Process** should be called with three arguments: i and the two numbers in columns A and B of row i. The Process sub should enter the larger of the two numbers in column C of row i, and it should color its font red if the number in row A is the larger. Otherwise, it should color the font blue.

11. The file **Customer Lists.xlsx** contains lists of customers from last year and this year in columns A and B. Write a sub called **FindMatch** that takes a single argument customerName (a string variable). It checks whether this customer is in both lists. If so, it displays a message to this effect, and it boldfaces both instances of the customer's name. Otherwise, it displays a message that the customer's name is *not* on both lists. Next, write a **Main** sub that uses an input box to ask for a customer name. Then it calls FindMatch with this customer's name as the argument.

12. The file **Stock Prices.xlsx** contains monthly adjusted closing prices, adjusted for dividends and stock splits, for WalTech's stock from 2000 to early 2008. (WalTech is a fictitious company.)

   a. Write a sub called **RecordHigh1** that takes a single argument called search-Price. This sub searches down the list of prices for the first price that exceeds the searchPrice argument. If it finds one, it displays the corresponding date in a message, something similar to, "The first date WalTech stock price exceeded _ was _." If the price never exceeded the argument searchPrice, it displays a message to this effect. Next, write a **Main** sub that uses an input box to ask the user for a price and then calls RecordHigh1 with this price as the argument.

b. Write another sub called **RecordHigh2** that takes a single argument called specifiedMonth. This sub searches down the list of prices for the last time up until (and including) the specified month where the stock reached a record high (that is, it was larger than all prices before it, going back to the beginning of 2000). It then displays a message such as, "The most recent record, up until _, was in _, when the price reached _." (Note that Jan-2000 is a record high by default, so at least one record high will always be found.) Change the Main sub from part **a** so that the input box now asks for a month and then calls RecordHigh2 with this month as an argument.

13. The file **Boy Girl Finished.xlsm** contains a sheet with scores for boys and girls. Open the file and click on the button. You'll see that it asks the user for 1 (boys) or 2 (girls). It then names the range of the scores for the chosen gender as DataRange, it enters a label and the average score for the chosen gender (as a *formula*) in cells D9 and E9, and it formats the D9:E9 range appropriately (blue font for boys, red font for girls). The code in this file is password-protected. Now open the **Boy Girl.xlsx** file, which contains only the data, and write your own code to perform the same tasks. It should contain a **Main** sub that calls the following subs: (1) **GetResponse** (to show the input box and get the user's response), (2) **NameGenderRange** (to name the appropriate range as DataRange), (3) **FormatOutputRange** (to format the output range D9:E9 appropriately), and (4) **EnterOutput** (to enter a label in D9 and a formula in E9). Write your subs so that there are no module-level variables. Instead, a string variable gender should be an argument of each called sub, where gender can be "boys" or "girls". Also, write the program so that it will work even if more data are added to the data set.

14. Open a new workbook and write a sub called **GetWorkbookInfo** that takes an argument called fileName (a string). This sub attempts to open the file called fileName. Assuming that it is successful (the file exists), a message box displays the creator of the file and the number of worksheets in the file. It then closes the file. Next, write a **Main** sub that uses an input box to ask for the name of a file, including its path and then calls GetWorkbookInfo with this file name as the argument. (Your GetWorkbookInfo will have one serious deficiency—it will bomb if the requested file doesn't exist, at least not in the specified path. Don't worry about this for now. You will see how to check for it in Chapter 12.)

15. The program in the **Merge Lists.xlsm** file from the previous chapter (see Example 9.4) is written as a single sub.

a. Break it into several shorter subs, all called from a **Main** sub. The called subs should be (1) **ClearOld** (to clear the old merged list in column D, if any), (2) **GetData** (to put the data in the current lists in arrays), and (3) **CreateMergedList** (to create the merged list in column D). Don't pass any variables; use all module-level variables for any shared variables.

b. Repeat part **a**, but pass variables. In particular, the listSize1 and listSize2 variables and the list1 and list2 arrays should be arguments of both GetData and CreateMergedList. (*Hint*: Refer to the section in this chapter dealing with passing arrays as arguments.)

16. The program in the **Product Sales.xlsx** file from the previous chapter (see Example 9.2) is written as a single sub. Break it into at least three shorter subs, all called from a **Main** sub. You can decide how to break it up and whether you want to use module-level variables or pass arguments.

17. The file **Recent Sales Finished.xlsm** contains a list of a company's sales reps in the SalesReps sheet. For each of several Midwest states, there is a sheet showing recent sales by the sales reps in that state. Open this file and click on the button on the SalesReps sheet. You'll see that it asks for a sales rep and then a state, and it summarizes sales by that rep in that state in a message box. Run this several times (including queries for reps and states not in the company's list) to see all the functionality built in to it. The code in this file is password-protected. Now open the file **Recent Sales.xlsm**, which contains only the data and a **Main** sub that calls some yet-to-be-written subs. Your job is to write the subs, using the arguments indicated in the Main sub, to achieve the same functionality. (Note: Make sure that when you do a search for, say, Arnett, you don't also find information for Barnett. Check out the various arguments for the Find function in VBA.)

18. The file **Transactions Finished.xlsm** contains two sheets. The CustomersProducts sheet lists a company's customers and its products. The Transactions sheet lists information about recent transactions involving these customers and products. Open this file and click on the button on the CustomersProducts sheet. You'll be asked for a last name and a first name of a customer. If this customer is found on the list, you'll be asked for the name of a product. If this product is found on the list, a message will be displayed summarizing the sales of this product to this customer. Try it a few times (including queries for customers or products not in the lists) to see how it works. The code in this file is password-protected. Now open the file **Transactions.xlsm**, which contains only the data and a **Main** sub that calls some yet-to-be-written subs. Your job is to write the subs, using the arguments indicated in the Main sub, to achieve the same functionality.

19. The file **Errors 1.xlsx** contains a list of forecasting errors in column A made by some forecasting method. Write a function subroutine called **MAE** that finds the mean absolute error, that is, the average of the absolute values of the errors. It should be written to work on *any* range of errors such as the one in column A. Then try it out by entering the appropriate formula in cell E1.

20. The file **Errors 2.xlsx** contains a time series of monthly sales in column A and a series of forecasts of these sales in column B. Write a function subroutine called **MAPE** that finds the mean absolute percentage error of the forecasts, that is, the average of the absolute percentage errors. For example, the absolute percentage error in row 2 is $|713 - 738|/713 = 0.035$, or 3.5%. Write this function so that it will work with *any* two ranges of observations and corresponding forecasts. Then try it out by entering the appropriate formula in cell E1.

21. The **triangular** distribution is a probability distribution that is commonly used in business spreadsheet simulations. It is literally triangularly shaped. There are three

parameters to this distribution, labeled a, b, and c. The parameters a and c are the minimum and maximum possible values, and the parameter b is the most likely value (where you see the high point of the triangle). This is a simple distribution for people to understand, but it is not straightforward to generate random numbers from this distribution. The method is as follows:

- Calculate $d = (b - a)/(c - a)$
- Generate a uniformly distributed random number U between 0 and 1 (with VBA's Rnd function).
- If $U \leq d$, return $a + (c - a)\sqrt{dU}$ as the random number.
- If $U > d$, return $a + (c - a)[1 - \sqrt{(1 - d)(1 - U)}]$ as the random number.

(Note that VBA has a built-in sqr function for taking square roots.) Write a function subroutine called **Triangular** that takes three arguments corresponding to a, b, and c and returns a triangularly distributed random number. (Use the Application.Volatile and Randomize statements that were used in Example 10.4.) Then try out your random number generator in a worksheet by entering the formula and copying it down to generate a large number of these random numbers. You might also want to create a histogram of these random numbers, just to see if it has an approximate triangular shape.

User Forms

11.1 Introduction

This chapter introduces user forms, or what you know as dialog boxes. Everyone who has ever used a Windows program is familiar with dialog boxes. They are the primary means for getting users' inputs. In fact, they are so familiar that you probably take them for granted, never stopping to think how they actually work. This chapter explains how to create user forms for your own applications.[1] This entails two distinct operations. First, you have to *design* the user form to have the required functionality and look attractive. Second, you have to write **event handlers** that sit behind the user form waiting to respond appropriately to whatever the user does. For example, most user forms have OK and Cancel buttons. During the design stage, you have to place and resize these buttons on the form. You then have to write VBA code to respond appropriately when a user clicks on one of these buttons. Specifically, when the user clicks on the Cancel button, you typically want the dialog box to disappear. When the user clicks on the OK button, you typically want to capture the user's inputs and then have the dialog box disappear.

Working with user forms is arguably the most fun part of VBA application development. You can use your creative and artistic talents to design the dialog boxes that users will interact with. You can then use your logical skills to ensure that everything works properly when users click on buttons, select items from a list box, check "radio" buttons, fill in text boxes, and so on. In short, you get to *create* what you have been using for years—dialog boxes—and you start to see why there is a "V" in VBA.

11.2 Exercise

Working with user forms is not difficult, but there are many small steps to master, and practice is the key to mastering these. The following exercise is typical. It requires very little in the way of calculation, but you must put all of the pieces of the application together in just the right way. By the time you have read through

---

[1] Throughout this chapter, the terms "dialog box" and "user form" are used interchangeably. The former term is used by most users, whereas the latter term is used by programmers. In fact, many programmers spell "user form" as UserForm, all one word with two capital letters. I will use the less formal spelling here. Also, any a reference to a "form" is really to a "user form."

the rest of this chapter and have studied its examples, this exercise will be fairly straightforward—but it is exactly the type your boss will appreciate!

Exercise 11.1   Summarizing Monthly Sales

Consider a company that has regional stores in Atlanta, Charlotte, and Memphis. Each region sells a variety of products, although the products vary from region to region. The file **Sales Summary.xlsm** contains a separate sheet for each region that shows monthly sales for a 3-year period for each product the region sells. Part of the Atlanta sheet appears in Figure 11.1. Note that the product codes sold in any region always appear in row 4.

The file also contains an Explanation sheet, as shown in Figure 11.2. This summarizes what the exercise is supposed to accomplish. (Similar Explanation sheets appear in all of the applications in the second part of the book. It is always good to tell the user right away what an application is all about.) The button on this sheet should eventually be attached to a macro that runs the application.

It is easier to show what this application is supposed to do than to explain it in detail. In fact, you can try it out yourself by opening the **Sales Summary Finished.xlsm** file and clicking on the button. The user form in Figure 11.3 is first displayed, where the user must select a region and a set of summary measures. By default, the Atlanta button and the Median and Average boxes should be selected when the user sees this form. The user can then make any desired selections.

Next, the user sees the user form in Figure 11.4. It contains a message specific to the region chosen and a list of all products sold in that region. (When you write the program, you must find this list of product codes by scanning across row 4 of the region's sales sheet.) By default, the first product code should be selected. The user can then select any product code by scrolling through the list.

When the user clicks on the OK button, the application should summarize the sales of the product and region chosen, and display the results in a message box. For example, if the user chooses Charlotte, product L769C61, and *all* of the summary measures, the message in Figure 11.5 should appear.

To develop this application, you need to create the two user forms in Figures 11.3 and 11.4, place the appropriate controls on them, give these controls appropriate properties, and write appropriate event handlers. You also have to insert a module that contains the non-event code. Specifically, this code must "show" the user forms, perform any necessary calculations, and display the final message box. One hint that will come in handy is the following. To calculate the required summary measures, you can borrow any of Excel's worksheet functions: Count, Average, Median, Stdev, Min, or Max. For example, to calculate the average for some range, you can use Application.WorksheetFunction.Average(*range*), where *range* is a reference to the range you want to average. (Remember Application.WorksheetFunction from Chapter 5?)

Figure 11.1 Sample Data for Atlanta

	A	B	C	D	E	F	G	H
1	Sales for Atlanta							
2								
3		Product code						
4	Month	U394K71	B350B99	Y342H72	Q253I61	W311E65	F822G38	M228M28
5	Jan-03	105	477	492	873	424	97	582
6	Feb-03	102	433	528	904	445	111	1149
7	Mar-03	99	591	612	835	553	87	917
8	Apr-03	116	538	546	1143	571	84	898
9	May-03	52	670	573	987	536	97	994
10	Jun-03	97	671	520	720	507	82	1069
11	Jul-03	82	398	501	701	402	95	1170
12	Aug-03	92	559	523	966	388	142	396
13	Sep-03	107	402	432	1161	506	116	881
14	Oct-03	98	419	448	1232	454	116	1138

Figure 11.2 Explanation Sheet

Monthly Sales

The next three sheets show monthly sales of various products for a company's three sales regions. The purpose of this application is to summarize the sales for a particular region and a particular product. The scores can be summarized by any of the following: count, average, median, standard deviation, minimum, and maximum. The user first chooses a region and a set of summary measures. Then the user chooses a product from a list of products for that region. The results should be shown in a message box.

[Find summary measures]

Figure 11.3 First User Form

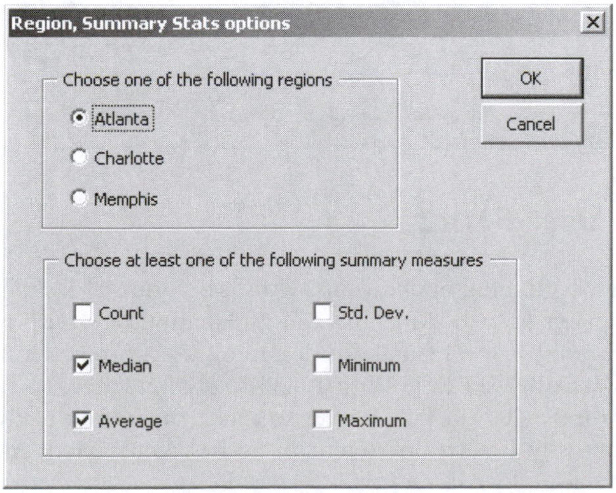

Figure 11.4 Second User Form

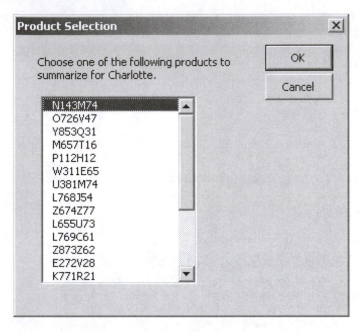

Figure 11.5 Results

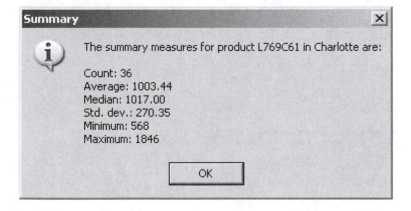

11.3 Designing User Forms

The first step in developing applications with user forms is designing the forms. This section explains how to do it, but the explanations are purposely kept fairly brief. The more you have to read about designing user forms, the harder you will think it is. It is actually very easy. With a half hour of practice, you can learn how to design user forms. (It will take longer to make them look really professional, but that too is mostly a matter of practice.) So let's get started. As you read this section, you should follow along on your own PC.

Figure 11.6 New User Form

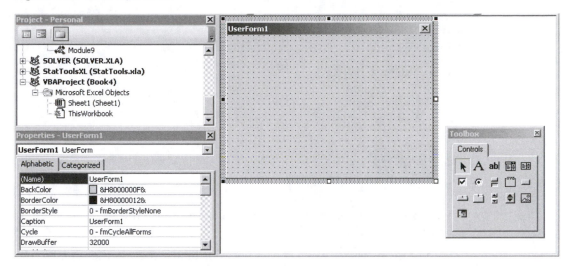

First, open a new workbook in Excel, get into the VBE, and make sure the Project Explorer and Properties windows are visible. (If they aren't visible, click on the appropriate buttons on the Standard toolbar or use the appropriate menu items from the View menu.) To add a user form, use the **Insert → UserForm** menu item. A blank user form will appear, and your screen will appear as in Figure 11.6. If it doesn't look exactly like this, you can resize windows and "dock" the Project Explorer and Properties windows at the left side of the screen. In fact, you can move and resize windows any way you like. Also, when you insert the user form, the **Toolbox** at the bottom right should appear. If it ever disappears, you can always redisplay it by selecting the **View → Toolbox** menu item or clicking on the "hammer and wrench" button on the Standard toolbar.

To design user forms, you need to know three things:

1. Which **controls** are available
2. How to place, resize, and line up controls on a user form
3. How to give controls properties in the **Properties window**

Available Controls

The available controls are those shown in the Toolbox. (See Figure 11.7.) The arrow at the top left is used only for pointing. The rest, starting with the A and going from left to right, have the following generic names:[2]

- First row—Label, TextBox, ComboBox, ListBox
- Second row—CheckBox, OptionButton, ToggleButton, Frame, Command-Button

---

[2]This list uses the technical single-word names for the controls, such as TextBox. Throughout the discussions, I often revert to less formal names, such as text box.

Figure 11.7 Toolbox

- Third row—TabStrip, MultiPage, ScrollBar, SpinButton, Image
- Fourth row—RefEdit

Each of these controls has a certain behavior built into it. Without going into details, I will simply state that this standard behavior is the behavior you are familiar with from working with dialog boxes in Windows applications. For example, if there are several option (radio) buttons on a user form and you click on one of them, then the others are automatically unchecked. The following list describes the functionality of the most frequently used controls.

- **CommandButton**—used to run subs (the user clicks on a button and a sub runs)
- **Label**—used mainly for explanations and prompts
- **TextBox**—used to obtain any type of user input (the user types something in the box)
- **ListBox**—used to let the user choose one or more items from a list
- **ComboBox**—similar to a list box, except that the user can type an item that isn't on the list in a box
- **CheckBox**—lets the user check whether an option is desired or not (any or all of a set of check boxes can be checked)
- **OptionButton**—often called a radio button, lets the user check which of several options is desired (only one of a set of option buttons can be checked)
- **Frame**—usually used to group a related set of options buttons, but can be used to organize any set of controls into logical groups
- **RefEdit**—similar to a TextBox control, but used specifically to let the user select a worksheet range

The controls in Figure 11.7 are the "standard" controls that are available to everyone who uses Excel. However, there are actually many more controls you might want to experiment with. Right-click on any of the controls in Figure 11.7 and select **Additional Controls.** You will see a fairly long list. Just check any that look interesting, and they will be added to your Toolbox.

A particularly useful control is the **Calendar** control. It not only allows you to put a calendar on a form, but this calendar is smart, so it needs virtually no programming on your part. If you add a calendar control to a form, you can find information about its properties and methods by going to Object Browser and viewing the MSACAL library. Check it out. My students love it!

Adding Controls to a User Form

To add any control to a user form, click on the control in the Toolbox and then drag a shape on the form. That's all there is to it. Try the following step-by-step exercise, and don't be afraid to experiment. When you are finished, your user form should appear approximately like the one in Figure 11.8.

1. **Resize form.** Resize the user form (make it considerably wider).
2. **Command button.** Add a command button at the top right. While it is still selected, press the Ctrl key and drag the button down to make a copy. You will know you are copying, not moving, when you see a plus sign as you drag. This is the general way to copy controls—select them and then drag them with your finger on the Ctrl key. (Don't take your finger off the Ctrl key too early, or you will move, not copy. I make this mistake all the time.)
3. **Explanation label.** Add a wide label to the left of the command buttons. This is a good place for explaining what your dialog box does.
4. **Text box and corresponding label.** Add a label (shown as Label2) and a corresponding text box to its right. A text box typically has a corresponding label that acts as a prompt for what the user should enter in the text box.
5. **Frame and option buttons.** Add a fairly large frame below the text box. Next, add an option button inside the frame, and make a copy of this option button. Make sure that . . . both option buttons fit entirely within the frame boundary.
6. **Copy frame and option buttons.** Drag over the frame to select it, put your finger on the Ctrl key, and drag the whole thing to the right to make a copy. Note that you get not only a new frame but also a new set of option buttons.

Figure 11.8 Controls on Practice User Form

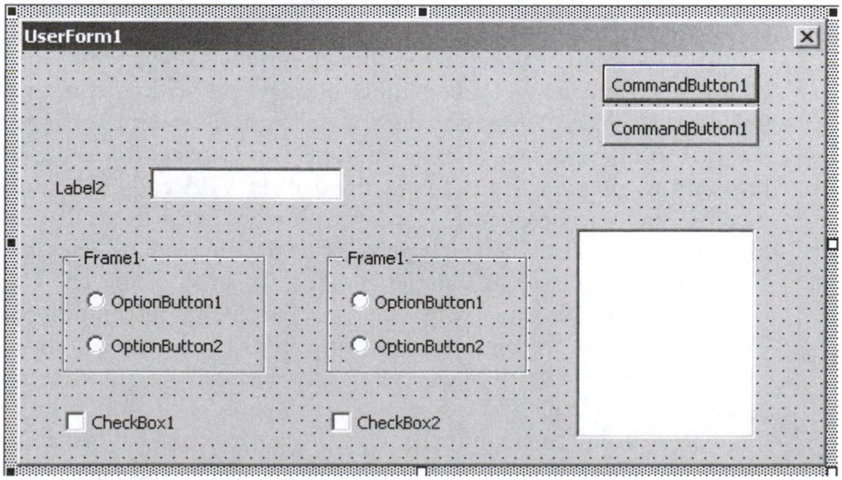

The option buttons in a frame are essentially part of the frame, so when you copy the frame, you also copy the option buttons. In addition, the option buttons in any frame are a "logical set" in the sense that only one button *in each frame* can be checked. For example, the top button in the left frame could be checked, *and* the bottom button in the right frame could be checked. If option buttons are not inside frames, then only one option button on the whole user form can be checked.

7. **Check box.** Add a check box at the lower left and make a copy of it to its right. Any number of these can be checked, including none of them.
8. **List box.** Add a list box at the bottom right. It doesn't look like a "list" box yet, because there is no list. This will be added later.
9. **Resize and align.** Resize and align the controls to make the form visually appealing. This is quite easy (if a bit tedious). Just experiment with the menu items under the Format menu, such as **Format → Align** and **Format → Make Same Size**. The key is that you can drag over several controls to select them. The selected controls are then treated as a group for the purpose of aligning and resizing. Also, the *first* one selected is the one with which the others are aligned or resized to. (It is the one with the white handles; the others have black handles.)

11.4 Setting Properties of Controls

The user form in Figure 11.8 doesn't do anything yet. In fact, it isn't even clear what it is supposed to do. You can fix the latter problem by setting some properties of the controls. You do this in the **Properties** window. Like Excel ranges, worksheets, and workbooks, controls are objects with properties, and these are listed in the Properties window. The items in the Properties window change depending on which control is selected, because different types of controls have different sets of properties. Figure 11.9 shows the Properties window for the user form itself. (To select the user form, click somewhere on it where there are no controls.) The names of the properties are listed on the left, and their values are listed on the right.

Microsoft has provided a bewildering number of properties for user forms and controls. Fortunately, you can ignore most properties and concentrate on the few you need to change. For example, you will typically want to change the Name and Caption properties of a user form. The Name property is used in general for referring to the user form (or any control) in VBA code. The default names are generic, such as UserForm1, CommandButton1, and so on. It is typically a good idea to change the Name property only if you plan to refer to the object in VBA code; otherwise, you can let the default name stand. The Caption property is what you see on the screen. On a user form, the caption appears in the title bar. For now, go through the following steps to change certain properties. (See Figure 11.10 for the finished user form.) For each step, select the control first (click on it), so that the Properties window shows the properties for *that* control.

Before going through these steps, I want to make a point about naming user forms and controls. In Chapter 5, I mentioned several conventions for naming

Figure 11.9 Properties Window for User Form

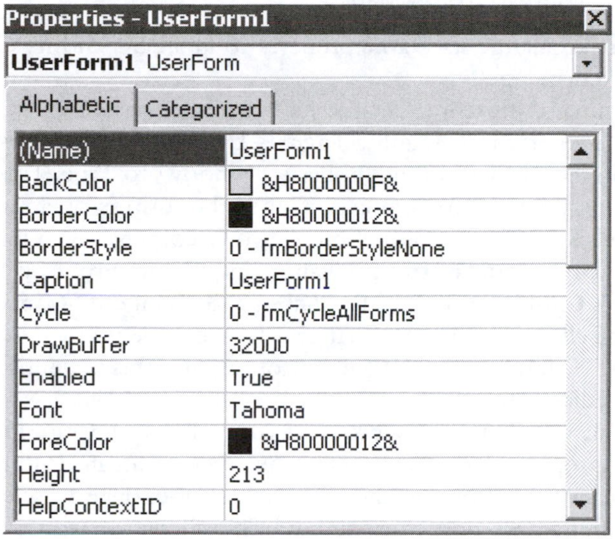

Figure 11.10 User Form with Changed Properties

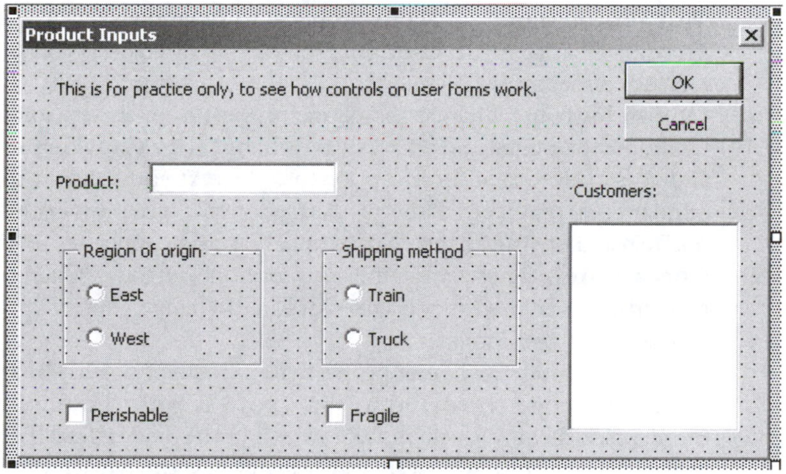

variables, and I said I favored the camel convention, with names such as unitCost. I have been using that convention consistently ever since, and I intend to continue it in the rest of the book. However, when it comes to user forms and controls, I favor the Hungarian convention, which uses short prefixes in the name to indicate what type of control it is. I adopt this convention because it is in common use by most programmers. Here are some common prefixes: **frm** for user form, **lbl** for label, **btn** for command button (some people prefer **cmd**), **txt** for text box, **lb** for list box, **cbo** for combo box, **opt** for option button, **chk** for check box, and **rfe** for ref edit. These prefixes make your code much more readable. They not only distinguish one type of control from another, but perhaps more important, they distinguish controls from variables.

1. **User form.** Change its **Name** property to frmInputs and its **Caption** property to Product Inputs.
2. **Top command button.** Change its **Name** property to btnOK, change its **Caption** property to OK, and change its **Default** property (yes, it is listed as Default in the left pane of the Properties window) to True. This gives the OK button the functionality you expect once the form is operational—namely, you can click on it *or* press the Enter key to accomplish the same thing.
3. **Bottom command button.** Change its **Name** property to btnCancel, change its **Caption** property to Cancel, and change its **Cancel** property to True. The effect of this latter change is to allow the user to press the Esc key instead of clicking on the Cancel button. Again, this is standard behavior in Windows dialog boxes.
4. **Top label.** Often, the only property you will ever change for a label is its **Caption** property—what appears in the label. You can do this through the Properties window, or you can click on the label once to select it and then again to put a dark border around it.[3] This allows you to type the label "in place." For this label, enter the caption "This is for practice only to see how controls on user forms work." (Don't include the quotes.)
5. **Label to the left of the text box.** Change its **Caption** property to Product:.
6. **Text box.** Change the **Name** property to txtProduct.
7. **Frames.** Change their **Caption** properties to Region of Origin and Shipping Method, respectively.
8. **Option buttons.** Change the **Name** properties of the option buttons in the left frame to optEast and optWest, and change their **Caption** properties to East and West. (Note that these captions are the text you see next to the buttons.) Similarly, change the Name properties of the other two option buttons to optTrain and optTruck, and change their Caption properties to Train and Truck.
9. **Check boxes.** These are similar to option buttons. Change their **Name** properties to chkPerish and chkFragile, and change their **Caption** properties to Perishable and Fragile.
10. **List box.** Change its **Name** property to lbCustomer. A list box does not have a Caption property, so add a label above it with the caption Customers:. Otherwise, the user will not know what the list is for. There is another property you should be aware of for list boxes: the **MultiSelect** property. Its default value is **0–fmMultiSelectSingle**. This means that the user is allowed to select only one item from the list. Many times you will want the user to be able to select *more* than one item from a list. If so, you should select option **2–fmMultiSelectExtended**. (See Figure 11.11.) For now, accept the first (default) option. (The middle option is virtually never used. I have no idea why they even include it.)

---

[3]If you accidentally double-click on the label or any other controls during the design stage, you will open the event code window, which is discussed later in the chapter. To get back to the user form design, select the **View → Object** menu item.

Figure 11.11 MultiSelect Property for List Boxes

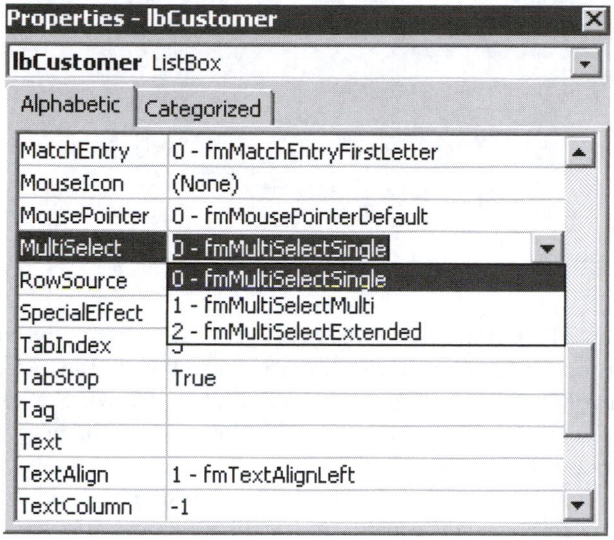

Tab Order

There is one final touch you can add to make your user form more professional—the **tab order.** You are probably aware that most dialog boxes allow you to move from one control to another by pressing the Tab key. To give your user form this functionality, all you need to do is change the **TabIndex** property of each control, using any ordering you like and starting with index 0. There are two things you should know about tabbing.

- Any control with the **TabStop** property set to False cannot be tabbed to. This is typically the case for labels.
- When there is a frame with "embedded" controls such as option buttons, you set the TabIndex for the *frame* relative to the order of the other controls on the form, but the tab order for the controls within the frame is set separately. For example, a frame might have index 6 in the tab order of *all* controls, but its two option buttons would have indexes 0 and 1. Essentially, the user first tabs to the frame and then tabs through the controls inside the frame.

The easiest way to set the tab order is to select the **View → Tab Order** menu item. This allows you to move any of the controls up or down in the tab order. Just remember that if you select **View → Tab Order** when a frame is selected, you will see the tab order only for the controls inside that frame.

Testing the Form

Now that you have designed the form, you can see how it will look to the user. To do this, make sure the user form, not some control on the form, is selected, and click on the **Run Sub/UserForm** button (the blue triangle button) or

Figure 11.12 User Form Template

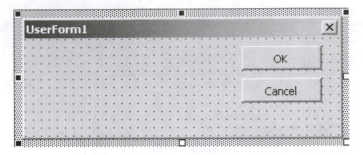

press the F5 key. This displays the user form. It doesn't *do* anything yet, but it should at least look nice. You should note that the **focus** (the cursor location) is set to the control at the top of the tab order (tab index 0). For example, if you set the tab index of the text box to 0, then the cursor will be in the text box, waiting for the user to type something. You can see how the tab order works by pressing the Tab key repeatedly. To get back to design view, click on the Close button of the form (the X button). Note that you cannot yet close the user form by clicking on the Cancel button, because the Cancel button is not yet "wired." You will make it functional shortly.

11.5 Creating a User Form Template

If you design a lot of user forms, you will quickly get tired of always having to design the same OK and Cancel buttons that appear on most forms. This section illustrates a handy shortcut. Open a new workbook and go through the procedure in the previous two sections to design a user form with an OK and a Cancel button and having the properties listed earlier in steps 2 and 3. It should look something like Figure 11.12. Now select the **File → Export File** menu item, and save the form under a name such as **OK_Cancel.frm** in some convenient folder.[4] Later on, whenever you want a user form with ready-made OK and Cancel buttons, select the **File → Import File** menu item and open the **OK_Cancel. frm** file. This can save you about a minute each time you design a form.

11.6 Writing Event Handlers

Much of Windows programming is built around **events**, where an event occurs whenever the user does something. This could mean clicking on a button, entering text in a text box, clicking on an option button, selecting a worksheet, right-clicking on a cell—in short, doing just about anything. Each of these events has a

---

[4]You'll note that this also saves a file called **OK_Cancel.frx** in your folder. You don't need to be concerned about this file, except that if you ever move the .frm file to a different folder, you should also move the .frx file to the same folder.

built-in **event handler**. This is a sub where you can add code so that appropriate actions are taken when the event occurs. These subs are always available—*if* you want the program to respond to certain events. Of course, there are many events that you don't want to bother responding to. For example, you *could* respond to the event where the mouse is dragged over a command button, but you probably have no reason to do so. In this case, you simply ignore the event. On the other hand, there are certain events you *do* want to respond to. For these, you have to write the appropriate code. This section illustrates how to do this in the context of user forms.

First, you have to understand where the event handler is placed. Also, you have to understand naming conventions. All of the VBA code to this point has been placed in modules, which are inserted into a project with the **Insert** → **Module** menu item. Event handlers are *not* placed in these modules. Instead, they are placed in a user form's **code window**. To get to a user form's code window, make sure you are viewing the form's design window, and select the **View** → **Code** menu item. In general, the **View** → **Code** and **View** → **Object** menu items (or F7 and Shift-F7 keys, if you prefer shortcut keys) toggle between the form's design and its code window.

Another way to get from the design window to the code window is to double-click on a control. (You might already have experienced this by accident.) This not only opens the code window, but it inserts a "stub" for event code. For example, by clicking on the OK button in design view, the code window opens and the following stub is inserted:

```
Private Sub btnOK_Click()

End Sub
```

Each control has many such subs available. The sub names all start with the name of the control, followed by an underscore and an event type. The one you get by double-clicking on the control depends on which event is the *default* event for that control. To understand this better, get into the code window for the user form you created in Section 11.3. You will see two dropdown lists at the top of the window. The one on the left lists all controls on the form, including the form itself, as shown in Figure 11.13. Select any of these and then look at the dropdown list on the right. It lists all events the selected control can respond to. Figure 11.14 illustrates this list for a command button.

If you double-click on any of the items in the list in Figure 11.14, you get a sub into which you can write code. For example, if you double-click on the MouseUp item, you will get the following sub:

```
Private Sub btnOK_MouseUp(ByVal Button As Integer, ByVal Shift As Integer,
   ByVal X As Single, ByVal Y As Single)

End Sub
```

Figure 11.13 List of Controls

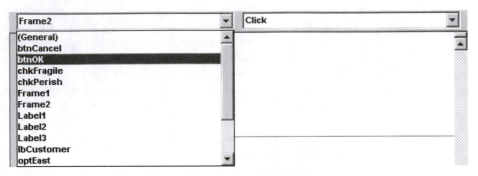

Figure 11.14 List of Events for a Command Button

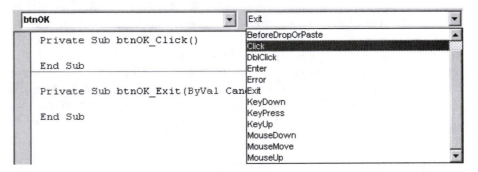

You have no choice over the format of the Sub line. The sub must be named as shown (control name, underscore, event type), and it must contain any arguments that are given. But how would you ever know what this sub responds to (what is a MouseUp event, anyway?), and how would you know what the arguments are all about? The best way is to consult the **Object Browser**. Try it out. Open the Object Browser and select the **MSForms** library. This library provides help for all objects in user forms. Specifically, it provides a list of controls on the left and their properties, methods, and events on the right, as shown in Figure 11.15. The events are designated by lightning icons. By selecting any of these and clicking on the question mark button, you can get plenty of help. For example, help for the MouseUp and MouseDown events appears in Figure 11.16. (You don't need to bother reading this now; just remember how to get to it through the Object Browser.)

This information about getting help works for most controls, but not for the RefEdit control (the one that allows a user to select a range). For some reason, there is no information about the RefEdit control in the MSForms library, evidently because it is not part of that library. Instead, it is in its own RefEdit library, with itself as the only member and with virtually no online help! If you want to use RefEdit controls, your best bet is to Google for information about them.

In general, you need to decide which events you want to respond to with code. This chapter illustrates the ones that are used most often for the applications

Figure 11.15 Object Browser

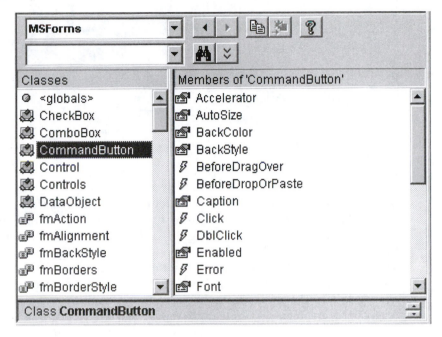

Figure 11.16 Help for MouseUp and MouseDown events

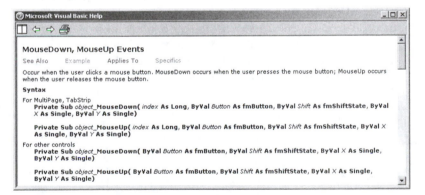

in later chapters, but you should realize that the floodgates are wide open—you can respond to just about any action the user takes. This can be bewildering at first, but it is the reason Windows programming is so powerful. The following example illustrates some possibilities.

EXAMPLE 11.1

Consider the dialog box in Figure 11.17. (See the file **StatPro Location Form. xlsm.**) It gives the user three choices of where to place results from some analysis—to

Figure 11.17 Location Dialog Box

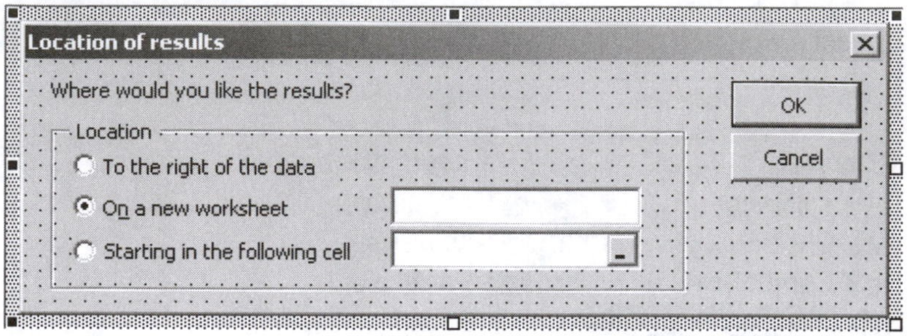

the right of a data set, on a new worksheet, or in a selected cell. (It is taken from my old StatPro add-in, available free from http://www.kelley.iu.edu/albrightbooks. However, I am no longer supporting this add-in, and the free version works only for Excel 2003 and earlier.) The three option buttons are named optToRight, opt-NewSheet, and optCell. If the user chooses the second option, the text box next to this option (named txtNewSheet) is enabled so that the user can type the name of the new worksheet. Otherwise, this text box is disabled. Similarly, if the user chooses the third option, the refedit control next to this option (named rfeCell) is enabled so that the user can select the desired cell. Otherwise, this control is disabled.

The following three event handlers implement the desired logic. Each responds to the Click event of an option button. They set the Enabled property of the txtNewSheet and rfeCell controls to True or False, and they use the SetFocus method to place the cursor in the appropriate control. For example, if the user clicks on the optNewSheet button, the txtNewSheet text box is enabled, with the cursor inside it, and the rfeCell box is disabled. These subs should give you a taste of the power you have over your applications.

```
Private Sub optToRight_Click()
    txtNewSheet.Enabled = False
    rfeCell.Enabled = False
End Sub

Private Sub optNewSheet_Click()
    With txtNewSheet
        .Enabled = True
        .SetFocus
    End With
    rfeCell.Enabled = False
End Sub

Private Sub optCell_Click()
    txtNewSheet.Enabled = False
    With rfeCell
        .Enabled = True
        .SetFocus
    End With
End Sub
```

EXAMPLE 11.2

This example illustrates event handlers for the user form you created in Sections 11.3 and 11.4. (The completed version is in the file **Practice Form.xlsm.**) It is typical of the forms you will see in later chapters. There are three event handlers: **UserForm_Initialize, btnOK_Click**, and **btnCancel_Click**. The first determines how the user form will look when the user first sees it, and the latter two determine what occurs when the user clicks on the OK and Cancel buttons.[5]

UserForm_Initialize Code

For this application, I want the following behavior when the user form initially appears: the East and Truck buttons should be checked, the Perishable box should be unchecked, the Fragile box should be checked, and the CustomerList should be filled with a list of customers. (Of course, the programmer gets to make these decisions, which the user can then override.) Except for the last requirement, this is easy. Each control has properties that can be set with VBA code. Also, each type of control has a default property.[6] If you want to set the default property, you don't even have to list the property's name. For example, the **Value** property is the default property of an option button and a check box. It is True or False, depending on whether the control is checked or not. To set this property, you can write

```
optEast.Value = True
```

or you can use the shortened version

```
optEast = True
```

Similarly, the **Value** property is the default property of a text box control. It indicates the value, treated as a string, in the box.[7] For example, to make a text box blank, you can write

```
txtProduct.Value = ""
```

or

---

[5]Unlike what you might expect, the initialize sub is called **UserForm_Initialize**, not **frmInputs_ Initialize**. It always has this generic name, regardless of how you name the form.

[6]The default property for a control has a small blue dot above it in the Object Browser. For example, if you select OptionButton in the Object Browser and scan its list of properties, you will see a blue dot above the Value property.

[7]A text box also has a **Text** property. From what I can uncover in online help, the Text and Value properties are virtually identical for a text box. You can use either.

Figure 11.18 Customer List on a Worksheet

	A
1	Customer list
2	Adobe
3	Altaire
4	Canon
5	Compaq
6	Diamond
7	Epson
25	Symantec
26	Toshiba
27	Visioneer
28	Xerox

```
txtProduct = ""
```

I strongly prefer the first version in each case. Even though the default property can be omitted, I believe the code is much more readable if the default property is shown explicitly.

List boxes are a bit trickier. You can populate them in several ways. Two methods are illustrated here. For both, I assume that there is a worksheet with a list of customers in a range named Customers. This list might appear as in Figure 11.18, where the Customers range is A2:A28.

Then the **AddItem** method of the list box can be used inside a For loop to add the customers to the list box, one at a time. The only required argument of the AddItem method is the name of the item to be added.

The completed UserForm_Initialize code appears below.

```
Private Sub UserForm_Initialize()
    Dim cell As Range

    txtProduct.Text = ""
    optEast.Value = True
    optTruck.Value = True
    chkPerish.Value = False
    chkFragile.Value = True

    ' Populate the list box from the data in the Customers range.
    For Each cell In Range("Customers")
        lbCustomer.AddItem cell.Value
    Next
End Sub
```

Alternatively, the **RowSource** property of the list box can be set to Customers at design time (through the Properties window). This tells VBA to populate the list box with the list in the Customers range. As a result, the For Each loop in the above code would not be necessary.

When the user form is shown initially, it will appear as in Figure 11.19. Of course, the user is then free to make any desired selections.

btnCancel_Click Code

There is usually not much you want to happen when the user clicks on the Cancel button. This is the user's way of saying she doesn't want to continue, so the typical btnCancel_Click code is as follows.

```
Private Sub btnCancel_Click()
    Unload Me
        End
End Sub
```

The first line says to unload the user form (which is referred to with the keyword Me). This makes the form disappear. The second line says to end the program.

btnOK_Click Code

Usually the lengthiest event handler, this is where you capture the user's inputs. Typically, the inputs are stored in public variables, declared in a module, so that they can be used by the module code later on, but they are also recognized by the event handlers. Also, as explained in more detail in the next chapter, this code generally performs some error checking to ensure that

Figure 11.19 Initialized User Form

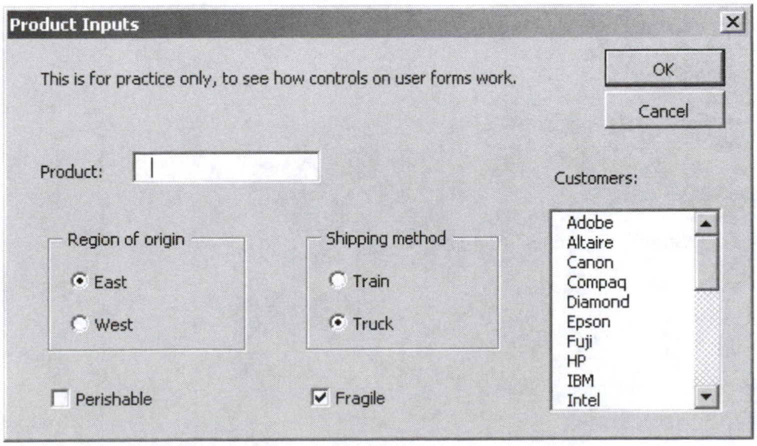

the user provides "valid" inputs. For the user form used here, the only things the user could do wrong are (1) leave the product box blank, (2) enter an invalid product in the product box, or (3) fail to select a customer in the list box. For illustration, I assume that the company's products are indexed from 1 to 1000. Any number not in this range, or any nonnumeric value, should not be accepted in the product box. The following event handler does the job.

```vb
Private Sub btnOK_Click()
    ' Capture the value in the text box, but make sure it is from 1 to 1000.
    With txtProduct
        If .Value = "" Or Not IsNumeric(.Value) Then
            MsgBox "Enter a product number from 1 to 1000."
            .SetFocus
            Exit Sub
        End If
        productIndex = .Text
        If productIndex < 1 Or productIndex > 1000 Then
            MsgBox "Enter a product number from 1 to 1000."
            .SetFocus
            Exit Sub
        End If
    End With

    ' Capture region (in a string variable).
    If optEast.Value Then
        region = "East"
    Else
        region = "West"
    End If

    ' Capture shipping method (in a string variable).
    ' The Select Case method is an option to the above If method.
    Select Case True
        Case optTruck.Value
            shipping = "Truck"
        Case optTrain.Value
            shipping = "Train"
    End Select

    ' Capture check box settings (in Boolean variables).
    isPerishable = chkPerish.Value
    isFragile = chkFragile.Value

    ' Capture customer (in a string variable).
    With lbCustomer
        If .ListIndex <> -1 Then
            customer = .Value
        Else
            MsgBox "Select a customer from the list."
            .SetFocus
            Exit Sub
        End If
    End With

    ' Unload the form.
    Unload Me
End Sub
```

Most of this code is straightforward, but you should note the following.

- The user inputs are captured in the variables productIndex, region, customer, shipping, isPerishable, and isFragile. These must be declared as **Public** variables at the top of the module where they will be used, as illustrated below. The idea is that the values of these variables are captured in the user form event handlers, and then they are used later on in the module code.

```
' Public variables captured from the user form.
Public productIndex As Integer
Public region As String
Public customer As String
Public shipping As String
Public isPerishable As Boolean
Public isFragile As Boolean
```

- The first error check made on txtProduct uses VBA's **IsNumeric** function to check whether an input is numeric. This and the **IsDate** function are very handy for error checking.
- If an error check is not passed, a message box displays an error message, the focus is set to the offending control, and the sub is exited immediately with the **Exit Sub** statement, *without* unloading the user form. This last part is important. It guarantees that the user form does not disappear and that the user has to try again.
- When you have a set of option buttons, where only one can be checked, you can use an If construction to find which of them is checked (which has its Value property set to True), or you can use a Select Case construction. The code above illustrates both; you can choose the one you prefer.
- The **Value** property of a list box indicates the item selected—in this case, the name of the customer. The **ListIndex** property indicates the position in the list of the selected item, starting with 0. For example, it returns 3 if the fourth item is chosen. If no item is selected, ListIndex is –1. This explains the error check. It ensures that *some* item has been selected. (To make your code more bulletproof, you can set ListIndex equal to 0 in the UserForm_Initialize code. Then the first item in the list is selected automatically, and it is impossible for the user to *not* select an item.)
- You *must* unload the user form at the end of the sub, but this is surprisingly easy to forget. If you forget to do this and then test your dialog box by clicking the OK button (in run mode), nothing will happen—the dialog box will just sit there! I guarantee that this will happen to you at least once, so you are warned.

A Note on Extraneous Event Handler "Stubs"

Don't be surprised if you find a couple of lines like the following in your event code:

```
Private Sub txtProduct_Change()

End Sub
```

Figure 11.20 Display of User's Inputs

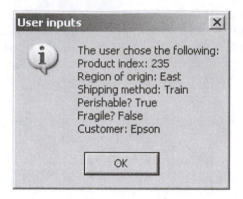

I got these by inadvertently double-clicking on the txtProduct text box while in design mode. This happens frequently. Whenever you do it, you get the beginnings of an event handler for the control's default event, in this case the Change event. This "stub" causes no harm if you leave it in your program; but if you don't really need it, you should get rid of it. I wouldn't be surprised if I have one or two of these "stubs" in the files included in this book. If so, I simply forgot to delete them.

11.7 Displaying a User Form

You have probably been wondering how the user form is displayed in the first place. This is easy. Each user form has a **Show** method that displays the form (and immediately runs its **UserForm_Initialize** event handler). To illustrate, the **Practice Form.xlsm** file from the previous example has a module containing the following **Main** sub, which is attached to a button on a worksheet. When the user clicks on the button, the Main sub runs. The **frmInputs.Show** line displays the user form. Execution of the Main sub is then suspended until the user is finished entering inputs and clicks on the OK button or the Cancel button. If the user clicks on Cancel, the program simply ends. If the user clicks on OK, the Main sub resumes and displays the user's inputs in a message box, as in Figure 11.20. Of course, a real application would then use these inputs in some further analysis. That is, there would be additional code in the module.

```
Sub Main()
    frmInputs.Show
    MsgBox "The user chose the following:" & vbCrLf _
        & "Product index: " & productIndex & vbCrLf _
        & "Region of origin: " & region & vbCrLf _
        & "Shipping method: " & shipping & vbCrLf _
        & "Perishable? " & isPerishable & vbCrLf _
        & "Fragile? " & isFragile & vbCrLf _
        & "Customer: " & customer, vbInformation, "User inputs"
    ' The rest of the program would then act on the user's inputs.
End Sub
```

11.8 Looping Through the Controls on a User Form

There are many times when you place several related controls on a user form and would then like to loop through them to perform some action. For example, you might have a group of check boxes, one for each region of the country, and you would like to use event code to see which of them are checked. The easiest way to do this would be to form an *array* of controls and then go through the array elements with a For loop. Unfortunately, however, VBA does not allow you to form arrays of controls. An alternative method that *is* possible is to use a For Each loop to loop through the **Controls** collection on the user form. This loops through *all* controls—text boxes, labels, command buttons, and so on. If you want to perform some action on only a particular type of control, such as the text boxes, you can use the **TypeName** function, as illustrated in the following code.

```
Dim ctl As Control

For Each ctl In Me.Controls
    If TypeName(ctl) = "TextBox" Then
        If ctl.Value = "" Or Not IsDate(ctl) Then
            MsgBox "Enter valid dates in the text boxes.", _
                vbInformation, "Invalid entry"
            ctl.SetFocus
            Exit Sub
        End If
    End If
Next
```

Note that ctl is declared as a generic control. The For Each loop goes through all controls in the collection Me.Controls (where Me is a reference to the user form). The If TypeName(ctl) = "TextBox" statement then checks whether the control is a text box. (Note that it requires the formal name, TextBox, spelled exactly as shown.) If it is, certain actions are taken. If it is not, no actions are taken. This looping method is probably not as convenient as being able to loop through an array of controls, but it is the best method available—at least with the current version of VBA. (Note that you will *not* get Intellisense when you type ctl and then a period. This is because the different types of controls have different properties and methods, and with ctl being a *generic* control, VBA doesn't know which list of properties and methods to show.)

11.9 Working with List Boxes

List boxes are among the most useful controls for user forms, but they are also tricky to work with. This section explains methods for populating list boxes and capturing users' choices.

First, list boxes come in two basic types: **single** and **multi**. The type is determined by the **MultiSelect** property. A single-type list box allows the user to select only one item from the list, whereas a multi-type list box allows the user to select *any* number of items from the list. Of course, the context of the application determines which type to use, but you should know how to work with both.

Single List Boxes

If you want a list box to be of the single type, you do *not* have to change its **MultiSelect** property. By default, a list box is of the single type (the MultiSelect setting is **0–fmMultiSelectSingle** in the Properties window). There are then two properties you are likely to use: the **Value** property and the **ListIndex** property. These properties were illustrated in Example 11.2. For example, if the user selects Compaq from the list in Figure 11.19, which is the fourth customer in the list, then the Value property is the string "Compaq" and the ListIndex property is 3. (It is 3, not 4, because indexing always starts with 0.) If no item is selected, then ListIndex is –1, which can be used for error checking. (You typically want the user to select *some* item.)

Multi List Boxes

Multi list boxes are slightly more complex. First, you have to set the **MultiSelect** property appropriately (the correct setting is **2–fmMultiSelectExtended** in the Properties window) at design time. Second, it no longer makes much sense to use Value and ListIndex properties. Instead, you need to know *which* items the user has selected. You do this with the **Selected** property of the list box, which acts as a 0-based Boolean array, as illustrated below. You can also take advantage of the **ListCount** property, which returns the number of items in the list. The following sample code is typical. It uses a public Boolean array variable isChosen (declared in a module) to capture the user's choices for later use. Because I prefer 1-based arrays, isChosen starts with index 1. Unfortunately, it is not possible to make the built-in Selected array 1-based; it is *always* 0-based. This accounts for the difference between the indexes of Selected and isChosen in the code.

```
For i = 1 To lbProducts.ListCount
    isChosen(i) = lbProducts.Selected(i - 1)
Next
```

For example, if there are five items in the list and the user selects the first, second, and fifth, then isChosen(1), isChosen(2), and isChosen(5) will be True, and isChosen(3) and isChosen(4) will be False. This information can then be used in the rest of the program.

There is more to say about list boxes. For example, they can have multi-column lists. However, this is enough information for now. Other list box features are explained as needed in later chapters.

11.10 **Working with Excel Controls**

By now, you are probably used to placing buttons on your worksheets. As described in Chapter 3, you typically click on the upper-left button icon in Figure 11.21, drag a button on your sheet, and assign a macro to the button. The

Figure 11.21 Excel Controls

controls shown in Figure 11.21 are accessed from the Insert dropdown on the Developer ribbon in Excel 2007. (They were in two separate toolbars in Excel 2003 and earlier.) These controls have the same purposes and functionality as those from the VBE, but they are placed directly in Excel worksheets.

The "Forms" controls at the top of Figure 11.21 are a leftover from older versions of Excel (version 95 and before). These controls are simple and easy to use. Microsoft changed its Excel programming environment rather dramatically in version 97, but it decided to keep the Forms controls for backward compatibility—and because users liked them. Fortunately (in my opinion), these Forms controls are still around.

You don't need to do any VBA programming to make the Forms controls useful. All you need to do is click on one of them, drag it on a worksheet, and then right-click on it to change a few properties. The following example is typical of the useful applications you can create with the Forms controls.

The file **Home Loan.xlsx** is a template for the monthly mortgage payment for a home loan. (Note that it is an .xlsx file, not an .xlsm file. It contains *no* VBA.) As shown in Figure 11.22, the user enters inputs in cells B3, B4, and B5, and the monthly payment is calculated in cell B7 with the PMT function. With the Forms controls in Figure 11.21 visible, drag a spinner control (fourth from the left in the top row) approximately as in the figure. Then right-click on it, select Format Control, select the Control tab, and set its properties as shown in Figure 11.23. This says that the

Figure 11.22 Home Loan Calculation

	A	B	C	D	E
1	Home loan application				
2					
3	Amount financed	$125,000		Spinner for term	
4	Annual interest rate	6.25%		▲	
5	Term (years)	15		▼	
6					
7	Monthly payment	$1,071.78			

Figure 11.23 Spinner Properties

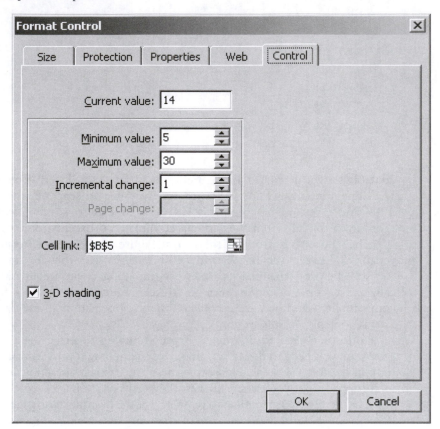

spinner's possible values are integers from 5 to 30, in increments of 1, and that the spinner's value is stored in cell B5, the term of the loan. Now click anywhere else on the worksheet to deselect the spinner. Finally, click on the up or down arrows of the spinner and watch what happens. The term increases or decreases, and the monthly payment changes accordingly—all with no programming!

Now you should understand why Microsoft kept the Forms controls. They are extremely easy to use, and users like to employ them to automate their worksheets, as in the home loan example. However, these controls are not "modern" controls because they do not respond to events as discussed earlier in this chapter. Therefore, beginning in version 97 of Excel, Microsoft introduced the ActiveX controls listed at the bottom of Figure 11.21. They have the same basic functionality as the Forms controls, but they behave quite differently.

To see how the ActiveX controls work, click on the ActiveX spinner control, and drag it to a worksheet. You will get a spinner in **design mode**. There will be "handles" around the spinner, and the Design Mode button on the Developer ribbon will be highlighted, as shown in Figure 11.24 This button toggles a given control, such as the spinner, in or out of design mode. You need to be in design

Figure 11.24 Design Mode Button Highlighted

mode to "wire up" the control. You need to be out of design mode to make it work—to make it "spin," for example.

In design mode, right-click on the control and select Properties from the resulting menu to see the Properties window in the VBE, as in Figure 11.25. This is exactly like the Properties window discussed earlier in this chapter. It is available for ActiveX controls, but not for Forms controls. You can experiment with the various properties. For example, you can change the Orientation property to make

Figure 11.25 Spinner Control and Associated Properties Window

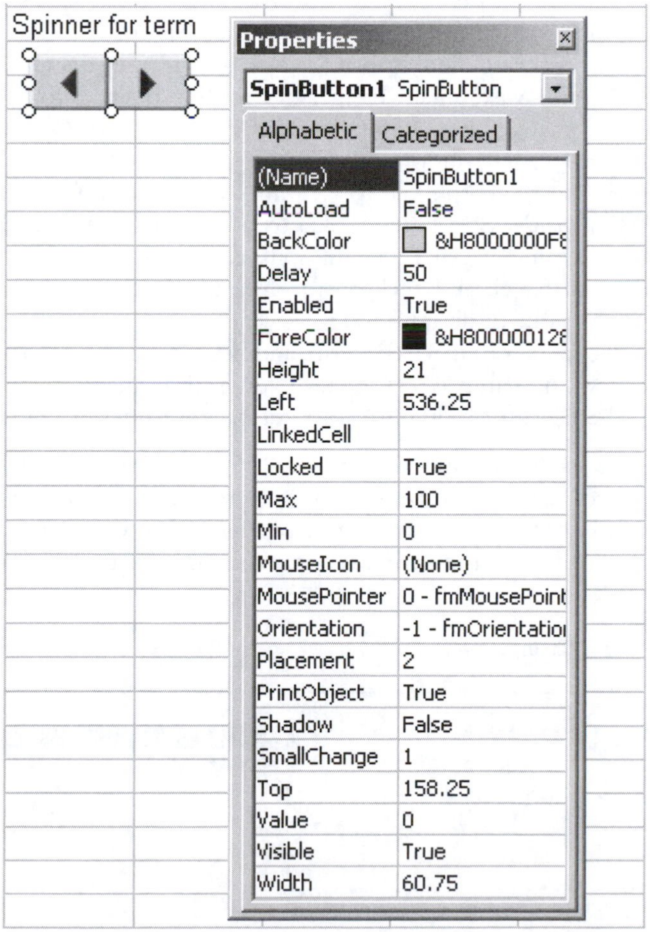

Spinner for term

Properties		✕
SpinButton1 SpinButton		▾
Alphabetic	Categorized	
(Name)	SpinButton1	
AutoLoad	False	
BackColor	☐ &H8000000F8	
Delay	50	
Enabled	True	
ForeColor	■ &H800000128	
Height	21	
Left	536.25	
LinkedCell		
Locked	True	
Max	100	
Min	0	
MouseIcon	(None)	
MousePointer	0 - fmMousePoint	
Orientation	-1 - fmOrientatio	
Placement	2	
PrintObject	True	
Shadow	False	
SmallChange	1	
Top	158.25	
Value	0	
Visible	True	
Width	60.75	

the spinner point north-south versus east-west (change it to 0–frmOrientation-Vertical), or you can change the Min, Max, SmallChange, and Value properties to mimic the behavior of the spinner used in the home loan example.

Next, close the Properties window and double-click on the spinner. You get an event handler for the Change event of the spinner. (See Figure 11.26.) In general, you get the event handler for the default event of the control you double-click on. The Change event is the natural default event for a spinner, because you want to react in some way when the user clicks on the up or down arrow of the spinner. You can write event handlers for other events associated with the spinner, however. Just select any of the other events from the list in Figure 11.26. The chances are that you won't have any reason to do so, but you can if you like. The point is that you have as much control over these ActiveX controls as you have in the controls you place in user forms in the VBE. The difference is that the controls discussed earlier in this chapter were placed on a user form. The ones from the Developer ribbon (Figure 11.21) are placed directly on a worksheet.

To use an ActiveX spinner in the home loan example, go through the following steps.

1. Drag a spinner to the worksheet, exactly as in Figure 11.22.
2. Right-click on the spinner, choose Properties from the resulting menu, and change the Min, Max, SmallChange, and Value properties to 5, 30, 1, and 15. If you like, change the Orientation property to 0–frmOrientationVertical. Close the Properties window.
3. Double-click on the spinner to get into the code window. Add the line Range("B5").Value = SpinButton1.Value to the sub in Figure 11.26. As before, this links the value in cell B5 to the spinner value.
4. Get back into Excel, and click on the Design Mode button on the controls toolbar to get out of design mode.
5. Click on the spinner to make the term, and hence the monthly payment, change.
6. The spinner is now fully operational. If you want to make any further changes, click on the Design Mode button to get back into design mode.

You might ask where the event handler lives. Go into the VBE and double-click on the sheet name in Project Explorer where the spinner resides, for example, Sheet1. You will see your event handler. In general, the event handlers for ActiveX controls reside "behind" the sheets they are on—not in modules.

Figure 11.26 Event Handler for Change Event

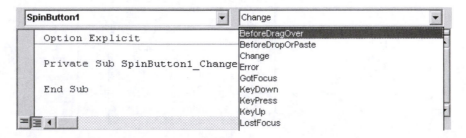

I will let you decide whether you want to use Forms controls or ActiveX controls—or both. Forms controls are definitely easier to work with, but ActiveX controls give you a much greater degree of control over their look and behavior. Besides, once you get used to working with controls in user forms, you should have no problems with ActiveX controls.

11.11 Summary

With the material in this chapter, you can finally become a real *Windows* programmer. I have discussed how to design user forms by placing various types of built-in controls on them, and I have illustrated how to write event handlers that respond to various events triggered by a user's actions. Once you have designed a user form and have made any necessary changes in the Properties window, it is then a matter of writing the appropriate event handlers in the form's code window. Typically, this means capturing user selections in publicly declared values that can later be analyzed with the code in a module. You will see many examples of how this is done in the second half of the book, most of which employ user forms. Finally, I compared the Forms and ActiveX controls you can place directly on your worksheets.

EXERCISES

1. Suppose you have a user form with quite a few text boxes and possibly some other controls. Write a **UserForm_Initialize** sub that loops through all controls and, if they are text boxes, sets their Value property to a blank string.
2. Create a user form that contains the usual OK and Cancel buttons. It also should contain two sets of option buttons, each set placed inside a frame. The captions on the first set should be Baseball, Basketball, and Football. The captions on the second set should be Watch on TV and Go to games. Then write the event handlers and code in a module so that when the program runs, the user sees the form. If the user makes a couple of choices, clicks on OK, he should see a message like, "Your favorite sport is basketball, and you usually watch on TV." If the user clicks on Cancel, the message "Sorry you don't want to play" should appear.
3. Repeat the previous exercise, but now make the controls checkboxes, not option buttons. Change the message in case the user clicks on OK to something appropriate, such as, "You like baseball and basketball, and you like to watch on TV and go to games." The message should be appropriate, regardless of which checkboxes are checked (including none being checked).
4. Create a user form that contains the usual OK and Cancel buttons. It should also contain a listbox of the type where the user is allowed to select only one item from the list. Write a **UserForm_Initialize** sub that populates the list with the states Illinois, Indiana, Iowa, Michigan, Minnesota, Ohio, Pennsylvania, and Wisconsin (in this order), and selects Indiana by default. Then write the event handlers for

the buttons and code in a module so that when the program runs, the user sees the form. If she chooses an item from the list and then clicks on OK, she should see a message such as, "You live in Ohio." If she clicks on Cancel, she should see the message, "You must not live in a Big Ten state."

5. Repeat the previous exercise, but now start with the file **Big Ten States.xlsx**, which contains a list of the states in a range named States. When you create the list box, set its RowSource property to States. This will populate the list box automatically, so that you don't need to do it in the **UserForm_Initialize** sub.

6. Repeat Exercise 4, but now change the listbox to the type where the user can select multiple items from the list. The resulting message for OK should now be something like, "You have lived in Indiana, Illinois, and Ohio." For Cancel, it should be "You have never lived in a Big Ten state."

7. The file **Big Ten Teams.xlsx** contains the school and mascot names for the Big Ten teams in a range named Teams. Create a user form that contains the usual OK and Cancel buttons. It should also contain a listbox of the type where the user is allowed to select only one item from the list. Set its RowSource property to Teams, so that the listbox is automatically populated from the list in this range. Also, set its ColumnCount property to 2, so that schools and mascots both appear in the listbox, and set its ColumnHeads property to True, so that each column has an appropriate heading. Write a **UserForm_Initialize** sub that selects Indiana by default. Then write the event handlers for the buttons and code in a module so that when the program runs, the user sees the form. If he chooses an item from the list and then clicks on OK, he should see a message such as, "You must root for the Indiana Hoosiers." If he clicks on Cancel, he should see the message, "You must not be a Big Ten fan." (*Hint*: In online help, look up the BoundColumn property of a list box and how it controls the Value property.)

8. The file **Receivables.xlsx** contains data on a company's receivables from its customers. Each row corresponds to a particular customer. It indicates the size of the customer (1 for small, 2 for medium, 3 for large), the number of days the payment has been outstanding, and the amount of the payment due. Develop a user form that has the usual OK and Cancel buttons, plus two sets of option buttons. The first set allows the user to choose the size of the customer (using captions Small, Medium, and Large), and the second set allows the user to choose the Days or the Amount column to summarize. Then write code in a module that takes these choices and displays a message listing the appropriate average. For example, if the user chooses Small and Amount, the message box should display the average amount owed by all small customers.

9. Repeat the preceding exercise, but now use check boxes instead of option buttons. Now a separate message should be displayed for each combination the user checks. For example, if the user checks the Small check box and the Days and Amount check boxes, one message should display the average of Days for the small customers and another should display the average of Amount for the small customers.

10. The file **Stock Returns.xlsx** contains stock returns for many large companies. Each sheet contains the returns over a 5-year period for a certain stock, with the ticker symbol of the stock used as the sheet name. Write a sub that presents the user with a

user form. This user form should have the usual OK and Cancel buttons, and it should have a list box with a list of all stocks (actually, their ticker symbols). The user should be allowed to choose only one stock in the list. The sub should then display a message box that reports the average monthly return for the selected stock.

11. Repeat the previous exercise, but now allow the user to select multiple stocks from the list. Use a For loop to display a message box for each selected stock separately.

12. The file **Exceptions Finished.xlsm** contains monthly sales totals for a number of sales regions. Open the file and click on the button. It allows you to choose two colors and two cutoff values. When you click on OK, all sales totals below the minimum cutoff are colored the first color, and all totals above the maximum cutoff are colored the other color. The VBA in this file has been password-protected. Your job is to create this same application, starting with the **Exceptions.xlsx** file. This file contains only the data. Make sure you do some error checking on the inputs in the user form. Specifically, the text boxes must have numeric values, the minimum cutoff should not exceed the maximum cutoff, and the two chosen colors should not be the same.

13. The file **Scores Finished.xlsm** contains scores for various assignments in three courses taught by an instructor. Open the file. You will see an Explanation sheet and a button. Click on the button to run the program. It shows one user form where you can choose a course and any of six summary measures. When you click on OK, you see a second user form where you can choose an assignment for that course. (Note the list of assignments varies from course to course. Also, the label at the top includes the course number chosen in the first user form.) When you click on OK, a message box is displayed summarizing the scores on that assignment. The VBA in this file has been password-protected. Your job is to create this same application, starting with the **Scores.xlsx** file. This file contains only the data.

14. The file **Book Reps Finished.xlsm** contains data on a number of sales representatives for a publishing company. The data on each rep include last name, first name, gender, region of country, age, years of experience, and performance rating. Open the file and click on the button. It presents two user forms. The first asks for the last name and first name of a rep. After the user enters these, the program searches for a rep with this name. If none is found, a message to this effect is displayed and the program ends. If the rep is found, a second user form is displayed with the rep's characteristics. The user can then change *any* of these and click on OK. The changes are then reflected in the database. The VBA in this file has been password-protected. Your job is to create this same application, starting with the **Book Reps.xlsx** file. This file contains only the data.

15. The file **Country Form Finished.xlsm** contains a user form. The user can click on any of three option buttons, named optUSA, optCanada, and optEurope. When any of these is selected, the labels and text boxes should change appropriately. Specifically, if the USA button is clicked, the caption of the top label, named lblLocation, should change to State, and the bottom text box, named txtLanguage, should be disabled, with English entered in the text box. (Presumably, English is the common language in the USA.) If the user chooses the Canada option, txtLanguage should be enabled, with the text box cleared, and the caption of

lblLocation should change to Province. Similarly, if the user chooses the Europe option, txtLanguage should be enabled, with the text box cleared, and the caption of lblLocation should change to Country. The code in this file has been password-protected. Starting with the "codeless" form in the file **Country Form.xlsm**, write event handlers for the Click event of the option buttons to guarantee this behavior.

16. Open a new workbook and develop a user form that asks for a beginning date and an ending date in text boxes. It should instruct the user (with an appropriate label) to enter dates from January 1, 1990, to the current date. The btnOK_Click event handler should then perform the following error checks: (1) the date boxes should not be blank; (2) they should contain valid dates (use the **IsDate** function for this); (3) the first date shouldn't be before January 1, 1990; (4) the last date shouldn't be after the current date (use the **Date** function for this—it returns the current date); and (5) the first date should be before the last date. If any one of these error checks is not passed, the **btnOK_Click** sub should be exited *without* unloading the user form, and the focus should be set to the offending text box so that the user can try again. If all error checks are passed, the dates should be displayed in an appropriate message box, such as "You chose the dates 1/1/2000 and 2/2/2002."

17. Continuing the previous exercise, if you are like me, it will probably take you several tries to get everything, especially the error checking, working properly. Dates are tricky! Once you go to all of this work, you shouldn't have to do it again. The purpose of this exercise, therefore, is to write a Public sub called **DateValidation** that does the error checking for this type of situation automatically. You could use this general sub any time you need it in the future. Structure it as follows. It should take four arguments: txtDate1 (a TextBox for the first date), txtDate2 (a TextBox for the second date), earliestDate (a Date variable, corresponding to the January 1, 1990, date in the previous exercise), latestDate (corresponding to the current date in the previous exercise), and isValid (a Boolean). This sub should check for all errors. If it finds any, it should set the focus to the offending text box, set isValid to False, and return control to the calling sub (which will probably be the **btnOK_Click** sub). Otherwise, it should set isValid to True and return control to the calling sub. The calling sub can then check the value of isValid passed back to see whether to exit without unloading the form. Write this DateValidation sub, which should be placed in a *module*, and then use it to solve the previous exercise. (*Hint*: If you try to make a TextBox the argument of a sub in a module, you can't just type something like txtDate1 As TextBox. You must also include a reference to the library that has information about text boxes. Therefore you must type txtDate1 As MSForms. TextBox. You learn such details through extensive trial and error!)

18. This chapter has explained only the most frequently used controls: command buttons, labels, text boxes, option buttons, check boxes, and so on. However, there are a few others you might want to use. This exercise and the next one let you explore two of these controls. In this exercise, you can explore the **SpinButton** control. Open a new workbook, get into the VBE, add a user form, and place a spin button on the form. You can probably guess the functionality this button should have. If the user clicks on the up arrow, a counter should increase. If the user clicks on

the down arrow, the counter should decrease. To operationalize the button, set its Min, Max, SmallChange, and Value properties to 1, 10, 1, and 5 in the Properties window. This will allow the user to change the counter from 1 to 10 in increments of 1, with an initial value of 5. But how would a user know the value of the counter? The trick is to put a text box right below the spin button and make the text box's Value property equal to the spin button's Value property (which is the counter). To keep them in sync, write a line of code in the spin button's Change event handler that sets the text box's value equal to the spin button's value. Similarly, write an event handler for the text box's Change event, so that if the user changes the value in the text box, the spinner's counter stays in sync with it. Try it out by running the form (by clicking on the blue triangle run button). How can you make sure that the two controls *start* in sync when the form is first displayed?

19. Continuing the previous exercise, put a spin button to work on the **Car Loan.xlsx** file. This file contains a template for calculating the monthly payment on a car loan, given the amount financed, the annual interest rate, and the term of the loan (the number of months to pay). Develop an application around this template that does the following: (1) It has a button on the sheet to run a **VaryTerm** sub in a module; (2) the VaryTerm sub "shows" a user form with the usual OK and Cancel buttons, a spin button and corresponding text box, and appropriate label(s) that allow(s) the user to choose a term for the loan (allow only multiples of 12, up to 60); and (3) the VaryTerm sub then places the user's choice of term in cell B5, which automatically updates the monthly payment.

20. This exercise continues the previous two exercises, but it now asks you to explore the **ScrollBar** control. Open a new workbook, get into the VBE, add a user form, and place a scrollbar on the form. (You can make it vertical or horizontal. Take your choice.) As you can probably guess, the scrollbar's Value property indicates the position of the slider. It can go from the Min value to the Max value. The SmallChange property indicates the change in the slider when the user clicks on one of the arrows. The LargeChange property indicates the change when the user clicks somewhere inside the scrollbar. You could proceed as with spin buttons to place a text box next to the scrollbar that shows the current value of the scrollbar. However, try another possibility this time. Place *labels* at the ends of the scrollbar and around the middle, as illustrated in Figure 11.27. These labels provide guidance

Figure 11.27 Scrollbar with Informational Labels

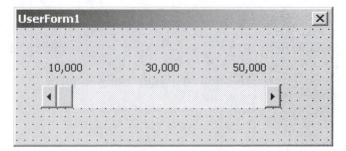

for the user. Now try all of this out on a variation of the previous exercise, using the same **Car Loan.xlsx** file. Write a **VaryAmount** sub that shows a user form with a scrollbar. The Min, Max, SmallChange, LargeChange, and Value properties of the scrollbar should be 10000, 50000, 500, 2000, and 30000 (by using the Properties window at design time). The goal is the same as in the previous exercise, except that now the sensitivity analysis is on the amount financed. When the form first shows, make the value of the scrollbar whatever value is in cell B3 of the spreadsheet.

21. The previous two exercises employed a user form with either a spinner or a scrollbar. In this exercise, don't use a user form. Instead, obtain the same functionality with controls from the Forms controls on the Developer ribbon. Then repeat, using ActiveX controls.

22. When you use text boxes, you often do some error checking in the **btnOK_Click** sub to ensure that the user enters something appropriate. For example, if you ask for a date, then "12/46/1996" is clearly not appropriate. In this case, you typically have code something like the following:

```
If Not isValid Then
    MsgBox "Please enter a valid date.", vbExclamation
    txtDate.SetFocus
    Exit Sub
End If
```

This indicates what was wrong, puts the cursor back in the date box, and makes the user try again. For example, if the user entered "12/46/1996", the cursor will be right after 1996. You can add an even more professional touch by having your code highlight the whole "12/46/1996". Then the user can just start typing to enter a new date. Create a small application that does this. (*Hint*: Get into the Object Browser and check the properties of a TextBox object that start with "Sel". Note that online help in Object Browser is available for controls from the MSForms library, and this library is in the list only when your project contains a user form.)

23. Open the file **Baseball Favorites Finished.xlsm** and click on the button. The user form should be self-explanatory, but notice what is enabled and what is disabled, and how this changes as you make selections. For example, you can't type in the "Other" text boxes until you choose an "Other below" option. Eventually, make a choice and click on OK to see a resulting message. The code in this finished version is password-protected. Now open the file **Baseball Favorites.xlsm**. The form has been designed and the module code that shows the form and displays a message has been written. Your job is to write the event handlers for the form—and quite a few are necessary to make sure everything is enabled or disabled at the appropriate times. (*Note*: My finished version doesn't check that any text is in the text box in case the user clicks on an "Other below" option and then clicks on OK. You might want to error check for this.)

Error Handling

12.1 Introduction

The important topic of debugging was discussed in Chapter 5. You debug to find and fix the errors in your code. Unfortunately, you have to be concerned about more than your *own* errors. The applications you will be developing are typically inter-active. An application displays one or more dialog boxes for the user to fill in, and it then responds to the user's inputs with appropriate actions. But what if the user is asked to enter a percentage as a decimal between 0 and 1, and he enters 25? Or what if a user is asked for a date and she enters 13/35/99? Your code should check for these types of errors that a *user* might make. VBA will not do it automatically for you. It is up to you to include the appropriate "error-trapping" logic.

In addition to watching for inappropriate user inputs, you must be on the watch for situations where your code performs an action that cannot be performed in the current context. For example, you might have a line that deletes a worksheet named Results. But suppose that when this line executes, there is no worksheet named Results. If you, the programmer, do not include error-trapping logic, this line will cause your program to bomb.

12.2 Error Handling with On Error Statement

This section discusses methods for trapping the types of errors discussed in the previous paragraph. The most common way to do this is with the **On Error** statement. There are several forms of this statement. They all essentially watch for errors and then respond in some way. The following lines provide a simple example.

```
On Error Resume Next
Application.DisplayAlerts = False
Worksheets("Results").Delete
MsgBox "Now the program can continue."
```

The objective here is to delete the Results sheet. However, there might not *be* a Results sheet, in which case the Delete line will cause a run-time error. The On Error Resume Next statement says, "If an error is encountered, just ignore it and go on to the next statement." In this case, if there is no Results sheet, no error message is displayed, and the MsgBox statement is executed.

Figure 12.1 Error Code Message

More specifically, when you include an On Error Resume Next statement, the program is in error-checking mode from that point on. If it comes to a statement that would lead to an error, it essentially ignores that statement—doesn't try to execute it—and goes on to the next statement.

A variation of this is listed below. If an error is encountered, control still passes to the next statement, but the default **Number** property of the built-in **Err** object has a *nonzero* value that an If statement can check for. Actually, each specific type of error has a particular error code that is stored in the Err object. For example, this particular error (trying to delete a worksheet that doesn't exist) returns error code 9. You can discover this by running the following code to obtain the message box in Figure 12.1. However, unless you plan to do *a lot* of programming, you don't need to learn these error codes. Just remember that Err.Number is nonzero if an error occurs, and it is 0 if there is no error. (Because Number is the default property of the Err object, you could write If Err <> 0, rather than If Err.Number <> 0. You will often see the shortened version.)

```
On Error Resume Next
Application.DisplayAlerts = False
Worksheets("Results").Delete
If Err.Number <> 0 Then MsgBox "The Results worksheet couldn't be deleted because it " _
    & "doesn't exist. This is error code " & Err.Number
```

The On Error Resume Next statement is useful when you want to ignore an "unimportant" error. However, there are some errors that you definitely do *not* want to ignore. The following code illustrates a typical method that programmers use to handle errors.

```
Sub TryToOpen()
    On Error GoTo ErrorHandling
    Workbooks.Open "C:\VBABook\Ranges.xlsm"
    Statements
    Exit Sub

ErrorHandling:
    MsgBox "The Ranges.xlsm file could not be found."
    End
End Sub
```

The purpose of this sub is to open the **Ranges.xlsm** file, located in the VBABook folder on the C drive, and then perform some actions on this file (designated by the *Statements* line). However, there is always the possibility that this file does not exist, at least not in the specified location. The On Error GoTo ErrorHandling line handles this possibility. It says, "Watch for an error. If an error is encountered, go to the ErrorHandling **label** farther down in the sub. Otherwise, continue with the normal sequence of statements." You can have any number of labels in a sub, each followed by a colon, and you can give them any names you like. Each label acts like a bookmark that you can "GoTo." (Note: Many programs from a few decades ago contained multiple GoTo statements, resulting in code that was practically impossible to decipher. GoTo statements are now frowned upon, except in these special error handling situations. Even here, many programmers try to avoid GoTo statements. In Microsoft's newest programming environment, .NET, there is a better error handling structure called Try/Catch that avoids GoTo statements altogether.)

The Exit Sub statement is necessary in case there is no error. Without it, the Ranges.xlsm file would be opened and the *Statements* lines would be executed—so far, so good. But then the MsgBox statement would be executed, and the program would end—not exactly what the programmer has in mind.

If you have an On Error GoTo statement somewhere in a sub, it is active throughout the entire sub, always monitoring for errors. If you want to turn off this monitoring, you can use the On Error GoTo 0 statement. This disables any error checking.

12.3   Handling Inappropriate User Inputs

In addition to On Error statements, you should check explicitly for invalid user inputs. This is done in most of the btnOK_Click event handlers in later chapters to check that the user has entered appropriate values in a user form. A typical example of this is the following. The dialog box in Figure 12.2 contains two text boxes that the user must fill in. They are named txtDate1 and txtDate2. There are several inappropriate inputs that could be given: the boxes could be left blank, the entries could be invalid dates such as 6/31/1999 (or not dates at all), or the beginning date could be *after* the ending date. You hope that the user will not provide any such invalid inputs, but you as a programmer should not leave it to chance.

The following code uses no error checking. It simply captures the user's inputs in the public variables begDate and endDate and hopes for the best. If invalid dates are supplied, there is no telling what might go wrong in the rest of the program.

```
Private Sub btnOK_Click()
    begDate = txtDate1.Value
    endDate = txtDate2.Value
    Unload Me
End Sub
```

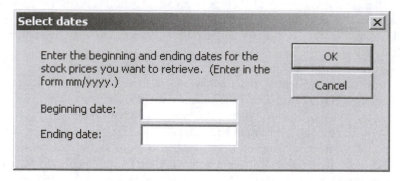

Figure 12.2 Dialog Box for Dates

A much better way is to check for possible invalid dates, as illustrated in the code below. It goes through all of the controls on the user form and checks whether they are text boxes. For the text boxes, it checks whether they are blank or contain invalid dates (with VBA's *very* handy IsDate function). In either case, an error message is displayed, focus is set to the offending text box, and the sub is exited *without* unloading the user form. This means that the user has to try again. If these error checks are passed, a later error check is performed to see if the beginning date is after the ending date. If it is, another error message is displayed, the focus is set to the first date box, and the sub is again exited without unloading the user form. By the time this user form is eventually unloaded, the programmer can be sure that begDate and endDate contain valid dates.

```
Private Sub OKButton_Click()
    Dim ctl As Control
    Dim begDate as Date, endDate as Date

    For Each ctl In Me.Controls
        If TypeName(ctl) = "TextBox" Then
            If ctl.Value = "" Or Not IsDate(ctl.Value) Then
                MsgBox "Enter a valid date.", vbInformation, "Invalid entry"
                ctl.SetFocus
                Exit Sub
            End If
        End If
    Next

    begDate = txtDate1.Value
    endDate = txtDate2.Value

    If begDate >= endDate Then
        MsgBox "The beginning date should be before the ending date.", _
            vbInformation, "Invalid dates"
        txtDate1.SetFocus
        Exit Sub
    End If

    Unload Me
End Sub
```

Writing this error-checking code is not a lot of fun, but it is necessary for any professional program. It not only prevents the program from accepting invalid inputs and then proceeding blindly, but it also provides users with helpful error messages so that they can change their responses appropriately. You might not be able to check for all conceivable errors, but you should attempt to anticipate the most likely ones.

12.4 Summary

Error handling is probably no one's favorite programming topic, but it is necessary if you want to consider yourself a professional programmer. You need to include code that anticipates things that could go wrong, anything from an attempt to open a file that doesn't exist to a user providing an input of "abc" when asked for a birth date. To write bulletproof code—code that (almost) never bombs—you have to take an active role in defeating Murphy's law (If it *can* go wrong, it *will* go wrong). Otherwise, Murphy's law will bite you!

EXERCISES

1. Open a new workbook and make sure it has two sheets in it named Sheet1 and Sheet2. Write a sub that has three lines. The first should be Application. DisplayAlerts = False. (See Section 5.10 to recall what this does.) The second line should delete Sheet2, and the third should similarly delete Sheet3. What happens when you run the program? Change your code so that if it tries to delete a sheet that doesn't exist, nothing happens—and no error message is given.

2. Open a new workbook and make sure it has two sheets named Sheet1 and Sheet2. Write a sub that has three lines. The first should be Application.DisplayAlerts = False. (See Section 5.10 to recall what this does.) The second line should delete Sheet2, and the third should delete Sheet1. What happens? The problem is that Excel won't allow you to delete a sheet if it's the only sheet left. Restore Sheet2. Then add an appropriate On Error GoTo line and an associated label in your sub to trap for the error. Take an appropriate action when it occurs. Use a message box to learn the code for this error (from the **Number** property of the built-in **Err** object).

3. Open a new workbook, insert a module, and write a sub that does the following: (1) it uses an input box to ask the user for the path and name of an Excel file to open, and (2) it then tries to open the file. Run this sub and enter the name of a file that you know exists. It should open the file with no problem. Then run it again and enter a file that you know does not exist. What happens? Rewrite the sub with the appropriate error-handling capability to take care of this possibility—and present a "nice" message to the user in either case.

4. The file **Shaq.xlsm** contains hypothetical data on Shaquille O'Neal's success from the free throw line. (In case you are not a basketball fan, Shaq is a notoriously poor free throw shooter.) For each of several games, it lists the number of free throws attempted and the number made. It then divides the number made by the number

attempted to calculate his free throw percentage for that game. Unfortunately, this results in a #DIV/0! error in games where he didn't take any free throws. The question explored here is how you can recognize and react to this cell error in VBA code. There is already a **DisplayPcts** sub in this file that goes through each cell in the Pct Made column and displays the cell's value in a message box. Run the sub and watch how it bombs. Now rewrite the code so that if this error ever occurs, a message is displayed to the effect that no percentage can be reported because no free throws were attempted—and no nasty error messages are displayed. Do this by checking only the cell in column D; don't check the cell in column B. (*Hint*: Use VBA's **IsError** function.)

5. Open a new workbook, get into the VBE, insert a user form, add a text box named txtLastName, and add a Last Name label to its left. This text box is supposed to capture a person's last name. Therefore, it should contain alphabetical characters only. You could perform an error check in the btnOK_Click event handler, but you might want to check for nonalphabetical characters at the same time the user is typing the name. You can do this with the **Change** event for a text box. In this case, the event handler's name is txtLastName_Change. This event "fires" each time any change occurs to the contents of the text box, including the insertion of a new character. Write the appropriate code for this event handler. It should check whether the *last* character is alphabetical. If not, it should display an appropriate message box telling the user to type alphabetical characters only, set the focus to the text box, and exit the sub. For example, if the user types Smi7, it should recognize that the fourth character is nonalphabetical and respond accordingly.

The following five problems exercises deal with debugging. Although this is not exactly the topic of the current chapter, it is still in the spirit of error handling.

6. The file **State Sales.xlsm** lists sales by some company in a number of states. Each state has its own sheet, with the name of the state used as the sheet name. There is a module that contains the sub **ListStates**. The purpose of this sub is to display a message that lists all of the states. Unfortunately, it has a few bugs. Find them and correct them.

7. Continuing the previous exercise, the module in **State Sales.xlsm** contains the subs **StateSearch** and **FindState**. The StateSearch sub should get the name of a state from the user, call the FindState sub, and then display a message saying whether that state is one of the sheets in the workbook. The FindState sub searches for the state passed to it and returns the Boolean variable isFound, which should be True if the state is found and False otherwise. Again, these subs have bugs. Find them and correct them.

8. Continuing Exercise 6 once more, the module in **State Sales.xlsm** contains the sub **CountSales**. The purpose of this sub is to ask the user for a state and a sales rep. It should then count the number of sales by this sales rep in this state and report the result in a message box. An On Error statement is supposed to trap for the error that the given state is not one of the states in the workbook. As you can see, this sub is in bad shape. The red lines indicate syntax errors. Find and fix all of the errors, syntax and otherwise.

9. Continuing Exercise 6 again, the module in **State Sales.xlsm** contains the sub **TotalSales1**. The purpose of the sub is to ask the user for a date. Then the total of all sales in all states up to (and including) this date should be found and displayed in a message box, with the date and the total suitably formatted. Again, this sub is full of bugs, including syntax errors. Find and fix all of the errors, syntax and otherwise.

10. Continuing Exercise 6 one *last* time, the module in **State Sales.xlsm** contains a sub **TotalSales2**. There is also a user form called frmInputs. The purpose of these is to let the user choose a state and a sales rep from list boxes on the user form. The TotalSales2 sub should then calculate the total of all sales made by this sales rep in the selected state and display it in a message box. Before showing the user form, the TotalSales2 sub creates an array of all states and an array of all sales reps (in all sheets). It uses these to populate the list boxes. The logic in the TotalSales2 sub and the event handlers for the user form is basically correct, but there are numerous small errors that keep the program from running correctly. Find all of them and fix them. When you think you have everything fixed and running correctly, check your total sales (for some state and some rep) manually, just to make *sure* you have it correct!

13

Working with Files and Folders

13.1 Introduction

The focus of this chapter is on working with files and folders, not on manipulating Excel objects. There are many times when you need to find a file or folder and, perhaps, manipulate it. For example, you might want to check whether a particular file exists, or you might want to rename a file in a particular folder. Of course, you can open Windows Explorer (or My Computer) and perform the required file or folder operations there. However, you can also perform these operations with VBA, as discussed in this chapter. You might also want to work with text files. For example, you might want to import the contents of a text file into Excel, or you might want to write the contents of an Excel worksheet into a text file for use by some other program. These text file operations can also be performed with VBA and are discussed here.

13.2 Exercise

The following exercise requires the types of file operations that you will learn in this chapter.

Exercise 13.1   Retrieving SoftBed Sales Data

The SoftBed Company has historical sales data for several of its customers for the years 2008 and 2009. They are stored in tab-delimited text files in various folders. Each file has a name such as **Clark Sales Q1 2008.txt**, which identifies the customer name, the quarter, and the year. Each file is structured as shown in Figure 13.1. The first row identifies product numbers, such as P3254, and the other rows list the date and sales figures. Your boss would like you to write a program that asks for a customer name, a product code, a quarter, and a year, imports the appropriate data from the text file into an Excel workbook, and saves it under a name such as **Clark Sales P3254 Q3 2008.xlsx**. The resulting file should be structured as shown in Figure 13.2. You can assume that all text files for a given customer are in the same folder, but you don't know which folders contain which files. Therefore, you should present your boss with a dialog box for finding the appropriate folder for any selected customer.

Figure 13.1 Text File Data

```
Clark Sales Q1 2008.txt - Notepad                    _ □ ×
File   Edit   Format   View   Help
Date      P3254      P7417      P3416
25-Jan-08      1960      2710      1850
26-Jan-08      2290      2640      2170
27-Jan-08      2610      2270      2370
28-Jan-08      3130      2720      2650
31-Jan-08      2500      2610      2540
01-Feb-08      3430      2360      3040
02-Feb-08      3480      3140      1920
03-Feb-08      2050      2460      3100
04-Feb-08      3170      1840      2210
07-Feb-08      2050      2830      1680
08-Feb-08      2390      2920      2020
09-Feb-08      1320      2930      2390
10-Feb-08      2060      2360      1700
11-Feb-08      1670      2930      2550
14-Feb-08      1740      2490      2810
15-Feb-08      1330      2700      3640
```

Figure 13.2 Imported Data in Excel File

	A	B	C
1	Clark sales of P3254 for Q3 2008		
2			
3	Date	Sales	
4	7/18/2008	$2,530	
5	7/19/2008	$2,780	
6	7/20/2008	$2,880	
7	7/21/2008	$2,310	
8	7/24/2008	$1,780	
9	7/25/2008	$2,910	
10	7/26/2008	$2,030	
53	9/25/2008	$2,870	
54	9/26/2008	$1,560	
55	9/27/2008	$2,760	
56	9/28/2008	$2,650	
57	9/29/2008	$2,740	

This exercise illustrates the type of operations discussed in this chapter. First, it requires you to obtain a dialog box for finding the appropriate folder. Next, it requires you to find the appropriate files in the selected folder. Finally, it requires you to import the appropriate data into Excel format. By the time you have read this chapter, you will be able to perform all of these operations in VBA. Eventually, you should try doing this application on your own, but if you want to see the finished application, it is in the file **Sales Import Finished.xlsm.** (Note: If you used the second edition of this book, you will see significant differences in the code for this example. In the second edition, I used the very handy **FileSearch** object to find a file with a given name and given content. For reasons that are not clear, Microsoft not only discontinued FileSearch in Office 2007, but it broke all existing applications like mine that use FileSearch. The current application is forced to use a workaround: the VB Script object **FileSystemObject**. I will explain it in Section 13.4.)

13.3 Dialog Boxes for File Operations

Creating dialog boxes can be fun and rewarding, but it definitely takes time. Fortunately, VBA includes a few built-in dialog boxes that you can use "off the shelf." You are already well aware of two of these dialog boxes: InputBox and MsgBox. Neither is a very fancy way of getting a user input or displaying output, but they are certainly easy to use. In this section I will briefly describe several additional built-in dialog boxes you can use for performing common file or folder operations. The first of these, **FileDialog**, is the most powerful. It is actually part of the Office object model, so that it can be used in any Office VBA application. However, it was introduced only in Excel XP (version 2002). Therefore, for backward compatibility, I will also discuss two methods of the Application object that were available before Excel XP and are still available: **GetOpenFileName** and **GetSaveAsFileName**. (You can find help for them in the Object Browser by going to the Excel library and searching for methods of the Application object.)

FileDialog

The FileDialog object provides file functionality similar to that of the standard Open and Save As dialog boxes in all Microsoft Office applications. With these dialog boxes, users can easily specify the files and folders that they wish to use. There are actually four versions of FileDialog specified by the following constants (where **mso** stands for Microsoft Office):

- msoFileDialogOpen—lets the user select one or more files that can then be opened in Excel with the **Execute** method
- msoFileDialogSaveAs—lets the user select a pathname that the current file can be saved as using the **Execute** method
- msoFileDialogFilePicker—lets the user select one or more files that are stored in the **SelectedItems** collection
- msoFileDialogFolderPicker—lets the user select a folder that is stored in the **SelectedItems** collection (as item 1)

Figure 13.3 File Open Dialog Box

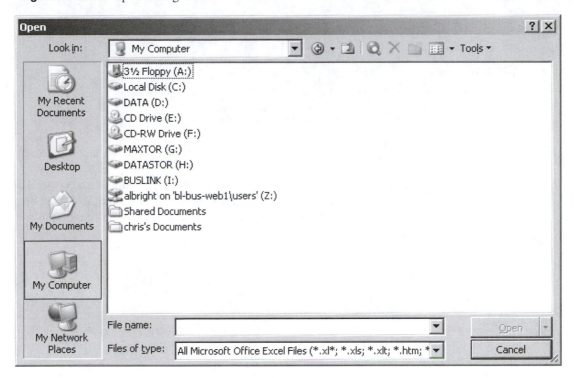

The following sub is typical. (This sub and the others in this section are in the **FileDialog Examples.xlsm** file.) It allows a user to select one or more files and then open each file selected. Note that fd is first declared as an Office.FileDialog object. It is then set to an Application.FileDialog of type **msoFileDialogOpen**. The **Show** method opens the familiar File Open dialog box in Figure 13.3, at which time the user can select one or more files in the usual way. The Show method returns True or False depending on whether the user clicks on Open or Cancel in the dialog box. If the user clicks on Open, the **Execute** method opens each of the selected files in Excel. (If the user selects a file type such as a .docx file that Excel doesn't recognize, an error occurs.[1]) If the user clicks on Cancel, the sub is exited quietly. Note that the files the user selects are in the **SelectedItems** collection, and a typical file in this collection *must* be declared as Variant, not as String.

---

[1]If this *same* code were used, say, in a Word application, then the Application in the Set fd = Application.FileDialog statement would refer to Word, and any selected files not recognized by Word would cause an error.

```
Sub OpenFiles()
    Dim fd As Office.FileDialog
    Dim file As Variant

    Set fd = Application.FileDialog(msoFileDialogOpen)
    With fd
        If .Show Then
            For Each file In .SelectedItems
                .Execute
            Next
        End If
    End With
End Sub
```

The following sub allows the user to save the file that contains the code in a selected folder with a specified name. It opens the usual File Save As dialog box seen in Figure 13.4, and, unless the user clicks on Cancel, it saves the file with the **Execute** method.

```
Sub SaveFileAs()
    Dim fd As Office.FileDialog

    Set fd = Application.FileDialog(msoFileDialogSaveAs)
    With fd
```

Figure 13.4 File Save Dialog Box

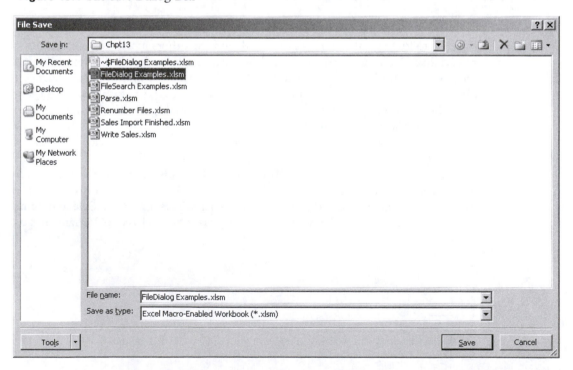

```
        If .Show Then
            .Execute
        End If
    End With
End Sub
```

The **msoFileDialogFolderPicker** version of FileDialog is especially useful. (It is also welcome. Before Excel XP, only a difficult workaround was available.) The following sub allows the user to select a folder from the dialog box in Figure 13.5, and, unless the user clicks on Cancel, stores it as SelectedItems(1). Based on the folder chosen in the figure, the message would appear as in Figure 13.6.

Figure 13.5 Folder Picker Dialog Box

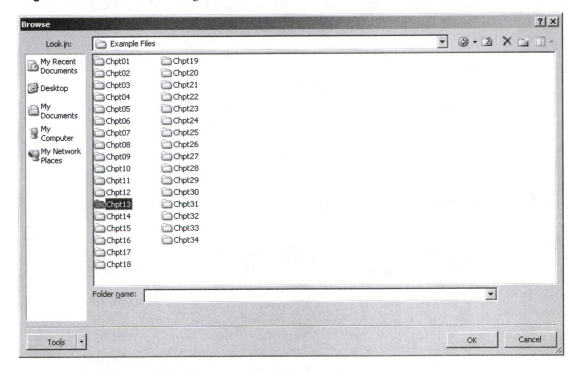

Figure 13.6 Selected Folder

```
Sub  FolderPicker()
    Dim  fd  As  Office.FileDialog
    Dim  path  As  String

    Set fd = Application.FileDialog(msoFileDialogFolderPicker)
    With fd
        If .Show Then
            path = .SelectedItems(1)
            MsgBox "The selected folder is " & path, vbInformation
        End If
    End With
End Sub
```

The **msoFilePicker** option is similar to the msoFolderPicker option, except that the user can select multiple files, not just a single folder. All selected files are stored in the **SelectedItems** collection and can be looped through with a For Each construction, just as in the earlier FileOpen sub.

GetOpenFileName Method[2]

The **GetOpenFileName** method displays the usual Open dialog box you see when you click on the Open button menu item in Excel. Although there are a number of optional arguments for this method (see online help), you can call it without any arguments, as in the following line:

```
Application.GetOpenFileName
```

The user then sees the typical Open dialog box, such as in Figure 13.7, and he can maneuver around in it in the usual way to find the file he wants to open.

However, the behavior is not quite what you might expect. If the user selects a file and then clicks on Open, the selected file is *not* opened. Instead, the GetOpenFileName method returns the file name of the selected file, as a string. Therefore, the typical way you would use this method is illustrated in the following code lines.

```
Dim fileToOpen as String

fileToOpen = Application.GetOpenFileName
Workbooks.Open fileToOpen
```

---

[2]If you own Excel XP (version 2002) or a later version, you can skip this section, since FileDialog is superior to the GetOpenFileName method.

Figure 13.7 Open Dialog Box

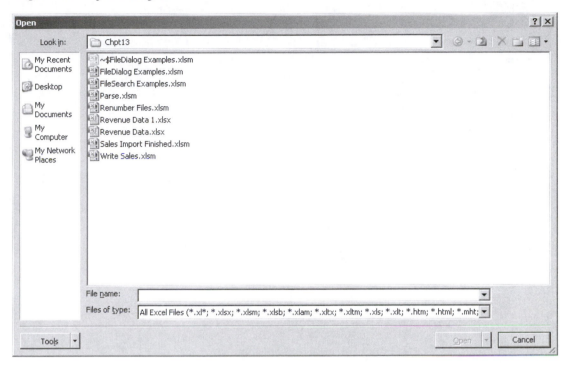

In this case, fileToOpen holds the name of the selected file (actually, the full path name to this file). The last line actually opens this file in Excel.

GetSaveAsFileName[3]

Similarly, the **GetSaveAsFileName** method mimics Save As in Excel. It opens the usual Save As dialog box, as shown in Figure 13.8. Now the user maneuvers to where she wants to save the file and enters a file name in the File name box. When she clicks on Save, the file is not actually saved. Instead, the full path name of her selection is stored as a string. Then an extra line of code is required to actually save the file. The typical use of this method is illustrated in the following code lines:

```
Dim nameToSaveAs As String

nameToSaveAs = Application.GetSaveAsFilename
ActiveWorkbook.SaveAs Filename:=nameToSaveAs
```

---

[3]If you own Excel XP (version 2002) or a later version, you can skip this section, since FileDialog is superior to the GetSaveAsFileName method.

Figure 13.8 Save As Dialog Box

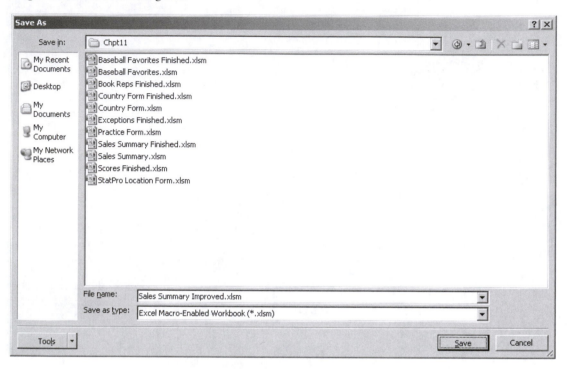

The next-to-last line opens the Save As dialog box and captures the name of the file to be saved. The last line actually saves the file with this name. Assuming the selection made in Figure 13.8, the active workbook (the one holding the code) would be saved as **Sales Summary Improved.xlsm**.

Other Built-In Dialog Boxes

There are many dialog boxes you see when you select various Excel menu items. You can get to these dialog boxes in VBA with the Dialogs property of the Application object. The code in Figure 13.9 indicates how to do it. When you type Application. Dialogs(, you see a list of all available dialog boxes from Excel—and there are a lot of them. Once you select an available dialog box, you can then use the Show method to display it. For example, the following line shows the Page Setup dialog box, at which time the user can make the usual choices for printing. Eventually, the user will click on OK or Cancel. The variable result will be True (for OK) or False (for Cancel).

```
result = Application.Dialogs(xlDialogPageSetup).Show
```

You might not use these built-in dialog boxes very often in your VBA code. After all, once the Page Setup (or whatever) dialog box appears, the user is free to make any

Figure 13.9 Dialogs Property

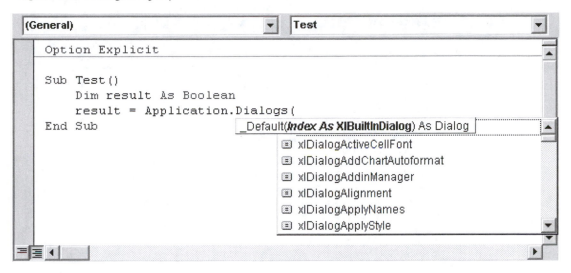

choices she likes, and you (the programmer) have no control over her choices. Nevertheless, you might want to experiment with these built-in dialog boxes.

13.4 The FileSystemObject Object

There are many times when we would like to write code to check whether a file exists, rename a file, or other common file operations. In Excel 2003, there was a very handy object, **FileSearch**, part of the Office library, that could be used to perform file operations easily. I discussed the FileSearch capabilities in the second edition of this book. Unfortunately, Microsoft discontinued the FileSearch object in Excel 2007. It is simply *gone*, and any applications that used it, such as a few files in the second edition, are now broken—they give an error message when you try to run them. If you Google for "FileSearch Office 2007," you will see that a number of programmers are not very happy about this unfortunate state of affairs. Why did Microsoft do it, and how do we fix the broken code? I can't answer the first question, but I will offer some advice on workarounds in this section.

From what I have discovered, there are at least two workarounds. The first is to find similar functionality developed by third-party companies. For example, Codematic, a software company in the UK, has developed a class called **AltFile-Search** that does much of what FileSearch did. You can purchase it online for about $30 and then add it to your programs. However, it lacks at least one feature that was in FileSearch: the ability to find a file containing specific text. For example, in the opening example of this chapter, FileSearch was able to look inside a text file and determine whether it contained a given product code, all with a single line of code. This is not possible with AltFileSearch. You can purchase this alternative and experiment with it if you like, but I won't discuss it further here.

Figure 13.10 Setting Reference to Scripting Library

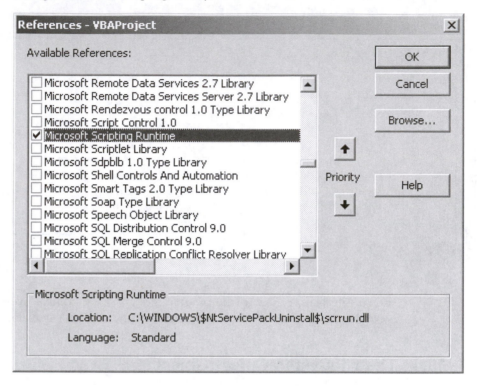

The second workaround is to use a library that has been around for a long time and comes with Windows, so that you already own it. This is the **Scripting** library. In particular, it contains a **FileSystemObject** object that has much of the functionality of FileSearch. To use the Scripting library in a VBA project, you must first set a reference to it. To do so, select the **Tools → References** menu item in the VBE, scroll down the list for **Microsoft Scripting Runtime**, and check it (see Figure 13.10). As you can see, this functionality is stored in a file called **scrrun.dll**, located somewhere in your Windows folder. Once you set this reference, you can visit the Object Browser to learn more about the Scripting library. Figure 13.11 shows the objects available, including **FileSystemObject**, the one we want. As usual, you can select a property or method of this object and then click on the question mark to get help. Actually, if you click on the question mark, you are taken to a generic help screen, but if you then search for **FileSystemObject**, you will get real help.

I will not try to explain all of the functionality of the FileSystemObject object, but I will show how I used it in the opening example of this chapter. The relevant part of the code is listed below. The declarations section illustrates two ways to declare the FileSystemObject (or, to be more precise, to create an *instance* of the FileSystemObject class). You can do it all in one line, using the **New** keyword, or you can do it in two lines, first declaring the fso variable and then *setting* it with the **CreateObject** function. The only use I make of the fso variable is when I use

Figure 13.11 Scripting Library Objects

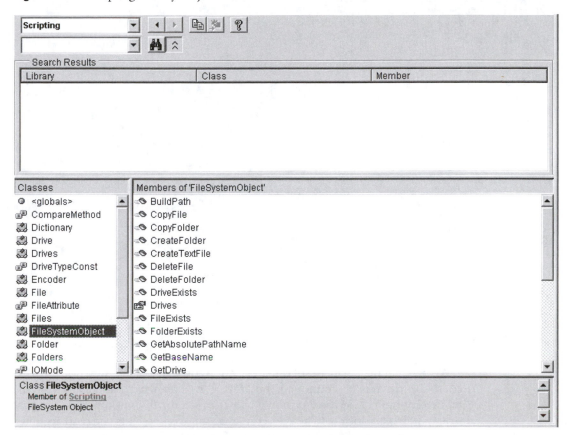

the **FileExists** method later on to check whether a file of a given name exists in a specified folder. The FileExists method returns True or False. If it returns False, I provide a message to this effect and then quit. If it returns True, I then open the text file and search for the given product code. With the (now discontinued) FileSearch object, it was possible to perform this latter search *inside* the file with a line or two of code. However, the FileSystemObject object doesn't have this capability, so the only alternative is to open the text file and parse through it with the last few lines of code. I will discuss parsing in detail in Section 13.6.

```
Dim fso As New Scripting.FileSystemObject
' The following two lines are an alternative to the
' preceding line for declaring the FileSystemObject.
' You tend to see the following version in online help.
'Dim fso
'Set fso = CreateObject("Scripting.FileSystemObject")

' Get the user inputs (customer, product, quarter, year).
frmInputs.Show
```

```
' Get the folder where the files are stored.
MsgBox "In the following dialog box, browse for the " _
    & "folder where the " & customer & " sales files are stored."
Set FD = Application.FileDialog(msoFileDialogFolderPicker)
With FD
    If .Show Then
        path = .SelectedItems(1)
    Else
        Exit Sub
    End If
End With

Application.ScreenUpdating = False
With fso
    ' First check whether there is a customer file in the selected location
    ' for this quarter and year.
    textFile = path & "\" & customer & " Sales Q" & quarter & " " & year & ".txt"
    isFound = .FileExists(textFile)
    If Not isFound Then
        MsgBox "There is no sales file in this location for customer " & customer & _
            " in Q" & quarter & " " & year & ".", vbInformation, "No file"
        Exit Sub
    Else
        ' File is found, so now open it and search for selected product code.
        Open textFile For Input As #1
        Line Input #1, dataLine
        Call GetProductIndex(dataLine, index)
    End If
End With
```

We programmers hate to see our applications broken because functionality that used to be there is discontinued, but this is exactly what happened with the **FileSearch** object. Microsoft certainly had a reason for discontinuing it, but that reason is difficult to locate. (The Web contains a lot of complaints and workarounds, but no reasons I could find for Microsoft's decision.) In the meantime, we can get most of the same functionality with the Scripting library's **FileSystemObject**.

13.5 A File Renumbering Example

The application in this section is one I have used to automate renumbering of files. You might be able to modify it to suit your own situation. When writing books such as this one, I like to keep a folder for each chapter that stores the screen capture files numbered consecutively. For example, the figures in this chapter are named Figure13_01.gif, Figure13_02.gif, and so on.[4] Sometimes I revise a chapter by adding a new section in the middle with several figures. Suppose the current figures are numbered 1 through 25, and I then add four new figures, 5 through 8. To make room for these, I have to renumber the current files Figure13_05.gif to Figure13_25.gif as Figure13_09.gif to Figure13_29.gif. This is quite tedious to do in Windows Explorer, especially if I have to do it very often.

---

[4]Can you guess why I use numbering such as Figure13_02.gif instead of Figure13_2.gif? It's simple. With the extra 0, Windows Explorer lists the files in consecutive order.

Figure 13.12 File Renumbering Dialog Box

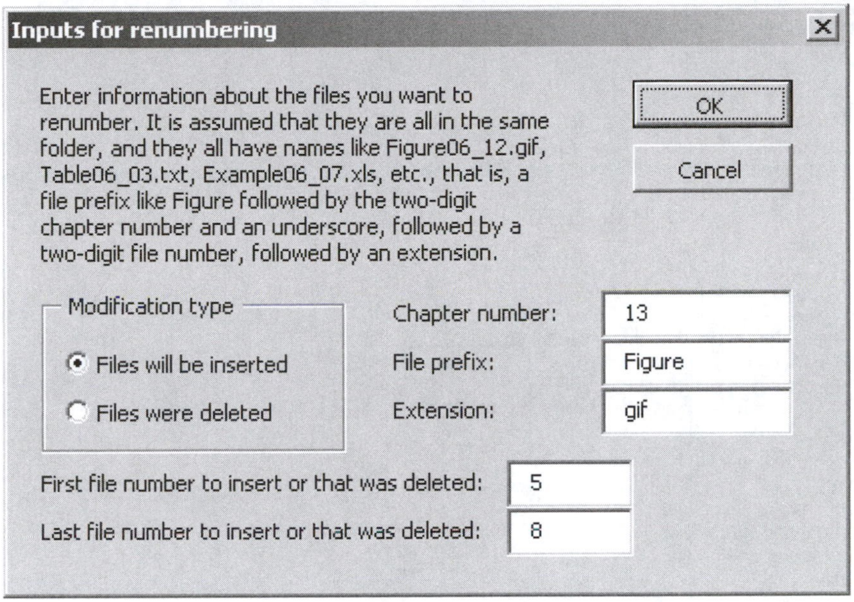

Alternatively, suppose I decide to delete a section that has figures 5 through 8. I first delete these .gif files, which is easy to do manually, and then I need to renumber the remaining files to "fill in the holes." Specifically, I need to renumber the files Figure13_09.gif to Figure13_25.gif as Figure13_05.gif to Figure 13_21.gif. Again, this is tedious to do in Windows Explorer.

The file **Renumber Files.xlsm** takes care of the renumbering automatically. It first uses a FileDialog object to allow the user to specify the folder where the files to be renumbered are stored. It then opens the user form shown in Figure 13.12. The settings shown here will renumber all files Figure13_05.gif and higher by adding 4 to each file number. When the user clicks on OK, all of the renumbering is performed automatically. (Note: The version of this file in the second edition used the now defunct FileSearch object. The new code uses the FileSystemObject object, as discussed in Section 13.4. Also, this new version renumbers correctly even if there are "holes" in the file numbering. For example, if I have files numbered 1, 2, 3, 5, 9, and I want to insert files with indexes 3 and 4, this version will renumber the last three existing files with indexes 5, 7, and 11.)

The event handlers for the form are straightforward and are listed below. The **btnOK_Click** sub captures the user's inputs in the public variables chapterNumber, filePrefix, extension, firstFileNumber, and lastFileNumber. Note that if a single digit such as 8 is entered in any of the "number" boxes, it is changed to the string "08". This is because my file numbering convention uses two-digit numbers in the file names. Also, the extension is converted to .gif (with the period) regardless of whether the user enters gif or .gif.

```
Private Sub btnCancel_Click()
    Unload Me
    End
End Sub

Private Sub btnOK_Click()
    ' If input is a single digit such as 3, change it to 03.
    If Len(txtChapterNumber.Text) = 1 Then
        chapterNumber = "0" & txtChapterNumber.Text
    Else
        chapterNumber = txtChapterNumber.Text
    End If

    filePrefix = txtFilePrefix.Text

    ' extension will include the period, such as .gif, even
    ' if input didn't include it.
    If Left(txtExtension.Text, 1) = "." Then
        extension = txtExtension.Text
    Else
        extension = "." & txtExtension.Text
    End If

    If optInsert.Value Then
        operation = "Insert"
    Else
        operation = "Delete"
    End If

    ' Again, change any single digit such as 3 to 03.
    If Len(txtFirstFileNumber.Text) = 1 Then
        firstFileNumber = "0" & txtFirstFileNumber.Text
    Else
        firstFileNumber = txtFirstFileNumber.Text
    End If
    If Len(txtLastFileNumber.Text) = 1 Then
        lastFileNumber = "0" & txtLastFileNumber.Text
    Else
        lastFileNumber = txtLastFileNumber.Text
    End If

    Unload Me
End Sub

Private Sub UserForm_Initialize()
    Dim ctl As Control
    optInsert.Value = True
    For Each ctl In Me.Controls
        If TypeName(ctl) = "TextBox" Then
            ctl.Text = ""
        End If
    Next
End Sub
```

The **RenumberFiles** sub in the module performs the actual renumbering. It first uses a FileDialog object of the folder picker type to capture the folder variable. It then shows the form (frmInputs) in Figure 13.12. Next, a FileSystemObject object is used to look for all existing files that match a pattern such as Figure13_*.gif. Specifically (and I found a lot of this on online help), I use the GetFolder method of the FileSystemObject to return a folder object. Then I fill a files array with all files from this folder that match the pattern. The renumbering code depends on whether files are being inserted or deleted. This code is tricky, but it is basically just string operations and careful arithmetic. I first rename all the files with the new numbering and a "t" appended to the extension. This appendix is used to ensure that new files don't try to overwrite other new files. Then I get rid of the "t" in the extensions. Finally, there is a VBA statement called **Name** that is used to rename the files. Its syntax is Name *oldfilename* As *newfilename*.[5]

```
Option Explicit
Option Base 1

Public chapterNumber As String
Public filePrefix As String
Public extension As String
Public operation As String
Public firstFileNumber As Integer
Public lastFileNumber As Integer

Sub RenumberFiles()
  Dim fso As New Scripting.FileSystemObject
  Dim fd As FileDialog
  Dim searchFolder As String
  ' In the next two lines, I've declared the variables as "generic"
  ' Object types. Maybe I could be more specific, but I'm not sure how.
  ' Online help doesn't help! Anyway, this works.
  Dim folder As Object, file As Object
  Dim files() As Object
  Dim i As Integer
  Dim nFilesFound As Integer
  Dim oldName() As String, newName() As String
  Dim oldNumber As Integer, newNumber As Integer
  Dim newNumberString As String
  Dim numberPosition As Integer

  ' Open a dialog box to let user select folder
  ' where files to be renumbered are stored.
  MsgBox "In the next dialog box, select the folder where files to be renumbered " _
    & "are stored.", vbInformation
  Set fd = Application.FileDialog(msoFileDialogFolderPicker)
  If fd.Show Then
    ' Capture the selected folder.
    searchFolder = fd.SelectedItems(1)
  Else
    ' User clicked on Cancel, so end.
    Exit Sub
  End If
```

---

[5]I couldn't locate a Rename method in online help, and VBA's Name statement is pretty well hidden, but it does the job. By the way, if you want to delete a file, VBA has a Kill statement with syntax **Kill** *filename*.

```
' Get user inputs on which files to renumber.
frmInputs.Show

' Search for all files of desired type from selected folder.
Set folder = fso.GetFolder(searchFolder)
nFilesFound = 0
For Each file In folder.files
   ' The Like operator is good for comparing strings with wildcards.
   If file.Name Like filePrefix & chapterNumber _
       & "_*" & extension Then
     nFilesFound = nFilesFound + 1
     ReDim Preserve files(nFilesFound)
     Set files(nFilesFound) = file
   End If
Next

ReDim oldName(nFilesFound)
ReDim newName(nFilesFound)

If operation = "Insert" Then
   ' Renumber upward.
   For i = 1 To nFilesFound
     oldName(i) = files(i)
     ' Find the old number (just before the extension). This assumes
     ' the file numbers are all two digits.
     oldNumber = Mid(oldName(i), Len(oldName(i)) - Len(extension) - 1, 2)
     If oldNumber >= firstFileNumber Then
       newNumber = oldNumber + lastFileNumber - firstFileNumber + 1
       ' If the number is, say, 8, change it to 08.
       If newNumber <= 9 Then
         newNumberString = "0" & newNumber
       Else
         newNumberString = newNumber
       End If
       ' Find the index of the character before the file number.
       numberPosition = Len(oldName(i)) - Len(extension) - 2
       ' Build the new file name. Append "t" to it (for temporary)
       ' for now. This will be deleted later on.
       newName(i) = Left(oldName(i), numberPosition) _
           & newNumberString & extension & "t"
       ' Rename the file.
       Name oldName(i) As newName(i)
     End If
   Next

   ' Get rid of the "t" on the new file names.
   For i = 1 To nFilesFound
     ' Find the old number (just before the extension).
     oldNumber = Mid(oldName(i), Len(oldName(i)) - Len(extension) - 1, 2)
     If oldNumber >= firstFileNumber Then
       ' Rename the file (delete the appended "t").
       Name newName(i) As Left(newName(i), Len(newName(i)) - 1)
     End If
   Next
Else
   ' Renumber downward.
   For i = 1 To nFilesFound
     oldName(i) = files(i)
     ' Find the old number (just before the extension). This assumes
     ' the file numbers are all two digits.
     oldNumber = Mid(oldName(i), Len(oldName(i)) - Len(extension) - 1, 2)
     If oldNumber >= lastFileNumber + 1 Then
```

```
            newNumber = oldNumber - (lastFileNumber - firstFileNumber + 1)
            ' If the number is, say, 8, change it to 08.
            If newNumber <= 9 Then
               newNumberString = "0" & newNumber
            Else
               newNumberString = newNumber
            End If
            ' Find the index of the character before the file number.
            numberPosition = Len(oldName(i)) - Len(extension) - 2
            ' Build the new file name. Append "t" to it (for temporary)
            ' for now. This will be deleted later on.
            newName(i) = Left(oldName(i), numberPosition) _
               & newNumberString & extension & "t"
            ' Rename the file.
            Name oldName(i) As newName(i)
         End If
      Next

      ' Get rid of the "t" on the new file names.
      For i = 1 To nFilesFound
         ' Find the old number (just before the extension).
         oldNumber = Mid(oldName(i), Len(oldName(i)) - Len(extension) - 1, 2)
         If oldNumber >= lastFileNumber + 1 Then
            ' Rename the file (delete the appended "t").
            Name newName(i) As Left(newName(i), Len(newName(i)) - 1)
         End If
      Next
   End If
   MsgBox "Files have been renumbered successfully.", vbInformation
End Sub
```

13.6 Working with Text Files

The last type of file operation discussed in this chapter concerns importing text from a text file into Excel or exporting Excel data to a text file. It is not uncommon to find data in a text file because this format represents a lowest common denominator—all you need is NotePad (or any other text editor) to read a text file. Usually the extension for a text file is .txt, although .csv (comma-delimited), .dat, and .prn are also used. When data are stored in a text file, each line typically includes information about a particular record. This could be information about a particular order, a particular customer, a particular product, and so on. The individual pieces of data in a line, such as first name, last name, address, and so on, are typically separated with a **delimiter** character. The most common delimiters are the tab character and the comma, although others are sometimes used.

If you look at a line in a tab-delimited text file, it might look like

01-Feb-02   3430   2360   3040

This is a bit misleading. There are four pieces of data in this line, but there is only a *single* character between each piece of data—a tab character, or **vbTab** in VBA. If you want to import this line into the first four cells of a row in Excel, you must **parse** the line into its individual pieces of data. Essentially, you must go through the line, character by character, searching for vbTab characters. This parsing operation is at the heart of working with text files. (It is also at the heart of all word processors.)

Importing a Text File into Excel

To import a text file into Excel, perform the following steps.

1.   Open the text file for input with the line

```
Open file For Input As #1
```

Here, file is declared as String, which by this time has a value such as "D:\My Files\Sales.txt". You can have several text files open at the same time, in which case you number them consecutively as #1, #2, and so on.

2.   Loop over the the lines with the statements

```
Do  Until EOF(1)
      Line Input #1, dataLine
      ' Code for parsing the line
Loop
```

This loops until it reaches the end of file (EOF) for input file #1. The first line inside the loop reads a new line of data and stores it in the string variable dataLine. Then this line must be parsed appropriately.

3.   Close the text file with the line

```
Close #1
```

Parsing the line is where most of the work is involved. The following sub is fairly general. (It is stored in the file **Parse.xlsm**.) It accepts two arguments, a dataLine to be read and a delimiter character, and it returns two results, the number of pieces of data and an array of these pieces of data. The comments spell out the individual steps. Whether you use this sub as is or you write your own parser, the logic is always the same. You have to go through the line character by character, searching for the delimiters and the text between them. (This sub has been written for 1-based indexing.)

```
Sub ParseLine (dataLine As String, delimiter As String, nValues As Integer, returnArray() As String)
    ' This sub parses a line of data from the text file into individual pieces of data.
    ' It returns an array of the pieces of data and number of pieces (in nValues).

    Dim i As Integer
    Dim char As String
    Dim counter As Integer ' counts the pieces of data in the line
    Dim currentText As String ' text since last delimiter
```

```
' Counter counts the number of pieces of data in the line.
counter = 1
ReDim returnArray(counter)

' currentText is any piece of data in the line, where the pieces
' are separated by commas.
currentText = ""

' Go through the string a character at a time.
For i = 1 To Len(dataLine)

    ' Get the character in position i.
    char = Mid(dataLine, i, 1)

    ' Check if the character is a delimiter, such as a comma, or the last character in the string.
    If char = delimiter Then
        returnArray(counter) = currentText

        ' Get ready for the next piece of data.
        currentText = ""
        counter = counter + 1
        ReDim Preserve returnArray(counter)

    ElseIf i = Len(dataLine) Then
        ' Capture this last piece of data and return the number of pieces.
        currentText = currentText & Mid(dataLine, i, 1)
        returnArray(counter) = currentText
        nValues = counter

    Else
        ' Add this character to the currentText string.
        currentText = currentText & Mid(dataLine, i, 1)
    End If
Next i
End Sub
```

Exporting Excel Data to a Text File

Writing Excel data to a text file is not as common as reading from a text tile, but it is sometimes useful. The steps required are as follows.

1. Open the text file for output with the line

```
Open txtFile For Output As #1
```

Here, txtFile is declared as String, which by this time has a value such as "D: \Sales.txt". As with importing, you can have several text files open at the same time, in which case you number them consecutively as #1, #2, and so on.

2. Loop over the lines you will be storing. Inside the loop create a line (in the dataLine variable), and store it with the code

```
Write #1, dataLine
```

Figure 13.13 Excel Data to be Exported

	A	B	C	D
1	Date	P3254	P7417	P3416
2	25-Jan-09	1960	2710	1850
3	26-Jan-09	2290	2640	2170
4	27-Jan-09	2610	2270	2370
5	28-Jan-09	3130	2720	2650
6	31-Jan-09	2500	2610	2540

Figure 13.14 Resulting Text File

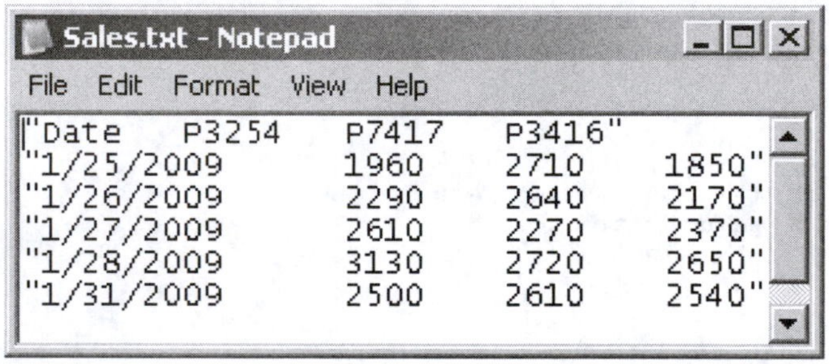

```
Sales.txt - Notepad
File  Edit  Format  View  Help
"Date      P3254      P7417      P3416"
"1/25/2009      1960      2710      1850"
"1/26/2009      2290      2640      2170"
"1/27/2009      2610      2270      2370"
"1/28/2009      3130      2720      2650"
"1/31/2009      2500      2610      2540"
```

3. Close the text file with the line

```
Close #1
```

In this case there is no parsing. Each dataLine is typically created by reading cells from an Excel worksheet and separating them with a delimiter. For example, suppose the Excel file is structured as in Figure 13.13. Then the following **Write-SalesToText** sub could be used to store the data in the file D:\Sales.txt. (This sub is stored in the file **Write Sales.xlsm**.)

The resulting text file is shown in Figure 13.14. Note that double-quotes are automatically inserted around each line of text (because each line is considered a string by VBA). These double-quotes could be a potential nuisance for a programmer who later intends to *import* this text data into Excel. The moral is that you should always check text files before you try to import the data. Text files are notorious for containing messy data.

```
Sub WriteSalesToText( )
    Dim txtFile As String
    Dim row As Integer, column As Integer
    Dim nRows As Integer, nColumns As Integer
    Dim dataLine As String
```

```
        txtFile = "D:\Sales.txt"
        Open txtFile For Output As #1

        With Range("A1")
            nRows = Range(.Offset(0, 0), .End(xlDown)).Rows.Count
            nColumns = Range(.Offset(0, 0), .End(xlToRight)).Columns.Count
            For row = 1 To nRows
                ' Build data line from data in this row, separated by tabs.
                dataLine = ""
                For column = 1 To nColumns
                    dataLine = dataLine & .Cells(row, column)
                    ' Don't add a tab after the last piece of data in the row.
                    If column < nColumns Then _
                        dataLine = dataLine & vbTab
                Next
                ' Write this line to the text file.
                Write #1, dataLine
            Next
        End With
        Close #1
End Sub
```

13.7 Summary

Although this chapter is not geared as specifically to Excel operations as the other chapters, it provides a lot of useful information for dealing with files and folders. For example, by using the FileDialog object, you can easily let a user specify a folder to look in. Or by using the FileSystemObject object, you can easily test whether a file exists in a specific folder. In addition to the file/folder operations you typically perform in Windows Explorer, this chapter has briefly illustrated how to work with text files, either for importing or exporting. An example of importing text data for use in an optimization model appears in Chapter 32.

EXERCISES

1. Write an application that uses a FileDialog object of the File Picker type. It should allow the user to select one or more files, and then it should list the chosen files in column A of a worksheet. (The worksheet should be in the same workbook as your code. A typical file name will include the path, such as **D:\My Files\Sales.xlsx.**)

2. Write an application that uses a FileDialog object of the File Open type. It should allow the user to select a *single* Excel (.xlsx) file, which should then be opened in Excel. (*Hint*: Look up the AllowMultiSelect and Filters properties of the FileDialog object in the Object Browser.)

3. Write an application that uses a FileDialog object of the File Save As type. After it saves the file in a name chosen by the user, it should display the new file name in a message box.

4. Write an application that uses a FileDialog object of the Folder Picker type. After the user selects a folder, the application should then use a FileSystemObject object

to find all of the files in that folder (and its subfolders) with extension .xls or .doc., and these files should all be listed in column A of a worksheet. (The worksheet should be in the same workbook as your code. A typical file name will include the path, such as **D:\My Files\Sales.xlsx**.)

5. (Note: I left this exercise from the second edition here to illustrate how much we are missing by not having FileSearch. There is no easy way to do it! My solution uses the AltFileSearch object from Codematics, which you have to purchase. Even with it, there is no easy way to answer the second part of the exercise.) Write an application that asks the user for an extension, such as .xlsx, and then uses a FileSearch object to count the number of files on the C drive with this extension. The count should be displayed in a message box. Try it out on your own PC, say, with the extension .docx. Then modify the application so that only files that have been modified during the current month are listed.

6. Write an application that asks the user to pick a folder. The application should then open all Excel files (.xls or .xlsx) in that folder, if any, with "Forecast" in the file name. For example, these would include **Forecasting the Weather.xls** and **Company Forecasts for March.xlsx.**

7. Suppose a company has a lot of Excel files for its customers. In particular, assume that all files for a given customer are in the same folder, and all of these customer files begin the customer's name, such as **Davidson_Sales_2003.xls.** You don't know the exact naming convention; you only know that the file begins with the customer's name. Write an application that asks for a customer's name and the folder where this customer's files are stored and then lists all of the file names for this customer in column A of a worksheet. (The worksheet should be in the same workbook as your code. A typical file name will include the path, such as D:\My Files\Davidson_Sales_2003.xls.)

8. Starting with the same setup as in the previous exercise, suppose that a customer's name changes. Create an application that asks for the customer's old name, new name, and the folder where this customer's files are stored, and then renames all of the files appropriately.

9. Sometimes I renumber entire chapters. For example, Chapter 14 might become Chapter 17. Then various files for the chapter need to be renumbered. If there are a lot of files of the form Figure 14_xx.gif, say, they would all need to renumbered as Figure 17_xx.gif. Revise the **Renumber Files.xlsm** application to take care of this type of renumbering.

10. Use NotePad to create a text (.txt) file that contains one long list of words, where the individual words are separated by the space character. (In NotePad, use the Format menu to turn word wrap off, so your text will physically appear in one long line.) Write a sub that opens this text file, parses the single line with the space character as the delimiter, returns the number of words in a message box, returns the number of words with more than five characters in a second message box, and finally closes the file.

11. The file **Revenue Data.xlsx** has a single worksheet. This sheet has headings in row 1 and revenues for various products on various dates in the remaining rows. Write

a sub that exports this data in tab-delimited format to a text file that should be named **Revenue Data.txt** and stored in the same folder as the Excel file. Once you get the data exported, write another sub that imports the tab-delimited data back into an Excel file, just like the original Excel file, but with name **Revenue Data1.xlsx**. You can create this new file manually, name it, and make sure it contains only a single sheet named Revenues, but your code should open it before doing the importing.

14 Importing Data into Excel from a Database

14.1 Introduction

An important theme throughout this book is that Excel applications often need to access data. Sometimes the data is obtained from one or more user forms, and sometimes the data resides in an Excel worksheet, either in the application's workbook or in another Excel file. However, in the corporate world, the chances are that the data is stored in a relational database, possibly on a database server. Therefore, applications typically need to import data into Excel for analysis. This chapter illustrates how to do this with VBA code. Fortunately, because this is such a common need, Microsoft has developed several technologies for importing data from relational databases. In fact, an "alphabet soup" of technologies for importing data has emerged over the past 20 years: ODBC, DAO, RDO, OLE DB, ADO, and ADO.NET. This chapter discusses the most recent technology that is available with Excel VBA: ActiveX Data Objects (ADO).[1]

14.2 Exercise

The **Sales Orders.mdb** file is an Access database included in the book's "CD". (Access files created in Access 2007 have a new .accdb extension. However, I'll continue to use files with the old .mdb extensions here.) As discussed in the next section, this database includes a number of related tables that store information about a company's orders for its products. The structure of this database appears in Figure 14.1. Specifically, there is a row in the Orders table for each order taken by the company, there is a row in the Products table for each product the company sells, and there is a row in the LineItems table for each line item in each order. For example, if a customer places an order for 3 units of product 7 and 2 units of product 13, there will be a single row in the Orders table for this order, and there will be two rows in the LineItems table, one for each of the two products ordered.

The purpose of this exercise is to develop an application where a user can select a product from a list box in a user form (see Figure 14.2) and then see details about all orders that include this product (see Figure 14.3, which shows the first few rows). This exercise requires two uses of the material in this chapter. It must first

---

[1] A more recent technology is ADO.NET, part of Microsoft's .NET initiative. Although ADO.NET *can* be used to develop VBA applications for Excel, it requires more software than simply Microsoft Office, so it is not covered here. The "old" ADO works just fine.

Figure 14.1 Structure of SalesOrders Database

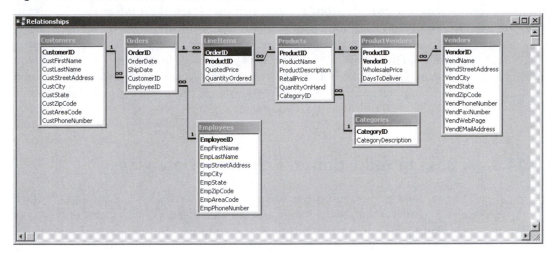

Figure 14.2 Dialog Box with List of Products

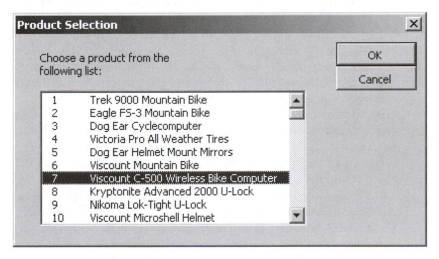

Figure 14.3 Information on Orders for Selected Product

	A	B	C	D	E	F	G	H	I
1	Orders for product:	Viscount C-500 Wireless Bike Computer							
2									
3	Order ID	Order Date	Unit Price	Quantity	Extended Price				
4	6	1-Jul-1999	$49.00	2	$98.00		Show orders for a selected product		
5	17	2-Jul-1999	$47.53	6	$285.18				
6	22	3-Jul-1999	$47.53	6	$285.18				
7	26	4-Jul-1999	$47.53	6	$285.18				
8	27	4-Jul-1999	$49.00	3	$147.00				
9	28	4-Jul-1999	$49.00	4	$196.00				
10	32	5-Jul-1999	$49.00	1	$49.00				
11	33	5-Jul-1999	$47.53	6	$285.18				
12	44	7-Jul-1999	$49.00	1	$49.00				
13	58	9-Jul-1999	$49.00	4	$196.00				

query the Products table to populate the list box in Figure 14.2. Then, once the user selects a product from the list, it must query the Orders and LineItems tables to obtain the order information for this product in Figure 14.3.

As you read through this chapter, you can try to develop this application on your own. The details will eventually be discussed in Section 14.5. Once you understand the material in the next two sections—relational databases, **Structured Query Language** (SQL), and ADO—you will see that applications such as this one are not as difficult to develop as you might expect.

14.3 A Brief Introduction to Relational Databases

The two main purposes of databases are to (1) store data efficiently, and (2) allow users to request the data they want, in a suitable form. Various forms of databases have existed, including those that predate computers. Approximately 30 years ago, researchers formalized the **relational** form of databases that is still the predominant method of storing data electronically. Many packages have been developed by various companies to implement relational databases, and many are in daily use in organizations. Some packages, such as the well-known Microsoft Access package, are **desktop** systems. If you own Microsoft Office (for Windows), then you own Access. It resides on your desktop (or laptop) machine, and you can create databases as files that reside on your hard drive. Other more "heavy-duty" software packages, referred to as **relational database management systems** (**RDBMS**), are **server-based**. The software and the associated databases are not likely to reside on an individual's PC, except possibly as a scaled-down version for testing purposes. Instead, they reside on a central server, where users can access the data through network connections. Three well-known server-based packages are Microsoft's SQL Server, Oracle, and IBM's DB2—and there are others.

The purpose of this section is to describe the essential ideas behind relational databases. These ideas are relevant regardless of the software package that implements them, although I illustrate the concepts with Microsoft Access so that you can follow along on your PC. The basic ideas are so intuitive that it is hard to believe that relational databases have been around for only about 30 years. However, this is the case; relational databases are a relatively new concept.

Tables, Fields, and Records

The essential element of any relational database is a **table**. A table stores data in a rectangular array of rows and columns—yes, much like a spreadsheet. In database terminology, however, the rows are usually called **records**, and the columns are usually called **fields**. If you were storing information about customers in a table, each field would include some characteristic of a customer, so you might have fields such as FirstName, LastName, BirthDate, Address, City, State, Phone, EMailAddress, and possibly others. Any row (record) contains all of this information for a particular

Figure 14.4 Customers Table

CustomerID	CustFirstName	CustLastName	CustStreetAddress	CustCity	CustState	CustZipCode	CustAreaCode	CustPhoneNumber
1	Suzanne	Viescas	15127 NE 24th, #383	Redmond	WA	98052	425	555-2686
2	Will	Thompson	122 Spring River Drive	Duvall	WA	98019	425	555-2681
3	Gary	Hallmark	Route 2, Box 203B	Auburn	WA	98002	253	555-2676
4	Michael	Davolio	672 Lamont Ave	Houston	TX	77201	713	555-2491
5	Kenneth	Peacock	4110 Old Redmond Rd.	Redmond	WA	98052	425	555-2506
6	John	Viescas	15127 NE 24th, #383	Redmond	WA	98052	425	555-2511
7	Laura	Callahan	901 Pine Avenue	Portland	OR	97208	503	555-2526
8	Neil	Patterson	233 West Valley Hwy	San Diego	CA	92199	619	555-2541

Record: 28 of 28

customer. In other words, each row has to do with a single customer, whereas each field lists a particular characteristic of the customers. Part of the Customers table from the Sales Orders database is shown in Figure 14.4.

Many databases consist of a single table. These types of databases are usually called **flat files**. Suppose you want to store information about all of the books you read. You might store the title, the author (or authors, one per field), the year you read it, and whether it is fiction or nonfiction. A single-table database for such a simple collection of data would probably suffice. (I have such a flat-file database for all the books I have read.)

However, most real-world databases contain multiple tables, sometimes *many* tables. These tables are typically related in some way, which leads to concept of the *relational* database. In a well-designed relational database, each table should have information about a particular type of entity. For example, in the Sales Orders database discussed in the previous section, the data center around a company's orders for its products. Several tables include: (1) the Customers table, with information about the customers who place the orders, (2) the Employees table, with information about the employees who take the orders, (3) the Orders table, with information about the orders taken, (4) the Products table, with information about the products the company sells, and (5) the Vendors table, with information about the company's suppliers.

Why isn't all of this data stored in a *single* table? This is the crucial question. Presumably, if a single table were used, each record would have data about a single order: which customer placed the order, which employee took the order, when the order was placed, and so on. Now imagine that customer Jim Smith has placed 100 orders. If the database includes personal information about the customers, then that information for Jim Smith will be repeated in 100 records of the single table. This introduces an immense amount of redundancy. Not only will the size of the database be much larger than necessary, but there will be many possibilities for errors. First, if you are a data entry person, you will need to enter Jim Smith's personal data many times, and you are likely to make errors. Second, what if Jim Smith's phone number changes? You will then have to search through all of the records for Jim Smith and change the phone number in each. This means a lot of work and many chances for errors.

You probably do not need to be convinced that this level of redundancy—storing a customer's personal information in multiple places—is a bad idea, but what is the alternative? The answer is to have a Customers table that stores *only* information about customers, with one record per customer. Then if Jim Smith's phone number changes, you need to change it in exactly one place—in the single record for Jim Smith. This sounds like a great idea for avoiding redundancy and errors, and it is, but it causes a potential problem. In the Orders table, where information about orders is stored, how do you know which customers placed which orders? This question is answered next. It is the key to relational databases.

Many-to-One Relationships, and Primary and Foreign Keys

Consider the Categories and Products tables in the Sales Orders database. The Categories table lists all product categories, and the Products table lists information about each product, including its category. The relationship between these tables is called a **many-to-one** relationship, because each product is in exactly *one* category, but each category can contain *many* products.

The two tables are related by fields called **keys**. Let's start with the Categories table, the "one" side of the many-to-one relationship. It contains a field called a **primary key**. A primary key is any *unique identifier* of the records in the table. In other words, no two records are allowed to have the same value in the primary key field. For some entities, there are "natural" primary keys. For example, a unique identifier for U.S. citizens is their Social Security Number (SSN). For books, a unique identifier is their ISBN. But even if there is no ready-made unique identifier, it is always possible to generate one as an **autonumber** field. This is a field that numbers the records consecutively—1, 2, 3, and so on— as the data are entered into the table. If the most recently entered record has autonumber 347, then the next one will automatically have autonumber 348. This guarantees uniqueness and provides an easy way to create a primary key. The primary key for the Categories table is indeed an autonumber field named CategoryID.

To relate the Categories and Products table, a **foreign key** field, also called CategoryID, is placed in the Products table.[2] For example, it turns out that the category Clothing has CategoryID 3. Therefore, for every product in the Clothing category, the foreign key value is 3. This clearly indicates that foreign key fields are not unique. If there are, say, 250 products in the Clothing category, then there will be 250 rows in the Products table with CategoryID equal to 3.

The actual data for these two tables appears in Figure 14.5 and 14.6 (with the first few of the rows showing for the Products table). Note how the CategoryID field in Figure 14.6 allows you to perform a "table lookup" in Figure 14.5 to find the category for any given product. Alternatively, you could use the primary key values in Figure 14.5 to find all products, say, in the Clothing category.

---

[2]The field names of the primary key and associated foreign key are often the same, simply to avoid confusion. However, there is no requirement that they be the same. For example, the primary key could be named CategoryID and the foreign key could be named CatID.

Figure 14.5 Categories Table

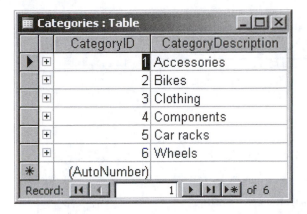

Figure 14.6 Products Table

	ProductID	ProductName	ProductDescription	RetailPrice	QuantityOnHand	CategoryID
	1	Trek 9000 Mountain Bike		$1,200.00	6	2
	2	Eagle FS-3 Mountain Bike		$1,800.00	8	2
	3	Dog Ear Cyclecomputer		$75.00	20	1
	4	Victoria Pro All Weather Tires		$54.95	20	4
	5	Dog Ear Helmet Mount Mirrors		$7.45	12	1
	6	Viscount Mountain Bike		$635.00	5	2
	7	Viscount C-500 Wireless Bike Computer		$49.00	30	1
	8	Kryptonite Advanced 2000 U-Lock		$50.00	20	1

Record: 1 of 40

Referential Integrity

An extremely important idea in relational databases is that of keeping the links between primary and foreign keys valid. The technical term for this is **referential integrity**. Again, consider the Clothing category with primary key 3. Referential integrity could be violated in the following ways:

- The Clothing row in the Categories table could be deleted. Then there would be a lot of "dangling" products, with links to a category that is no longer in the database.
- The primary key value for Clothing in the Categories table could be changed to, say, 9. Then all of the clothing products with foreign keys equal to 3 would be wrong; they should now also be 9.
- Some product's foreign key could be changed from 3 to a new value. This might or might not violate referential integrity. If we realize that this product's category is not Clothing but is instead Accessories, with primary key 1, then the foreign key *should* be changed to 1. However, if the foreign key is changed to a value such as 15, which is not the primary key for *any* category, this will violate referential integrity.

Figure 14.7 Dialog Box with Referential Integrity Option

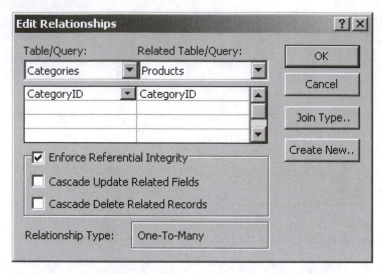

Fortunately, database packages such as Access allow you to check an option that enforces referential integrity. (See Figure 14.7, the dialog box from Access.) With this option checked, you will not be *allowed* to inadvertently make a change that would violate referential integrity. There are usually additional options, such as **cascading deletions**. With this option checked, if you delete the Clothing record in the Categories table, then all of the associated clothing products in the Products table will also be deleted automatically. For obvious reasons, you want to be sure you know what you are doing before you check this option.

Many-to-Many Relationships

Not all entities are related in a many-to-one manner. There are also **many-to-many** relationships. (In addition, there are **one-to-one** relationships, but they are less common, and I will not discuss them here.) A perfect example of a many-to-many relationship is the relationship between orders and products. Any order can include several products, and any product can be included in multiple orders.

The way to deal with such relationships again uses primary and foreign keys, but now an extra table is required. This table is often called a **linking** table. The Orders table has primary key OrderID, and the Products table has primary key ProductID. Then the linking table, which has been named LineItems, has two foreign keys, OrderID and ProductID. The linking table for this database has a couple of extra fields, QuotedPrice and QuantityOrdered, but it is often just a set of foreign keys. There is a row in this linking table for *each* combination of order and product. So, for example, if an order is for four products, there will be four associated rows in the linking table. Or if a product is a part of 25 orders, there will be 25 associated rows in the linking table. Because of this, linking tables tend to be tall and narrow.

The linking table allows you to look up information on orders or products. For example, if you want to know when the product King Cobra Helmet has been ordered, you look up its ProductID in the Products table, which happens to be 25. Then you search the ProductID column of the LineItems table for values of 25 and keep track of the corresponding OrderID values. Then you look up these latter values in the Orders table to find the order dates.

Many database experts insist that all tables have a primary key. What is the primary key for the LineItems table? It cannot be OrderID because of duplicates in this field. For the same reason, it cannot be ProductID. In this case, a *combination* of fields, OrderID and ProductID, is used to form the primary key. This works fine, because no two records in the LineItems table have the same combination of these two fields. The point is that if there is no single field with unique values, it is usually possible to find a combination of fields that can serve as the primary key.

14.4 A Brief Introduction to SQL

As relational databases became the standard several decades ago, a language called **Structured Query Language**, or **SQL**, was developed to retrieve data from relational databases. In database terminology, SQL statements are used to **query** a database. The SQL language, known as "the language of databases," applies in some form to all database systems, whether they be Access, SQL Server, Oracle, or others. If you have worked with Access, you are probably not familiar with SQL because Access provides a user-friendly graphical interface for developing queries. However, when you use this interface, an SQL statement is actually created in the background, and this SQL statement is used by Access to find the data you want.

Whole books (thick ones at that) have been written on SQL, but you can learn the essentials of SQL pretty quickly. First, there are several types of SQL statements. The most common type is called a SELECT query. A SELECT query asks for certain data from the database. For example, a SELECT statement would be used to find information on all orders placed after the year 2003. A SELECT statement allows you to view data; it doesn't *change* the data. Other SQL statements allow you to change the data. These include INSERT, UPDATE, and DELETE queries. This section, however, discusses SELECT queries only.

A SELECT query is analogous to a single sentence with several clauses. There are only a few possible types of clauses:

- The SELECT clause lists the fields you want data on.
- The FROM clause specifies the table or tables that hold the data you want.
- The WHERE clause lists criteria that you specify. Only the data that meet the criteria are returned.
- The GROUP BY clause allows you to get subtotals, such as the total revenue from each order. In this case, you "group by" the orders.[3]
- The ORDER BY clause allows you to specify sort orders for the data returned.

---

[3]There is also a HAVING clause that can follow a GROUP BY clause, but I won't discuss it here.

Figure 14.8 Relationships Diagram for "Sales Orders" Database

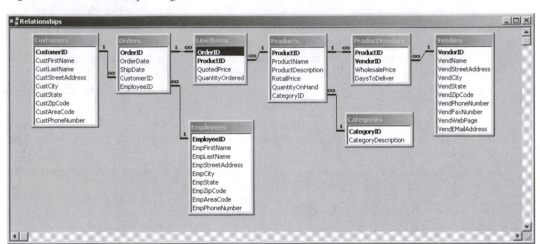

Only the SELECT and FROM clauses are necessary. If any of the others are used, they must be listed in the above order.

Single-Table Queries

The simplest SELECT statements are queries from a single table, such as the information on all customers who live in California. Because all of this information resides in the Customers table, the query is called a **single-table query**. (See the relationships diagram in Figure 14.8, a copy of Figure 14.1 repeated here for convenience.) The corresponding SQL statement might look something like the following:[4]

```
SELECT CustFirstName, CustLastName, CustPhoneNumber
FROM Customers
WHERE CustState = 'CA'
ORDER BY CustLastName, CustFirstName
```

Although this is a *single* SELECT statement, it is customary to put each clause on one or more separate lines to improve readability. The SELECT clause lists the fields you are interested in seeing. The FROM clause lists the single table that contains the customer data. The WHERE clause includes a criterion: the customer's state should be 'CA'. Finally, the ORDER BY clause states that data should be returned alphabetically on last name, and in case of ties, on first name. Note the single quotes around CA in the WHERE clause. The rules in

---

[4]Case is not important in SQL statements, but it is common, especially when learning the language, to capitalize keywords such as SELECT. I will do so in this section.

SQL for Access are that (1) single quotes should be placed around literal text, such as CA; (2) pound signs (#) should be placed around literal dates, such as **WHERE OrderDate > #12/31/2001#;** and (3) nothing should placed around numbers, as in **WHERE QuantityOrdered >= 5.**

There are many variations of single-table SQL statements. Rather than present a long list here, I refer you to the file **Sales Order Queries.docx** on the CD-ROM. This file presents a number of examples, along with some explanation. I will just mention two variations here. First, you can include **calculated fields** in the SELECT clause. Here are two examples:

```
SELECT QuotedPrice * QuantityOrdered AS ExtendedPrice
```

and

```
SELECT CustFirstName & ' ' & CustLastName AS CustName
```

The first example calculates the product of QuotedPrice and QuantityOrdered and calls the result ExtendedPrice. Then ExtendedPrice acts just like any other field. The second example concatenates CustFirstName and CustLastName, with a literal space in between, and calls the result CustName.

The second variation is to use aggregate functions in the SELECT clause. The aggregate functions available are COUNT, SUM, AVERAGE, MIN, MAX, and a few others. For example, suppose you want to show the number of line items and the total amount spent in the order corresponding to OrderID 17. Then the following SQL statement does the job:

```
SELECT COUNT(ProductID) AS NumberItems, SUM(QuotedPrice * QuantityOrdered) AS TotalSpent
FROM LineItems
WHERE OrderID = 17
```

The COUNT function counts the rows in the LineItems table where OrderID equals 17, and the SUM function sums the products of QuotedPrice and QuantityOrdered for these line items. For the Sales Orders database, this query returns a single row with two numbers: 6 and 4834.98.

Often a SELECT statement with aggregate functions is accompanied by a GROUP BY clause. For example, suppose you want to know how many of the company's customers are in each state. Then the following SQL statement is appropriate:

```
SELECT CustState, COUNT(CustomerID) AS CustomerCount
FROM Customers
GROUP BY CustState
```

Figure 14.9 Results of GROUP BY Query

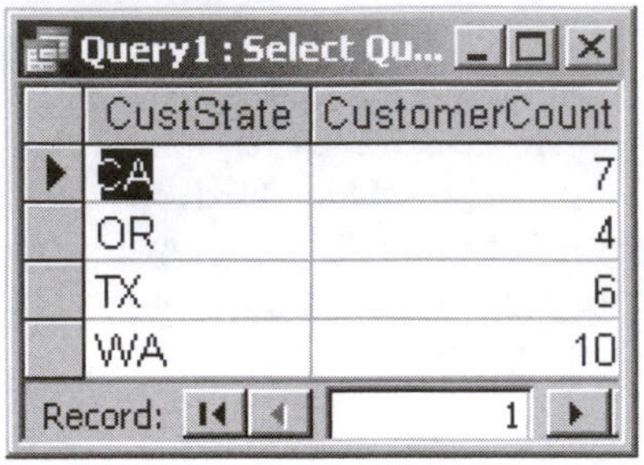

Note that the SELECT clause includes a mix: an individual field name (CustState) and an aggregate (the COUNT function). In this case, the rule is that you *must* GROUP BY each individual field in the list. The result of this query for the Sales Orders database is shown in Figure 14.9. It shows a count of customers in each of the four states represented in the database.

Multitable Queries and Joins

One principal goal of relational databases is to separate data into individual, but related, tables so that data redundancy can be avoided. However, queries often need to access data from two or more tables. In database terminology, the related tables must be **joined**. For example, if you want information on all orders that include the King Cobra Helmet product, a quick look at the relationships diagram in Figure 14.8 shows that you need data from three tables: Orders, LineItems, and Products. The resulting SQL statement might look as follows:

```
SELECT Orders.OrderDate, LineItems.QuotedPrice, LineItems.QuantityOrdered
FROM (Orders INNER JOIN LineItems ON Orders.OrderID = LineItems.OrderID)
    INNER JOIN Products ON LineItems.ProductID = Products.ProductID
WHERE Products.ProductName = 'King Cobra Helmet'
```

The middle two lines make up the FROM clause. The basic syntax for joining two tables is:

```
Table1 INNER JOIN Table2 ON Table1.KeyField1 = Table2.KeyField2
```

The two key fields are typically the primary key from one table and the corresponding foreign key from the other table. Note that each field in the above SQL statement is preceded by a table name and a period, as in **Orders. OrderDate**. This avoids ambiguity, in case the same field name is used in more than one table, and it is a good practice in all multitable queries.

Because this SQL requires a lot of typing, it is common to use **aliases** (short nicknames) for tables, as in the following version of the preceding query.

```
SELECT O.OrderDate, L.QuotedPrice, L.QuantityOrdered
FROM (Orders O INNER JOIN LineItems L ON O.OrderID = L.OrderID)
    INNER JOIN Products P ON L.ProductID = P.ProductID
WHERE P.ProductName = 'King Cobra Helmet'
```

Here, the aliases O, L, and P are defined in the FROM clause. The rule is that if table aliases are defined in a FROM clause, they *must* be used throughout the entire SQL statement.

One final note about multitable queries is that Access requires parentheses in the FROM clause, as shown in the preceding query, if more than two tables are being joined. Essentially, these parentheses indicate that *two* tables are joined at a time. If you wanted information on customers in addition to information on orders and products, the following FROM clause, including the parentheses, would be relevant.

```
FROM ((Customers C INNER JOIN Orders O ON C.CustomerID = O.CustomerID)
    INNER JOIN LineItems L ON O.OrderID = L.OrderID)
    INNER JOIN Products P ON L.ProductID = P.ProductID
```

Admittedly, the syntax takes a bit of getting used to, but the idea is fairly simple. You check which tables hold the data you need, you consult the relationships diagram, and you follow the links.

Again, it can take some time to master SQL, but it is time well spent. If you study the sample queries in the Sales Orders Queries.docx file, you will see that SQL is a relatively simple language, at least for the majority of common queries.

14.5 The Technology: DAO and ADO

To understand the code in this chapter, you must understand relational databases and SQL, but you must also understand the way Microsoft allows VBA programmers to retrieve data from an external database. Its current standard is called **OLE DB**. This is a library of code written in a more complex language (C++) that retrieves data from practically any type of database and transforms the results into a common row-column format. Because OLE DB is too complex for most programmers to work with, several technologies, including **Data Access Objects** (**DAO**) and **ActiveX Data Objects** (**ADO**), have been developed as a go-between. Each of these exposes an object model to VBA programmers. DAO came first, and there are still many corporate applications that use it. Later, Microsoft developed ADO. Its object model is "flatter" than DAO's—there are fewer objects to learn. Both of these technologies allow a developer to write relatively simple code in VBA to retrieve data from an

Figure 14.10 Setting Reference to the ADODB Library

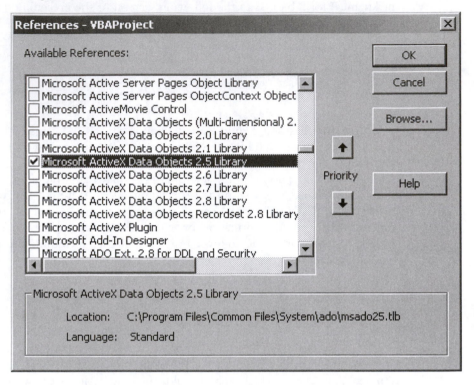

external database. Because ADO is both simpler and more "modern," this chapter focuses entirely on it.

It is important to realize that neither DAO nor ADO is part of the Excel (or Office or VBA) object model. Therefore, the first step in using either DAO or ADO in your VBA code is to set a reference in the VBE. Try it now. Open a blank workbook, get into the VBE, and select the **Tools → References** menu item. You will see a long list of libraries, with a few items at the top checked by default. Now scroll down to the Microsoft ActiveX Data Objects 2.x Library items. As the technology evolves, newer versions are added to this list. My PC lists versions 2.0, 2.1, 2.5, 2.6, 2.7 and 2.8; yours might list others. (See Figure 14.10.)[5] You can check any of these and click on OK. Now you have access to the ADO object model. However, to avoid confusion with other possible libraries, you should refer to ADO objects with the prefix ADODB, such as **ADODB.Connection**. (Why ADODB and not simply ADO? I have no idea.) In fact, once you set a reference to the library and then type ADODB and a period in your code, you will get help about this library from Intellisense. (Also, once you set the reference, the Object Browser provides help about the ADODB library.)

---

[5]If you wanted to use the older DAO technology, you would set a reference to the Microsoft DAO x.x Object Library.

Once a reference to ADO is set, you need to create a **connection** to the database. This requires, at the very least, a reference to the name and location of the database file and information above the **data provider**. Each type of database has a data provider. A data provider is code stored somewhere on your PC that knows how to deal with a particular type of database. It is analogous to the drivers that are provided for various types of printers. There is a provider for Access, Oracle, SQL Server, and other database systems. The provider for Access is called **Microsoft Jet 4.0 OLE DB Provider.**[6]

Once a connection is formed, the next step is usually to open a **recordset** based on an SQL statement. A recordset is a temporary database table (temporary in the sense that it resides only in memory, not as a file on a hard drive). It can be an entire table from the database, or it can be the result of a query.

After the recordset is opened, it is easy to go through its records with a Do loop and retrieve information from any of its fields. A common practice is to use code such as the following:

```
With rs
    Do Until .EOF
        Statements
        .MoveNext
    Loop
End With
```

Here, rs is a **Recordset** object variable. One of its properties is **EOF** (end of file), and one of its methods is **MoveNext**. Very simply, these lines tell the program to go through the rows of the recordset, one at a time, taking some actions in the part called *Statements*, and quitting when the end of the file is reached. The MoveNext method moves to the next row of the table. To capture the data in a field named ProductName, say, a reference to .Fields("ProductName") can be made inside this loop.

A Note on MoveNext Statement. If you use a Do loop in this manner, the .MoveNext line is crucial—and easy to forget. If you forget to include it, as I have done many times, the loop will stay forever in the *first* row of the table, and you will have created an infinite loop. Remember, press Ctrl-Break to exit the infinite loop if this happens to you.

How to Open a Connection

To open a connection to a database, you first declare a **Connection** object, as in the following line:

```
Dim cn as ADODB.Connection
```

---

[6]Version 4.0 is the latest version at the time of this writing. A later version might be available when you read this. However, 4.0 should still work.

Here, cn is the name of the Connection object variable—any generic name could be used—and ADODB indicates that this Connection object comes from the ADODB library. Second, the line

```
Set cn = New ADODB.Connection
```

creates a new instance of a Connection object. Alternatively, these two lines can be combined into the single line.

```
Dim cn as New ADODB.Connection
```

This single line performs two actions: (1) it declares cn as an ADODB. Connection object, and (2) it creates a new **instance** of a Connection object. We say that it **instantiates** a Connection object. Whether you use two separate lines or a single line, the keyword **New** is required. This is an object-oriented programming concept. Before you can work with an object from the ADODB library, you must create an instance of one.

Next, the **ConnectionString** and **Provider** properties are used to specify information about the connection (what type of database it is and where it lives), and the **Open** method of the Connection object is used to actually open the connection. The next few lines illustrate how to open the connection to the **Sales Orders.mdb** file. (Note that this code resides in an Excel file, so **ThisWorkbook.Path** refers to the folder where the Excel file lives. For the connection to succeed, the Access file must be in the *same* folder as the Excel file. Alternatively, you could replace ThisWorkbook.Path with the actual path to the mdb file, assuming you know what it is.)

```
With cn
    .ConnectionString = "Data Source=" & ThisWorkbook.Path & "\SalesOrders.mdb"
    .Provider = "Microsoft Jet 4.0 OLE DB Provider"
    .Open
End With
```

The **ConnectionString** property in the second line must begin with "Data Source=" and be followed by the path and name of the Access database file. The Provider property is the name of the data provider for Access. The Open method opens the connection. Once the data have been obtained, the following line should be used to close the connection.

```
cn.Close
```

How to Open a Recordset

Similarly, a new **Recordset** object with a generic name such as rs must be declared and instantiated with the lines

```
Dim rs as ADODB.Recordset
Set rs = New ADODB.Recordset
```

or the single line

```
Dim rs as New ADODB.Recordset
```

It can then be opened with the line

```
rs.Open SQL, cn
```

Here, SQL is a string variable that contains an SQL statement. In general, the first two arguments of a recordset's Open method are an SQL string (or a table name) and the Connection object that has already been opened. (There are other optional arguments, but they are not discussed here.) As with a Connection object, a Recordset object should be closed with the line

```
rs.Close
```

Then the Close method of the Connection object should be called.

Note that Access does not need to be open to do any of this. In fact, you don't even need to have Access installed on your PC. All you require is the Access database file (the .mdb file) and the knowledge of its location on your hard drive and its structure (table names and field names). Of course, if you want to create your own Access database, you *do* need Access.

On a first reading, this business about connections, recordsets, data providers, and so on, can be intimidating. However, the code varies very little from one application to the next, so there is not as much to learn as you might expect. Besides, the effort required to learn ADO is well worth it due to the power it provides for retrieving external data for your Excel applications.

Importing from Other Database Packages

The examples in this book retrieve data only from Access databases. However, you should be aware that most corporate databases are not stored in Access files that reside on an employee's PC. They are typically stored on a database server—not on a desktop—using either SQL Server, Oracle, or some other server-based database system.[7] Fortunately, ADO can be used with these server-based database

---

[7]SQL Server is Microsoft's server-based database system, whereas Oracle is the flagship product of Oracle Corporation. Oracle holds the largest market share of the database market, but SQL Server is not too far behind.

systems as well as with Access. The only differences are in the ConnectionString and Provider properties of the Connection object. For the ConnectionString, you must specify the server name, the database name, credentials (username and password), and possibly other information. For the Provider, you must specify the type of database system (SQL Server, Oracle, or whatever.)

The credentials in the ConnectionString are particularly important. A company doesn't want unauthorized people accessing its corporate data, so it is the job of the database administrator (DBA) to set up various permissions for company employees. Then, once you enter your username and password in the ConnectionString, the settings in the database system check whether you have permission to do what you are trying to do. For example, you might have permission to run SQL queries that *retrieve* data from tables in a database, but not to run queries that *change* data in tables.

The main point, however, is that once you set the ConnectionString and Provider properties for a particular database, whatever type of database it might be, the rest of the ADO code is *exactly the same* as illustrated in this chapter for Access databases. This is why ADO is so powerful—it applies with very few changes to all relational database systems.

14.6 Discussion of the SalesOrders Exercise

Now that you know the steps required to use ADO in an Excel VBA application, this section explains how to create the Sales Orders application described in Section 14.2. (If you want to follow along on your PC, open the file **Sales Orders.xlsx**, which contains a template for getting started. Otherwise, you can open the **Sales Orders Finished.xlsm** file, which contains the completed application.)

The first step is to design and write event handlers for the user form, called frmProducts, so that it appears as in Figure 14.11 (a copy of Figure 14.2 repeated here for convenience). This form includes the usual OK and Cancel buttons, as well as a list box named lbProducts. You should set the list box's ColumnCount to 2 so that the user sees both the product ID and the product name. This is not just for cosmetic purposes. The rest of the application uses both the ProductID and ProductName fields from the Products table of the database, so they need to be shown in the list box.

The event handlers for this form are listed below. By the time the dialog box appears, code in the **Main** sub (shown later) will have filled the recordset object variable rs with product IDs and product names from the Products table. The **Userform_Initialize** sub populates the list box with the contents of rs. This is a bit tricky. According to online help, a multicolumn list box should be populated by setting its List property to a variant array. Therefore, a 100×2 array, productArray, is first filled by looping through the rows of the recordset. The first column of the array is filled with the ProductID field, and the second column is filled with the ProductName field. (Note that the rows and columns of a list box are necessarily indexed starting at 0, not 1.)

Figure 14.11 Product Selection Dialog Box

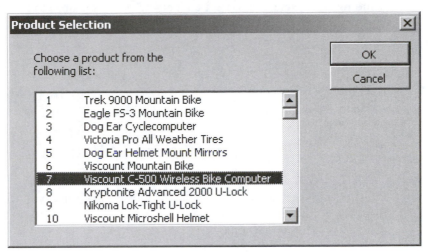

The last line of this sub selects the *first* product in the list by default. Then the **btnOK_Click** sub stores the contents of the selected row of the list box in the Public variables productID and productName for use in the Main sub. Recall from Chapter 11 that the selected row of the list box is provided by the ListIndex property.

```
Private Sub btnCancel_Click()
    Unload Me
    End
End Sub

Private Sub btnOK_Click()
    productID = lbProducts.List(lbProducts.ListIndex, 0)
    productName = lbProducts.List(lbProducts.ListIndex, 1)
    Unload Me
End Sub

Private Sub UserForm_Initialize()
    Dim rowCount As Integer
    Dim productArray(100, 2) As Variant ' Assume no more than 100 products.

    ' Populate the two-column list box with items from the recordset.
    rowCount = 0
    With rs
        Do Until .EOF
            productArray(rowCount, 0) = .Fields("ProductID")
            productArray(rowCount, 1) = .Fields("ProductName")
            rowCount = rowCount + 1
            .MoveNext
        Loop
    End With
    lbProducts.List = productArray
    lbProducts.ListIndex = 0
End Sub
```

The application's single module begins by declaring several Public variables, including the connection object cn and the recordset object rs. Note that these objects are both declared and instantiated in single lines of code.

```
Option Explicit

Public cn As New ADODB.Connection
Public rs As New ADODB.Recordset
Public productID As Integer
Public productName As String
Public topCell As Range
```

The **Main** sub clears any possible previous results (refer back to Figure 14.3), opens the connection to the database, calls a couple of subs to do the work, and finally closes the connection.

```
Sub Main()
    ' Delete any previous results.
    Range("C1") = ""
    Set topCell = Worksheets("Orders").Range("A3")
    With topCell
        Range(.Offset(1, 0), .Offset(1, 4).End(xlDown)).ClearContents
    End With

    ' Open connection to database.
    With cn
        .ConnectionString = "Data Source=" & ThisWorkbook.Path & "\Sales Orders.mdb"
        .Provider = "Microsoft Jet 4.0 OLE DB Provider"
        .Open
    End With

    Call GetProductList
    Call GetOrderInfo

    ' Close the connection.
    cn.Close

    Range("A2").Select
End Sub
```

The **GetProductList** sub creates a straightforward SQL string to obtain the ProductID and ProductName fields from the Products table. Then it opens a recordset, based on this SQL string and the already opened connection, to get the data. When it "shows" frmProducts, the contents of rs are used to populate the form's list box, as discussed earlier. After the form is unloaded (when the user clicks on its OK button), the recordset is closed, but the connection remains open.

```
Sub GetProductList()
    Dim SQL As String

    ' Import product info and use it to populate the list box.
    ' After frmProducts is unloaded, we will know the productID
    ' and productName for the selected product.
    SQL = "SELECT ProductID, ProductName FROM Products"
    rs.Open SQL, cn
    frmProducts.Show
    rs.Close
End Sub
```

Finally, the **GetOrderInfo** sub queries the database for information on all orders that include the selected product. It then uses this data to fill the Orders worksheet. It begins by putting the selected product's name in cell B1. Then it defines an SQL statement. Note that the required data is stored in two related tables, Orders and LineItems. (Refer back to Figure 14.8 for table names and field names.) Therefore, an inner join of these tables is required. (Because the product ID is *known*, there is no need to include the Products table in the join.) To save typing, I use the aliases O and L for the two tables. The SELECT clause lists the desired fields, including the calculated ExtendedPrice field (price times quantity). The WHERE clause indicates that results should be returned only for the selected product. Pay particular attention to the WHERE clause condition. The variable productID contains the ProductID field's value for the selected product, and this field is a foreign key in the LineItems table. Hence, the condition is on this foreign key field. Finally, the ORDER BY clause sorts the returned rows by OrderDate and then OrderID.

```
Sub GetOrderInfo()
    Dim SQL As String
    Dim rowCount As Integer

    Range("B1") = productName

    ' Define SQL statement to get order info for selected product.
    SQL = "SELECT O.OrderID, O.OrderDate, L.QuantityOrdered, " _
        & "L.QuotedPrice, L.QuantityOrdered * L.QuotedPrice AS ExtendedPrice " _
        & "FROM Orders O Inner Join LineItems L ON O.OrderID = L.OrderID " _
        & "WHERE L.ProductID=" & productID & " " _
        & "ORDER BY O.OrderDate, O.OrderID"

    ' Run the query and use results to fill Orders sheet.
    With rs
        .Open SQL, cn
        rowCount = 0
        Do While Not .EOF
            rowCount = rowCount + 1
            topCell.Offset(rowCount, 0) = .Fields("OrderID")
            topCell.Offset(rowCount, 1) = .Fields("OrderDate")
            topCell.Offset(rowCount, 2) = .Fields("QuotedPrice")
```

```
            topCell.Offset(rowCount, 3) = .Fields("QuantityOrdered")
            topCell.Offset(rowCount, 4) = .Fields("ExtendedPrice")
            .MoveNext
        Loop
        .Close
    End With
End Sub
```

The last half of this sub opens the recordset rs, based on the SQL statement and the still-open connection and then loops through its rows to enter the data from the five fields into the Orders worksheet. All cell references are relative to cell A3, indicated by the range variable topCell. Once the results have been transferred to the worksheet, the recordset is closed. Then, in the Main sub, the connection to the database is closed.

A Common Error. When building a fairly long SQL string by string concatenation across several lines, a common error is to run clauses together. In the above SQL statement, note the " " at the end of the next-to-last line. I initially forgot to include this literal space, so the last part of the SQL statement became something like WHERE L.ProductID=6ORDER BY O.OrderDate, O.OrderID. This created a syntax error—there must be spaces between the clauses—and it caused the program to bomb. Unfortunately, this common error can be hard to locate!

Opening and Closing Recordsets. Note that I have used the Public variable rs for both queries in this application. This double use of a recordset variable is perfectly legal, and it is common practice, but you have to remember to close the first use of rs before you can open it for a second use. If you forget to close rs after its first use, you will get the error message "Operation is not allowed when the object is open." Therefore, you should get in the habit of closing a recordset as soon as you have stored its data in variables or in a worksheet.

Although there are a number of details that you have to get just right to make this type of application work properly (such as populating the two-column list box correctly), it is amazing that so much can be accomplished with so little code. As you see, ADO is not only powerful, but it results in very compact VBA code.

14.7   Summary

As demonstrated throughout this book, the ability to automate Excel with VBA programs makes you a very useful employee. Given the importance of corporate databases in today's business environment, your usefulness elevates to a whole new level when you can write programs to import external data into your Excel applications. Fortunately, a little knowledge of relational databases, SQL, and ADO goes a long way toward getting you to this level.

EXERCISES

1. Based on the Sales Orders database, write SQL statements to implement the following queries. Run them in Access to ensure that they work properly.
   a. Find the OrderDate for all orders placed by the customer with CustomerID 13.
   b. Find the OrderDate for all orders placed by the customer with first name Mark and last name Rosales.
   c. Find the number of orders placed by the customer in part **b**.
   d. Find the ProductName for all products supplied by the vendor with VendorID 3.
   e. Find the ProductName for all products supplied by the vendor Armadillo Brand.
   f. Find the number of products in each product category.
   g. Find the total dollar value of all products in each product category (RetailPrice times QuantityOnHand). The results should be grouped by category. That is, there should be a row in the result for each category.

2. The trickiest part of the Sales Orders application (at least for me) was filling the two-column list box correctly in the **Userform_Initialize** sub. Here is an alternative. In the Properties window for the list box, set the **RowSource** property to ProductList. Then write code in the **GetProductList** sub (before the **frmProducts.Show** line) to fill a range starting in cell AA1 of the Orders sheet with the product numbers (column AA) and product names (column AB) from the Products table. Then name the resulting two-column range ProductList. Now all of the code in the Userform_Initialize sub can be omitted except the last line that sets the ListIndex property to 0.

3. Change the Sales Orders application so that it asks the user for the location and name of the database file. After all, there is no reason to believe that it resides in the same folder as the application itself. You could do this with an input box (and risk having the user spell something wrong), but Excel provides an easier way with the **FileDialog** object as illustrated in Chapter 13 (or the **GetOpenFilename** method of the **Application** object if you prefer). Use either of these to change the application so that it prompts the user for the name and location of the database file. Actually, you should probably precede the above line with a MsgBox statement so that the user knows she's being asked to select the file with the data. Then try the modified application with a renamed version of the .mbd file, stored in a folder *different* from the folder containing the Excel application.

4. Develop an application similar to the Sales Orders application that again uses data from the Sales Orders database. This application should show a user form that lists the CategoryID and CategoryDescription fields from the Categories table in a two-column list box. Once the user selects a category, the application should display all information about the products (all fields in the Products table) for the

selected product category. This information should be placed in a worksheet called Products.

5. Develop an application similar to the Sales Orders application that again uses data from the Sales Orders database. This application should show a user form that lists the CustomerID field and a CustomerName calculated field from the Customers table in a two-column list box. (The calculated field should be a concatenation of the CustFirstName and CustLastName fields. It should be defined in an SQL statement.) Once the user selects a customer, the application should display all information about the orders placed by the selected customer. Specifically, it should show the OrderDate and TotalCost for each order, sorted by OrderDate. TotalCost should be a calculated field, the sum over all items in the LineItems table of QuantityOrdered times QuotedPrice. In other words, for each order, TotalCost is the total amount the customer spent for the order. This information should be placed in a worksheet called CustomerOrders.

6. Develop an application that is a combination of the application in the chapter and the previous problem. Specifically, a userform should show two two-column list boxes, one for customers (as in the previous problem) and one for products. When the user selects a customer and a product, the application should display OrderDate, QuotedPrice, QuantityOrdered, and ExtendedPrice for each order for the selected product placed by the selected customer.

Working with Pivot Tables and Excel 2007 Tables

15.1 Introduction

Excel's pivot tables and associated pivot charts are among its best features. They let you view data sets in all sorts of ways. For example, if a data set shows a daily company's sales in each state where it has stores, you can easily view sales totals by month, by state, or by both. Pivot tables are not only useful, but they are extremely powerful, and they are very easy to use. All you need to do is drag and drop to obtain summary results in a matter of seconds. With such a simple user interface, it might appear that there is no need to manipulate pivot tables with VBA code, and this is often the case. However, everything you can do manually with pivot tables, you can also do with VBA. This could be particularly useful if your job is to develop an executive information system for your boss, who wants to obtain results quickly and easily with the click of a button or two. In this chapter I briefly discuss the manual way of creating and manipulating pivot tables, just in case you have never been introduced to them, and then I illustrate the pivot table "object model" that allows you to create and manipulate pivot tables with VBA.

In addition to pivot tables, Microsoft introduced **tables** in Excel 2007. These are especially useful for sorting and filtering a data set. Much of the functionality of tables has been in Excel for years, but it is now more powerful and easier to use. Interestingly, there is no new Table object in the Excel 2007 object model, but there is a **ListObject** object for working with tables, and this ListObject object is *not* new to Excel 2007. "Tables" were referred to as **lists** in previous versions of Excel, and it was possible to manipulate them with VBA. Now there are more possibilities, as I will discuss briefly in this chapter.

15.2 Working with Pivot Tables Manually

To create a pivot table, you must start with a data set. This data set can reside in an Excel worksheet or in an external database, such as Access, SQL Server, or Oracle. For simplicity, I assume in this chapter that the data set resides in an Excel worksheet. In that case, it should be in the form shown in Figure 15.1 (with many rows hidden). This data set contains sales transactions, one per row, for a direct marketing company over some period of time. (It is in the **Sales Data.xlsx** file.) There is one row for each transaction, and each column contains some attribute of the transaction. In database terminology, the columns are often called **fields**.

This is the typical type of data set where pivot tables are useful. There are some numeric fields, such as NumberOrders and AmountSpent, that you would

Figure 15.1 Sales Data Set

	A	B	C	D	E	F	G	H
1	Age	Gender	OwnHome	Married	Salary	Catalogs	NumberOrders	AmountSpent
2	Young	Female	No	No	Low	12	4	$1,508
3	Middle-aged	Female	Yes	Yes	High	18	3	$651
4	Middle-aged	Male	Yes	Yes	High	12	4	$1,045
5	Senior	Male	Yes	Yes	Low	12	1	$175
6	Young	Male	No	No	Low	6	2	$432
7	Middle-aged	Female	No	No	Medium	12	1	$62
8	Middle-aged	Female	No	No	Medium	18	3	$890
999	Middle-aged	Male	Yes	Yes	High	18	5	$1,505
1000	Middle-aged	Female	No	Yes	High	24	6	$824
1001	Middle-aged	Male	Yes	Yes	High	24	1	$258

Figure 15.2 Pivot Table Dialog Box

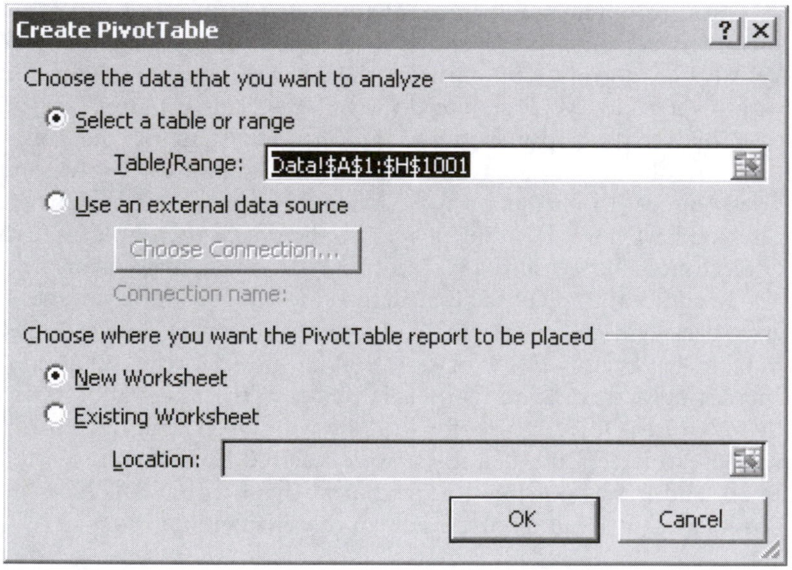

like to summarize, and there are categorical fields, such as Age and Gender, that you would like to break the summary measures down by.

To create a pivot table, make sure your cursor is inside the data range, and click on the PivotTable button on the Insert ribbon.[1] You will see the dialog box in Figure 15.2. Fill it out as shown. The data set in this example lives in an Excel worksheet (you can override Excel's guess for the data range, but it's usually correct), and you want the results to be placed on a new worksheet. (This dialog box replaces a three-step wizard in previous versions of Excel.)

When you click on Finish, you get a new worksheet with a blank pivot table, shown on the left of Figure 15.3. (This worksheet has a generic sheet name, which

---

[1]The user interface for creating and working with pivot tables changed significantly in Excel 2007. All screen shots and explanations in this chapter are geared to Excel 2007.

Figure 15.3 Blank Pivot Table and PivotTable Field List Pane

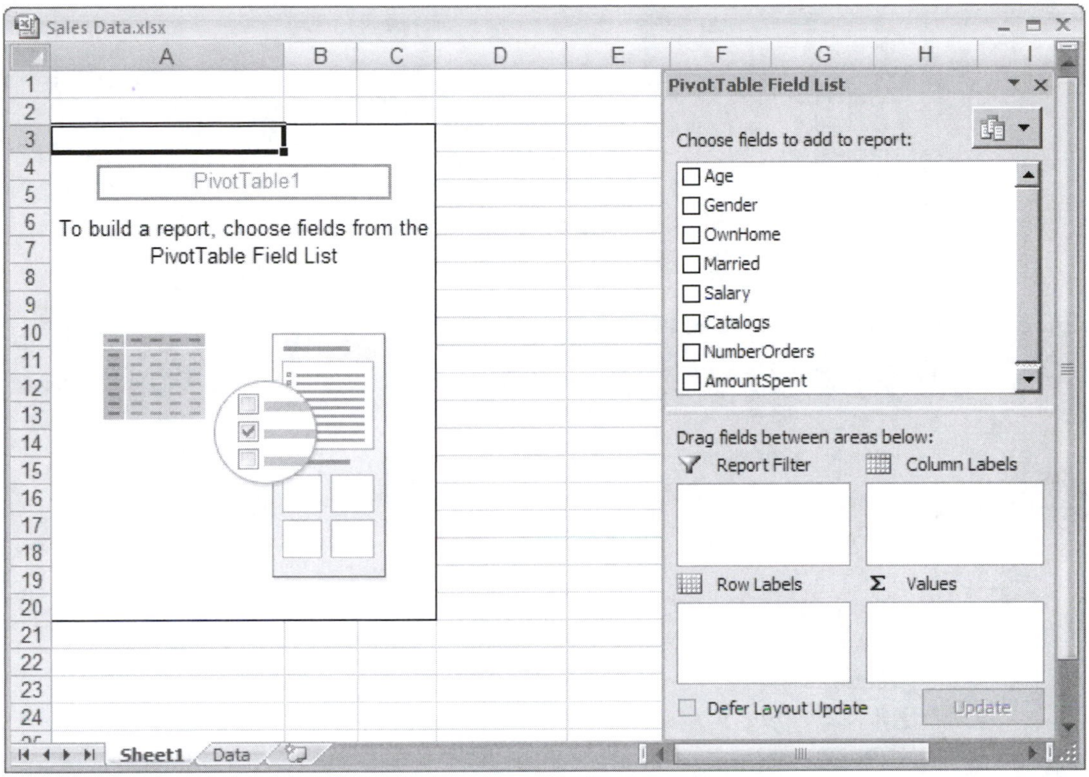

Figure 15.4 PivotTable Tools Ribbons

you'll probably want to change.) This blank pivot table sheet is accompanied by the PivotTable Field List pane on the right of Figure 15.3 and two new PivotTable Tools ribbons, Options and Design, in Figure 15.4. (If you ever lose either of these just put the cursor inside the pivot table, and they will reappear.) The pivot table has four "areas": Row, Column, Report Filter, and Values. The first three are typically for categorical fields you want to summarize by. The Values area is typically for numeric fields you want to summarize. You can move any of the fields to any of the areas by dragging from the field list to the appropriate pivot table area.

The pivot table in Figure 15.5 is typical. I dragged Age to the row area, Gender to the column area, Married to the report filter area, and AmountSpent to the values area. (See Figure 15.6.) The results show the sum of amount spent for each combination of Age and Gender. For example, the total of all orders from

Figure 15.5 Typical Pivot Table

	A	B	C	D
1	Married	(All) ▼		
2				
3	Sum of AmountSpent	Column Labels ▼		
4	Row Labels ▼	Female	Male	Grand Total
5	Middle-aged	178087	267211	445298
6	Senior	109529	64067	173596
7	Young	156296	102596	258892
8	Grand Total	443912	433874	877786

Figure 15.6 Corresponding Field List Pane

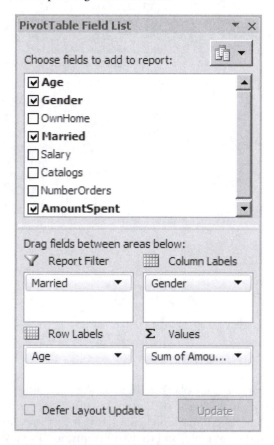

middle-aged females was $178,087, whereas the total of all orders from young people of both genders was $258,892.

If you want this breakdown only for married people, click on the dropdown arrow in cell B1 and select Yes. The results for this subset of married people appears in Figure 15.7, which illustrates the role of the report filter area. However, the report filter field is optional; you don't have to have a field in this area.

If you don't care about Gender, drag Gender from the pivot table field list to get the results in Figure 15.8. This illustrates that you don't need both a row field

Figure 15.7 Results for Married People Only

	A	B	C	D
1	Married	Yes		
2				
3	Sum of AmountSpent	Column Labels		
4	Row Labels	Female	Male	Grand Total
5	Middle-aged	102809	156800	259609
6	Senior	64468	48479	112947
7	Young	36709	39193	75902
8	**Grand Total**	203986	244472	448458

Figure 15.8 Relsults After Dragging Gender Off Column Area

	A	B
1	Married	Yes
2		
3	Row Labels	Sum of AmountSpent
4	Middle-aged	259609
5	Senior	112947
6	Young	75902
7	**Grand Total**	448458

Figure 15.9 Value Field Settings Dialog Box

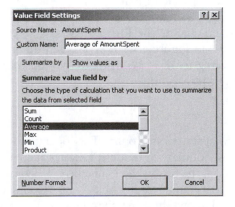

and a column field; you can have only one or the other. Actually, you can have more than one row or column field, but the pivot table becomes more difficult to read when you have multiple fields in either area.

If you'd rather have Gender in the row area and Age in the column area, it's easy. Just drag Gender to the row area and then drag Age to the column area. Now you should be starting to see why pivot tables are so powerful and easy to use.

Recall that AmountSpent was dragged to the values area. When you do this with a numeric variable such as AmountSpent, it is automatically summarized by the Sum operator. There are several other possible summary operators. Right-click on any number in the pivot table, and select the **Value Field Settings** menu item. (I have boldfaced this item because you will use it often.) This brings up the dialog box in Figure 15.9. You can choose any of the

Figure 15.10   Average of AmountSpent Formatted as Currency

	A	B
1	Married	Yes
2		
3	Row Labels ▼	Average of AmountSpent
4	Middle-aged	$883.02
5	Senior	$882.40
6	Young	$948.78
7	**Grand Total**	**$893.34**

Figure 15.11   Pivot Table with Counts

	A	B	C	D
1	Married	(All)		
2				
3	Count	Column Labels ▼		
4	Row Labels ▼	Female	Male	Grand Total
5	Middle-aged	206	302	508
6	Senior	129	76	205
7	Young	171	116	287
8	**Grand Total**	**506**	**494**	**1,000**

summary operators, such as Average. The text in the Custom Name box changes accordingly. Note, however, that this text is just the label you see at the top of the pivot table; you can change it if you like. Also, if you want to change the number formatting in the pivot table, here is the place to do so. Click on the Number button and change the formatting, say, to currency with two decimals. The results appear in Figure 15.10. Now each dollar figure is an average of the corresponding category. For example, the young married people spent an average of $948.78 per transaction.

Working with Counts

Note that one of the summary operators is Count. This operator requires some explanation. If you summarize by Count, then it doesn't matter at all which variable is in the values area. For this reason, the text in the Name box in Figure 15.9 can be misleading. I like to change it to "Count" rather than, say, "Count of Amount-Spent". For example, Figure 15.11 shows the same pivot table as in Figure 15.5, but summarized by Count, not Sum. Each number in the pivot table is now a count of the transactions for each category combination. For example, 116 of the 1000 transactions were made by young males, and 205 of the transactions were made by seniors. The variable in the values area is still AmountSpent, but this is completely irrelevant; any other variable in the data area would produce exactly the same counts.

Suppose you want to know the percentage of transactions made by females versus males for each age group. Starting from the pivot table in Figure 15.11, right-click on any of the counts and select Value Field Settings. In the resulting dialog box, select the **Show values as** tab, and select % **of row** in the dropdown (see Figure 15.12). (You can experiment with the other options.) This produces the results in Figure 15.13. For example, almost 63% of all transactions made by seniors were made by females.

Figure 15.12 Changing the Show Data As Option

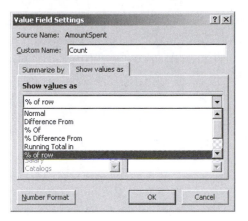

Figure 15.13 Counts Shown as Percentages of Row

	A	B	C	D
1	Married	(All)		
2				
3	Count	Column Labels		
4	Row Labels	Female	Male	Grand Total
5	Middle-aged	40.55%	59.45%	100.00%
6	Senior	62.93%	37.07%	100.00%
7	Young	59.58%	40.42%	100.00%
8	**Grand Total**	**50.60%**	**49.40%**	**100.00%**

As mentioned earlier, it is common to put categorical variables in the row and column areas and numeric variables in the values area. But this is not required. Try the following. Drag everything off the current pivot table, and then drag Amount-Spent to the row area and any categorical variable such as Salary to the values area. Note that when you drag a categorical (nonnumeric) variable to the values area, it is automatically summarized by Count, which is what you want here. Unfortunately, the resulting pivot table isn't very informative. Every distinct value of AmountSpent is listed in column A, so you get a very "tall" pivot table. Fortunately, this can be fixed. Right-click on any value in column A, and select Group to bring up the dialog box in Figure 15.14. You can change the default settings if you like. For example, I changed the bottom entry to 200 and obtained the pivot table shown in Figure 15.15.

Remember that when the data area is summarized by Count, the variable in the data area is irrelevant. So although the label in cell A3 is "Count of Salary", the numbers in column B are really just counts of the various AmountSpent groupings. For example, 116 of the transactions had an amount spent from $1024 to $1223 (inclusive). For this reason, it would be better to get into the Field Settings

Figure 15.14 Group Dialog Box

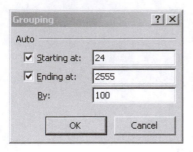

Figure 15.15 Pivot Table Grouped By AmountSpent

	A	B
1		
2		
3	Row Labels ▾	Count of Salary
4	24-223	91
5	224-423	142
6	424-623	142
7	624-823	108
8	824-1023	131
9	1024-1223	116
10	1224-1423	104
11	1424-1623	79
12	1624-1823	52
13	1824-2023	24
14	2024-2223	6
15	2224-2423	4
16	2424-2623	1
17	**Grand Total**	**1000**

dialog box and change the text in the Custom Name box from "Count of Salary" to "Count", as discussed earlier.

Pivot Charts

Once you have a pivot table, you can easily create a corresponding **pivot chart**. To do so, make sure the cursor is inside the pivot table, and click on the PivotChart button on the PivotTable Tools/Options ribbon. (See Figure 15.4.) From there, you can choose the type of chart you want. When you make changes to the pivot table, the pivot chart updates accordingly—and automatically. For example, the pivot chart corresponding to the pivot table in Figure 15.15 is shown in Figure 15.16. This pivot chart is every bit as "interactive" as the pivot table. You can drag fields to or from its areas, and you can select items from its dropdowns. Whatever changes you make to the pivot chart are made to the pivot table as well. In addition, the chart is just like any other Excel chart, so, for example, you can change the type of chart from a column chart to a line chart if you like, you can change the chart title, and so on.

This discussion has barely scratched the surface of what you can do with pivot tables. However, it has already given you a glimpse of how powerful they are and how easy they are to manipulate. In the next section I illustrate how these same operations can be performed with VBA.

Figure 15.16   Pivot Chart

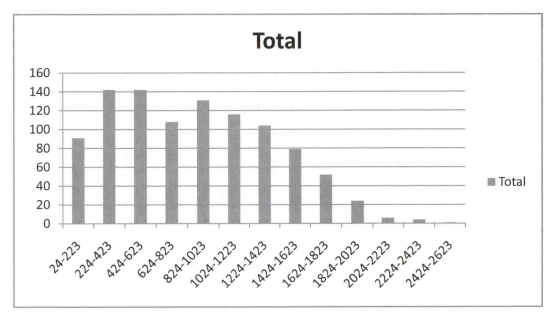

15.3 Working with Pivot Tables Using VBA

You might remember the discussion of charts and VBA in Chapter 8. I mention this discussion because you can manipulate so many parts of charts in so many ways. The part of Excel's object model that deals with charts is quite complex. There are numerous of objects and each has many properties and methods. The same applies to pivot tables and pivot charts. If you want to learn the part of VBA that deals with pivot tables, you could spend a lot of time exploring the various objects and their properties and methods. I will try to keep it simple here, exploring only the parts you are most likely to use in applications.

First, just as with charts, you can use VBA to build a pivot table from scratch and then manipulate it. Alternatively, and more easily, you can form a blank pivot table (as in Figure 15.3) manually and then use VBA to populate it. I will briefly illustrate pivot table creation with VBA, and then I will discuss pivot table manipulation with VBA in a bit more depth.

Creating a Pivot Table with VBA

When you create a pivot table manually, Excel actually stores the data that the pivot table is based on in a cache (short-term memory). The notion of a cache for your pivot table data is important in understanding the VBA required to create a pivot table. There are two key objects: the **PivotCache** object and the **PivotTable** object. To create a pivot table in VBA, you first create a PivotCache object, and then you create a PivotTable object based on the PivotCache object. Actually, you can create multiple pivot tables from the *same* cache.

The code below is a slightly modified version I obtained by turning the recorder on and creating a pivot table. This pivot table was based on a data set with range name Data. There were no pivot tables yet in this workbook, so a PivotCache had to be created first. Then the pivot table was created from the cache. Although I named both the new worksheet and the new pivot table as PT1, they could have different names. (Note that version 12 refers to Excel 2007. The Version and DefaultVersion arguments are optional.)

```
Sub CreatePivotTable()
    Sheets.Add
    ActiveSheet.Name = "PT1"
    ActiveWorkbook.PivotCaches.Create(SourceType:=xlDatabase, _
            SourceData:="Data", Version:=xlPivotTableVersion12) _
        .CreatePivotTable TableDestination:=Range("A3"), _
            TableName:="PT1", DefaultVersion:=xlPivotTableVersion12
    Range("A3").Select
End Sub
```

I then recorded code to create another pivot table, with the results below. Note that it uses the pivot cache associated with PT1 to create the second pivot table. I could have based it on a new cache, but this would be a waste of memory.

```
Sub CreateAnotherPivotTable()
    Sheets.Add
    ActiveSheet.Name = "PT2"
    ActiveWorkbook.Worksheets("PT1").PivotTables("PT1").PivotCache _
        .CreatePivotTable TableDestination:=Range("A3"), _
            TableName:="PT2", DefaultVersion:=xlPivotTableVersion12
    Range("A3").Select
End Sub
```

The resulting pivot tables from these two subs have nothing in them. Each is just a "shell" of a pivot table. However, now it is possible to use the properties and methods of PivotTable objects to populate a blank pivot table. This is discussed next.

Manipulating Pivot Tables

To manipulate an existing pivot table, you rely heavily on the **PivotFields** collection. This is a list of all fields from the data set. There is also an **AddFields** method of a PivotTable object. This generally gives you two ways to add a field to an area of a pivot table. Specifically, suppose PT has been set equal to an existing pivot table. Then either of the following two lines adds Gender to the row area:

```
PT.AddFields RowFields:="Gender"
```

or

```
PT.PivotFields("Gender").Orientation = xlRowField
```

The first statement uses the AddFields method, which takes arguments such as RowFields to specify where the added fields are placed. The second statement sets the **Orientation** property of a **PivotField** object to one of several possibilities: xlRowField, xlColumnField, xlPageField, xlDataField, and xlHidden.

The first statement can be generalized to add several fields at once, as in

```
PT.AddFields RowFields:="Gender", ColumnFields:="Age", PageFields:="Married"
```

In fact, you can even use it to add multiple fields to a given area by specifying an array, as in

```
PT.AddFields RowFields:=Array("Gender","Age"), ColumnFields:="Married"
```

However, the AddFields method cannot be used to place fields in the data area. To do this, you must use the Orientation property, as in

```
PT.PivotFields("AmountSpent").Orientation = xlDataField
```

As long as you are at it, you might also want to set other properties of a data field. These include the **Function** property, which specifies how the variable is summarized (Sum, Count, and so on), and the **NumberFormat** property, which uses the same format codes as regular number formatting. Here is one possibility.

```
With  PT.PivotFields("AmountSpent")
    .Orientation = xlDataField
    .Function = xlSum
    .NumberFormat = "$#,##0.0"
End  With
```

If you want to get rid of a field in some area on the pivot table, set its orientation to **xlHidden**, as in

```
PT.PivotFields("Gender").Orientation = xlHidden
```

If you have several fields in the data area, you can get rid of all of them with the line

```
PT.PivotFields("Data").Orientation = xlHidden
```

Figure 15.17 Variable Selection Dialog Box

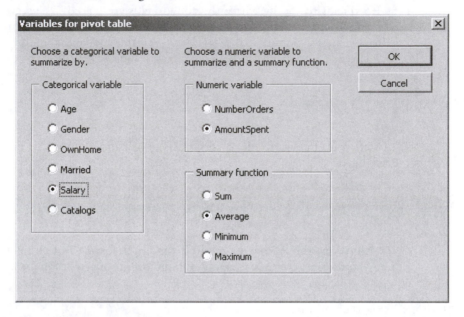

Figure 15.18 Item Selection Dialog Box

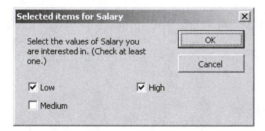

15.4 An Example

Using the same sales data as in the Section 15.2, I now illustrate a simple but useful application. (It is stored in the file **Sales Data with VBA.xlsm**.) It first uses the code illustrated in the previous section to create a pivot table named Pivot-Table1 on a sheet of the same name. Alternatively, this step could be done manually. At this point there is a blank pivot table. The user then clicks on a button on the Data sheet that runs a Report sub (listed later). This sub first shows two user forms, frmVariables and then frmItems. The first form, shown in Figure 15.17, allows the user to select a categorical variable for the row area, a numeric variable for the data area, and a function to summarize by.

The second form, shown in Figure 15.18, lets the user select any of the items (categories) for the selected categorical variable. Note that the categories and the prompt are both based on the variable selected in the first form.

Figure 15.19 Typical Result

Figure 15.20 Pivot Table Results Are Based On

	A	B
1	Average of AmountSpent	
2	Salary ▼	Total
3	High	$916.19
4	Low	$889.15
5	Medium	$850.67
6	Grand Total	$877.79

The program then fills a pivot table (behind the scenes), and for each item checked in the second form, it displays a message box like the one shown in Figure 15.19. The pivot table itself is shown in Figure 15.20.

The first form, frmVariables, is straightforward. Its event handlers are listed below. The btnOK_Click sub captures three public variables, rowVariable, dataVariable, and summaryFunction, for later use.

```
Private Sub btnCancel_Click()
    Unload Me
    End
End Sub

Private Sub btnOK_Click()
    Select Case True
        Case optAge.Value
            rowVariable = "Age"
        Case optGender.Value
            rowVariable = "Gender"
        Case optMarried.Value
            rowVariable = "Married"
        Case optOwnHome.Value
            rowVariable = "OwnHome"
        Case optSalary.Value
            rowVariable = "Salary"
        Case optCatalogs.Value
            rowVariable = "Catalogs"
    End Select
    Select Case True
        Case optNOrders.Value
            dataVariable = "NumberOrders"
        Case optAmtSpent.Value
```

```
            dataVariable = "AmountSpent"
    End Select
    Select Case True
        Case optSum.Value
            summaryFunction = "Sum"
        Case optAvg.Value
            summaryFunction = "Average"
        Case optMin.Value
            summaryFunction = "Min"
        Case optMax.Value
            summaryFunction = "Max"
    End Select
    Unload Me
End Sub

Private Sub UserForm_Initialize()
    optGender.Value = True
    optAmtSpent.Value = True
    optAvg.Value = True
End Sub
```

The second form, frmItems, is listed below. The UserForm_Initialize sub sets up the checkboxes depending on the value of rowVariable. Note that the most categories in any categorical variable is 4, so the form has four checkboxes. However, some of these are hidden in case rowVariable has fewer than four categories. Then the btnOK_Click sub captures the items checked and the number checked in the array rowItem and the variable nChecked. This sub also ensures that the user selects at least one item.

```
Private Sub btnCancel_Click()
    Unload Me
    End
End Sub
Private Sub btnOK_Click()
    Dim iItem As Integer
    Dim ctl As Control

    For Each ctl In Me.Controls
        If TypeName(ctl) = "CheckBox" Then
            If ctl.Value Then
                nChecked = nChecked + 1
            End If
        End If
    Next

    If nChecked = 0 Then
        MsgBox "You must check at least one."
        Exit Sub
    End If

    iItem = 0
    For Each ctl In Me.Controls
        If TypeName(ctl) = "CheckBox" Then
            If ctl.Value Then
                iItem = iItem + 1
                ReDim Preserve rowItem(iItem)
                rowItem(iItem) = ctl.Caption
            End If
```

```
        End If
    Next
    Unload Me
End Sub

Private Sub UserForm_Initialize()
    Me.Caption = "Selected items for " & rowVariable
    lblPrompt.Caption = "Select the values of " & rowVariable _
        & " you are interested in. (Check at least one.)"
    chk1.Value = True
    chk2.Value = False
    chk3.Value = False
    chk4.Value = False
    Select Case rowVariable
        Case "Age"
            chk1.Caption = "Young"
            chk2.Caption = "Middle-aged"
            chk3.Caption = "Senior"
            chk3.Visible = True
            chk4.Visible = False
        Case "Gender"
            chk1.Caption = "Male"
            chk2.Caption = "Female"
            chk3.Visible = False
            chk4.Visible = False
        Case "Married"
            chk1.Caption = "Yes"
            chk2.Caption = "No"
            chk3.Visible = False
            chk4.Visible = False
        Case "OwnHome"
            chk1.Caption = "Yes"
            chk2.Caption = "No"
            chk3.Visible = False
            chk4.Visible = False
        Case "Salary"
            chk1.Caption = "Low"
            chk2.Caption = "Medium"
            chk3.Caption = "High"
            chk3.Visible = True
            chk4.Visible = False
        Case "Catalogs"
            chk1.Caption = "6"
            chk2.Caption = "12"
            chk3.Caption = "18"
            chk4.Caption = "24"
            chk3.Visible = True
            chk4.Visible = True
    End Select
End Sub
```

The Report sub, listed below, shows the two forms and then fills the already existing pivot table. It first clears all fields in the data area by setting the Orientation property to xlHidden. It then adds the rowVariable field to the row area, and it adds the dataVariable field to the data area, formatting it appropriately and setting its summarizing function to summaryFunction. For each item selected in the second form, it then uses the GetPivotData method of a

PivotTable object. This method allows you to set a reference to a particular cell in the pivot table. You must supply enough information to specify the cell: the data variable, the row variable, and the particular item for the row variable. (If there were also a column variable, you would have to specify information about it as well.) Finally, a message box is displayed for each item the user specified in the second form.

```vba
Sub Report()
    Dim PT As PivotTable
    Dim tableItemCell() As Range
    Dim iItem As Integer

    ' Get user's choices.
    frmVariables.Show
    frmItems.Show

    ReDim tableItemCell(nChecked)

    ' The pivot table is already created. Its default name is PivotTable1.
    Set PT = Worksheets("PivotTable1").PivotTables("PivotTable1")
    With PT
        ' Clear any old items in the Data area. Note that this would cause
        ' an error if there is currently no item in the Data area.
        On Error Resume Next
        .PivotFields("Data").Orientation = xlHidden

        ' Add the selected row (categorical) field
        .AddFields RowFields:=rowVariable

        ' Add the selected data field, formatted and summarized appropriately.
        With .PivotFields(dataVariable)
            .Orientation = xlDataField
            If dataVariable = "NumberOrders" Then
                .NumberFormat = "0.0"
            Else
                .NumberFormat = "$#,##0.00"
            End If
            Select Case summaryFunction
                Case "Sum"
                    .Function = xlSum
                Case "Average"
                    .Function = xlAverage
                Case "Min"
                    .Function = xlMin
                Case "Max"
                    .Function = xlMax
            End Select
        End With

        ' Get the single summary data item from the pivot table.
        For iItem = 1 To nChecked
            Set tableItemCell(iItem) = _
                    .GetPivotData(dataVariable, rowVariable, rowItem(iItem))
        Next
    End With

    ' Display the results.
    For iItem = 1 To nChecked
```

```
        MsgBox "The " & summaryFunction & " of " _
            & dataVariable & " for the " & rowItem(iItem) _
            & " category of the variable " & rowVariable & " is " _
            & IIf(dataVariable = "NumberOrders", Format(tableItemCell(iItem), "0.0"), _
            Format(tableItemCell(iItem).Value, "$#,##0")) & ".", vbInformation
    Next
End Sub
```

Note the **IIf** (Immediate If) function in the MsgBox statement. This is a very handy VBA function that works just like Excel's If function. You supply a condition and then two arguments—one for when the condition is true and one for when it is false. This immediate If is used to format as decimal or currency depending on whether the dataVariable is NumberOrders or AmountSpent.

Clearly, if you know how to work with pivot tables manually, you could get these types of results much more easily than by writing a lot of VBA code. However, if your boss wants the results and doesn't know a thing about pivot tables, then he will really appreciate this type of application. In fact, you could hide the pivot table sheet, and your boss would never even know that it exists.

15.5 Working with Excel Tables Manually

As I stated in the introduction to this chapter, a **table** is a new feature of Excel 2007. Tables have always been around, and they were referred to as **lists**, **data sets**, or even **tables** in previous versions of Excel, but Microsoft has now given them "official" status with plenty of useful functionality. Tables are used primarily to sort, filter and summarize data. They don't replicate the functionality of pivot tables—not by a long shot—but they enable you to perform relatively simple data analysis very easily. In this section, I will illustrate some of the main features of Excel tables and how you can work with them manually. Then in the next section, I will illustrate how you can automate these tasks with VBA. As with pivot tables, you might never need to use VBA to manipulate tables, given the ease of working with them through Excel's user interface, but it is good to know that everything you can do manually, you can also do with VBA.

The file I will use for illustration is **MBA Students.xlsx**. It contains information on a sample of 1000 (fictional) MBA students, a small subset of which is shown in Figure 15.21. This is exactly what I mean by a *table*: a rectangular array of data, where each row has information about a student, each column is an attribute of the students, and the columns have names at the top. However, before you can use the new functionality of tables, you must *designate* the data set as a table. To do so, click on the **Table** button on the Insert ribbon. (Make sure your cursor is somewhere inside the data set when you do so.) This does four things: (1) it colors the range nicely, (2) it inserts dropdown arrows next to each column name (see Figure 15.22), (3) it gives the resulting table a generic name such as Table 1 (which you can change to something more descriptive), and (4) it gives you a new **Table Tools Design** ribbon that is visible when your cursor is inside the table (see Figure 15.23).

Figure 15.21 MBA Student Data

	A	B	C	D	E	F	G	H	I	J	K	L
1	Student	Age	Gender	Nationality	Married	Children	Year in program	Undergrad major	GMAT score	Previous salary	Monthly expenses	School debt
2	1	28	Female	South America	No	0	2	Finance		55000	1210	32200
3	2	27	Male	US	No	0	2	Other business	663	44600	570	20000
4	3	28	Female	US	No	0	2	Engineering		43500	1850	53500
5	4	26	Male	China	Yes	1	2	Other business		37000	1300	91300
6	5	36	Male	US	No	0	1	Marketing	666	88600	1420	11100
7	6	29	Female	Europe	No	0	2	Marketing	658	41900	1310	49000
8	7	33	Female	US	Yes	1	1	Marketing		59000	1950	30400
9	8	37	Male	US	Yes	0	2	Other non-business	750	60400	870	19000
10	9	31	Male	Japan	No	0	2	Other business		49500	1090	32900
11	10	29	Female	US	Yes	1	1	Finance	669	65700	1570	18700

Figure 15.22 Table with Dropdown Arrows

	A	B	C	D	E	F	G	H	I	J	K	L
1	Student	Age	Gender	Nationality	Married	Children	Year in program	Undergrad major	GMAT score	Previous salary	Monthly expenses	School debt
2	1	28	Female	South America	No	0	2	Finance		55000	1210	32200
3	2	27	Male	US	No	0	2	Other business	663	44600	570	20000
4	3	28	Female	US	No	0	2	Engineering		43500	1850	53500
5	4	26	Male	China	Yes	1	2	Other business		37000	1300	91300
6	5	36	Male	US	No	0	1	Marketing	666	88600	1420	11100
7	6	29	Female	Europe	No	0	2	Marketing	658	41900	1310	49000
8	7	33	Female	US	Yes	1	1	Marketing		59000	1950	30400
9	8	37	Male	US	Yes	0	2	Other non-business	750	60400	870	19000
10	9	31	Male	Japan	No	0	2	Other business		49500	1090	32900
11	10	29	Female	US	Yes	1	1	Finance	669	65700	1570	18700

Figure 15.23 Table Tools Design Ribbon

Although there are many things you can now do with the table, I will illustrate only the most common, and these are so easy that you can learn them with just a few minutes of practice. In the rest of this section, I will lead you through some operations. After you try these, you should be comfortable experimenting on your own.

Sorting

Suppose you want to sort first on Nationality, then (in case of ties) on Gender, with Males at the top, and finally (again in case of ties) on Age. To do this, you go in *backwards* order. First, click on the Age dropdown and select the A-Z option. Next, click on the Gender dropdown and select the Z-A option (because we want Males at the top). Finally, click on the Nationality dropdown and select the A-Z option. If you'd rather get back to the original sort order, just sort on the Student dropdown in column A. (An index for the records, as this data set has in column A, is useful for exactly this purpose: to get data back in an original sort order.)

Note that you can even sort by color. I guess this could come in handy, and it certainly sounds cool, but unfortunately, I haven't yet found an example where it is useful.

Filtering

You might have used Excel's Autofilter in previous versions of Excel. This is basically what you get "for free" with Excel 2007 tables. Try the following.

- Filter out all but the US students. To do so, click on the Nationality drop-down and uncheck all nationalities but US. (A quicker way is to uncheck the Select All item and then check US.) You will see blue row numbers, meaning that some rows have been hidden, that is, filtered out. You will also see a filter icon in the Nationality dropdown, indicating that a filter is in place. You could get clear this filter by clicking on the Nationality dropdown and selecting the Clear Filter option, but don't do so yet.
- Filter out all students with "business" in the name of their undergraduate major. To do this, you could click on the Undergrad Major dropdown and uncheck the Other business and Other non-business items, but there is an alternative way to be aware of. Select Text Filters to see a number of possibilities for filtering text. For now, select **Does not contain**, and enter **business**.
- Filter out all students who are age 30 or older. To do this, click on the Age dropdown, and under the Number Filters, select **Less than** and enter **30**.

Note that you are now seeing only US students with undergraduate majors in Finance, Marketing, or Engineering who are not yet 30 years old. That is, the filters build upon themselves.

These few examples indicate just a few of the possibilities for filtering. Excel provides most of the options you will ever need, and they are very easy to implement. If you have a number of filters in place and you want to clear all of them, go to the Data ribbon and click on Clear in the Sort & Filter group. (This is also available on the Home ribbon.)

Summarizing

Once you have filtered data, you might want to create summary measures for one or more columns *based on the filtered data only.* This was rather difficult in earlier versions of Excel, but now it is really easy. First, it is useful to split the screen horizontally so that you can see the top and bottom of the table on the screen. Then in the Table Tools Design ribbon, check the **Total Row** option. You will see a new blue row at the bottom of the table. By default, it summarizes the *last* variable with the Sum function, but you can summarize *any* variable with any of several functions. As an example, click on the total row cell for the Previous Salary variable and select the Average function from the resulting dropdown. As another example, select the Count Numbers option for the GMAT column to see the number of non-missing values. (If you look at the formulas entered in these cells, you will see that they use the SUBTOTAL function, along with a numeric code for the operation. For example, 101 corresponds to Average, 102 corresponds to Count Numbers, and so on.)

Again, these summary values are for the filtered data only, so if you change the filter, the summary measures will change. And if you don't want the total row, you can simply uncheck the Total Row option in the Table Tools Design ribbon.

Expandability

One final property of tables is an extremely useful one. As you add data to a table, either to the right or to the bottom, the table automatically expands. Try the following. Enter **Marketing major** in cell M1. It automatically gets its own dropdown arrow, meaning that it is automatically part of the table. Next, in the cell below, enter an IF formula to record a 1 if the student's undergraduate major is Marketing or a 0 otherwise. When you enter this formula, don't type the cell reference (H6, because rows 2–5 have been filtered out), but instead point to it. You will see the following formula: **=IF(Table1[[#This Row], [Undergrad major]] = "Marketing", 1, 0)**. Although the usual **=IF(H6 = "Marketing", 1, 0)** would still work fine, this new syntax indicates exactly what the formula means. Also, notice that as soon as you enter this formula, it automatically copies down. This is another advantage of a table. Finally, if you enter data for a new student at the bottom of the table, it will automatically be added to the table. (You might want to clear filters and remove the table row before doing this.)

This automatic expandability has a very important implication. Suppose you build a pivot table from a table. When you insert the pivot table, don't enter a range such as A1:L1001 for the pivot table range; enter the name of the table (Table1 in this case) instead. Now if you add more data, either to the right or to the bottom of the table, you can refresh the pivot table simply by clicking the pivot table Refresh button; you do *not* need to rebuild the pivot table. The same is true of a chart based on a table. It refreshes automatically as the table expands. People in the business world will *love* this new feature, at least once they learn that it exists!

15.6 Working with Excel Tables with VBA

When I say that tables were given "official" status in Excel 2007, this isn't entirely true. The Excel object model in previous versions of Excel had a **ListObject** object for working with lists—that is, tables. I didn't explore this object then, so I am not familiar with its original properties and methods, but there must have been a number of additions in Excel 2007 given the new functionality available with tables. In any case, the ListObject object is the key to creating or manipulating tables with VBA.

To keep this section reasonably short, I will simply show the VBA code I obtained when I went through the exercises in the previous section with the VBA recorder on. Then I will show equivalent code I obtained by cleaning up the recorded code. Here is the recorded code.

```
Sub RecordedCode()
    ActiveSheet.ListObjects.Add(xlSrcRange, Range("$A$1:$L$1001"), , xlYes).Name = _
        "Table1"
    Range("Table1[#All]").Select
    ActiveWorkbook.Worksheets("Data").ListObjects("Table1").Sort.SortFields.Clear
    ActiveWorkbook.Worksheets("Data").ListObjects("Table1").Sort.SortFields.Add _
        Key:=Range("Table1[[#All],[Age]]"), SortOn:=xlSortOnValues, Order:= _
        xlAscending, DataOption:=xlSortNormal
    With ActiveWorkbook.Worksheets("Data").ListObjects("Table1").Sort
        .Header = xlYes
        .MatchCase = False
        .Orientation = xlTopToBottom
        .SortMethod = xlPinYin
        .Apply
    End With
    ActiveWorkbook.Worksheets("Data").ListObjects("Table1").Sort.SortFields.Clear
    ActiveWorkbook.Worksheets("Data").ListObjects("Table1").Sort.SortFields.Add _
        Key:=Range("Table1[[#All],[Gender]]"), SortOn:=xlSortOnValues, Order:= _
        xlDescending, DataOption:=xlSortNormal
    With ActiveWorkbook.Worksheets("Data").ListObjects("Table1").Sort
        .Header = xlYes
        .MatchCase = False
        .Orientation = xlTopToBottom
        .SortMethod = xlPinYin
        .Apply
    End With
    ActiveWorkbook.Worksheets("Data").ListObjects("Table1").Sort.SortFields.Clear
    ActiveWorkbook.Worksheets("Data").ListObjects("Table1").Sort.SortFields.Add _
        Key:=Range("Table1[[#All],[Nationality]]"), SortOn:=xlSortOnValues, Order _
        :=xlAscending, DataOption:=xlSortNormal
    With ActiveWorkbook.Worksheets("Data").ListObjects("Table1").Sort
        .Header = xlYes
        .MatchCase = False
        .Orientation = xlTopToBottom
        .SortMethod = xlPinYin
        .Apply
    End With
    ActiveWorkbook.Worksheets("Data").ListObjects("Table1").Sort.SortFields.Clear
    ActiveWorkbook.Worksheets("Data").ListObjects("Table1").Sort.SortFields.Add _
        Key:=Range("Table1[[#All],[Student]]"), SortOn:=xlSortOnValues, Order:= _
        xlAscending, DataOption:=xlSortNormal
    With ActiveWorkbook.Worksheets("Data").ListObjects("Table1").Sort
        .Header = xlYes
        .MatchCase = False
        .Orientation = xlTopToBottom
        .SortMethod = xlPinYin
        .Apply
    End With
    ActiveSheet.ListObjects("Table1").Range.AutoFilter Field:=4, Criteria1:= _
        "US"
    ActiveSheet.ListObjects("Table1").Range.AutoFilter Field:=8, Criteria1:= _
        "<>*business*", Operator:=xlAnd
    ActiveSheet.ListObjects("Table1").Range.AutoFilter Field:=2, Criteria1:= _
        "<30", Operator:=xlAnd
    ActiveSheet.ListObjects("Table1").ShowTotals = True
    ActiveWindow.Panes(3).Activate
    Range("Table1[[#Totals],[Previous salary]]").Select
    ActiveSheet.ListObjects("Table1").ListColumns("Previous salary"). _
        TotalsCalculation = xlTotalsCalculationAverage
```

```
    Range("Table1[[#Totals],[GMAT score]]").Select
    ActiveSheet.ListObjects("Table1").ListColumns("GMAT score").TotalsCalculation _
        = xlTotalsCalculationCountNums
    ActiveWindow.Panes(1).Activate
    Range("M1").Select
    ActiveCell.FormulaR1C1 = "Marketing major"
    Range("M4").Select
    ActiveCell.FormulaR1C1 = _
        "=IF(Table1[[#This Row],[Undergrad major]]=""Marketing"",1,0)"
    Range("A11").Select
    ActiveSheet.ListObjects("Table1").ShowTotals = False
    ActiveWorkbook.Worksheets("Data").ListObjects("Table1").Sort.SortFields.Clear
    ActiveSheet.ShowAllData
    ActiveWindow.Panes(3).Activate
    Range("A1002").Select
    ActiveCell.FormulaR1C1 = "1001"
    Range("B1002").Select
    ActiveCell.FormulaR1C1 = "30"
    Range("C1002").Select
    ActiveCell.FormulaR1C1 = "Female"
    Range("D1002").Select
    ActiveCell.FormulaR1C1 = "US"
    Range("E1002").Select
    ActiveCell.FormulaR1C1 = "No"
    Range("F1002").Select
    ActiveCell.FormulaR1C1 = "0"
    Range("G1002").Select
    ActiveCell.FormulaR1C1 = "2"
    Range("H1002").Select
    ActiveCell.FormulaR1C1 = "Marketing"
    Range("J1002").Select
    ActiveCell.FormulaR1C1 = "51000"
    Range("K1002").Select
    ActiveCell.FormulaR1C1 = "850"
    Range("L1002").Select
    ActiveCell.FormulaR1C1 = "23000"
    Range("M1002").Select
End Sub
```

As usual, this recorded code is pretty ugly, and it is filled with unnecessary Select lines, but you can probably learn what you need from it for working with tables in your own code. Here is my cleaned up version.

```
Sub CleanedUpCode()
    Dim ws As Worksheet
    Dim tbl As ListObject
        Set ws = Worksheets("Data") ' Do this to get Intellisense.

    'Create the table and give it a name.
    Set tbl = ws.ListObjects.Add(Source:=Range("$A$1:$L$1001"), _
        XlListObjectHasHeaders:=xlYes)
    tbl.Name = "MBA_Table"

    With tbl
        With .Sort
            ' For each sort, first clear the SortFields list, then Add one,
            ' and then Apply it.
```

```
            .SortFields.Clear
            .SortFields.Add Key:=Range("MBA_Table[[#All],[Age]]"), _
                Order:=xlAscending
            .Apply
            .SortFields.Clear
            .SortFields.Add Key:=Range("MBA_Table[[#All],[Gender]]"), _
                Order:=xlDescending
            .Apply
            .SortFields.Clear
            .SortFields.Add Key:=Range("MBA_Table[[#All],[Nationality]]"), _
                Order:=xlAscending
            .Apply
            .SortFields.Clear

            ' Restore original sort order.
            .SortFields.Add Key:=Range("MBA_Table[[#All],[Student]]"), _
                Order:=xlAscending
            .Apply
            .SortFields.Clear
        End With

        ' Apply filters.
        With .Range
            .AutoFilter Field:=4, Criteria1:="US"
            .AutoFilter Field:=8, Criteria1:="<>*business*"
            .AutoFilter Field:=2, Criteria1:="<30"
        End With

        ' Show Total Row and create a couple totals.
        .ShowTotals = True
        .ListColumns("Previous salary") _
            .TotalsCalculation = xlTotalsCalculationAverage
        .ListColumns("GMAT score") _
            .TotalsCalculation = xlTotalsCalculationCountNums

        ' Remove Total Row.
        .ShowTotals = False

End With

' Clear filters.
ws.ShowAllData

' Create a new variable in column M.
Range("M1").Value = "Marketing major"
Range("M2").Formula = _
    "=IF(MBA_Table[[#This Row],[Undergrad major]]=""Marketing"",1,0)"

' Enter a new student at the bottom of the table.
With Range("A1").End(xlDown).Offset(1, 0)
    .Value = .Offset(-1, 0).Value + 1
    .Offset(0, 1).Value = 30
    .Offset(0, 2).Value = "Female"
    .Offset(0, 3).Value = "US"
    .Offset(0, 4).Value = "No"
    .Offset(0, 5).Value = 0
    .Offset(0, 6).Value = 2
    .Offset(0, 7).Value = "Marketing"
    .Offset(0, 8).Value = ""
```

```
        .Offset(0, 9).Value = 51000
        .Offset(0, 10).Value = 850
        .Offset(0, 11).Value = 23000
    End With

    Range("A1").Select
End Sub
```

This is actually a great way to learn about a complex object such as the ListObject object. Turn on the recorder and record a number of typical operations. Then try to clean up the recorded code by eliminating everything but the essentials. (This will take some trial and error; at least it did for me.) You will not only realize how much unnecessary code the recorder adds, but you will learn a lot about the properties and methods of the object. For example, I learned that a ListObject object has a Sort property. From this, you move down the hierarchy to the SortFields collection to add a field to sort on. But you must Clear the SortFields collection from one sort to the next, and you must use the Apply method to actually implement the sort. As another example, I tried to enter the typical IF formula in cell M2 *before* removing the filter. This produced an error because at that time, row 2 was filtered out. So evidently, you can't use VBA to enter a formula in a hidden cell. Live and learn!

15.7 Summary

If you have never explored pivot tables, you should take some time to do so. They provide one of the most powerful but yet simplest methods for analyzing data. Although you might never feel the need to create or manipulate pivot tables with VBA—because Excel's tools for doing it manually are so simple—just remember that everything you can do manually, you can also do with VBA. It just takes some practice, experimentation, and a few trips to the Object Browser for help on the details. The same comments apply verbatim to Excel 2007's tables.

EXERCISES

1. A human resources manager at Beta Technologies has collected current annual salary figures and related data for 52 of the company's full-time employees. The data are listed in the file **Beta.xlsx**. They include the employee's gender, age, number of years of relevant work experience prior to employment at Beta, number of years employed at Beta, number of years of postsecondary education, and annual salary. Use pivot tables and pivot charts to answer the following questions.
   a. What proportion of these employees are female?
   b. Is there evidence of salary discrimination against women at Beta?
   c. Is additional postsecondary education positively associated with higher average salaries at Beta?
   d. Is there evidence of salary discrimination against older employees at Beta?

2. The file **BusinessSchools.xlsx** contains enrollment data on the top-rated graduate business programs in the United States, as reported by *Business Week's Guide to the Best Business Schools*. Specifically, it reports the percentages of women, minority, and international students enrolled in each program, as well as the number of full-time students enrolled in each. Use pivot tables and pivot charts to answer the following questions.
   a. Do graduate business programs with higher proportions of female student enrollments tend to have higher proportions of minority student enrollments?
   b. Do graduate business programs with higher proportions of female student enrollments tend to have higher proportions of international student enrollments?
3. The file **HyTex.xlsx** contains data on the HyTex Company, a direct marketer of stereophonic equipment, personal computers, and other electronic products. HyTex advertises entirely by mailing catalogs to its customers, and all of its orders are taken over the telephone. The company spends a great deal of money on its catalog mailings, and it wants to be sure that this is paying off in sales. Therefore, it has collected data on 1000 customers at the end of the current year. Use pivot tables and pivot charts to find the following information about these customers.
   a. Find the percentage of homeowners, broken down by age, marital status, and gender.
   b. Find the percentage married, broken down by age, homeowner status, and gender.
   c. Find the average salary broken down by age, gender, marital status, and homeowner status.
   d. Find the percentages in the "History" categories, broken down by number of children and whether they live close to retail stores.
   e. Find the percentage receiving the various numbers of catalogs for each value of the History variable.
   f. Analyze the average amount spent in the current year, broken down by History, number of catalogs, and the various demographic variables.
4. Change the application in the file **Sales Data with VBA.xlsm** so that the user has no choice of summarizing function—it is always by Average—but the user gets to choose a column field as well as a row field, each from the same list. Write code in the btnOK_Click event handler of frmVariables that prevents the user from choosing the *same* variable for both row and column. Then there should another user form, just like frmItems, for the column variable.
5. Change the application in the file **Sales Data with VBA.xlsm** so that the user sees only a single form, frmVariables. It is an expanded version of the current frmVariables, where the user can also choose a column field and a page field. Write code in the btnOK_Click event handler that prevents the user from choosing the *same* variable for row, column, and page—they should all be different. Then, instead of reporting the results in one or more message boxes, simply allow the user to see the resulting pivot table.

16 Working with Menus and Toolbars

16.1 Introduction

In revising the second edition of this book, this chapter is the most problematic. As you are probably aware, the most obvious change in Excel 2007 is the introduction of tabs and ribbons, replacing the old menus and toolbars. When I wrote the second edition (for Excel 2003 and earlier), menus and toolbars were fully customizable, either through a user interface or with VBA. In Excel 2007, all of this changed. The items on the various ribbons are fixed, as are the tabs, and you cannot change them at all.[1] The only thing you can change is the Quick Access Toolbar (QAT), and even this can be done only through the user interface, not with VBA.

So my dilemma was whether to keep this chapter at all. I decided to keep it, with very few changes, for two reasons. First, there are probably many of you who have not switched to Excel 2007. For you, this chapter is as relevant as ever. Second, the object model for changing menus and toolbars, starting with the CommandBar object (explained in this chapter), is amazingly still intact in Excel 2007. Some of it is irrelevant and doesn't actually do anything in Excel 2007, but it is still there. So what happens, say, if you write code to create a new toolbar in Excel 2007? The answer is that it will show up in the Custom Toolbars group on the Add-Ins ribbon. Or if you create a new menu structure with VBA, it will show up in the Menu Commands group on the Add-Ins ribbon. So in this sense, things still work; they just don't work the way you might expect them to work.

If you are an Excel 2007 user, you can skip most of this chapter. However, the object model in Section 16.3 still works with Excel 2007, and the Grading application in Section 16.4 is still useful and still works fine with exactly the same code. The only difference is that its custom toolbar will now show up in the Add-Ins ribbon.

16.2 Using Excel's GUI (for Pre-2007 Version only)

Many Excel users are not aware that the Excel menus and toolbars they see "right out of the box" are fully customizable. For example, you can hide toolbars, you can make built-in toolbars visible that you might not even know you have, you can add or delete buttons from existing toolbars, and you can even create your own toolbars

---

[1]Well, this isn't quite true. There is a technology called RibbonX that can be used to manipulate the ribbons with XML code. However, it is beyond the scope of this book. If you are interested, my Web site at http://www.kelley.iu.edu/albrightbooks has more information about using RibbonX.

with your own buttons. Similar operations are possible with menus. There are actually two ways to make these changes: (1) with Excel's graphical user interface (GUI) and (2) with VBA. I illustrate both methods in this chapter. The GUI method is useful if you want to make relatively minor changes, such as getting rid of a toolbar button you never use or constructing a toolbar with your favorite buttons. The VBA method is useful for making your own toolbars or menus magically appear when your custom application opens—and magically disappear when it closes.

Excel shows two toolbars by default: the Standard and Formatting toolbars. They are typically located just below Excel's menu bar, although you can reposition them wherever you like. You are probably aware that there are quite a few other "prepackaged" toolbars available for use. To see the list, just right-click on any toolbar. Alternatively, select the **View → Toolbars** menu item. If a toolbar is checked, then it is visible. If you want a toolbar that isn't visible, just check it. A couple of toolbars I usually like to have handy are the Drawing and Formula Auditing toolbars, but you can experiment to find your favorites.

There is much more you can do to customize your toolbars. The key is the **Tools → Customize** menu item. When you select it, you go into "customize mode" and see the dialog box shown in Figure 16.1, with the Commands tab showing. If you click on the Toolbars tab, you see the dialog box in Figure 16.2. The Options tab, not shown here, lets you check or uncheck a few useful options. For example, it has an Always Show Full Menus check box. If you don't like Excel deciding which menu items to show and which to hide, just check this box. From then on, you will always the *full* set of menu items.

If you want to change anything about your menus or toolbars, you need to get into customize mode. I'll give you a few directions and then let you experiment. First, in Figure 16.1 you see a number of categories on the left and a number of commands, many with associated icons, on the right. Some of these icons are

Figure 16.1 Customize Dialog Box with Commands Tab Showing

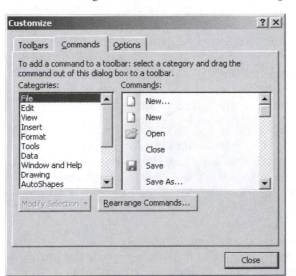

Figure 16.2   Customize Dialog Box with Toolbars Tab Showing

familiar, such as Open and Save. However, if you scroll through the categories and associated commands, you'll run into quite a few that are unfamiliar and possibly useful. For example, you'll find a Paste Values button under the Edit category. If you use the **Edit → Paste Special** menu item with the Values option a lot (like I do), this Paste Values button gives you the same functionality with a single click.

The important thing is that all of these command buttons are already "wired" to perform some task. If you find some you like, all you need to do is drag them up to one of the existing toolbars. This gives you the button's functionality. In the other direction, if there are buttons on existing toolbars that you never use, you can just drag them off and they'll disappear. (You can do this only in customize mode.) Furthermore, when you close Excel and then open it sometime later, the toolbars and menus are the same way you left them—your changes are remembered.

The discussion to this point is about existing toolbars and prewired buttons that ship with Excel. Fortunately, you can go much farther, with little or no programming. Try the following. The goal is to create your own toolbar with your own favorite macros attached to toolbar buttons.

1. Get to the Toolbars tab in Figure 16.2 and click on the New button to create a new toolbar. Name it something like My Favorites.
2. Record a macro that does some task you do repeatedly and make sure you save it in your **Personal.xls** workbook. (This was discussed in Chapter 4.) For example, I like to record creating a red border around a range. I select any range, turn on the recorder, create a red border, and turn off the recorder. I call this macro RedBorder.
3. Get to the Commands tab seen in Figure 16.1 and scroll down the Categories list to find the Macros category. You'll see two Command items: a custom menu item and a custom "happy face" button. This happy face button is generic—it has no code behind it. Drag it to your new toolbar.

Figure 16.3 Properly Menu for Toolbar Button

4. Right-click on your new happy face button to obtain the menu in Figure 16.3. This menu allows you to set properties of your button. The most important property is the macro assigned to it. Select Assign Macro and then choose the macro you just recorded. (Actually, you could assign *any* macro to this button.) You can then experiment with other menu items to personalize your button. For example, if you want a "toolbar tip" to appear when you hover the mouse over the button, change the Name property to something like &Red Border. (The & symbol designates the next character R as a "hot key." The key combination Ctrl-Shift-R will then run the macro.) If you don't want the generic happy face icon, select Edit Button Image. This takes you to a primitive paint program where you can use your artistic abilities to design an appropriate icon. Alternatively, right-click on some existing button whose icon you would like to borrow and select Copy Button Image. Then right-click on your button and select Paste Button Image, at which time you can modify the icon you just borrowed.

By repeating steps 2–4, you can quickly develop a toolbar that has buttons for macros you have developed. Alternatively, you can drag Excel's existing toolbar buttons onto your toolbar. For example, I like to have the "Command button" button from the Forms toolbar handy, whether or not the Forms toolbar is visible, so I just drag it to my favorites toolbar. Just remember that you must be in customize mode to do any of this. If you try dragging buttons off toolbars when you are *not* in customize mode, it won't work.

This discussion has focused on toolbars. You can also manipulate existing menus or create new menus while in customize mode. I'll let you explore the possibilities. (*Hint*: The bottom category in Figure 16.1 is New Menu. Also, the Rearrange Commands button in Figure 16.1 is useful.)

16.3 Relevant Objects for Menus and Toolbars[2]

Virtually anything you can do through Excel's GUI you can also do with VBA. First, because all Office products have menus and toolbars, the object model you need to learn is the Office object model, not Excel's. A portion of this object model appears in Figures 16.4 and 16.5. (As explained in the introduction, this object model still exists in Excel 2007, although some parts of it no longer do anything.)

CommandBar Objects

The first thing you need to understand is that VBA treats menus and toolbars as basically the same thing. To VBA, they are both **CommandBar** objects, members of the **CommandBars** collection. There are three types of CommandBar objects: toolbars, menu bars (such as those you see at the top of the Excel screen), and shortcut menus (such as those you see when you right-click on a cell).

Because the terminology can be confusing, let's try some simple programs to explore these objects. Open a new workbook with a single worksheet, get into the VBE, and insert a module into this workbook. Then enter the following code. (All of the code in this section is in the file **Toolbar and Menu Lists.xls** on the CD-ROM.)

```
Sub ListCommandBars()
    Dim cb As CommandBar
    Dim counter As Integer

    With Range("A1")
        ' Clear old list, if any.
        .CurrentRegion.ClearContents
        For Each cb In CommandBars
            .Offset(counter, 0) = cb.Index
            .Offset(counter, 1) = cb.Name
            If cb.Type = msoBarTypeMenuBar Then
                .Offset(counter, 2) = "Menu bar"
            ElseIf cb.Type = msoBarTypeNormal Then
                .Offset(counter, 2) = "Toolbar"
            ElseIf cb.Type = msoBarTypePopup Then
                .Offset(counter, 2) = "Shortcut menu"
            End If
            counter = counter + 1
        Next
    End With
End Sub
```

You'll notice as you are typing this that Intellisense helps. For example, as soon as you type cb.Type =, Intellisense shows that there are three possibilities: msoBarTypeMenuBar, **msoBarTypeNormal**, and **msoBarTypePopup**. (Well,

---

[2]As indicated in the introduction, this section was written primarily for Excel 2003 and earlier. However, the object model still applies to Excel 2007. The difference is that new menus or buttons now show up in the Add-Ins ribbon.

Figure 16.4 Office Objects for Menus and Toolbars

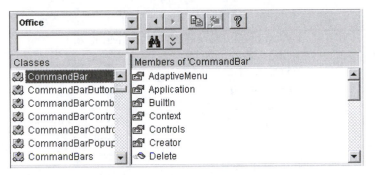

Figure 16.5 Part of Office Object Model

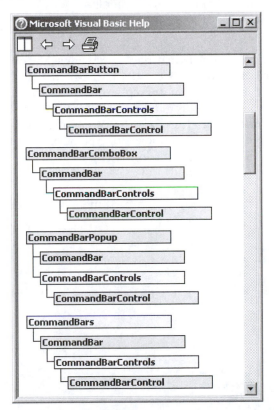

this help was provided in Excel 2003. It seems to have disappeared in Excel 2007.) As with Excel and VBA built-in constants that start with xl and vb, these are Microsoft Office built-in constants—hence the prefix mso.

The results of this program will depend on your Excel setup, but they will look something like those in Figure 16.6, which shows the first 12 items. Actually, the list on my PC contains 129 items! These items are obviously not all visible in Excel,

Figure 16.6 List of CommandBar Objects

	A	B	C
1	1	Worksheet Menu Bar	Menu bar
2	2	Chart Menu Bar	Menu bar
3	3	Standard	Toolbar
4	4	Formatting	Toolbar
5	5	PivotTable	Toolbar
6	6	Chart	Toolbar
7	7	Reviewing	Toolbar
8	8	Forms	Toolbar
9	9	Stop Recording	Toolbar
10	10	External Data	Toolbar
11	11	Formula Auditing	Toolbar
12	12	Full Screen	Toolbar

but they are all available and they all have names. For example, the two menu bars at the top are called **Worksheet Menu Bar** and **Chart Menu Bar**. The first is the menu bar usually displayed in Excel, but it is replaced by the second when a chart is selected. Also, you can see from this list (and the code) that two of the toolbars are called **Standard** and **Formatting**. These are the two toolbars that are visible in Excel by default. Each is a CommandBar object of type **msoBarTypeNormal**.

Note that you can refer to a CommandBar by its name or its index. For example, CommandBars(2) and CommandBars("Chart Menu Bar") both refer to the same thing.

If you want a list of the *visible* command bars, modify the code as follows.

```
Sub ListVisibleCommandBars()
    Dim cb As CommandBar
    Dim counter As Integer

    With Range("A1")
        ' Clear old list, if any.
        .CurrentRegion.ClearContents
        For Each cb In CommandBars
            If cb.Visible Then
                .Offset(counter, 0) = cb.Index
                .Offset(counter, 1) = cb.Name
                If cb.Type = msoBarTypeMenuBar Then
                    .Offset(counter, 2) = "Menu bar"
                ElseIf cb.Type = msoBarTypeNormal Then
                    .Offset(counter, 2) = "Toolbar"
                ElseIf cb.Type = msoBarTypePopup Then
                    .Offset(counter, 2) = "Shortcut menu"
                End If
                counter = counter + 1
            End If
        Next
    End With
End Sub
```

Figure 16.7 List of Visible CommandBar Objects

	A	B	C
1	1	Worksheet Menu Bar	Menu bar
2	3	Standard	Toolbar
3	4	Formatting	Toolbar
4	26	Drawing	Toolbar

Now the list is much shorter. The list for my PC is shown in Figure 16.7.

CommandBarControl Objects

Next in the hierarchy, CommandBar objects have **CommandBarControl** objects.[3] For example, the CommandBarControl objects in a toolbar are the toolbar buttons. In contrast, the CommandBarControl objects in a menu bar are the menus, menu items, and submenu items. Unlike CommandBar objects that are one of only three types, CommandBarControl objects come in many types. Even the "simple" Standard toolbar has four types of controls. To list them, modify the previous code as follows.

```
Sub ListToolbarButtons()
    Dim cb As CommandBar
    Dim cbc As CommandBarControl
    Dim counter As Integer

    Set cb = CommandBars("Standard")
    With Range("A1")
        ' Clear old list, if any.
        .CurrentRegion.ClearContents
        For Each cbc In cb.Controls
            .Offset(counter, 0) = cbc.Index
            .Offset(counter, 1) = cbc.Caption
            If cbc.Type = msoControlButton Then
                .Offset(counter, 2) = "Regular button"
            ElseIf cbc.Type = msoControlComboBox Then
                .Offset(counter, 2) = "Combo box"
            ElseIf cbc.Type = msoControlSplitDropdown Then
                .Offset(counter, 2) = "Split dropdown"
            ElseIf cbc.Type = msoControlSplitButtonPopup Then
                .Offset(counter, 2) = "Split button popup"
            Else
                .Offset(counter, 2) = "Some other type"
            End If
            counter = counter + 1
        Next
    End With
End Sub
```

---

[3] To be precise, a CommandBarControl can be one of three flavors: **CommandBarButton**, **CommandBarComboBox**, and **CommandBarPopup** (see Figures 16.4 and 16.5). Each of these has slightly different functionality and properties. As illustrated in the next section, it is sometimes useful to refer to the specific type of control, such as CommandBarButton, rather than the generic CommandBarControl.

Figure 16.8 Controls on Standard Toolbar

	A	B	C
1	1	&New	Regular button
2	2	Open	Regular button
3	3	&Save	Regular button
4	4	Permission (Unrestricted Acc	Regular button
5	5	&Mail Recipient	Regular button
6	6	Print (Adobe PDF)	Regular button
7	7	Print Pre&view	Regular button
8	8	&Spelling...	Regular button
9	9	&Research...	Regular button
10	10	Cu&t	Regular button
11	11	&Copy	Regular button
12	12	&Paste	Split button popup
13	13	&Format Painter	Regular button
14	14	&Undo	Split dropdown
15	15	&Redo	Split dropdown
16	16	Ink &Annotations	Regular button
17	17	Hyperl&ink...	Regular button
18	18	&AutoSum	Split button popup
19	19	Sort &Ascending	Regular button
20	20	Sort Des&cending	Regular button
21	21	&Chart Wizard	Regular button
22	22	&Drawing	Regular button
23	23	&Zoom:	Combo box
24	24	Microsoft Excel &Help	Regular button

Note that cb is set to the Standard toolbar. Then this cb object has a Controls collection that you can loop through. Each CommandBarControl (cbc) in this collection has, among other things, a **Caption** and a **Type**. (Surprisingly, there is no Name property for a CommandBarControl.) After some detective work in Object Browser, I found that the four types in the Standard toolbar are those shown in the code.[4] The most common type is **msoControlButton**, the common toolbar button. The results of this sub appear in Figure 16.8. (Compare this list to the Standard toolbar you see every day in Excel, and you'll get a better appreciation for the different types of functionality its buttons possess.)

Note that a CommandBarControl can be referred to by its caption (without the & symbol) or its index. For example, CommandBars("Standard").Controls ("Save") and CommandBars("Standard").Controls(3) refer to the same thing.

---

[4]To find a list of constants such as msoControlSplitButtonPopup, go to the Object Browser, select the Office library, and look for **MsoControlType** in the left pane. The right pane then shows a list of mso constants. Each item with prefix Mso (note the upper case M) in the left pane is called an **enumeration**, which is simply a list of built-in constants. All such constants have prefix mso (with lowercase m).

Figure 16.9 Controls on Worksheet Menu Bar

	A	B	C
1	1	&File	Menu popup
2	2	&Edit	Menu popup
3	3	&View	Menu popup
4	4	&Insert	Menu popup
5	5	F&ormat	Menu popup
6	6	&Tools	Menu popup
7	7	&Data	Menu popup
8	8	A&ction	Menu popup
9	9	&Window	Menu popup
10	10	&Help	Menu popup

Next, try this same type of sub for the Worksheet Menu Bar. It also has controls, but it turns out that they are all of type **msoControlPopup**, as the following modification of the previous code and the associated results in Figure 16.9 indicate. As you can see, this list is the familiar list of menus at the top of Excel. (I must admit, however, that I have no idea what the Action menu is. I've never seen it.)

```
Sub ListMenuBarControls()
    Dim cb As CommandBar
    Dim cbc As CommandBarControl
    Dim counter As Integer

    Set cb = CommandBars("Worksheet Menu Bar")
    With Range("A1")
        ' Clear old list, if any.
        .CurrentRegion.ClearContents
        For Each cbc In cb.Controls
            .Offset(counter, 0) = cbc.Index
            .Offset(counter, 1) = cbc.Caption
            If cbc.Type = msoControlPopup Then
                .Offset(counter, 2) = "Menu popup"
            Else
                .Offset(counter, 2) = "Some other type"
            End If
            counter = counter + 1
        Next
    End With
End Sub
```

As you know, menus such as the File menu have menu items, and some of these have submenu items. How do you get to them? The answer is that each CommandBarControl object can have a Controls collection consisting of its CommandBarControl objects, and each of these can have a Controls collection consisting of *its* CommandBarControl objects, and so on.

Figure 16.10 Menu Structure

	A	B	C	D	E	F
61	&File	E&xit		10	1	
62	&Edit	Can't &Undo		10	1	
63	&Edit	&Repeat Clear		10	1	
64	&Edit	Cu&t		10	1	
65	&Edit	&Copy		10	1	
66	&Edit	Office Clip&board...		10	1	
67	&Edit	&Paste		10	1	
68	&Edit	Paste &Special...		10	1	
69	&Edit	Paste as &Hyperlink		10	1	
70	&Edit	F&ill	&Down	10	10	1
71	&Edit	F&ill	&Right	10	10	1
72	&Edit	F&ill	&Up	10	10	1
73	&Edit	F&ill	&Left	10	10	1
74	&Edit	F&ill	&Across Worksheets...	10	10	1

The following code illustrates the structure of the Worksheet Menu Bar. Note that there is first a loop through all the controls listed in Figure 16.9. Inside this, there is a loop over the menu items for each menu. Finally, inside this there is a loop over all submenu items for each menu item. Figure 16.10 shows a few of the results. On my PC, the entire list has 292 items!

```
Sub ListMenuInfo()
    Dim menuBar As CommandBar
    Dim menu As CommandBarControl
    Dim menuItem As CommandBarControl
    Dim subMenuItem As CommandBarControl
    Dim counter As Integer

    Set menuBar = CommandBars("Worksheet Menu Bar")
    With Range("A1")
        ' Clear old list, if any.
        .CurrentRegion.ClearContents
        On Error Resume Next
        For Each menu In menuBar.Controls
            For Each menuItem In menu.Controls
                For Each subMenuItem In menuItem.Controls
                    .Offset(counter, 0) = menu.Caption
                    .Offset(counter, 1) = menuItem.Caption
                    .Offset(counter, 2) = subMenuItem.Caption
                    .Offset(counter, 3) = menu.Type
                    .Offset(counter, 4) = menuItem.Type
                    .Offset(counter, 5) = subMenuItem.Type
                    counter = counter + 1
                Next
            Next
        Next
    End With
End Sub
```

Note that I requested the Type property for each item. They are all 10 or 1. Some investigation in online help (refer back to footnote 2) shows that 10 corresponds to **msoControlPopup**, and 1 corresponds to **msoControlButton**. This is useful information if you want to create your own menus, as illustrated in the next section. It also makes sense. Get into Excel and click on the Edit menu. A menu list pops up. Then click on the Fill menu item. A submenu list pops up. However, if you click on any of the items in this submenu, nothing pops up. Instead, you get "button" functionality, the same as when you click on a button to run a macro. Similarly, if you click on the Paste menu item under the Edit menu, nothing pops up. You again get button functionality.

16.4 Modifying Menu Bars and Toolbars

Now that you have had a glimpse of the labyrinth of CommandBars and CommandBarControls, it's time to try modifying existing menu bars and toolbars or creating new ones. Specifically, suppose you develop an application—an Excel file—that requires a special toolbar and an extra menu. Whenever a user opens this application, you would like your toolbar and menu to appear, but when the user closes the application, you would like your toolbar and menu to disappear. In other words, you want your toolbar and menu to be present when your application is open and you want to clean up when your application closes.

The best way to proceed is to develop event handlers for the Open and BeforeClose events of the ThisWorkbook item of your application. In the This-Workbook_Open sub, you write code to set up your toolbar and menu. In the ThisWorkbook_BeforeClose sub, you make the toolbar and menu disappear.[5] I'll illustrate how to do it in this section.

A Grading Program Example

For my own use as an instructor, I have developed a grading program. It is stored as **Grader.xlsm** on the CD-ROM, and other instructors can actually use it for grading assignments or exams. (It is accompanied by a **Grader Instructions.htm** help file and several associated .gif screenshot files.) When it opens, a toolbar (in the middle left) and a corresponding menu appear in Excel. (See Figure 16.11. Keep in mind that this toolbar will show up in the Add-Ins ribbon in Excel 2007, but the buttons will still work fine.)

To learn how to use this program, you can click on the question mark button or select the last menu item. Then to use the program, you begin by clicking on the "1" button or selecting the first menu item. Each of the buttons and menu items runs a macro in the program. (These macros are not discussed here.) The toolbar and menu are set up as in many custom applications. Specifically, each

---

[5]This is not a foolproof solution. Suppose Excel crashes while your application is open—and we all know that this is possible. Then the BeforeClose event will not fire at crash time, and your toolbar and menu will still be there when Excel is reopened. In fact, you will have *two* of everything when you open your application again.

Figure 16.11 Toolbar and Menu for Grader Program

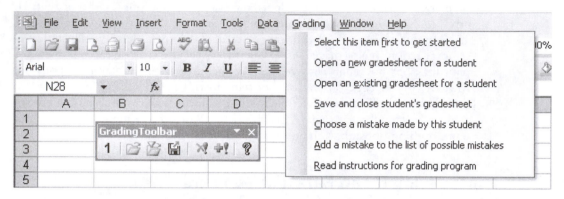

button on the toolbar corresponds to a menu item. This allows users to use the menu or the toolbar, whichever they prefer.

The ThisWorkbook item in the application has the following two event handlers:

```
Private Sub Workbook_Open()
    Call CreateToolbar
    Call CreateMenu
End Sub
```

```
Private Sub Workbook_BeforeClose(Cancel As Boolean)
    Call DeleteToolbar
    Call DeleteMenu
End Sub
```

Each of these calls a couple of subs in a module to create or delete the toolbar and menu. The delete subs are simple. Each uses an On Error statement, just in case the item it is trying to delete does not exist. Note that the DeleteToolbar sub deletes a CommandBar object—a toolbar. In contrast, the DeleteMenu sub deletes a CommandBarControl object—a menu from the Worksheet Menu Bar.

```
Sub DeleteToolbar()
    ' This sub is called in the Workbook_BeforeClose sub.
    On Error Resume Next
    CommandBars("GradingToolbar").Delete
End Sub
```

```
Sub DeleteMenu()
    ' This sub is called in the Workbook_BeforeClose sub.
    On Error Resume Next
    CommandBars("Worksheet Menu Bar").Controls("Grading").Delete
End Sub
```

The create subs are much longer, but each is very repetitive. The Create-Toolbar sub, listed below, first creates a new toolbar called "GradingToolbar", then it creates a few buttons (CommandBarButton objects) on the toolbar, and finally it sets a few properties of the buttons. Note that each button is a generic CommandBarControl object, and they could all be declared as such. However, it is useful to declare them more specifically as CommandBarButton objects. By being more specific, you obtain more help from Intellisense.

```vba
Sub CreateToolbar()
    ' This sub is called by the Workbook_Open sub.
    Dim gradingToolbar As CommandBar

    ' The following could all be declared as CommandBarControl objects,
    ' but by being more specific, you get Intellisense help for
    ' controls of the CommandBarButton type.
    Dim getStartedButton As CommandBarButton
    Dim openNewButton As CommandBarButton
    Dim openOldButton As CommandBarButton
    Dim closeSaveButton As CommandBarButton
    Dim chooseMistakeButton As CommandBarButton
    Dim addMistakeButton As CommandBarButton
    Dim helpButton As CommandBarButton

    ' Create the toolbar and dock it at the top of the screen.
    Set gradingToolbar = CommandBars.Add(Name:="GradingToolbar", Position:=msoBarTop)

    ' By default, the new toolbar is NOT visible.
    gradingToolbar.Visible = True

    ' Create the buttons on the toolbar.
    With gradingToolbar
        Set getStartedButton = .Controls.Add
        Set openNewButton = .Controls.Add
        Set openOldButton = .Controls.Add
        Set closeSaveButton = .Controls.Add
        Set chooseMistakeButton = .Controls.Add
        Set addMistakeButton = .Controls.Add
        Set helpButton = .Controls.Add
    End With
    ' Give buttons properties
    With getStartedButton
        .FaceId = 71
        .Caption = "Start here: open gradebook, identify gradesheet template"
        .OnAction = "GetStarted"
    End With
    With openNewButton
        .BeginGroup = True
        .FaceId = 23
        .Caption = "Open a new gradesheet for a student"
        .OnAction = "OpenNewGradesheet"
    End With
    With openOldButton
        .FaceId = 1791
        .Caption = "Open an existing gradesheet for a student"
        .OnAction = "OpenExistingGradesheet"
    End With
    With closeSaveButton
        .FaceId = 270
        .Caption = "Save and close student's gradesheet"
        .OnAction = "SaveAndCloseGradesheet"
```

```
      End With
      With chooseMistakeButton
         .BeginGroup = True
         .FaceId = 536
         .Caption = "Choose a mistake made by this student"
         .OnAction = "ChooseMistake"
      End With
      With addMistakeButton
         .FaceId = 535
         .Caption = "Add a mistake to the list of possible mistakes"
         .OnAction = "AddMistake"
      End With
      With helpButton
         .BeginGroup = True
         .FaceId = 926
         .Caption = "Read instructions for grading program"
         .OnAction = "ReadInstructions"
      End With
End Sub
```

Here are a few things to notice about this code.

- To create a new toolbar and set it to the variable gradingToolbar, use the line:

```
Set gradingToolbar = CommandBars.Add(Name:="GradingToolbar", Position:=msoBarTop)
```

This adds a new item to the CommandBars collection, gives it a name, and docks it at the top of the screen, just below existing toolbars. If you wanted a "floating" toolbar, you would set the Position to msoBarFloating.

- To add a button to the toolbar, you Add a CommandBarButton to the toolbar's Controls collection.
- The toolbar buttons have a number of properties you can set. The most important is the **OnAction** property. This is set to the name of a sub that you assign to the button. If you want to "group" the buttons, you can set the **BeginGroup** property of the first button in any group to True. This adds a gray vertical bar to the toolbar. (See Figure 16.11.) The **Caption** property is the tool tip you see when you hover the mouse above a button. It also provides a means to refer to the control later on. Finally, the **FaceId** property is the index of the icon you want to use, where you can choose from all available Windows icons. But how did I know, for example, to use the index 926 for a question mark icon? This takes some detective work. I have included a file **FaceI Ds.xlsm** on the CD-ROM that lets you view all available icons and find the corresponding FaceId indexes.

The CreateMenu sub is very similar and is listed below.

```
Sub CreateMenu()
   ' This sub is called by the Workbook_Open sub.
   Dim gradingMenu As CommandBarControl
   Dim windowMenu As CommandBarControl
```

```
' Again, the following could all be declared as CommandBarControl
' objects, but by being more specific, we get Intellisense help for
' controls of the CommandBarButton type.
Dim getStartedMenuItem As CommandBarButton
Dim openNewMenuItem As CommandBarButton
Dim openOldMenuItem As CommandBarButton
Dim closeSaveMenuItem As CommandBarButton
Dim chooseMistakeMenuItem As CommandBarButton
Dim addMistakeMenuItem As CommandBarButton
Dim helpMenuItem As CommandBarButton

' Create new menu just to the left of the Window menu.
Set windowMenu = CommandBars("Worksheet Menu Bar").Controls("Window")
Set gradingMenu = CommandBars("Worksheet Menu Bar") _
    .Controls.Add(Type:=msoControlPopup, Before:=windowMenu.Index)

' Add menu items to the new menu.
With gradingMenu
    .Caption = "&Grading"
    Set getStartedMenuItem = .Controls.Add
    Set openNewMenuItem = .Controls.Add
    Set openOldMenuItem = .Controls.Add
    Set closeSaveMenuItem = .Controls.Add
    Set chooseMistakeMenuItem = .Controls.Add
    Set addMistakeMenuItem = .Controls.Add
    Set helpMenuItem = .Controls.Add
End With


' Set properties of new menu items.
With getStartedMenuItem
    .Caption = "Select this item &first to get started"
    .OnAction = "GetStarted"
End With
With openNewMenuItem
    .Caption = "Open a &new gradesheet for a student"
    .OnAction = "OpenNewGradesheet"
End With
With openOldMenuItem
    .Caption = "Open an &existing gradesheet for a student"
    .OnAction = "OpenExistingGradesheet"
End With
With closeSaveMenuItem
    .Caption = "&Save and close student's gradesheet"
    .OnAction = "SaveAndCloseGradesheet"
End With
With chooseMistakeMenuItem
    .Caption = "&Choose a mistake made by this student"
    .OnAction = "ChooseMistake"
End With
With addMistakeMenuItem
    .Caption = "&Add a mistake to the list of possible mistakes"
    .OnAction = "AddMistake"
End With
With helpMenuItem
    .Caption = "&Read instructions for grading program"
    .OnAction = "ReadInstructions"
End With
End Sub
```

The main things to notice from this sub are the following.

- The Worksheet Menu Bar already exists; it is the menu you are used to seeing at the top of Excel. So unlike the CreateToolbar sub, this sub only needs to add controls to an existing CommandBar object.
- I decided to add the Grading menu just to the left of the Window menu. Therefore, the following lines first set a reference to the Window menu and then add a menu of type msoControlPopup to the left of the Window menu. Later, this new menu is given the caption &Grading. Again, the & symbol signifies that G is a hot key.

```
Set windowMenu = CommandBars("Worksheet Menu Bar").Controls("Window")
Set gradingMenu = CommandBars("Worksheet Menu Bar") _
    .Controls.Add(Type:=msoControlPopup, Before:=windowMenu.Index)
```

- The OnAction properties of the menu items are exactly the same—they refer to the same subs—as the corresponding toolbar buttons. This allows users to access the same functionality from either the toolbar or the menu.

This example is typical, but it merely scratches the surface of what you can do with VBA to create and modify toolbars and menus. For example, the first menu item in the Grading program runs a GetStarted sub. In the program, this sub actually performs three tasks. Therefore, it might make sense to allow the user to choose any one of these three tasks. So instead of making the first menu item a CommandBarButton, it could be a CommandBarPopup menu item with three CommandBarButton submenu items. The relevant code would then look something as follows.

```
Dim getStartedMenuItem As CommandBarPopup
Dim task1SubMenuItem As CommandBarButton
Dim task2SubMenuItem As CommandBarButton
Dim task3SubMenuItem As CommandBarButton

With getStartedMenuItem
    Set task1SubMenuItem = .Controls.Add
    Set task2SubMenuItem = .Controls.Add
    Set task3SubMenuItem = .Controls.Add
End With

With task1SubMenuItem
    .OnAction = "Task1"
    .Caption = "Task&1"
End With
With task2SubMenuItem
    .OnAction = "Task2"
    .Caption = "Task&2"
End With
With task3SubMenuItem
    .OnAction = "Task3"
    .Caption = "Task&3"
End With
```

The point is that the first menu item now has three submenu items, and each of these runs the sub that corresponds to its OnAction property. If you think about it, this is exactly the way many of the menu items you see every day work.

Hiding and Restoring All Toolbars

Some programmers like their Excel applications to replace all of Excel's toolbars and menu bars with their own custom versions. Essentially, they want their users to forget that they are really in Excel. This is not difficult to do, again with code in the Workbook_Open sub, but you should definitely restore everything back to normal in the Workbook_BeforeClose sub. Otherwise, users will curse you for "breaking" Excel.

Here is a sub you could call from the Workbook_Open sub to hide all visible toolbars. Note how it uses a "very hidden" sheet named ToolbarSheet to store a list of all visible toolbar names. This list allows the application to restore the hidden toolbars when it closes. (This code is stored in the **Hide and Restore.xls** file on the CD-ROM. It won't bomb in Excel 2007, but it won't do anything useful.) Note that it loops through the CommandBars collection. However, it makes two checks before setting the Visible property to False. First, the Command-Bar must be of type msoBarTypeNormal. Recall from the previous section that this is the toolbar type. Second, the toolbar must currently be visible; otherwise, there is no point in hiding it.

```
Sub HideToolbars()
    Dim tb As CommandBar
    Dim nToolbars As Integer
    Dim tbSheet As Worksheet

    Set tbSheet = Worksheets("ToolbarSheet")
    ' The xlSheetVeryHidden setting means the sheet can be unhidden only with VBA code.
    ' It can't be unhidden with the Format→Sheet→Unhide menu item.
    With tbSheet
        .Visible = xlSheetVeryHidden
        .Cells.Clear
    End With

    ' Hide all visible toolbars and store them in the hidden sheet.
    For Each tb In CommandBars
        If tb.Type = msoBarTypeNormal Then
            If tb.Visible Then
                nToolbars = nToolbars + 1
                tbSheet.Cells(nToolbars, 1) = tb.Name
                tb.Visible = False
            End If
        End If
    Next
End Sub
```

To restore the hidden toolbars once the application closes, you should call the following code from the Workbook_BeforeClose sub. This sub searches the list in the hidden sheet for toolbar names and reveals all of the corresponding toolbars. This means the Excel workspace is restored to its condition before the application was opened. Except for the strange requirement mentioned in the comments, this sub is straightforward.

```
Sub RestoreToolbars()
    Dim tb As CommandBar
    Dim nToolbars As Integer, i As Integer
    Dim tbSheet As Worksheet
    Dim tbRange As Range, cell As Range

    Set tbSheet = Worksheets("ToolbarSheet")

    ' For some obscure reason, the cells that store the
    ' toolbar names have to be treated as "special cells."
    Set tbRange = tbSheet.Range("A1").CurrentRegion _
        .SpecialCells(xlCellTypeConstants)

    ' Unhide each toolbar in the list.
    For Each cell In tbRange
        CommandBars(cell.Value).Visible = True
    Next
End Sub
```

Similar subs could be used to hide and then restore Excel's Worksheet Menu Bar, freeing the programmer to add his own custom menu bar.

16.5 Summary

Working with menus and toolbars via VBA was always a tricky undertaking. It is easy to get lost in the CommandBar labyrinth. So in one sense, maybe we are fortunate that Microsoft went to tabs and ribbons in Excel 2007, which can be manipulated only with an advanced RibbonX technology. However, be aware that you can still create custom menus and toolbars with the CommandBar object hierarchy, as I did in the Grader application. The difference is that they now show up in the Add-Ins ribbon in Excel 2007.

EXERCISES

Note: All of these exercises are geared to pre-2007 versions of Excel.

1. Are there buttons on your Standard and Formatting toolbars that you absolutely never use? If so, get into Customize mode and drag them off, freeing up space for some you might find more useful. Then, still in Customize mode, explore the various categories of toolbar buttons in the Commands tab. You're bound to find a few that you could be useful to you. Drag them up to one of the visible toolbars. Now close Excel and reopen it. The work you just performed should be preserved.

2. Create (or record) one or more macros that do something you do often, such as formatting a cell as a number with 0 decimals or using the File → Page Setup to specify print settings. Store the macros in your **Personal.xls** file so that they are always available. Then get into Customize mode, create a new toolbar with name My Favorites, and populate it with buttons that run your new macros. Change the happy faces on your buttons to something more meaningful, and give your buttons tool tips (change their Name property).

3. In spreadsheet optimization models, it is helpful to designate input cells, changing cells, and the target cell in some way. I like to put blue borders around input cells, red borders around changing cells, and a black border around the target cell, but there is nothing special about my system. Devise your own color-coding scheme or borrow mine. Then proceed as in the previous exercise to create macros that color code any selected range in the way you want (recording is a good option here), create a new toolbar named My Formatting, and add buttons to it with appropriate images and tool tips that run your macros. Finally, record one last button, and create an extra toolbar button for it that removes the formatting from any selected range. That way, you can remove any formatting you don't want. (*Hint*: Select a range *before* recording any macro. Then your formatting macros will work on *any* range you select.)

4. For either of the two preceding problems, get into Customize mode and add a new menu called My Menu to the left of the Window menu. Then add menu items to this menu that correspond to the buttons on your toolbar. This will allow you to access the functionality of your macros from either a toolbar or a menu. (*Hint*: Examine the Macros and New Menu categories of the Commands tab in the Customize dialog box.)

5. Starting with a blank workbook, add code to the Workbook_Open and Workbook_BeforeClose event handlers in the ThisWorkbook object. The code in the Workbook_Open sub should hide the Standard and Formatting toolbars that are usually visible. The code in the Workbook_BeforeClose sub should make these toolbars visible. Save this workbook, close it, and then reopen it. The toolbars should be missing. Then close it and open another workbook. This time the two toolbars should be visible. (If your code messes everything up and you can't get the toolbars back, you can always do so manually through the View → Toolbars menu item.)

6. Starting with the macros from either exercise 2 or 3, write a VBA sub that creates the toolbar in the earlier exercise and populates it with buttons that run the macros. (If you like, use the **Face IDs.xls** file to borrow appropriate "faces" for your buttons.)

7. Do the same as in the previous exercise, but this time use VBA code to create the menu requested in exercise 4.

17

Automating Solver and Palisade Add-Ins

17.1 Introduction

There are many add-ins for Excel that have been developed by third-party software companies. Many of these companies have provided VBA capabilities that programmers can use to manipulate the add-ins. Specifically, this is true of the Solver optimization add-in that is part of Microsoft Office. Solver can be manipulated not only through the familiar menu interface, but it can also be manipulated "behind the scenes" with VBA code. This chapter explains how to do it.

Besides the Solver add-in, you should be aware that many other add-ins can also be manipulated with VBA—and the number will certainly continue to grow. One example is the Analysis ToolPak that is part of Microsoft Office.[1] Two others are add-ins from Palisade Corp: @RISK for simulation and StatTools for statistical analysis. In each case, programmers must search for help (online help) that specifies the VBA functions available with the add-in. These functions are *not* part of Excel VBA, and they are not always well documented by the companies that have developed them. However, I will illustrate some of the possibilities for both @RISK and StatTools.

17.2 Exercise

This exercise requires you to run Solver on an existing model with VBA code. Because the size of the problem can change based on the value of a user input, the VBA code must respecify the Solver settings before running Solver.

Exercise 17.1   Scheduling Production

Consider a company that must plan its monthly production of footballs. It begins month 1 with a given number of footballs on hand, and at the beginning of each month it must decide how many footballs to produce. There are three constraints: (1) The quantity on hand after production must be at least as large as that month's (known) demand, (2) production in a month can never exceed production

---

[1] If you have ever loaded the Analysis ToolPak and have then looked at the add-ins list, you have probably noticed that there is an "Analysis ToolPak – VBA" box you can check. This gives you access to the VBA functions that accompany the Analysis ToolPak.

Figure 17.1 Production Model

	A	B	C	D	E	F	G	H	I	J	K	L	M
1	Multiperiod production model												
2													
3	Input data												
4	Initial inventory	5000											
5	Holding cost as % of production cost	5%											
6													
7	Month	1	2	3	4	5	6	7	8	9	10	11	12
8	Unit production cost	$12.50	$12.55	$12.70	$12.80	$12.85	$12.95	$12.95	$13.00	$13.00	$13.10	$13.10	$13.20
9													
10	Production schedule												
11	Month	1	2	3	4	5	6						
12	Units produced	5000	20000	30000	30000	25000	10000	15000	30000	30000	30000	30000	25000
13		<=	<=	<=	<=	<=	<=	<=	<=	<=	<=	<=	<=
14	Production capacity	30000	30000	30000	30000	30000	30000	30000	30000	30000	30000	30000	30000
15													
16	On hand after production	10000	20000	35000	35000	25000	10000	15000	33000	32000	37000	31000	25000
17		>=	>=	>=	>=	>=	>=	>=	>=	>=	>=	>=	>=
18	Demand	10000	15000	30000	35000	25000	10000	12000	31000	25000	36000	31000	25000
19													
20	Ending inventory	0	5000	5000	0	0	0	3000	2000	7000	1000	0	0
21		<=	<=	<=	<=	<=	<=	<=	<=	<=	<=	<=	<=
22	Storage capacity	10000	10000	10000	10000	10000	10000	10000	10000	10000	10000	10000	10000
23													
24	Summary of costs												
25	Month	1	2	3	4	5	6	7	8	9	10	11	12
26	Production cost	$62,500	$251,000	$381,000	$384,000	$321,250	$129,500	$194,250	$390,000	$390,000	$393,000	$393,000	$330,000
27	Holding cost	$0	$3,138	$3,175	$0	$0	$0	$1,943	$1,300	$4,550	$655	$0	$0
28													
29	Total cost	$3,634,260											

capacity, and (3) the ending inventory in any month can never exceed the storage capacity. We assume that production and storage capacity remain constant through the planning period. There are two costs: (1) the unit production cost, which increases gradually through the planning period, and (2) the unit holding cost, which is a percentage of the unit production cost and is charged on each month's ending inventory.

The file **Production Scheduling.xlsx** contains a model for finding the company's minimum-cost production schedule for any planning period up to 12 months. (See Figure 17.1.) The inputs are in blue cells, the decision variables (changing cells) are in row 12, and cell B29 shows the total cost. The current model uses a planning period of 12 months, and the solution shown in Figure 17.1 is optimal for this planning period. The Solver settings appear in Figures 17.2 and 17.3. Note that rows 12, 14, 16, 18, 20, 22, 26, and 27 (columns B to M) have been range-named Produced, ProdCap, Onhand, Demand, EndInv, StorCap, ProdCosts, and HoldCosts, respectively. Also, cell B28 has the range name TotalCost. These range names are provided to make the Solver setup in Figure 17.2 and the formula for total cost easier to read.

The purpose of the exercise is to develop a sub that asks the user for a planning period from 4 to 12 months. (You can also have it ask for other inputs, such as the initial inventory and the holding cost percentage, if you like.) Based on the length of the planning period, the sub should then rename the ranges in rows 14 to 22 appropriately (using only the months in the planning period) and reset Solver (the VBA equivalent of clicking on the Reset All button in Figure 17.2). It should then respecify the Solver settings in Figure 17.2 and 17.3, and finally it should run Solver. Note that if you rename the ranges appropriately, the Solver window will always end

Figure 17.2 Solver Dialog Box

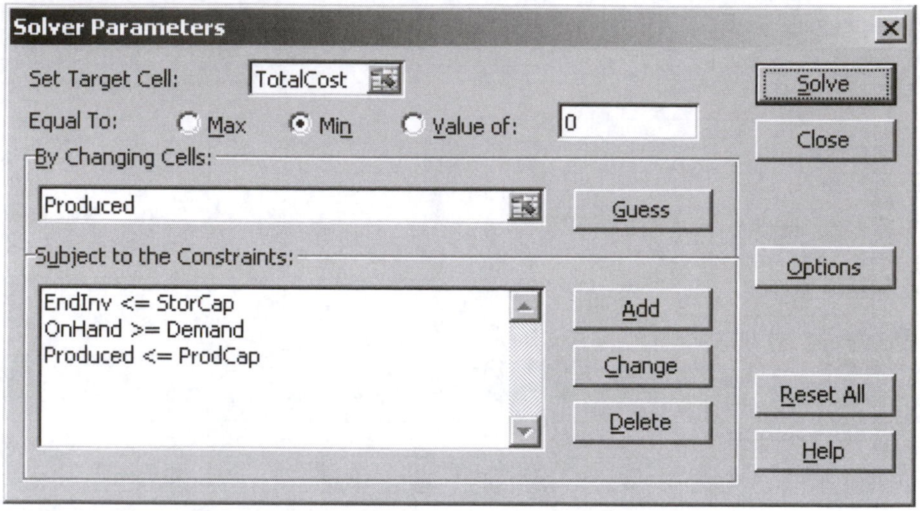

Solver Parameters				
Set Target Cell:	TotalCost			Solve
Equal To: ○ Max ● Min ○ Value of:	0			Close
By Changing Cells:				
Produced			Guess	
Subject to the Constraints:				Options
EndInv <= StorCap		Add		
OnHand >= Demand		Change		Reset All
Produced <= ProdCap		Delete		Help

Figure 17.3 Solver Options

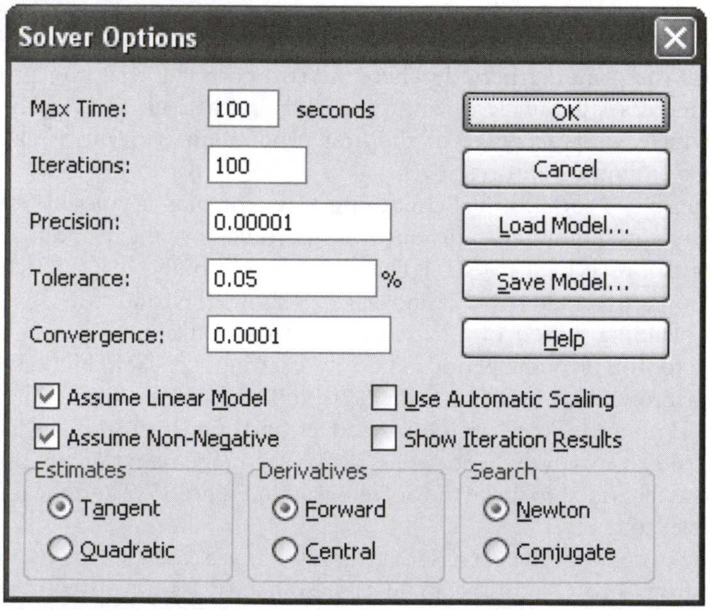

Solver Options		
Max Time: 100 seconds		OK
Iterations: 100		Cancel
Precision: 0.00001		Load Model...
Tolerance: 0.05 %		Save Model...
Convergence: 0.0001		Help
☑ Assume Linear Model	☐ Use Automatic Scaling	
☑ Assume Non-Negative	☐ Show Iteration Results	
Estimates	Derivatives	Search
● Tangent	● Forward	● Newton
○ Quadratic	○ Central	○ Conjugate

up looking like the one in Figure 17.2, but it *is* necessary to reset and then respecify the settings when the physical ranges change. As an added touch, you might try "hiding" the columns that are not used—for example, columns L and M for a 10-month model.

The file **Production Scheduling Finished.xlsm** contains one possible solution. Feel free to open it and click on its button to run it. However, do not look at the VBA code until you have tried writing it yourself.

17.3 Invoking Solver in VBA

Many of the applications in the remaining chapters are optimization models, where Excel's Solver is invoked to obtain an optimal solution. This section explains briefly how to do this. It makes two important assumptions. First, it assumes that you have some familiarity with Solver and know how to use it in the usual way through the Excel interface. Second, it assumes that an optimization model already exists. That is, the inputs and the formulas relating all quantities must already have been entered in a worksheet. This section deals only with specifying the Solver settings and running Solver; it does not deal with the optimization model itself.

Solver is an add-in written by Frontline Systems, *not* by Microsoft. It has a user-friendly Excel interface, shown by the dialog boxes in Figure 17.2 and 17.3, where you describe the model, set options, and eventually click on the Solve button. If all goes well, you obtain the dialog box in Figure 17.4, indicating that an optimal solution has been found.

Fortunately, Frontline Systems has written several VBA functions that allow developers to operate Solver "behind the scenes" with code. These functions enable you to specify the model (target cell, changing cells, and constraints), set options, optimize, and even capture the message in Figure 17.4 (which might say that there is no feasible solution, for example).

Setting a Reference

To use these functions in an application, the first step is to set a **reference** to the Solver add-in in the VBE. Otherwise, VBA will not recognize the Solver functions and you will get a "Sub or function not defined" error message. You set the

Figure 17.4 Solver Results Dialog Box

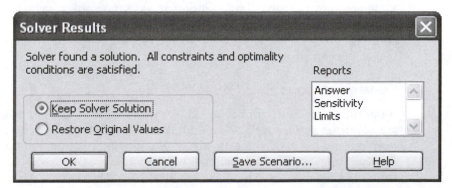

Figure 17.5 List of Potential References

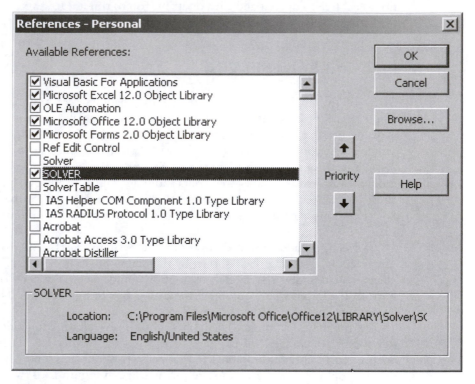

reference with the **Tools → References** menu item in the VBE. This brings up a long list of possible "libraries" of code to choose from. One of these should be **SOLVER**, as shown in Figure 17.5. (Your list might differ from the one shown here, depending on the software versions on your PC. Also, you'll notice that Figure 17.5 has two Solver items. The uppercase version is for the built-in Solver, the one I'm discussing in this chapter. The lowercase version is for Premium Solver, a somewhat more powerful Solver also developed by Frontline Systems and available with this book. I will say more about programming for Premium Solver shortly.) To add the reference, simply check its box. The reference will then appear in the Project Explorer window, as shown in Figure 17.6. Again, if you forget to set this reference and then try to use Solver functions in your code, you will get an error message.

Solver Functions

All of the Solver functions begin with the word Solver. The ones used most often are SolverReset, SolverOk, SolverAdd, SolverOptions, and SolverSolve. This section explains each of these briefly. For more information, go to the Object Browser (after you've set a reference to Solver), select the Solver library and then the VBA_Functions group. (See Figure 17.7.) This shows the names of the

Figure 17.6 Reference in Project Explorer window

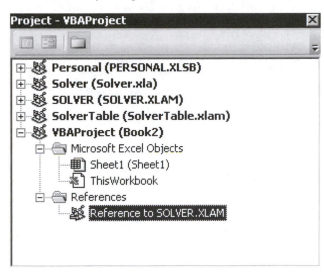

Figure 17.7 Solver Help in Object Browser

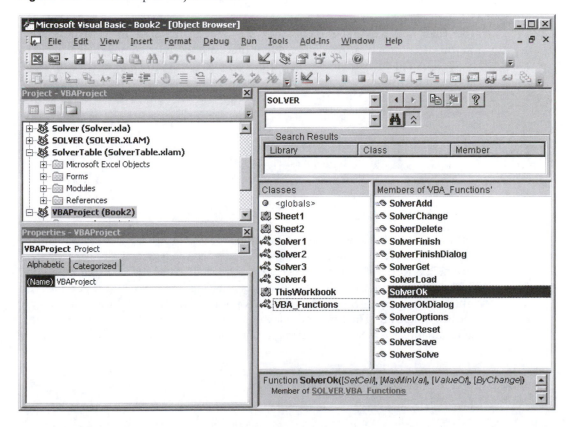

functions and the arguments each expects, but not much else. If you need more help, go to the Frontline Systems Web site and search there.

SolverReset Function

To reset Solver (which is equivalent to clicking on the Reset All button in Figure 17.2), use the line

```
SolverReset
```

This clears all previous settings and lets you start with a clean slate.

SolverOk Function

This function does three things: (1) it identifies the target cell (the objective); (2) it specifies whether the problem is a maximization or minimization problem; and (3) it identifies the changing cells. The following line is typical:

```
SolverOk SetCell:=Range("Profit"), MaxMinVal:=1, ByChange:=Range("Quantities")
```

Note that the **MaxMinVal** argument is 1 for a maximization problem and 2 for a minimization problem. Also, note that if there are several changing cell ranges (so that you would enter them, separated by commas, in the usual Solver dialog box), you can use **Union** in the **ByChange** argument. For example, you could write the following to indicate that there are two ranges of changing cells: the Quantities range and the Prices range.

```
SolverOk SetCell:=Range("Profit"), MaxMinVal:=1, _
   ByChange:=Union(Range("Quantities"), Range("Prices"))
```

SolverAdd Function

This function adds a new constraint each time it is called. It takes three arguments: a left-hand side, a relation index, and a right-hand side. The relation index is 1 for "<=", 2 for "=", 3 for ">=", 4 for "integer", and 5 for "binary". (This is the same order in which they appear in the Solver Add Constraint dialog box. Also, note that there is no right-hand-side argument for the latter two options.) The first and third arguments are specified differently. The left-hand side must be specified as a range, whereas the right-hand side must be specified as a string or a number. Here are several possibilities:

```
SolverAdd CellRef:=Range("Used"), Relation:=1, FormulaText:="Available"
SolverAdd CellRef:=Range("EndInventory"), Relation:=3, FormulaText:=0
SolverAdd CellRef:=Range("Investments"), Relation:=5
```

The first states that the Used range must be less than or equal to the Available range. The second states that the EndInventory range must be greater than or equal to 0. The third states that the Investments range must be binary.

SolverOptions Function

This function allows you to set any of the options in Figure 17.3. The two you will probably set most frequently are the Assume Linear Model and Assume Non-Negative options. They can be set as follows, where I have also changed the Precision option.

```
SolverOptions AssumeLinear:=True, AssumeNonneg:=True, Precision:=0.00001
```

This is equivalent to checking the Assume Linear Model and Assume Non-Negative boxes in Figure 17.3, and changing the precision setting to 0.00001. In general, *any* number of options can follow the SolverOptions function (all separated by commas). When you type SolverOptions and then a space, Intellisense will indicate the names of the various arguments. Because they are all optional, you can list only the ones you want, and you can list them in any order. But to do so, you must specify the name and then :=, as in Precision:=0.000001.

SolverSolve Function

This function is equivalent to clicking the Solve button in the usual Solver dialog box—it performs the optimization. There are two things you should know about SolverSolve. First, if it is used with the argument **UserFinish:=True**, then the dialog box in Figure 17.4 will *not* appear. This dialog box could be a nuisance to a user, so it is often convenient to keep it from appearing with the line

```
SolverSolve UserFinish:=True
```

If you *want* the dialog box in Figure 17.6 to appear, just delete the UserFinish:= True part (or use UserFinish:=False, the default value).

Second, the SolverSolve function returns an integer value that indicates Solver's Outcome. If this integer is 0, it means that Solver was successful, with the message in Figure 17.4. Actually, the integers 1 and 2 also indicate success, with slightly different messages. In contrast, the integer 4 means that Solver did not converge, and the integer 5 means that there are no feasible solutions. (More details can be found at Frontline Systems' Web site.) You can check for any of these and proceed accordingly. For example, the following lines are common. They run Solver, check for feasibility, and display an appropriate message if there are no feasible solutions.

```
Dim result As Integer
result = SolverSolve(UserFinish:=True)
If result = 5 Then
    MsgBox "There are no feasible solutions."
    End
Else
    Worksheets("Report").Activate
End If
```

Note that when the result is captured in a variable, the UserFinish:=True part must be inside parentheses. Actually, the result variable is not really necessary in this code; an alternative is the following:

```
If SolverSolve(UserFinish:=True) = 5 Then
    MsgBox "There are no feasible solutions."
    End
Else
    Worksheets("Report").Activate
End If
```

Some applications require *only* the SolverSolve function. Their Solver settings can be set up manually (with the Solver dialog box, not with VBA) at design time. Then all that is required at run time is to optimize with SolverSolve. Other applications, such as Exercise 17.1, require a SolverReset line, and then SolverOk, SolverAdd, and SolverOptions lines, before SolverSolve can be called. That is, they must set up the model completely—at run time—before they can optimize. This is usually the case when the *size* of the model changes from run to run.

EXAMPLE 17.1 Optimal Product Mix

The file **Product Mix.xlsm** contains a typical product mix linear programming model. A company must decide how many frames of four different types to produce to maximize profit. There are two types of constraints: (1) resources used (labor hours, glass, and metal) must not exceed resources available, and (2) production must not exceed maximum quantities that can be sold. The model appears in Figure 17.8 with an optimal solution. (You can open the file and examine the various formulas. They are all quite straightforward.) The Solver dialog box, filled in manually, appears in Figure 17.9.

The purpose of the example is to generate a sensitivity table in the range G4: L12, as indicated in Figure 17.8. Specifically, for each multiple in column G, we want to replace the original maximum sales values in row 18 by the multiple of these values, run Solver, and report the numbers of frames produced and the corresponding profit in the sensitivity table. Note that when the multiple is "unlimited," there is no maximum sales constraint at all. In this case, there should be only one constraint in the Solver dialog box. The results will appear as in Figure 17.10.

Figure 17.8 Model with Optimal Solution

	A	B	C	D	E	F	G	H	I	J	K	L
1	Product mix model											
2												
3	Input data						Sensitivity to multiples of maximum sales					
4	Hourly wage rate	$8.00		Run sensitivity analysis			Multiple	Frame1	Frame2	Frame3	Frame4	Profit
5	Cost per oz of metal	$0.50					0.50					
6	Cost per oz of glass	$0.75					0.75					
7							1.00					
8	Frame type	1	2	3	4		1.25					
9	Labor hours per frame	2	1	3	2		1.50					
10	Metal (oz.) per frame	4	2	1	2		1.75					
11	Glass (oz.) per frame	6	2	1	2		2.00					
12	Unit selling price	$28.50	$12.50	$29.25	$21.50		Unlimited					
13												
14	Production plan						Range names uses:					
15	Frame type	1	2	3	4		Available	=Model!$D$21:$D$23				
16	Frames produced	1000	800	400	0		MaxSales	=Model!$B$18:$E$18				
17		<=	<=	<=	<=		Multiples	=Model!$G$5:$G$12				
18	Maximum sales	1000	2000	500	1000		Produced	=Model!$B$16:$E$16				
19							Profit	=Model!$F$32				
20	Resource constraints	Used		Available			Used	=Model!$B$21:$B$23				
21	Labor hours	4000	<=	4000								
22	Metal (oz.)	6000	<=	6000								
23	Glass (oz.)	8000	<=	10000								
24												
25	Revenue, cost summary											
26	Frame type	1	2	3	4	Totals						
27	Revenue	$28,500	$10,000	$11,700	$0	$50,200						
28	Costs of inputs											
29	Labor	$16,000	$6,400	$9,600	$0	$32,000						
30	Metal	$2,000	$800	$200	$0	$3,000						
31	Glass	$4,500	$1,200	$300	$0	$6,000						
32	Profit	$6,000	$1,600	$1,600	$0	$9,200						

Figure 17.9 Solver Dialog Box

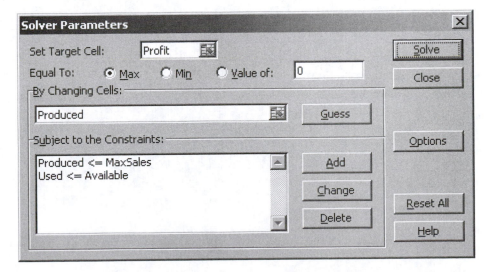

Figure 17.10 Completed Sensitivity Table

	G	H	I	J	K	L
3	Sensitivity to multiples of maximum sales					
4	Multiple	Frame1	Frame2	Frame3	Frame4	Profit
5	0.50	500	1000	250	500	$7,500
6	0.75	750	1250	375	62	$8,688
7	1.00	1000	800	400	0	$9,200
8	1.25	1250	300	400	0	$9,700
9	1.50	1400	0	400	0	$10,000
10	1.75	1400	0	400	0	$10,000
11	2.00	1400	0	400	0	$10,000
12	Unlimited	1400	0	400	0	$10,000

To develop this project, the first step is to open the VBE and add a reference to Solver. Then the following VBA code does the job. The "main" sub, called **Sensitivity**, is attached to the button in Figure 17.9. Its basic function is to call a number of other subs to perform the various tasks. Note that three of these subs, **ChangeModel**, **RunSolver**, and **StoreResults**, are called within a For Each loop that loops over all cells in the Multiples range. Also, note how an argument is passed to each of these subs. More explanation on the various subs is provided below.

```
Option Explicit
Option Base 1

Dim maxSales(4) As Single

Sub Sensitivity()
    Dim cell As Range
    Dim multiple As Variant
    Dim iModel As Integer
    Dim includeConstraint As Boolean

    Application.ScreenUpdating = False
    Call SaveOriginalValues
    iModel = 0
    For Each cell In Range("Multiples")
        iModel = iModel + 1
        multiple = cell.Value
        If IsNumeric(multiple) Then includeConstraint = True
        Call ChangeModel(multiple)
        Call RunSolver(includeConstraint)
        Call StoreResults(iModel)
    Next
    Call RestoreOriginalValues
End Sub
```

The first sub called, **SaveOriginalValues**, stores the original maximum sales values in the maxSales array for later use.

```
Sub SaveOriginalValues()
    Dim i As Integer
    For i = 1 To 4
        maxSales(i) = Range("MaxSales").Cells(i)
    Next
End Sub
```

The **ChangeModel** sub takes the multiple argument and checks whether it is numeric with VBA's handy **IsNumeric** function. If it is, the sub multiplies the original maximum sales values by multiple and places these multiples in the Max-Sales range.

```
Sub ChangeModel(multiple As Variant)
    Dim i As Integer
    If IsNumeric(multiple) Then
        For i = 1 To 4
            Range("MaxSales").Cells(i) = multiple * maxSales(i)
        Next
    End If
End Sub
```

The **RunSolver** sub first resets Solver and then sets it up from scratch. It takes a Boolean argument, includeConstraint. If this value is True (because mulitple is numeric), then the maximum sales constraint is included; otherwise, it is not included. Note that if *all* values of multiple in column G were numeric, then only the SolverSolve line of this sub would be required. This is because the Solver setup, developed manually as in Figure 17.9, would never change. You might argue that with only one possible change (the inclusion or exclusion of the maximum sales constraint), it should not be necessary to reset and then respecify the Solver setup *entirely*. This argument is correct. It is indeed possible to delete or add a single constraint to an existing Solver setup, but I have taken the "reset" route here, primarily to illustrate the various Solver functions.

```
Sub RunSolver(includeConstraint As Boolean)
    SolverReset
    SolverOk SetCell:=Range("Profit"), MaxMinVal:=1, ByChange:=Range("Produced")
    SolverAdd CellRef:=Range("Used"), Relation:=1, FormulaText:="Available"
    If includeConstraint Then
        SolverAdd CellRef:=Range("Produced"), Relation:=1, FormulaText:="MaxSales"
    End If
    SolverOptions AssumeLinear:=True, AssumeNonNeg:=True
    SolverSolve UserFinish:=True
End Sub
```

The **StoreResults** sub takes the Solver results in the Produced and Profit ranges and transfers them to the sensitivity table. It takes a single argument, iModel, that specifies how far down the table to place the results. Note that iModel is increased by 1 each time through the For Each loop in the Sensitivity sub.

```
Sub StoreResults(iModel As Integer)
    Dim i As Integer
    With Range("G4")
        For i = 1 To 4
            .Offset(iModel, i) = Range("Produced").Cells(i)
        Next
            .Offset(iModel, 5) = Range("Profit")
    End With
End Sub
```

Finally, the **RestoreOriginalResults** sub places the original maximum sales values back in the MaxSales range and runs Solver one last time. This is not absolutely necessary—by the time this sub is called, the sensitivity table is complete—but it is a nice touch. This way, the final thing the user sees is the solution to the original problem.

```
Sub RestoreOriginalValues()
    Dim i As Integer
    For i = 1 To 4
        Range("MaxSales").Cells(i) = maxSales(i)
    Next
    Call RunSolver(UserFinish:=True)
End Sub
```

17.4 Possible Solver Problems

There are a couple of peculiarities you should be aware of when you use Solver with VBA.

Using a Main Sub

The problem described in this section has evidently been fixed in Excel 2007's Solver. But I'll retain this section for pre-Excel 2007 users.

It is common to name your "control center" sub **Main**. This causes a strange problem in a program that has a reference to Solver. Try the following. Open a new workbook, get into the VBE, add a module, and add a reference to Solver (in Tools → References). Then add a sub in the module called Main. It doesn't have to do anything interesting, but it should be called Main. Now get back into Excel and open Solver from the Data ribbon. You will *not* see the Solver dialog box. To go one step farther, add a user form to your program (you can keep the generic name UserForm1), and add the following line to your Main sub:

```
UserForm1.Show
```

Again, get back into Excel and open Solver. Your new userform will appear!

What's going on? The problem is that Solver has its own Main sub. So when you open Solver in Excel, it gets confused and invokes *your* Main sub instead of its Main sub. The fix is easy. If your program sets a reference to Solver, don't use the name Main for any of your subs. If you still like Main, use a name like MainProductMix or something similar. This is my convention in all applications in the second part of the book that invoke Solver.

Missing Solver Reference

Let's say that someone (like me) writes a program that sets a reference to Solver. They give you that program, and you try running it—and you get an error. The chances are that you have a "missing Solver reference" problem. This is a common problem, one that I have gotten numerous e-mails about over the past few years. I finally went to the source—technical support at Frontline Systems—and got what I believe is a simple and reliable fix.

According to my source at Frontline Systems,[2]

> This problem happens because the Solver is a 'smart' add-in, which does not get loaded until you use it. (This stems back from the days where start-up time and memory usage was an issue). When Solver has not been used in an Excel session, and the **Solver.xla** is therefore not opened yet, the following can happen. A user can open a workbook with a reference to the solver add-in (because VBA uses Solver in the workbook). Excel tries to restore the reference by opening the **Solver.xla**, and it does this by following the path to the solver add-in stored in the workbook. If the user's solver add-in is located in a different place, Excel will fail, and produce a "Missing: solver.xla" in the references list, and the program won't run.
>
> By far the simplest solution is to start Excel with a blank workbook, and just open the Solver dialog box once. When this is done, **Solver.xla** gets loaded, and when your workbook now gets opened, the reference to the solver add-in will be updated to the loaded solver add-in. If the user now saves the workbook, the reference is updated permanently, and he will not have any problems in the future.

The point is that the cricital file **Solver.xla** is not stored in the same location on all PCs. This is the source of the "missing Solver reference" problem. (Actually, this missing reference can occur for other reasons that I won't go into here.) However, to avoid this problem, all you have to do is open Solver and then close it. Then all of the VBA applications that come from this book should work fine.

To help you remember this fix, all later applications in this book that require a reference to Solver show a message similar to that in Figure 17.11 when the application opens. This message is actually a user form, and it is always called **frmSolver**.

---

[2]Replace **Solver.xla** with **Solver.xlam** in the following discussion if you are using Excel 2007.

Figure 17.11 Solver Message in Solver Applications

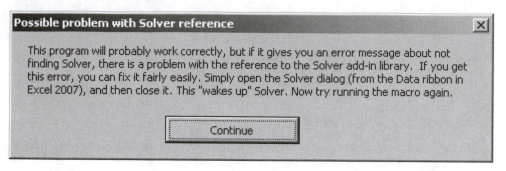

17.5 Programming with Advanced Versions of Solver

Writing programs to automate Solver should be straightforward, and it often is. But as I have found from experience with my SolverTable add-in (see http://www.kelley.iu.edu/albrightbooks/Free_downloads.htm), it can also be a never-ending source of headaches. The problem is that a programmer has to go by the rules Microsoft has set up for add-ins like Solver. But as Microsoft develops new versions of Excel, these rules change. Besides that, the rules have not always been obvious, and it is difficult to find them written down anywhere. This is the reason for many of the "fixes" described on my Web site.

Fortunately, there is now an alternative that I will briefly describe in this section. Frontline Systems has many products besides the "standard" Solver that ships with Excel. In particular, it has a Risk Solver Platform (and Risk Solver Platform for Education, that is available with this book) that is *much* more powerful than Excel's built-in Solver. Better yet, Risk Solver Platform has an improved API (application programming interface) for VBA programmers. This new API has an object model for controlling Solver models that is much more like other object models such as Excel's, complete with Intellisense. It takes some experimentation to get your code to work—the online help is not as thorough as it eventually will be—but the structure is more logical than the Solver functions discussed in previous sections. And best of all, the code is much more stable than the original Solver code. For example, you don't have to "wake up" Solver or worry about where the user's Solver folder is located.

To take advantage of this new API, you must first install Risk Solver Platform for Education. (This is available as a download for everyone who purchases a *new* version of this book.) Next, you must set a reference to **Risk Solver Platform 9.5 Type Library** from the **Tools → References** menu item in the VBE. (See Figure 17.12.)

Once you do this, you can get help from the Object Browser by selecting the RSP library. Some of this is shown in Figure 17.13. As usual, you can select an object or enumeration on the left and see more information on the right. Unfortunately, no extra help appears if you click on the question mark, but I will try to supply the information you need here.

Figure 17.12 Reference for Risk Solver Platform Library

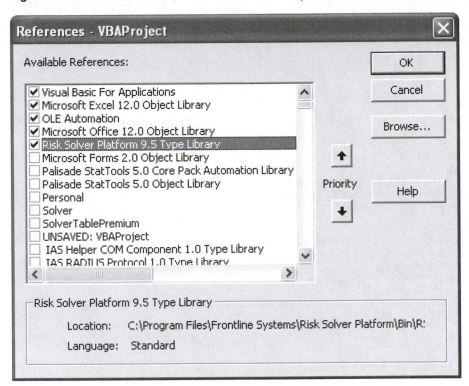

The "top-level" object for Risk Solver Platform models is the **Problem** object. It essentially refers to an optimization model on a worksheet. Other key objects are the **Solver**, **Function**, and **Variable** objects. The Solver object contains all of the information about the optimizer used to optimize the model. A Function object refers to either the objective (target) to be optimized or a group of constraint function cells. A Variable object refers to a range of changing cells. There is also a **Variables** collection object, the set of all changing cell ranges, and a **Functions** collection object, the set of all objective and constraint functions.

To illustrate how it all works, I developed the following code that can be used instead of the RunSolver code from Section 17.3 for the product mix application.

```
Sub RunSolver(includeConstraint As Boolean)
    Dim prob as New RSP.Problem

    With prob
        .Variables.Clear
        .Functions.Clear

        ' Objective
        Dim obj As New RSP.Function
        obj.Init Range("Profit")
```

```
            obj.FunctionType = Function_Type_Objective
            .Functions.Add obj

            ' Changing cells
            Dim chCells As New RSP.Variable
            chCells.Init Range("Produced")
            chCells.NonNegative
            .Variables.Add chCells

            ' MaxMin value
            .Solver.SolverType = Solver_Type_Maximize

            ' Constraints
            Dim constr1 As New RSP.Function
            constr1.Init Range("Used")
            constr1.FunctionType = Function_Type_Constraint
            constr1.UpperBound.Array = "Available"
            .Functions.Add constr1

            If includeConstraint Then
                Dim constr2 As New RSP.Function
                constr2.Init Range("Produced")
                constr2.FunctionType = Function_Type_Constraint
                constr2.UpperBound.Array = "MaxSales"
                .Functions.Add constr2
            End If
            .Solver.Optimize
        End With
    End Sub
```

Figure 17.13 Object Browser for RSP Library

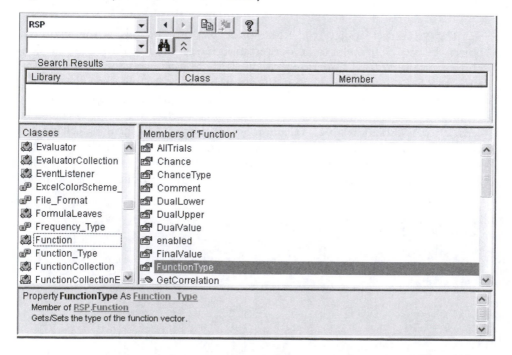

Although this code is quite readable, here are a few comments.

- Each Problem, Function, and Variable object must be *instantiated*, which is done with the keyword **New**. The prefix RSP is used to indicate that these objects are part of the RSP library.
- The Functions and Variables collections should first be cleared.
- Note how the objective (target) is set up. First, a new Function object is instantiated. Then the **Init** method is used to specify its range. Next, the **FunctionType** property is set. In this case, it is the Objective type, but later on in the code, it is the Constraint type. Finally, this function is added to the Functions collection of the Problem object.
- There is only one changing cell range in this model, so only one Variable object is required. If there were more changing cell ranges, extra Variable objects would be required. The **Nonnegative** property is used to ensure that the changing cells are nonnegative. After the properties of the Variable object are set, it is added to the Variables collection of the Problem object.
- The Problem object has a **Solver** property that returns the Solver that does the optimization. It has a **SolverType** property to specify whether the problem is a minimization or maximization, and it has an **Optimize** method to run the optimization.
- As in Section 17.3, the left and right sides of the constraints are treated differently. The **Init** method of a constraint function specifies the left side of the constraint as a range. The right side is specified by the **UpperBound. Array** (or **LowerBound.Array**) property, which is set to a string (either a range name or an address). Of course, UpperBound indicates a "<=" constraint, whereas LowerBound indicates a ">=" constraint. And if you want an equality constraint, you can set the LowerBound *and* UpperBound to the same value.

The above code is required if you need to reset the Solver settings several times through a loop, as in the product mix application. However, if the Solver settings never change during the execution of the program, you can set them up at design time interactively through the user interface. Then the only code you need is the following:

```
Dim prob as New RSP.Problem
Prob.Solver.Optimize
```

For all Solver models in this chapter and later chapters, I will use the original Solver functions (SolverSolver, SolverOK, and so on) in the code that appears in the book. However, there will be two files included with the book for each such model: a file like **Product Mix.xlsm** and a file like **Product Mix RSP.xlsm**. The latter indicates that Risk Solver Platform code is used. Most of the code in these latter files is a simple variation of the code illustrated here. However, there are a few twists, such as how to specify integer-constrained or binary-constrained variables. I urge you to learn by my examples—and to experiment.

Before leaving this section, I'd like to make several other comments about Risk Solver Platform.

- For most of you who are used to the Excel Solver dialog boxes, or even previous Premium Solver dialog boxes, the user interface will be quite new. There is a Risk Solver Platform tab, and when you click on it, you will see something like shown in Figures 17.14 and 17.15. You can define the Solver model from the buttons in the ribbon or through the new Model pane on the right. I won't try to explain the options, but I can assure you that they are quite straightforward. Also, if you prefer the "old" look, you can get something very close it by clicking on the small arrow at the bottom right of the Optimization Model group in Figure 17.14.

- When I claim that the Risk Solver Platform is much more powerful than Excel's Solver, I am not exaggerating. For many of you who are running small linear models, the difference will probably not be apparent. But optimization models in real applications are often much more complex. They can have a large number of integer or binary variables, and they can have complex nonlinear, maybe even nonsmooth, functions. Such problems are very difficult to solve and are often impossible for Excel's Solver. The chances are much better that Risk Solver Platform can solve them.

- As Figures 17.14 and 17.15 indicate, Risk Solver Platform can do much more than optimization. It can run simulations (hence the reason for Risk in its name), it can perform optimization on models with uncertainty, and it can run decision trees for making decisions under uncertainty. Its goal is to provide "one-stop shopping" for the serious modeler.

- The software world is constantly changing, so be ready for more changes. Specifically, a new version of Excel is due out soon after the third edition of this book appears, and Frontline Systems will undoubtedly adapt its software to the new Excel. Will the current Solver programs in this book still work? I hope so, but I won't guarantee it. If changes are required, I will post them on my Web site at http://www.kelley.iu.edu/albrightbooks. (The same comments apply to the Palisade add-ins discussed in the next section.)

Figure 17.14 Risk Solver Platform Toolbar

Figure 17.15 Risk Solver Platform Model Pane

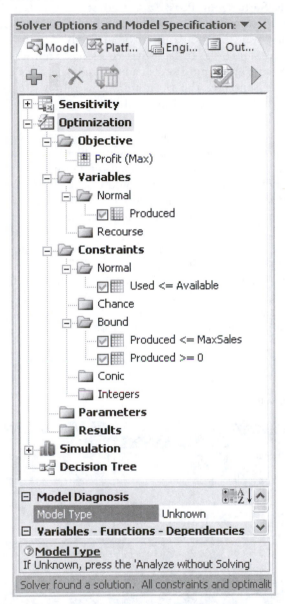

17.6 Programming with Palisade Add-Ins

The advantage of working with Solver is that it ships with Excel. When you purchase Microsoft Office, you get Solver as part of the deal. However, there are many other Excel add-ins that can be purchased separately. Some of these add-ins (but certainly not all) expose VBA programming capabilities, just as

I discussed with Solver. One set of add-ins I am particularly familiar with is the Decision Tools Suite from Palisade Corporation.[3] This suite includes, among others, @RISK for simulation modeling and StatTools for statistical analysis. In the same way that you can automate Solver with VBA, you can automate @RISK and StatTools. In fact, StatTools has been written so that a statistician with some programming skills can actually write his own advanced statistical routines. Essentially, the programmer would write the statistical logic in VBA but would still get to take advantage of the underlying Stat-Tools framework.

How would you learn how to do this? This depends entirely on the reference materials that accompany the add-in. For example, when you install the Palisade suite, you can go to the Windows Start button and find online reference manuals, as shown in Figure 17.16. For @RISK, you would choose **@RISK 5.0 for Excel Developer Kit Manual** on the right. These developer kit manuals explain how to manipulate the add-ins with VBA, and they are quite thorough.

To use @RISK functionality in a VBA program, say, you must first use the **Tools → References** menu item to set a reference to the @RISK object library, just as you do with Solver. For StatTools, you would do the same. (See the bottom two checked items in Figure 17.17 for the references you should add.) This allows you to take advantage of everything that is explained in the manuals. It is then "just" a matter of learning the functionality that @RISK or StatTools provides. The rest of this section illustrates some possibilities.

Figure 17.16 Palisade Reference Manuals

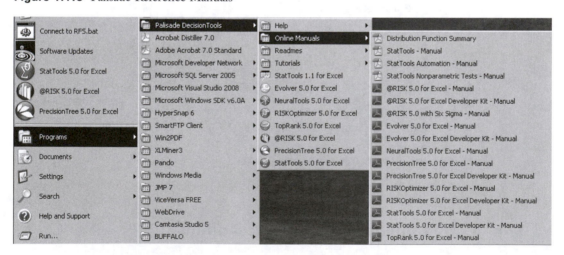

---

[3]The academic version of this suite is available with my *Practical Management Science* and *Data Analysis and Decision Making* books.

Figure 17.17 @RISK and StatTools References

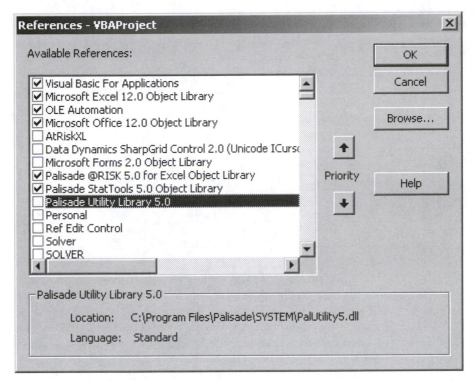

Automating @RISK

If you have used @RISK 5.0 (or the newer 5.5 version), you are aware that it has a number of ways to produce results from a simulation. In fact, the variety of possibilities can be bewildering. Therefore, I wrote a template to automate one variation of the process. You can find this in the file **Simulation Template.xlsm**. There is only one worksheet in this file, the Model sheet shown in Figure 17.18. It is quite generic and is set up so that you can enter any number of inputs in the Inputs section, any number of outputs in the Outputs section, and any simulation model in the Simulation section. I assume that you would like to run a number of simulations, one for each combination of input values to be tested, as listed in the Inputs section. In the case shown, there are $1 \times 2 \times 3 = 6$ input combinations, so 6 different simulations will be run. The program does this in a clever way with @RISK's **RiskSimtable** function. In the Outputs section, you can designate any statistical outputs desired, including percentiles and targets. (@RISK uses the term **target** to mean a probability of the "less than or equal to" variety. So, for example, row 15 is requesting the probability that the Output3 is less than or equal to 4.) The program runs the required number of simulations, each for the requested number of iterations, and creates a worksheet for means, a worksheet for standard deviations, and so on.

Figure 17.18 Simulation Template Setup

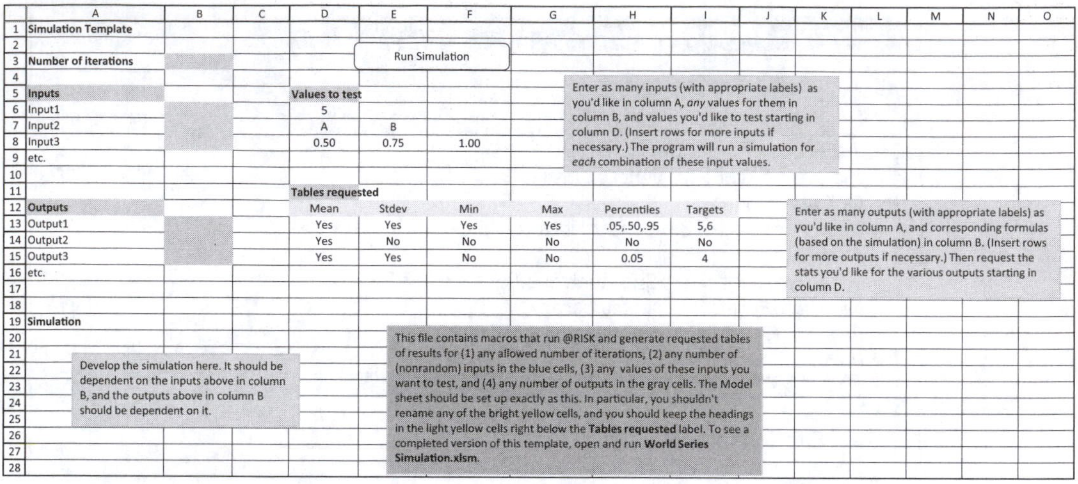

A lot of the code for this template contains nothing new, so I won't show it here. But here is part of the code, where I have boldfaced the lines that rely on the @RISK object model. (There aren't many.) Note that I first had to set a reference to the @RISK object library through the **Tools → References** menu item, as explained earlier. Otherwise, the boldfaced lines below wouldn't be recognized by VBA.

The first section of code illustrates how to change some @RISK simulation settings and how to designate cells as @RISK output cells. (There is no automatic way to perform this latter task. You just have to manipulate the formula for the output to include RISKOUT(*outputname*)+).

```
' Change some settings.
With Risk.Simulation.Settings
    .AutomaticResultsDisplay = RiskNoAutomaticResults
    .NumIterations = Range("Number_of_iterations").Value
    .NumSimulations = nSimulations
End With

' Designate output cells as @RISK output cells if they're not already designated.
For i = 1 To nOutputs
    If InStr(1, outputCell(i).Formula, "RiskOutput") = 0 Then
        outputCell(i).Formula = "=RiskOutput(""" & outputName(i) & """)+" _
            & Right(outputCell(i).Formula, Len(outputCell(i).Formula) - 1)
    End If
Next
```

To run the simulation once it has been set up, only one line of code is necessary:

```
Risk.Simulation.Start
```

Finally, to get the requested statistical results in various worksheets, the following code is used. Most of this is just careful bookkeeping, but the key is Risk.Simulation.Results.GetSimulatedOuput(*output*). This returns a particular set of results, those for the designated output, from the Results collection of the Simulation object. From there, you can ask for the mean, the standard deviation, or other statistical summary measures.

```
Select Case statType
    Case "Mean", "Stdev", "Min", "Max"
        For i = 1 To nOutputs
            If Range("Tables_Requested") _
                    .Offset(i + 1, index - 1).Value = "Yes" Then
                nRequested = nRequested + 1
                With Range("A1").Offset(0, j)
                    .Value = outputName(i)
                    For k = 1 To nSimulations
                        If statType = "Mean" Then
                            .Offset(k, 0).Value = Risk.Simulation.Results _
                                .GetSimulatedOutput(outputName(i), k).Mean
                        ElseIf statType = "Stdev" Then
                            .Offset(k, 0).Value = Risk.Simulation.Results _
                                .GetSimulatedOutput(outputName(i), k).StdDeviation
                        ElseIf statType = "Min" Then
                            .Offset(k, 0).Value = Risk.Simulation.Results _
                                .GetSimulatedOutput(outputName(i), k).Minimum
                        ElseIf statType = "Max" Then
                            .Offset(k, 0).Value = Risk.Simulation.Results _
                                .GetSimulatedOutput(outputName(i), k).Maximum
                        End If
                    Next
                End With
                j = j + 1
            End If
        Next
    Case "Percentiles", "Targets"
        For i = 1 To nOutputs
            statString = Range("Tables_Requested") _
                .Offset(i + 1, index - 1).Value
            If statString <> "No" Then
                nRequested = nRequested + 1
                ' Parse the string of comma-delimited values.
                Call GetArrays(statString, arrayString, arrayNumber)
                For l = 1 To UBound(arrayString)
                    With Range("A1").Offset(0, j)
                        If statType = "Percentiles" Then
                            .Value = "Pctile " & arrayString(l) _
                                & " " & outputName(i)
                        ElseIf statType = "Targets" Then
                            .Value = "P(" & outputName(i) _
                                & " <= " & arrayString(l) & ")"
                        End If
                        For k = 1 To nSimulations
                            If statType = "Percentiles" Then
                                .Offset(k, 0).Value = Risk.Simulation.Results _
                                    .GetSimulatedOutput(outputName(i), k) _
                                        .PToX(arrayNumber(l))
                            ElseIf statType = "Targets" Then
                                .Offset(k, 0).Value = Risk.Simulation.Results _
```

```
                              .GetSimulatedOutput(outputName(i),  k)  _
                                  .XToP(arrayNumber(l))
                    End If
                 Next
             End With
              j = j + 1
          Next
        End If
     Next
 End Select
```

The code in this template can be used, exactly as is, on *any* simulation model that is set up as instructed in Figure 17.18. I have included two examples on the CD-ROM: **World Series Simulation.xlsm** and **Newsvendor Simulation.xlsm**. Open them and try them out. Just remember that @RISK must be loaded for them to work properly.

Automating StatTools

StatTools is an add-in that contains a number of common statistical procedures. These include scatterplots, histograms, confidence intervals, hypothesis tests, regression analysis, and others. Palisade built this add-in with a very simple user interface, but it also provided VBA programmers with a lot of functionality. As with @RISK, you can automate any of the built-in statistical procedures. For example, with only a few lines of code, you can ask StatTools to run a hypothesis test for a particular variable. The code to do so is shown below. As you can see, it closely mimics the steps you would follow if you were doing it through the StatTools user interface.

```
'Scan this workbook to find the StatTools data sets.
StatTools.DataSets.Scan ThisWorkbook

'Optionally tell StatTools where to place reports.
StatTools.Settings.ReportPlacement = StatToolsPlaceInActiveWorkbook
StatTools.Settings.ReportOverwriteExisting = False

'Create object that is used to automate Hypothesis Test procedure.
Dim hypTestObj As New StatTools_HypothesisTest

'Define analysis parameters.
With hypTestObj
    .AnalysisType = StatToolsHypothesisTestOneSample
    .PerformMeanTest = True
    .MeanNullValue = 10
    .PerformStdDevTest = False
    .MeanAlternativeType = StatToolsAlternativeLessThan
    'Select a particular variable
    .VariableList.Add StatTools.DataSets(1).Variables(2)
    .GenerateReport
End With
```

For a more ambitious example of automating StatTools, see the file **StatTools Automated Analysis.xlsm**. Although the code is fairly straightforward, the application is quite useful. It assumes you start with any data set with upper left corner in cell A1 and that you designate by formatting (boldface, italics, underlining) which variables you want summary measures for, which you want histograms for, and which you want scatterplots for. Then with the click of a button, it designates the data set as a StatTools data set, and it creates the requested summary measures, histograms, and scatterplots. This is the initial analysis most of us perform when we are exploring data, so why not automate it!

Creating New StatTools Procedures

The feature of StatTools that has real potential for a statistician/programmer is that *new* statistical procedures can be developed. Fortunately, these can build on the structure that StatTools already has in place. For example, virtually all StatTools procedures start with a dialog box as in Figure 17.19, where (in the top part) the user must select one or more variables from a data set to analyze. This variable selection part of the dialog box is actually a control, just like the controls discussed in Chapter 11, except that Palisade developed it. In fact, their programmers undoubtedly spent many, many hours perfecting this control. Fortunately,

Figure 17.19 Typical StatTools Dialog Box

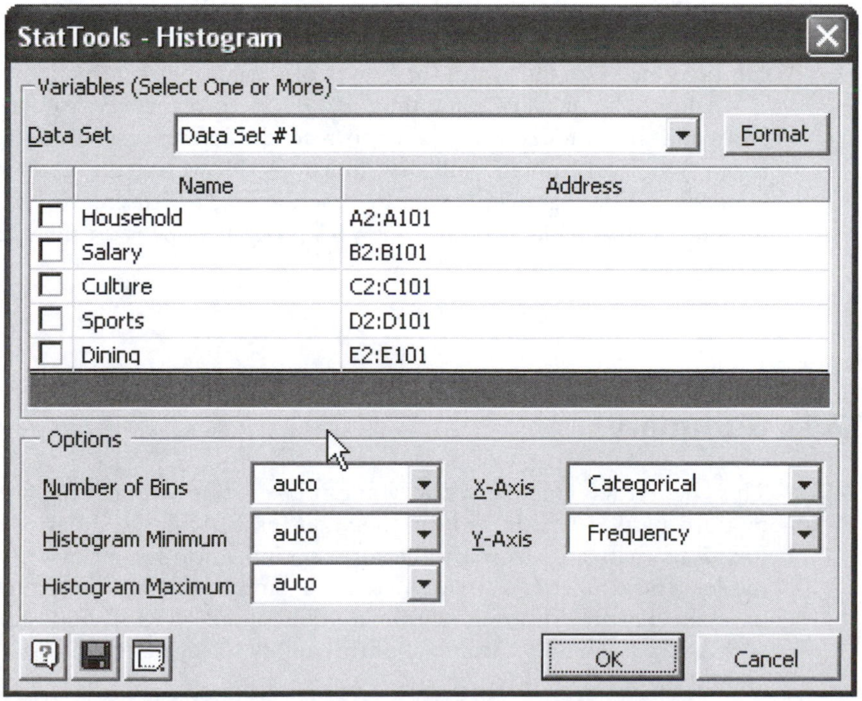

you can now create an instance of this control on your own user forms and tap into all the functionality it contains. In other words, you can borrow Palisades work, so that you dont have to reinvent the wheel on each new project.

I tried building a new statistical procedure, one that is not already included in StatTools. This is a confidence interval for a proportion. (Based on my prototype, Palisade is including this and other similar procedures for proportions in version 5.5 of StatTools.) The coding isnt exactly easy—you have to follow the rules Palisade has set up—but they have provided a template to make the process a lot easier than it would be otherwise. (This **Template.xls** file is located in the C:\Program Files\Palisade\StatTools5\Examples\English\Developer Kit folder.) It took me about a day to learn the rules and create my confidence interval procedure. I wont show the code here, but you can find it in the **CI_Proportion.xla** file.

To try out my new procedure, you might first want to open the **CI_Proportion.xls** file. It has the same code as the **CI_Proportion.xla** file, but it is not saved as an add-in (.xla) file. Its single worksheet indicates how the data should be set for my confidence interval procedure. Then go to the C:\Program Files\Palisade\StatTools5\Analyses folder, create a new subfolder with a name such as NewProcedures, and copy the **CI_Proportion.xla** and **CI_Proportion_Menu.xla** files to this new folder. (This latter file just creates a menu item for my procedure.) Now open StatTools in Excel, and open the **CI_Proportion_Menu.xla** file. You will see a new item in the Add-Ins ribbon (*not* the StatTools ribbon). Check it out on your own data set. You will still need to go through the usual StatTools Data Set Manager to designate your data set, but then you can run my procedure on it.

A Palisade colleague told me that I am the first programmer he knows who has taken advantage of this ability to create new StatTools procedures. However, it can be done. This illustrates the power of a true object model!

Admittedly, it takes some time and effort to learn how to automate a third-party add-in with VBA. You have to read the reference manual (assuming there is one!) and experiment with new functions. However, the good news is that it is possible. For example, if you are a serious @RISK user, the fact that you can fine-tune your simulation runs with VBA programs opens up a whole new realm of possibilities.

17.7 Summary

This chapter has illustrated how you can take advantage of VBA functions written by third-party developers to run their add-ins. Specifically, I have discussed Solver functions that can be used to perform optimization for an existing optimization model. These functions allow you to set up and run Solver completely with VBA. I have also illustrated how to automate the Palisade @RISK and StatTools add-ins with VBA. I will take advantage of this ability in several of the applications in the second half of the book.

EXERCISES

1. The file **Product Mix.xlsx** contains a typical product mix model. A company needs to decide how many of each type of picture frame to produce, subject to constraints on resource availabilities and upper bounds on production quantities. The objective is to maximize profit. The model is set up appropriately, although the current solution is not optimal. The cells in blue are inputs, and the cells in red are changing cells. The ranges names being used are listed. Write a sub that sets up Solver and then runs it.

2. The file **Production Scheduling.xlsx** contains a multiperiod production scheduling model. A company has to schedule its production over the next several months to meet known demands on time. There are also production capacity and storage capacity constraints, and the objective is to minimize the total cost. The model is currently set up (correctly) for a 12-month planning horizon. The cells in blue are inputs, and the cells in red are changing cells. The range names currently being used are listed. This model can easily be changed, by deleting columns or copying across to the right, to make the planning horizon longer or shorter. Suppose someone else does this. Your job is to write a sub that renames ranges appropriately, sets up Solver correctly, and then runs it. That is, your sub should optimize the model in the worksheet, regardless of how many months its planning horizon is.

3. The file **Facility Location.xlsx** contains a model for locating a central warehouse. There are four customers that send shipments to this warehouse. Their coordinates are given, as well as their numbers of annual shipments. The objective is to minimize the annual distance traveled, and there are no constraints. The cells in blue are inputs, and the cells in red are changing cells. The range names being used are listed. This is a nonlinear model, so it is conceivable that there is a local minimum in addition to the global minimum. If there is, then it is possible that the Solver solution could depend on the initial solution used (in the red cells). To test this, write two short subs and attach them to the buttons. The first should generate "reasonable" random initial solutions. (Use VBA's Rnd function, which generates a uniformly distributed random number from 0 to 1, in an appropriate way. Make sure to put a **Randomize** statement at the top of the sub so that you get different random numbers each time you run the sub.) The second sub should then run Solver. (It doesn't need to set up Solver. You can do that manually, once and for all.) Then repeatedly click the left button and then the right button. Do you always get the same Solver solution?

4. The file **Transport.xlsx** contains a transportation model where a product must be shipped from three plants to four cities at minimal shipping cost. The constraints are that no plant can ship more than its capacity, and each city must receive at least what it demands. The model has been developed (correctly) on the Model sheet. The company involved wants to run this model on five scenarios. Each of these scenarios, shown on the Scenarios sheet, has a particular set of capacities and demands. Write a sub that uses a For loop over the scenarios to do the following: (1) it copies the data for a particular scenario to the relevant parts of the Model sheet; (2) it runs Solver; and (3) it copies selected results to the Results sheet. To

get you started, the Results sheet currently shows the results for scenario 1. This is the format you should use for all scenarios.

5. The file **Pricing.xlsx** contains a model for finding the optimal price of a product. The product is made in America and sold in Europe. The company wants to set the price, in Euros, so that its profit, in dollars, is maximized. The demand for the product is a function of price, and it is assumed that the elasticity of demand is constant. This leads to the formula for demand in cell B14, which depends on the parameters in row 10. (These parameters are assumed to be known.) The revenue, in dollars, equals price multiplied by demand. Of course, this depends on the exchange rate in cell B4. The company wants to perform a sensitivity analysis on the exchange rate. The results will be placed in the Sensitivity sheet, which already lists the exchange rates the company wants to test. Do the following: (1) Enter *any* data in columns B, C, and D of the Sensitivity sheet and use them to create three line charts (to the right of the data) that show price, demand, and profit versus the exchange rate; and (2) write a sub that substitutes each exchange rate into the model, runs Solver, and transfers the results to the Sensitivity sheet. When you run your sub, the charts should update automatically with the new data. (That's why you manually set up the chart and link it to data columns—so that you don't have to do with it VBA code.)

6. The file **Stocks.xls** contains stock price returns for many large companies for a 5-year period. (Feel free to download more recent stock price data if you prefer.) Each company has its own sheet, with the stock's ticker symbol as the name of the sheet. There is also an S&P500 sheet with the market returns. The Model sheet uses the market returns and the returns from a given stock to estimate the equation **Market = Alpha + Beta * Stock**, where Market and Stock are the returns and Alpha and Beta are parameters to be estimated. The estimated Beta is especially useful to financial analysts. It is a measure of the volatility of the stock. The model is set up correctly (currently with data from American Express). The Alpha and Beta parameters are found by minimizing the sum of squared errors in cell E4. Write a sub that does the following: (1) It uses a For Each loop to go through all sheets except the Results, Model, and S&P500 sheets, that is, all stock sheets; (2) it copies the stock's returns to column C of the Model sheet; (3) it runs Solver; and (4) it reports the results in a new line in the Results sheet. At the end, the Results sheet should have the ticker symbol and the Alpha and Beta for each stock. (*Note*: Your sub doesn't need to set up Solver. You can do that once and for all at design time, manually.)

7. The file **Planting.xlsx** contains a very simple model that a farmer could use to plant his crops optimally. The inputs are in blue, and the changing cells are in red. The purpose of this exercise is to develop a VBA application that allows the user to (1) choose any of the input cells as the cell to vary in a sensitivity analysis, (2) choose a range over which to vary this cell, (3) run Solver over this range, and (4) report the results in the Sensitivity sheet. Here are some guidelines. For (1), you should develop a user form that has a list box with descriptive names of all input cells, such as Profit per acre of wheat, Workers used per acre of wheat, and so on. The user should be allowed to choose only one item from this list. For (2), you should develop a second user form where the user can enter a minimum value, a maximum value, and an increment. For example, the user might specify that she

wants to vary the profit per acre of wheat from $150 to $350 in increments of $50. Perform error checks to ensure that numerical values are entered, the minimum value is less than the maximum value, and the increment is positive. For (3), store the current values of the selected input in a variable, run the sensitivity analysis, and then restore the current value. For (4), make sure you adjust the labels in cells A1 and A3 of the Sensitivity sheet for the particular input chosen.

8. The Solver add-in contains some hidden secrets that can come in handy if you know them. (You might have to develop a friendship with someone in Frontline Systems' technical support group to learn them!) Here is one such secret. The changing cells in any Solver model are given the range name "solver_adj". This name won't appear in the list of range names when you use Excel's Name Manager, but it's there. You can use it as follows. Open the file **Plant Location.xlsx**. This is a fairly large Solver model that can be used to find optimal locations of plants and warehouses. It is currently set up correctly, but it is not obvious where the changing cells are. (I didn't color the changing cells red as I usually do.) You could peek at the Solver dialog box to find the changing cells, but don't do so. Instead, write a sub that displays, in a message box, the address of the range with name "solver_adj".

9. Continuing the previous exercise, you might wonder whether there are any other "hidden" Solver range names. Open the **Plant Location.xlsx** file again. You'll notice some headings out in columns AA and AB. Enter the following sub and run it. It finds all range names that start with "Model!solver". You'll see that Solver has stored quite a lot of information! What range name is given to the objective cell? (The part of the code that deals with errors is necessary because some of Solver's defined "names" do not refer to *ranges*. The On Error Resume Next statement says to ignore errors that would result because of these names.)

```
Sub ShowSolverRangeNames()
    Dim nm As Name
    Dim counter As Integer

    counter = 1
    With Range("AA1")
        For Each nm In ActiveWorkbook.Names
            On Error Resume Next
            If Left(nm.Name, 12) = _
                    "Model!solver" And Range(nm.Name).Address <> "" Then
                If Err.Number = 0 Then
                    .Offset(counter, 0) = nm.Name
                    .Offset(counter, 1) = Range(nm.Name).Address
                    counter = counter + 1
                End If
            End If
        Next
    End With
End Sub
```

Part II

VBA Management Science Applications

This part of the book builds upon the VBA fundamentals in the first 17 chapters by presenting a series of management science applications. I have two objectives in this part of the book. First, I have attempted to present applications that are interesting and useful in the business world. Most of these are derived from similar models in my Practical Management Science and Spreadsheet Modeling and Applications books. Even if readers want to ignore the VBA code in these applications completely, they can still benefit from the applications themselves. For example, they can use the transportation application in Chapter 23 to solve practically any transportation model, they can use the queueing simulation in Chapter 28 to simulate a wide variety of multiple-server queues, they can use the stock option model in Chapter 29 to price European and American options, they can use the portfolio application in Chapter 31 to find the efficient frontier for any group of stocks, using live stock data from the Web, and they can use the AHP application in Chapter 33 to make a job decision.

The second objective in this part of the book is to illustrate a number of ways VBA can be used to convert a spreadsheet model into a decision support system (DSS). This is not always easy. Businesses want powerful applications, and power is not always easy to achieve. However, the VBA techniques illustrated in these applications are within the grasp of anyone who is armed with the VBA fundamentals from the earlier chapters and who is willing to make the effort. This effort should pay off handsomely in the job market.

The chapters in this part of the book can be read in practically any order, depending on your interests. The only exception is Chapter 18, which should be read first. It presents a number of guidelines for application development, and it illustrates these guidelines in a reasonably straightforward car loan application.

18
Basic Ideas for Application Development with VBA

18.1 Introduction

It is now time to start using the elements of VBA from the first part of the book to develop modeling applications. This chapter establishes some guidelines for application development, and it also introduces a car loan application to illustrate some of these guidelines. The guidelines discussed here leave much room for creativity. There are many ways to develop a successful application. From the user's standpoint, the main criteria for a successful application are that it be useful, clear, and, of course, correct. Beyond this, users like an application that has the familiar look and feel of a Windows application. As later chapters illustrate, this leaves the door wide open for many possibilities, but it still provides some useful guidance.

I tend to use the term "application" for the programs in the second part of this book. As discussed briefly in Chapter 1, most of them could also be also called **decision support systems** (or **DSSs**). They provide easy access to helpful information that could then be used by a decision maker to make well-informed decisions.

18.2 Guidelines for Application Development

The topic of software application development is a huge one, and whole courses are devoted to discussions of it. If you are a software developer in a large or even a small company, there are important issues you must be aware of, and there are important procedures you must follow. You are typically *not* the only person who is, or ever will be, working on any particular application. Other programmers are often working with you, and future programmers might need to update your programs to meet new requirements. Therefore, your programs must be readable and understandable by other programmers. Also, whenever possible, you should program with future extensions in mind. If new functionality is required of the program you write, another programmer should not have to start from scratch to incorporate this new functionality. In short, you need to write programs that are readable and reasonably easy to maintain.

This section is certainly not a complete manual on the application development process; this is well beyond the scope of the book. However, there are several simple guidelines provided here—and illustrated later on—that will help you write programs that are readable and maintainable. They are as follows.

1. **Decide clearly what you want the application to accomplish.**

   This is probably the single most important guideline. It is particularly important if you are developing the application for a client, but it is important even if you are working only for yourself. Application development can be a lengthy process, and you certainly do not want to spend that time going in the wrong direction. Decide ahead of time exactly what functionality your application should have and how you plan to implement it. For example, where will the input data come from—dialog boxes, worksheets, text files, or database files? What information will be reported? Will it be reported in tables or charts, or in both? Programming is always challenging, but if you don't even know which direction you are heading, it is impossible. And be on the watch for "feature creep." Most software developers (including myself) have a tendency to add more and more features to their programs as time evolves. At some point, you have to stop and get your software out the door to your customers!

2. **Communicate clearly to the user what the application does and how it works.**

   You cannot assume that the eventual users will know what your application does and how it works. After all, the users have not been working on this application for several days (or weeks or months or years) as you have. The users need a road map. In real applications, this is often done through printed materials and/or online help. Because the applications in this book are somewhat limited, their explanations are provided in an explanation sheet that the user sees *first* upon opening the Excel files. If more explanation is required later on, it is provided, for example, in dialog boxes. The users might have no idea what is going on behind the scenes—the technical part—but the explanations should leave no doubt about the *objectives* of the application and what the users need to do to make it work.

3. **Provide plenty of comments.**

   The best way to document your programs is to insert plenty of comments. It is a natural human tendency to plow through the coding process as quickly as possible and get the program to work, thereby omitting the comments until the last minute—or altogether. Try to fight this impulse. Comments are useful not only to the next programmer who will have to read and maintain your code, but they are also useful to you as you are writing it. They remind you of the logical thought process you should be following. In this way, comments are analogous to an outline for an English composition—an organizational structure. Besides that, they are invaluable when you revisit your own program in a week or a month. It might be crystal clear to you, at the time you are writing, why you have done something in a certain way, but it is often a complete mystery a month later. And if it is a mystery to you, the programmer, think how mysterious it will be to another programmer (or your instructor). So when there is any possibility for confusion, add comments. Of course, you can overdo it. As an example, the comment in the following lines is a waste of typing.

```
' Add 1 to the counter.
counter = counter + 1
```

4. Use meaningful names for variables, subs, and other programming elements.

There are unfortunately many existing programs that *consistently* use variable names such as i, j, k, n, and nn. They tend to be completely unreadable. (I confess that I still frequently use i, j, and k for loop counters, but otherwise I try to avoid meaningless variable names.) Fortunately, programmers are becoming increasingly fussy about using meaningful names for variables and other programming elements. Names such as unitCost and totalProfit tend to make a program self-documenting. You can look at the names and figure out exactly what is going on.

As with comments, you can overdo naming. For example, if you want a variable name for the price paid by the first customer to enter your store, you could use priceForFirstCustomerToEnterStore. Unless you love to type, you will probably want to shorten this name to something like priceCust1 or price1.

5. Use a modular approach with multiple short subs instead of one long sub.

Beginning programmers tend to write one long sub to do everything. As discussed in Chapter 10, this is a bad habit for at least two reasons. First, it is hard to read one long sub that goes on and on, even if it is well documented with comments. It is much easier to read short subs, especially when each of them has a very specific objective. Second, programs are much easier to maintain, extend, and debug when they are written in a modular fashion. For example, suppose you have written a program that creates a sensitivity table of some type. Later on, you decide to accompany this with a chart. If your program has a **Main** sub that calls several other subs to do the work, then all you need to do is create a **CreateChart** sub that has the specific objective of creating the chart and then call CreateChart from the Main sub. The rest of your program, if written properly, should not be affected at all.

6.   **Borrow from other programs that you or others have developed.**

The concept of "shared" code is becoming increasingly important among programmers. The idea is that there is no need to reinvent the wheel each time you write a program. There are almost certainly elements of any program you write that are common to other programs you have written. Sometimes entire subs can be copied and pasted from one program to another. If this is not possible, it is still probably possible to copy and paste specific lines of code. As for "borrowing" code written by others, this is a gray area from a legal/ethical standpoint. You should certainly not borrow a whole program or significant portions of a program written by someone else and claim it as your own. However, many programmers make much of their code available for others to use—with no strings attached.[1] If you know that this is the case, then you can feel free to borrow (and adapt) this code for your own purposes, possibly with a comment or two to acknowledge the original programmer.

7.   **Decide how to obtain the required input data.**

Almost every application you write (and almost all of the ones in this book) require input data. For example, the car loan application illustrated later in this chapter requires four inputs: the price of the car, the down payment, the annual interest rate, and the term of the loan. The question is how to obtain the data in the application. Perhaps the most natural way is to use one or more dialog boxes. This method is especially convenient when there are just a few data inputs, such as in the car loan application. However, there are times when it would be impractical to ask the user to type *numerous* inputs into a bulky dialog box. For example, the logistics model discussed in Chapter 23 can have literally hundreds of input values. The dialog box approach makes no sense in this case.

When there is a lot of input data, the chances are that the data are stored in some type of database. Several possibilities are illustrated in later chapters. Each represents a different database format, and each must be handled in a particular way by the VBA code. The possible data locations include (1) a "data" worksheet in the same (or a different) file as the application itself, (2) a text (.txt) file, (3) one or more tables in an Access (or other database) file, as discussed in Chapter 14, and (4) a Web page.

Getting the required data for an application is an extremely important issue, and several applications in later chapters have purposely been included to illustrate some of the possibilities. Of course, you should be aware that in many real applications, you have no control over where the data are located. For example, your company might have the data you require in a SQL Server database file. If this is the case, then you must learn how to retrieve the required SQL Server data into Excel for your application.

---

[1]If programmers really want to keep other users from borrowing their code, they will probably password-protect it. This can be done easily with the Protection tab under the **Tools** → **VBA Project** menu item in the VBE.

8. ## Decide what can be done at design time rather than at run time.

This is a very important issue for you as a developer. Your skills with the Excel interface are probably greater than your programming skills. Therefore, you should develop as much of your application as possible with the Excel interface at *design* time. You then can write VBA to take care of other necessary details that are implemented at *run* time.

To illustrate, suppose you want to develop a linear programming model and then an accompanying report sheet and chart sheet based on the results of the model. It is certainly possible to do *all* of this with VBA code. Before the user runs the application, there would be blank Model, Report, and Chart sheets, and your VBA code would be responsible for filling them completely when the program runs. This is a demanding task! It is much easier for you to develop "templates" for these sheets at design time, using the Excel tools you are familiar with. Of course, you cannot fill in these templates completely because parts of them will depend on the inputs used in any particular run of the application. However, using VBA to fill in the missing pieces of a partially completed template is much easier than having to start from scratch with blank sheets.

This point is discussed for each of the applications in the following chapters. In each case, I indicate what can be created at design time—without any VBA.

9. ## Decide how to report the results.

The models in this book typically follow a three-step approach: (1) inputs are obtained; (2) a model is created to transform inputs into outputs; and (3) the outputs are reported. There are many ways to implement the third step. The two basic possibilities are to report the results in tabular and in graphical form. You must decide which is more appropriate for your application. Often you will decide to do both. But even then, you must decide what information to report in the table(s) and what types of charts to create. A reasonable assumption is that many users are nontechnical, so they want the results reported in a user-friendly, nontechnical manner. A simple table and an accompanying chart frequently do the job, but you must use discretion in each application.

As for charts, there is a tendency among many beginning developers to create the fanciest charts possible—wild colors, 3-dimensional design, and other "cool" elements. My personal suggestion is to keep your charts as simple as possible. A 3-dimensional chart might look great, but it sometimes portrays the underlying data less clearly than a "boring" 2-dimensional chart. And please, use common sense with color combinations. Red lettering on a purple background might work in an art course, but most business users do not appreciate garish color combinations.

A final issue concerning charts is where they should be placed—on the same worksheet as the underlying data or on separate chart sheets. This is entirely a matter of taste. Many developers tend to favor separate chart sheets (along with navigational buttons, discussed in the next point) to reduce the clutter. You might disagree. However, if you do decide to place charts on the same worksheets as the underlying data, you must decide whether to let them "cover up" the data. In other words, you will have to decide on proper placement (and sizing) of the charts on the worksheets. This can be tedious—and it might make you decide to place charts on separate chart sheets after all!

10. Add appropriate finishing touches.

There are a number of finishing touches you can add to make your applications more professional, although some are ultimately a matter of taste. Here are several possibilities.

- Add navigational buttons. For example, if there is a worksheet with tabular results and a chart sheet that contains a chart of the same results, it is useful to put a button on each sheet that, when clicked, takes the user to the other sheet. The code behind these buttons is simple, with lines such as

```
Sub ViewReportSheet()
    Worksheets("Report").Activate
    Range("A1").Select
End Sub
```

- Hide sheets until the user really needs to see them. For example, there might be a Report sheet that contains results from a previous run of the application (if any). There is no point in letting users see this sheet until the application is run and *new* results are obtained. To implement this idea, the following code could be used to hide all sheets except for the Explanation sheet when the application workbook is opened. Then the **Visible** property of the Report sheet could be changed to True at run time, right after the new results are obtained.

```
Private Sub Workbook_Open()
    Dim sht As Object
    Worksheets("Explanation").Activate
    Range("F4").Select
    For Each sht In ActiveWorkbook.Sheets
        If sht.Name <> "Explanation" Then sht.Visible = False
    Next
End Sub
```

- Use the View tab to change some of the default settings on selected sheets. For example, it is possible to turn off gridlines, the formula bar, and/or row and column headers. Some programmers like to do this to make their applications look less like they actually reside in Excel. You might want to experiment with these options.

18.3 A Car Loan Application

This section presents a rather simple application for calculating the monthly payments on a car loan. This calculation is very easy to perform in Excel with the PMT function, but there are undoubtedly Excel users who are unaware of the this function. Besides, these users might just want a point-and-click application that gets them results with no Excel formulas required. The car loan application does this, and it illustrates many of the guidelines discussed above. In addition, it has purposely been left incomplete. You will have a chance to fill in the missing pieces and thereby practice your VBA skills in the exercises.

Objectives of the Application

The car loan application has three primary functions:

1. It calculates the monthly payment and total interest paid for any car loan, given four inputs: the price of the car, the down payment, the annual interest rate, and the term (number of monthly payments) of the loan.
2. It performs a sensitivity analysis on any of the four inputs, showing how the monthly payment and total interest paid vary, both in tabular and graphical form.
3. It creates an amortization table and accompanying chart showing how the loan payment each month is broken down into principal and interest.

Basic Design of the Application

The application is stored in the file **Car Loan.xlsm**. (As you read the rest of this section, you should open the file and follow along.) The file consists of four worksheets and two chart sheets. The worksheets are named Explanation, Model, Sensitivity, and Amortization. The two chart sheets are named SensitivityChart and AmortizationChart. All of these except the Explanation sheet are hidden when the user opens the file. The others (except the Model sheet) are revealed when necessary. The Explanation sheet, shown in Figure 18.1, describes the application, and it has a button that the user clicks to run the application. (I like this design, so I use it in all of the applications in later chapters.)

There are three user forms that allow the user to select options or provide inputs. The first, named **frmOptions** and shown in Figure 18.2, provides users with the application's three basic options.

If the user selects the first option, the dialog box in Figure 18.3 appears, requesting the inputs for the car loan. (This user form is named **frmInputs**.) The initial values in this dialog box are those from the previous run, if any, and come from the hidden Model sheet. Of course, users can modify any of these inputs. Then the message box in Figure 18.4 displays the monthly payment and total interest paid for this loan.

Figure 18.1 Explanation Sheet

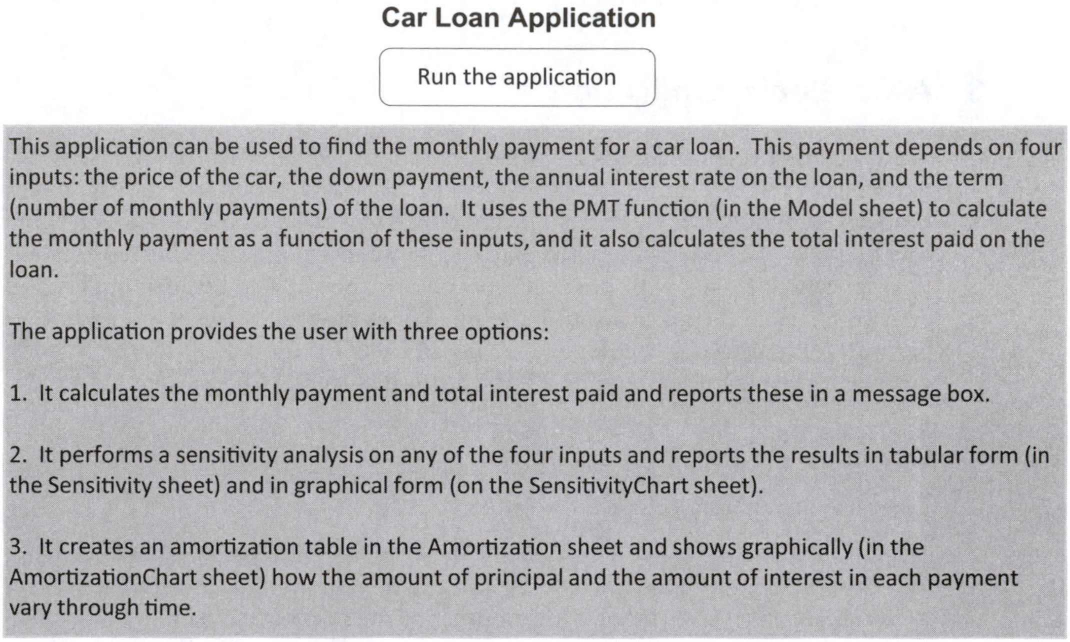

Car Loan Application
Run the application
This application can be used to find the monthly payment for a car loan. This payment depends on four inputs: the price of the car, the down payment, the annual interest rate on the loan, and the term (number of monthly payments) of the loan. It uses the PMT function (in the Model sheet) to calculate the monthly payment as a function of these inputs, and it also calculates the total interest paid on the loan.
The application provides the user with three options:
1. It calculates the monthly payment and total interest paid and reports these in a message box.
2. It performs a sensitivity analysis on any of the four inputs and reports the results in tabular form (in the Sensitivity sheet) and in graphical form (on the SensitivityChart sheet).
3. It creates an amortization table in the Amortization sheet and shows graphically (in the AmortizationChart sheet) how the amount of principal and the amount of interest in each payment vary through time.

Figure 18.2 Options Form

Application Options
Select one of the following basic options that are available with this application.
OK
Cancel
Options
Find monthly car payment for given inputs
Perform sensitivity analysis on selected input
Create amortization table

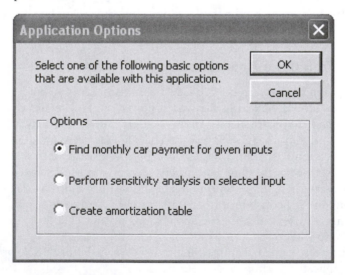

If the user selects the second basic option, the sensitivity option, the dialog box in Figure 18.5 asks the user to indicate which of the four inputs to vary for the analysis. (This user form is named **frmSensitivity**.) It then displays frmInputs shown earlier in Figure 18.3. However, frmInputs is now slightly different, as indicated in Figure 18.6. Specifically, the explanation label at the top

Figure 18.3 Inputs Form

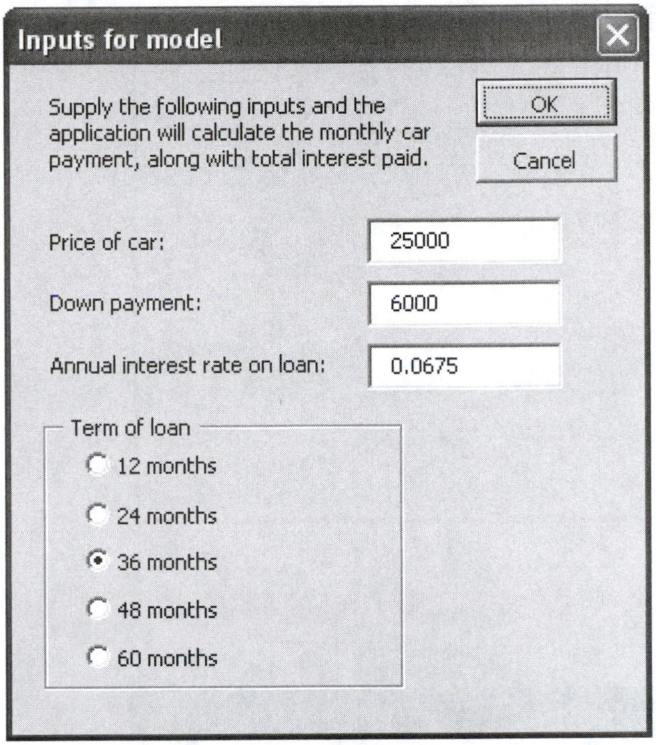

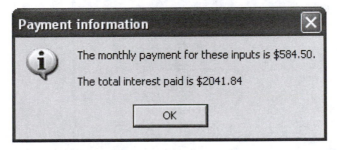

Figure 18.4 Payment information

indicates that these inputs will now be used in a sensitivity analysis. (The labels in dialog boxes should always be as clear as possible, to avoid any possible confusion.)

Now that the user has asked to perform a sensitivity analysis on the price of the car, what price range should be used? This is an application design issue. The application could ask the user for this range, or it could choose a default range. This application uses the latter option, primarily to make the application easier to develop. The range chosen is displayed next in an informational message box (see Figure 18.7). The results are displayed graphically in the SensitivityChart sheet (see Figure 18.8) and in tabular form in the Sensitivity

Figure 18.5 Sensitivity Form

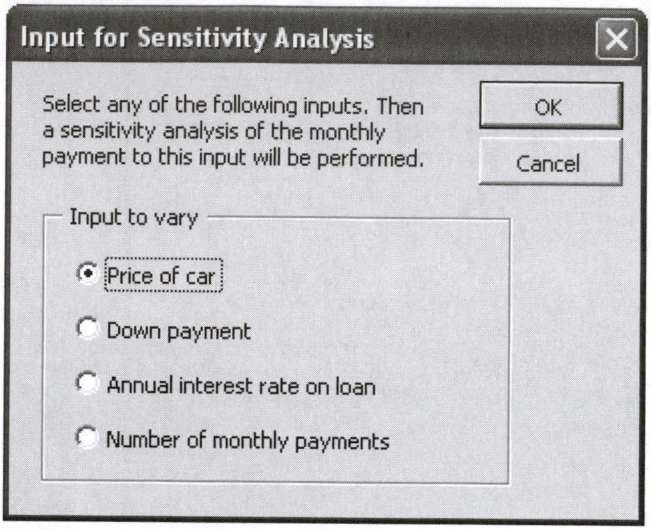

Figure 18.6 Inputs Form with a Different Label

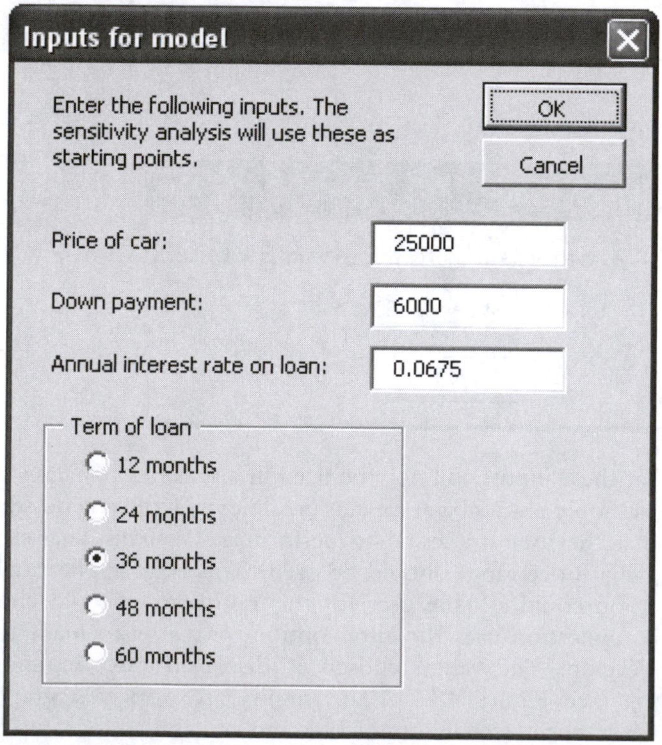

Figure 18.7 Information on Sensitivity Range

Figure 18.8 Sensitivity Chart

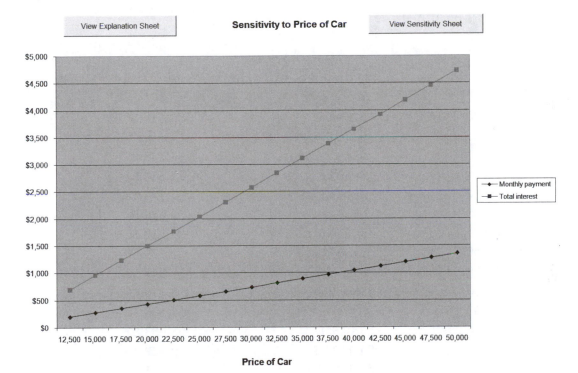

sheet (see Figure 18.9). Note how the buttons in these figures allow for easy navigation through the application.

Finally, if the user selects the application's third option, an amortization table, frmInputs in Figure 18.3 is again displayed, using a slightly different explanation label appropriate for the amortization objective. (This version of the form is not shown here.) The amortization information is shown graphically in the AmortizationChart sheet (see Figure 18.10) and in tabular form in the Amortization sheet (see Figure 18.11). The results shown here are for a 24-month loan.

Design Templates

Most of this application can be set up at design time, using only the Excel interface—no VBA. The Model sheet, shown in Figure 18.12, is never displayed

Figure 18.9 Sensitivity Table

Sensitivity analysis		

Basic inputs		
Price of car	$25,000	View Sensitivity Chart
Down payment	$6,000	
Annual interest rate	6.75%	View Explanation Sheet
Term (months to pay)	36	

Input to vary   Price

Price	Monthly payment	Total interest
$12,500.00	$199.96	$698.52
$15,000.00	$276.87	$967.19
$17,500.00	$353.77	$1,235.85
$20,000.00	$430.68	$1,504.51
$22,500.00	$507.59	$1,773.18
$25,000.00	$584.50	$2,041.84
$27,500.00	$661.40	$2,310.50
$30,000.00	$738.31	$2,579.16
$32,500.00	$815.22	$2,847.83
$35,000.00	$892.12	$3,116.49
$37,500.00	$969.03	$3,385.15
$40,000.00	$1,045.94	$3,653.82
$42,500.00	$1,122.85	$3,922.48
$45,000.00	$1,199.75	$4,191.14
$47,500.00	$1,276.66	$4,459.80
$50,000.00	$1,353.57	$4,728.47

to the user, but it is the key to the application. It can be set up completely at design time, including range names and formulas, using any trial values in the input cells. The key formula in cell B11 is **=PMT(IntRate/12,Term,-Loan)**. (If you want to examine this sheet more closely, you will need to unhide it. To do so, use Excel's Format dropdown on the Home ribbon. In Excel 2003 and earlier, go to the **Format→Sheet→Unhide** menu item.)

In addition, templates can be created in the Sensitivity and Amortization sheets, as shown in Figures 18.13 and 18.14. The inputs in both of these sheets are linked to the input cells in the Model sheet. For example, the formula in cell C4 of Figure 18.13 is **=Price**. Therefore, when the user fills in frmInputs in

Figure 18.10 Amortization Chart

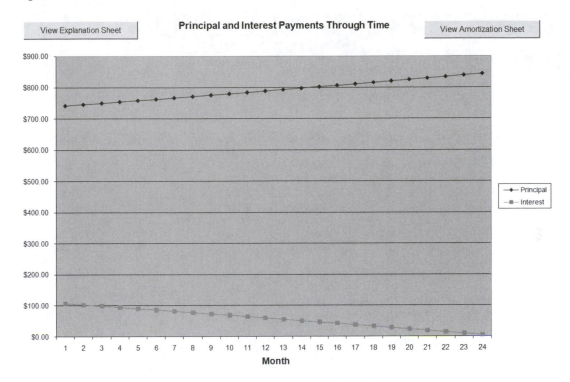

Figure 18.3, the values are transferred to the Model sheet, and they are then immediately available in the Sensitivity and Amortization sheets. Also, note the partially filled-in section of the Amortization table (rows 10 and 11). It is a good idea to enter the appropriate *formulas* at the top of this table at design time. VBA can then simply copy them down at run time. As an example, the formula for interest in cell F10 is **=IntRate/12*C10**. (You can examine the **Car Loan. xlsm** file for more details on the formulas.)

I will now examine how the inner details of the application work, starting with the user forms and their event handlers.

frmOptions and Event Handlers

The design of frmOptions appears in Figure 18.15. It includes the usual OK and Cancel buttons, an explanation label, a frame for grouping, and three option buttons named optPayment, optSensitivity, and optAmortization. Of course, these controls have to be positioned and named appropriately (through the Properties window) at design time. The **UserForm_Initialize** sub checks the first option by default. The **btnOK_Click** sub captures the user's choice in the public variable analysisOption, which is 1, 2, or 3. The **btnCancel_Click** sub unloads the dialog box and terminates the program. These subs are straightforward and are listed below.

Figure 18.11 Amortization Table

Amortization schedule				

Basic inputs	
Price of car	$25,000
Down payment	$6,000
Annual interest rate	6.75%
Term (months to pay)	24

View Amortization Chart

View Explanation Sheet

Month	Beginning balance	Payment	Principal	Interest	Ending balance
1	$19,000.00	$848.53	$741.65	$106.88	$18,258.35
2	$18,258.35	$848.53	$745.82	$102.70	$17,512.52
3	$17,512.52	$848.53	$750.02	$98.51	$16,762.50
4	$16,762.50	$848.53	$754.24	$94.29	$16,008.27
5	$16,008.27	$848.53	$758.48	$90.05	$15,249.79
6	$15,249.79	$848.53	$762.75	$85.78	$14,487.04
7	$14,487.04	$848.53	$767.04	$81.49	$13,720.00
8	$13,720.00	$848.53	$771.35	$77.18	$12,948.65
9	$12,948.65	$848.53	$775.69	$72.84	$12,172.96
10	$12,172.96	$848.53	$780.05	$68.47	$11,392.90
11	$11,392.90	$848.53	$784.44	$64.09	$10,608.46
12	$10,608.46	$848.53	$788.85	$59.67	$9,819.61
13	$9,819.61	$848.53	$793.29	$55.24	$9,026.31
14	$9,026.31	$848.53	$797.75	$50.77	$8,228.56
15	$8,228.56	$848.53	$802.24	$46.29	$7,426.32
16	$7,426.32	$848.53	$806.75	$41.77	$6,619.56
17	$6,619.56	$848.53	$811.29	$37.24	$5,808.27
18	$5,808.27	$848.53	$815.86	$32.67	$4,992.42
19	$4,992.42	$848.53	$820.44	$28.08	$4,171.97
20	$4,171.97	$848.53	$825.06	$23.47	$3,346.91
21	$3,346.91	$848.53	$829.70	$18.83	$2,517.21
22	$2,517.21	$848.53	$834.37	$14.16	$1,682.84
23	$1,682.84	$848.53	$839.06	$9.47	$843.78
24	$843.78	$848.53	$843.78	$4.75	$0.00

A note on using colons in statements. VBA allows you to write two or more statements on a single line, provided that they are separated by colons. This is often done with **Case** statements, as shown below, provided that the statement after each Case is short. The resulting code simply takes up less space.

```
Private Sub btnCancel_Click()
    Unload Me
    End
End Sub

Private Sub btnOK_Click()
    ' Capture the option in the public variable appOption.
    Select Case True
        Case optPayment.Value: analysisOption = 1
        Case optSensitivity.Value: analysisOption = 2
        Case optAmortization.Value: analysisOption = 3
    End Select
End Sub
```

Figure 18.12 Model Sheet

	A	B
1	**Car loan model**	
2		
3	**Inputs**	
4	Price of car	$25,000
5	Down payment	$6,000
6	Annual interest rate	6.75%
7	Term (months to pay)	24
8		
9	**Outputs**	
10	Amount financed	$19,000
11	Monthly payment	$848.53
12	Total interest paid	$1,364.65

Figure 18.13 Sensitivity Template

Sensitivity analysis

Basic inputs

Price of car	$25,000
Down payment	$6,000
Annual interest rate	6.75%
Term (months to pay)	24

View Sensitivity Chart

View Explanation Sheet

Input to vary   Price

Price	Monthly payment	Total interest

Figure 18.14 Amortization Template

Amortization schedule

Basic inputs

Price of car	$25,000
Down payment	$6,000
Annual interest rate	6.75%
Term (months to pay)	24

View Amortization Chart

View Explanation Sheet

Month	Beginning balance	Payment	Principal	Interest	Ending balance
1	$19,000.00	$848.53	$741.65	$106.88	$18,258.35
2	$18,258.35				

Figure 18.15 frmOptions Design

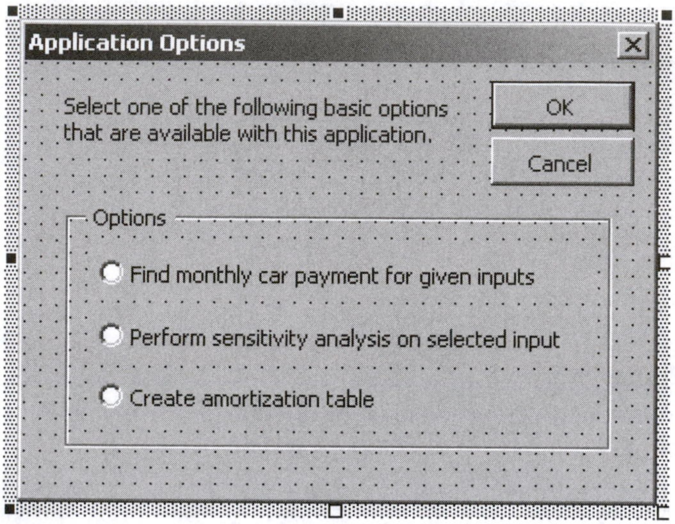

```
    Unload Me
End Sub

Private Sub UserForm_Initialize()
    optPayment.Value = True
End Sub
```

frmInputs Design and Event Handlers

The design of frmInputs appears in Figure 18.16. It includes the usual OK and Cancel buttons, a label named lblExplanation at the top, three text boxes named txtPrice, txtDownPayment, and txtInterest (and corresponding labels), a frame for grouping, and five option buttons named opt12, opt24, opt36, opt48, and opt60. (Note that it was a *design* decision to limit the term of the loan to multiples of 12 months.) The lblExplanation at the top of the form has a blank caption at design time. The explanation that is inserted at run time depends on which option the user chooses. (Compare the labels in Figures 18.3 and 18.6, for example.)

The **UserForm_Initialize** sub for this user form fills the three text boxes with the values currently in the Model sheet. (Alternatively, some program-mers might elect to leave these boxes blank.) It also checks the appropriate option button, depending on what term is currently in the Model sheet, and it sets the **Caption** property of lblExplanation to explanation, a public string variable that has, by this time, been defined in the module code (shown later on).

Figure 18.16 frmInputs Design

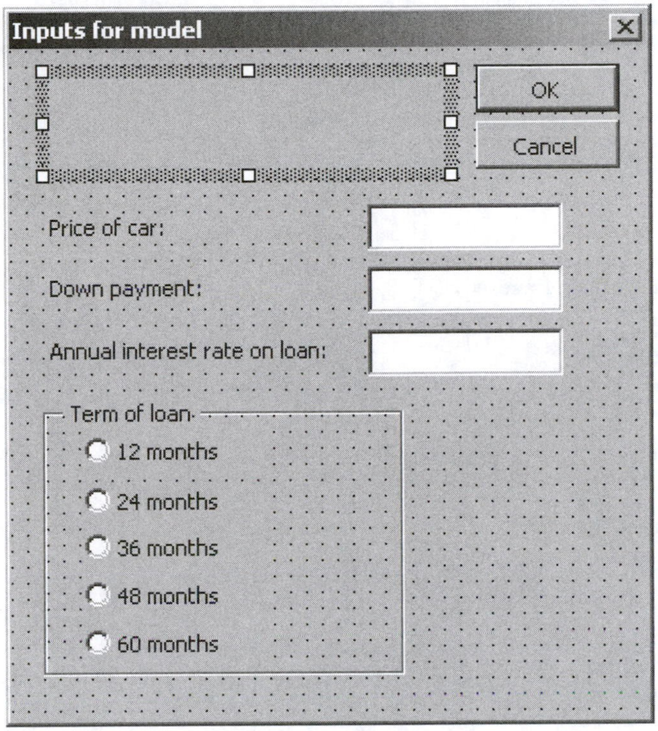

```
Private Sub UserForm_Initialize()
    ' Enter the values from the Model sheet (from a previous run, if any)
    ' in the text boxes.
    lblExplanation.Caption = explanation
    txtPrice.Text = Format(Range("Price").Value, "0")
    txtDownPayment.Text = Format(Range("DownPay").Value, "0")
    txtInterest.Text = Format(Range("IntRate").Value, "0.0000")

    ' Check the appropriate option button, depending on the Term value from the Model sheet.
    Select Case Range("Term").Value
        Case 12: opt12.Value = True
        Case 24: opt24.Value = True
        Case 36: opt36.Value = True
        Case 48: opt48.Value = True
        Case 60: opt60.Value = True
        Case Else: opt36.Value = True
    End Select
End Sub
```

The **btnOK_Click** sub then goes the other direction, placing the user's choices into the input cells of the Model sheet. (It first performs some error checking for invalid inputs. This error checking actually makes up the majority of the sub and is tedious to write, but it avoids problems later on.)

```
Private Sub btnOK_Click()
    Dim ctl As Control, response As Variant

    For Each ctl In Me.Controls
        If TypeName(ctl) = "TextBox" Then
            If ctl = "" Or Not IsNumeric(ctl) Then
                MsgBox "Enter a positive number in each box.", _
                    vbInformation, "Improper input"
                ctl.SetFocus
                Exit Sub
            End If
            If ctl <= 0 Then
                MsgBox "Enter a positive number in each box.", _
                    vbInformation, "Improper input"
                ctl.SetFocus
                Exit Sub
            End If
        End If
    Next

    If Val(txtDownPayment.Value) > Val(txtPrice.Value) Then
        MsgBox "The down payment can't be greater than the price " _
            & "the car!", vbInformation, "Improper input"
        txtDownPayment.SetFocus
        Exit Sub
    End If

    If Val(txtInterestRate.Value) > 0.25 Then
        response = MsgBox("You entered an annual interest rate greater than 25%. " _
            & "Do you really mean this?", vbYesNo, "Abnormal interest rate")
        If response = vbNo Then
            txtInterestRate.SetFocus
            Exit Sub
        End If
    End If

    Range("Price").Value = Val(txtPrice.Value)
    Range("DownPayment").Value = Val(txtDownPayment.Value)
    Range("InterestRate").Value = Val(txtInterestRate.Value)

    Select Case True
        Case opt12.Value: Range("Term").Value = 12
        Case opt24.Value: Range("Term").Value = 24
        Case opt36.Value: Range("Term").Value = 36
        Case opt48.Value: Range("Term").Value = 48
        Case opt60.Value: Range("Term").Value = 60
    End Select

    Unload Me
End Sub
```

The **btnCancel_Click** sub unloads the form and terminates the program.

```
Private Sub btnCancel_Click()
    Unload Me
    End
End Sub
```

Figure 18.17 frmSensitivity Design

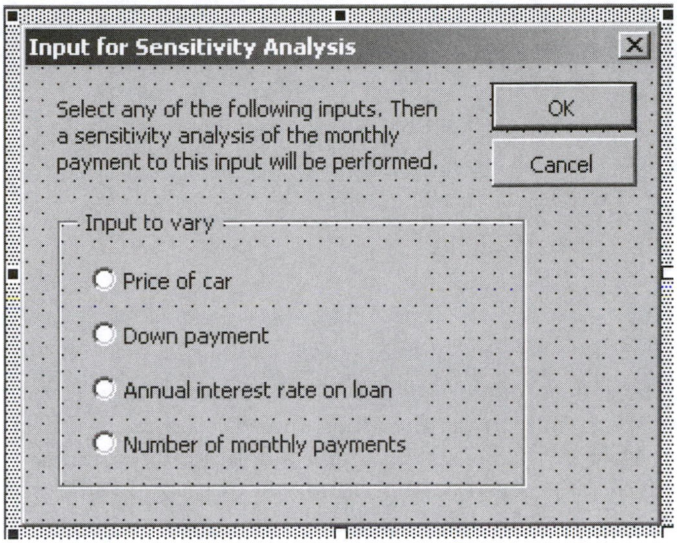

frmSensitivity Design and Event Handlers

There are no new concepts in frmSensitivity, so I will simply display its design in Figure 18.17 and list its code below. Its purpose is to capture the public variable sensitivityOption, which has possible values 1, 2, 3, 4.

```
Private Sub btnCancel_Click()
    Unload Me
    End
End Sub

Private Sub btnOK_Click()
    Select Case True
        Case optPrice.Value: sensitivityOption = 1
        Case optDownPayment.Value: sensitivityOption = 2
        Case optInterestRate.Value: sensitivityOption = 3
        Case optTerm.Value: sensitivityOption = 4
    End Select

    Unload Me
End Sub

Private Sub UserForm_Initialize()
    optPrice.Value = True
End Sub
```

Module Code

The module contains the VBA code that does most of the work. It begins with declaration of a few public variables, along with comments that explain these variables.

```
Option Explicit

' Definitions of public variables
'    analysisOption - 1, 2, or 3, depending on which option the user chooses in frmOptions
'    sensitivityOption - 1, 2, 3, or 4, depending on which input the user chooses
'         to vary in frmSensitivity
'    explanation - an explanation string that will be used in the frmInputs.
'         It varies depending on the value of analysisOption.

Public analysisOption As Integer
Public sensitivityOption As Integer
Public explanation As String
```

Main Code

To make the code as modular as possible, a **Main** sub is used as a control center. Its primary purpose is to call the other, shorter subs that perform the individual tasks. This Main sub begins by showing frmOptions. Based on the user's response, it then uses a Case construct to perform one of three possible actions: (1) show frmInputs and calculate the monthly payment and total interest paid, (2) show frmSensitivity and perform a sensitivity analysis on the selected input, or (3) create an amortization table. Note that frmInputs is shown in each case, although the explanation string variable varies slightly. Also, note that for the sensitivity option, there is a nested Case construct that is based on the input variable chosen. (The comments in the code provide further details.)

```
Sub Main()
    ' See which option of the application the user wants to run.
    frmOptions.Show
    Select Case analysisOption

        Case 1
            ' This explanation string will appear at the top of frmInputs.
            explanation = "Supply the following inputs and the application " _
                & "will calculate the monthly car payment, along with total " _
                & "interest paid."

            ' Get the user inputs and display the results in a message box.
            frmInputs.Show
            MsgBox "The monthly payment for these inputs is " _
                & Format(Range("Payment").Value, "$0.00") & "." & vbCrLf _
                & vbCrLf & "The total interest paid is " _
                & Format(Range("TotalInterest").Value, "$0.00"), _
                vbInformation, "Payment information"

        Case 2
            ' First, see which input to vary.
            frmSensitivity.Show

            ' This explanation string will appear at the top of frmInputs.
            explanation = "Enter the following inputs. The sensitivity analysis " _
                & "will use these as starting points."
```

```
                ' Get the user's inputs.
                frmInputs.Show

                ' Perform the sensitivity analysis for the selected input.
                Select Case sensitivityOption
                        Case 1: Call PriceSensitivity
                        Case 2: Call DownPaymentSensitivity
                        Case 3: Call InterestRateSensitivity
                        Case 4: Call TermSensitivity
                End Select

            Case 3
                ' This explanation string will appear at the top of frmInputs.
                explanation = "Enter the following inputs. The amortization table will be based on these."
                frmInputs.Show
                Call Amortization
        End Select
End Sub
```

A Note on Screen Updating. You'll note a couple of lines in the above code that turn off screen updating. This is something you typically do as an afterthought when you run your program and see that the screen updates continuously, causing a lot of flickering. In such cases, I like to turn screen updating off until the end, at which time I turn it back on. Your application will then proceed a lot more "quietly."

PriceSensitivity Code

The **PriceSensitivity** sub is called if the user wants a sensitivity analysis on the price of the car. It first unhides and activates the Sensitivity sheet. Next, it clears the contents from the previous run, if any. Then it uses a For loop to cycle through prices as low as half the current price and as high as double the current price. For each of these, it substitutes the price into the Price cell of the Model sheet, captures the monthly payment and total interest paid from the corresponding cells of the Model sheet, and places these values in the Sensitivity sheet. Note how the "counter" variable rowOffset keeps track of where to place these values in the Sensitivity sheet. At the end of this loop, it puts the original price back in the Price cell of the Model sheet. Finally, it sets range variables for the ranges of the sensitivity data, and it calls the UpdateSensitivityChart sub (discussed below) with these ranges as arguments.

```
Sub PriceSensitivity()
    Dim currentPrice As Currency
    Dim price As Currency
    Dim rowOffset As Integer
    Dim i As Integer
    Dim dataRange As Range
    Dim xRange As Range

    With Worksheets("Sensitivity")
        .Visible = True
```

```
        .Activate
    End With

    ' Enter some labels and clear the sensitivity table from a previous run, if any.
    Range("C9").Value = "Price"
    With Range("B11")
        .Value = "Price"
        Range(.Offset(1, 0), .Offset(1, 2).End(xlDown)).ClearContents
    End With

    ' Capture the current price.
    currentPrice = Range("Price").Value
    MsgBox "The price will be varied from half the current price " _
        & "to double the current price, in increments of 10% of the " _
        & "current price. (But it will never be less than the current " _
        & "down payment.)", vbInformation, "Price range"

    ' For each possible price, enter it in the Price cell (in the Model sheet)
    ' and then store the corresponding payment and total interest values in
    ' the sensitivity table.
    rowOffset = 0
    With Range("B11")
        For i = -5 To 10
            price = currentPrice * (1 + i / 10)
            If price >= Range("DownPayment").Value Then
                rowOffset = rowOffset + 1
                Range("Price").Value = price
                .Offset(rowOffset, 0).Value = Format(price, "$0.00")
                .Offset(rowOffset, 1).Value = Format(Range("Payment").Value, "$0.00")
                .Offset(rowOffset, 2).Value = Format(Range("TotalInterest").Value, "$0.00")
            End If
        Next
    End With

    ' Restore the current price to the Price range (in the Model sheet).
    Range("Price").Value = currentPrice

    ' Set the ranges for the sensitivity chart and then update the chart.
    With Range("B11")
        Set dataRange = Range(.Offset(1, 1), .Offset(1, 2).End(xlDown))
        Set xRange = Range(.Offset(1, 0), .End(xlDown))
    End With
    Call UpdateSensitivityChart("Price of Car", dataRange, xRange)
End Sub
```

UpdateSensitivityChart Code

The **UpdateSensitivityChart** sub takes three arguments: a string for chart titles, a range for the source data, and another range for the horizontal axis variable. (Note how Range object variables can be passed as arguments, just like any other variables.) It then updates the already existing SensitivityChart sheet with these arguments. (If you are not sure exactly what part of the chart each of the lines changes, set a breakpoint at the Sub line. Then when you run the application, it will stop here, allowing you to step through the sub with the F8 key and examine the effect of each line.)

Keep in mind that the SensitivityChart sheet and the AmortizationChart sheet discussed below are created at design time, using Excel's chart tools in the usual way. Therefore, the only task required of VBA is to populate these charts with the current data, and this is relatively simple. It would be a lot more tedious to create the chart sheets from scratch with VBA.

```vba
Sub UpdateSensitivityChart(inputParameter As String, dataRange As Range, _
        xRange As Range)
    With Charts("SensitivityChart")
        .Visible = True
        .Activate
        .SetSourceData dataRange
        .SeriesCollection(1).Name = "Monthly payment"
        .SeriesCollection(2).Name = "Total interest"
        .SeriesCollection(1).XValues = xRange
        .Axes(xlCategory).AxisTitle.Caption = inputParameter
        .ChartTitle.Text = "Sensitivity to " & inputParameter
        .Deselect
    End With
End Sub
```

DownPaymentSensitivity, InterestRateSensitivity, and TermSensitivity Code

The next three subs are analogous to the PriceSensitivity sub. They are relevant for sensitivity analyses on the down payment, the interest rate, and the term, respectively. Their code has purposely *not* been supplied. They are left to you as an exercise. (Right now, they contain only messages that you can delete when you write your code.) Note that you should call the UpdateSensitivityChart sub from each of them, using appropriate arguments in each case.

```vba
Sub DownPaymentSensitivity()
    MsgBox "The code for this sensitivity analysis is not yet written. " _
    & "Try writing it on your own.", vbInformation, "Incomplete"
End Sub

Sub InterestRateSensitivity()
    MsgBox "The code for this sensitivity analysis is not yet written. " _
    & "Try writing it on your own.", vbInformation, "Incomplete"
End Sub

Sub TermSensitivity()
    MsgBox "The code for this sensitivity analysis is not yet written. " _
    & "Try writing it on your own.", vbInformation, "Incomplete"
End Sub
```

Amortization Code

The **Amortization** sub creates an amortization table. It first unhides and activates the Amortization table and clears the contents of the previous run, if any.

Because the amortization table will have as many rows as the term of the loan, the variable term is defined to help fill the table, and then the table is built. Its first column, the month number, is filled with the DataSeries method of a Range object. (This is equivalent to Excel's **Fill** tool. You can learn the syntax for the DataSeries line by using this tool with the macro recorder on.) The rest of the table is filled by copying the relevant formulas down their respective columns. (These formulas were entered in the template at design time. See rows 10 and 11 of Figure 18.14.) Finally, the sub sets range variables for the ranges of the amortization table, and it calls the UpdateAmortizationChart sub with these ranges as arguments.

```
Sub Amortization()
    Dim term As Integer
    Dim dataRange As Range
    Dim xRange As Range

    With Worksheets("Amortization")
        .Visible = True
        .Activate
    End With

    ' Clear out old table (but leave a few key formulas as is).
    With Range("B10")
        Range(.Offset(2, 0), .Offset(2, 1).End(xlDown)).ClearContents
        Range(.Offset(1, 2), .Offset(1, 5).End(xlDown)).ClearContents
    End With

    ' Capture the term in a variable. It is the "length" of the amortization table.
    term = Range("Term").Value

    ' Autofill the first column of the table (1,2,3,etc.). Then copy the
    ' formulas already supplied down the other columns.
    With Range("B10")
        .DataSeries Rowcol:=xlColumns, Step:=1, Stop:=term
        .Offset(1, 1).Copy Range(.Offset(2, 1), .Offset(term - 1, 1))
        Range(.Offset(0, 2), .Offset(0, 5)).Copy _
            Range(.Offset(1, 2), .Offset(term - 1, 5))
    End With

    ' Set the ranges for the amortization chart and then update the chart.
    With Range("B9")
        Set dataRange = Range(.Offset(1, 3), .Offset(1, 4).End(xlDown))
        Set xRange = Range(.Offset(1, 0), .End(xlDown))
    End With
    Call UpdateAmortizationChart(dataRange, xRange)
End Sub
```

UpdateAmortizationChart Code

The **UpdateAmortizationChart** sub takes two arguments: a range for the source data, and another range for the horizontal axis variable. It then updates the already existing AmortizationChart with these arguments.

```
Sub UpdateAmortizationChart(dataRange As Range, xRange As Range)
  ' This sub updates the (already created) chart based on the amortization table.
  With Charts("AmortizationChart")
    .Visible = True
    .Activate
    .SetSourceData dataRange
    .SeriesCollection(1).Name = "Principal"
    .SeriesCollection(2).Name = "Interest"
    .SeriesCollection(1).XValues = xRange
    .Deselect
  End With
End Sub
```

Navigational Code

The remaining subs are attached to the buttons on the various sheets. They are for navigational purposes only.

```
Sub ViewExplanation()
  Worksheets("Explanation").Activate
  Range("F4").Select
End Sub

Sub ViewSensitivitySheet()
  Worksheets("Sensitivity").Activate
  Range("B1").Select
End Sub

Sub ViewSensitivityChart()
  Charts("SensitivityChart").Activate
End Sub

Sub ViewAmortizationSheet()
  Worksheets("Amortization").Activate
  Range("B1").Select
End Sub

Sub ViewAmortizationChart()
  Charts("AmortizationChart").Activate
End Sub
```

18.4 Summary

The car loan application is not the simplest one you will ever encounter, and there is no way you could develop it in, say, an hour. There are admittedly many details to take care of. As a tactical issue, you might want to try developing this application (on your own) in pieces. For example, you might omit the parts on sensitivity analysis and amortization, along with their charts, and develop only the part that displays the message box for the monthly payment in Figure 18.4. Once you get this working properly, you can try developing the sensitivity analysis part of the application. You can then tackle the amortization table. The advantage of this approach is that you can work on several small and relatively easy subprojects, rather than one daunting large project, and gain confidence with your successes along the way. In addition, if you keep these small subprojects in separate subs, you can test them independently of one another, thereby eliminating bugs as you proceed.

If you keep this "divide and conquer" approach in mind, you will probably agree that there is no single piece of the application that you cannot master with some practice. Many applications in later chapters are like this one. They are somewhat *long*, but they are not necessarily *difficult*. Just remember the claim in Chapter 1—you can be a successful programmer if you persevere.

EXERCISES

1. Complete the DownPaymentSensitivity, InterestRateSensitivity, and TermSensitivity subs that were left incomplete.
2. The charts in the application are currently line charts. Suppose the initial reaction from users is that they would rather see some other chart type such as stacked columns. Make the necessary changes. (Do you need to rewrite any of the code?)
3. Change the application so that the term of the loan can be *any* number of months from 12 to 60. Note that option buttons are no longer practical. Use a text box instead to capture the term of the loan.
4. Suppose all car loans are for 36 months. In that case, there is no need to obtain this input from the user, although it would be nice to inform the user of the term in a message box. Change the application appropriately to handle this situation.
5. Suppose a down payment of 20% is required for all car loans. In that case there is no need to obtain this input from the user, although it would be nice to inform the user of the down payment in a message box. Change the application appropriately to handle this situation.
6. Change the application so that it is relevant for home loans (mortgages). Assume that the term of the loan can be any number of *years* from 5 to 30 (although you make *monthly* payments) and that a downpayment of *at least* 10% of the price of the home is required. Make sure there are no leftover references to cars!

A Blending Application

19.1 Introduction

This application illustrates how a typical linear programming model, in this case an oil blending model, can be transformed into an impressive decision support system with very little VBA coding. The key to the application is that it is for a *fixed-size* model. Specifically, it works only if there are three types of crude oils blended into three gasoline products. This is certainly a limiting feature of the application. However, the fixed-size property allows the entire application to be set up at design time, without any VBA. The linear programming model can be developed, a report can be created, and several charts can be created. The only VBA tasks are to get the user's inputs for the model and to run Solver. There are many *Excel* details to take care of at design time, but the finished application is very straightforward, with a minimal amount of VBA code.

New Learning Objective: VBA

- To see how VBA can be used to develop a complete decision support system around a fixed-size optimization model by supplying input dialog boxes and charts and reports for the results.

New Learning Objective: Non-VBA

- To develop an understanding of linear programming blending models.

19.2 Functionality of the Application

The application provides the following functionality:

1. The application is based on a typical oil-blending model with three crude oils blended into three gasoline products. There are many inputs to the model, including crude oil availabilities, gasoline demands, minimum octane and maximum sulfur percentage requirements on the gasoline products, and others, all of which can change each time the model is run. The user has a chance to view all of these inputs and make any desired changes.

2. The model is developed in a Model sheet and is optimized by Solver. The key outputs are reported in a Report sheet. Various aspects of the solution

are also displayed on several charts. The user can view these charts by clicking on navigational buttons on the Report sheet.

19.3   Running the Application

The application is stored in the file **Blending Oil.xlsm**. When this file is opened, the Explanation sheet in Figure 19.1 is displayed. When the user clicks on the button on this sheet, the dialog box in Figure 19.2 appears, which indicates that the inputs to the model are grouped into three categories. The user can view (and then change, if desired) the inputs in any of these categories by checking the appropriate options. If they are all checked, the dialog boxes in Figures 19.3, 19.4, and 19.5 appear sequentially. The inputs that appear initially in the boxes are those from the previous run of the model (if any). Of course, any of these inputs can be changed.

Solver Warning

Actually, the first thing the user sees upon opening the file is a Solver warning. This warning appears in all future applications that invoke Solver. It addresses the "missing Solver reference" problem discussed in Chapter 17. It indicates the necessary fix in case of a Solver problem.

When the user has finished viewing/changing inputs, these inputs are substituted into the model in the (hidden) Model sheet, and the model is optimized with Solver. The important inputs and outputs are displayed in a Report sheet, as shown in Figure 19.6. This sheet contains several buttons for navigating to the various chart sheets and back to the Explanation sheet.

The available charts appear in Figures 19.7–19.13. Each of these charts contains a button that navigates back to the Report sheet.

19.4   Setting Up the Excel Sheets

The **Blending Oil.xlsm** file contains three worksheets and seven chart sheets. *All* of these can be developed at design time, without any VBA. The three worksheets are the Explanation sheet in Figure 19.1, the Model sheet in Figure 19.14, and the Report sheet in Figure 19.6. Because of the fixed size of the problem (always three crude oils and three gasoline products), the structure of the model never changes; the only changes are new input values. Therefore, this model can be developed *completely*, including the Solver dialog box, at design time. Any inputs can be used for testing the model. (The model itself is a straightforward application of linear programming. You can open the **Blending Oil.xlsm** file, unhide the Model sheet, and examine its formulas if you like.) Similarly, the Report sheet can be developed, with links to appropriate cells in the Model sheet, once and for all at design time. Finally, the charts in Figures 19.7–19.13 can be developed and linked to appropriate ranges in the Report sheet at design time. After these worksheets and chart sheets are developed, they are ready and waiting for user inputs.

Figure 19.1 Explanation Sheet

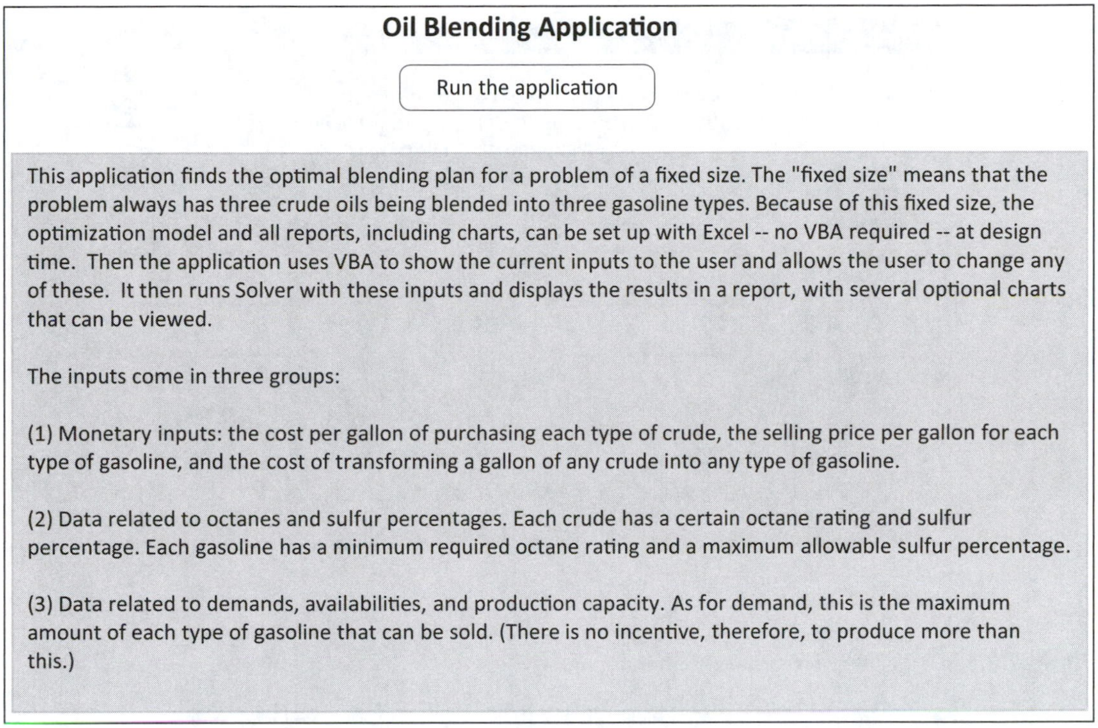

Oil Blending Application
Run the application
This application finds the optimal blending plan for a problem of a fixed size. The "fixed size" means that the problem always has three crude oils being blended into three gasoline types. Because of this fixed size, the optimization model and all reports, including charts, can be set up with Excel -- no VBA required -- at design time. Then the application uses VBA to show the current inputs to the user and allows the user to change any of these. It then runs Solver with these inputs and displays the results in a report, with several optional charts that can be viewed.
The inputs come in three groups:
(1) Monetary inputs: the cost per gallon of purchasing each type of crude, the selling price per gallon for each type of gasoline, and the cost of transforming a gallon of any crude into any type of gasoline.
(2) Data related to octanes and sulfur percentages. Each crude has a certain octane rating and sulfur percentage. Each gasoline has a minimum required octane rating and a maximum allowable sulfur percentage.
(3) Data related to demands, availabilities, and production capacity. As for demand, this is the maximum amount of each type of gasoline that can be sold. (There is no incentive, therefore, to produce more than this.)

Figure 19.2 Initial Dialog Box

Input options
You can view/change any of the inputs for this model in the following groups. Check the group(s) you want to view.
OK
Cancel
Monetary inputs
Data on octane ratings, sulfur contents
Data on demands, availabilities, capacity

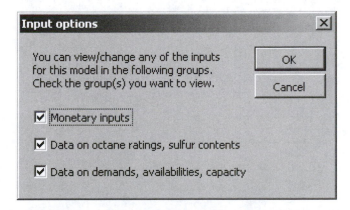

19.5 Getting Started with the VBA

The application includes four user forms, named frmInputTypes, frm-Inputs1, frmInputs2, and frmInputs3, a single module, and, because this application will be invoking Solver VBA functions, a reference to

Figure 19.3 Dialog Box for Monetary Inputs

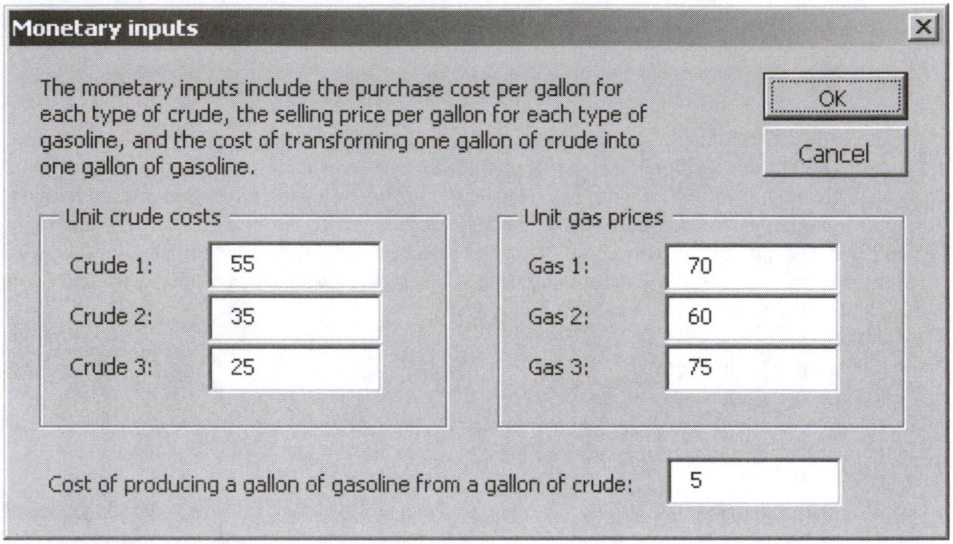

Figure 19.4 Dialog Box for Octane, Sulfur Inputs

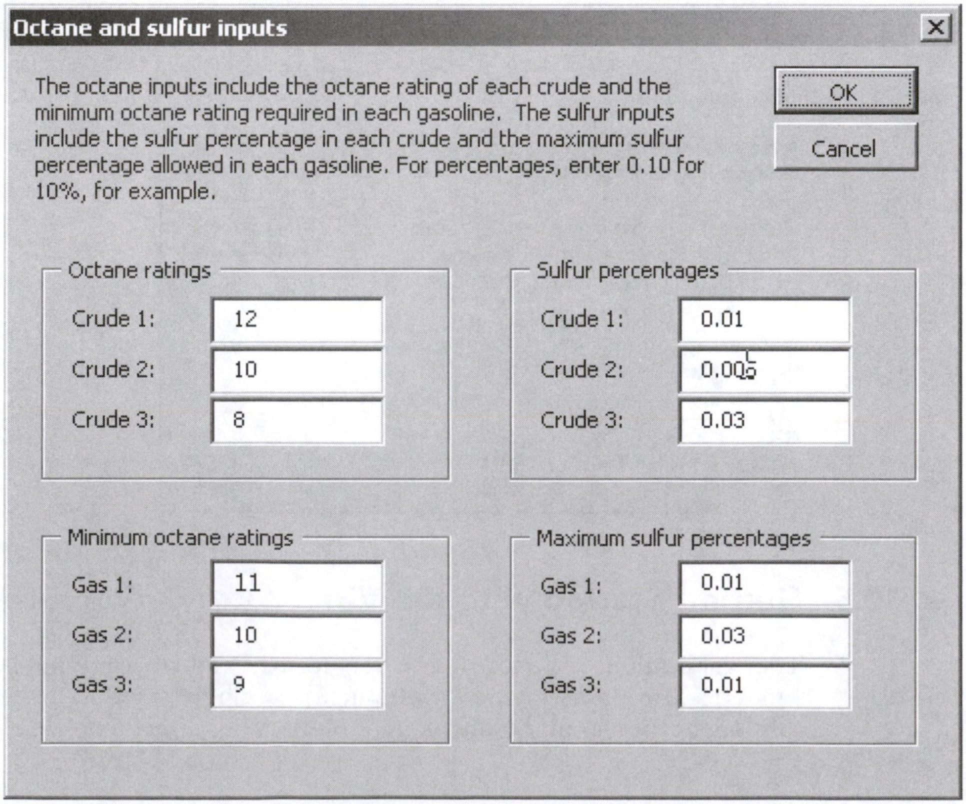

Figure 19.5 Dialog Box for Remaining Inputs

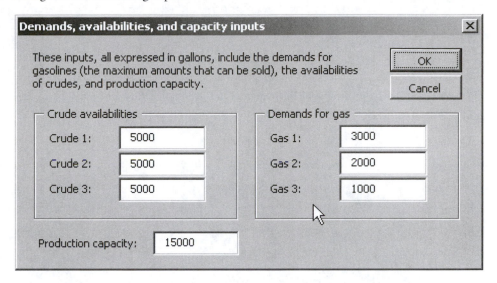

Figure 19.6 Report Sheet

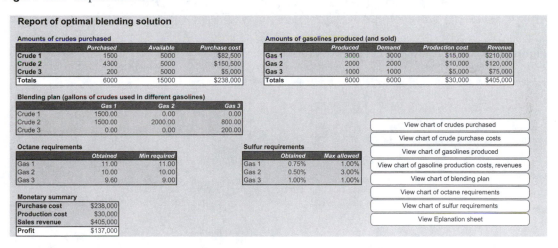

Solver.[1] (Remember that you set a reference with the **Tools→References** menu item in the VBE.) Once these items are added, the Project Explorer window will appear as in Figure 19.15.

Workbook_Open Code

To guarantee that the Explanation sheet appears when the file is opened, the following event handler is placed in the **ThisWorkbook** code window. Note that it uses a For Each loop to hide all sheets except the Explanation sheet.

---

[1]It also contains the one other user form, frmSolver, that simply displays a message about possible Solver problems when the workbook is opened. This is included in all of my Solver applications.

Figure 19.7 Chart of Crude Oils Purchased

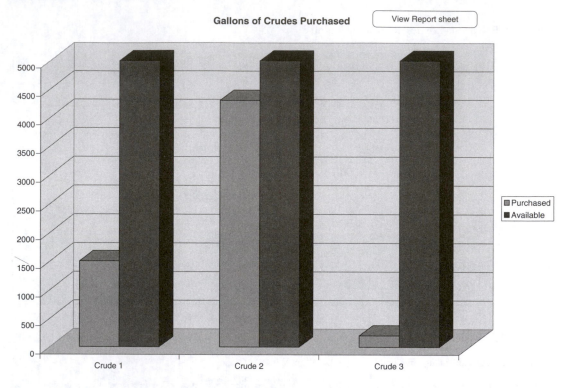

Figure 19.8 Chart of Crude Oil Purchase Costs

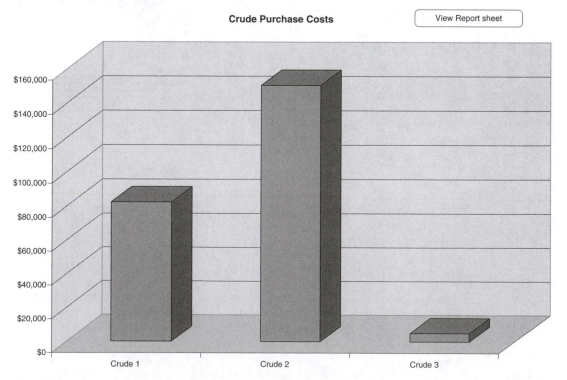

Figure 19.9 Chart of Gasolines Produced and Demands

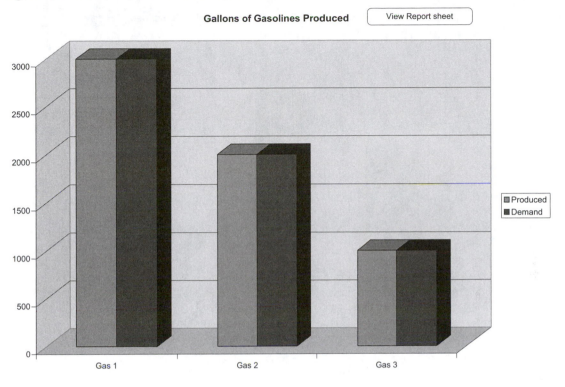

Figure 19.10 Chart of Production Costs and Gasoline Revenues

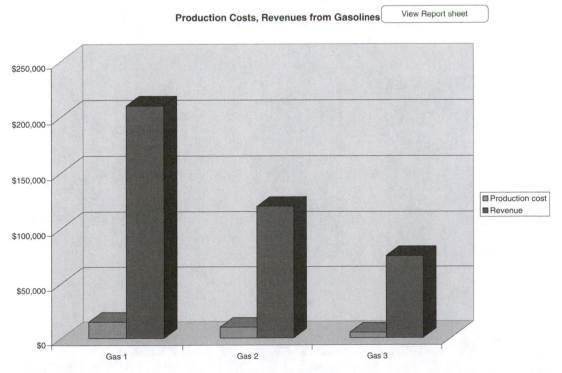

Figure 19.11 Chart of the Blending Plan

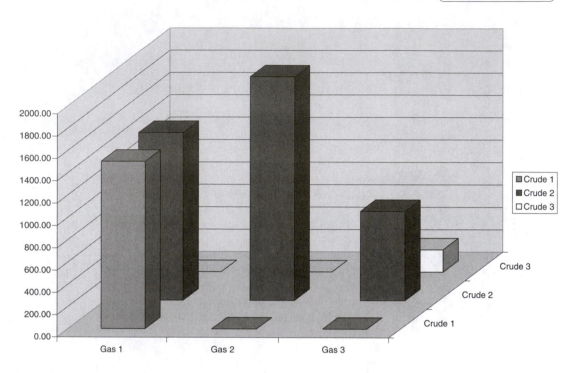

Blending Plan: Gallons of Crudes Used in Gasolines — View Report sheet

Figure 19.12 Chart of Octane Requirements

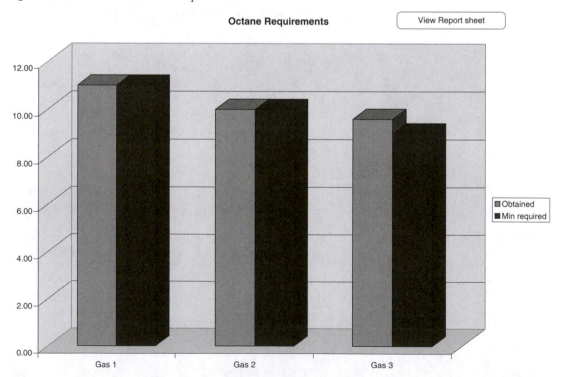

Octane Requirements — View Report sheet

Figure 19.13 Chart of Sulfur Percentage Requirements

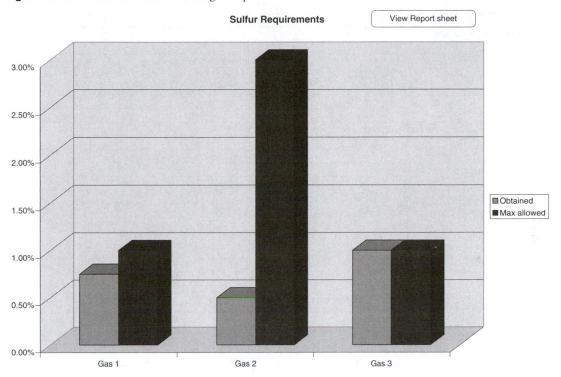

(The **Sheets** collection is appropriate here. This collection includes both worksheets and chart sheets. In contrast, the **Worksheets** collection includes only worksheets, and the **Charts** collection includes only chart sheets.)

```
Private Sub Workbook_Open()
    Dim sht As Object
    Worksheets("Explanation").Activate
    Range("F4").Select
    For Each sht In ActiveWorkbook.Sheets
        If sht.Name <> "Explanation" Then sht.Visible = False
    Next
    frmSolver.Show
End Sub
```

19.6 The User Forms and Their Event Handlers

frmInputTypes

The design of frmInputTypes is shown in Figure 19.16. It contains the usual OK and Cancel buttons, an explanation label, and three check boxes named chkInputs1, chkInputs2, and chkInputs3. The design of the user forms for this application is completely straightforward. The text boxes must be positioned and named, the labels must be positioned and captioned, and so on—straightforward operations.

Figure 19.14 Blending Model

	A	B	C	D	E	F	G
1	**Oil blending model**						
2							
3	Purchase prices per gallon of crude			Sale price per barrel of gasoline			
4	Crude 1	$55		Gas 1	Gas 2	Gas 3	
5	Crude 2	$35		$70	$60	$75	
6	Crude 3	$25					
7							
8	Cost to transform one barrel of crude into one barrel of gasoline						
9		$5					
10							
11	Requirements for gasolines						
12		Gas 1	Gas 2	Gas 3			
13	Minimum octane	11	10	9			
14	Maximum sulfur	1%	3%	1%			
15							
16	Octane ratings			Sulfur content			
17	Crude 1	12		Crude 1	1.0%		
18	Crude 2	10		Crude 2	0.5%		
19	Crude 3	8		Crude 3	3.0%		
20							
21	Purchase/production plan						
22		Gas 1	Gas 2	Gas 3	Total purchased		Max Available
23	Crude 1	1500.00	0.00	0.00	1500	<=	5000
24	Crude 2	1500.00	2000.00	800.00	4300	<=	5000
25	Crude 3	0.00	0.00	200.00	200	<=	5000
26							
27	Demand for gasolines						
28		Gas 1	Gas 2	Gas 3			
29	Amount produced	3000	2000	1000			
30		<=	<=	<=			
31	Maximum Demand	3000	2000	1000			
32							
33	Constraint on total production						
34		Total produced		Max Capacity			
35		6000	<=	15000			
36							
37	Octane constraints	Gas 1	Gas 2	Gas 3			
38	Actual total octane	33000	20000	9600			
39		>=	>=	>=			
40	Required	33000	20000	9000			
41							
42	Sulfur constraints	Gas 1	Gas 2	Gas 3			
43	Actual total sulfur	22.5	10	10			
44		<=	<=	<=			
45	Required	30	60	10			
46							
47	Purchase costs	$238,000					
48	Production costs	$30,000					
49	Sales revenue	$405,000					
50							
51	Profit	$137,000					

Figure 19.15 Project Explorer Window

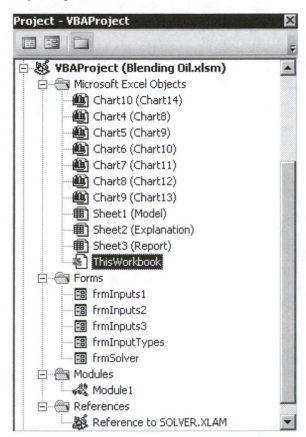

Figure 19.16 Design of frmInputTypes

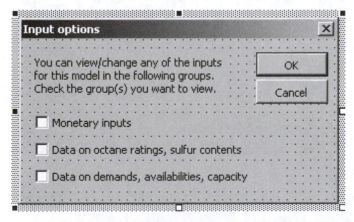

The event handlers for this user form are listed below. The **Userform_Initialize** sub checks each of the check boxes by default. The **btnOK_Click** sub captures the user's entries in the check boxes in the public Boolean variables blnInputs1, blnInputs2, and blnInputs3. The **btnCancel_Click** sub unloads the user form and terminates the program.

Event Handlers for frmInputs

```
Private Sub btnCancel_Click()
    Unload Me
    End
End Sub

Private Sub btnOK_Click()
    ' Capture the status of the checkboxes in Boolean variables.
    blnInputs1 = chkInputs1.Value
    blnInputs2 = chkInputs2.Value
    blnInputs3 = chkInputs3.Value
    Unload Me
End Sub

Private Sub Userform_Initialize()
    ' Have all boxes checked initially.
    chkInputs1.Value = True
    chkInputs2.Value = True
    chkInputs3.Value = True
End Sub
```

frmInputs1

The design of frmInputs1 is shown in Figure 19.17. It contains OK and Cancel buttons, an explanation label, two frames for grouping inputs, and seven text boxes and corresponding labels. The three text boxes in the Unit crude costs

Figure 19.17 Design of frmInputs1

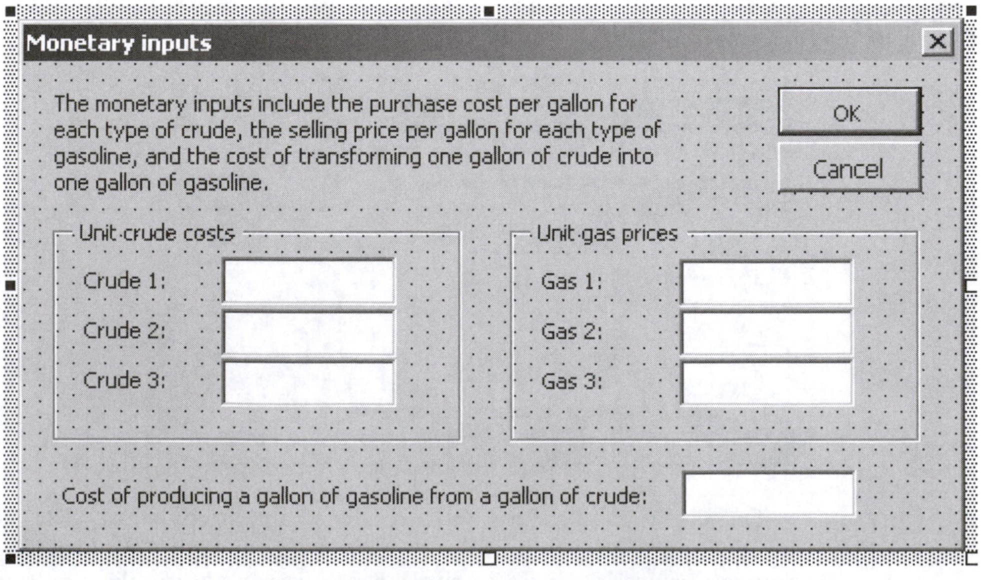

group are named txtCrude1, txtCrude2, and txtCrude3. The three text boxes in the Unit gas prices group are named txtGas1, txtGas2, and txtGas3. Finally, the production cost text box is named txtProdCost.

The **Userform_Initialize** sub captures the values in the Model sheet (from a previous run, if any) and enters them in the text boxes, and then the **btnOK_Click** sub takes the user's choices and places them back in the Model sheet. It also performs some error checking on the user's inputs to ensure that they are numeric and positive. Note that it also uses the **Val** function to convert a string (which is always the result from a text box) to a numeric value (which is what we want in the worksheet). Otherwise, arithmetic operations couldn't be performed on these cells in the worksheet.

Event Handlers for frmInputs1

```vba
Private Sub btnCancel_Click()
    Unload Me
End Sub

Private Sub btnOK_Click()
    ' Check that the text boxes are not empty, have numeric values, and
    ' have positive values.
    Dim ctl As Control
    For Each ctl In Me.Controls
        If TypeName(ctl) = "TextBox" Then
            If ctl.Value = "" Or Not IsNumeric(ctl) Then
                MsgBox "Enter positive numeric values in all boxes.", _
                    vbInformation, "Invalid entry"
                ctl.SetFocus
                Exit Sub
            End If
            If ctl.Value < 0 Then
                MsgBox "Enter positive numeric values in all boxes.", _
                    vbInformation, "Invalid entry"
                ctl.SetFocus
                Exit Sub
            End If
        End If
    Next

    ' Capture the user inputs in the various ranges in the (hidden) Model sheet.
    With Range("PurchCosts")
        .Cells(1).Value = Val(txtCrude1.Text)
        .Cells(2).Value = Val(txtCrude2.Text)
        .Cells(3).Value = Val(txtCrude3.Text)
    End With
    With Range("SellPrices")
        .Cells(1).Value = Val(txtGas1.Text)
        .Cells(2).Value = Val(txtGas2.Text)
        .Cells(3).Value = Val(txtGas3.Text)
    End With
    Range("ProdCost").Value = Val(txtProdCost.Text)
    Unload Me
End Sub
```

```
Private Sub Userform_Initialize()
    ' Initialize with the current values in the various ranges from the
    ' (hidden) Model sheet.
    With Range("PurchCosts")
        txtCrude1.Text = .Cells(1).Value
        txtCrude2.Text = .Cells(2).Value
        txtCrude3.Text = .Cells(3).Value
    End With
    With Range("SellPrices")
        txtGas1.Text = .Cells(1).Value
        txtGas2.Text = .Cells(2).Value
        txtGas3.Text = .Cells(3).Value
    End With
    txtProdCost.Text = Range("ProdCost").Value
End Sub
```

frmInputs2 and frmInputs3

The other two input forms, frmInputs2 and frmInputs3, shown in Figures 19.4 and 19.5, are very similar. For example, frmInputs2 contains OK and Cancel buttons, an explanation label, four frames for grouping the inputs, and 12 text boxes and corresponding labels. The event handlers for these two forms are very similar to those in frmInputs1, so they are not listed here.

19.7 The VBA Code in the Module

In most applications, the VBA code in the module does the majority of the work. However, this is not the case here. There is a **MainBlending** module that "shows" the appropriate forms. The **btnOK_Click** event handlers for these forms store the user's inputs in public variables declared in the Model sheet. Therefore, all the Main sub needs to do is show the forms and then run Solver. (Note that it must first unhide the Model sheet. Solver cannot be run on a model in a hidden sheet.) Other than this, the module contains only "navigational" subs. These are attached to the buttons on the Report sheet and the various chart sheets. There is also a **RepositionButtons** sub described below.

Option Statement and Public Variables

```
' These Boolean variables indicate which types of inputs the user
' wants to view/change.
Public blnInputs1 As Boolean
Public blnInputs2 As Boolean
Public blnInputs3 As Boolean
```

MainBlending Code

```
Sub MainBlending()
    ' This sub runs when the user clicks on the button on the Explanation sheet.
    Dim solverStatus As Integer
```

```
' Find which types of inputs the user wants to view/change.
frmInputTypes.Show

' Show the input forms the user has requested.
If blnInputs1 Then frmInputs1.Show
If blnInputs2 Then frmInputs2.Show
If blnInputs3 Then frmInputs3.Show

Application.ScreenUpdating = False

' Unhide and activate the Model sheet, and run Solver.
With Worksheets("Model")
    .Visible = True
    .Activate
End With

' Call Solver and check for no feasible solutions.
solverStatus = SolverSolve(UserFinish:=True)
If solverStatus = 5 Then
    ' There are no feasible solutions, so report this and quit.
    MsgBox "There is no feasible solution to the problem with these " _
        & "inputs. Try again with different inputs.", vbInformation, "Not feasible"
    Worksheets("Model").Visible = False
    Call ViewExplanation

Else
    ' There is a solution, so report it in the Report sheet.
    Worksheets("Model").Visible = False
    With Worksheets("Report")
        .Visible = True
        .Activate
    End With
    Range("A1").Select
End If

Application.ScreenUpdating = True
End Sub
```

Navigational Code

The following subs are for navigational purposes. Note that the chart sheets are initially hidden. Each of them has a button that runs the ViewReport sub. When this sub runs, it hides the active chart sheet.

```
Sub ViewReport()
    ActiveChart.Visible = False
    Worksheets("Report").Activate
    Range("A1").Select
End Sub

Sub ViewExplanation()
    Worksheets("Explanation").Activate
    Range("F4").Select
End Sub
```

```
Sub ViewCrudePurch()
    With Charts("CrudePurch")
        .Visible = True
        .Activate
    End With
End Sub

Sub ViewCrudeCosts()
    With Charts("CrudeCosts")
        .Visible = True
        .Activate
    End With
End Sub

Sub ViewGasProduced()
    With Charts("GasProduced")
        .Visible = True
        .Activate
    End With
End Sub

Sub ViewProdCostsRevs()
    With Charts("ProdCostsRevs")
        .Visible = True
        .Activate
    End With
End Sub

Sub ViewBlendPlan()
    With Charts("BlendPlan")
        .Visible = True
        .Activate
    End With
End Sub

Sub ViewOctane()
    With Charts("Octane")
        .Visible = True
        .Activate
    End With
End Sub

Sub ViewSulfur()
    With Charts("Sulfur")
        .Visible = True
        .Activate
    End With
End Sub
```

Repositioning the Buttons

As one final touch, the **RepositionButtons** sub, listed below, ensures that the eight buttons on the Report sheet (see Figure 19.6) are lined up, have the same size, and have the same spacing. (It is tricky to do this manually!) This sub needs to be run only once, at design time. The key to it is that each "shape" floating above a worksheet has **Top**, **Left**, **Height**, and **Width** properties. (Buttons are members of the **Shapes** collection. They are the *only* shapes in the Report sheet.) By manipulating these properties, the buttons can be positioned exactly as desired. Note that measurements for these properties are in **points**, where one point is 1/72 inch.

This sub was run once to line up the eight buttons on the Report sheet. When this sub was run, the buttons had already been created on the sheet, and the first (top) button was positioned and sized correctly.

```
Sub RepositionButtons()
    ' This sub was run once to line up the 8 buttons on the Report sheet. When
    ' this sub was run, the buttons had already been created on the sheet,
    ' and the first (top) button was positioned and sized correctly.
    Dim i As Integer
    Dim t, l, h, w
    With Worksheets("Report")
        ' Get the coordinates of the top button.
        With .Shapes(1)
            t = .Top
            l = .Left
            h = .Height
            w = .Width
        End With

        ' Make sure each succeeding button is the same size as the top button
        ' and is positioned slightly (2/72 inch) below the previous button.
        For i = 2 To 8
            With .Shapes(i)
                .Top = Worksheets("Report").Shapes(i - 1).Top + h + 2
                .Left = l
                .Height = h
                .Width = w
            End With
        Next
    End With
End Sub
```

19.8 Summary

This application is a great example of the functionality you can achieve with very little VBA code. Although I don't necessarily encourage you to create all of the applications, starting from scratch, in the remaining chapters, I urge you to try developing this blending application on your own. There are at least two ways you can proceed. First, you can open a new, blank workbook and create the *entire* application—model, user forms, and code. Alternatively, you can make a copy of the **Blending Oil.xlsm** file. Then you can delete the user forms and the module from your copy and recreate them on your own, using the explanations in this chapter as a guide. In either case, you will find that there are no *difficult* steps in this application; there are just a lot of relatively simple steps. In fact, you will find that many of these steps are rather repetitive. Therefore, you should look for any possible shortcuts, such as copying and pasting, to reduce the development time.

EXERCISES

1. All of the charts in this application are types of 3-dimensional column charts. Change the application so that they are different chart types. (You can decide which you prefer.) Do you need to rewrite any of the VBA code?

2. Continuing Exercise 1, suppose you want to give the *user* the choice of chart types. For example, suppose you want to give the user two choices: the current chart types or some other chart type. (You can choose the other type.) Change the application to allow this choice. Now you *will* have to add some new VBA code, along with another user form. However, you should never need to create any charts from scratch with VBA; you only need to modify existing charts.

3. Suppose there is another chemical additive—let's call it Excron—that is part of each crude oil. You know what percentage of each crude oil is Excron, and you know the *minimum* percentages of each gasoline product that must be Excron. That is, all of these percentages are inputs. Change the optimization model and the application to take Excron into account. (Expand the appropriate user form to capture the Excron inputs, and make all other necessary modifications.)

4. (More difficult) Changing the size of a model like this one can be quite tedious. Try the following to see what is involved. Assume that the model can have either two or three crude oils, and it can have either two or three gasoline products. First, create a new user form called frmSize to capture these size options. Then modify the rest of the application accordingly. (*Hints:* You can change the **Visible** property of controls on the user forms to hide them or unhide them, depending on whether they are needed. With VBA you can change the range names of the parts of the Model sheet that will appear in the Solver dialog box. As discussed in Chapter 17, this will make all Solver setups *look* the same, but you will have to do a SolverReset and then respecify all settings because of changes in the physical locations of the ranges. Finally, you might want to remove the formatting from the Report sheet (make it less fancy) to make modifications easier.)

A Product Mix Application

20.1 Introduction

This application is an example of the product mix model. It is a prototpye model often used to introduce linear programming. The products illustrated here are custom-made pieces of wood furniture that require labor hours from senior and junior woodworkers, machine hours, and wood (measured in board feet). There are constraints on the availability of the resources. For some of the products, there are also constraints on the minimum and/or maximum production levels. The objective is to maximize profit: revenues minus costs.

The linear programming model in this application is, if anything, simpler than the blending model in the previous chapter. However, the VBA requirements are considerably more extensive. The model is no longer fixed in size, because the user is allowed to include any number of products in the potential product mix. This means, for example, that the number of changing cells in the optimization model can change from one run to another. From a decision support point of view, this is much more realistic, but it also complicates the VBA. Only a limited part of the optimization model can be set up at design time. The rest must be developed at run time with VBA code.

New Learning Objectives: VBA

- To see how VBA can be used to get the data inputs from one worksheet and use them to build an optimization model in another worksheet.
- To illustrate how VBA can be used to develop an optimization model of varying size.
- To illustrate how a VBA program that must perform many tasks can be divided into many relatively small subroutines.
- To better understand how VBA can be used to enter formulas into cells.

New Learning Objectives: Non-VBA

- To develop an understanding of a prototype linear programming model: the product mix model.

20.2 Functionality of the Application

The application provides the following functionality:

1. It provides a database (on the Data sheet) of all required inputs for the model. Before running the application, the user can change these inputs. In fact, it is possible to manually add or delete products and resources in the list. The VBA code will always capture the current data in the Data sheet when it develops and solves the optimization model in the Model sheet.

2. Given the set of all products listed in the Data sheet, the user can select the products that will be included in the product mix model. If a product is not selected, it will not even be considered in the product mix.

3. Once the user selects the products to be included in the model, a product mix model is developed in the (hidden) Model sheet, and Solver is invoked to find the optimal product mix. The key results are then listed in a Report sheet.

20.3 Running the Application

The application is in the file **Product Mix.xlsm**. When this file is opened, the explanation in Figure 20.1 appears.

The data for the products and the data for the resources appear in Figures 20.2 and 20.3. The unit costs in column D of Figure 20.2 are actually calculated from formulas: Each is a sum of products of the unit usages in a product row of Figure 20.2 multiplied by the unit resource costs in column N of Figure 20.3. All other data are given values. The MinUnits and MaxUnits in columns E and F of Figure 20.2 prescribe lower and upper limits on the quantities of the products that can be produced. If a MinUnits value is blank, it is replaced by 0 in the model. If a MaxUnits value is blank, it is replaced by a suitably large value in the model (so that there is effectively no upper limit).

When the user clicks on the button in Figure 20.1, the dialog box in Figure 20.4 appears. This allows the user to select the products that will be included in the model.

Once the products have been selected, VBA is used to develop the Model sheet. Any results on this sheet from a previous run are cleared. Then a new model is developed, and Solver is set up and run. Finally, VBA unhides the Report sheet, clears any results from a previous run, and reports the new solution. Typical Model and Report sheets appear in Figures 20.5 and 20.6. I will not spell out the formulas in the Model sheet; it is a straightforward linear programming model. (If you are interested, open the file, run the application once, unhide the Model sheet, and examine its formulas.)

Figure 20.1 Explanation Sheet

Product Mix Application

The Woodworks Company manufactures and sells custom-made furniture.The products, their unit prices, their unit resource usages, and their minimum and maximum production quantities for the next month appear on the data sheet. This sheet also lists the resources, their availabilities for the next month, and their unit costs. The problem is to find the mix of products that maximizes profit.

This application allows the user to choose which of the potential products to include in the product mix. (If a product is not chosen, it won't even be considered for the optimal product mix.) The product mix model is then formulated on a Model sheet, it is solved with Solver, and a report describing the optimal product mix is presented on a Report sheet.

The application searches the Data sheet for all product and resource data. Therefore, the user can add products and/or resources to this sheet, along with the corresponding data, and the application will include these new entries when it runs.

Figure 20.2 Data for the Products

	A	B	C	D	E	F	G	H	I	J	K
3	Data on products: unit price, resources required per unit, minimum and maximum units										
4	Product code	Description	UnitPrice	UnitCost	MinUnits	MaxUnits	SrLaborHrs	JrLaborHrs	MachineHrs	OakFt	CherryFt
5	1243	Oak end table	$190	$130	20	40	0.5	1.3	0.4	2.8	0
6	2243	Cherry end table	$203	$146		30	0.7	1.2	0.4	0	2.8
7	1456	Oak rocking chair	$371	$277	5	20	2.1	2.9	1.2	5.2	0
8	2456	Cherry rocking chair	$407	$308	5	15	2.5	2.7	1.2	0	5.2
9	1372	Oak coffee table	$238	$167	10	30	1.3	1.7	0.6	3.2	0
10	2372	Cherry coffee table	$259	$185		10	1.5	1.5	0.6	0	3.2
11	1531	Oak dining table	$837	$648	5		1.9	3.2	1.7	15.6	0
12	2531	Cherry dining table	$964	$724		10	2.1	2.8	1.6	0	15.6
13	1635	Oak desk	$1,084	$841	5	15	4.3	5.8	3.2	18.2	0
14	2635	Cherry desk	$1,214	$938	5		4.5	5.6	3.5	0	18.2
15	1367	Oak bookshelves	$401	$315	15	30	1.8	2.5	2.1	6.2	0
16	2367	Cherry bookshelves	$455	$349		40	1.9	2.5	2.2	0	6.2

Figure 20.3 Data for the Resources

	M	N	O
3	Data on resources		
4	Resource	UnitCost	Availability
5	SrLaborHrs	$20	263
6	JrLaborHrs	$12	450
7	MachineHrs	$15	225
8	OakFt	$35	488
9	CherryFt	$40	638

Figure 20.4 Dialog Box for Selecting Products in the Model

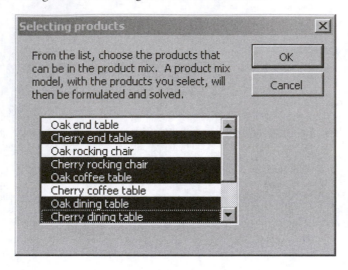

Figure 20.5 Model Sheet

	A	B	C	D	E	F	G	H	I	J	K	L	M	N
1	Model formulation													
2														
3	Product mix													
4	Product code	2243	2456	1372	1531	2531								
5	Min	0	5	10	5	0								
6		<=	<=	<=	<=	<=								
7	Produced	30	15	30	25	10								
8		<=	<=	<=	<=	<=								
9	Max	30	15	30	31	10								
10														
11	UnitPrice	$203.00	$407.00	$238.00	$837.00	$964.00								
12	UnitCost	$146.40	$308.40	$167.40	$647.90	$723.60								
13	UnitProfit	$56.60	$98.60	$70.60	$189.10	$240.40								
14														
15	Resource usage					Monetary summary			Resources used per unit of products					
16	Resource	Used		Available		Total revenue	$49,900		Resource/Product code	2243	2456	1372	1531	2531
17	SrLaborHrs	166.0	<=	263.0		Total cost	$37,474		SrLaborHrs	0.7	2.5	1.3	1.9	2.1
18	JrLaborHrs	235.5	<=	450.0		Total profit	$12,427		JrLaborHrs	1.2	2.7	1.7	3.2	2.8
19	MachineHrs	106.5	<=	225.0					MachineHrs	0.4	1.2	0.6	1.7	1.6
20	OakFt	486.0	<=	488.0					OakFt	0	0	3.2	15.6	0
21	CherryFt	318.0	<=	638.0					CherryFt	2.8	5.2	0	0	15.6

Figure 20.6 Report Sheet

	A	B	C	D	E	F	G	H	I	J	K
1	Optimal product mix										
2											
3	Monetary summary										
4	Total revenue	$49,900									
5	Total cost	$37,474									
6	Total profit	$12,427									
7											
8	Product data							Resource data			
9	Product code	Description	Units produced	Revenue	Cost	Profit		Resource	Used	Available	Left over
10	2243	Cherry end table	30	$6,090	$4,392	$1,698		SrLaborHrs	166.0	263.0	97.0
11	2456	Cherry rocking chair	15	$6,105	$4,626	$1,479		JrLaborHrs	235.5	450.0	214.5
12	1372	Oak coffee table	30	$7,140	$5,022	$2,118		MachineHrs	106.5	225.0	118.5
13	1531	Oak dining table	25	$20,925	$16,198	$4,728		OakFt	486.0	488.0	2.0
14	2531	Cherry dining table	10	$9,640	$7,236	$2,404		CherryFt	318.0	638.0	320.0

20.4 Setting Up the Excel Sheets

The Model and Report sheets cannot be set up entirely at design time because the number of products and the number of resources could change, depending on the data entered in the Data sheet and the user's choice of potential products from the user form. However, these sheets can be set up partially, and certain cells can be designated as "anchors" (for use in the VBA code) and assigned range names. (I like to use upper-left corner "anchor" cells and offset everything with respect to them.) The names and addresses of the anchor cells for this application are listed here for later reference. Take a look at Figures 20.2, 20.3, 20.5, and 20.6 to familiarize yourself with the locations of these cells.

- ProdAnchor (cell A4 of Data sheet)
- ResAnchor (cell M4 of Data sheet)
- ProdMixAnchor (cell A3 of Model sheet)
- ResUseAnchor (cell A16 of Model sheet)
- MonSummAnchor (cell F15 of Model sheet)
- UnitUseAnchor (cell I16 of Model sheet)
- ProdRepAnchor (cell A9 of Report sheet)
- ResRepAnchor (cell H9 of Report sheet)

The templates for the Model and Report sheets appear in Figures 20.7 and 20.8.

20.5 Getting Started with the VBA

This application requires a user form named frmProducts, a single module, and a reference to Solver. Once these items are added, the Project Explorer window will appear as in Figure 20.9.[1]

Workbook_Open Code

To guarantee that the Explanation sheet appears when the file is opened, the following code is placed in the ThisWorkbook code window. Note that it also hides the Model and Report sheets.

```
Private Sub Workbook_Open()
    Worksheets("Explanation").Activate
    Range("F4").Select
    Worksheets("Model").Visible = False
    Worksheets("Report").Visible = False
    frmSolver.Show
End Sub
```

---

[1]It also contains the usual frmSolver that displays a message about possible Solver problems when the workbook is opened.

Figure 20.7 Model Sheet Template

	A	B	C	D	E	F	G	H	I	J	K
1	Model formulation										
2											
3	**Product mix**										
4	Product code										
5	Min										
6											
7	Produced										
8											
9	Max										
10											
11	UnitPrice										
12	UnitCost										
13	UnitProfit										
14											
15	**Resource usage**					Monetary summary			Resources used per unit of products		
16	Resource	Used		Available		Total revenue			Resource/Product code		
17						Total cost					
18						Total profit					
19											

Figure 20.8 Report Sheet Template

	A	B	C	D	E	F	G	H	I	J	K
1	Optimal product mix										
2											
3	**Monetary summary**										
4	Total revenue										
5	Total cost										
6	Total profit										
7											
8	**Product data**							Resource data			
9	Product code	Description		Units produced	Revenue	Cost	Profit		Resource	Used	Available	Left over
10											

Figure 20.9 Project Explorer Window

20.6 The User Form and Its Event Handlers

The design of frmProducts is shown in Figure 20.10. It has the usual OK and Cancel buttons, a label for explanation at the top, and a list box named lbProduct. The **MultiSelect** property for this list box should be changed to option 2 in the Properties window (see Figure 20.11). This enables the user to select *multiple* products from the list, not just a single product.

Once the user form has been designed, the appropriate event handlers can be written. The **UserForm_Initialize** sub indicates how the form should be presented initially to the user. It fills the list box with the product array (which will have been populated by this time with code in the module), and it selects the first product as the default. (Remember once again that the **Selected** array for a multi-type list box is 0-based. The first item in the list has index 0, the second has index 1, and so on.) The **btnOK_Click** sub captures the user's selections in a public Boolean isSelected array (1-based) and then unloads the dialog box. The **btnCancel_Click** sub unloads the dialog box and terminates the application.

Event Handlers for frmProducts

```
Private Sub btnCancel_Click()
    ' Unload the dialog box and quit.
    Unload Me
    End
End Sub

Private Sub btnOK_Click()
    ' Go through the items in the list box to see which have been selected,
    ' and use these to form the Boolean isSelected array. Note that the items
    ' in a list box always start with index 0, whereas the isSelected array
    ' starts with index 1.
    With lbProducts
        Dim p As Integer ' product index, 0-based
        For p = 0 To nProducts - 1
            isSelected(p + 1) = .Selected(p)
        Next
    End With

    Unload Me
End Sub

Private Sub UserForm_Initialize()
    ' Add the product descriptions to the list.
    Dim p As Integer ' product index
    For p = 1 To nProducts
        lbProducts.AddItem product(p)
    Next
    ' Select the first item (so that it will be impossible for the user
    ' to select no items).
    lbProducts.Selected(0) = True
End Sub
```

Figure 20.10 frmProducts Design

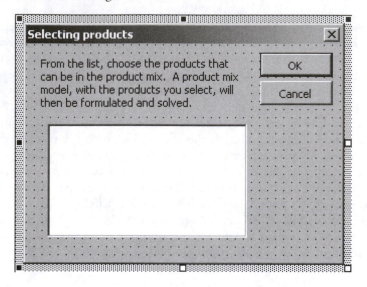

Figure 20.11 Changing the MultiSelect Property of the List Box

Properties - lbProducts	

lbProducts ListBox

Alphabetic | Categorized

Font	Tahoma
ForeColor	&H80000008&
Height	84.05
HelpContextID	0
IMEMode	0 - fmIMEModeNoControl
IntegralHeight	True
Left	16.5
ListStyle	0 - fmListStylePlain
Locked	False
MatchEntry	0 - fmMatchEntryFirstLetter
MouseIcon	(None)
MousePointer	0 - fmMousePointerDefault
MultiSelect	2 - fmMultiSelectExtended
RowSource	
SpecialEffect	2 - fmSpecialEffectSunken
TabIndex	3
TabStop	True
Tag	
Text	
TextAlign	1 - fmTextAlignLeft

20.7 The VBA Code in the Module

Most of the work is performed by the VBA code in the module. This code is listed below. The application uses a modular design, as described in Chapter 10. After declaring the public variables at the top, a **Main** sub calls several other subs in a logical order. Some of these subs call other subs. Again, the purpose of dividing the overall program into so many small subs is to make it more readable—and easier to debug.

Option Statements and Public Variables

```
Option Explicit
Option Base 1

' Definition of main variables:
'    nProducts - number of products listed in Data sheet
'    nResources - number of resources listed in Data sheet
'    product() - array of product names
'    resource() - array of resource names
'    isSelected() - Boolean array that indicates which products are selected
'        from the user form
Public nProducts As Integer, nResources As Integer
Public product() As String, resource() As String
Public isSelected() As Boolean
```

MainProductMix Code

The **MainProductMix** sub is the control center. It calls all of the other subs that do the real work. The button on the Explanation sheet (see Figure 20.1) has the MainProductMix macro assigned to it.

```
Sub MainProductMix()
    ' This sub runs when the user clicks on the button on the Explanation sheet.
    Call GetProducts
    Call GetResources
    frmProducts.Show
    Application.ScreenUpdating = False
    Call SetupModel
    Call RunSolver
    Call CreateReport
End Sub
```

GetProducts, GetResources Code

The **GetProducts** and **GetResources** subs find the numbers of products and resources from the Data sheet, redimension the product, resource, and isSelected arrays appropriately, and fill them with the product and resource names from the

Data sheet. Note how the "anchor" cells are used. Everything is offset relative to them. This occurs many times throughout the application.

```
Sub GetProducts()
    ' This sub finds the number of products and their corresponding data.
    With Range("ProdAnchor")
        nProducts = Range(.Offset(1, 0), .End(xlDown)).Count
        ReDim product(nProducts)
        ReDim isSelected(nProducts)
        Dim p As Integer ' product index
        For p = 1 To nProducts
            product(p) = .Offset(p, 1).Value
        Next
    End With
End Sub

Sub GetResources()
    ' This sub finds the number of resources and their corresponding data.
    With Range("ResAnchor")
        nResources = Range(.Offset(1, 0), .End(xlDown)).Count
        ReDim resource(nResources)
        Dim r As Integer ' resource index
        For r = 1 To nResources
            resource(r) = .Offset(r, 0).Value
        Next
    End With
End Sub
```

SetupModel Code

The **SetupModel** sub first unhides and activates the Model sheet (which at this point is only a template or contains data from a previous run), and then it calls seven other subs to develop the optimization model.

```
Sub SetupModel()
    ' This sub develops the optimization model through a series of subroutines.
    With Worksheets("Model")
        .Visible = True
        .Activate
    End With
    Call ClearOldModel
    Call EnterProductData
    Call EnterResourceData
    Call EnterUsageData
    Call CalcMaxProduction
    Call CalcResourceUsages
    Call CalcMonetaryValues
End Sub
```

ClearOldModel Code

The **ClearOldModel** sub clears out data, if any, from a previous run to return the Model sheet to its "template" form. Note that it uses the **ClearContents** method.

This deletes all values but leaves old formatting in place. Again, note how the "anchor" cells are used with offsetting.

```
Sub ClearOldModel()
    ' This sub clears all of the old data, but not formatting, from any previous model.
    With Range("ProdMixAnchor")
        Range(.Offset(1, 1), .Offset(10, 1).End(xlToRight)).ClearContents
    End With
    With Range("ResUseAnchor")
        Range(.Offset(1, 0), .Offset(1, 0).End(xlDown).Offset(0, 3)).ClearContents
    End With
    With Range("MonSummAnchor")
        Range(.Offset(1, 1), .Offset(3, 1)).ClearContents
    End With
    With Range("UnitUseAnchor")
        Range(.Offset(0, 0), .End(xlDown).End(xlToRight)).ClearContents
        .Value = "Resource/Product code"
    End With
End Sub
```

EnterProductData Code

The **EnterProductData** sub enters data about the selected products in the Model sheet. It also names a few ranges for later reference.

```
Sub EnterProductData()
    ' This sub enters the product data for all products selected in the
    ' Product Mix part of the Model sheet.
    Dim p1 As Integer ' product index, selected products only
    Dim p2 As Integer ' product index, all products
    Dim minVal As Single

    ' Enter data only for the selected products
    p1 = 0
    With Range("ProdMixAnchor")
        For p2 = 1 To nProducts
            If isSelected(p2) Then
                p1 = p1 + 1

                ' Enter product code.
                .Offset(1, p1).Value = Range("ProdAnchor") _
                    .Offset(p2, 0).Value

                ' Enter minimum production level.
                ' (Enter 0 if one isn't given in the Data sheet).
                If Range("ProdAnchor").Offset(p2, 4).Value = "" Then
                    minVal = 0
                Else
                    minVal = Range("ProdAnchor").Offset(p2, 4).Value
                End If
                .Offset(2, p1).Value = minVal

                ' Set the initial values of the changing cells to 0.
                .Offset(4, p1).Value = 0
```

```
                    ' Enter labels to identify constraints.
                    .Offset(3, p1).Value = "<="
                    .Offset(5, p1).Value = "<="

                    ' Enter unit price and unit cost.
                    .Offset(8, p1).Value = Range("ProdAnchor") _
                        .Offset(p2, 2).Value
                    .Offset(9, p1).Value = Range("ProdAnchor") _
                        .Offset(p2, 3).Value

                    ' Calculate unit profit.
                    .Offset(10, p1).FormulaR1C1 = "=R[-2]C-R[-1]C"
            End If
        Next

        ' Name various ranges.
        Range(.Offset(2, 1), .Offset(2, 1).End(xlToRight)).Name = "MinProd"
        Range(.Offset(4, 1), .Offset(4, 1).End(xlToRight)).Name = "Produced"
        Range(.Offset(8, 1), .Offset(8, 1).End(xlToRight)).Name = "UnitRev"
        Range(.Offset(9, 1), .Offset(9, 1).End(xlToRight)).Name = "UnitCost"
        Range(.Offset(10, 1), .Offset(10, 1).End(xlToRight)).Name = "UnitProfit"
    End With
End Sub
```

EnterResourceData Code

The **EnterResourceData** sub enters the resource names and availabilities in the Model sheet and names a couple of ranges for later use.

```
Sub EnterResourceData()
    ' This sub enters the resources availabilities in the Resource
    ' Usage part of the Model sheet.
    Dim r As Integer ' resource index

    With Range("ResUseAnchor")
        For r = 1 To nResources
            ' Enter name of resource.
            .Offset(r, 0).Value = resource(r)

            ' Enter label to identify constraint.
            .Offset(r, 2).Value = "<="

            ' Enter resource availability.
            .Offset(r, 3).Value = Range("ResAnchor").Offset(r, 2).Value
        Next

        ' Name resource ranges.
        Range(.Offset(1, 1), .Offset(nResources, 1)).Name = "Used"
        Range(.Offset(1, 3), .Offset(nResources, 3)).Name = "Available"
    End With
End Sub
```

EnterUsageData Code

The **EnterUsageData** sub enters the table of unit resource usages (how much of each resource is used by a unit of each product) in the Model sheet.

```
Sub EnterUsageData()
    ' This sub enters the unit usages of resources for selected products
    ' in the resource usage part of the Model sheet.
    Dim p1 As Integer ' product index, selected products only
    Dim p2 As Integer ' product index, all products
    Dim r As Integer ' resource index

    With Range("UnitUseAnchor")
        ' Enter resource names.
        For r = 1 To nResources
            .Offset(r, 0).Value = resource(r)
        Next

        ' Enter data only for selected products.
        p1 = 0
        For p2 = 1 To nProducts
            If isSelected(p2) Then
                p1 = p1 + 1

                ' Enter product code.
                .Offset(0, p1).Value = Range("ProdAnchor") _
                    .Offset(p2, 0).Value

                ' Enter unit usages of all resources used by this product.
                For r = 1 To nResources
                    .Offset(r, p1).Value = Range("ProdAnchor") _
                        .Offset(p2, 5 + r).Value
                Next
            End If
        Next
    End With
End Sub
```

CalcMaxProduction Code

The **CalcMaxProduction** sub finds the maximum limit on production for each selected product and enters it in the Model sheet. If no explicit maximum limit is given for a product in the Data sheet, a suitable maximum limit is calculated in this sub by seeing which of the resources would be most constraining if *all* of the resource were committed to this particular product.

```
Sub CalcMaxProduction()
    ' This sub calculates the max production levels for all selected products.
    Dim p1 As Integer ' product index, selected products only
    Dim p2 As Integer ' product index, all products
    Dim r As Integer ' resource index
    Dim maxVal As Single
    Dim unitUse As Single
    Dim ratio As Single

    ' Enter data only for selected products, where p1 is a counter for these.
    p1 = 0
```

```
        With Range("ProdMixAnchor")
            For p2 = 1 To nProducts
                If isSelected(p2) Then
                    p1 = p1 + 1
                    If Range("ProdAnchor").Offset(p2, 5).Value = "" Then

                        ' No maximum production level was given, so find how much of
                        ' this product could be produced if all of the resources were
                        ' devoted to it, and use this as a maximum production level.
                        maxVal = 1000000
                        For r = 1 To nResources
                            unitUse = Range("UnitUseAnchor").Offset(r, p1).Value
                            If unitUse > 0 Then
                                ratio = Range("Available").Cells(r).Value / unitUse
                                If ratio < maxVal Then maxVal = ratio
                            End If
                        Next

                        ' Enter calculated maximum production level
                        ' (rounded down to nearest integer).
                        .Offset(6, p1).Value = Int(maxVal)

                    Else
                        ' The maximum production level was given, so enter it.
                        .Offset(6, p1).Value = Range("ProdAnchor") _
                            .Offset(p2, 5).Value
                    End If
                End If
            Next

            ' Name the range of maximum production levels.
            Range(.Offset(6, 1), .Offset(6, 1).End(xlToRight)).Name = "MaxProd"
        End With
End Sub
```

CalcResourceUsages Code

The **CalcResourceUsages** sub calculates the amount of each resource used by the current product mix and enters it in the Model sheet. Pay particular attention to the following two lines, which are inside the For loop on r.

```
unitUseAddress = Range(.Offset(r, 1), .Offset(r, 1).End(xlToRight)).Address
Range("Used").Cells(r).Formula = "=Sumproduct(Produced," & unitUseAddress & ")"
```

I want to enter a formula such as **=Sumproduct(Produced,J17:N17)** in a cell. (For example, if r=1, this would be the formula in cell B17 for the model in Figure 20.5.) To do this, I find the address for the second argument of the Sumproduct function from the first line and store it in the string variable unitUseAddress. Then I use string concatenation to build the formula in the second line. Entering formulas in cells with VBA can be tricky, and it often involves similar string concatenation to piece together a combination of literals and string variables.

```
Sub CalcResourceUsages()
    ' This sub calculates the resource usage for each resource by using a Sumproduct function.
    ' Note how the address of the row of unit usages for resource i is found first,
    ' then used as part of the formula string.
    Dim r As Integer ' resource index
    Dim unitUseAddress As String

    With Range("UnitUseAnchor")
        For r = 1 To nResources
            unitUseAddress = Range(.Offset(r, 1), .Offset(r, 1).End(xlToRight)).Address
            Range("Used").Cells(r).Formula = "=Sumproduct(Produced," & unitUseAddress & ")"
        Next
    End With
End Sub
```

CalcMonetaryValues Code

The **CalcMonetaryValues** sub uses Excel's SUMPRODUCT function to calculate the total revenue, total cost, and total profit from the current product mix. It also names the corresponding cells for later reference.

```
Sub CalcMonetaryValues()
    ' This sub calculates the summary monetary values.
    With Range("MonSummAnchor")
        .Offset(1, 1).Formula = "=Sumproduct(Produced,UnitRev)"
        .Offset(2, 1).Formula = "=Sumproduct(Produced,UnitCost)"
        .Offset(3, 1).Formula = "=Sumproduct(Produced,UnitProfit)"

        ' Name the monetary cells.
        .Offset(1, 1).Name = "TotRev"
        .Offset(2, 1).Name = "TotCost"
        .Offset(3, 1).Name = "TotProfit"
    End With
End Sub
```

RunSolver Code

The **RunSolver** sub sets up Solver and then runs it.[2] It checks whether there are no feasible solutions. (Remember from Chapter 17 that the numerical code for no feasible solutions in the SolverSolve function is 5.) If the model has no feasible solutions, the Model and Report sheets are hidden, the Explanation sheet is activated, an appropriate message is displayed, and the application is terminated. Note that this code imposes integer constraints on the changing cells. Of course, if

---

[2]Even though the Solver setup will always *look* the same—for example, it will always have the constraint Used<=Available—it must be reset and then set up from scratch each time the application is run. If this is not done and the *size* of the model is different from the previous run, the Solver settings will be interpreted incorrectly.

you do not want to impose integer constraints, you can delete (or comment out) the appropriate line in this sub.

```
Sub RunSolver()
    ' This sub sets up and runs Solver.
    Dim solverStatus As Integer

    ' Reset Solver settings, then set up Solver.
    SolverReset
    SolverOk SetCell:=Range("TotProfit"), MaxMinVal:=1, ByChange:=Range("Produced")

    ' Add constraints.
    SolverAdd CellRef:=Range("Produced"), Relation:=3, _
        FormulaText:=Range("MinProd").Address
    SolverAdd CellRef:=Range("Produced"), Relation:=1, _
        FormulaText:=Range("MaxProd").Address
    SolverAdd CellRef:=Range("Used"), Relation:=1, _
        FormulaText:=Range("Available").Address

    ' Comment out the next line if you don't want integer constraints on production.
    SolverAdd CellRef:=Range("Produced"), Relation:=4
    SolverOptions AssumeLinear:=True, AssumeNonNeg:=True

    ' Run Solver and check for infeasibility.
    solverStatus = SolverSolve(UserFinish:=True)
    If solverStatus = 5 Then
        ' There is no feasible solution, so report this, tidy up, and quit.
        MsgBox "This model has no feasible solution. Change the data " _
            & "in the Data sheet and try running it again.", _
            vbInformation, "No feasible solution"
        Worksheets("Explanation").Activate
        Range("A1").Select
        Worksheets("Model").Visible = False
        Worksheets("Report").Visible = False
        End
    End If
End Sub
```

CreateReport Code

The **CreateReport** sub first unhides and activates the Report sheet (which at this point is only a template or contains results from a previous run). It then clears any previous results and transfers the important results from the Model sheet to the appropriate places in the Report sheet through a series of three short subs.

```
Sub CreateReport()
    ' This sub fills in the Report sheet, mostly by transferring the
    ' results from the Model sheet.

    ' Hide Model sheet.
    Worksheets("Model").Visible = False

    ' Unhide and activate Report sheet.
    With Worksheets("Report")
        .Visible = True
        .Activate
    End With
```

```
    ' Enter results in three steps.
    Call EnterMonetaryResults
    Call EnterProductResults
    Call EnterResourceResults

    ' Make sure columns B and H are wide enough, then select cell A1.
    Columns("B:B").Columns.AutoFit
    Columns("H:H").Columns.AutoFit
    Range("A1").Select
End Sub
```

EnterMonetaryResults, EnterProductResults, and EnterResourceResults Code

These three short subs do exactly what their names imply: They transfer the key results from the Model sheet to the Report sheet.

```
Sub EnterMonetaryResults()
    ' This sub transfers the total revenue, total cost, and total profit.
    Dim i As Integer
    With Range("B3")
        For i = 1 To 3
            .Offset(i, 0).Value = Range("MonSummAnchor").Offset(i, 1).Value
        Next
    End With
End Sub
```

In addition to transferring the production quantities to the Report sheet, the **EnterProductResults** sub also performs simple calculations to report the revenue, cost, and profit for each product individually.

```
Sub EnterProductResults()
    ' This sub transfers results for the products in the optimal product mix.
    Dim p1 As Integer ' product index, selected products only
    Dim p2 As Integer ' product index, all products

    With Range("ProdRepAnchor")
        ' Clear old data (if any).
        Range(.Offset(1, 0), .Offset(1, 0).End(xlDown).End(xlToRight)) _
            .ClearContents

        ' Enter results for selected products only, where p is a counter for these.
        p1 = 0
        For p2 = 1 To nProducts
            If isSelected(p2) Then
                p1 = p1 + 1

                ' Enter product code, description, and number of units produced.
                .Offset(p1, 0).Value = Range("ProdAnchor").Offset(p2, 0).Value
```

```
            .Offset(p1, 1).Value = Range("ProdAnchor").Offset(p2, 1).Value
            .Offset(p1, 2).Value = Range("Produced").Cells(p1).Value
            ' Calculate revenue, cost, and profit for the product.
            .Offset(p1, 3).Value = Range("Produced").Cells(p1).Value * _
                Range("UnitRev").Cells(p1).Value
            .Offset(p1, 4).Value = Range("Produced").Cells(p1).Value * _
                Range("UnitCost").Cells(p1)
            .Offset(p1, 5).Value = Range("Produced").Cells(p1).Value * _
                Range("UnitProfit").Cells(p1).Value
        End If
      Next
   End With
End Sub
```

In addition to transferring the resource usages and availabilities to the Report sheet, the **EnterResourceResults** sub also calculates the amount of each resource left over.

```
Sub EnterResourceResults()
   ' This sub transfers results about resource usage.
   Dim r As Integer ' resource index

   With Range("ResRepAnchor")
      ' Clear old data (if any).
      Range(.Offset(1, 0), .Offset(1, 0).End(xlDown).End(xlToRight)).ClearContents
      For r = 1 To nResources

         ' Enter resource name, amount used, and amount available.
         .Offset(r, 0).Value = Range("ResAnchor").Offset(r, 0).Value
         .Offset(r, 1).Value = Range("Used").Cells(r).Value
         .Offset(r, 2).Value = Range("Available").Cells(r).Value

         ' Calculate amount left over.
         .Offset(r, 3).FormulaR1C1 = "=RC[-1]-RC[-2]"
      Next
   End With
End Sub
```

20.8 Summary

I promised in the introduction that this application is considerably more complex from a VBA point of view than the previous chapter's blending application. Although most of it involves Excel manipulations that are easy to do manually, a significant amount of programming is required to perform these same operations with VBA. After all, an entire optimization model must be developed "on the fly" at run time. You can learn a lot of Excel VBA by carefully studying the code in this application. Better yet, open the file, split the screen so that you can see the Excel worksheets on one side and the VBA code on the other, step through the program with the F8 key, and keep watches on a few key variables. This can be *very* instructive. Finally, pay particular attention to how the overall program has been structured as a series of fairly small subs. This, taken together with a liberal dose of comments, makes the program much easier to read, understand, and debug.

EXERCISES

1. The application will work with *any* number of products in the Data sheet, provided the data are entered appropriately. Convince yourself of this by adding a few more products to the section shown in Figure 20.2 and then rerunning the application.

2. Continuing the previous exercise, the application will also work for any number of resources, provided that you make space for them in the sections shown in Figures 20.2 and 20.3. Convince yourself of this by adding a new resource (glue, for example). What changes do you have to make to the overall file?

3. As the previous exercise illustrates, it might be inconvenient (and confusing) to the user to have to insert new columns if more resources are added. I originally thought of putting the resource data in Figure 20.3 *below*, not to the right of, the product data in Figure 20.2, but this could also cause a problem if more products were added. (Then the user might need to insert extra rows.) Try the following alternative approach. Create *two* data sheets, one for the product data in Figure 20.2, called ProductData, and one for the resource data in Figure 20.3, called ResourceData. Transfer the current data to these two sheets, and make any necessary changes to the application. Now users will never have to insert any new rows or columns. Do you believe this new design has any drawbacks (from a user's, not a programmer's) point of view? Which design do you like best?

4. Change the application so that the user has no choice of the potential products in the product mix. That is, all products listed in the Data sheet will be in the product mix model, and the user form in Figure 20.4 will no longer be necessary. However, the application should still be written to adapt to any number of products that might be listed in the Data sheet.

5. Continuing the previous exercise, continue to assume that all products in the Data sheet are potential products in the product mix. However, the company now wants, in addition to the current Report sheet, a second report sheet that shows how the optimal profit changes as the availability of all resources increases. Specifically, it should show a table and a corresponding chart, such as in Figure 20.12, on a SensitivityReport sheet. This table shows, for example, that when all of the resource availabilities increase by 30%, the new optimal profit is $23,392. Of course, your data might differ, depending on which products are on your Data sheet. (*Hint:* Do as much as you can at design time. Then write VBA code to handle any tasks that must take place at run time.)

6. This application currently has no charts; it currently displays the outputs in tabular form only. Change the application so that it also displays a column chart (on a separate chart sheet) similar to the one in Figure 20.13, showing the amounts of the various products produced. As part of your changes, create buttons on the Report

Figure 20.12 Sensitivity Analysis for Exercise 5

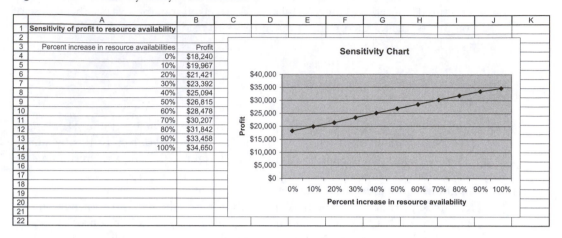

Figure 20.13 Chart of Optimal Production Levels for Exercise 6

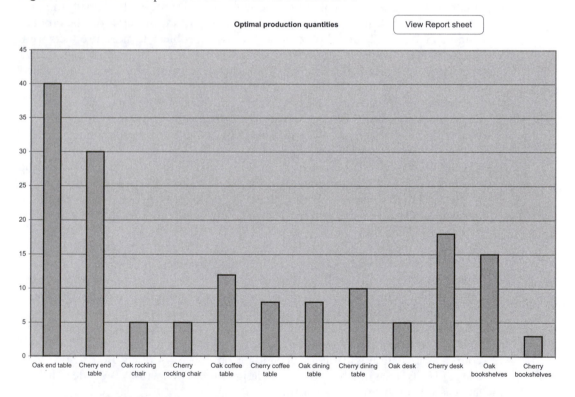

sheet and the chart sheet, and write navigational subs to attach to them to allow the user to go back and forth easily. (*Hint*: Create the chart with Excel's chart tools only, not VBA, using representative data from the Report sheet to populate it at design time. Then write VBA code to modify it appropriately at run time.)

21

An Employee-Scheduling Application

21.1 Introduction

This application is based on a model for scheduling workers. A company needs to schedule its workers to meet daily requirements for a seven-day week, and each worker must work five days per week. Some of the workers can have nonconsecutive days off. For example, a worker could be assigned to work Monday, Wednesday, Thursday, Friday, and Sunday. This worker's two days off, Tuesday and Saturday, are nonconsecutive. However, there is a constraint that no more than a certain percentage of all workers can be assigned to nonconsecutive days-off shifts, where this maximum percentage is an input to the model. The objective is to minimize the weekly payroll, subject to meeting daily requirements, where the hourly wage rate on weekdays can differ from the wage rate on weekends.

New Learning Objectives: VBA

- To see how VBA can be used to conduct a sensitivity analysis for an optimization model.

New Learning Objectives: Non-VBA

- To learn how employee scheduling can be performed with an optimization model and how a sensitivity analysis can be performed on a key input parameter.

21.2 Functionality of the Application

This application provides the following functionality:

1. It allows a user to view and change the following inputs: daily requirements, weekday and weekend wage rates, and maximum percentage of nonconsecutive days off. For these given inputs, it finds the optimal solution to the model and reports it in a user-friendly form.
2. For given daily requirements and wage rates, it performs a sensitivity analysis on the maximum percentage of nonconsecutive days off and displays the results graphically.

Figure 21.1 Explanation Sheet

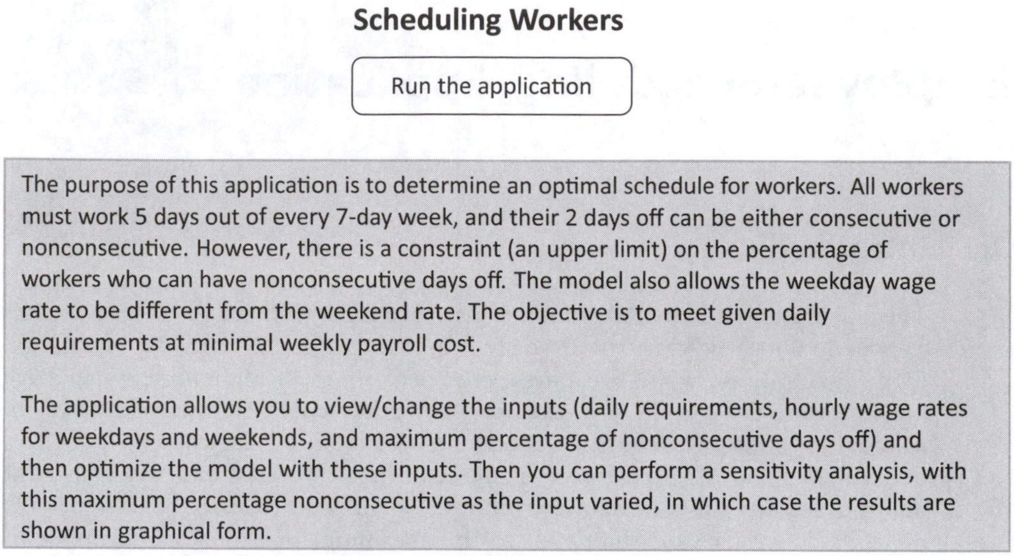

Scheduling Workers

> Run the application

The purpose of this application is to determine an optimal schedule for workers. All workers must work 5 days out of every 7-day week, and their 2 days off can be either consecutive or nonconsecutive. However, there is a constraint (an upper limit) on the percentage of workers who can have nonconsecutive days off. The model also allows the weekday wage rate to be different from the weekend rate. The objective is to meet given daily requirements at minimal weekly payroll cost.

The application allows you to view/change the inputs (daily requirements, hourly wage rates for weekdays and weekends, and maximum percentage of nonconsecutive days off) and then optimize the model with these inputs. Then you can perform a sensitivity analysis, with this maximum percentage nonconsecutive as the input varied, in which case the results are shown in graphical form.

Figure 21.2 Daily Requirements Dialog Box

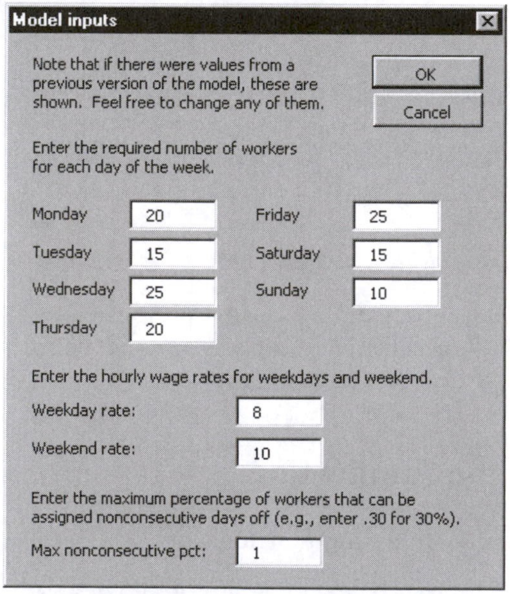

Model inputs

Note that if there were values from a previous version of the model, these are shown. Feel free to change any of them.

> OK
> Cancel

Enter the required number of workers for each day of the week.

Monday	20	Friday	25
Tuesday	15	Saturday	15
Wednesday	25	Sunday	10
Thursday	20		

Enter the hourly wage rates for weekdays and weekend.

Weekday rate: 8

Weekend rate: 10

Enter the maximum percentage of workers that can be assigned nonconsecutive days off (e.g., enter .30 for 30%).

Max nonconsecutive pct: 1

21.3 Running the Application

The application is in the file **Worker Scheduling.xlsm**. When this file is opened, the explanation and button in Figure 21.1 appear. By clicking on the button, the user can view and change the inputs in Figure 21.2. (The values shown are from

Figure 21.3 Report of Optimal Solution

	A	B	C	D	E	F	G	H	I	J
1	Report of optimal solution									
2										
3	Weekly costs			Worker availabilities				Number of workers:		
4	Weekday	$6,720		Day	Available	Required		With consecutive days off		11
5	Weekend	$2,400		Mon	20	20		With nonconsecutive days off		15
6	Total	$9,120		Tue	15	15		Total		26
7				Wed	25	25				
8	Optimal assignments (positive assignments only)			Thu	20	20				
9	Days off	Number assigned		Fri	25	25				
10	Mon, Tue	3		Sat	15	15				
11	Mon, Sun	3		Sun	10	10				
12	Tue, Sun	8								
13	Wed, Sun	1			Return to Explanation Sheet		Perform Sensitivity Analysis			
14	Thu, Sat	6								
15	Fri, Sat	1								
16	Sat, Sun	4								
17										
18										

the previous run, if any.) When the OK button is clicked, the user's inputs are placed in the appropriate range of the (hidden) Model sheet (see Figure 21.6 later in the chapter).

Once these inputs are entered and the user clicks on OK, Solver is invoked and the optimal solution is reported in a Report sheet, as shown in Figure 21.3

If the user then clicks on the Perform Sensitivity button, Solver is invoked several times, once for each maximum nonconsecutive percentage from 0% to 100% in increments of 10%, and important aspects of the optimal solutions appear graphically, as shown in Figure 21.4 Specifically, for each maximum percentage of nonconsecutive days off, the report shows the total number of workers required and the number of these who are assigned nonconsecutive days off. As an aid to the user, the reminder in Figure 21.5 is also displayed.

All of these results are based on the prebuilt model in the Model sheet, shown in Figure 21.6. (Although the formulas for this model are reasonably straightforward, you might want to examine them. To do so, you will need to unhide the Model sheet.)

21.4 Setting Up the Excel Sheets

This optimization model always has the same size because there are always seven days in a week. Therefore, most of the application can be developed with the Excel interface—without any VBA. It contains the following four sheets.

1. The Explanation sheet in Figure 21.1 contains an explanation of the application in a text box, and it has a button for running the application.
2. The Model sheet, shown in Figure 21.6, can be set up completely at design time, using any sample input values. Also, the Solver settings can

Figure 21.4 Results of Sensitivity Analysis

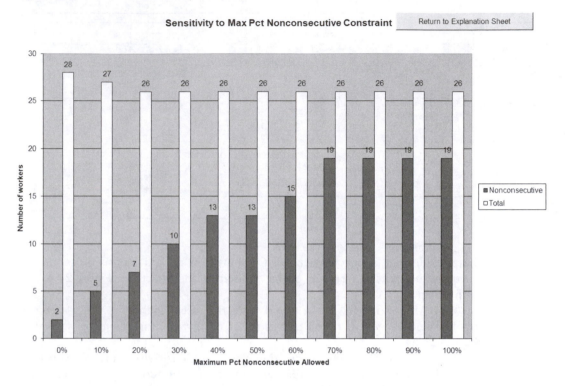

Figure 21.5 Reminder about Possible Multiple Optimal Solutions

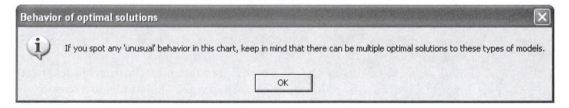

be entered. Again, this is possible because the model itself will never change; only the inputs to it will change. You can look through the logic of this model in the **Worker Scheduling.xlsm** file. Most of it is straightforward. Pay particular attention to the formulas for worker availabilities in row 32. For example, the formula in cell E32 is **=SUM (AvailThu)**. Here, AvailThu is the range name used for a set of *non*-contiguous cells, namely, those changing cells where Thursday is *not* a day off. Giving range names to noncontiguous ranges is indeed possible and can sometimes be useful.

3. A template for the report shown in Figure 21.4 can be developed in the Report sheet. This template appears in Figure 21.7. The costs section, worker availabilities section, and numbers of workers section have

Figure 21.6 Scheduling Model

	A	B	C	D	E	F	G	H
1	Worker scheduling problem							
2								
3	Maximum percent with nonconsecutive days off					Hourly wage rates		
4		100%				Weekday	$8.00	
5						Weekend	$12.00	
6	Assignment of workers to days off pairs							
7	Days off	Consecutive	Assignments					
8	Mon, Tue	1	0					
9	Mon, Wed	0	0					
10	Mon, Thu	0	0					
11	Mon, Fri	0	0					
12	Mon, Sat	0	0					
13	Mon, Sun	1	6					
14	Tue, Wed	1	0					
15	Tue, Thu	0	0					
16	Tue, Fri	0	0					
17	Tue, Sat	0	4					
18	Tue, Sun	0	7					
19	Wed, Thu	1	0					
20	Wed, Fri	0	0					
21	Wed, Sat	0	0					
22	Wed, Sun	0	1					
23	Thu, Fri	1	0					
24	Thu, Sat	0	6					
25	Thu, Sun	0	0					
26	Fri, Sat	1	0					
27	Fri, Sun	0	1					
28	Sat, Sun	1	1					
29			26	<-- Total workers				
30	Daily constraints on workers							
31		Mon	Tue	Wed	Thu	Fri	Sat	Sun
32	Available	20	15	25	20	25	15	10
33		>=	>=	>=	>=	>=	>=	>=
34	Required	20	15	25	20	25	15	10
35								
36	Consecutive days off constraint							
37	Number nonconsecutive	19						
38		<=						
39	Maximum	26.00						
40								
41	Payroll							
42	Weekday	$6,720						
43	Weekend	$2,400						
44	Total	$9,120						

formulas linked to the Model sheet, so they show the results from a previous run, if any. However, the optimal assignments section is left blank. It will contain the *positive* assignments only, and these will not be known until run time. The VBA code takes care of transferring the positive assignments from the Model sheet to this section of the Report sheet.

Figure 21.7 Report Template

	A	B	C	D	E	F	G	H	I	J
1	Report of optimal solution									
2										
3	Weekly costs			Worker availabilities				Number of workers:		
4	Weekday	$6,720		Day	Available	Required		With consecutive days off		11
5	Weekend	$2,400		Mon	20	20		With nonconsecutive days off		15
6	Total	$9,120		Tue	15	15		Total		26
7				Wed	25	25				
8	Optimal assignments (positive assignments only)			Thu	20	20				
9	Days off	Number assigned		Fri	25	25				
10				Sat	15	15				
11				Sun	10	10				
12										
13										
14				Return to Explanation Sheet			Perform Sensitivity Analysis			
15										

Figure 21.8 Data for Chart

	AA	AB	AC
1	Sensitivity of solutions to maxpct		
2	MaxPct	0	29
3	0%	2	28
4	10%	5	27
5	20%	7	26
6	30%	10	26
7	40%	13	26
8	50%	13	26
9	60%	15	26
10	70%	19	26
11	80%	19	26
12	90%	19	26
13	100%	19	26

4. The chart in Figure 21.4 is located on a separate Chart sheet. This chart is linked to the data in a remote area of the Model sheet (see Figure 21.8). This area contains the percentages in column AA and the counts from the optimization model in columns AB and AC. Columns AB and AC contain, respectively, the numbers of workers with nonconsecutive days off and the numbers of workers total in the optimal solutions. Any reasonable values can be used in columns AB and AC initially for the purpose of building the chart with Excel's chart tools. They will eventually be replaced with the optimal values by VBA when the sensitivity analysis is run.

21.5   Getting Started with the VBA

This application requires a user form named frmInputs, a module, and a reference to Solver. Once these items are added, the Project Explorer window will appear as in Figure 21.9.[1]

---

[1]It also contains the usual frmSolver that displays a message about possible Solver problems when the workbook is opened.

Figure 21.9 Project Explorer Window

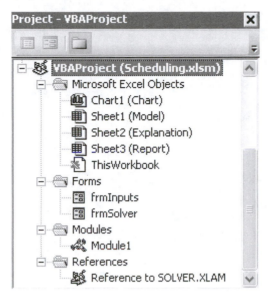

Workbook_Open Event Handler

To guarantee that the Explanation sheet appears when the file is opened, the following code is placed in the ThisWorkbook code window. The **GoToExplanation** sub is actually in the module (see below), but it is perfectly acceptable to call a sub from a module in the Workbook_Open sub.

```
Private Sub Workbook_Open( )
    Call GoToExplanation
    frmSolver.Show
End Sub
```

21.6 The User Form and Its Event Handlers

The design of frmInputs uses 10 text boxes and accompanying labels, as shown in Figure 21.10, along with the usual OK and Cancel buttons and a couple of explanation labels to their left. The "day" boxes are named txtDay1 to txtDay7 (for Monday to Sunday), the wage rate boxes are named txtWeekday and txtWeekend, and the percentage box is named txtMaxPct.

Figure 21.10 frmInputs Design

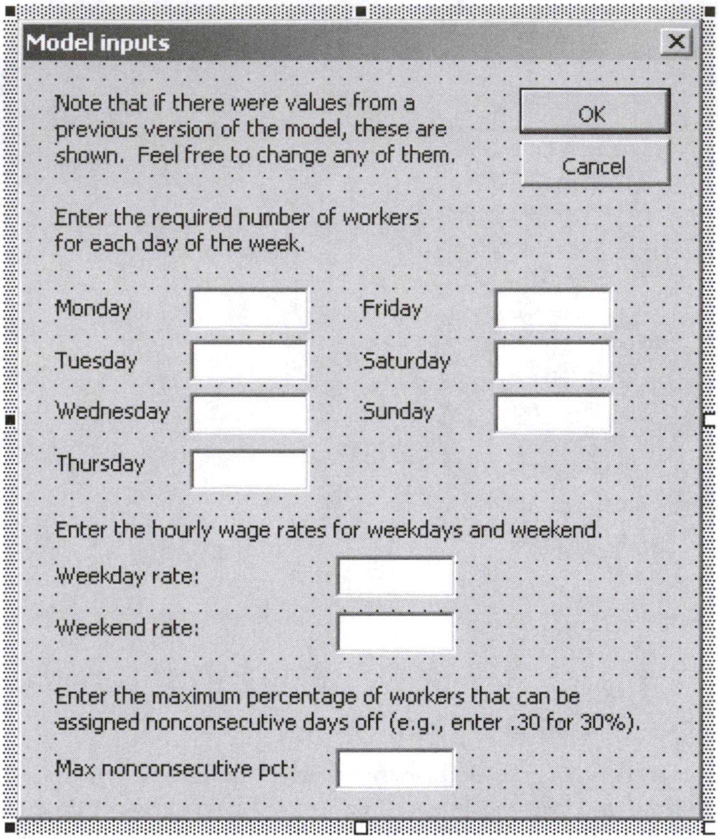

The event handlers for frmInputs are listed below. The **UserForm_Initialize** sub captures the existing inputs, if any, from the Model sheet and uses them as starting values in the text boxes. The **btnOK_Click** sub then captures the user's inputs, subject to passing the usual types of error checks. Note that the **Val** function converts user responses (treated as *strings*) to numbers, which are placed in the appropriate cells of the Model sheet.

Event Handlers for frmInputs

```
Private Sub btnCancel_Click( )
    Unload Me
    End
End Sub

Private Sub btnOK_Click( )
```

```
            ' Check for improper entries in the text boxes. If any entries are improper,
            ' exit this sub without unloading the dialog box.
            Dim ctl As Control
            Dim day As Integer ' day index, 1 to 7

            For Each ctl In Me.Controls
                If TypeName(ctl) = "TextBox" Then
                    If ctl.Text = "" Or Not IsNumeric(ctl.Text) Then
                        MsgBox "Enter a numeric value in each box.", _
                            vbInformation, "Improper entry"
                        ctl.SetFocus
                        Exit Sub
                    ElseIf InStr(1, ctl.Name, "Day") > 0 And ctl.Text < 0 Then
                        MsgBox "Enter a nonnegative integer in each day box.", _
                            vbInformation, "Improper entry"
                        ctl.SetFocus
                        Exit Sub
                    ElseIf InStr(1, ctl.Name, "Week") > 0 And ctl.Text <= 0 Then
                        MsgBox "Enter a positive wage rate in each wage box.", _
                            vbInformation, "Improper entry"
                        ctl.SetFocus
                        Exit Sub
                    ElseIf ctl.Name = "txtMaxPct" And (ctl.Text < 0 Or ctl.Text > 1) Then
                        MsgBox "Enter a percentage between 0 and 1 in the percentage box.", _
                            vbInformation, "Improper entry"
                        ctl.SetFocus
                        Exit Sub
                    End If

                    ' The entry is valid, so put it in the appropriate cell in the Required
                    ' range or MaxPct range of the Model sheet. Note that a textbox always
                    ' returns a string. The Val function converts it to a number.
                    If InStr(1, ctl.Name, "Day") > 0 Then
                        day = Right(ctl.Name, 1)
                        Range("Required").Cells(day).Value = Val(ctl.Text)
                    ElseIf ctl.Name = "txtWeekday" Then
                        Range("WeekdayRate").Value = Val(ctl.Text)
                    ElseIf ctl.Name = "txtWeekend" Then
                        Range("WeekendRate").Value = Val(ctl.Text)
                    Else
                        Range("MaxPct").Value = Val(ctl.Text)
                    End If
                End If
            Next

            Unload Me
        End Sub

        Private Sub UserForm_Initialize( )
            ' Enter values in the text boxes, if any, from the Required, BonusPct,
            ' and MaxPct ranges.
            Dim ctl As Control
            Dim day As Integer

            For Each ctl In Me.Controls
                If TypeName(ctl) = "TextBox" Then
                    ' Note that the boxes for Monday through Sunday have been named txtDay1
                    ' through txtDay7. Therefore, these names all contain "Day" and the
                    ' last character goes from 1 to 7.
                    If InStr(1, ctl.Name, "Day") > 0 Then
                        day = Right(ctl.Name, 1)
                        ctl.Text = Range("Required").Cells(day).Value
```

```
            ElseIf ctl.Name = "txtWeekday" Then
                ctl.Text = Range("WeekdayRate").Value
            ElseIf ctl.Name = "txtWeekend" Then
                ctl.Text = Range("WeekendRate").Value
            Else
                ctl.Text = Range("MaxPct").Value
            End If
        End If
    Next
End Sub
```

21.7 The VBA Code in the Module

Most of the work in this application is performed by the VBA code in the module. This code is listed below. It proceeds in a modular manner, as described in Chapter 10.

MainScheduling Code

This **MainScheduling** sub is the control center and is assigned to the button on the Explanation sheet. It calls other subs to do the real work.

```
Sub MainScheduling( )
    ' This sub runs when the button on the Explanation sheet is clicked.
    frmInputs.Show
    Call RunSolver
    Call CreateReport
End Sub
```

RunSolver Code

The **RunSolver** sub unhides and activates the Model sheet, and then it runs Solver. Note that Solver is already set up (this was done at design time), so the SolverSolve function is the only Solver function required. Also, note that there is no need to check for feasibility because it is always possible to hire enough workers to meet all daily requirements—it might just cost a lot.

```
Sub RunSolver( )
    ' The Solver settings are already in place, so this sub just runs Solver.
    Application.ScreenUpdating = False
    With Worksheets("Model")
        .Visible = True
        .Activate
    End With
    SolverSolve userfinish:=True

    Worksheets("Model").Visible = False
End Sub
```

CreateReport Code

This **CreateReport** sub unhides and activates the Report sheet, clears old assignments, and then transfers *positive* assignments from the Model sheet to the appropriate cells (below A9) in the Report sheet.

```vba
Sub CreateReport( )
    ' This sub transfers the optimal results from the Model sheet to the Report sheet.
    Dim iPair As Integer ' index of days off pair
    Dim nPositive As Integer
    Const nDaysOffPairs = 21

    Application.ScreenUpdating = False

    ' Unhide the Report sheet and activate it.
    With Worksheets("Report")
        .Visible = True
        .Activate
    End With

    ' Clear out old assignments from a previous run (the part below A9).
    With Range("A9")
        Range(.Offset(1, 0), .Offset(1, 1).End(xlDown)).ClearContents
    End With

    ' Transfer the positive assignments from the Model sheet to the Report sheet.
    ' nPositive counts the positive assignments.
    nPositive = 0
    With Range("A9")
        For iPair = 1 To nDaysOffPairs
            If Range("Assignments").Cells(iPair).Value > 0 Then
                nPositive = nPositive + 1

                ' Record the names of the days off and the number of workers assigned.
                .Offset(nPositive, 0).Value = Range("Assignments") _
                    .Cells(iPair).Offset(0, -2).Value
                .Offset(nPositive, 1).Value = Range("Assignments") _
                    .Cells(iPair).Value
            End If
        Next
    End With

    Range("A1").Select
End Sub
```

Sensitivity Code

The **Sensitivity** sub unhides and activates the Model sheet, and then it runs Solver 11 times for equally spaced values of the maximum percentage of nonconsecutive days off. The results are stored in cells under cell AA1 (in the Model sheet). Because the prebuilt chart is linked to the data in these cells, the chart updates automatically.

```
Public Sub Sensitivity( )
    ' This sub performs sensitivity analysis on the maximum percentage
    ' nonconsecutive by running Solver repeatedly and reporting the results.
    Dim iProblem As Integer ' index of problem
    Const nProblems = 11

    Application.ScreenUpdating = False

    ' Unhide and activate the Model sheet.
    With Worksheets("Model")
        .Visible = True
        .Activate
    End With

    ' Solve problems for maximum percentage from 0 to 1 in increments of 0.1.
    For iProblem = 1 To nProblems
        Range("MaxPct").Value = (iProblem - 1) * 0.1

        ' Enter the maximum percentage of days off, and reset all assignments
        ' (changing cells) to 0. Then run Solver.
        Range("Assignments").Value = 0
        SolverSolve userfinish:=True

        ' Store the results in the range that the existing chart is linked to.
        With Range("AA1")
            .Offset(iProblem, 1).Value = Range("Nonconsec").Value
            .Offset(iProblem, 2).Value = Range("TotalWorkers").Value
        End With
    Next

    ' Show the results.
    Worksheets("Model").Visible = False

    Application.ScreenUpdating = True
    With Sheets("Chart")
        .Visible = True
        .Activate
    End With
    MsgBox "If you spot any 'unusual' behavior in this chart, keep in mind that " _
        & "there can be multiple optimal solutions to these types " _
        & "of models.", vbInformation, "Behavior of optimal solutions"
End Sub
```

GoToExplanation Code

The **GoToExplanation** sub is for easy navigation. It is attached to the corresponding buttons on the Model, Report, and Chart sheets.

```
Public Sub GoToExplanation( )
    Worksheets("Explanation").Activate
    Range("E4").Select
    ' Hide other sheets.
    Worksheets("Model").Visible = False
    Worksheets("Report").Visible = False
    Charts("Chart").Visible = False
End Sub
```

21.8   Summary

This application is similar to the blending optimization model in Chapter 19, in that the size of the model never changes. Therefore, most of the application, including the entire optimization model, can be set up at design time. This decreases the amount of VBA code necessary. One objective here has been to show how to build sensitivity analysis into an application. This has been done for the maximum percentage of workers with nonconsecutive days off, but in general it can be done for any key input parameters. It is basically just a matter of running Solver inside a For loop and reporting the results.

EXERCISES

1. Change the application so that there is another button on the Report sheet. This is the option to perform a sensitivity analysis on the ratio of the weekend wage rate to the weekday wage rate. When you implement this, use the current value of the weekday wage rate from the Model sheet, and let the ratio vary from 1 to 2 in increments of 0.1. In each case, capture the total cost. Then show the results of this sensitivity analysis (total weekly payroll cost versus the ratio) in graphical form, similar to that shown in Figure 21.4. (You can use the same general location of the Model sheet, starting in column AF, say, to store your sensitivity results and a new chart sheet to show the results graphically. It should be transparent to the user.)

2. Repeat the previous exercise, but now add a third button on the Report sheet that performs a sensitivity analysis on both parameters simultaneously. That is, it should use a nested pair of For loops to vary the maximum percentage of nonconsecutive days off from 0% to 100%, in increments of 10%, *and* to vary the ratio from the previous problem from 1 to 2, in increments of 0.1. (This will result in 11(11) = 121 Solver runs, and it will take awhile) The total weekly payroll cost from each run should be captured and stored in some remote location of the Model sheet, and a chart based on these results should be created and displayed. You can decide on the most appropriate chart type. One possibility might look like the chart in Figure 21.11.

3. Change the application so that there is no longer a sensitivity option. However, the user should now be allowed to select from approximately 10 different preset patterns of weekly requirements. For example, one pattern might be the weekend-heavy pattern 10, 10, 10, 10, 10, 30, 30 (where these are the requirements for Monday through Sunday), whereas another pattern might be the more stable pattern 15, 15, 15, 15, 20, 20, 15. You can make up any patterns you think might be reasonable. Then allow the user to choose a pattern, along with weekday and weekend wage rates and the maximum percentage of nonconsecutive days off allowed, solve this particular problem, and present the results in a Report sheet.

Figure 21.11
Sensitivity Chart for Exercise 2

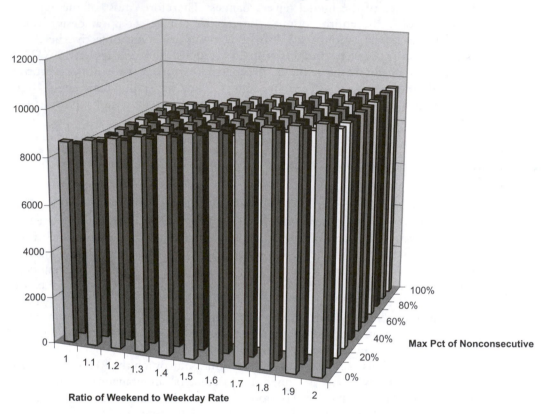

4. Change the model on the Model sheet, and make any necessary modifications to the application as a whole when each worker works only four days of the week, not five.

22

A Production-Planning Application

22.1 Introduction

This application finds an optimal multiperiod production plan for a single product. The objective is to minimize the sum of production and inventory costs, subject to meeting demand on time and not exceeding production and inventory capacities. This model is discussed in all management science textbooks, where the future demands and unit production costs are generally assumed to be known. In reality, these quantities, particularly the demands, must be forecasted from historical data. This application uses exponential smoothing to forecast future demands and unit production costs from historical data. Then it bases the optimal production plan on the forecasted values.

In addition, users can enter new data, update the forecasts, and then run the optimization model again. This allows the application to implement a rolling planning horizon. For example, it can optimize for January through June, then observe actual data for January and update forecasts, then optimize for February through July, then observe actual data for February and update forecasts, and so on. Because of these powerful features, this application is by far the most ambitious application discussed so far.

New Learning Objectives: VBA

- To learn how an application with several user forms, worksheets, charts, and various user options can be integrated within one relatively large VBA program.

New Learning Objectives: Non-VBA

- To learn how forecasts can be made with exponential smoothing methods and then used as inputs to a production-planning optimization model.
- To see how a rolling planning horizon can be implemented.

22.2 Functionality of the Application

The application has the following functionality:

1. It finds the optimal production plan for a 3- to 12-month planning horizon, using the data observed to date.

2. It allows users to view the historical data, along with the exponentially smoothed forecasts, in tabular and graphical form.

3. It allows users to append new demand and unit production cost data to the end of the historical period and update the forecasts.

4. It allows users to change any of the smoothing constants and update the forecasts.

The historical data included in the application are fictional monthly data for a period of several years. Demands are seasonal with an upward trend, so it is appropriate to use Winters' exponential smoothing method. Unit production costs are not seasonal, but they have an upward trend. Therefore, it is appropriate to use Holt's exponential smoothing method for the cost data. Users can replace these data with their own data (in the Data sheet).

22.3 Running the Application

The application is stored in the file **Production Planning.xlsm**. When the file is opened, the Explanation sheet in Figure 22.1 appears. This explanation indicates two nonstandard features of the optimization model. First, the percentage of any month's production that is available to satisfy that month's demand can be *less* than 100%. For example, if this percentage is 70%, then 70% of this month's production can be used to satisfy this month's demand. The other 30% of this month's production is then available for future months' demands. Second, the inventory cost in any month can be based on the ending inventory for the month (the usual assumption), or it can be based on the average of the beginning and ending inventories for the month. Note also that the production and inventory capacities are assumed to be *constant* throughout the planning horizon. This assumption could be relaxed, but it would require additional user inputs.

When the button on the Explanation sheet is clicked, the dialog box in Figure 22.2 appears. It indicates the four basic options for the application.

First Option

If the user selects the first option, the dialog box in Figure 22.3 appears. It requests the inputs for the production-planning model. It then develops this model on the (hidden) Model sheet, sets up and runs Solver, and reports the optimal solution in tabular and graphical form, as shown in Figure 22.4.

Second Option

Historical data are stored in the Data sheet. The second option in Figure 22.2 allows users to view these data, as shown in Figure 22.5 (where several rows have been hidden). Note that the historical data appear in columns B and C, and their exponentially smoothed forecasts appear in columns G and J.

Figure 22.1 Explanation Sheet

Production planning, using exponential smoothing for demand and cost forecasts

Run the application

This application uses exponential smoothing to forecast future demands and unit production costs from historical data. The future forecasts are inputs to a production planning optimization model, where the production quantities are the changing cells, total cost is the target, and the constraints are that demand must be met from available inventory, production cannot exceed production capacity, and ending inventory cannot exceed storage capacity.

The user has four basic options:
1. Find an optimal production plan, with demand and unit cost forecasts based on all observed data so far.
2. View the demand and unit cost data, along with their forecasts.
3. Enter new observed demand and unit cost data, as would be done in a rolling planning horizon procedure.
4. Change the smoothing constants for forecasting.

Some other information about the model:
1. The Data sheet currently includes severalyears of monthly data on demands and unit production costs in columns B and C. Demand is assumed to be seasonal, with an upward trend. Unit production costs are not seasonal, but they are trending upward through time. To the right on the Data sheet (starting in column AA), parameters for the Winters' and Holt's exponential smoothing methods are listed (smoothing constants and initialization constants). If you like, you can enter new demand and unit cost data, as well as new smoothing constants and appropriate initilization constants, in place of the data here.

2. The unit holding cost is assumed to be a percentage of the unit production cost, where this percentage is a user input. The holding cost can be based on ending inventory or on the average of beginning and ending inventories.

3. Only a percentage of a month's production can be used to meet that month's demand. The rest goes into ending inventory. (This percentage can be 100%.)

4. Production capacity and storage capacity are assumed to be constant through time.

5. The planning horizon for the optimization model can be from 3 to 12 months.

Figure 22.2 Options Dialog Box

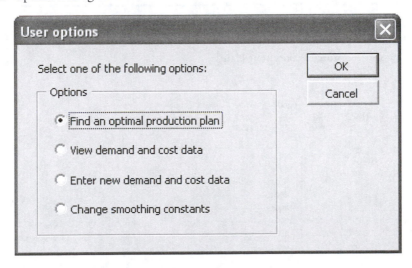

The hidden columns in between contain the exponential smoothing calculations. (You can unhide them if you like.) Note that cell A3 has the range name DataAnchor. This is used later in the VBA code.

Figure 22.3 Inputs for Production-Planning Model

Input data for planning optimization model

The production planning model will be based on the following inputs:

Planning horizon (number of months): 6

Initial inventory: 500

Percentage of production in a month ready to meet demand in that month: 0.80   E.g. enter .75 for 75%

Unit holding cost percentage (of unit production cost): 0.10   E.g. enter .05 for 5%

Holding cost options
- ⦿ Based on ending inventory
- ○ Based on average of beginning and ending inventories

The following are assumed to remain constant through the entire planning horizon.

Production capacity: 2000

Storage capacity: 500

OK

Cancel

Figure 22.4 Report of Optimal Production Plan

Summary of optimal production plan

Month	Feb-09	Mar-09	Apr-09	May-09	Jun-09	Jul-09
Production	370.8	1044.7	884.2	1125.8	1632.7	1735.3
Ending inventory	74.2	208.9	176.8	225.2	500.0	347.1

Total production cost	$841,017
Total holding cost	$18,985
Total cost	$860,002

View Explanation Sheet

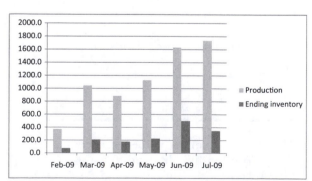

Figure 22.5 Data Sheet with Forecasts

	A	B	C	G	J	M	N	O	P	Q
1	Historical data on demands and unit production costs									
2		View Demand Forecast Chart		View Unit Cost Forecast Chart		View Explanation Sheet		Find Optimal Production Plan		
3	Month	Demand	UnitCost	FCastDemand	FCastUnitCost		MAPE for historical data			
4	Jan-04	376	55.50	366.10	57.20		Demand	9.0%		
5	Feb-04	394	61.00	375.98	58.14		Unit cost	2.7%		
6	Mar-04	416	63.42	443.25	60.53					
7	Apr-04	437	57.17	446.69	63.02		The exponential smoothing calculations and the absolute percentage errors are hidden in columns D-F, H-I, and K-M. Unhide them if you like. Smoothing constants and initialization constants are out in column AA.			
8	May-04	524	62.62	510.13	62.71					
9	Jun-04	672	65.66	697.29	64.13					
10	Jul-04	930	64.18	881.44	66.08					
11	Aug-04	945	69.37	908.26	66.94					
12	Sep-04	719	66.96	684.53	69.17					
13	Oct-04	444	65.87	448.77	69.95					
14	Nov-04	402	62.01	456.49	70.04					
60	Sep-08	1208	115.17	1217.22	111.68					
61	Oct-08	667	114.29	721.82	113.61					
62	Nov-08	760	113.09	842.77	114.72					
63	Dec-08	1885	120.58	1412.91	115.09					
64	Jan-09	920	122	861.84	117.76					

When the left two buttons on the Data sheet are clicked, the charts in Figure 22.6 and 22.7 appear. They show the actual data with the forecasts superimposed.

Third Option

If the user selects the third option in Figure 22.2, the dialog box in Figure 22.8 appears. It asks for the number of months of new data. Then the dialog box in Figure 22.9 is shown repeatedly, once for each new month.

The new data are automatically appended to the bottom of the historical period in the Data sheet (see Figure 22.10), and the exponential smoothing calculations are extended for this new period. If the user then asks for the new optimal production plan, the planning horizon starts *after* the period of the new data, as illustrated in Figure 22.11.

Fourth Option

Finally, if the user selects the fourth option in Figure 22.2, the dialog box in Figure 22.12 appears. It requests new smoothing constants. The updated MAPE (mean absolute percentage error) values are then reported in a message box, as

Figure 22.6 Demand Data and Forecasts

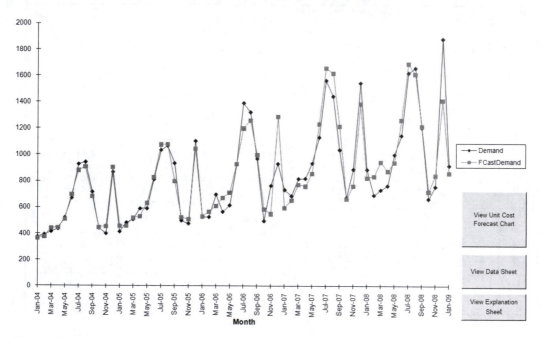

Figure 22.7 Unit Production Cost Data and Forecasts

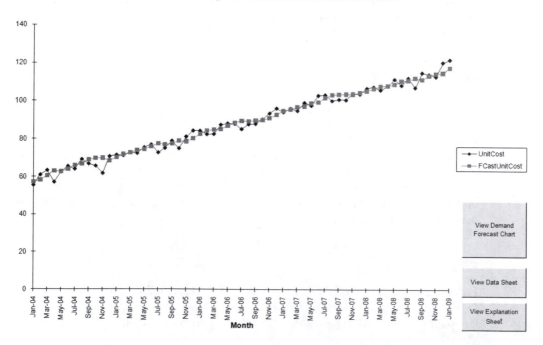

Figure 22.8 First New Data Dialog Box

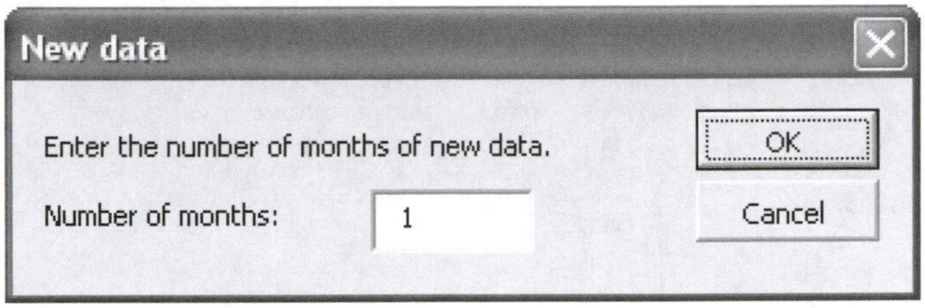

Figure 22.9 Second New Data Dialog Box

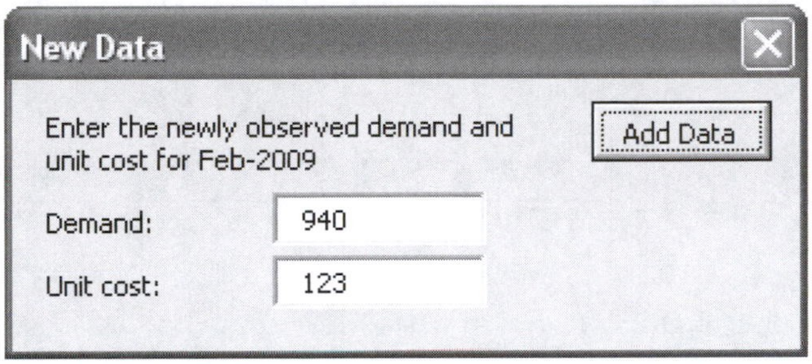

Figure 22.10 Appended Data in Data Sheet

	A	B	C	G	J
61	Oct-08	667	114.29	721.82	113.61
62	Nov-08	760	113.09	842.77	114.72
63	Dec-08	1885	120.58	1412.91	115.09
64	Jan-09	920	122	861.84	117.76
65	Feb-09	940	123	796.65	120.18

shown in Figure 22.13. The smoothing constants, along with initialization values for Winters' method and Holt's method, are stored in a remote location in the Data sheet, as shown in Figure 22.14.

Possibility of No Feasible Solutions

There is always the possibility that the production-planning model has no feasible solutions. This typically occurs when there is not enough production capacity to meet forecasted demands on time. In this case, the message box in Figure 22.15 is displayed.

Figure 22.11 New Production Plan Report

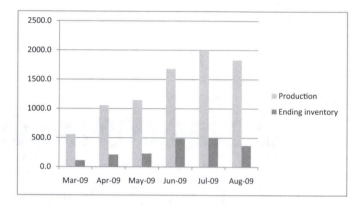

Summary of optimal production plan

Month	Mar-09	Apr-09	May-09	Jun-09	Jul-09	Aug-09
Production	557.0	1054.7	1144.5	1680.7	2000.0	1828.9
Ending inventory	111.4	210.9	228.9	485.7	500.0	365.8

Total production cost	$1,042,057
Total holding cost	$23,997
Total cost	$1,066,054

View Explanation Sheet

Figure 22.12 Smoothing Constant Dialog Box

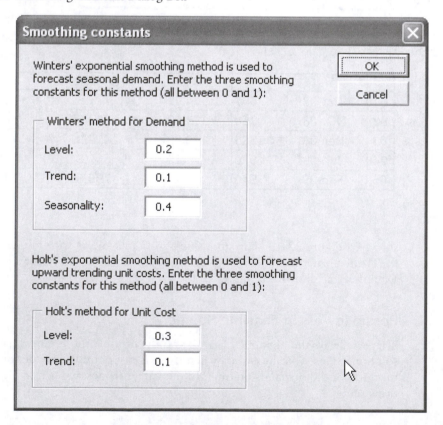

Figure 22.13 Updated MAPE Values

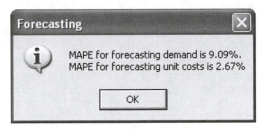

Figure 22.14 Exponential Smoothing Information

	AA	AB	AC	AD	AE	AF	AG
3	Smoothing parameters for exponential smoothing						
4							
5	Winters' method (for demand)			Holt's method (for unit cost)			
6	Level	0.2		Level	0.3		
7	Trend	0.1		Trend	0.1		
8	Seasonality	0.4					
9							
10	Initialization values for Winters'method			Initialization values for Holt's method			
11	Level	512		Level	55.7		
12	Trend	11		Trend	1.5		
13							
14	Seasonal factors						
15	Jan	0.7					
16	Feb	0.7					
17	Mar	0.8					
18	Apr	0.8					
19	May	0.9					
20	Jun	1.2					
21	Jul	1.5					
22	Aug	1.5					
23	Sep	1.1					
24	Oct	0.7					
25	Nov	0.7					
26	Dec	1.4					

Figure 22.15 No Feasible Solutions Message

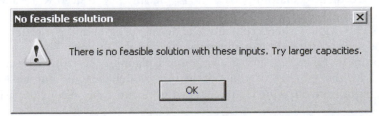

Figure 22.16 Completed Model Sheet

	A	B	C	D	E	F	G
1	Production planning model						
2							
3	**Inputs**						
4	Planning horizon	6					
5	Beginning inventory	500					
6	Production pct	80.0%					
7	Holding cost pct	10.0%					
8	Holding cost option	1					
9	Production capacity	2000					
10	Storage capacity	500					
11							
12	**Production plan**						
13	Month	Mar-09	Apr-09	May-09	Jun-09	Jul-09	Aug-09
14	Beginning inventory	500.0	111.4	210.9	228.9	485.7	500.0
15	Production	557.0	1054.7	1144.5	1680.7	2000.0	1828.9
16		<=	<=	<=	<=	<=	<=
17	Production capacity	2000	2000	2000	2000	2000	2000
18							
19	Available to meet demand	945.6	955.2	1126.6	1573.4	2085.7	1963.1
20		>=	>=	>=	>=	>=	>=
21	Demand	945.6	955.2	1126.6	1423.9	1985.7	1963.1
22							
23	Ending inventory	111.4	210.9	228.9	485.7	500.0	365.8
24							
25	Storage capacity	500	500	500	500	500	500
26	Average inventory	305.7	161.2	219.9	357.3	492.9	432.9
27							
28	**Cost summary**						
29	Month	Mar-09	Apr-09	May-09	Jun-09	Jul-09	Aug-09
30	Forecasted unit production costs	$122.26	$123.49	$124.72	$125.96	$127.19	$128.42
31							
32	Total production cost	$1,042,057					
33	Total holding cost	$23,997					
34	Total cost	$1,066,054					

22.4 Setting Up the Excel Sheets

The **Production Planning.xlsm** file contains four worksheets, named Explanation, Data, Model, and Report, and two chart sheets, named Demand_Forecast and Cost_Forecast. The Data sheet can be set up completely at design time, as shown in Figures 22.5 and 22.14. Note that, the hidden columns in Figure 22.5 must contain the exponential smoothing formulas for Winters' and Holt's methods. (See the **Production Planning.xlsm** file for details. If you need to review exponential smoothing, see Chapter 16 of *Practical Management Science.*)

The Model sheet contains the linear programming production-planning model. It must be developed almost entirely at run time. The completed version appears in Figure 22.16 for a six-month planning horizon (starting in March). Clearly, the number of columns in this model depends on the length of the planning horizon, which is not known until run time. About the only parts that

Figure 22.17 Template for Report Sheet

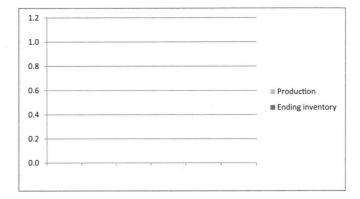

Summary of optimal production plan

Month
Production
Ending inventory

Total production cost	$1,042,057
Total holding cost	$23,997
Total cost	$1,066,054

View Explanation Sheet

can be entered at design time are the labels in column A. (The formula in cell B34 is the one exception. It is always the sum of cells B32 and B33.)

A template for the Report sheet (shown earlier in Figure 22.4) *can* be developed at design time, as shown in Figure 22.17. In particular, the embedded chart can be created with Excel's chart tools. It can then be linked to the appropriate data in rows 3–5 at run time. Also, formulas in cells B7 to B9 can be entered at design time. These formulas are links to the appropriate Model sheet cells.

Similarly, the chart sheets shown earlier in Figures 22.6 and 22.7 can be created at design time. Then they are linked to the appropriate data from the Data sheet at run time.

22.5 Getting Started with the VBA

The application includes five user forms, named frmOptions, frmInputs, frmNewData1, frmNewData2, and frmSmConst, a single module, and a reference to Solver. Once these are inserted, the Project Explorer window will appear as in Figure 22.18.[1]

Workbook_Open Code

To guarantee that the Explanation sheet appears when the file is opened, the following code is placed in the ThisWorkbook code window. It also hides all sheets except for the Explanation sheet. (The Sheets collection, not the Worksheets collection, is appropriate here because it includes both worksheets and chart sheets.)

---

[1]It also contains the usual frmSolver that displays a message about possible Solver problems when the workbook is opened.

Figure 22.18 Project Explorer Window

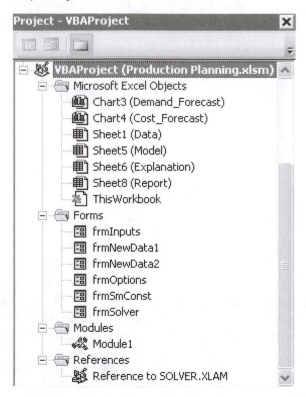

```
Private Sub Workbook_Open()
    Dim sht As Object
    Worksheets("Explanation").Activate
    Range("F4").Select
    For Each sht In ActiveWorkbook.Sheets
        If sht.Name <> "Explanation" Then sht.Visible = False
    Next
    frmSolver.Show
End Sub
```

22.6 The User Forms and Their Event Handlers

frmOptions

This form has the usual OK and Cancel buttons, an explanation label, a frame for grouping, and four option buttons named optOptimize, optViewData, optNewData, and optSmConst. Its design appears in Figure 22.19.

Event Handlers for frmOptions

The event handlers for frmOptions are straightforward and are listed below. The whole purpose of the btnOK_Click sub is to capture the user's choice in the public variable choice, which has possible values 1–4.

Figure 22.19 frmOptions Design

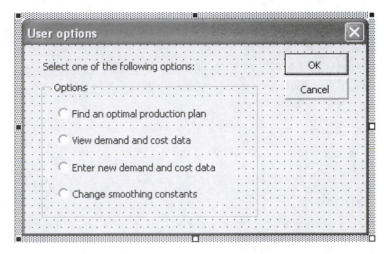

```
Private Sub btnCancel_Click()
    Unload Me
    End
End Sub

Private Sub btnOK_Click()
    ' Capture the user's choice in the choice variable.
    If optOptimize.Value Then
        choice = 1
    ElseIf optViewData.Value Then
        choice = 2
    ElseIf optNewData.Value Then
        choice = 3
    Else
        choice = 4
    End If
    Unload Me
End Sub

Private Sub UserForm_Initialize()
    optOptimize.Value = True
End Sub
```

frmInputs

This form contains the usual OK and Cancel buttons; several explanation labels; a frame that contains two options buttons named optEndInv and optAvgInv; and six text boxes, named txtNMonths, txtInitInv, txtProdPct, txtHoldPct, txtProd-Cap, and txtInvCap. Its design appears in Figure 22.20.

Event Handlers for frmInputs

The event handlers for frmInputs are rather lengthy, but this is mostly because of error checking for the text boxes. The **UserForm_Initialize** sub fills the dialog box with the previous settings from the Model sheet. Then the **btnOK_Click** sub captures the user's settings in public variables (declared in the module), and

Figure 22.20 frmInputs Design

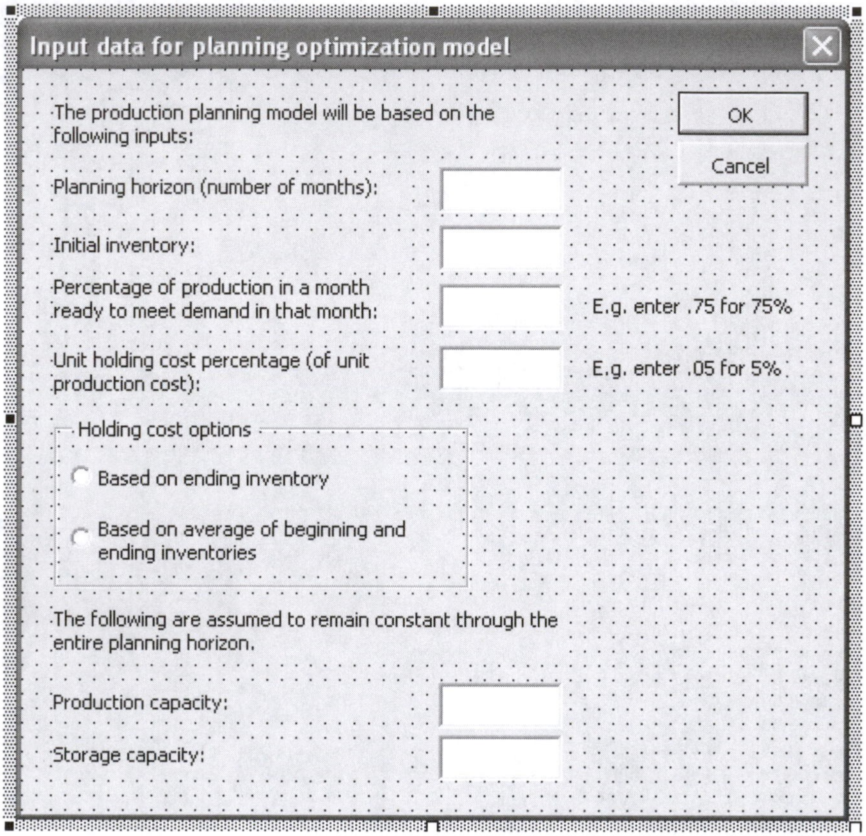

it enters these values in the appropriate cells of the Model sheet. The **btnCancel_Click** sub unloads the dialog box and terminates the program.

```
Private Sub btnCancel_Click()
    Unload Me
    End
End Sub

Private Sub btnOK_Click()
    ' Most of this sub is error checking. First check that all of the text
    ' boxes are not blank and have numeric values.
    Dim ctl As Control
    For Each ctl In Me.Controls
        If TypeName(ctl) = "TextBox" Then
            If ctl.Value = "" Or Not IsNumeric(ctl.Value) Then
                MsgBox "Enter a numeric value in each box.", _
                    vbInformation, "Invalid entry"
                ctl.SetFocus
                Exit Sub
            End If
        End If
    Next

    ' This If-End If block is typical. Check whether txtNMonths has a
```

```
' valid entry (between 3 and 12). If not, let the user try again. If the
' entry is valid, capture the value in the nMonths variable and put it
' in the appropriate cell in the Model sheet.
If txtNMonths.Text < 3 Or txtNMonths.Text > 12 Then
    MsgBox "Make the planning horizon at least 3 months " _
        & "and no more than 12 months.", vbInformation, "Invalid entry"
    txtNMonths.SetFocus
    Exit Sub
Else
    nMonths = txtNMonths.Text
    Range("NMonths").Value = nMonths
End If


' Initial inventory cannot be negative.
If txtInitInv.Text < 0 Then
    MsgBox "Enter a nonnegative initial inventory.", _
        vbInformation, "Invalid entry"
    txtInitInv.SetFocus
    Exit Sub
Else
    initInv = txtInitInv.Text
    Range("InitInv").Value = initInv
End If


' The production percentage must be from 0 to 1.
If txtProdPct.Text < 0 Or txtProdPct.Text > 1 Then
    MsgBox "Enter a percentage (in decimal form) between 0 " _
        & "and 1.", vbInformation, "Invalid entry"
    txtProdPct.SetFocus
    Exit Sub
Else
    prodPct = txtProdPct.Text
    Range("ProdPct").Value = prodPct
End If


' The holding cost percentage must be from 0 to 1.
If txtHoldPct.Text < 0 Or txtHoldPct.Text > 1 Then
    MsgBox "Enter a percentage (in decimal form) between 0 " _
        & "and 1.", vbInformation, "Invalid entry"
    txtHoldPct.SetFocus
    Exit Sub
Else
    holdPct = txtHoldPct.Text
    Range("HoldPct").Value = holdPct
End If


' Store the holding cost option, 1 or 2, in the holdOpt variable.
If optEndInv.Value Then
    holdOpt = 1
Else
    holdOpt = 2
End If
Range("HoldOpt").Value = holdOpt


' Production capacity cannot be negative.
If txtProdCap.Text < 0 Then
    MsgBox "Enter a nonnegative production capacity.", _
        vbInformation, "Invalid entry"
    txtProdCap.SetFocus
    Exit Sub
```

```
        Else
            prodCap = txtProdCap.Text
            Range("ProdCap").Value = prodCap
        End If

        ' Storage capacity cannot be negative.
        If txtInvCap.Text < 0 Then
            MsgBox "Enter a nonnegative storage capacity.", _
                vbInformation, "Invalid entry"
            txtInvCap.SetFocus
            Exit Sub
        Else
            invCap = txtInvCap.Text
            Range("InvCap").Value = invCap
        End If

        ' Unload the userform. This statement is run only if all user inputs
        ' are valid.
        Unload Me
End Sub

Private Sub UserForm_Initialize()
    ' Use the current values from the Model sheet to initialize the form.
    txtNMonths.Text = Range("NMonths").Value
    txtInitInv.Text = Range("InitInv").Value
    txtProdPct.Text = Format(Range("ProdPct").Value, "0.00")
    txtHoldPct.Text = Format(Range("HoldPct").Value, "0.00")
    If Range("HoldOpt").Value = 1 Then
        optEndInv.Value = True
    Else
        optAvgInv.Value = True
    End If
    txtProdCap.Text = Range("ProdCap").Value
    txtInvCap.Text = Range("InvCap").Value
End Sub
```

frmNewData1 and frmNewData2

The two user forms for new data, shown earlier in Figures 22.8 and 22.9, are straightforward, so their event handlers are not listed here. The only new wrinkle is that an Add Data button replaces the usual OK and Cancel buttons on frmNewData2. Actually, this button has exactly the same functionality as the usual OK button; only its name and caption are different. The Cancel button is purposely omitted. By this time, new data rows have been added to the Data form, so the user *must* enter demand and cost data for them!

frmSmConst

The form for the smoothing constants, shown earlier in Figure 22.12, also contains no new ideas, so its event handlers are not listed here. It is initialized with the previous smoothing constants from the Model sheet (see Figure 22.14). It then places the user's choice of smoothing constants in these same cells.

22.7　The VBA Code in the Module

The module contains the code that does most of the work. As usual, the button on the Explanation sheet is attached to a MainProductionPlanning sub that first shows frmOptions and then calls the appropriate sub, depending on the value of the public variable choice. The public variables and the code for the MainProductionPlanning sub are listed below.

Option Statements and Public Variables

```
Option Explicit
Option Base 1

' Definitions of public variables:
'   choice: 1, 2, or 3, depending on which basic option the user requests
'   nMonthsNew: number of new data entries
'   nMonths: number of months in planning horizon
'   initInv: initial inventory in first month of planning horizon
'   prodPct: percentage of a month's production that can be used to meet
'       that month's demand
'   holdPct: percentage of unit production cost used for unit holding cost
'   holdOpt: 1 or 2, depending on whether holding cost is based on ending
'       inventory or average of beginning and ending inventory
'   prodCap: production capacity, assumed constant each month
'   invCap: storage capacity, assumed constant each month
'   newMonth: month for new data
'   newDemand: newly observed demand for newMonth
'   newUnitCost: newly observed unit cost for newMonth

Public choice As Integer
Public nMonthsNew As Integer, nMonths As Integer
Public initInv As Long, prodPct As Single
Public holdPct As Single, holdOpt As Integer
Public prodCap As Long, invCap As Long
Public newMonth As Date, newDemand As Long, newUnitCost As Single
```

Main Code

```
Sub MainProductionPlanning()
    ' This is the main program that runs when the user clicks on the button
    ' on the Explanation sheet.
    frmOptions.Show
    Select Case choice
        Case 1
            Call ProdModel
        Case 2
            Call ViewData
        Case 3
            Call NewData
        Case 4
            Call SmConstants
    End Select
End Sub
```

ProdModel Code

The **ProdModel** sub "shows" frmInputs, activates the Model sheet, clears the contents of any previous model, and calls several subs (**EnterForecasts, EnterFormulas, RunSolver, and CreateReport**) to develop and optimize the production-planning model and report the results.

```
Sub ProdModel()
    ' This sub is run when the user wants to find an optimal production plan,
    ' based on the historical data observed so far.

    frmInputs.Show
    Application.ScreenUpdating = False

    ' Activate the Model sheet and get rid of any old model.
    With Worksheets("Model")
        .Visible = True
        .Activate
    End With
    Range("B13:M33").ClearContents

    ' Develop the model and optimize with Solver.
    Call EnterForecasts
    Call EnterFormulas
    Call RunSolver

    ' Transfer selected results to the Report sheet.
    Call CreateReport
    Worksheets("Model").Visible = False
    Application.ScreenUpdating = True
End Sub
```

EnterForecasts Code

The purpose of the **EnterForecasts** sub is to calculate *future* forecasts of demands and unit costs, based on the data in the Data sheet, and then enter these in the Model sheet. Note that the Data sheet contains forecasts for the *historical* period only. Therefore, forecasts for the planning horizon must be calculated in this sub. (Also, remember when reading the code that the DataAnchor cell is cell A3 of the Data sheet, the cell just above the first data entry.)

Unless you thoroughly understand Holt's and Winters' forecasting models, you will probably not understand all of the details in this sub. In that case, it suffices to know that the relevant formulas have *already* been entered in the Data sheet for the historical period. (This was done at design time.) This sub copies these formulas down for the planning period.

```
Sub EnterForecasts()
    ' This sub enters the forecasts of demand and unit cost in the Model sheet.
    ' They are calculated by Winters' and Holt's exponential smoothing models.
    Dim i As Integer
    Dim levelCell1 As Range, levelCell2 As Range, level1 As Single, level2 As Single
    Dim trend1 As Single, trend2 As Single
    Dim seasFactor As Single

    ' The levelCell1 and levelCell2 cells are the last values of "smoothed level"
    ' for demand and unit cost, respectively, in the Data sheet.
    Set levelCell1 = Range("DataAnchor").Offset(0, 3).End(xlDown)
    Set levelCell2 = Range("DataAnchor").Offset(0, 7).End(xlDown)

    ' The next four values are the basis for future forecasts.
    level1 = levelCell1.Value
    trend1 = levelCell1.Offset(0, 1).Value
    level2 = levelCell2.Value
    trend2 = levelCell2.Offset(0, 1).Value

    ' Fill up rows 13 and 29 of the Model sheet with the appropriate dates in the
    ' planning horizon. Dates are tricky to work with, but an easy way to do it here
    ' is to temporarily put the last historical date in cell A13, then use the
    ' AutoFill method to fill up the future dates in row 13, then replace the date
    ' in A13 with the label "Month", then copy row 13 to row 29.
    With Range("A13")
        .Value = Range("DataAnchor").End(xlDown)
        .AutoFill Destination:=Range(.Offset(0, 0), .Offset(0, nMonths)), Type:=xlFillDefault
        .Value = "Month"
        Range(.Offset(0, 1), .Offset(0, nMonths)).Copy Destination:=Range("B29")
    End With

    ' For demand forecasts in row 21, project the most recent level upward by i
    ' times the most recent trend, then multiply by the appropriate seasonal factor.
    ' Do the same for unit costs in row 30, except that there is no seasonality.
    For i = 1 To nMonths
        seasFactor = levelCell1.Offset(i - 12, 2).Value
        Range("A21").Offset(0, i).Value = (level1 + i * trend1) * seasFactor
        Range("A30").Offset(0, i).Value = level2 + i * trend2
    Next

    ' Name some ranges for later use.
    With Range("A13")
        Range(.Offset(0, 1), .Offset(0, nMonths)).Name = "Months"
    End With
    With Range("A21")
        Range(.Offset(0, 1), .Offset(0, nMonths)).Name = "FDemands"
    End With
    With Range("A30")
        Range(.Offset(0, 1), .Offset(0, nMonths)).Name = "FCosts"
    End With
End Sub
```

EnterFormulas Code

The **EnterFormulas** sub is rather lengthy because it has to develop the optimization model on the fly at run time. It enters all of the formulas in the Model sheet and names ranges appropriately. The comments spell out the details. (It is helpful to refer to Figure 22.16 when reading this code.)

```
Sub EnterFormulas()
    ' This sub enters all of the formulas for the production planning model.
    ' It uses the Formula or FormulaR1C1 property, depending on which is most natural.
    Dim i As Integer

    For i = 1 To nMonths
        ' Calculate beginning inventories in row 14. Other than the first, these equal
        ' the previous ending inventory (9 rows below).
        If i = 1 Then
            Range("A14").Offset(0, i).Formula = "=InitInv"
        Else
            Range("A14").Offset(0, i).FormulaR1C1 = "=R[9]C[-1]"
        End If

        ' Row 15 contains the production quantities, the changing cells. Enter 0's initially.
        Range("A15").Offset(0, i).Value = 0

        ' Enter <= labels in row 16 to denote constraints.
        Range("A16").Offset(0, i).Value = "<="

        ' Enter a link to the ProdCap cell throughout row 17.
        Range("A17").Offset(0, i).Formula = "=ProdCap"

        ' Calculate onhand inventory (available to meet demand) in row 19 as beginning
        ' inventory (5 rows up) plus production percentage times production (4 rows up).
        Range("A19").Offset(0, i).FormulaR1C1 = "=R[-5]C+ProdPct*R[-4]C"

        ' Enter >= labels in row 20 to denote constraints.
        Range("A20").Offset(0, i).Value = ">="

        ' Calculate ending inventory in row 23 as the difference between onhand inventory
        ' (4 rows up) and demand (2 rows up), plus (1 minus the production percentage)
        ' times the production (8 rows up).
        Range("A23").Offset(0, i).FormulaR1C1 = "=R[-4]C-R[-2]C+(1-ProdPct)*R[-8]C"

        ' Enter a link to the InvCap cell throughout row 25.
        Range("A25").Offset(0, i).Formula = "=InvCap"

        ' Calculate the average of beginning inventory (12 rows up) and ending inventory
        ' (3 rows up) in row 26.
        Range("A26").Offset(0, i).FormulaR1C1 = "=(R[-12]C+R[-3]C)/2"
    Next

    ' Name some ranges for later use.
    With Range("A15")
        Range(.Offset(0, 1), .Offset(0, nMonths)).Name = "Production"
    End With
    With Range("A17")
        Range(.Offset(0, 1), .Offset(0, nMonths)).Name = "ProdCaps"
    End With
    With Range("A19")
        Range(.Offset(0, 1), .Offset(0, nMonths)).Name = "Onhand"
    End With
    With Range("A23")
        Range(.Offset(0, 1), .Offset(0, nMonths)).Name = "EndInv"
    End With
    With Range("A25")
        Range(.Offset(0, 1), .Offset(0, nMonths)).Name = "InvCaps"
    End With
    With Range("A26")
```

```
          Range(.Offset(0, 1), .Offset(0, nMonths)).Name = "AvgInv"
    End With

    ' Calculate the total production cost.
    Range("B32").Formula = "=Sumproduct(Production,FCosts)"

    ' Calculate the total holding cost.
    If holdOpt = 1 Then
        Range("B33").Formula = "=Sumproduct(EndInv,HoldPct*FCosts)"
    Else
        Range("B33").Formula = "=Sumproduct(AvgInv,HoldPct*FCosts)"
    End If

    ' The total cost in cell B34 already has a formula in it, which never changes.
End Sub
```

RunSolver Code

The **RunSolver** sub resets the Solver dialog box, sets it up appropriately, and runs Solver. A check is made for feasibility. If there are no feasible solutions, a message to this effect is displayed and the ProdModel sub is called. The effect is to let the user try again with new inputs.

```
Sub RunSolver()
    Dim solverStatus As Integer

    SolverReset
    SolverOK SetCell:=Range("TotalCost"), MaxMinVal:=2, _
        ByChange:=Range("Production")
    SolverAdd CellRef:=Range("Production"), Relation:=1, _
        FormulaText:="ProdCaps"
    SolverAdd CellRef:=Range("OnHand"), Relation:=3, _
        FormulaText:="FDemands"
    SolverAdd CellRef:=Range("EndInv"), Relation:=1, _
        FormulaText:="InvCaps"
    SolverOptions AssumeLinear:=True, AssumeNonNeg:=True

    ' Solve. If the result code is 5, this means there is no feasible solution, so
    ' display a message to that effect and call ProdModel (to try again).
    solverStatus = SolverSolve(UserFinish:=True)
    If solverStatus = 5 Then
        MsgBox "There is no feasible solution with these inputs. Try " _
            & "larger capacities.", vbExclamation, "No feasible solution"
        Call ProdModel
        End
    End If
End Sub
```

CreateReport Code

The **CreateReport** sub copies the data on months, production quantities, and ending inventory levels from the Model sheet to the Report sheet. In the case of ending inventory levels, the Model sheet contains formulas, so these are pasted as *values* in the Report sheet. Finally, this sub updates the embedded chart on the Report sheet with the new data.

```vba
Sub CreateReport()
    ' The Report sheet is already set up (at design time), so just copy (with
    ' PasteSpecial/Values when formulas are involved) selected quantities to
    ' the Report sheet.
    Dim i As Integer

    ' Unhide and activate the Report sheet.
    With Worksheets("Report")
        .Visible = True
        .Activate
    End With

    ' Clear old values.
    Range("B3:M5").ClearContents

    ' Copy results from named ranges in Model sheet to rows 3-5 of Report sheet.
    Range("Months").Copy Destination:=Range("B3")
    Range("Production").Copy Destination:=Range("B4")
    Range("EndInv").Copy
    Range("B5").PasteSpecial xlPasteValues

    ' Name some ranges for later use.
    With Range("A3")
        Range(.Offset(0, 1), .Offset(0, nMonths)).Name = "RepMonths"
        Range(.Offset(1, 0), .Offset(1, nMonths)).Name = "RepProd"
        Range(.Offset(2, 0), .Offset(2, nMonths)).Name = "RepEndInv"
    End With

    ' Update the embedded chart on the Report sheet.
    With ActiveSheet.ChartObjects(1).Chart
        .SetSourceData Source:=Union(Range("RepProd"), Range("RepEndInv"))
        .SeriesCollection(1).XValues = Range("RepMonths")
    End With

    ' Color the whole sheet blue.
    ActiveSheet.Cells.Interior.ColorIndex = 37

    Range("B14").Select
End Sub
```

NewData Code

The **NewData** sub "shows" frmNewData1 and frmNewData2 and appends the new data to the bottom of the historical data range in the Data sheet. It then copies the exponential smoothing formulas down to these new rows, and it renames ranges to include the new rows. Finally, it calls the UpdateCharts sub to update the two chart sheets that show historical data with superimposed forecasts. Remember that the charts themselves were created with the Excel's chart tools at design time.

```
Sub NewData()
    ' This sub allows the user to enter newly observed demand and unit cost data.
    Dim i As Integer
    Dim lastMonth As Date

    ' Unhide and activate the Data sheet.
    With Worksheets("Data")
        .Visible = True
        .Activate
    End With

    ' Get the number of new data values from the user.
    frmNewData1.Show

    With Range("DataAnchor").End(xlDown)
        ' Enter new dates in column A with the AutoFill method.
        .AutoFill Range(.Offset(0, 0), .Offset(nMonthsNew, 0))

        ' Get demand and unit cost data for new months and enter them below old data.
        For i = 1 To nMonthsNew
            newMonth = .Offset(i, 0).Value
            frmNewData2.Show
            .Offset(i, 1).Value = newDemand
            .Offset(i, 2).Value = newUnitCost
        Next
    End With

    ' Copy the formulas in columns D through L of the Data sheet down for the new data.
    ' These implement the exponential smoothing methods.
    With Range("DataAnchor").Offset(0, 3).End(xlDown)
        Range(.Offset(0, 0), .Offset(0, 8)).Copy _
            Destination:=Range(.Offset(1, 0), .Offset(nMonthsNew, 8))
    End With

    ' Rename the ranges for various columns in the Data sheet.
    With Range("DataAnchor")
        Range(.Offset(1, 0), .End(xlDown)).Name = "Month"
        Range(.Offset(0, 1), .Offset(0, 1).End(xlDown)).Name = "Demands"
        Range(.Offset(0, 2), .Offset(0, 2).End(xlDown)).Name = "UnitCosts"
        Range(.Offset(0, 6), .Offset(0, 6).End(xlDown)).Name = "DemFCasts"
        Range(.Offset(0, 9), .Offset(0, 9).End(xlDown)).Name = "CostFCasts"
        Range(.Offset(1, 10), .Offset(1, 10).End(xlDown)).Name = "_APE1"
        Range(.Offset(1, 11), .Offset(1, 11).End(xlDown)).Name = "_APE2"
    End With

    ' Update the charts to include all data observed so far.
    Call UpdateCharts

    Range("N9").Select
End Sub
```

UpdateCharts Code

The **UpdateCharts** sub resets the links to the data for the two chart sheets. This is done to accommodate the new data that were just appended to the historical data range.

```
Sub UpdateCharts()
    ' This sub updates the source data ranges for the two chart sheets.
    ' It is called only when the user enters new data.
    With Charts("Demand_Forecast")
        .SetSourceData Source:=Union(Range("Demands"), Range("DemFCasts"))
        .SeriesCollection(1).XValues = Range("Month")
    End With
    With Charts("Cost_Forecast")
        .SetSourceData Source:=Union(Range("UnitCosts"), Range("CostFCasts"))
        .SeriesCollection(1).XValues = Range("Month")
    End With
End Sub
```

SmConstants Code

The **SmConstants** sub "shows" frmSmConst and displays a message about the updated MAPE values. (Remember that the btnOK_Click event handler for frmSmConst performs the task of entering the new smoothing constants in the Data sheet.)

```
Sub SmConstants()
    ' This sub allows the user to change the smoothing constants. After choosing them,
    ' everything on the Data sheet recalculates automatically and a message box shows the
    ' updated MAPE values.
    frmSmConst.Show
    MsgBox "MAPE for forecasting demand is " & Format(Range("MAPE1"), "0.00%") & "." _
        & vbCrLf & "MAPE for forecasting unit costs is " _
        & Format(Range("MAPE2"), "0.00%"), vbInformation, "Forecasting"
End Sub
```

Navigational Code

The rest of the subs listed below are for navigational purposes. They are attached to the buttons on the various sheets.

```
Sub ViewData()
    With Worksheets("Data")
        .Visible = True
        .Activate
    End With
    Range("N9").Select
End Sub

Sub ViewDemFCasts()
    With Charts("Demand_Forecast")
        .Visible = True
        .Activate
    End With
End Sub

Sub ViewCostFCasts()
    With Charts("Cost_Forecast")
```

```
        .Visible = True
        .Activate
    End With
End Sub

Sub ViewExplanation()
    Dim sht As Object
    Worksheets("Explanation").Activate
    Range("F4").Select
    For Each sht In ActiveWorkbook.Sheets
        If sht.Name <> "Explanation" Then sht.Visible = False
    Next
End Sub

Sub ViewReport()
    Worksheets("Report").Activate
    Range("B14").Select
    Charts("Demand_Forecast").Visible = False
    Charts("Cost_Forecast").Visible = False
End Sub
```

22.8 Summary

This forecasting/optimization application is admittedly fairly long and complex, but this is the price paid for accomplishing so much. The application combines two traditional areas of management science. First, it implements exponential smoothing forecasting methods. Second, it uses the exponential smoothed forecasts as inputs to a production-planning optimization model. In this way, the application can be used to implement the rolling planning horizon method used by many organizations.

EXERCISES

1. The application currently creates a column chart of production quantities and ending inventories on the Report sheet. (See Figure 22.4.) Change it so that two *separate* charts are created on the Report sheet: one of production quantities and one of ending inventories. Also, make each of them *line* charts.

2. The planning horizon can currently be any number of months from 3 to 12. Suppose the company involved insists on a 6-month planning horizon—no more, no less. Would this make your job as a programmer easier or harder? Explain in words what basic changes you would make to the application.

3. Some programmers might object to our EnterFormulas sub, arguing that it is too long and should be broken up into smaller subs. Try doing this. You can decide how many smaller subs to use and what specific task each should have. Then test the application with your new code. It should still work correctly!

4. I have used my own (fictional) historical data to illustrate the application. Try using your own. Specifically, enter your own data in columns A, B, and C of the

Data sheet (see Figure 22.5), and make sure the columns next to them (D–J) have the same number of rows as your new data. (Delete rows or copy down if necessary.) You'll also have to enter "reasonable" initialization values for the smoothing methods. (See Figure 22.14 for the cells involved.) Now run the application. Does it work correctly? It should!

5. The third basic option in the application allows the user to enter *any* number of new observations. Change this so that only *one* new observation (of demand and unit cost) can be added on a given run. In this case, you won't need frmNewData1.

6. (More difficult, and only for those familiar with exponential smoothing) The fourth basic option in the application allows the user to enter *any* smoothing constants from 0 to 1. Delete this option. Instead, have the application choose the smoothing constants to minimize the root mean square error (RMSE), which is defined as the square root of the sum of squared differences between observations and forecasts. You will need to write code to set up and run Solver for this minimization. Write this as two subs, one for the demands and one for the unit costs (since each has its own set of smoothing constants). Then decide when these subs should be called and update other subs accordingly.

7. (More difficult, and only for those familiar with exponential smoothing) The application is written for a product with seasonal demand. This is the reason for using Winters' method. Change the application so that the user can choose (in an extra user form) which of three exponential smoothing methods to use for forecasting demand: simple, Holt's, or Winters'. Then the appropriate formulas should be used. (*Hint:* There are probably fewer required modifications than you might expect because the formulas for simple exponential smoothing and Holt's methods are special cases of the built-in Winters' method.

A Logistics Application

23.1 Introduction

This application solves a well-known management science problem called the transportation problem. A company needs to ship a product from it plants to its retailers. Each route from a plant to a retailer has a unit shipping cost. The problem is to develop a shipping plan that gets the product from the plants to the retailers at minimum cost. There are plant capacity constraints and retailer demand constraints. There can be as many as 200 routes in the network (only because this is the maximum number of changing cells allowed by Solver).[1] In the usual management science terminology, the plants and retailers are called **nodes**, and the routes from plants to retailers are called **arcs**.

This problem requires extensive input data, including node data (names of plants and retailers, as well as capacities and demands) and arc data (unit costs for all plant/retailer combinations). The data for a real problem of this type might well reside on a database, not within Excel, so this possibility is illustrated here. The data are in three related tables (Capacity, Demand, and UnitCost) of an Access database called **Transportation.mdb**. This application illustrates how the Access data can be imported into an Excel worksheet to create a Solver model, which can then be optimized in the usual way. To do so, it uses Microsoft's **ActiveX Data Objects** (**ADO**) technology, as discussed in Chapter 14, to import the data into Excel. You do not even need to own Access to make it work. Fortunately, ADO is quite easy to implement in VBA, as this chapter illustrates. This gives the developers of decision support systems a whole new level of power—the ability to access external databases from Excel.

New Learning Objective: VBA

- To learn how to import data from Access into an Excel application by using ADO, and to use the imported data to set up a model on the fly.

New Learning Objective: Non-VBA

- To learn about transportation models and how they can be optimized with Solver.

---

[1]The 200 changing cell limit is for the version of Solver that is built into Excel. Frontline Systems offers commercial versions of Solver with much larger limits.

23.2 Functionality of the Application

The application performs the following functions:

1. It presents a dialog box where the user can choose from two lists: a list of plants and a list of retailers. These lists are populated using ADO, which reads all of the plants from the Capacity table and all of the retailers from the Demand table. The resulting transportation model uses only the *selected* plants and retailers.
2. It again uses ADO, through VBA, to retrieve the data on capacities, demands, and unit costs from the Access tables to develop a transportation model for the selected plants and retailers. It then uses Solver to optimize this model.
3. It reports the minimum total cost and the positive amounts shipped on all arcs in a Report sheet.

23.3 Running the Application

The application is in the Excel file **Transportion.xlsm**. When this file is opened, the Explanation sheet in Figure 23.1 appears. When the button is clicked, the user sees the dialog box in Figure 23.2. It has a list of all plants and retailers in the database, and the user can select any number of them from the lists. The data from the database for the selected plants and retailers are then imported into the (hidden) Model sheet (see Figure 23.3), the transportation model is developed, Solver is set up and run, and the results are

Figure 23.1 Explanation Sheet

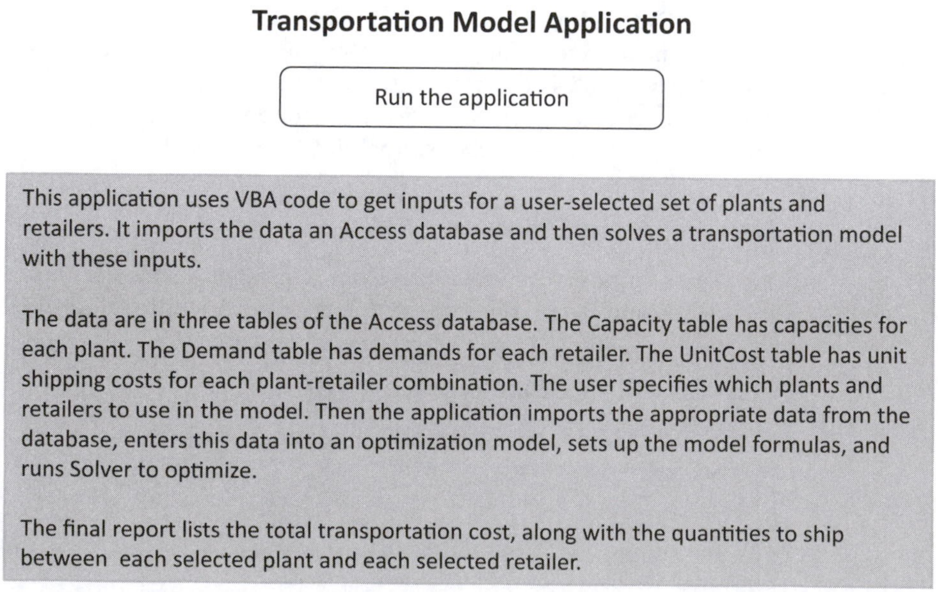

Transportation Model Application

Run the application

This application uses VBA code to get inputs for a user-selected set of plants and retailers. It imports the data an Access database and then solves a transportation model with these inputs.

The data are in three tables of the Access database. The Capacity table has capacities for each plant. The Demand table has demands for each retailer. The UnitCost table has unit shipping costs for each plant-retailer combination. The user specifies which plants and retailers to use in the model. Then the application imports the appropriate data from the database, enters this data into an optimization model, sets up the model formulas, and runs Solver to optimize.

The final report lists the total transportation cost, along with the quantities to ship between each selected plant and each selected retailer.

Figure 23.2 Dialog Box for Selecting Plants and Retailers

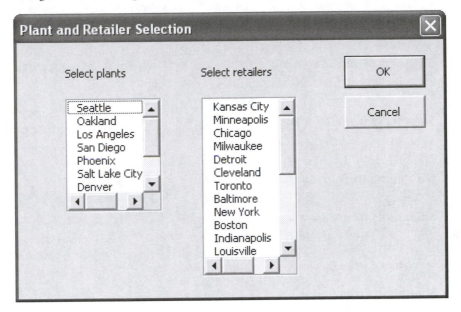

Figure 23.3 Model Sheet

	A	B	C	D	E	F	G	H	I	J	K	L
1	Transportation Model											
2												
3		Unit Costs		Retailers								
4				Chicago	Detroit	Cleveland	Toronto	New York	Boston	Indianapolis		Capacity
5		Plants	Seattle	$23.34	$27.14	$14.38	$19.76	$18.46	$24.64	$30.39		1300
6			Oakland	$16.67	$22.42	$24.09	$12.23	$10.48	$21.97	$25.16		1200
7			Los Angeles	$25.45	$31.54	$26.49	$27.70	$16.70	$25.81	$16.09		1000
8			San Diego	$26.41	$20.58	$21.70	$10.68	$17.67	$21.15	$15.25		1500
9			Phoenix	$23.36	$23.03	$22.62	$14.83	$14.31	$12.25	$20.55		1300
10			Salt Lake City	$13.11	$18.50	$18.44	$21.11	$21.98	$12.65	$20.07		1000
11												
12			Demand	500	450	200	500	500	300	450		
13												
14		Shipments									Sent out	
15				0	0	200	0	0	0	0	200	
16				0	0	0	0	500	0	0	500	
17				0	0	0	0	0	0	0	0	
18				0	0	0	500	0	0	450	950	
19				0	0	0	0	0	300	0	300	
20				500	450	0	0	0	0	0	950	
21			Sent in	500	450	200	500	500	300	450		
22												
23		Total Cost		$38,874								

transferred to the Report sheet. This Report sheet, an example of which is shown in Figure 23.4, indicates all positive shipments, along with the total shipping cost. At this point, the user can run another problem (with a different selection of plants and/or retailers).

Figure 23.4 Report of Optimal Solution

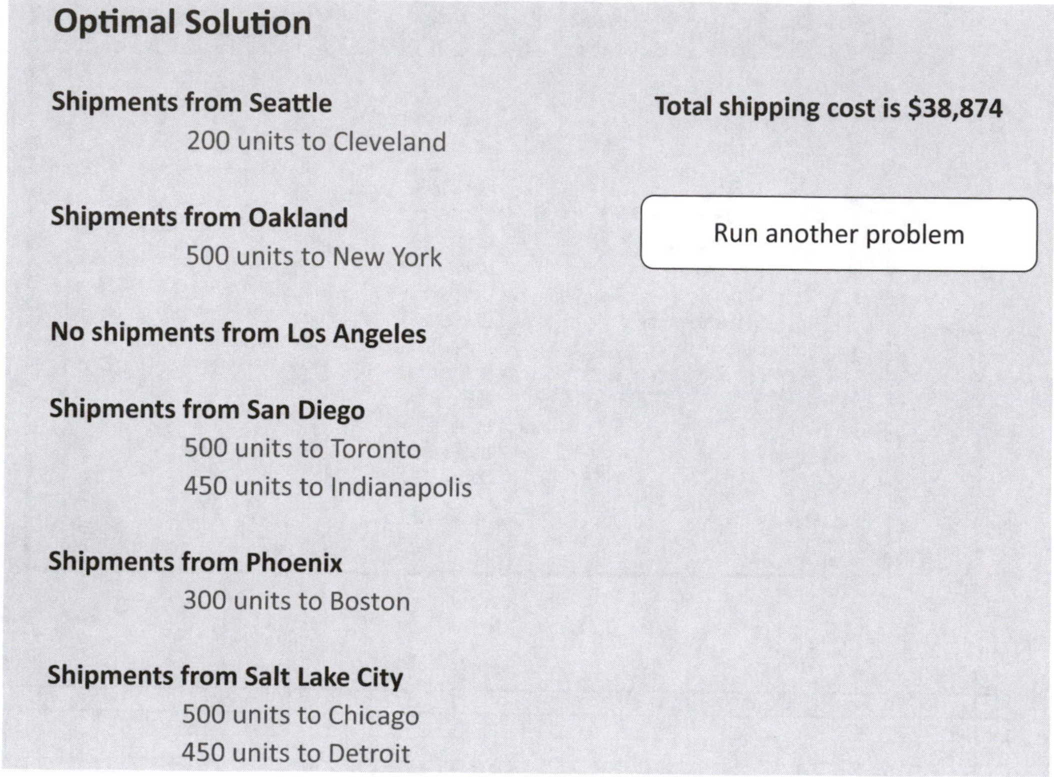

Optimal Solution

Shipments from Seattle
> 200 units to Cleveland

Total shipping cost is $38,874

Shipments from Oakland
> 500 units to New York

> Run another problem

No shipments from Los Angeles

Shipments from San Diego
> 500 units to Toronto
> 450 units to Indianapolis

Shipments from Phoenix
> 300 units to Boston

Shipments from Salt Lake City
> 500 units to Chicago
> 450 units to Detroit

23.4   Setting Up the Access Database

The application depends entirely on the Access database. The application uses the database with the Capacity, Demand, and UnitCost tables shown in Figures 23.5, 23.6, and 23.7 (with some hidden rows in the latter). The tables are related through the PlantID and RetailerID fields, as indicated by the relationships diagram in Figure 23.8. The application will work for any database structured this way, provided the following are true:

- It should be named **Transportation.mdb**, and it should be located in the *same* folder as the **Transportation.xlsm** Excel file. Actually, the file name could be changed, but the appropriate line in the VBA module code, where the name of the file is specified, would have to be changed accordingly.
- It should have three tables named Capacity, Demand, and UnitCost.
- The Capacity table should be structured as in Figure 23.5. It should have a record (row) for each plant, and it should have three fields (columns) named PlantID, Plant, and Capacity. The PlantID field is an AutoNumber **primary key** field, used to index the plants. (This means that it is automatically populated with consecutive integers.) The Plant field contains the name of

Figure 23.5 Capacity Table in Access Database

	PlantID	Plant	Capacity
+	1	Seattle	1300
+	2	Oakland	1200
+	3	Los Angeles	1000
+	4	San Diego	1500
+	5	Phoenix	1300
+	6	Salt Lake City	1000
+	7	Denver	1500
+	8	Tucson	1200
+	9	Santa Fe	1000
+	10	Sacramento	1300
*	(AutoNumber)		0

Record: 1 of 10

Figure 23.6 Demand Table in Access Database

	RetailerID	Retailer	Demand
+	1	Kansas City	300
+	2	Minneapolis	500
+	3	Chicago	500
+	4	Milwaukee	400
+	5	Detroit	450
+	6	Cleveland	200
+	7	Toronto	500
+	8	Baltimore	400
+	9	New York	500
+	10	Boston	300
+	11	Indianapolis	450
+	12	Louisville	300
+	13	Cincinnati	400
+	14	St. Louis	350
+	15	Nashville	500
+	16	Pittsburgh	400
+	17	Philadelphia	450
+	18	Charlotte	300
+	19	Orlando	500
+	20	Miami	500
+	21	Tampa	400
+	22	Jacksonville	250
+	23	Memphis	300
+	24	Little Rock	400
+	25	New Orleans	500
*	(AutoNumber)		0

Record: 1 of 25

Figure 23.7 UnitCost Table in Access Database

PlantID	RetailerID	UnitCost
1	1	$13.24
1	2	$20.04
1	3	$23.34
1	4	$14.30
1	5	$27.14
1	6	$14.38
1	7	$19.76
1	8	$21.31
1	9	$18.46
1	10	$24.64
1	11	$30.39
1	12	$24.55
1	13	$15.26
1	14	$16.30
1	15	$25.30
1	16	$24.00
1	17	$20.88
1	18	$15.68
1	19	$18.43
1	20	$21.87
1	21	$23.01
1	22	$22.68
1	23	$20.76
1	24	$21.07
1	25	$23.59
2	1	$21.43
2	2	$22.37

Record: 1 of 250

Figure 23.8 Relationships Diagram for Database

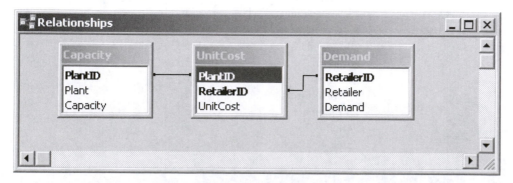

the plant, and the Capacity field contains the capacity of the plant. The Demand table should be structured similarly for the retailers.

- The UnitCost table should be structured as in Figure 23.7. It should have a record for each plant–retailer pair, and it should have three fields named PlantID, RetailerID, and UnitCost. The PlantID and RetailerID fields are **foreign keys**. They reference the corresponding rows in the Capacity and Demand tables. The UnitCost field contains the unit shipping cost for the associated plant–retailer route.

- The tables should be related as indicated in Figure 23.8.

23.5   Setting Up the Excel Worksheets

The **Transportation.xlsm** file contains three worksheets: the Explanation sheet in Figure 23.1, the Model sheet in Figure 23.3, and the Report sheet in Figure 23.4. The Model sheet must be set up almost completely at run time because its size depends on the plants and retailers selected by the user. Therefore, the only template that can be formed in the Model sheet at design time is shown in Figure 23.9. Similarly, the only template that can be set up in the Report sheet at design time is shown in Figure 23.10.

Figure 23.9 Template for Model Sheet

	A	B	C	D	E
1	Transportation Model				
2					
3		Unit Costs		Retailers	
4					
5		Plants			
6					

Figure 23.10 Template for Report Sheet

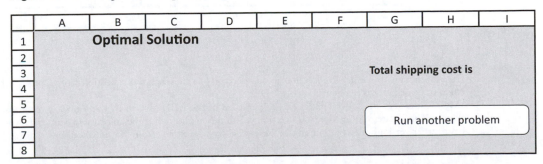

	A	B	C	D	E	F	G	H	I
1		**Optimal Solution**							
2									
3							**Total shipping cost is**		
4									
5									
6							Run another problem		
7									
8									

23.6　Getting Started with the VBA

This application requires a module and a user form named frmInputs.[2] In addition, two references must be set. First, because Solver functions are used, a reference must be set to Solver. Also, because the ADO object model is being used, a reference must be set to it. To do so, select the **Tools→References** menu item in the VBE, scroll down the list for the **Microsoft ActiveX Data Objects 2.5 Library**, and check its box.[3] (See Figure 23.11.) After this is done, the Project Explorer will look as shown in Figure 23.12. Note that there is no reference showing for ADO, only for Solver. Evidently, Microsoft lists only the *non*-Microsoft references in the Project Explorer.

Figure 23.11　References Dialog Box

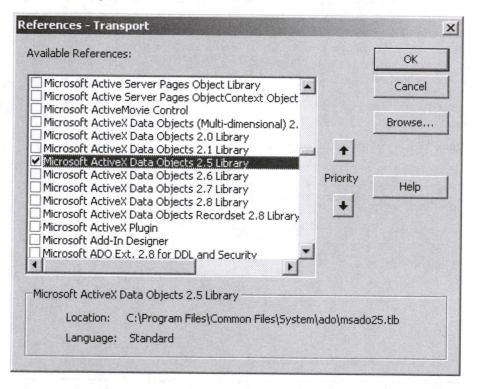

---

[2]It also contains the usual frmSolver that simply displays a message about possible Solver problems when the workbook is opened.

[3]My PC lists versions 2.0, 2.1, 2.5, 2.6, 2.7, and 2.8 of the ADO library. By the time you read this, there might be later verions. I've used version 2.5 in this application to be compatible with users who have earlier versions of Excel, but any of these versions, at least any from 2.5 on, should work fine.

Figure 23.12 Project Explorer Window

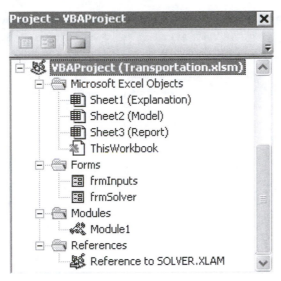

Workbook_Open Code

To guarantee that the Explanation sheet appears when the file is opened, the following code is placed in the ThisWorkbook code window. It also hides the Model and Report sheets.

```
Private Sub Workbook_Open()
    Worksheets("Model").Visible = False
    Worksheets("Report").Visible = False
    Worksheets("Explanation").Activate
    Range("G18").Select
End Sub
```

23.7 The User Form and Its Event Handlers

The user form allows the user to select any subsets of plants and retailers from the sets of all plants and retailers in the database. It uses two list boxes, named lbPlants and lbRetailers, to do this. Each has its MultiSelect property set to **2–fmMultiSelectExtended** so that the user can indeed select *several* items from each list. The design of this form is shown in Figure 23.13.

Code for frmInputs Event Handlers

The **btnCancel_Click** sub performs its usual tasks of unloading the form and terminating the application. For the **btnOK_Click** sub, recall from Chapter 11

Figure 23.13 frmInputs Design

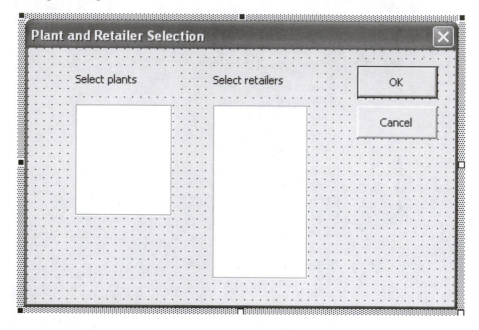

that "multiselect" list boxes have a Selected property that is essentially a 0-based Boolean array. Each element indicates whether the corresponding item in the list has been selected. The **btnOK_Click** sub uses this property to capture the selected plants and retailers in 1-based Public arrays, selectedPlant and selected-Retailer, that are declared in the module. (It also checks that the user selects at least one item from each list.) After it captures these arrays, it builds two strings, plantList and retailerList, that are used in a later SQL statement to get the required unit costs from the UnitCost table. For example, if the user selects the plants Seattle, Oakland, and Dallas, then plantString is "('Seattle','Oakland','Dallas')". The **Userform_Initialize** sub populates the list boxes with *all* of the plants and retailers from the database, which by this time have been stored in the Public arrays existingPlants and existingRetailers.

```
Private Sub btnCancel_Click()
    Unload Me
    End
End Sub

Private Sub btnOK_Click()
    ' Fill an array, selectedPlant, of the plants selected.
    nSelectedPlants = 0
    For i = 1 To lbPlants.ListCount
        If lbPlants.Selected(i - 1) Then
            nSelectedPlants = nSelectedPlants + 1
            ReDim Preserve selectedPlant(nSelectedPlants)
            selectedPlant(nSelectedPlants) = lbPlants.List(i - 1)
        End If
    Next
```

```
    If nSelectedPlants = 0 Then
        MsgBox "Please select at least one plant.", vbExclamation, _
            "Selection required"
        Exit Sub
    End If

    ' Build a string, plantList, that looks something like
    ' ('Seattle','Oakland','Dallas'), depending on plants selected.
    plantList = "("
    For i = 1 To nSelectedPlants
        If i < nSelectedPlants Then
            plantList = plantList & "'" & selectedPlant(i) & "',"
        Else
            plantList = plantList & "'" & selectedPlant(i) & "')"
        End If
    Next

    ' Fill an array, selectedRetailer, of the retailers selected.
    nSelectedRetailers = 0
    For i = 1 To lbRetailers.ListCount
        If lbRetailers.Selected(i - 1) Then
            nSelectedRetailers = nSelectedRetailers + 1
            ReDim Preserve selectedRetailer(nSelectedRetailers)
            selectedRetailer(nSelectedRetailers) = lbRetailers.List(i - 1)
        End If
    Next
    If nSelectedRetailers = 0 Then
        MsgBox "Please select at least one retailer.", vbExclamation, _
            "Selection required"
        Exit Sub
    End If

    ' Build a similar string, retailerList, depending on retailers selected.
    retailerList = "("
    For i = 1 To nSelectedRetailers
        If i < nSelectedRetailers Then
            retailerList = retailerList & "'" & selectedRetailer(i) & "',"
        Else
            retailerList = retailerList & "'" & selectedRetailer(i) & "')"
        End If
    Next

    Unload Me
End Sub

Private Sub UserForm_Initialize()
    ' Populate the listboxes with the arrays.
    lbPlants.List = existingPlant
    lbRetailers.List = existingRetailer
End Sub
```

23.8 The VBA Code in the Module

The Public and module-level variables are listed below. Pay particular attention to the way the cn and rs variables are declared. First, they use the **New** keyword. As discussed in Chapter 14, this keyword is required to *instantiate* new ADO objects, in this case, a connection object and a recordset object. Also, the ADODB prefixes let VBA know that these types of objects come from the ADO library.

Option Statements and Public and Module-Level Variables

```
Option Explicit
Option Base 1

Public existingPlant() As String, existingRetailer() As String
Public nSelectedPlants As Integer, nSelectedRetailers As Integer
Public selectedPlant() As String, selectedRetailer() As String
Public plantList As String, retailerList As String

' Instantiate connection and recordset objects for later use.
Dim cn As New ADODB.Connection, rs As New ADODB.Recordset
```

The button on the Explanation sheet is attached to the **MainTransport** sub in the module. This sub calls other subs to retrieve the data from the Access database, develop the transportation model, run Solver, and report the results.

MainTransport Code

```
Sub MainTransport()
    ' This is the main macro that is run when the button on the
    ' Explanation sheet is clicked.
    Application.ScreenUpdating = False

    ' Open a connection to the database. It is assumed that this Excel workbook
    ' and the Access database are in the same folder.
    With cn
        .ConnectionString = "Data Source=" & ThisWorkbook.Path & "\Transportation.mdb"
        .Provider = "Microsoft Jet 4.0 OLE DB Provider"
        .Open
    End With

    ' Import the required data from the database.
    Call GetPlantAndRetailers
    frmInputs.Show
    Call CheckSolverLimit
    Call EnterModelData

    ' Close the connection to the database.
    cn.Close

    ' Set up and solve the model.
    Call EnterFormulas
    Call SetupAndRunSolver
End Sub
```

GetPlantsAndRetailers Code

The **GetPlantsAndRetailers** sub imports the data from the Capacity and Demand tables of the Access database. Because a connection to the **Transportation.mdb** database file is already open (see the MainTransport code above), it can immediately open a recordset based on a simple SQL statement: **Select Plant**

From Capacity. Once this recordset is open, the code loops through the records and stores the plant names in the existingPlant array for later use in the Model sheet. Then it performs similar steps for retailers.

You should refer to the general discussion of ADO in Chapter 14 as you examine this code. However, it is actually very straightforward once you see the big picture. Once a recordset based on a SQL statement is open, you move through each record of the recordset and extract data from its fields. For example, you reference .Fields("Plant").Value to get the value of the Plant field in the current record. Note that this reference is inside a With rs construction, where rs is the recordset. This means that the reference is really to rs.Fields("Plant").Value. Therefore, you see that the familiar "dot" notation used for Excel objects and properties carries over to ADO.

Several things are worth mentioning about this code. First, it uses a Do loop to step through the records (rows) of the recordset. The stopping condition is While Not .EOF, which is really short for While Not rs.EOF. This means to keep going until you reach the end of file. Second, there *must* be a .MoveNext line inside the loop. Otherwise, the recordset will be stuck on its *first* record, creating an infinite loop. Finally, you should always close a recordset (rs.Close) when you're finished getting its data.

```vba
Sub GetPlantAndRetailers()
    ' This sub gets the potential plants and retailers from the database so that
    ' they can be entered in the listboxes.
    Dim nExisitingPlants As Integer, nExisitingRetailers As Integer
    Dim i As Integer, j As Integer
    Dim SQL As String

    ' Get the plants from the Capacity table to populate the array existingPlant.
    SQL = "Select Plant From Capacity"
    With rs
        .Open SQL, cn
        nExisitingPlants = 0
        Do While Not .EOF
            nExisitingPlants = nExisitingPlants + 1
            ReDim Preserve existingPlant(nExisitingPlants)
            existingPlant(nExisitingPlants) = .Fields("Plant").Value
            .MoveNext
        Loop
        .Close
    End With

    ' Get the retailers from the Demand table to populate the array existingRetailer.
    SQL = "Select Retailer from Demand"
    With rs
        .Open SQL, cn
        nExisitingRetailers = 0
        Do While Not .EOF
            nExisitingRetailers = nExisitingRetailers + 1
            ReDim Preserve existingRetailer(nExisitingRetailers)
            existingRetailer(nExisitingRetailers) = .Fields("Retailer").Value
            .MoveNext
        Loop
        .Close
    End With

End Sub
```

CheckSolverLimit Code

After the user has selected plants and retailers from frmInputs, the **CheckSolver-Limit** sub checks whether the Solver limit of 200 changing cells has been exceeded. If so, the user is asked to make other selections.

```
Sub CheckSolverLimit()
    Dim nChangingCells As Integer
    nChangingCells = nSelectedPlants * nSelectedRetailers
    If nChangingCells > 200 Then
        MsgBox "With your selections, there are " & nChangingCells _
            & " changing cells in the model (" & nSelectedPlants & " x " _
            & nSelectedRetailers & "). The most Solver can handle is 200. " _
            & "Choose fewer plants or retailers.", _
            vbExclamation, "Model too large"
        frmInputs.Show
    End If
End Sub
```

EnterModelData Code

The **EnterModelData** sub does the hard work. It uses three SQL statements to import the unit costs, the capacities, and the demands corresponding to the plants and retailers selected from frmInputs. It then places the imported data into the appropriate ranges of the Model sheet (consult Figure 23.3.) The hardest part of this sub is the SQL statement for obtaining the unit costs. Although the unit costs obviously come from the UnitCost table, the SQL statement requires inner joins with the Capacity and Demand tables. This is because the UnitCost table stores only IDs (indexes) for the plants and retailers, whereas we need to access them by names such as Seattle. Also, the Where clause of this SQL statement uses the plantList and retailerList strings created earlier. It will look something like: **Where Plant In ('Seattle', 'Oakland', 'Dallas') And Retailer In ('Chicago', 'New York', 'Miami', 'Orlando', 'Little Rock', 'New Orleans')**. This clause filters out all unit costs except those for the cities listed. The rest of the code is reasonably straightforward and is explained by the comments.

```
Sub EnterModelData()
    ' The following macro uses ADO to place the appropriate data
    ' from the database in the appropriate cells of the Model sheet.
    Dim SQL As String
    Dim i As Integer, j As Integer
    Dim topCell As Range

    ' Clear everything from Model sheet (including formatting).
    With Worksheets("Model")
        .Cells.Clear
        .Activate
    End With

    ' Enter labels.
    Range("A1").Value = "Transportation Model"
```

```
Range("B3").Value = "Unit Costs"
Range("B5").Value = "Plants"
Range("D3").Value = "Retailers"

Set topCell = Range("C4")

' Add headings.
With topCell
    For i = 1 To nSelectedPlants
        .Offset(i, 0).Value = selectedPlant(i)
    Next
    For j = 1 To nSelectedRetailers
        .Offset(0, j).Value = selectedRetailer(j)
    Next
End With

' Get the data with the following SQL statement, and use the
' data to fill in the UnitCost range. The SQL statement requires a couple
' of inner joins. The reason is that the UnitCost table lists only the
' IDs of the plants and retailers. Their names, required in the Where clause,
' are stored in the Capacity and Demand tables.
SQL = "Select UC.UnitCost " _
    & "From (UnitCost UC Inner Join Capacity C On UC.PlantID = C.PlantID) " _
    & "Inner Join Demand D On UC.RetailerID = D.RetailerID " _
    & "Where C.Plant In " & plantList & " And D.Retailer In " & retailerList
With rs
    .Open SQL, cn
    For i = 1 To nSelectedPlants
        For j = 1 To nSelectedRetailers
            topCell.Offset(i, j).Value = .Fields("UnitCost").Value
            .MoveNext
        Next
    Next
    .Close
End With

' Name the range
With topCell
    Range(.Offset(1, 1), .Offset(nSelectedPlants, nSelectedRetailers)) _
        .Name = "UnitCosts"
End With

' Do the same type of operation to fill in the capacities.
Set topCell = Range("C4").Offset(0, nSelectedRetailers + 2)
topCell.Value = "Capacity"
SQL = "Select Capacity From Capacity " & _
    "Where Plant In " & plantList
With rs
    .Open SQL, cn
    For i = 1 To nSelectedPlants
        topCell.Offset(i, 0).Value = .Fields("Capacity").Value
        .MoveNext
    Next
    .Close
End With
With topCell
    Range(.Offset(1, 0), .Offset(nSelectedPlants, 0)).Name = "Capacities"
End With

' Do the same type of operation to fill in the demands.
Set topCell = Range("C4").Offset(nSelectedPlants + 2, 0)
```

```
    topCell.Value = "Demand"

    SQL = "Select Demand From Demand " & _
        "Where Retailer In " & retailerList
    With rs
        .Open SQL, cn
        For j = 1 To nSelectedRetailers
            topCell.Offset(0, j).Value = .Fields("Demand").Value
            .MoveNext
        Next
        .Close
    End With
    With topCell
        Range(.Offset(0, 1), .Offset(0, nSelectedRetailers)).Name = "Demands"
    End With

End Sub
```

EnterFormulas Code

By this time, ADO has done its job and is no longer needed. The required data from the database have now been placed in the Model sheet. The **EnterFormulas** sub finishes the model by adding formulas to the Model sheet. These are straightforward. (Again, consult Figure 23.3.) Specifically, sum formulas are required to calculate the total amounts shipped out of any plant and into any retailer. Also, a "sumproduct" formula is needed to find the total cost—the sum of unit costs times amounts shipped.

```
Sub EnterFormulas()
    ' This sub puts the various formulas in the Model sheet, including
    ' the total shipped out of each plant and the total shipped into
    ' each retailer.
    Dim outOfRange As Range, intoRange As Range
    Dim topCell As Range

    Worksheets("Model").Activate

    ' Set up changing cells (Shipments) range and enter 0's as initial values.
    Range("B4").Offset(nSelectedPlants + 4, 0).Value = "Shipments"
    Set topCell = Range("C4").Offset(nSelectedPlants + 4, 0)
    With Range(topCell.Offset(1, 1), _
        topCell.Offset(nSelectedPlants, nSelectedRetailers))
        .Name = "Shipments"
        .Value = 0
        .BorderAround Weight:=xlMedium, ColorIndex:=3
    End With

    ' Enter formulas for row and column sums for "SentOut" and "SentIn" ranges.
    Set topCell = Range("Shipments").Cells(1)
    With topCell
        .Offset(-1, nSelectedRetailers).Value = "Sent out"
        .Offset(nSelectedPlants, -1).Value = "Sent in"
        Set outOfRange = Range(.Offset(0, nSelectedRetailers), _
            .Offset(nSelectedPlants - 1, nSelectedRetailers))
        Set intoRange = Range(.Offset(nSelectedPlants, 0), _
            .Offset(nSelectedPlants, nSelectedRetailers - 1))
```

```
        End With
        With outOfRange
            .Name = "SentOut"
            .FormulaR1C1 = "=SUM(RC[-" & nSelectedRetailers & "]:RC[-1])"
        End With
        With intoRange
            .Name = "SentIn"
            .FormulaR1C1 = "=SUM(R[-" & nSelectedPlants & "]C:R[-1]C)"
        End With

        ' Calculate total cost in "TotalCost" range.
        Set topCell = Range("SentIn").Item(1).Offset(2, 0)
        With topCell
            .Formula = "=SumProduct(UnitCosts,Shipments)"
            .Name = "TotalCost"
            .NumberFormat = "$#,##0_);($#,##0)"
            .Offset(0, -2).Value = "Total Cost"
        End With

        Range("A1").Select
End Sub
```

SetupAndRunSolver Code

The **SetupAndRunSolver** sub sets up and then runs Solver. It checks for infeasibility (code 5 of the SolverSolve function). If there are no feasible solutions, a message to that effect is displayed and the user is asked to make different input selections.

```
Sub SetupAndRunSolver()
    Dim solverStatus As Integer

    With Worksheets("Model")
        .Visible = True
        .Activate
    End With

    SolverReset
    SolverAdd Range("SentOut"), 1, "Capacities"
    SolverAdd Range("SentIn"), 3, "Demands"
    SolverOptions AssumeLinear:=True, AssumeNonNeg:=True
    SolverOk SetCell:=Range("TotalCost"), MaxMinVal:=2, _
        ByChange:=Range("Shipments")

    ' Run Solver. If there are no feasible solutions (code 5), call the
    ' MainTransport sub. The effect is to let the user try again.
    solverStatus = SolverSolve(UserFinish:=True)
    If solverStatus = 5 Then
        MsgBox "There is no feasible solution. Try a different combination of " _
            & "plants and retailers.", vbExclamation, "Infeasible"
        Call MainTransport
    Else
        Worksheets("Model").Visible = False
        Call CreateReport
    End If
End Sub
```

CreateReport Code

Finally, the **CreateReport** sub transfers the total shipping cost and the information about all routes with *positive* flows to the Report sheet. If there are no shipments out of a particular plant, a note to this effect is included in the report. (See Figure 23.4 for an example.)

```
Sub CreateReport()
    ' Finally, Report the results in the Report sheet.
    Dim i As Integer, j As Integer
    Dim nShippedTo As Integer, amountShipped As Integer
    Dim topCell As Range

    ' Clear everything from Report sheet (including formatting), but not the button.
    With Worksheets("Report")
        .Cells.Clear
        .Visible = True
        .Activate
    End With

    ' Enter heading and format.
    With Range("B1")
        .Value = "Optimal Solution"
        With .Font
            .Size = 14
            .Bold = True
        End With
    End With
    With ActiveWindow
        .DisplayGridlines = False
        .DisplayHeadings = False
    End With
    Cells.Interior.ColorIndex = 40
    Columns("B:B").Font.ColorIndex = 1
    Columns("C:C").Font.ColorIndex = 5
    Range("B1").Font.ColorIndex = 1

    ' For each route that ships a positive amount, record how much is shipped.
    Set topCell = Range("B3")
    For i = 1 To nSelectedPlants
        If Range("SentOut").Cells(i).Value > 0.1 Then
            With topCell
                .Value = "Shipments from " & selectedPlant(i)
                .Font.Bold = True
            End With
            nShippedTo = 0
            For j = 1 To nSelectedRetailers
                amountShipped = Range("Shipments").Cells(i, j).Value
                If amountShipped > 0.01 Then
                    nShippedTo = nShippedTo + 1
                    topCell.Offset(nShippedTo, 1).Value = _
                        amountShipped & " units to " & selectedRetailer(j)
                End If
            Next
            Set topCell = topCell.Offset(nShippedTo + 2, 0)
        Else
            With topCell
                .Value = "No shipments from " & selectedPlant(i)
                .Font.Bold = True
```

```
            End With
            Set topCell = topCell.Offset(2, 0)
        End If
    Next

    ' Record the total shipping cost.
    With Range("G3")
        .Value = "Total shipping cost is " & _
            Format(Range("TotalCost").Value, "$#,##0;($#,##0)")
        .Font.Bold = True
    End With

    Range("A1").Select
End Sub
```

23.9   Summary

Virtually all of the VBA applications you will develop in Excel will require data, and it is very possible that the required data will reside in an external database format such as Access. (Actually, it is more likely that the data will reside in a server-based database such as SQL Server or Oracle, but the code would not change much from what I have presented here.) This chapter has demonstrated how to import the data from an Access database into Excel for use in a transportation model. This requires you to use the basic functionality of a new object model, ADO. It also requires you to know how to write SQL statements, the "language of databases." However, the effort required to learn these is well spent. Knowing how to import data from an external database is an extremely valuable skill in today's business world, and it is likely to become even more valuable in the future.

EXERCISES

1.   The application currently has no charts. Change it so that the user can view two charts (each on a separate chart sheet) after Solver has been run. The first should be a column chart showing the total amount shipped and the total capacity for each selected plant, something similar to Figure 23.14. Likewise, the second chart should show the total amount shipped to each selected retailer and the retailer's demand. (Actually, the latter two should be equal, given the way the transportation problem has been modeled. There is absolutely no incentive to send a retailer *more* than it demands.) As always, do as much at design time, and write as little VBA code, as possible.

2.   I claimed that this application works with any data, provided that the database file is structured properly. Try it out. Open the **Transportation.mdb** file in Access and change its data in some way. (You can change names of plants, unit costs, and so on. You can even add some plants or retailers. Just be sure that there is a row in the UnitCost table for each plant–retailer pair.) Then rerun the application to see if it still works properly.

Figure 23.14 Shipments from Plants for Exercise 1

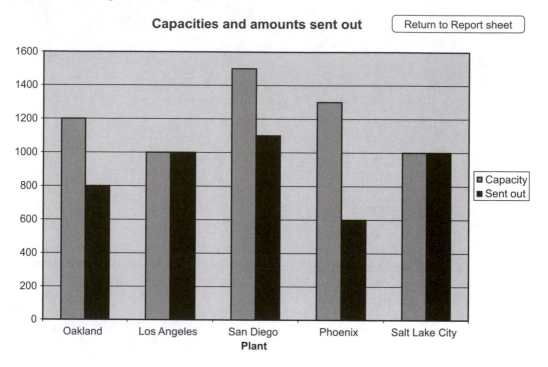

3. Repeat the previous exercise, but now create a *new* Access file called **MyData. mdb** (stored in the same folder as the Excel application), structured exactly as **Transportation.mdb**, and add some data to it. Then rerun the application to see if it still works properly. (Note that you will have to change one line of the VBA code so that it references the correct name of your new Access file.)

4. The previous problem indicates a "fix" that no business would ever tolerate—they would never be willing to get into the VBA code to change a file name reference. A much better alternative is to change the VBA code in the first place so that it asks the user for the location and name of the database file. You could do this with an input box (and risk having the user spell something wrong), but Excel provides an easier way with the **FileDialog** object, as illustrated in Chapter 13 (or the **GetOpenFilename** method of the **Application** object if you have Excel 2000 or an earlier version). Use either of these to change the application, so that it prompts the user for the name and location of the database file. Actually, you should probably precede the above line with a MsgBox statement so that the user knows she is being asked to select the file with the data. Then try the modified application with your own Access file, stored in a folder *different* from the folder containing the Excel application.

A Stock-Trading Simulation Application

24

24.1 Introduction

In *Practical Management Science*, we illustrate two ways to run spreadsheet simulations. Each method starts with a spreadsheet model that includes random quantities in selected cells. The first method creates a data table to replicate desired outputs. Summary measures and charts can then be obtained manually from this data table. The second method uses a simulation add-in such as @RISK. Once the user designates desired output cells, the add-in runs all of the replications and automatically creates summary measures, including charts, for these outputs. This application illustrates how VBA can be used to automate a simulation model, similar to the way @RISK does it. However, no data tables are created, and no add-ins are required.

The model itself simulates the trading activity of an investor in the stock market over the period of a year (250 trading days). This investor starts with a certain amount of cash and owns several shares of a stock. The investor then uses a "buy low/sell high" trading strategy. The trading strategy implemented in the model is as follows. If the price of the stock increases two days in a row, the investor sells 10% of his shares. If it increases three days in a row, he sells 25% of his shares. In the other direction, if the price decreases two days in a row, the investor buys 10% more shares. For example, if he owns 500 shares, he buys 50 more shares. If the price decreases three days in a row, he buys 25% more shares. The only restriction on buying is that the investor cannot spend more than his current cash. The price of the stock is generated randomly through a **lognormal** model used by many financial analysts.

The simulation keeps track of five output measures: (1) the investor's cash at the end of the year, (2) the value of the investor's stock at the end of the year, (3) the gain (or loss) from the investor's cash/stock portfolio at the end of the year, relative to what he owned at the beginning of the year, (4) the lowest price of the stock during the year, and (5) the highest price of the stock during the year.

New Learning Objectives: VBA

- To illustrate how to automate a spreadsheet simulation model with VBA.
- To illustrate how the run time of a simulation can be affected by the recalculation mode.
- To show how to use VBA to enter an array function into an Excel range.

New Learning Objective: Non-VBA

- To show how simulation can be used to measure the effectiveness of a stock market trading strategy.

24.2 Functionality of the Application

The application has the following functionality:

1. It allows the user to specify a trading strategy. As written, the user can change the percentages to sell if the stock price increases two or three days in a row and the similar percentages to buy if the price decreases two or three days in a row. The model could be modified slightly to examine other types of trading strategies (buy high, sell low, for example)—without any changes in the VBA code.
2. The simulation can be run for up to 1000 replications. (This limit could easily be changed.) As it runs, it keeps track of the five outputs listed in the introduction. It then reports summary measures for these outputs (minimum, maximum, average, standard deviation, median, and 5th and 95th percentiles), and it creates histograms of the outputs. The application could be modified fairly easily to incorporate other outputs from the simulation.

24.3 Running the Application

The application is stored in the file **Stock Trading.xlsm**. When this file is opened, the user sees the Explanation sheet in Figure 24.1.

If the user clicks on the left button, the Inputs sheet in Figure 24.2 appears. The various inputs appear in blue. The user can change any of these before running the simulation. In particular, a different trading strategy can be examined by changing the percentages in column J. Also, note that the current price (on day 1) and the prices on the three previous days are shown in column E. Because the investor's trading strategy depends on the three previous price changes, these past prices are required for the trading decisions on the first few days.

When the user clicks on the button in Figure 24.2 (or the right button in Figure 24.1), the input box in Figure 24.3 is displayed. Here the user can choose any number of replications, up to 1000, for the simulation.

After the user clicks on OK, the simulation runs. It recalculates the random numbers on the hidden Model sheet (more about this sheet later) for each replication, stores the outputs on a (hidden) Replications sheet, and calculates summary measures, which are stored on a Summary sheet, shown in Figure 24.4. This can take quite a while, so a replication counter placed on the Explanation sheet shows the progress. (This counter is certainly not necessary for the proper running of the simulation, but it is a nice touch for the user.)

Each output has a corresponding histogram worksheet. These are created at design time, and they are then updated at the end of the simulation. As an example, the histogram for the cumulative gain/loss output appears in Figure 24.5.

Figure 24.1 Explanation Sheet

Stock Market Trading Simulation

View/change inputs   Run the simulation

This application simulates the stock market and the trading strategy of an investor. The investor owns some cash and shares of a stock at the beginning of day 1. From then on, the investor uses a buy/sell strategy that depends on the recent stock price changes. The current strategy, described on the Inputs sheet, is a version of "buy low/sell high." The only constraint is that the investor can't buy more shares than he can afford with the current cash on hand.

The stock price changes according to a "lognormal model," a model commonly used by financial analysts.

The user can view/change the inputs first or run the simulation with the current inputs. A summary of the results are shown on the Summary sheet, and corresponding histograms are shown on the histogram sheets. The results of the individual replications of the simulation are available on the (hidden) Replications sheet.

Figure 24.2 Inputs Sheet

	A	B	C	D	E	F	G	H	I	J	K	L
1	Inputs to simulation											
2												
3	Inputs			Recent stock prices				Trading strategy				
4	Initial cash	$75,000		3 days ago	$49.86			Buying: if change is negative				
5	Initial shares owned	500		2 days ago	$49.79			3 days in a row, buy		25%	of current shares	
6				1 day ago	$49.95			2 days in a row, buy		10%	of current shares	
7	Daily growth rate of stock price			Current	$50.00			Selling: if change is positive				
8	Mean	0.01%						3 days in a row, sell		25%	of current shares	
9	StDev	2.0%						2 days in a row, sell		10%	of current shares	
10												
11	Implication for the year (assuming 250 trading days per year)											
12	Mean	2.50%	(average annual growth rate of stock price)									
13	StDev	31.62%	(standard deviation of annual growth rate)									
14												
15												
16					Enter any new inputs in the blue cells. Then click on the button							
17					below to run the simulation with these inputs.							
18												
19					Run the simulation							
20												

Figure 24.3 Input Box for the Number of Replications

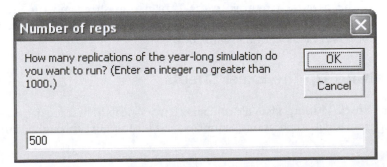

Figure 24.4 Summary Results from the Simulation

	A	B	C	D	E	F
1	Summary results from the simulation					
2						
3		Ending cash	Ending stock value	Cum gain/loss	Min price	Max price
4	Min	$4	$33	($54,237)	$18.41	$50.00
5	Max	$122,875	$106,724	$27,187	$50.00	$125.09
6	Average	$90,863	$9,945	$808	$40.07	$64.60
7	Stdev	$22,513	$18,101	$8,939	$7.02	$13.16
8	Median	$100,192	$1,639	$2,245	$40.81	$61.26
9	5th percentile	$38 399	$52	($17,327)	$27.77	$50.56
10	95th percentile	$106,678	$48,836	$11,502	$49.50	$91.49
11						
12		For further results, take a look at any of the histogram sheets. They show				
13		histograms of the various output measures.				
14						

Figure 24.5 Histogram for Cumulative Gain/Loss

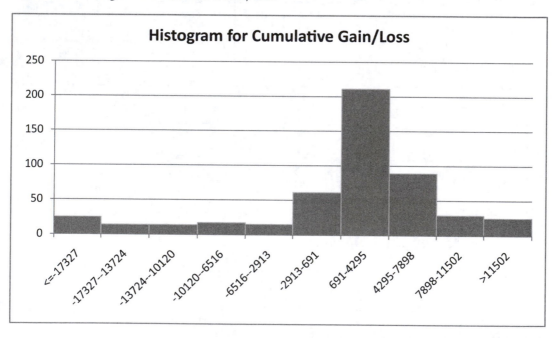

If the user then returns to the Explanation sheet and runs the simulation again, the results will differ, even if the same inputs are used, because *new* random numbers will be used in the simulation.

24.4 Setting Up the Excel Sheets

The **Stock Trading.xlsm** file contains 10 worksheets. These are named Explanation, Inputs, Model, Replications, Summary, and Histogram1 through Histogram5.

The Model Sheet

The Model sheet, shown in Figure 24.6 (with many hidden rows), can be set up *completely* at design time.

From row 10 down, this sheet models the trading activity for a 250-day period. I will discuss a few of the formulas in this sheet; you can open the file and examine the rest. First, the stock prices in column B are determined from the well-known lognormal stock price model. Specifically, the formula in cell B17, which is copied down column B, is

=ROUND(B16*EXP((GrMean-0.5*GrStdev^2)
+GrStdev*NORMINV(RAND(),0,1)),2)

This formula uses the daily mean growth rate and standard deviation of growth rate (GrMean and GrStdev, from cells B8 and B9 of the Inputs sheet), along with a standard normal random number—from **NORMINV(RAND(),0,1)**—to generate the day's price from the previous day's price in cell B16.

Second, the trading strategy is implemented in columns E and F with rather complex IF functions. For example, the number of shares bought in cell F16 uses the formula

=IF(AND(C14<0,C15<0,C16<0),MIN(ROUND(BuyPct3*D16,0),
INT(H16/B16)),IF(AND(C15<0,C16<0),MIN(ROUND
(BuyPct2*D16,0),INT(H16/B16)),0))

Here, BuyPct3 and BuyPct2 are 25% and 10%, respectively, from cells J5 and J6 of the Inputs sheet. The formula first checks whether the price has decreased three days in a row. If it has, the investor buys the smaller of two quantities—the number of shares he would like to buy (25% of what he owns), and the number of shares he has cash for (his cash divided by the current stock price, rounded down to the nearest integer). If the price has not decreased three days in a row, then the formula checks whether it has decreased two days in a row. If it has, the investor again purchases the smaller of two quantities. If it hasn't, the investor buys nothing.

Finally, the cumulative gain/loss in column L is the current value of the cash/stock portfolio minus the initial value on day 1. For example, the formula for the last day in cell L265 is

=(J265+K265)-(InitCash+InitShares*InitPrice)

where InitCash, InitShares, and InitPrice refer to cells B4, B5, and E7 of the Inputs sheet.

Once the 250-day model has been developed, the outputs in rows 4–8 can be calculated easily. For example, the formulas in cells B6 and B7 are **=L265** and **=MIN (B16:B265)**. Note that these outputs summarize a *single* 250-day replication.

The Replication Sheet

When the simulation runs for, say, 500 replications, the VBA code forces the model to recalculate 500 times, each time producing new random numbers and therefore new outputs in the Model sheet. It captures these outputs and stores

Figure 24.6 Simulation Model and Outputs

	A	B	C	D	E	F	G	H	I	J	K	L
1	Stock Market Simulation											
2												
3	Outputs from one year-long simulation											
4	Ending cash	$89,215										
5	Ending value of stock owned	$13,347										
6	Cumulative gain/loss	$2,562										
7	Lowest stock price	$42.56										
8	Highest stock price	$65.24										
9												
10	Simulation											
11		Stock price		Trading activity				Value of stock/cash portfolio				
12	Day	Beginning price	Change from previous day	Beginning shares	Shares sold	Shares purchase	Ending shares	Beginning cash	Change in cash	Ending cash	Worth of shares	Cumulative gain/loss
13		$49.86										
14		$49.79	-$0.07									
15		$49.95	$0.16									
16	1	$50.00	$0.05	500	50	0	450	$75,000	$2,500	$77,500	$22,500	$0
17	2	$50.77	$0.77	450	113	0	337	$77,500	$5,737	$83,237	$17,109	$347
18	3	$49.89	-$0.88	337	0	0	337	$83,237	$0	$83,237	$16,813	$50
19	4	$51.12	$1.23	337	0	0	337	$83,237	$0	$83,237	$17,227	$464
20	5	$52.01	$0.89	337	34	0	303	$83,237	$1,768	$85,005	$15,759	$764
261	246	$45.40	-$0.75	250	0	0	250	$91,572	$0	$91,572	$11,350	$2,922
262	247	$44.93	-$0.47	250	0	25	275	$91,572	($1,123)	$90,449	$12,356	$2,804
263	248	$46.30	$1.37	275	0	0	275	$90,449	$0	$90,449	$12,733	$3,181
264	249	$45.50	-$0.80	275	0	0	275	$90,449	$0	$90,449	$12,513	$2,961
265	250	$44.05	-$1.45	275	0	28	303	$90,449	($1,233)	$89,215	$13,347	$2,562

Figure 24.7 Replications Sheet

	A	B	C	D	E	F
1	Results of individual replications					
2						
3	Replication	Ending cash	Ending stock value	Cum gain/loss	Min price	Max price
4	1	$102,824	$54	$2,878	45.93	68.81
5	2	$99,126	$3,194	$2,320	46.49	63.51
6	3	$102,994	$57	$3,051	47.21	75.83
7	4	$103,677	$4,733	$8,410	39.1	56.35
501	498	$102,547	$83	$2,630	48.34	94.57
502	499	$103,367	$1,260	$4,627	45.66	62.64
503	500	$89,215	$13,347	$2,562	42.56	65.24

them in the (hidden) Replications sheet, as shown in Figure 24.7 (with many hidden rows). These outputs are then summarized in the Summary sheet at the end of the simulation. Note that the Replications sheet and the Summary sheet (in Figure 24.4) have only labels, no numbers, at design time.

Data Sheets for Histograms

The histogram for each output is formed from a column of data in Figure 24.7 and from information on categories (usually called "bins"). The individual data, such as ending cash amounts, are placed into these bins and are then counted to obtain the histogram. The application uses 10 bins for each histogram. The first bin extends up to the 5th percentile for the output, the last extends beyond the 95th percentile, and the other 8 bins are of equal width between the extremes. This information is summarized in a histogram sheet for each output at the end of the simulation.

Figure 24.8 Data for Cumulative Gain/Loss Histogram

	A	B	C
1	**Frequency table for Cum gain/loss**		
2			
3	Upper limit	Category	Frequency
4	-17327	<=-17327	25
5	-13724	-17327--13724	14
6	-10120	-13724--10120	14
7	-6516	-10120--6516	17
8	-2913	-6516--2913	15
9	691	-2913-691	61
10	4295	691-4295	211
11	7898	4295-7898	89
12	11502	7898-11502	29
13		>11502	25

For example, Figure 24.8 shows the data for the Cumulative Gain/Loss output. Column A contains the upper limit of each bin (other than the rightmost), column B contains horizontal axis labels (where −19611−15861, for example, means "from minus 19611 to minus 15861"), and column C contains the frequencies (obtained with Excel's FREQUENCY function, as discussed below).

Note that sample data can be placed in these data sheets, and histograms can be created from the sample data, at design time. The data in the histogram sheets can then be updated at run time, and the histograms will change automatically.

24.5 Getting Started with the VBA

This application includes only a module—no user forms and no references. Once the module is inserted, the Project Explorer window will appear as in Figure 24.9.

Workbook_Open Code

The following code is placed in the ThisWorkbook code window. It activates the Explanation sheet and hides all other sheets.

```
Private Sub Workbook_Open()
    Dim ws As Worksheet
    Worksheets("Explanation").Activate
    Range("G4").Select
    For Each ws In ActiveWorkbook.Worksheets
        If ws.Name <> "Explanation" Then ws.Visible = False
    Next
End Sub
```

Figure 24.9 Project Explorer Window

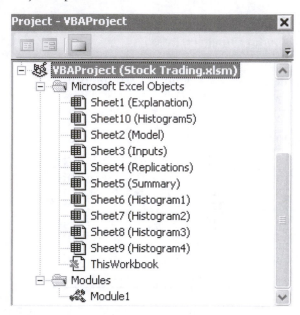

24.6 The VBA Code in the Module

The module contains a **Main** sub, which calls several subs to do most of the work. The Main sub also does some work itself. It gets the number of desired replications from an input box, it clears the contents from the Replications sheet from any previous run, and it places some (temporary) labels in row 21 of the Explanation sheet. These are used to show the progress of the simulation as it runs.[1]

Option Statement and Module-Level Variable

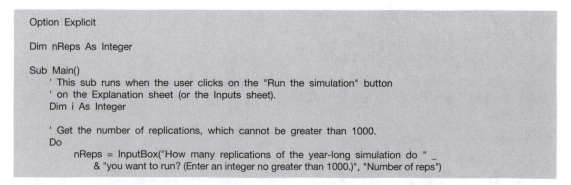

```
Option Explicit

Dim nReps As Integer

Sub Main()
    ' This sub runs when the user clicks on the "Run the simulation" button
    ' on the Explanation sheet (or the Inputs sheet).
    Dim i As Integer

    ' Get the number of replications, which cannot be greater than 1000.
    Do
        nReps = InputBox("How many replications of the year-long simulation do " _
            & "you want to run? (Enter an integer no greater than 1000.)", "Number of reps")
```

---

[1]I intended to put this "progress report" in Excel's status bar at the bottom of the screen, but Excel claims the status bar for its own message, as you will see when you run the simulation.

```
            If nReps > 1000 Then MsgBox "The number of reps should not exceed 1000.", _
                vbExclamation, "Too many reps"
    Loop Until nReps <= 1000

    ' Clear previous results.
    With Worksheets("Replications").Range("A3")
        Range(.Offset(1, 0), .Offset(0, 5).End(xlDown)).ClearContents
    End With

    ' Enter labels for a replication counter on the Explanation sheet.
    Worksheets("Explanation").Activate
    Range("D21").Value = "Simulating replication"
    Range("G21").Value = "of"
    Range("H21").Value = nReps

    ' Run the simulation and collect the stats.
    Call RunSimulation

    ' Delete counters and turn off screen updating.
    Range("D21:H21").ClearContents
    Application.ScreenUpdating = False

    Call CollectStats

    ' Delete the replication counter on the Explanation sheet.
    Range("D18:H18").ClearContents

    ' Update the histogram data.
    Call UpdateHistograms

    ' Show the results.
    With Worksheets("Summary")
        .Visible = True
        .Activate
        .Range("A2").Select
    End With

    ' Unhide the histogram chart sheets.
    For i = 1 To 5
        Worksheets("Histogram" & i).Visible = True
    Next

    Application.ScreenUpdating = True
End Sub
```

RunSimulation Code

The **RunSimulation** sub runs the simulation for the desired number of replications and stores the outputs in the Replications sheet for later summarization. The key to this sub is the **Calculate** method of the **Application** object (which is Excel). Each time this method is called, it forces a recalculation of the workbook, which generates new random numbers in the simulation model. It's that simple!

A note on Recalculation. Each workbook recalculation takes a fraction of a second, but these fractions add up. The recalculations take place each time the Calculate method is called from VBA code, but also each time any change is made to the workbook. This means, for example, that each of the Offset lines below causes a recalculation—each time through the loop! The effect is that the simulation runs rather slowly. Fortunately, it is possible to change Excel's recalculation mode from Automatic, the default mode, to Manual. (To do this click on the Office button, then Excel Options, and then the Formulas tab). In Manual mode, recalculations take place only when the Calculate method is called from VBA (or the F9 key is pressed). I originally ran the simulation in Automatic mode. However, when I converted to Manual mode, the run time decreased dramatically (by a factor of about 7 for a 500-replication run). Try it yourself.

```
Sub RunSimulation()
    ' This sub runs the replications of the simulation. The simulation
    ' model is already set up, so all this sub has to do is force a
    ' recalculation of the sheet and record the results.

    ' Loop over the replications.
    Dim i As Integer
    For i = 1 To nReps

        ' Show the current replication number on the Explanation sheet.
        Range("RepNumber").Value = i

        ' Force a recalculation.
        Application.Calculate

        ' Record outputs on the Replication sheet.
        With Worksheets("Replications").Range("A3")
            .Offset(i, 0).Value = i
            .Offset(i, 1).Value = Range("EndCash").Value
            .Offset(i, 2).Value = Range("EndStockVal").Value
            .Offset(i, 3).Value = Range("CumGainLoss").Value
            .Offset(i, 4).Value = Range("MinPrice").Value
            .Offset(i, 5).Value = Range("MaxPrice").Value
        End With
    Next
End Sub
```

CollectStats Code

The **CollectStats** sub uses a For loop to go through the simulation outputs, one at a time. For each, it "sets" the repRange object variable to the range of data in the Replications sheet to be summarized. It then uses Excel functions to calculate the summary measures and places them in the Summary sheet. For example, Application.WorksheetFunction.Average(repRange) uses Excel's Average function to calculate the average of the data in repRange.

```
Sub CollectStats()
    ' This sub summarizes the results of all replications of the simulation.
    Dim i As Integer
    Dim repRange As Range

    ' Loop over the output measures.
    For i = 1 To 5
```

```
' RepRange is the range on the Replications sheet to summarize.
With Worksheets("Replications").Range("A3")
    Set repRange = Range(.Offset(1, i), .Offset(nReps, i))
End With

' Use Excel's functions to calculate summary measures, and put
' them on the Summary sheet.
With Worksheets("Summary").Range("A3")
    .Offset(1, i).Value = Application.WorksheetFunction.Min(repRange)
    .Offset(2, i).Value = Application.WorksheetFunction.Max(repRange)
    .Offset(3, i).Value = Application.WorksheetFunction.Average(repRange)
    .Offset(4, i).Value = Application.WorksheetFunction.StDev(repRange)
    .Offset(5, i).Value = Application.WorksheetFunction.Median(repRange)
    .Offset(6, i).Value = Application.WorksheetFunction.Percentile(repRange, 0.05)
    .Offset(7, i).Value = Application.WorksheetFunction.Percentile(repRange, 0.95)
End With
Next
End Sub
```

UpdateHistograms Code

The **UpdateHistograms** sub also loops over the simulation outputs. For each, it updates the appropriate histogram sheet (see Figure 24.8), using the results from the simulation.

A note on Array Functions. Pay particular attention to the line.

```
Range(.Offset(1, 2), .Offset(10, 2)).FormulaArray = _
    "=Frequency(Replications!" & repRange.Address & "," & binRange.Address & ")"
```

Excel's Frequency function is called an **array function.** To enter it manually in a worksheet, you need to highlight the range where the frequencies will be placed, type the formula, and press Ctrl-Shift-Enter. To do this in VBA, you specify the range where it will be entered and then use the **FormulaArray** property. Two other points about this formula are worth noting. First, it is not enough to specify RepRange.Address in the first argument. Because this range is on a *different* worksheet from where the formula is entered, its worksheet name and an exclamation point must precede its address. Second, the bin range required in the second argument is the range of upper limits for the bins. These are the values in column A of the relevant histogram sheet.

```
Sub UpdateHistograms()
' This sub changes the settings for histograms of simulation data appropriately.

Dim i As Integer, j As Integer
Dim pct5 As Single, pct95 As Single, increment As Single
Dim repRange As Range, binRange As Range

' Loop over the output measures.
For i = 1 To 5

    ' The histograms each have 10 "bins". The lowest extends up to the
    ' 5th percentile, the last extends beyond the 95th percentile, and the
```

```
' remaining ones are equal-length beyond these extremes.
pct5 = Worksheets("Summary").Range("A9").Offset(0, i).Value
pct95 = Worksheets("Summary").Range("A10").Offset(0, i).Value
increment = (pct95 - pct5) / 8
' RepRange contains the data for the histogram.
With Worksheets("Replications").Range("A3")
    Set repRange = Range(.Offset(1, i), .Offset(nReps, i))
End With

' The histogram sheets contain the data for building the histograms.
' Column A has the bins, column B has labels for the horizontal axis, and
' column C has the frequencies (for the heights of the bars).
With Worksheets("Histogram" & i).Range("A3")
    .Offset(1, 0).Value = Round(pct5, 0)
    .Offset(1, 1).Value = "<=" & .Offset(1, 0)
    For j = 2 To 9
        .Offset(j, 0).Value = Round(pct5 + (j - 1) * increment, 0)
        .Offset(j, 1).Value = Round(.Offset(j - 1, 0), 0) _
            & "-" & Round(.Offset(j, 0).Value, 0)
    Next
    .Offset(10, 1).Value = ">" & Round(.Offset(9, 0).Value, 0)
    Set binRange = Range(.Offset(1, 0), .Offset(9, 0))

    ' Excel's Frequency function is an array formula, so the appropriate property
    ' is the FormulaArray property.
    Range(.Offset(1, 2), .Offset(10, 2)).FormulaArray = _
        "=Frequency(Replications!" & repRange.Address & "," & binRange.Address & ")"
End With
Next
End Sub
```

ViewChangeInputs Code

The **ViewChangeInputs** sub unhides and activates the Inputs sheet, allowing the user to view the inputs or enter different inputs before running the simulation.

```
Sub ViewChangeInputs()
    ' This sub runs when the user clicks on the "View/change inputs" button
    ' on the Explanation sheet.

    ' Unhide and activate the Inputs sheet so that the user can view or change them.
    With Worksheets("Inputs")
        .Visible = True
        .Activate
    End With
End Sub
```

24.7 Summary

This application illustrates how to run a spreadsheet simulation model with VBA. You first develop a spreadsheet simulation model, including one or more cells with random functions, in a Model sheet. To replicate this model, you use a For loop, inside which you call the **Calculate** method of the **Application** object to force a recalculation with new random numbers. The rest is a simple matter of recording selected outputs on a Replications sheet and then summarizing them as desired at the end of the simulation. Because all of this can take a while, especially with many replications of a complex model, it is a good idea to set Excel's calculation mode to Manual, rather the Automatic, before running the simulation.

EXERCISES

1. Prove to yourself that the simulation runs much faster when Excel's calculation mode is set to Manual. Run the simulation in the current **Stock Trading.xlsm** file for about 250 replications. (This file has calculation mode set to Manual.) Then change the calculation mode to Automatic and run the simulation again. Keep track of the run time for each—you should see a noticeable difference.

2. Experiment with the same basic buy-low/sell-high trading strategy, but with different percentages in column J of the Inputs sheet. Can you find any strategies that consistently outperform others?

3. Repeat the previous exercise, but now change the basic type of strategy to buy high/sell low. That is, if the price goes up, you buy more shares, whereas if it goes down, you sell. What changes do you need to make to the simulation model? Do you need to make any changes to the VBA code? Do these strategies tend to do better or worse than those in the previous exercise?

4. Change the application so that there is no limit on the shares the investor can buy. For example, if his strategy tells him to buy 25% more shares but he doesn't have enough cash to do so, he *borrows* the cash he needs. Now his cash positions in columns H and J of the Model sheet can be negative, indicating that he owes money to the lender. Capture the maximum he ever owes during the year in an extra output cell, keep track of it, and summarize it, just like the other outputs, with your VBA code.

5. Change the application so that if the investor ever gets to a point where his cumulative gain for the year is above some threshold level, he sells his stock and does no more trading for the rest of the year. Your revised application should ask for the threshold with an input box. Also, it should add an extra output cell: the number of days it takes to reach the threshold (which is defined as 251 in case he never gets there). Keep track of this output and summarize it, just like the other outputs, with your VBA code.

25 A Capital-Budgeting Application

25.1 Introduction

This application illustrates how VBA can be used to compare an optimal procedure with a good but nonoptimal heuristic procedure. This is done for a capital-budgeting problem, where a company must decide which of several projects to undertake. Each project incurs an initial cost and provides a stream of future cash flows, summarized by a net present value (NPV). Each project is an all-or-nothing proposition—it cannot be undertaken part way. Other than that, the only constraint is that the sum of the initial costs of the projects undertaken cannot exceed a given budget. The objective is to find the subset of projects that maximizes the total NPV and stays within the budget.

One solution method is to solve the problem optimally with Excel's Solver, using binary changing cells to decide which projects to undertake. Another possibility is to use an intuitive heuristic procedure that operates as follows. It first ranks the projects in decreasing order of the ratio of NPV to initial cost ("bang for buck"). Then it goes through the list of projects in this order, adding each as long as there is enough money left in the budget. The application compares the total NPVs obtained by these two methods.

New Learning Objectives: VBA

- To illustrate how a simple heuristic can be implemented in VBA with looping and arrays.
- To illustrate how random inputs for a model can be generated by VBA as formulas in a worksheet and how they can then be "frozen" with the Copy and PasteSpecial methods of Range objects.

New Learning Objectives: Non-VBA

- To compare a simple but reasonable heuristic solution method with an optimal integer programming method.
- To show the effect of the Solver's Tolerance setting in an integer programming model.

25.2 Functionality of the Application

The application has the following functionality:

1. It first asks the user for the total number of projects, which can be any number up to 30. It then randomly generates the inputs for a model with this many projects—the initial costs, the NPVs, and the budget. It does this so that there is a large enough budget to undertake many, but not all, of the projects.
2. Given the inputs, a capital-budgeting model is developed in the (hidden) Model sheet, and it is solved as a 0–1 integer programming model with Solver. The heuristic procedure is also used to solve the same problem. The outputs from both procedures are shown in the Report sheet, including the heuristic's total NPV as a percentage of Solver's total NPV.
3. The program can be repeated as often as the user desires, using different random inputs on each run.
4. To show the effect of the Solver's Tolerance option (which is set to 0 in all of the Solver runs), a sheet named Interesting accompanies the file. It shows one problem where the optimal solution was *not* found by Solver when the Tolerance setting was at its default value of 5. (This sheet is not really part of the VBA application, but it illustrates an interesting aspect of Solver.)

25.3 Running the Application

The application is stored in the **Capital Budgeting.xlsm** file. Upon opening it, the user sees the Explanation sheet in Figure 25.1. When the button on this sheet is clicked, the dialog box in Figure 25.2 appears and asks the user for a number of projects up to 30. It then randomly generates the inputs for a capital-budgeting model with this many projects in the Model sheet, solves it optimally with Solver, performs the heuristic on this same problem, and reports the results in the Report sheet.

Typical Report sheets from two separate runs of the application appear in Figures 25.3 and 25.4. Each of these problems has 30 potential projects. The first is a case where the heuristic obtains the optimal solution. The second is a case where the heuristic's NPV is 97.04% as large as the optimal NPV. By running the application on many problems of varying sizes, it becomes apparent that the heuristic is very good, often finding the optimal solution and almost always coming within a few percentage points of the optimal solution.

The three buttons at the bottom of the Report sheet give the user three options. The user can solve another problem by clicking on the left button. Alternatively, the user can view the (hidden) Model sheet, shown below in Figure 25.5 (with several hidden columns), or the Interesting sheet (not shown here). Each of these sheets has a button that leads back to the Report sheet.

Figure 25.1 Explanation Sheet

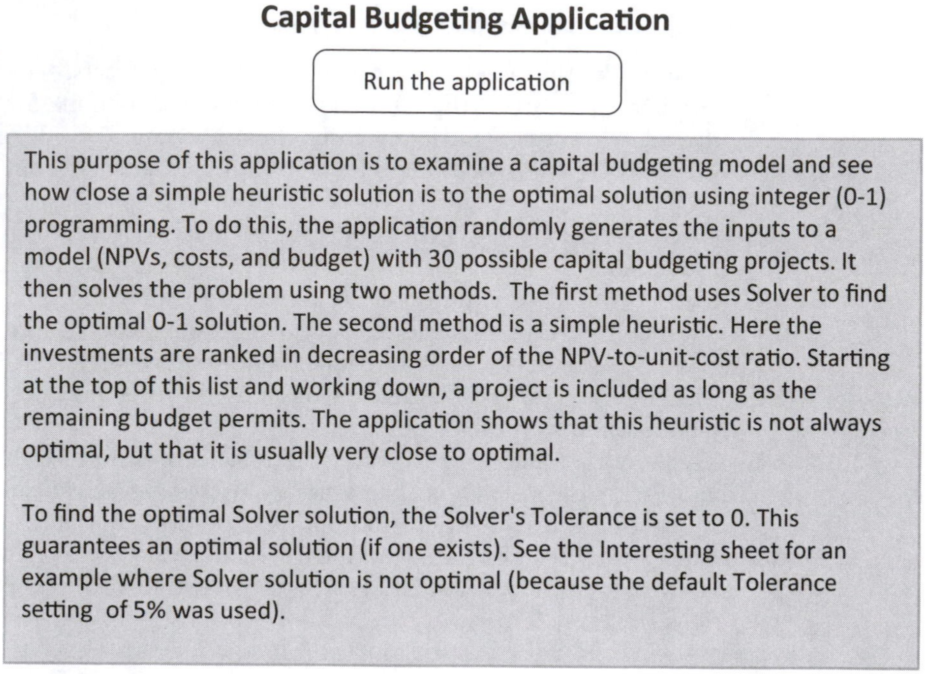

Capital Budgeting Application
Run the application
This purpose of this application is to examine a capital budgeting model and see how close a simple heuristic solution is to the optimal solution using integer (0-1) programming. To do this, the application randomly generates the inputs to a model (NPVs, costs, and budget) with 30 possible capital budgeting projects. It then solves the problem using two methods. The first method uses Solver to find the optimal 0-1 solution. The second method is a simple heuristic. Here the investments are ranked in decreasing order of the NPV-to-unit-cost ratio. Starting at the top of this list and working down, a project is included as long as the remaining budget permits. The application shows that this heuristic is not always optimal, but that it is usually very close to optimal.
To find the optimal Solver solution, the Solver's Tolerance is set to 0. This guarantees an optimal solution (if one exists). See the Interesting sheet for an example where Solver solution is not optimal (because the default Tolerance setting of 5% was used).

Figure 25.2 Number of Projects Input Box

Number of projects
Enter the number of potential capital budgeting projec
OK
Cancel
Number of projects (up to 30):
30

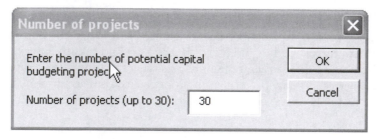

25.4 Setting Up the Excel Sheets

The **Capital Budgeting.xlsm** file has four worksheets: the Explanation sheet in Figure 25.1, the Report sheet in Figures 25.3 and 25.4, the Model sheet in Figure 25.5, and the Interesting sheet (not shown here, but just another version of the Model sheet). The Model and Report sheets cannot be set up completely at design time because they depend on the number of projects. This number determines the number of columns that are necessary in the model. (See rows 4–8 in Figure 25.5.) However, it is possible to develop templates for these sheets. The Model template is shown in Figure 25.6, where the range names that can be created in the Model sheet at design time are listed.

Figure 25.3 An Example Where the Heuristic Is Optimal

Optimal Investment Policy

Investments	11,12,13,14,15,16,17,18,19,20,21,22,23,24,25,26,27,28,29,30
Leftover cash	$200
Total NPV	$409,000

Investment Policy from Heuristic Policy

Investments	11,12,13,14,15,16,17,18,19,20,21,22,23,24,25,26,27,28,29,30
Leftover cash	$200
Total NPV	$409,000

Suboptimal NPV as a % of optimal NPV

100.00%

Run another problem with new inputs	View Model sheet	View Interesting sheet

Figure 25.4 An Example Where the Heuristic Is Not Optimal

Optimal Investment Policy

Investments	5,10,11,12,13,14,15,16,17,18,19,20,21,22,23,24,25,26,27,28,29,30
Leftover cash	$100
Total NPV	$523,900

Investment Policy from Heuristic Policy

Investments	9,10,11,12,13,14,15,16,17,18,19,20,21,22,23,24,25,26,27,28,29,30
Leftover cash	$5,800
Total NPV	$508,400

Suboptimal NPV as a % of optimal NPV

97.04%

Run another problem with new inputs	View Model sheet	View Interesting sheet

Figure 25.5 Model Sheet

	A	B	C	D	E	F	AD	AE
1	Capital Budgeting Model							
2								
3	Model							
4	Investment	1	2	3	4	5	29	30
5	Investment level	0	0	0	0	0	1	1
6	NPV	20800	14700	$41,100	$17,600	26900	13000	39600
7	Investment cost	7900	5400	$14,500	$6,200	9000	1500	4100
8	Bang-for-buck	$2.63	$2.72	$2.83	$2.84	$2.99	$8.67	$9.66
9								
10	Budget constraint	Spent		Available				
11		$82,500	<=	$82,700				
12								
13	Total NPV	$409,000						
14								
15	Note that the Solver Tolerance has been set to 0.							
16								
17			Return to the Report sheet					
18								

Figure 25.6 Model Sheet Template

	A	B	C	D	E	F	G
1	Capital Budgeting Model				Range names at design time:		
2					Budget	=Model!$D$11	
3	Model				TotCost	=Model!$B$11	
4	Investment				TotNPV	=Model!$B$13	
5	Investment level						
6	NPV						
7	Investment cost						
8	Bang-for-buck						
9							
10	Budget constraint	Spent		Available			
11			<=				
12							
13	Total NPV						
14							
15	Note that the Solver Tolerance has been set to 0.						
16							
17			Return to the Report sheet				
18							

Figure 25.7 Report Sheet Template

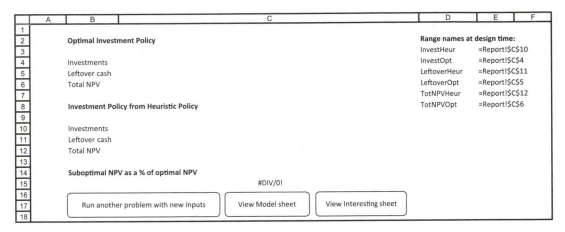

The Report sheet template is shown in Figure 25.7, again with the range names used. Note that cell C15 contains the formula **=TotNPVHeur/TotNPVOpt**. Its current value is undefined (0 divided by 0) because both total NPVs are currently 0, but it reports correctly when the application runs.

VBA is then used to fill in these templates at run time. (Again, the Interesting sheet is not really an integral part of the application; it is appended only to illustrate the effect of Solver's Tolerance option. Therefore, it was created at design time and never changes.)

25.5 Getting Started with the VBA

This application requires a user form named frmProjects, a module, and a reference to Solver.[1] Once these items are added, the Project Explorer window appears as in Figure 25.8.

Workbook_Open Code

To guarantee that the Explanation sheet appears when the file is opened, the following code is placed in the ThisWorkbook code window. It uses a For Each loop to hide all sheets except the Explanation sheet.

```
Private Sub Workbook_Open()
    Dim sht As Worksheet
    Worksheets("Explanation").Activate
    Range("F4").Select
    For Each sht In ActiveWorkbook.Worksheets
        If sht.Name <> "Explanation" Then sht.Visible = False
    Next
    frmSolver.Show
End Sub
```

[1]It also contains the usual frmSolver that displays a message about possible Solver problems when the workbook is opened.

Figure 25.8 Project Explorer Window

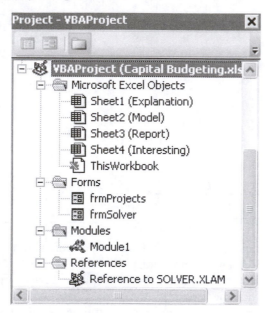

25.6   The User Form and Its Event Handlers

The user form, shown in Figure 25.9, contains the usual OK and Cancel buttons, an explanation label, and a text box named txtNProjects and an accompanying label. The event handlers, listed below, are completely straightforward. The whole purpose is to capture the number of projects in the public variable nProjects, a number that should be no larger than 30.

Figure 25.9 frmProjects Design

Event Handlers for frmProjects

```
Private Sub btnCancel_Click()
    Unload Me
    End
End Sub

Private Sub btnOK_Click()
    ' Make sure the box is not empty and is numeric.
    If txtNProjects.Text = "" Or Not IsNumeric(txtNProjects.Text) Then
        MsgBox "Enter a positive number of projects.", _
            vbInformation, "Invalid entry"
        txtNProjects.SetFocus
        Exit Sub
    End If
    nProjects = txtNProjects.Text

    ' Check that the number of projects is from 1 to 30, the most
    ' allowed in this application.
    If nProjects < 1 Or nProjects > 30 Then
        MsgBox "Enter a number from 1 to 30.", _
            vbInformation, "Invalid entry"
        txtNProjects.SetFocus
        Exit Sub
    End If

    ' Hide the dialog box.
    Unload Me
End Sub

Private Sub UserForm_Initialize()
    txtNProjects.Text = ""
End Sub
```

25.7   The VBA Code in the Module

The main work is performed by the code in the module. When the user clicks on the button on the Explanation sheet (or the left button on the Report sheet), the **MainCapitalBudgeting** sub runs. It "shows" frmProjects and then calls other subs that perform the individual tasks.

Option Statements and Public Variables

```
Option Explicit
Option Base 1

' Definitions of public variables:
'    nProjects - number of potential projects (<=30)
'    zeroOne - binary array, indicates which projects are chosen by the heuristic
'    leftoverHeur - amount of budget left over using heuristic
'    totalNPVHeur - total NPV using heuristic
'    leftoverOpt - amount of budget left over from the optimal solution
'    totalNPVOpt - total NPV from the optimal solution
```

```
Public nProjects As Integer
Public zeroOne(30) As Integer
Public leftoverHeur As Single, totalNPVHeur As Single
Public leftover0pt As Single, totalNPV0pt As Single
```

Main Code

```
Sub MainCapitalBudgeting()
    ' This macro runs when the user clicks on the button on the Explanation sheet.
    Application.ScreenUpdating = False

    ' Get the number of potential projects.
    frmProjects.Show
    ' Calculate random inputs for the model (NPVs, costs, and budget).
    Call GetInputs
    ' Sort projects on "bang for buck".
    Call SortProjects
    ' Calculate the optimal investments.
    Call RunSolver
    ' Calculate the investments based on the heuristic.
    Call Heuristic
    ' Report the results.
    Call CreateReport
End Sub
```

GetInputs Code

The **GetInputs** sub uses the combination of Excel's **RAND** and **NORMINV** functions to generate normally distributed values for the budget and for the initial costs and NPVs of the projects. The details are described in the comments below. Actually, this sub enters *formulas* for these random values, and it then "freezes" them with the Copy and PasteSpecial/Values method. (There is no particular reason for using the *normal* distribution here. I simply want to generate "representative" problems randomly, and the normal distribution works as well as any other distribution.) Finally, an initial solution of all 1's is used, so that all projects are initially undertaken. Actually, any other initial solution could be used, and the one used here almost certainly overspends the budget.

```
Sub GetInputs()
    ' This sub randomly generates inputs for a new version of the capital
    ' budgeting model.
    Dim i As Integer

    ' Unhide and activate the Model sheet.
    With Worksheets("Model")
        .Visible = True
        .Activate
    End With

    With Range("A4")
        ' Clear previous data and name some ranges.
        Range(.Offset(0, 1), .Offset(4, 1).End(xlToRight)).ClearContents
        For i = 1 To nProjects
            .Offset(0, i).Value = i
```

```
            Next
            Range(.Offset(1, 1), .Offset(1, nProjects)).Name = "InvLevel"
            Range(.Offset(2, 1), .Offset(2, nProjects)).Name = "NPV"
            Range(.Offset(3, 1), .Offset(3, nProjects)).Name = "InvCost"

            ' Calculate the ratio of NPV to investment cost (bang for buck).
            Range(.Offset(4, 1), .Offset(4, nProjects)).FormulaR1C1 = "=R[-2]C/R[-1]C"
    End With

    ' Randomly generate NPVs, costs, and budget. Use the Round function,
    ' with second argument -2, to round these to the nearest $100. The
    ' parameters used here have been chosen to generate "interesting" models.

    ' Each NPV is normal, mean $25000, standard deviation $6000.
    Range("NPV").Formula = "=Round(NORMINV(RAND(),25000,6000),-2)"

    ' Each cost is between 10% and 40% of corresponding NPV.
    Range("InvCost").Formula = "=Round(NPV*(.1+.3*RAND()),-2)"

    ' The budget is between 30% and 90% of the total cost of all investments.
    Range("Budget").Formula = "=Round(SUM(InvCost)*(.3+.6*RAND()),-2)"

    ' "Freeze" the random numbers.
    With Union(Range("NPV"), Range("InvCost"))
        .Copy
        .PasteSpecial Paste:=xlValues
    End With
    With Range("Budget")
        .Copy
        .PasteSpecial Paste:=xlValues
    End With

    ' Get rid of the dotted line around the copy range.
    Application.CutCopyMode = False

    ' Use all 1's as an initial solution.
    Range("InvLevel").Value = 1

    ' Calculate the total investment cost and the total NPV.
    Range("TotCost").Formula = "=Sumproduct(InvCost,InvLevel)"
    Range("TotNPV").Formula = "=Sumproduct(NPV,InvLevel)"
End Sub
```

SortProjects Code

The **SortProjects** sub sorts the projects according to bang-for-buck, putting those with the largest ratios of NPV to investment cost to the right. Note that the **Orientation** argument of the **Sort** method must be used because the values are in a row, not a column.

```
Sub SortProjects()
    ' This sub sorts the projects in increasing order of "bang-for-buck".
    With Range("A4")
        Range(.Offset(1, 1), .Offset(4, nProjects)).Sort _
            Key1:=Range("B8"), Order1:=xlAscending, _
            Orientation:=xlLeftToRight, Header:=xlNo
    End With
End Sub
```

RunSolver Code

The **RunSolver** sets up and then runs Solver. It must be reset and then set up each time through, just in case the size of the problem (the number of projects) has changed. Note how the Tolerance is set to 0 in the SolverOptions statement. This guarantees that Solver will continue to search until it has found the optimal solution. (The nonoptimal solution on the Interesting sheet occurred because the Tolerance was set at its default value of 5.)

```vba
Sub RunSolver()
    ' Set up and run the Solver to find the optimal integer solution.
    SolverReset
    SolverOK SetCell:=Range("TotNPV"), MaxMinVal:=1, ByChange:=Range("InvLevel")
    SolverOptions IntTolerance:=0, AssumeLinear:=True
    SolverAdd CellRef:=Range("TotCost"), Relation:=1, FormulaText:="Budget"
    SolverAdd CellRef:=Range("InvLevel"), Relation:=5
    SolverSolve UserFinish:=True

    ' Capture the optimal total NPV and the amount of the budget left over.
    totalNPVOpt = Range("TotNPV").Value
    leftoverOpt = Range("Budget").Value - Range("TotCost").Value
End Sub
```

Heuristic Code

The **Heuristic** sub implements the heuristic. It is a perfect example of looping and arrays. The first For loop sets all zeroOne array elements to 0. Then a single pass through the second For loop checks whether there is enough money left in the budget for each project, where the projects are examined in decreasing order of bang-for-buck. If enough money is left, the project's zeroOne value is set to 1, its investment cost is subtracted from the remaining budget, and its NPV is added to the total NPV for the heuristic.

```vba
Sub Heuristic()
    ' This sub finds the heuristic solution by choosing the investments in decreasing
    ' order of bang-for-buck.
    Dim i As Integer

    ' Initialize values so that no projects are undertaken and the whole budget is available.
    For i = 1 To nProjects
        zeroOne(i) = 0
    Next
    totalNPVHeur = 0
    leftoverHeur = Range("Budget").Value

    ' Loop through all projects in decreasing order of "bang-for-buck."
    ' Include the project only if its cost is no more than the remaining budget.
    For i = nProjects To 1 Step -1
        If Range("InvCost").Cells(i).Value <= leftoverHeur Then
            leftoverHeur = leftoverHeur - Range("InvCost").Cells(i).Value
            totalNPVHeur = totalNPVHeur + Range("NPV").Cells(i).Value
            zeroOne(i) = 1
        End If
    Next
End Sub
```

CreateReport Code

The **CreateReport** sub places the results from Solver and the heuristic in the Report sheet. The main difficulty in doing this is creating *strings* that list the projects undertaken in each solution. (See the lists of investments in Figure 25.3, for example.) To see how this works, suppose the optimal solution undertakes projects 4, 6, 9, and 10. The string "4,6,9,10" is then created and placed in the InvestOpt cell of the Report sheet. This string and the similar string for the heuristic solution are "built" one step at a time by using string concatenation and the For loop in the middle of the sub. Note that the number of projects undertaken must be known so that the For loop knows when to stop adding a comma to the string. (There is no comma after 10 in the above string.) Therefore, the first For loop in the sub counts the number of projects undertaken by each solution. Then this count variable can be used in an If construction in the second For loop to indicate when to stop adding the comma.

```
Sub CreateReport()
    ' This sub shows the results, so that a comparison of the optimal and
    ' heuristic solutions can be made.
    Dim i As Integer
    Dim investOpt As String, investHeur As String
    Dim nOpt As Integer, nHeur As Integer
    Dim counter1 As Integer, counter2 As Integer

    ' Hide the Model sheet, then unhide and activate the Report sheet.
    Worksheets("Model").Visible = False
    With Worksheets("Report")
        .Visible = True
        .Activate
    End With
    Range("A1").Select

    ' Find the number of investments under the optimal plan (nOpt) and
    ' under the suboptimal plan (nHeur).
    nOpt = 0
    nHeur = 0
    For i = 1 To nProjects
        If Range("InvLevel").Cells(i).Value = 1 Then
            nOpt = nOpt + 1
        End If
        If zeroOne(i) = 1 Then
            nHeur = nHeur + 1
        End If
    Next

    ' Create strings investOpt and investHeur that list the investments undertaken
    ' by the two plans. First, initialize strings and counters.
    investOpt = ""
    investHeur = ""
    counter1 = 0
    counter2 = 0
```

```
' Loop through all projects.
For i = 1 To nProjects

    ' Check whether this project is in the optimal solution.
    If Range("InvLevel").Cells(i).Value = 1 Then
        counter1 = counter1 + 1
        ' Add a comma to the string only if this investment is not the last one.
        If counter1 < nOpt Then
            investOpt = investOpt & i & ","
        Else
            investOpt = investOpt & i
        End If
    End If

    ' Check whether this project is selected by the heuristic.
    If zeroOne(i) = 1 Then
        counter2 = counter2 + 1
        ' Add a comma to the string only if this investment is not the last one.
        If counter2 < nHeur Then
            investHeur = investHeur & i & ","
        Else
            investHeur = investHeur & i
        End If
    End If
Next

' Enter the results in the Report sheet, where the range names were created
' in this sheet at design time.
Range("InvestOpt").Value = investOpt
Range("InvestHeur").Value = investHeur
Range("LeftoverOpt").Value = leftoverOpt
Range("totalNPVOpt").Value = totalNPVOpt
Range("LeftoverHeur").Value = leftoverHeur
Range("totalNPVHeur").Value = totalNPVHeur
End Sub
```

Navigation Code

The following subs allow for easy navigation through the application. They are attached to the corresponding buttons on the Model, Interesting, and Report sheets.

```
Sub ViewReport()
    Worksheets("Report").Activate
    Range("A1").Select
End Sub

Sub ViewModel()
    With Worksheets("Model")
        .Visible = True
        .Activate
    End With
    Range("A2").Select
End Sub
```

```
Sub ViewInteresting()
    With Worksheets("Interesting")
        .Visible = True
        .Activate
    End With
    Range("A2").Select
End Sub
```

25.8 Summary

This application has illustrated how VBA can be used to generate representative problems of a certain type and then compare the optimal Solver solutions for these problems to heuristic solutions. The context here is capital budgeting, but the same approach could be used to evaluate heuristics to other types of management science problems.

EXERCISES

1. The RunSolver sub sets the Tolerance to 0 to ensure that it gets the optimal solution. Change the application so that instead of running the heuristic, Solver is run once with the Tolerance at 0, and it is run again with the Tolerance argument omitted in the SolverOptions statement (which will set the Tolerance to its default value). Also, change labels appropriately on the Report sheet. Now the report should compare a solution known to be optimal with one that might not be optimal. Then run the application a few times. Do the two solutions ever differ? (The solution on the Interesting sheet shows that they *can* differ, but it might not happen very often.)

2. The GetInputs sub generates random inputs with statements such as the following:

```
Range("NPV").Formula = "=ROUND(NORMINV(RAND(),25000,6000),-2)"
```

This formula fills the NPV range in the Model sheet with the specified formula. Later, it "freezes" these formulas by copying and then pasting special with the values option. Another possible approach is the following. Inside a For loop that goes over all investments, replace the above line by

```
randNPV = Round(Application.WorksheetFunction.NormInv(Rnd, 25000, 6000), -2)
```

This line also generates a random NPV and stores it in the variable randNPV. It does so with the VBA random number generator **Rnd**, not with Excel's RAND function, and it borrows Excel's NORMINV function to get a normally distributed random NPV. It should then place the randNPV value in the appropriate cell of the Model sheet. However, no copying and pasting are necessary now. Change the GetInputs sub to implement this approach for all random inputs. If you want *different* random numbers each time you run the application, you should also insert a **Randomize** line near the top of the MainCapitalBudgeting sub. (This approach is not necessarily better or worse than the formula approach; it is simply an alternative.)

3. Change the heuristic so that it works as follows. First, it orders the investments in increasing order of their investment costs. Then it proceeds as before, scanning from left to right and choosing each investment as long as there is enough budget left to afford it. How does this heuristic compare with the optimal solution? What would you expect?

4. Repeat the previous problem, but now use the heuristic that orders the investments in decreasing order of their NPVs.

5. (More difficult) Change the model so that some investments incur an investment cost right away, some incur an investment cost a year from now, and some incur an investment cost right away *and* a year from now. There are now two budget amounts: the amount available right away and another amount that is allocated for a year from now. A decision on each investment must be made right away—to invest (and gain an NPV) or not to invest. The amount that can be spent a year from now includes the budget set aside for a year from now, plus any of the current budget not used. The following heuristic is proposed. It sorts the investments in decreasing order of the ratio of NPV to the *total* investment cost. It then goes through the investments from left to right and chooses each investment as long as there is enough money in each year's budget to afford it. (It never considers the possibility of having leftover money from the year 1 budget in year 2.) Develop an application similar to the one in the chapter that implements this new model and compares the heuristic to the optimal Solver solution for randomly generated problems. (If you like, you can use the method described in Exercise 2 to generate the random inputs.)

A Regression Application

26.1 Introduction

This application estimates the relationship between any two variables, such as demand and price. It begins with data on these two variables. The Data sheet in the **Regression.xlsm** file contains sample data that can be used, or the user can supply new data. The application then copies the data to a Report sheet, creates four scatterplots on separate chart sheets, each with a different type of trend line (linear, power, exponential, and logarithmic) superimposed, and calculates the parameters and the mean absolute percentage error (MAPE) for the best-fitting trend line of each type.

New Learning Objectives: VBA

- To illustrate how RefEdit controls can be used in user forms to specify ranges from a worksheet.
- To show how formulas can be entered in cells with the FormulaR1C1 property, using a combination of absolute and relative addresses.

New Learning Objectives: Non-VBA

- To illustrate how the relationship between two variables can be estimated by well-known and widely accepted trend curves, and how the fits from these curves can be compared with a measure such as MAPE.

26.2 Functionality of the Application

This application provides the following functionality.

1. The user first selects data for two variables from the Data sheet. (The sample price/demand data can be used, or the user can enter new data. In the latter case, the new data should be entered in the Data sheet *before* running the application.) The data for the two variables should come in pairs (a price and a demand for each of several time periods, for example). One variable is designated as the horizontal axis variable; the other is designated as the vertical axis variable.

2. Four chart sheets named Linear, Power, Exponential, and Logarithmic are created. Each chart is a scatterplot of the two variables, with the appropriate trend line (linear, power, exponential, or logarithmic) superimposed.

3. All calculations are performed in a new worksheet named Report. This sheet contains a copy of the data, logarithms of the data (required for all but the linear case), formulas for the parameters of the best-fitting trend line of each type, columns of absolute percentage errors in predicting one variable from the other for each trend line, and the MAPE for each trend line.

26.3 Running the Application

The application is in the file **Regression.xlsm**. When this file is opened, the explanation in Figure 26.1 appears. When the user clicks on the button, the Data sheet and the dialog box in Figure 26.2 appear. The user must supply the ranges for the two variables, which should contain variable names at the top. Note that the data set can contain more than two variables, but this application works with only two of them. The only requirement is that the two ranges identified in the dialog box must have equal numbers of cells, because the data (price and demand, for example) must come in pairs.

Once the ranges are specified, the application performs calculations on the Report sheet and creates charts on four separate chart sheets named Linear, Power, Exponential, and Logarithmic. The completed Report sheet appears in Figure 26.3. It shows the absolute percentage errors for the four fits in columns H, I, J, and K, and it shows summary measures of the fits in the range C5:F7. (The comments in cells C4 through F4 remind the user what form each trend line takes.) Each chart sheet displays a scatterplot of the data, a superimposed trend line, and the equation of that trend line. For example, Figure 26.4 shows the scatterplot and the power trend line (really a trend *curve*) on the Power chart sheet.

Figure 26.1 Explanation Sheet

Estimating a relationship between two variables

Run the application

This application takes a set of data on two variables, such as prices and corresponding demands, and then estimates the best-fitting linear, power, exponential, and logarithmic curves for these data. It shows each fit superimposed on a scatterplot of the data and calculates the corresponding mean absolute percentage error (MAPE).

Sample demand-price data appear on the Data sheet, but any data on any two variables can be substituted for these sample data before running the application. The only restriction is that, because logarithmic transformations are required, none of the data should be negative or 0.

Figure 26.2 Variable Ranges Dialog Box

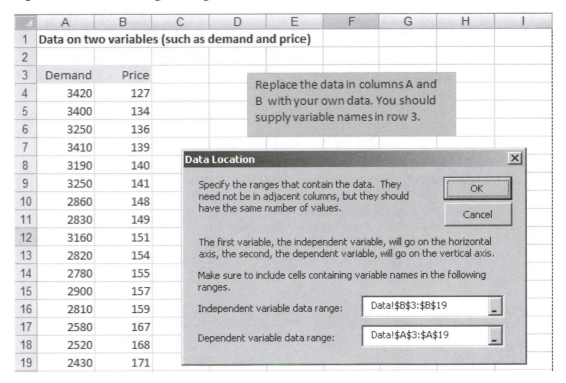

Figure 26.3 Report Sheet Results

	B	C	D	E	F	G	H	I	J	K
1	Calculations and report									
2							The values to the left and below show the parameters			
3	Parameters of best-fitting equations						of the best fits and the corresponding absolute			
4		Linear	Power	Exponential	Logarithmic		percentage errors and MAPEs. See the Linear, Power,			
5	a	6532.4110	1195683.7341	9925.9225	20645.2131		Exponential, and Logarithmic sheets for the			
6	b	-23.7515	-1.1990	-0.0081	-3530.0722		corresponding charts.			
7	MAPE	2.79%	2.97%	2.87%	2.86%					
8							Absolute percentage errors			
9	Price	Demand	Log(Price)	Log(Demand)			Linear	Power	Exponential	Logarithmic
10	127	3420	4.8442	8.1374			2.81%	4.97%	3.98%	3.65%
11	134	3400	4.8978	8.1315			1.48%	0.99%	1.16%	1.31%
12	136	3250	4.9127	8.0864			1.61%	1.75%	1.74%	1.64%
13	139	3410	4.9345	8.1345			5.25%	5.53%	5.36%	5.39%
14	140	3190	4.9416	8.0678			0.54%	0.12%	0.36%	0.34%
15	141	3250	4.9488	8.0864			2.05%	2.56%	2.29%	2.29%
16	148	2860	4.9972	7.9586			5.50%	4.48%	4.93%	5.06%
17	149	2830	5.0039	7.9480			5.78%	4.74%	5.18%	5.33%
18	151	3160	5.0173	8.0583			6.77%	7.69%	7.31%	7.16%
19	154	2820	5.0370	7.9445			1.94%	1.03%	1.38%	1.57%
20	155	2780	5.0434	7.9302			2.55%	1.69%	2.01%	2.21%
21	157	2900	5.0562	7.9725			3.33%	4.00%	3.78%	3.58%
22	159	2810	5.0689	7.9409			1.92%	2.42%	2.29%	2.08%
23	167	2580	5.1180	7.8555			0.55%	0.20%	0.25%	0.06%
24	168	2520	5.1240	7.8320			0.88%	1.86%	1.31%	1.48%
25	171	2430	5.1417	7.7956			1.68%	3.41%	2.54%	2.67%

Figure 26.4 Scatterplot and Power Trend Line

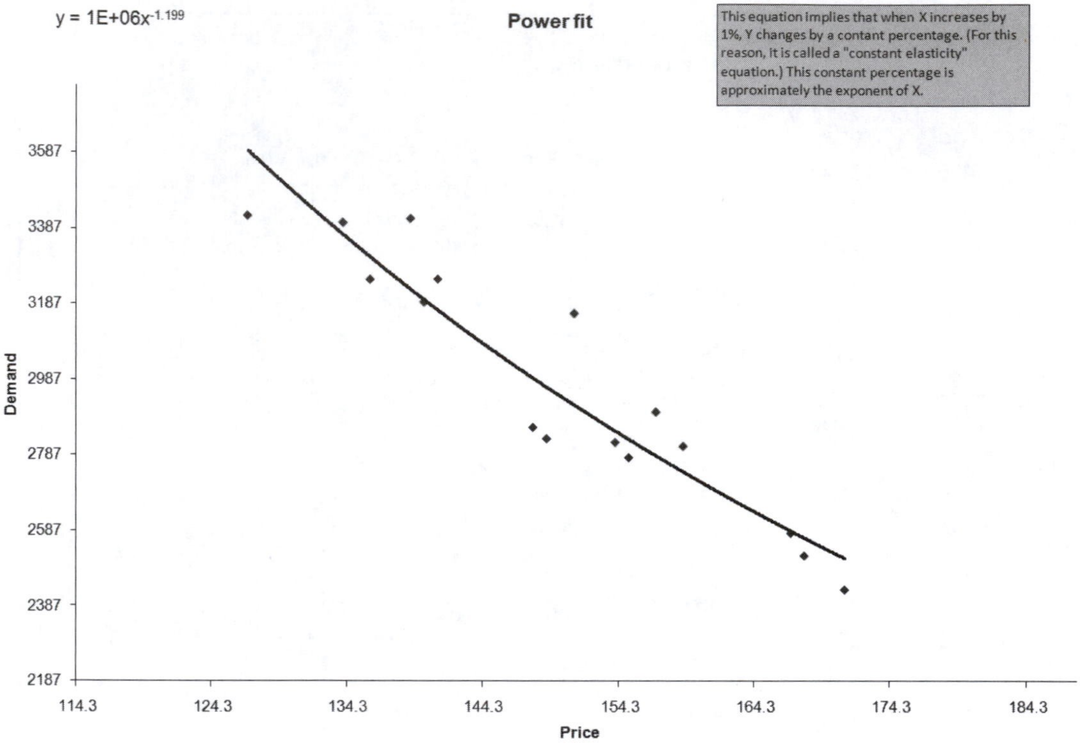

y = 1E+06x$^{-1.199}$

Power fit

> This equation implies that when X increases by 1%, Y changes by a contant percentage. (For this reason, it is called a "constant elasticity" equation.) This constant percentage is approximately the exponent of X.

26.4 Setting Up the Excel Sheets

This **Regression.xlsm** file contains three worksheets and four chart sheets. The worksheets are the Explanation sheet in Figure 26.1, the Data sheet in Figure 26.2, and the Report sheet in Figure 26.3. The Data sheet must contain data for at least two variables. A template in the Report sheet can be created at design time with *any* sample data, as indicated in Figure 26.5. The application always places the data in columns B and C of this sheet, starting in row 10 (with labels in row 9). Then four chart sheets, named Linear, Power, Exponential, and Logarithmic, can be created at design time with Excel's chart tools, using the sample data in columns B and C of the Report sheet template as the source data for XY charts. Also, the trend lines and the associated equations for them can be placed on the charts by using Excel's trendline option (found under the Chart Tools Layout ribbon in Excel 2007). The important point is that these charts can be created, along with any desired formatting, at design time. The only changes required at run time are to their source data, titles, and axis settings.

26.5 Getting Started with the VBA

This application requires a single user form named frmData and a module. Once they are inserted, the Project Explorer window will appear as in Figure 26.6.

Figure 26.5 Template for Report Sheet

	A	B	C	D	E	F	G	H	I	J	K
1		Calculations and report									
2											
3		Parameters of best-fitting equations									
4			*Linear*	*Power*	*Exponential*	*Logarithmic*					
5		a									
6		b									
7		MAPE									
8								Absolute percentage errors			
9		Price	Demand						Linear	Power	Exponential	Logarithmic
10		127	3420									
11		134	3400									
12		136	3250									
13		139	3410									
14		140	3190									
15		141	3250									
16		148	2860									
17		149	2830									
18		151	3160									
19		154	2820									
20		155	2780									
21		157	2900									
22		159	2810									
23		167	2580									
24		168	2520									
25		171	2430									

The values to the left and below show the parameters of the best fits and the corresponding absolute percentage errors and MAPEs. See the Linear, Power, Exponential, and Logarithmic sheets for the corresponding charts.

Figure 26.6 Project Explorer Window

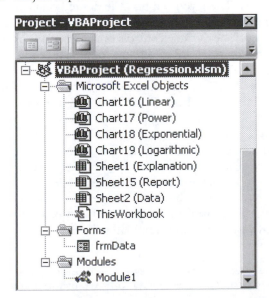

Workbook_Open Code

To guarantee that the Explanation sheet appears when the file is opened, the following code is entered in the ThisWorkbook code window. This code also hides most of the other sheets.

```
Private Sub Workbook_Open()
    Worksheets("Explanation").Activate
    Range("F4").Select
    Worksheets("Report").Visible = False
    Charts("Linear").Visible = False
    Charts("Power").Visible = False
    Charts("Exponential").Visible = False
    Charts("Logarithmic").Visible = False
End Sub
```

26.6   The User Form and Its Event Handlers

The design of frmData appears in Figure 26.7 It includes the usual OK and Cancel buttons, several labels, and two controls named rfeRange1 and rfeRange2 for the data ranges. These latter two boxes are called **RefEdit** controls. They are controls perfectly suited for allowing a user to select ranges. The RefEdit control is the lower left-hand control in the Control Toolbox in Figure 26.8.

A Note about RefEdit Controls. RefEdit controls act somewhat differently from the other controls on the Control Toolbox in Figure 26.8. Specifically, if you use the Object Browser to look for online help on the RefEdit control under the MSForms library, you won't find it. The RefEdit control has its *own* library, which you can open by using the **Tools → References** menu item in the VBE and checking the RefEdit Control box. There you can find the desired online help under the RefEdit library. This brings up another curious point. Do you have to set a reference to the RefEdit Control to *use* one of these controls on a user form? Fortunately, the answer is "no." As soon as you place a RefEdit control on a user form, the RefEdit Control box is automatically checked in the list of references![1]

The event handlers for frmData are listed below. The **UserForm_Initialize** sub clears the two range boxes. The **btnOK_Click** sub captures the user's inputs and checks for errors. (Other than checking for blank boxes, the only other error check is to ensure that the two specified ranges have the same number of cells.) Note that the specified ranges are captured in the range variables range1 and range2. Then the variable names are captured in the public variables var1Name and var2Name, and the data ranges are captured in the public variables var1Range and var2Range. (The latter two must be captured with the keyword Set because they are *object* variables.) The **btnCancel_Click** sub unloads the dialog box, activates the Explanation worksheet, and terminates the program.

---

[1]If you do a Web search for the RefEdit control, you'll see that they have some problems. In fact, some programmers offer their own replacements for this control. However, they have worked well enough for me.

Figure 26.7 frmData Design

Data Location

Specify the ranges that contain the data. They need not be in adjacent columns, but they should have the same number of values.

OK

Cancel

The first variable, the independent variable, will go on the horizontal axis, the second, the dependent variable, will go on the vertical axis.

Make sure to include cells containing variable names in the following ranges.

Independent variable data range:

Dependent variable data range:

Figure 26.8 Control Toolbox

Note that the **Value** (or **Text**) property of a **RefEdit** control returns the *address* of the designated range as a string. Then a line such as

```
Set range1 = Range(rfeRange1.Value)
```

can be used to define the Range object variable range1.

Event Handlers for frmData

```
Private Sub btnCancel_Click()
    ' Activate the Explanation sheet, unload the dialog box, and quit.
    Worksheets("Explanation").Activate
    Range("F4").Select
    Unload Me
    End
End Sub
```

```
Private Sub btnOK_Click()
    Dim ctl As Control
    Dim nCells1 As Integer, nCells2 As Integer
    Dim range1 As Range, range2 As Range
    ' Check whether any box is empty.

    For Each ctl In Me.Controls
        If TypeName(ctl) = "RefEdit" Then
            If ctl.Value = "" Then
                MsgBox "Enter a range in each box.", _
                    vbInformation, "Invalid entry"
                ctl.SetFocus
                Exit Sub
            End If
        End If
    Next

    ' Capture names and ranges.
    Set range1 = Range(rfeRange1.Value)
    Set range2 = Range(rfeRange2.Value)
    nCells1 = range1.Rows.Count
    nCells2 = range2.Rows.Count

    ' Check that both ranges are of the same length.
    If nCells1 <> nCells2 Then
        MsgBox "Make sure the two ranges have equal numbers " _
            & "of cells", vbExclamation, "Improper selections"
        rfeRange1.SetFocus
        Exit Sub
    End If

    var1Name = range1.Cells(1).Value
    var2Name = range2.Cells(1).Value
    Set var1Range = Range(range1.Cells(2), range1.Cells(nCells1))
    Set var2Range = Range(range2.Cells(2), range2.Cells(nCells2))
    nObs = nCells1 - 1

    ' Unload the dialog box only if the entries are valid.
    Unload Me
End Sub

Private Sub UserForm_Initialize()
    rfeRange1.Text = ""
    rfeRange2.Text = ""
End Sub
```

26.7 The VBA Code in the Module

Most of the work is performed by the VBA code in the module. This code is listed below. The **Main** sub is attached to the button on the Explanation sheet. In turn, it calls the four subs **GetData**, **TransferData**, **ModifyCharts**, and **DoCalculations**. The public variables are listed below. Just remember that index 1 is for the horizontal axis variable and index 2 is for the vertical axis variable. In regression terminology, variable 1 is the independent (or explanatory) variable, and variable 2 is the dependent variable.

Option Statement and Public Variables

```
Option Explicit

' Definitions of public variables
'    nObs - number of observations for each variable
'    var1Range - range of the data on the horizontal axis
'    var1LogRange - range of logs of data in var1Range
'    var1Min - smallest observation in var1Range
'    var1Max - largest observation in var1Range
'    var1Name - descriptive name of horizontal axis variable
'    var2Range, var2LogRange, var2Min, var2Max,
'         var2Name - similar for vertical axis variable
'    chartDataRange - range containing both variables for use in scatterplot

Public nObs As Integer
Public var1Range As Range, var1LogRange As Range
Public var1Min As Single, var1Max As Single, var1Name As String
Public var2Range As Range, var2LogRange As Range
Public var2Min As Single, var2Max As Single, var2Name As String
Public chartDataRange As Range
```

Main Code

```
Sub Main()
    ' This sub runs when the user clicks on the button on the Explanation sheet.

    ' Specify the data on the Data sheet to be used.
    Call GetData

    Application.ScreenUpdating = False

    ' Transfer the data to the Report sheet and perform the analysis.
    Call TransferData
    Call ModifyCharts
    Call DoCalculations

    Application.ScreenUpdating = True
End Sub
```

GetData Code

The GetData sub activates the Data sheet and "shows" frmData, so that the user can specify the price and demand ranges. If there is no Data sheet, an error message is displayed and the program terminates. Actually, this error check is not necessary, assuming that the user has not deleted or renamed the Data sheet that comes with the file, but I have included it here for illustration. Error checks such as this *are* often necessary.

```
Sub GetData()
    ' This sub gets the data on the two variables from the Data sheet.

    ' Make sure there is a Data sheet. If so, activate it.
    ' If not, display an error message and quit.
    On Error Resume Next
    Worksheets("Data").Activate
    If Err.Number <> 0 Then
        MsgBox "Make sure there is a Data sheet that contains the " _
            & "data you want to analyze.", vbExclamation, "Data sheet required"
        Worksheets("Explanation").Activate
        Range("F4").Select
        End
    End If

    ' Show the user input form.
    frmData.Show
End Sub
```

TransferData Code

The **TransferData** sub copies the selected data in the Data sheet to columns B and C of the Report sheet. When Excel creates a scatterplot (an XY chart), it automatically places the variable in the leftmost column on the horizontal axis. Therefore, the variable designated as the horizontal axis variable is copied to column B, and the variable designated as the vertical axis variable is copied to column C. Note that the var1Range and var2Range object variables are set to the data ranges in columns B and C. Then the chartDataRange variable is set to their union—both columns B and C—for later use as the source range of the scatterplots.

```
Sub TransferData()
    ' This sub transfers the data to the Report sheet, and sets up
    ' that sheet for further analysis.

    ' Unhide and activate the Report sheet.
    With Worksheets("Report")
        .Visible = True
        .Activate
    End With

    ' Clear any data from a previous run.
    Range("B9").CurrentRegion.ClearContents
    With Range("H9")
        Range(.Offset(1, 0), .End(xlDown).Offset(0, 3)).ClearContents
    End With

    ' Add and format some labels.
    Range("B9").Value = var1Name
    Range("C9").Value = var2Name

    ' Copy the Data from the Data sheet to the Report sheet, with the first
    ' variable selected in column B and the second variable in column C.
    var1Range.Copy Destination:=Range("B10")
    var2Range.Copy Destination:=Range("C10")
```

```
        ' Set the pasted ranges and the chart range to Range object variables.
        With Range("B9")
            Set var1Range = Range(.Offset(1, 0), .Offset(nObs, 0))
            Set var2Range = Range(.Offset(1, 1), .Offset(nObs, 1))
            Set chartDataRange = Union(var1Range, var2Range)
        End With
        ' Capture the min and max of the variables for charting purposes.
        var1Min = Application.Min(var1Range)
        var1Max = Application.Max(var1Range)
        var2Min = Application.Min(var2Range)
        var2Max = Application.Max(var2Range)
End Sub
```

ModifyCharts Code

The **ModifyCharts** sub modifies the properties of the charts that are affected by new data. (Recall that these charts are created at design time.) These properties include the source data, the titles, and the axes. For the latter, the application sets minimum and maximum values for the axes so that the data points fill up most of the chart. Specifically, it ensures that each axis extends from 10% below the smallest observation (on that axis) to 10% above the largest observation.

```
Sub ModifyCharts()
    ' This sub gets the chart sheets ready for the scatterplots of the
    ' data and the various trendlines.
    Dim cht As Chart

    ' Loop through all chart sheets.
    For Each cht In ActiveWorkbook.Charts

        ' Unhide and activate the chart.
        With cht
            .Visible = True
            .Activate

            ' Specify the source data for the chart.
            .SetSourceData Source:=chartDataRange, PlotBy:=xlColumns

            ' The xlCategory axis is the horizontal axis, and the xlValue axis is
            ' the vertical axis.
            With .Axes(xlCategory)
                .AxisTitle.Characters.Text = var1Name

                ' Set the min and max values on the horizontal axis. This is done
                ' so that the data will just about fill the chart.
                .MinimumScale = var1Min * 0.9
                .MaximumScale = var1Max * 1.1
            End With

            ' Set similar properties for the vertical axis.
            With .Axes(xlValue)
                .AxisTitle.Characters.Text = var2Name
                .MinimumScale = var2Min * 0.9
                .MaximumScale = var2Max * 1.1
            End With
```

```
                  ' Deselect the chart to remove the "handles" around it.
               .Deselect
           End With
       Next
   End Sub
```

DoCalculations Code

The **DoCalculations** sub enters formulas in the appropriate ranges of the Report sheet. It first creates logarithms of the data in columns D and E. Next, it uses formulas from regression to calculate the parameters of the best-fitting trend lines in the range C5:E6. It then calculates the absolute percentage errors in columns H, I, J, and K. Finally, it calculates the MAPE values in the range C7:F7.

A Note on the FormulaR1C1 Property. Pay particular attention to how the **FormulaR1C1** property of ranges is used several times to enter formulas with relative and absolute addresses. For example, the *relative* reference RC[-2] refers to the same row and two columns to the left of the cell it is referenced by. If this is called from cell E5, say, it refers to cell C5; if it is called from cell G23, it refers to cell E23; and so on. In contrast, the reference R5C3, without brackets, is an *absolute* reference to the cell in row 5 and column C. It is equivalent to $C$5. The formulas for calculating absolute percentage errors toward the bottom of this sub use a combination of relative and absolute references. The relative parts are for the actual and estimated values of the variable; the absolute parts are for the parameters of the fitted equation. The FormulaR1C1 property is somewhat more difficult to learn than the Formula property, but it is often more powerful—it enables you to fill an entire range with formulas with a *single* line of code—no loops are required.

```
Sub DoCalculations()
    ' This sub uses Excel's built-in regression functions to calculate
    ' the parameters of the various trendlines, and then it calculates some
    ' error measures to get the MAPEs.
    Dim parameterRange As Range, APERange As Range
    Dim i As Integer

    Worksheets("Report").Activate

    ' Enter labels for the log variables.
    Range("D9").Value = "Log(" & var1Name & ")"
    Range("E9").Value = "Log(" & var2Name & ")"

    ' Create logarithms of the two variables in columns D and E for later use.
    With Range("D9")
        Range(.Offset(1, 0), .Offset(nObs, 1)).FormulaR1C1 = "=Ln(RC[-2])"
        Set var1LogRange = Range(.Offset(1, 0), .Offset(nObs, 0))
        Set var2LogRange = Range(.Offset(1, 1), .Offset(nObs, 1))
    End With

    ' Calculate the best-fitting parameters with formulas using Excel's
    ' Intercept and Slope functions, and place them in parameterRange.
    ' (The details won't be clear unless you know regression.)
    Set parameterRange = Range("C5:E6")
    With parameterRange
```

```
                ' The linear fit uses original data.
                .Cells(1, 1).Formula = "=Intercept(" & var2Range.Address & "," _
                    & var1Range.Address & ")"
                .Cells(2, 1).Formula = "=Slope(" & var2Range.Address & "," _
                    & var1Range.Address & ")"
                ' The power fit uses logs of both variables.
                .Cells(1, 2).Formula = "=Exp(Intercept(" & var2LogRange.Address & "," _
                    & var1LogRange.Address & "))"
                .Cells(2, 2).Formula = "=Slope(" & var2LogRange.Address & "," _
                    & var1LogRange.Address & ")"

                ' The exponential fit uses original variable 1 and log of variable 2.
                .Cells(1, 3).Formula = "=Exp(Intercept(" & var2LogRange.Address & "," _
                    & var1Range.Address & "))"
                .Cells(2, 3).Formula = "=Slope(" & var2LogRange.Address & "," _
                    & var1Range.Address & ")"

                ' The logarithmic fit uses log of variable 1 and original variable 2.
                .Cells(1, 4).Formula = "=Intercept(" & var2Range.Address & "," _
                    & var1LogRange.Address & ")"
                .Cells(2, 4).Formula = "=Slope(" & var2Range.Address & "," _
                    & var1LogRange.Address & ")"
            End With

            ' Calculate the absolute percentage errors (with formulas) when predicting
            ' variable 2 from the four trend lines.
            With Range("H9")
                Range(.Offset(1, 0), .Offset(nObs, 0)).FormulaR1C1 = _
                    "=Abs(RC[-5]-(R5C3+R6C3*RC[-6]))/RC[-5]"
                Range(.Offset(1, 1), .Offset(nObs, 1)).FormulaR1C1 = _
                    "=Abs(RC[-6]-R5C4*RC[-7]^R6C4)/RC[-6]"
                Range(.Offset(1, 2), .Offset(nObs, 2)).FormulaR1C1 = _
                    "=Abs(RC[-7]-R5C5*Exp(R6C5*RC[-8]))/RC[-7]"
                Range(.Offset(1, 3), .Offset(nObs, 3)).FormulaR1C1 = _
                    "=Abs(RC[-8]-(R5C6+R6C6*RC[-7]))/RC[-8]"
                Set APERange = Range(.Offset(1, 0), .Offset(nObs, 3))
            End With

            ' Calculate the MAPE values for the four trend lines.
            With Range("B7")
                For i = 1 To 4
                    .Offset(0, i).Formula = _
                        "=Average(" & APERange.Columns(i).Address & ")"
                Next
            End With
End Sub
```

26.8 Summary

Finding a trend curve that relates two variables, or finding the best of several such trend curves, is an extremely important task in the business world. Excel has several built-in tools for estimating such curves, including the ability to superimpose trend curves and their equations on a scatterplot. This application illustrates how the whole process can be automated with VBA. The charts indicate visually how well the trend curves fit the data, and the numerical parameters of the curves can be used for forecasting.

EXERCISES

1. The application currently calculates the MAPE for each trend curve. Another frequently used measure of the goodness of fit is the mean absolute error (MAE). It is the average of the absolute differences between the actual and predicted values. Change the application so that it reports the MAE for each trend curve rather than the MAPE.

2. Repeat the previous exercise, but now report the root mean square error (RMSE) instead of the MAPE. This is defined as the square root of the average of squared differences between the actual and predicted values. It is another popular measure of the goodness of fit.

3. Change the application so that it reports all three goodness-of-fit measures for each trend curve: the MAPE, the MAE from Exercise 1, and the RMSE from Exercise 2.

4. The application currently shows only the absolute percentage errors in columns H, I, J, and K of the Report sheet. It doesn't explicitly show the predicted values from the trend equations, although it implicitly uses them in the equations for the absolute percentage errors. Change the application so that it enters the predicted values, with formulas, in columns H, I, J, and K, and then it enters the absolute percentage errors, again as formulas, in columns L, M, N, and O. Actually, you should be able to use a *single* FormulaR1C1 property to enter *all* of the errors in the latter four columns.

5. This application is typical in the sense that it requires input data. The question from the developer's point of view is where the data are likely to reside. Here I have assumed that the data reside in a Data sheet in the same file as the application. This exercise and the next one explore other possibilities. For this exercise, assume that the data reside in some other worksheet but in the same file as the application. Change the application so that it can locate the data, wherever they might be. (*Hint*: The RefEdit control allows a user to select a range from *any* sheet.)

6. For this exercise, assume that the data are in another Excel workbook. It will be up to the user to specify the workbook and then the data ranges in that workbook. Change the application so that (1) it informs the user with a message box that he is about to be prompted for the data file; (2) it uses the **FileDialog** object as illustrated in Chapter 13 (or the **GetOpenFilename** method of the **Application** object if you have Excel 2000 or an earlier version) to select the data file and then open this file; (3) it uses the same frmData as in Figure 26.7 to get the data ranges; (4) it enters the required data in the Report sheet of the application file; (5) it closes the data file; and (6) it proceeds as before to analyze the data.

An Exponential Utility Application

27.1 Introduction

This application illustrates a rather surprising result that can occur when a decision maker is risk averse.[1] Suppose you can enter a risky venture where there will be either a gain of G or a loss of L. The probability of the gain is p and the probability of the loss is $1 - p$. You can have any share s of this venture, where s is a fraction from 0 to 1. Then if there is a gain, you win sG; if there is a loss, you lose sL. You must decide what share you want, given that you are risk averse and have an exponential utility function with risk tolerance parameter R. (The larger your R is, the more willing you are to take risks.)

The surprising result is that if the gain G increases and all other parameters remain constant, your optimal share s might *decrease*! In other words, you might want a *smaller* share of a better thing. The intuition is that if you are risk averse, you do not like risky ventures. However, as G increases, you can have less exposure to risk by decreasing your share s and still expect to do better in the venture.

In case this argument does not convince you, the application calculates the optimal share s for varying values of G and plots them graphically. The resulting chart shows clearly, at least for some values of the parameters, that the optimal value of s can decrease as G increases.

New Learning Objectives: VBA

- To learn how a VBA application, especially one that uses a chart, can illustrate a result that might be very difficult to understand—or believe—in any other way.

New Learning Objectives: Non-VBA

- To illustrate the role of risk in decision making under uncertainty.

---

[1]It is based on the article "Too Much of a Good Thing?" by D. Clyman, M. Walls, and J. Dyer, in *Operations Research*, Vol. 47, No. 6 (1999).

27.2   Functionality of the Application

The application is slightly more general than explained in the introduction. It does the following:

1.   It first gets the inputs G, L, p, and R from the user in a dialog box. This dialog box also asks whether the user wants to vary G or L in a sensitivity analysis, and it asks for the range of values for the sensitivity analysis. Although the sensitivity analysis on the gain G is of primary interest, it might also be interesting to do a sensitivity analysis on the loss L.
2.   The user's expected utility from the risky venture, given a share s, is calculated in a Model sheet, and then it is maximized with Solver (as a nonlinear model) several times, once for each value of G (or L) in the sensitivity analysis.
3.   The Solver results are shown graphically in a chart sheet named SensitivityChart.
4.   The model and chart show the optimal share s. They also show the corresponding certainty equivalent. This is the dollar equivalent of the risky venture, using the optimal share s. More specifically, it is the dollar amount such that the decision maker is indifferent between (1) receiving this dollar amount for sure and (2) participating in the risky venture. This certainty equivalent should increase as G increases, even though s might decrease. The chart indicates that this is indeed the case.

27.3   Running the Application

The application is stored in the file **Exponential Utility.xlsm**. When this file is opened, the Explanation sheet in Figure 27.1 is displayed. Clicking on the button on this sheet produces the dialog box in Figure 27.2 Its top four boxes are filled with parameters from a previous run, if any. (To make things more interesting, you might want to think of the monetary amounts as expressed in *millions* of dollars.) The other options are set at chosen default values.

Once the OK button is clicked, the application runs Solver on a (hidden) Model sheet several times, once for each value in the sensitivity analysis, and reports the results in the SensitivityChart sheet. For the parameters in Figure 27.2, the chart appears as in Figure 27.3. This chart shows clearly that the optimal share reaches its maximum of about 0.46 when the gain G has increased by about 60% above its original value of $68 million. As G increases further, the optimal share *decreases* slightly. However, the certainty equivalent continues to increase. This simply means that as G increases, the decision maker values the risky venture more.

The Model sheet that is the basis for this chart appears in Figure 27.4. It is discussed in more detail below.[2]

If the second option button in Figure 27.2 is selected, then the sensitivity analysis is performed on the loss L, so that L varies and all other parameters remain

---

[2]I have experienced some strange behavior if I don't open the Solver dialog box *before* running this application. The left-most point in the chart is wrong, but it is then correct if I run the application a second time. This has to be a Solver problem.

Figure 27.1 Explanation Sheet

Risk Averseness: A Surprising Result

> Run the application

Consider a risk averse decision maker about to become a partner in a risky venture. The venture will be a success, earning G, or a failure, losing L. The probability of success is p. The decision maker can have any share s of this venture, where s is a fraction from 0 to 1. Then the possible gain to him is sG, and the possible loss is sL. The decision maker wants to choose the share s that maximizes his expected utility, where the utility function is of the exponential form, with risk tolerance R. Then he wants to perform a sensitivity analysis to see how the optimal share s changes as G or L changes.

This application has the decision maker's model in the Model sheet. It is a straightforward Solver application. When you click on the button above, you get to choose the input parameters: G, L, p, and R. You also get to choose the input parameter to change for sensitivity analysis, as well as the range of change (e.g., from 50% below to 100% above the current value). The application then runs Solver for each value inside this range (in 5% increments) and charts the results. The chart shows the optimal share s, as well as the associated "certainty equivalent." This is the equivalent dollar value, i.e., it is the value such that the decision maker would be indifferent between (1) taking the gamble (with the optimal s) and (2) getting the sure dollar value.

The surprising result is that for many input parameters, if you increase G (making the venture a more attractive one), the optimal shares decreases. In words, the decision maker wants a smaller percentage of a better deal! (However, the certainty equivalent always increases.) Here is the intuition behind this surprising result. Risk averse decision makers like to avoid risk, so they tend to prefer smaller shares of a risky venture. As the venture becomes more attractive (G increases), they can afford to have a smaller share and still make more money. Essentially, they can have their cake (smaller risk) and eat it too (higher certainty equivalent).

The idea for this application comes from the paper "Too Much of a Good Thing?" by Clyman, Walls, and Dyer, in Operations Research, Vol. 47, No. 6 (1999). They saw this phenomenon in the oil drilling industry, where they claim it is quite common.

constant. The chart from this analysis appears in Figure 27.5. This chart shows no surprises. As the loss increases, you want a smaller and smaller share of a bad thing, and your certainty equivalent also decreases steadily.

27.4 Setting Up the Excel Sheets

The **Exponential Utility.xlsm** file contains two worksheets: the Explanation sheet in Figure 27.1 and the Model sheet in Figure 27.4. It also contains the SensitivityChart chart sheet. Except for the sensitivity section (from row 17 down), a template for the Model sheet can be formed at design time, as shown in Figure 27.6. (The input cells are shaded with blue borders, and the changing cell has a red border.) The formula in cell B12 calculates the expected utility for any share in cell B11, and the formula in cell B13 calculates the corresponding certainty equivalent. These formulas are

```
=PrSuc*(1-EXP(-Share*Gain/RiskTol))+(1-PrSuc)*(1-EXP(-Share*(-Loss)/RiskTol))
```

and

```
=-RiskTol*LN(1-ExpUtil)
```

Figure 27.2 User Inputs Dialog Box

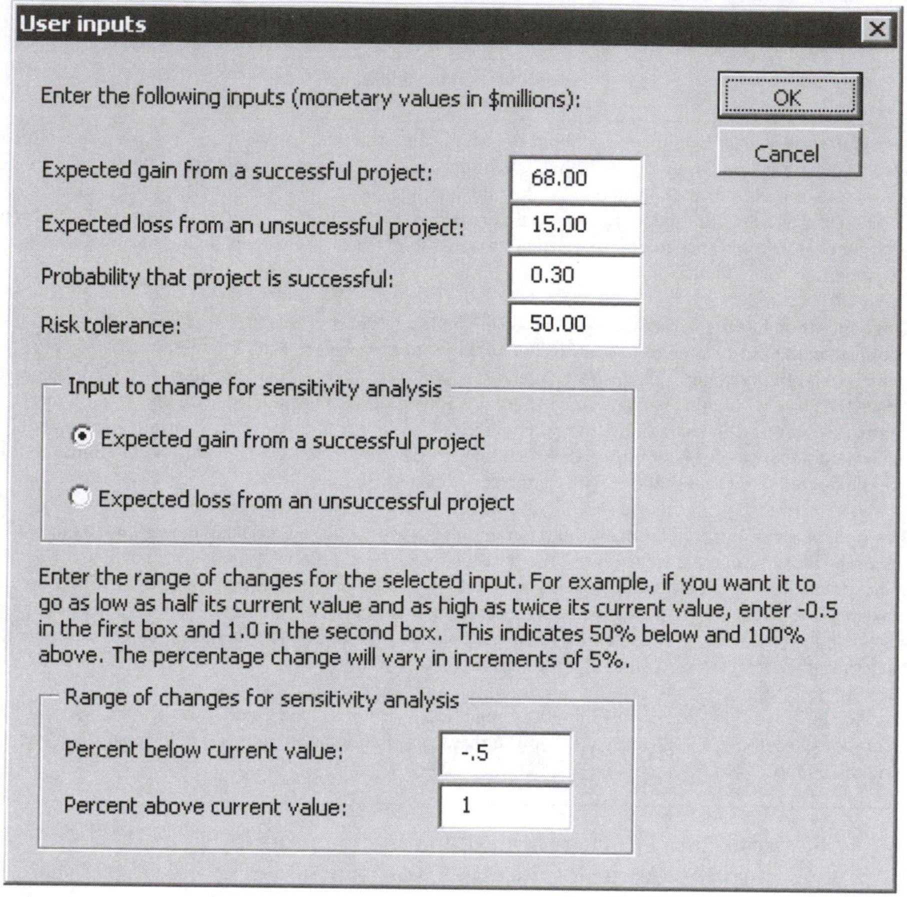

(See Chapter 10 of *Practical Management Science* for a discussion of expected utility and exponential utility functions.) Then Solver is set up to maximize cell B12, with the single changing cell B11 constrained to be between 0 and 1. Because of the exponential utility function, this model must be solved as a *nonlinear* model.

The chart sheet can also be created at design time. To do this, enter *any* trial values in columns A, B, and C of the sensitivity section of the Model sheet (see Figure 27.4) and then create the chart from these trial values. The VBA code will then update the chart with the appropriate values at run time.

Figure 27.3 Chart for Sensitivity Analysis on Gain G

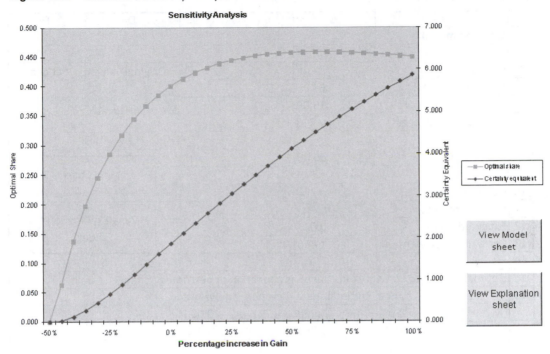

27.5 Getting Started with the VBA

This application requires a user form named frmInputs, a module, and a reference to Solver.[3] Once these items are added, the Project Explorer window will appear as in Figure 27.7.

Workbook_Open Code

To guarantee that the Explanation sheet appears when the file is opened, the following code is placed in the ThisWorkbook code window. It also uses a For Each loop to hide all sheets except the Explanation sheet.

```
Private Sub Workbook_Open()
    Dim sht As Object
    Worksheets("Explanation").Activate
    Range("F4").Select
    For Each sht In ActiveWorkbook.Sheets
        If sht.Name <> "Explanation" Then sht.Visible = False
    Next
    frmSolver.Show
End Sub
```

---

[3]It also contains the usual frmSolver that displays a message about possible Solver problems when the workbook is opened.

Figure 27.4 Model Sheet

	A	B	C	D	E
1	**Decision model**				
2					
3	**Inputs**			Original values	Pct change
4	Gain with success	68.00		68.00	0%
5	Loss with failure	15.00		15.00	0%
6	Probability of success	0.300			
7					
8	Risk tolerance	50.00			
9				View Chart	
10	**Decision**				
11	Share of project	0.400		View Explanation sheet	
12	Expected utility	0.037			
13	Certainty equivalent	1.866			
14					
15	Optimal share and certainty equivalent as a function of percentage change in Gain				
16	Percentage change	Optimal share	Certainty equivalent		
17	-50%	0.000	0.000		
18	-45%	0.063	0.023		
19	-40%	0.137	0.118		
20	-35%	0.197	0.267		
21	-30%	0.246	0.453		
36	45%	0.456	3.915		
37	50%	0.457	4.117		
38	55%	0.458	4.314		
39	60%	0.458	4.505		
40	65%	0.458	4.691		
41	70%	0.457	4.872		
42	75%	0.457	5.048		
43	80%	0.456	5.220		
44	85%	0.454	5.387		
45	90%	0.453	5.549		
46	95%	0.451	5.707		
47	100%	0.449	5.861		

Figure 27.5   Chart for Sensitivity Analysis on Loss L

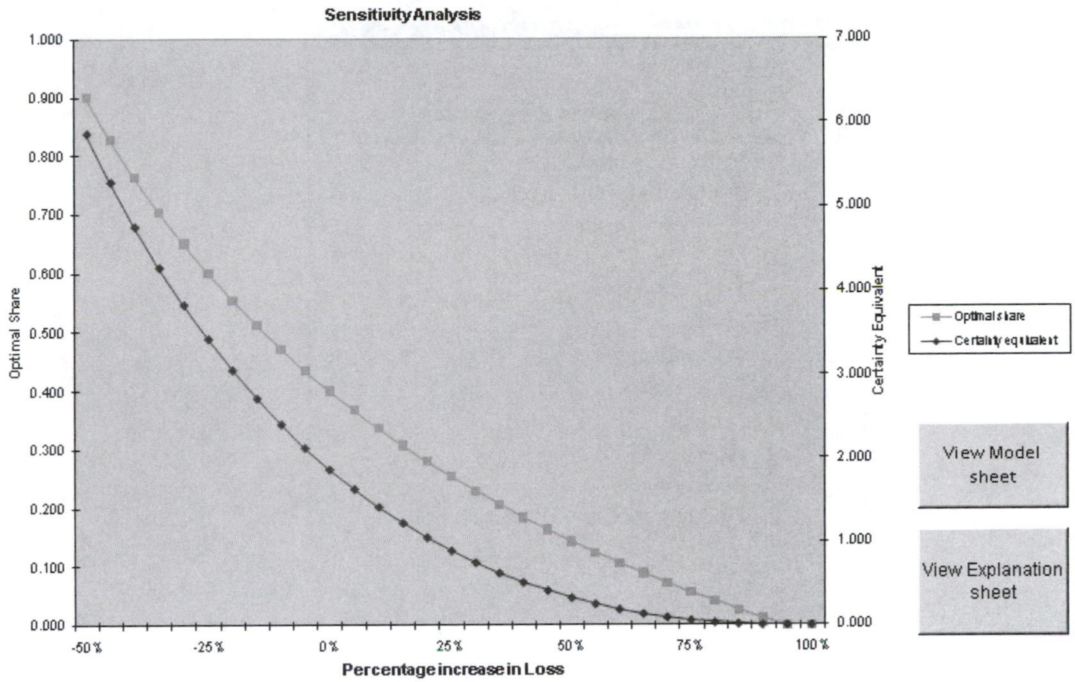

Figure 27.6   Template for Model Sheet

	A	B	C	D	E
1	**Decision model**				
2					
3	**Inputs**			Original values	Pct change
4	Gain with success	68.00		68.00	0%
5	Loss with failure	15.00		15.00	0%
6	Probability of success	0.300			
7					
8	Risk tolerance	50.00			
9				View Chart	
10	**Decision**				
11	Share of project	0.400		View Explanation	
12	Expected utility	0.037		sheet	
13	Certainty equivalent	1.866			
14					
15	Optimal share and certainty equivalent as a function of percentage change in Loss				
16	Percentage change	Optimal share	Certainty equivalent		

Figure 27.7 Project Explorer Window

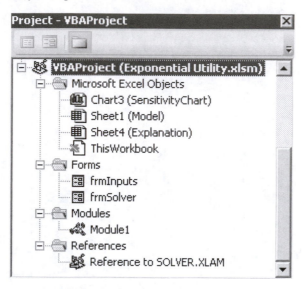

27.6 The User Form and Its Event Handlers

The design of frmInputs is shown in Figure 27.8. It includes the usual OK and Cancel buttons, two explanation labels, two frames for grouping controls, two option buttons named optGain and optLoss, and six text boxes with corresponding labels. These text boxes (from top to bottom) are named txtGain, txtLoss, txtPrSuccess, txtRiskTol, txtPctBelow, and txtPctAbove.

The event handlers for this user form are listed below. Note that the Userform_Initialize sub captures the values from the Model sheet from a previous run, if any, and places them in the top four text boxes. It then chooses the first option button by default, and it places the default values 0 and 1 in the bottom two text boxes. (Note how the Format function is used to ensure that the values in the top four text boxes are formatted as numbers with two decimals.) The btnOK_Click sub captures the user's inputs in public variables for later use in the module. It also does appropriate error checking for the various user inputs. The btnCancel_Click sub unloads the dialog box and terminates the program.

Figure 27.8 frmInputs Design

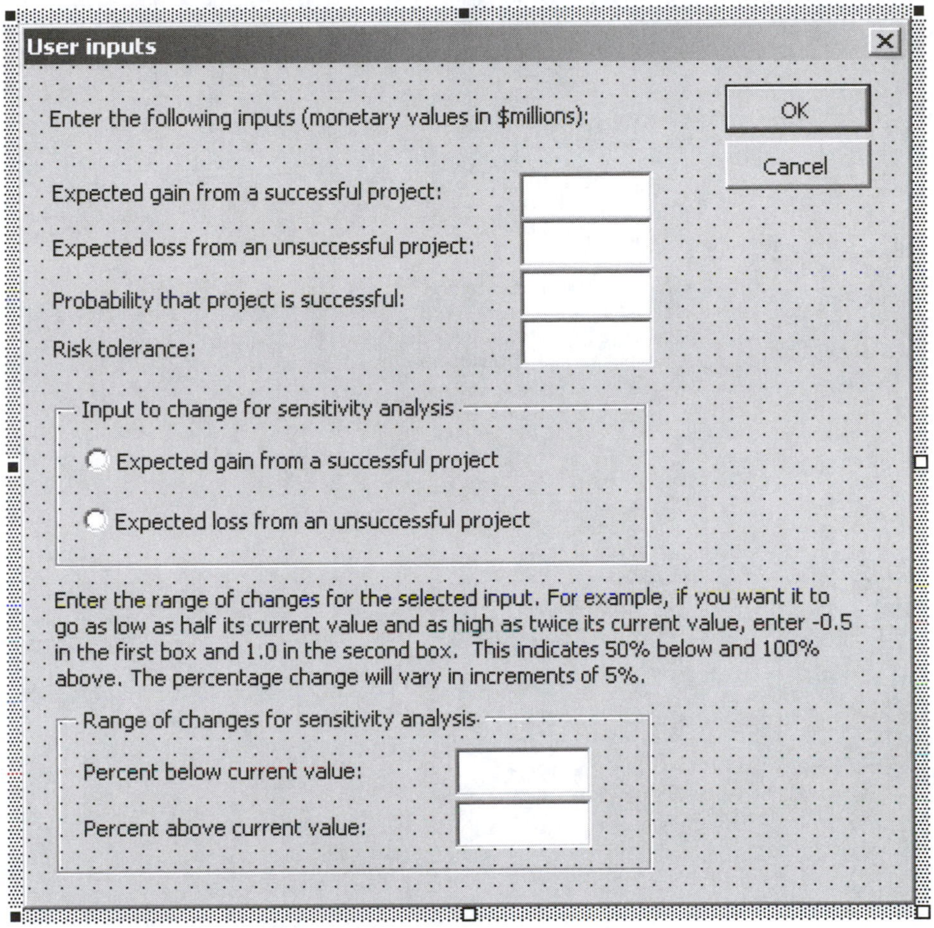

Event Handlers for frmInputs

```
Private Sub btnCancel_Click()
    Unload Me
    End
End Sub

Private Sub btnOK_Click()
    ' Perform error checking for inputs. Each text box must be nonblank and
    ' numeric, the PctBelow box must not be positive, the PrSuccess must be between
    ' 0 and 1, and the other boxes must not be negative.
    Dim ctl As Control
    For Each ctl In Me.Controls
        If TypeName(ctl) = "TextBox" Then
```

```vba
                If ctl.Value = "" Or Not IsNumeric(ctl) Then
                    MsgBox "Enter numerical values in all of the boxes.", _
                        vbInformation, "Invalid entry"
                    ctl.SetFocus
                    Exit Sub
                End If
                If ctl.Name = "txtPctBelow" Then
                    If ctl.Value > 0 Then
                        MsgBox "Enter a nonpositive value in this box.", _
                            vbInformation, "Invalid entry"
                        ctl.SetFocus
                        Exit Sub
                    End If
                ElseIf ctl.Name = "txtPrSuccess" Then
                    If ctl.Value < 0 Or ctl.Value > 1 Then
                        MsgBox "Enter a value between 0 and 1 in this box.", _
                            vbInformation, "Invalid entry"
                        ctl.SetFocus
                        Exit Sub
                    End If
                Else
                    If ctl.Value < 0 Then
                        MsgBox "Enter a nonnegative value in this box.", _
                            vbInformation, "Invalid entry"
                        ctl.SetFocus
                        Exit Sub
                    End If
                End If
            End If
        End If
    Next

    ' Capture the user's inputs in public variables.
    gain = txtGain.Text
    Loss = txtLoss.Text
    probSuccess = txtPrSuccess.Text
    riskTol = txtRiskTol.Text
    If optGain.Value Then
        inputToChange = "Gain"
    Else
        inputToChange = "Loss"
    End If
    pctBelow = txtPctBelow.Text
    pctAbove = txtPctAbove.Text

    ' Unload the userform.
    Unload Me
End Sub

Private Sub UserForm_Initialize()
    ' Capture the values from the Model sheet in the first four boxes, and
    ' use appropriate default values for the others.
    txtGain.Text = Format(Range("OrigGain").Value, "0.00")
    txtLoss.Text = Format(Range("OrigLoss").Value, "0.00")
    txtPrSuccess.Text = Format(Range("PrSuccess").Value, "0.00")
    txtRiskTol.Text = Format(Range("RiskTol").Value, "0.00")
    optGain.Value = True
    txtPctBelow.Text = 0
    txtPctAbove.Text = 1
End Sub
```

27.7   The VBA Code in the Module

The module contains a **Main** sub that first "shows" frmInputs and then calls several other subs to do the real work. The code is listed below.

Option Statement and Public Variables

```
Option Explicit

' The following variables capture the user's inputs. Note that
' inputToChange will be "Gain" or "Loss". Also, pctBelow and pctAbove
' are the extremes in percentage changes for the sensitivity analysis.
Public gain As Single, loss As Single, probSuccess As Single
Public riskTol As Single
Public inputToChange As String, pctBelow As Single, pctAbove As Single
```

Main Code

The **Main** sub gets the user inputs from frmInputs, enters these in the Model sheet, does the sensitivity analysis in the Model sheet, and finally updates the chart.

```
Sub MainExpUtility()
    ' This is the sub that the user runs by clicking on the button on
    ' the Explanation sheet.

    ' Get the user inputs.
    frmInputs.Show

    Application.ScreenUpdating = False

    ' Enter the user inputs into the Model sheet.
    Call EnterInputs
    ' Run the sensitivity analysis in the Model sheet.
    Call Sensitivity
    ' Show and update the chart.
    Call UpdateChart

    Application.ScreenUpdating = True
End Sub
```

EnterInputs Code

The EnterInputs sub enters the user's inputs from frmInputs and enters them into named ranges of the Model sheet. (Refer to Figure 27.4.) It enters an initial share of 0.5 in the changing cell, although any other initial share could be entered instead.

```
Sub EnterInputs()
    ' Enter the user inputs from the form into the Model sheet.

    ' Unhide and activate the Model sheet.
    With Worksheets("Model")
        .Visible = True
        .Activate
    End With

    ' Enter the user's inputs into cells (already range-named) in the Model sheet.
    Range("OrigGain").Value = gain
    Range("OrigLoss").Value = loss
    Range("PrSuccess").Value = probSuccess
    Range("RiskTol").Value = riskTol

    ' Set the initial share to 0.5; Solver will find the optimal share.
    Range("Share").Value = 0.5
End Sub
```

DoSensitivity Code

The DoSensitivity sub runs the sensitivity analysis on the chosen input parameter (gain or loss). To do this, it uses a Do loop to run through the various percentage changes for the selected input, and for each setting, it runs Solver to find the optimal share. As it does this, it records the optimal share and the corresponding expected utility and certainty equivalent in the sensitivity section of the Model sheet. These values are the basis for the chart.

```
Sub Sensitivity()
    ' This sub runs a sensitivity analysis on the percentage change in the
    ' input (gain or loss) being changed.

    Dim rowOffset As Integer
    Dim currentPct As Single

    ' Enter an appropriate label.
    Range("A15").Value = "Optimal share and certainty equivalent as a function " _
        & "of percentage change in " & inputToChange

    With Range("A16")
        ' Clear out old values, if any, from the previous sensitivity table.
        Range(.Offset(1, 0), .Offset(1, 2).End(xlDown)).ClearContents

        ' rowOffset is the current number of rows below row 16, i.e., where the results
        ' from the current Solver run will be placed.
        ' currentPct is the current percentage change in the input being changed.
        rowOffset = 1
        currentPct = pctBelow

        ' Loop through the percentages to change, incrementing by 5% each time.
        Do
            ' Enter the current percentage in the sensitivity table and up above
            ' (in the PctGain or PctLoss cell), which ties it to the model.
            .Offset(rowOffset, 0).Value = currentPct
            Range("Pct" & inputToChange).Value = currentPct
            ' Run Solver, which has already been set up.
            SolverSolve UserFinish:=True
```

```
        ' Enter the Solver results in the sensitivity table.
        .Offset(rowOffset, 1).Value = Range("Share").Value
        .Offset(rowOffset, 2).Value = Range("CertEquiv").Value

        ' Update rowOffset and currentPct for the next time through the loop (if any).
        rowOffset = rowOffset + 1
        currentPct = currentPct + 0.05

        ' The +0.001 in the next statement handles numerical roundoff. It ensures
        ' that the loop will be run when currentPct is equal to pctAbove.
    Loop While currentPct <= pctAbove + 0.001

        ' Run Solver one more time, using the original (user's input) values.
        ' (This isn't really necessary, but the user might want to see the model
        ' results with the original inputs.)
        Range("Pct" & inputToChange).Value = 0
        SolverSolve UserFinish:=True
    End With
    ' Hide the Model sheet.
    ActiveSheet.Visible = False
End Sub
```

UpdateChart Code

Recall that the chart has already been created (and formatted as desired) at design time. Therefore, the only purpose of the UpdateChart sub is to populate the chart with the data from the sensitivity analysis. It does this by using the SetSourceData method of the active chart. To label the horizontal axis appropriately, it sets the **Text** property of the Axes(xlCategory).AxisTitle.Characters object. To set the data range for the horizontal axis, that is, the range of percentage changes, it sets the **XValues** property of the SeriesCollection(1) object. (This object refers to the first of the two series plotted in the chart. Because they are both based on the same set of percentage changes, either could be used in this XValues statement.)

```
Sub UpdateChart()
    ' This sub updates the (already-created) chart to show the results of
    ' the sensitivity analysis.

    Dim chartData As Range, chartPcts As Range

    ' Define ranges for the parts of the sensitivity table used for the chart.
    With Worksheets("Model").Range("A16")
        Set chartData = Range(.Offset(0, 1), .Offset(0, 2).End(xlDown))
        Set chartPcts = Range(.Offset(1, 0), .End(xlDown))
    End With

    ' Unhide and activate the chart sheet.
    With Charts("SensitivityChart")
        .Visible = True
        .Activate
    End With
    ' Update the chart, which was already set up at design time.
    With ActiveChart
```

```
        .Axes(xlCategory).AxisTitle.Characters.Text = _
            "Percentage increase in " & inputToChange
        .SetSourceData chartData
        .SeriesCollection(1).XValues = chartPcts
        .Deselect
    End With
End Sub
```

Navigational Code

The following subs allow for easy navigation through the application. They are attached to the corresponding buttons on the Model and SensitivityChart sheets.

```
Sub ViewModel()
    With Worksheets("Model")
        .Visible = True
        .Activate
    End With
    Range("A2").Select
End Sub
Sub ViewExplanation()
    Worksheets("Explanation").Activate
    Range("F4").Select
    Worksheets("Model").Visible = False
    Charts("SensitivityChart").Visible = False
End Sub

Sub ViewChart()
    Worksheets("Model").Visible = False
    Charts("SensitivityChart").Activate
End Sub
```

27.8 Summary

This chapter has illustrated how a certain type of unexpected behavior can be demonstrated clearly to an unconvinced user. More generally, it has illustrated how a VBA application can perform a sensitivity analysis and present the results in a clear graphical format. This particular application allows users to run the sensitivity analysis with a variety of inputs to gain insight into the role risk aversion plays in risky ventures.

EXERCISES

1. Change the application so that it is possible to perform a sensitivity analysis on the probability p of gain G. In this case, the user should be asked to select the range that p can vary over, in increments of 0.05, where the lower and upper limits of this range must be multiples of 0.05 from 0 to 1. The resulting chart should be like the ones illustrated in the chapter except that the horizontal axis should now show p.

2. Change the application so that it is possible to perform a sensitivity analysis on the risk tolerance parameter R. In this case, the user should be asked to select the range that R can vary over. The resulting chart should be like the ones illustrated in the chapter except that the horizontal axis should now show R.

3. Change the application so that it is possible to perform a sensitivity analysis on both L and G simultaneously. Specifically, the user should be asked for values of these parameters (as well as p and R). Then it should perform a sensitivity analysis where the possible loss and gain are of the form mL and mG, where m is a multiple that varies from 1 to 10 in increments of 1. The resulting chart should be like the ones illustrated in the chapter except the horizontal axis should now show the multiple m.

4. Change the application so that the risky venture has three possible outcomes: a large gain G, a smaller gain g, and a loss L. The associated probabilities should be inputs that sum to 1. The user should now be allowed to perform a sensitivity analysis on G, g, or L. However, g should always be less than G.

28 A Queueing Simulation Application

28.1 Introduction

As Chapter 24 illustrated, spreadsheet simulation usually means creating a spreadsheet model with random numbers' in certain cells and then replicating the model with a data table, an add-in such as @RISK, or VBA. This chapter illustrates a simulation model that is very difficult to model with spreadsheet formulas because of the timing and bookkeeping involved. A more natural approach is to take care of all the model's logic in VBA and then simply report the results on a worksheet.

The model considered here is a multiserver queueing model. Customers arrive at random times to a service center, such as a bank. There are several identical servers (identical in the sense that they can all serve customers with the same mean service time). If a customer arrives and all servers are busy, the customer joins the end of a single queue. However, the model assumes that there is a maximum number of customers allowed in the queue. If the queue is already full when a customer arrives, this customer is turned away. At the beginning of the simulation, there are no customers in the system. The system is then simulated for a user-defined length of clock time. At this time, no further arrivals are allowed to enter the system, but customers already present are served. (This is analogous to a bank that locks its doors at 5:30 PM but allows customers already in the bank to finish.) The simulation terminates when the last customer departs. The model developed here assumes the times between arrivals and the service times are exponentially distributed, a very common assumption in queueing analysis.

The purpose of the simulation is to simulate the system for the pre-scribed amount of time and, as it runs, collect statistics on the system behavior. At the end, the application reports measures such as the average amount of time in queue for a typical customer, the fraction of time a typical server is busy, the fraction of all arriving customers who are turned away, and others.

New Learning Objectives: VBA

* To learn how to use VBA to take care of the timing and bookkeeping details in a queueing simulation.

New Learning Objectives: Non-VBA

- To understand the effect of system inputs (arrival rate, mean service time, number of servers) on system outputs (average time in queue, average number in queue, and others) in a typical queueing model.

28.2 Functionality of the Application

The application allows the user to change six inputs to the queueing model: (1) the time unit (minute or hour, say), (2) the customer arrival rate to the system, (3) the mean service time per customer, (4) the number of servers, (5) the maximum number of customers allowed in the queue, and (6) the closing time (the time when no more customers are allowed to enter the system). The simulation then runs for the specified amount of time and keeps track of many interesting output measures, such as the average amount of time in queue for a typical customer, the fraction of time a typical server is busy, and the fraction of all arriving customers who are turned away. It also tabulates the distribution of the number of customers in the queue and shows this distribution graphically.

28.3 Running the Application

The application is stored in the file **Queueing Simulation.xlsm**. Upon opening this file, the user sees the Explanation sheet in Figure 28.1. When the button on

Figure 28.1 Explanation Sheet

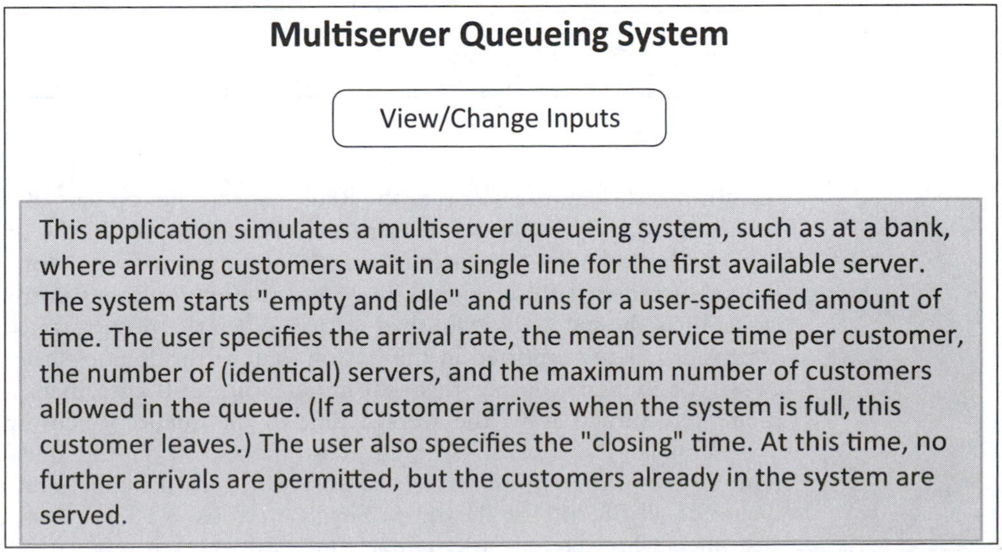

Multiserver Queueing System

View/Change Inputs

This application simulates a multiserver queueing system, such as at a bank, where arriving customers wait in a single line for the first available server. The system starts "empty and idle" and runs for a user-specified amount of time. The user specifies the arrival rate, the mean service time per customer, the number of (identical) servers, and the maximum number of customers allowed in the queue. (If a customer arrives when the system is full, this customer leaves.) The user also specifies the "closing" time. At this time, no further arrivals are permitted, but the customers already in the system are served.

Figure 28.2 Inputs Section of Report Sheet

	A	B	C	D	E	F	G
1	Multiple Server Queueing Simulation						
2				Change any of the inputs in the blue cells			
3	Inputs			and then click on the top button to run			
4	Time unit	minute		the simulation.			
5	Customer arrival rate	1.000	customers/minute				
6	Mean service time	2.700	minutes	Run the simulation			
7	Number of servers	3					
8	Maximum allowed in queue	10		Measure of system congestion			
9	Simulation run time	480	minutes	Traffic intensity	0.9		

Figure 28.3 Simulation Results

	A	B	C	D	E	F	G	H	I
11	Simulation Outputs								
12	Time last customer leaves	485.53	minutes						
13									
14	Average time in queue per customer	2.88	minutes						
15	Maximum time in queue for any customer	15.19	minutes						
16	Average number of customers in queue	2.78							
17	Maximum number in queue	10							
18									
19	Fraction of time each server is busy	85.1%							
20									
21	Number of customers processed	469							
22	Number of customers turned away	31							
23	Fraction of customers turned away	6.2%		Distribution of number in queue					
24									
25	Probability distribution of number in queue								
26	Number in queue	% of time							
27	0	38.26%							
28	1	9.53%							
29	2	10.14%							
30	3	9.98%							
31	4	5.66%							
32	5	6.06%							
33	6	4.24%							
34	7	3.48%							
35	8	3.09%							
36	9	4.48%							
37	10	5.07%							

this form is clicked, the user sees the Report sheet, the top part of which appears in Figure 28.2. This allows the user to change the inputs in the blue cells.

The button allows the user to run the simulation. It runs for the simulated time shown in cell B9 of Figure 28.2, and then it continues until all customers currently in the system have finished service. When this occurs, statistical measures are calculated and reported in the bottom half of the Report sheet, as in Figure 28.3. For example, during this 480-minute run, 500 customers arrived, 31 of them were turned away, the average time in the queue per customer was 2.78 minutes, and the longest time any customer spent in the queue was 15.19 minutes. Also, the typical server was busy 85.1% of the time, and there was no queue at all 38.26% of the time. Finally, it took 5.53 minutes to service all customers who were in the system at time 480.

These results are for a *single* replication of the 480-minute simulation. Clicking repeatedly on the Run button will cause different results to appear. As you can check, these results can differ dramatically, even with the same inputs. Some 480-minute days experience a lot of congestion, and some experience relatively little congestion—just as in real life! It would be possible to embed the current VBA code in a loop over a number of replications. For example, you could simulate 100 480-minute days, each starting empty and idle. Then you could summarize output measures across days. (You will get a chance to do this in an exercise at the end of the chapter.)

28.4 Setting Up the Excel Sheets

The **Queueing Simulation.xlsm** file contains two worksheets, named Explanation and Report. The Report sheet can be set up only as a template, with sample inputs in the inputs section and labels only in the outputs section. One measure, called the traffic intensity, can be calculated in cell E9 of the Report sheet (see Figure 28.2) with the formula

    =ArriveRate/(NServers/MeanServeTime)

This is actually the arrival rate divided by the *maximum* service rate of the system (when all servers are busy). If it is greater than 1 or only slightly below 1, the system is likely to experience long waiting times, and many arriving customers are likely to be turned away. However, if the traffic intensity is well less than 1, there will be very little waiting in line, and the servers will tend to have a lot of idle time. The sample results above show that considerable congestion can occur even when they traffic intensity is "only" 0.9. Of course, the simulation outputs show exactly what happens on any given run.

The chart can be created at design time with Excel's chart tools, using any sample data in rows 27 down in the Report sheet. Then it can be linked to the actual data at run time.

28.5 Getting Started with the VBA

The application includes only a module—no user forms and no references. Once the module is added, the Project Explorer window will appear as in Figure 28.4.

Workbook_Open Code

The Workbook_Open sub guarantees that the Explanation sheet appears when the file is opened, and it hides the Report sheet.

```
Private Sub Workbook_Open()
    Worksheets("Explanation").Activate
    Range("F4").Select
    Worksheets("Report").Visible = False
End Sub
```

Figure 28.4 Project Explorer Window

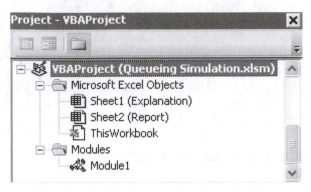

28.6 The Structure of a Queueing Simulation

As stated in the introduction, there is no Model sheet where the logic of the model is captured. Everything is done in memory with VBA. A worksheet is used only as a place to show the inputs and the eventual outputs. Therefore, the VBA code has to take care of all the timing and statistical bookkeeping as the simulation progresses. The general ideas are explained here before looking at the detailed code.

The key idea is one of scheduled events. At any point in time, there is a list of scheduled events of two types. The first type is an arrival. Each time an arrival occurs, the *next* arrival is scheduled at some random time in the future. When it occurs, *another* arrival is scheduled, and so on. The second type of event is a service completion. Each time a customer goes into service (possibly after waiting in the queue), a service completion is scheduled at a random time in the future.

It is important to understand that *nothing happens*, in terms of computer code, between events. There is a simulation "clock" that is updated from one event time to the next. All of the action occurs at these event times.

The overall logic of the simulation is placed inside a Do loop, which continues until the arrivals have been cut off (because they would occur after closing time) and all customers have been cleared from the system. Each pass through the loop deals with a single event—the next (most imminent) event. It is implemented with the following four subroutines.

FindNextEvent Sub

This sub is the key to any queueing simulation. It scans through the list of all scheduled events and finds the most imminent one. For example, it might find that the next event is a departure from server 3 that will occur at clock time 100.47. It would then reset the clock to time 100.47 and return the information about the next event (a service completion from server 3). The next time through, the clock would be reset from 100.47 to the time of the *next* event.

UpdateStatistics Sub

This sub, always called right after the FindNextEvent sub, updates any statistical counters with information since the previous event time. As an example, suppose the clock has just been reset to time 100.47 and that the previous clock time was 99.89. Also, suppose there were 3 customers in the queue from time 99.89 to time 100.47. (Remember that nothing happens between events, so the number in the queue has to remain constant during this time interval.) Then if there is a statistical variable that accumulates the total customer-minutes spent in the queue, the sub adds 3 times the difference $(100.47 - 99.89)$ to the previous value of this variable.

Arrival Sub

If the FindNextEvent sub determines that the next event is an arrival, the following logic is played out.

- Schedule the time of the next arrival. If this time is after closing time, disallow the next arrival and don't schedule any future arrivals.
- Check whether the queue is already full. If it is, turn this customer away, and add 1 to the number of customers turned away.
- Check whether all servers are busy. If they are, put this arrival at the end of the queue and keep track of his arrival time to the system (for later statistics). Otherwise, find an idle server, place this customer in service, and schedule a service completion.

Departure Sub

If the FindNextEvent sub determines that the next event is a departure from a particular server, the following logic is played out.

- Increase the number of completed customers by 1.
- Check whether there is anyone in the queue. If there is no queue, decrease the number of busy servers by 1, and do *not* schedule a new departure event for the server who just finished. Otherwise, if there is at least one customer in the queue, keep this server busy with the customer at the front of the queue, move all other customers up one space in the queue, and schedule a departure event for this server.

Outputs

Once the clock time is past closing time and all customers have departed, the only thing left to do is report the outputs for the simulation. Some outputs must be calculated first. Other than counters such as the number of customers turned away, the outputs are of two types: **customer averages** and **time averages**.

A typical customer average is the average time spent in queue per customer. To obtain this average, we keep track of a variable that sums the queueing times of all customers. Then at the end of the simulation, we divide it by the number of customers who have completed service to obtain the desired average.

A typical time average is the average number of customers in the queue. To obtain this average, we keep track of a variable that sums the total number of customer-minutes spent in the queue. For example, if six customers wait in queue for half a minute each, this contributes three customer-minutes to the total. Then at the end of the simulation, we divide this variable by the final clock time to obtain the desired average. (Can you convince yourself that this gives the desired average?)

Another typical time average is the average server utilization, defined as the fraction of time a typical server is busy. To obtain this average, we keep track of a variable that sums the total number of server-minutes spent serving customers. At the end of the simulation, we divide this variable by the final clock time to obtain the average number of servers busy, and we then divide this ratio by the number of servers to obtain the desired server utilization.

The Need for Careful Programming

The logic of most queueing simulations is really quite straightforward—we just play out the events as they occur through time. However, the devil is in the details! Queueing simulations are difficult to get correct. Part of the reason is that there are so many interrelated details. Perhaps an even more important reason is that we don't know what the "answers" ought to be, so it is often not clear whether a queueing simulation is working correctly or not! (I can only imagine how many supposedly correct simulations in the business world are really wrong.)

My intent is not to scare you away. Rather, it is to emphasize the need for careful programming. At the very least, variables and subroutines should be named meaningfully. A variable's name should leave little doubt about what it represents. Also, queueing simulations should probably be commented more extensively than any other programs in this book. This clearly helps people who read the program, but it also helps you, the programmer, to understand your own logic.

28.7 The VBA Code in the Module

Now let's take a look at the code for this application. The following list separates the module-level variables into three categories for ease of interpretation. The system parameters are the user inputs. The system status indicators define the current status of the system at any point in time. The statistical variables are the "bookkeeping" variables that are eventually used to calculate the simulation outputs. You should read these definitions carefully.

Option Statements and Public Variables

```
Option Explicit

' Declare system parameters.
'    meanIATime - mean interarrival time (reciprocal of arrival rate)
'    meanServeTime - mean service time
'    nServers - number of servers
```

```
'    maxAllowedInQ - maximum number of customers allowed in the queue
'    closeTime - clock time when no future arrivals are accepted

Dim meanIATime As Single
Dim meanServeTime As Single
Dim nServers As Integer
Dim maxAllowedInQ As Integer
Dim closeTime As Single


' Declare system status indicators.
'    nInQueue - number of customers currently in the queue
'    nBusy - number of servers currently busy
'    clockTime - current clock time, where the inital clock time is 0
'    eventScheduled(i) - True or False, depending on whether an event of type i is
'        scheduled or not, for i>=0, where i=0 corresponds to arrivals and i from
'        1 to nServers corresponds to server i service completions
'    timeOfLastEvent - clock time of previous event
'    timeOfNextEvent(i) - the scheduled clock time of the next event of type i
'        (only defined when eventScheduled(i) is True)

Dim nInQueue As Integer
Dim nBusy As Integer
Dim clockTime As Single
Dim eventScheduled() As Boolean
Dim timeOfLastEvent As Single
Dim timeOfNextEvent() As Single


' Declare statistical variables.
'    nServed - number of customers who have completed service so far
'    nLost - number of customers who have been turned away so far
'    maxNInQueue - maximum number in the queue at any point in time so far
'    maxTimeInQueue - maximum time any customer has spent in the queue so far
'    timeOfArrival(i) - arrival time of the customer currently in the i-th
'        place in the queue, for i>=1
'    totalTimeInQueue - total customer-time units spent in the queue so far
'    totalTimeBusy - total server-time units spent serving customers so far
'    sumOfQueueTimes - sum of all times in the queue so far, where sum is over
'        customers who have completed their times in the queue
'    queueTimeArray(i) - amount of time there have been exactly i customers
'        in the queue, for i>=0

Dim nServed As Long
Dim nLost As Integer
Dim maxNInQueue As Integer
Dim maxTimeInQueue As Single
Dim timeOfArrival() As Single
Dim totalTimeInQueue As Single
Dim totalTimeBusy As Single
Dim sumOfQueueTimes As Single
Dim queueTimeArray() As Single
```

The **Main** sub is attached to the button on the Report sheet. It runs the simulation. It first calls VBA's **Randomize** function to ensure that *different* random numbers are used for each simulation run, it clears old results from the Report sheet, it captures the inputs from the Model sheet, and it calls the **Initialize** sub to initialize the simulation (see explanation below). Then it enters a Do loop, as explained in the previous section. This loop processes one event after another until the arrivals have been cut off and all customers have been cleared from the system. Finally, it calls the **Report** sub to calculate the outputs and place them on the Report sheet.

Main Code

```
Sub Main()
    ' This sub runs when the user clicks on the "Run the simulation" button on
    ' the Simulation sheet. It sets up and runs the simulation.
    Dim nextEventType As Integer
    Dim finishedServer As Integer

    ' Always start with new random numbers.
    Randomize

    ' Clear previous results, if any, from the Report sheet.
    Call ClearOldResults

    ' Get inputs from the Report Sheet.
    meanIATime = 1 / Range("ArriveRate").Value
    meanServeTime = Range("MeanServeTime").Value
    nServers = Range("nServers").Value
    maxAllowedInQ = Range("MaxAllowedInQ").Value
    closeTime = Range("CloseTime").Value

    ' The next two arrays have an element for arrivals (index 0)
    ' and one for each server.
    ReDim eventScheduled(nServers + 1)
    ReDim timeOfNextEvent(nServers + 1)

    ' Set counters, status indicators to 0 and schedule first arrival.
    Call Initialize

    ' Keep simulating until the last customer has left.
    Do
        ' Find the time and type of the next event, and reset the clock.
        ' Capture the index of the finished server in case the next event
        ' is a service completion.
        Call FindNextEvent(nextEventType, finishedServer)

        ' Update statistics since the last event.
        Call UpdateStatistics

        ' nextEventType is 1 for an arrival, 2 for a departure.
        If nextEventType = 1 Then
            Call Arrival
        Else
            Call Departure(finishedServer)
        End If
    Loop Until Not eventScheduled(0) And nBusy = 0

    ' Report the results.
    Call Report
End Sub
```

ClearOldResults Code

The **ClearOldResults** sub clears all outputs from a previous run from the output section of the Report sheet.

```
Sub ClearOldResults()
    ' This sub clears the results from any previous simulation.
    With Worksheets("Report")
        .Range("B12:B23").ClearContents
        With .Range("A26")
            Range(.Offset(1, 0), .Offset(0, 1).End(xlDown)).ClearContents
        End With
    End With
End Sub
```

Initialize Code

Most of the **Initialize** sub involves setting status indicators and statistical variables to 0. (Remember that the simulation starts at clock time 0 with no customers in the system—empty and idle.) Note in particular how the array queueTimeArray is initialized. By the time the simulation has finished, there should be an element in this array for each number of customers that have ever been in the queue. At time 0, however, we don't know how long the queue will eventually grow. Therefore, we initialize queueTimeArray to have only one element, the 0 element. It will then be redimensioned appropriately as the queue grows later on.

The Initialize sub also schedules the first event—the time of the first arrival. It does this by setting eventScheduled(0) to True and generating a random time for this event in timeOfNextEvent(0). However, it sets eventScheduled(i) to False for i from 1 to nServers. This is because all of the servers are currently idle, so they should not have scheduled service completions.

```
Sub Initialize()
    ' This sub initializes the simulation to the "empty and idle" state and
    ' sets all statistical counters to 0. It then schedules the first arrival.
    Dim i As Integer

    ' Initialize system status indicators.
    clockTime = 0
    nBusy = 0
    nInQueue = 0
    timeOfLastEvent = 0

    ' Initialize statistical variables.
    nServed = 0
    nLost = 0
    sumOfQueueTimes = 0
    maxTimeInQueue = 0
    totalTimeInQueue = 0
    maxNInQueue = 0
    totalTimeBusy = 0
```

```
        ' Redimension the queueTimeArray array to have one element (the 0 element,
        ' for the amount of time when there are 0 customers in the queue).
        ReDim queueTimeArray(1)
        queueTimeArray(0) = 0

        ' Schedule an arrival from the exponential distribution.
        eventScheduled(0) = True
        timeOfNextEvent(0) = Exponential(meanIATime)

        ' Don't schedule any departures because there are no customers in the system.
        For i = 1 To nServers
            eventScheduled(i) = False
        Next
End Sub
```

A note on Generating Exponentially Distributed Random Numbers. The random interarrival times and service times in this simulation are all exponentially distributed.[1] (Again, this is an assumption frequently made in queueing models.) If an exponential distribution has mean m, then we can generate a random number from it with the VBA expression

```
- m * Log(Rnd)
```

Here, Rnd is VBA's function for generating *uniformly* distributed random numbers from 0 to 1, and Log is VBA's natural logarithm function. The minus sign is required because the logarithm of a number between 0 and 1 is *negative*. Because exponentially distributed random numbers are generated several times in the program, I wrote the following function subroutine to take care of it.

Exponential Function Code

```
Function Exponential(mean As Single) As Single
    ' This generates a random number from an exponential distribution
    ' with a given mean.
    Exponential = -mean * Log(Rnd)
End Function
```

FindNextEvent Code

The **FindNextEvent** sub is the key to the simulation. When it is called, there are typically several events scheduled to occur in the future (such as an arrival and several service completions). The nextEventTime variable captures the minimum of these—the time of the most imminent event. If the most

---

[1]The term *interarrival time* means the time between two successive customer arrivals.

imminent event is an arrival, nextEventType is set to 1. If it is a departure, nextEventType is set to 2, and finishedServer records the index of the server who just completed service. In either case, clockTime is reset to nextEventTime. This last operation is crucial. If clockTime were not updated, the simulation would never end!

```
Sub FindNextEvent(nextEventType As Integer, finishedServer As Integer)
    ' This sub finds the type (arrival, departure, or closing time) of the next
    ' event and advances the simulation clock to the time of the next event.
    Dim i As Integer
    Dim nextEventTime As Single

    ' nextEventTime will be the minimum of the scheduled event times.
    ' Start by setting it to a large value.
    nextEventTime = 10 * closeTime

    ' Find type and time of the next (most imminent) scheduled event. Note that
    ' there is a potential event scheduled for the next arrival (indexed as 0) and
    ' for each server completion (indexed as 1 to nServers).
    For i = 0 To nServers
        ' Check if there is an event schedule of type i.
        If eventScheduled(i) Then
            ' If the current event is the most imminent so far, record it.
            If timeOfNextEvent(i) < nextEventTime Then
                nextEventTime = timeOfNextEvent(i)
                If i = 0 Then
                    ' It's an arrival.
                    nextEventType = 1
                Else
                    ' It's a departure - record the index of the server who finished.
                    nextEventType = 2
                    finishedServer = i
                End If
            End If
        End If
    Next

    ' Advance the clock to the time of the next event.
    clockTime = nextEventTime
End Sub
```

UpdateStatistics Code

The **UpdateStatistics** sub first defines timeSinceLastEvent as the elapsed time since the previous event. At the end of the sub, it resets timeOfLastEvent to the current clock time (in anticipation of the *next* time this sub is called). In between, it updates any statistics with what has occurred during the elapsed time. For example, queueTimeArray(i) in general is the amount of time exactly i customers have been in the queue. During the time since the previous event, the number in the queue has been nInQueue, so timeSinceLastEvent is added to the array element queueTimeArray(nInQueue). The next two lines add the number of customer-time units in the queue and the number of server-time units being busy, respectively, to the totalTimeInQueue and totalTimeBusy variables. If there were other outputs we wanted to keep track of, they would be updated similarly in this sub.

```
Sub UpdateStatistics()
    ' This sub updates statistics since the time of the previous event.
    Dim timeSinceLastEvent As Single

    ' timeSinceLastEvent is the time since the last update.
    timeSinceLastEvent = clockTime - timeOfLastEvent

    ' Update statistical variables.
    queueTimeArray(nInQueue) = queueTimeArray(nInQueue) + timeSinceLastEvent
    totalTimeInQueue = totalTimeInQueue + nInQueue * timeSinceLastEvent
    totalTimeBusy = totalTimeBusy + nBusy * timeSinceLastEvent

    ' Reset timeOfLastEvent to the current time.
    timeOfLastEvent = clockTime
End Sub
```

Arrival Code

The **Arrival** sub plays out the logic described in the previous section for an arrival event. The comments clarify the details. Note in particular the case where the arrival must enter the queue. A check is made to see whether this makes the queue length longer than it has ever been before. If it is, the maxNInQueue variable is updated, and the queueTimeArray and timeOfArrival arrays are redimensioned (to have an extra element). You can think of the timeOfArrival values as "tags" placed on the customers. Each tag shows when the customer arrived to the system. When a customer eventually goes into service, his tag allows us to calculate how long he has spent in the queue: the current clock time minus his timeOfArrival value.

```
Sub Arrival()
    ' This sub takes care of all the logic when a customer arrives.
    Dim i As Integer

    ' Schedule the next arrival.
    timeOfNextEvent(0) = clockTime + Exponential(meanIATime)

    ' Cut off the arrival stream if it is past closing time.
    If timeOfNextEvent(0) > closeTime Then
        eventScheduled(0) = False
    End If

    ' If the queue is already full, this customer is turned away.
    If nInQueue = maxAllowedInQ Then
        nLost = nLost + 1
        Exit Sub
    End If

    ' Check if all servers are busy.
    If nBusy = nServers Then

        ' All servers are busy, so put this customer at the end of the queue.
        nInQueue = nInQueue + 1
```

```
        ' If the queue is now longer than it has been before, update maxNInQueue
        ' and redimension arrays appropriately.
        If nInQueue > maxNInQueue Then
            maxNInQueue = nInQueue

            ' queueTimeArray is 0-based, with elements 0 to maxNInQueue.
            ReDim Preserve queueTimeArray(0 To maxNInQueue)

            ' timeOfArrival is 1-based, with elements 1 to maxNInQueue.
            ReDim Preserve timeOfArrival(1 To maxNInQueue)
        End If

        ' Keep track of this customer's arrival time (for later stats).
        timeOfArrival(nInQueue) = clockTime

    Else
        ' The customer can go directly into service, so update the number of servers busy.
        nBusy = nBusy + 1

        ' This loop searches for the first idle server and schedules a departure
        ' event for this server.
        For i = 1 To nServers
            If Not eventScheduled(i) Then
                eventScheduled(i) = True
                timeOfNextEvent(i) = clockTime + Exponential(meanServeTime)
                Exit For
            End If
        Next
    End If
End Sub
```

Departure Code

The **Departure** sub plays out the logic described in the previous section for a service completion event. It takes one argument to identify the server who just completed service. Again, the comments clarify the details. The final For loop is important. We want the timeOfArrival "tags" to remain with the customers as they move up one space in the queue. Therefore, the timeOfArrival(1) value, the time of arrival of the first person in line becomes timeOfArrival(2) (because this person used to be second in line), timeOfArrival(2) becomes timeOfArrival(3), and so on.

```
Sub Departure(finishedServer As Integer)
    ' This sub takes care of the logic when a customer departs from service.
    Dim i As Integer
    Dim timeInQueue As Single

    ' Update number of customers who have finished.
    nServed = nServed + 1

    ' Check if any customers are waiting in queue.
    If nInQueue = 0 Then

        ' No one is in the queue, so make the server who just finished idle.
        nBusy = nBusy - 1
```

```
                eventScheduled(finishedServer) = False

        Else

            ' At least one person is in the queue, so take first customer
            ' in queue into service.
            nInQueue = nInQueue - 1

            ' timeInQueue is the time this customer has been waiting in line.
            timeInQueue = clockTime - timeOfArrival(1)

            ' Check if this is a new maximum time in queue.
            If timeInQueue > maxTimeInQueue Then
                maxTimeInQueue = timeInQueue
            End If

            ' Update the total of all customer queue times so far.
            sumOfQueueTimes = sumOfQueueTimes + timeInQueue

            ' Schedule departure for this customer with the same server who just finished.
            timeOfNextEvent(finishedServer) = clockTime + Exponential(meanServeTime)

            ' Move everyone else in line up one space.
            For i = 1 To nInQueue
                timeOfArrival(i) = timeOfArrival(i + 1)
            Next
        End If
End Sub
```

Report Code

The **Report** sub, called at the end of the simulation, calculates customer and time averages and then reports the results in named ranges in the Report sheet. It also names a couple of ranges where the distribution of queue length is stored, and it updates the chart.

```
Sub Report()
    ' This sub calculates and then reports summary measures for the simulation.
    Dim i As Integer
    Dim avgTimeInQueue As Single
    Dim avgNInQueue As Single
    Dim avgNBusy As Single

    ' Calculate averages.
    avgTimeInQueue = sumOfQueueTimes / nServed
    avgNInQueue = totalTimeInQueue / clockTime
    avgNBusy = totalTimeBusy / clockTime

    ' queueTimeArray records, for each value from 0 to maxNInQueue, the percentage
    ' of time that many customers were waiting in the queue.
    For i = 0 To maxNInQueue
        queueTimeArray(i) = queueTimeArray(i) / clockTime
    Next

    ' Enter simulate results in named ranges.
    Range("FinalTime").Value = clockTime
    Range("NServed").Value = nServed
```

```
        Range("AvgTimeInQ").Value = avgTimeInQueue
        Range("MaxTimeInQ").Value = maxTimeInQueue
        Range("AvgNInQ").Value = avgNInQueue
        Range("MaxNInQ").Value = maxNInQueue
        Range("AvgServerUtil").Value = avgNBusy / nServers
        Range("NLost").Value = nLost
        Range("PctLost").Formula = "=NLost/(NLost + NServed)"

        ' Enter the queue length distribution from row 27 down, and name the two columns.
        With Range("A27")
            For i = 0 To maxNInQueue
                .Offset(i, 0).Value = i
                .Offset(i, 1).Value = queueTimeArray(i)
            Next
            Range(.Offset(0, 0), .Offset(maxNInQueue, 0)).Name = "NInQueue"
            Range(.Offset(0, 1), .Offset(maxNInQueue, 1)).Name = "PctOfTime"
        End With

        ' Update the chart.
        With ActiveSheet.ChartObjects(1).Chart
            With .SeriesCollection(1)
                .Values = Range("PctOfTime")
                .XValues = Range("nInQueue")
            End With
        End With

        Range("A2").Select
End Sub
```

ViewChangeInputs Code

This last sub is for navigational purposes. It is attached to the button on the Explanation sheet. It unhides and activates the Report sheet so that the user can view and change any inputs before running the simulation. It also clears any old outputs from the Report sheet.

```
Sub ViewChangeInputs()
    ' This sub runs when the user clicks on the "View/Change Inputs" button on the
    ' Explanation sheet. It clears old results, if any, and lets the user see
    ' the Report sheet.
    With Worksheets("Report")
        .Visible = True
        .Activate
    End With
    Call ClearOldResults
End Sub
```

28.8 Summary

A typical queueing simulation program, as illustrated in this chapter, is considerably different from most of the other applications in this book. The reason is that all of the logic must be done behind the scenes in VBA code—there is no spreadsheet model. Although the overall flow of the program is conceptually straightforward, there are many timing and bookkeeping details to keep straight, which means that the programmer must be extremely careful. However, this type of program provides an excellent way to sharpen your programming skills. Besides, a successfully completed queueing simulation program can provide many important insights into the system being modeled.

EXERCISES

1. Change the simulation so that there is no upper limit on the number allowed in the queue. This means that no customers will be turned away because the system is full. (Make sure you delete any variables that are no longer needed.)

2. Continuing the previous exercise, assume that each customer who arrives to the system looks at the queue (if there is one) and then decides whether to join. Assume the probability that a customer joins the queue is of the form r^n, where r is an input between 0 and 1 (probably close to 1), and n is the current number of customers in the queue. We say that a customer **balks** if she decides not to join. Keep track of the number of customers who balk.

3. Change the simulation so that the servers have different mean service times, so that some tend to be faster than others. Assume that an arrival always chooses the fastest idle server (when more than one are idle). Now report the fraction of time *each* server is busy.

4. Change the simulation so that all activity stops at closing time—the customers currently in the system are *not* serviced any further. Report the number of customers still in the system at closing time. (Make sure you update statistics from the time of the last event until closing time.)

5. (More difficult) This exercise is based on the "express" lines you see at some service centers. Assume that arriving customers are designated as "regular" or "express" customers when they arrive. The probability that an arrival is an express customer is an input between 0 and 1. Express customers have a relatively small mean service time. The mean service time for regular customers is larger. One of the servers is an "express" server. This server handles only the express customers. The other servers can serve *either* type of customer. The customers wait (at least conceptually, if not physically) in two separate lines. They are served in first-come, first-served order as servers become available, although the express server cannot serve a regular customer. If an express customer enters, and a regular server and the express server are both idle, you can assume that the customer goes to the express server. Change the simulation appropriately to handle this situation, and keep track of separate statistics for express customers and regular customers, as well as for regular servers and the express server.

6. Change the program so that the current simulation is embedded in a For loop from 1 to 100. Each time through the loop, one simulation is run, and its outputs (you can select which ones) are reported on a Replications sheet. After all 100 simulations have run, summarize the selected outputs on a Summary sheet. For

each output, report the following summary measures: minimum, maximum, average, standard deviation, median, and 5th and 95th percentiles. For example, if one of your outputs on any replication is the maximum number in queue, then you will get 100 such maximums, one for each replication. The Summary sheet should summarize these 100 numbers: their average, their standard deviation, and so on. In this way, you can see how results vary from replication to another.

29

An Option-Pricing Application

29.1 Introduction

This application prices European and American call and put options. A European call option on a certain stock allows the owner of the option to purchase a share of the stock for a certain price, called the exercise (or strike) price, on a certain date in the future, called the exercise date. A put option is the same except that it allows the owner to *sell* a share on the exercise date. An American option is similar, but it can be exercised at *any* time between the current date and the exercise date.

The owner of a call option hopes that the price of the stock will *increase* above the exercise price. The option can then be exercised, and the owner can make the difference by buying the stock at the exercise price and immediately selling it back at the actual price. The opposite is true for a put option. For a put option the owner hopes that the price of the stock will *decrease* below the exercise price so that he can sell it for a relatively high price and immediately "cover his position" by buying it back at a cheaper price. The question answered by this application is how much these options are worth.

It is relatively easy to price European options. This is done with the famous Black–Scholes formula. American options are considerably more difficult to price. The usual method is to use a technique called **binomial trees**, as is done in this application. In addition, it can be shown that if no dividends are given, as is assumed here, then it is never optimal to exercise an American call option early (before the exercise date). However, this is not true for American put options. For American puts, there is an **early exercise boundary** that specifies when the put should be exercised. More specifically, this boundary consists of a cutoff price for each date in the future up until the exercise date. If the actual stock price falls below this cutoff price on any particular date, then the put should be exercised at that time. This application calculates the early exercise boundary for American put options (if the user requests it).

New Learning Objectives: VBA

- To gain practice working with dates, including the use of a user-defined function for calculating the number of days between two specified dates, excluding weekends, and to learn how to use the very handy calendar control in a user form.
- To learn how to manipulate Excel's status bar to indicate the progress of a program.
- To learn how to deal with literal double quotes inside a string.
- To learn how to use Excel's Goal Seek tool with VBA.

New Learning Objectives: Non-VBA

- To gain some knowledge of how options work and how they are priced, including the use of the Black-Scholes formula for European options and binomial trees for American options.

29.2 Functionality of the Application

The application has the following functionality:

1. It first asks the user for the inputs required to price any option. These include (1) the current price of the stock, (2) the exercise price, (3) the exercise date, (4) the annual risk-free rate of interest, (5) the volatility of the stock price (the standard deviation of its annual return), and (6) the type of option (European or American, call or put). It is assumed that the current date is the actual date the user runs the program, so that the exercise date must be *after* this. (Actually, the current date is taken to be the next Monday in case the user runs the program on a weekend day.) Note that the current date can be found with Excel's TODAY function.
2. It next calculates the price of the option and displays it in a message box.
3. If the option is an American put option, the user can also request the early exercise boundary.

There are two underlying assumptions. First, it is assumed that there are no dividends for the stock. If there were, the calculations would need to be modified. Second, it is assumed that trading days include weekdays but not weekends. This assumption is used to calculate the *duration* of the option, the number of trading days between the current date and the exercise date. It would be possible to exclude some weekdays as trading days (the Fourth of July, for example), but this would add complexity to the application, and it is not done here.

29.3 Running the Application

The application is stored in the file **Stock Options.xlsm**. Upon opening this file, the user sees the Explanation sheet in Figure 29.1. When the button on this form is clicked, the dialog box in Figure 29.2 appears. The inputs on the left are the current values in the EuroModel sheet (more about it below). Of course, any of these can be changed.

If the user selects any type of option other than an American put, the price of the option is calculated "behind the scenes" in the EuroModel or the AmerModel sheet and is displayed in a message box, as shown in Figure 29.3. (The examples in this chapter were run on 11/7/2008, a Friday.)

For an American put option, the message box in Figure 29.4 appears. If the user clicks on No, the same type of message as in Figure 29.3 appears. If the user clicks on Yes, then the early exercise boundary is calculated and is reported in the AmerPutReport sheet, as shown in Figure 29.5. This particular example assumes

Figure 29.1 Explanation Sheet

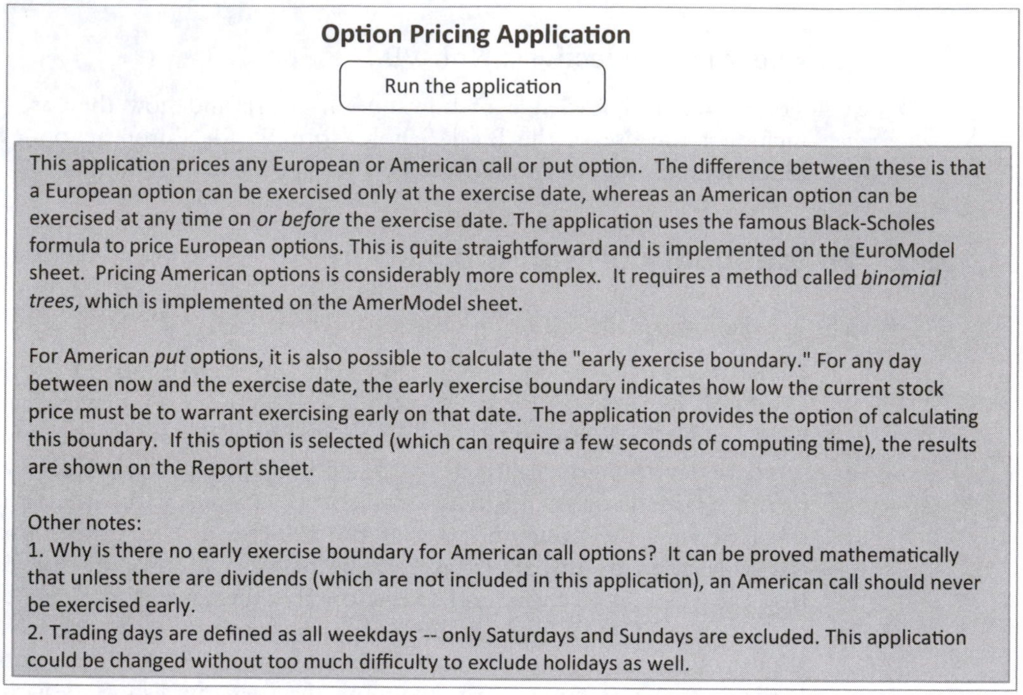

Option Pricing Application
Run the application
This application prices any European or American call or put option. The difference between these is that a European option can be exercised only at the exercise date, whereas an American option can be exercised at any time on *or before* the exercise date. The application uses the famous Black-Scholes formula to price European options. This is quite straightforward and is implemented on the EuroModel sheet. Pricing American options is considerably more complex. It requires a method called *binomial trees*, which is implemented on the AmerModel sheet.
For American *put* options, it is also possible to calculate the "early exercise boundary." For any day between now and the exercise date, the early exercise boundary indicates how low the current stock price must be to warrant exercising early on that date. The application provides the option of calculating this boundary. If this option is selected (which can require a few seconds of computing time), the results are shown on the Report sheet.
Other notes:
1. Why is there no early exercise boundary for American call options? It can be proved mathematically that unless there are dividends (which are not included in this application), an American call should never be exercised early.
2. Trading days are defined as all weekdays -- only Saturdays and Sundays are excluded. This application could be changed without too much difficulty to exclude holidays as well.

Figure 29.2 User Inputs Dialog Box

User inputs
Enter the follow inputs. Express rates and volatility in decimal form (e.g., enter 0.10 for 10%)
OK
Cancel
Current price
50
Exercise price
49
Stock volatility
.4
Riskfree rate
.1
Option Type
European Call
European Put
American Call
American Put
Select an exercise date. Make sure you select a day if you change the month or year.
Nov 2008
Nov
2008
Sun Mon Tue Wed Thu Fri Sat
26 27 28 29 30 31 1
2 3 4 5 6 7 8
9 10 11 12 13 14 15
16 17 18 19 20 21 22
23 24 25 26 27 28 29
30 1 2 3 4 5 6

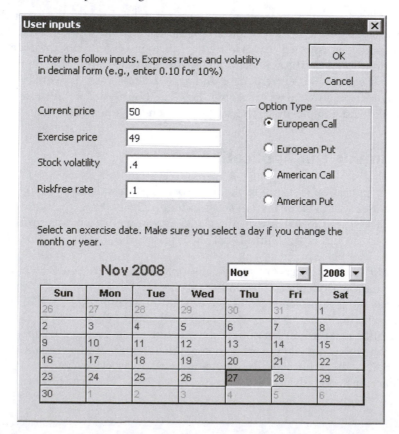

Figure 29.3 Message Box Display of Option Price

Figure 29.4 Request for Early Exercise Boundary

Extra info

Do you want to calculate the early exercise boundary? (If you click on No, you will get only the price of the option.)

Yes   No

Figure 29.5 Early Exercise Boundary Report

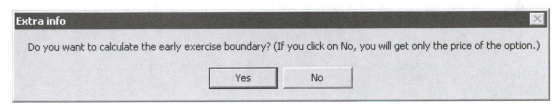

	A	B	C	D	E	F	G
1	Option price and early exercise boundary for the American put option						
2							
3	Price of option	$1.64		View Explanation Sheet			
4							
5	Early exercise boundary: exercise only if stock price on this day is below the value in column B.						
6	Trading date	Boundary price					
7	11/10/08	$53.70					
8	11/11/08	$53.71					
9	11/12/08	$53.99					
10	11/13/08	$54.14					
11	11/14/08	$54.33					
12	11/17/08	$54.76					
13	11/18/08	$54.78					
14	11/19/08	$55.15					
15	11/20/08	$55.67					
16	11/21/08	$55.68					
17	11/24/08	$56.20					
18	11/25/08	$56.98					
19	11/26/08	$57.91					
20	11/27/08	$58.93					
21	11/28/08	$60.00					

that the exercise date is November 28, 2008 and the exercise price is $60. If this were a European put, the owner would wait until November 28, 2008 and then exercise the option only if the actual stock price were less than $60. However, the report indicates that the American put should be exercised on, say, November 19 if it hasn't been exercised already and the actual price on November 19 is less than $55.15. By the way, the European put with these same inputs is priced at $1.59. The American option provides more flexibility, so it is priced slightly higher at $1.64.

29.4 Setting Up the Excel Sheets

The **Stock Options.xlsm** file contains four worksheets: the Explanation sheet, the EuroModel sheet, the AmerModel sheet, and the AmerPutReport sheet. The EuroModel sheet, shown in Figure 29.6, can be set up completely at design time, using any trial values in the input cells. The current date is calculated in cell B7 with Excel's TODAY function. Actually, it uses an IF formula together with Excel's WEEKDAY function to return today's date or the following Monday in case today is a weekend day. The formula is

=IF(WEEKDAY(TODAY())=1,TODAY()+1,IF(WEEKDAY(TODAY())=7, TODAY()+2,TODAY()))

Figure 29.6 EuroModel Sheet

	A	B	C	D	E
1	Black-Scholes model for pricing European puts, calls				
2					
3	Input data				
4	Type of option (1 for call, 2 for put)	2			
5	Stock price	$60.00			
6	Exercise price	$60.00			
7	Today's date	07-Nov-08			
8	Exercise date	28-Nov-08			
9	Riskfree interest rate	0.080			
10	StDev of annual return	0.300			
11					
12	Duration (trading days)	15			
13					
14	Quantities for Black-Scholes formula				
15	d1	0.10008009		N(d1)	0.46014
16	d2	0.02802242		N(d2)	0.488822
17					
18	Option price	$1.59			

Figure 29.7 Defining a Sheet-Level Range Name

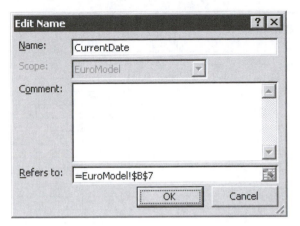

Note that WEEKDAY of any date returns 1 for Sunday and 7 for Saturday. The **duration** of the option (number of trading days until the exercise date) is calculated in cell B12 with a function called **TradeDays**, written just for this application (see the code at the end of the chapter). The formulas in cells B15, B16, E15, E16, and B18 implement the Black-Scholes formula. (These formulas are rather technical. See the **Stock Options.xlsm** file for the details.)

A Note on Range Names. The EuroModel and AmerModel sheets each have input sections that use several of the same range names, such as Riskfree-Rate for cell B9. If you want to use the *same* range names for different worksheets, you need to be careful. The best way is to precede them by their sheet name when they are defined. Specifically, to define the RiskfreeRate range name for the EuroModel sheet, first select cell B9 in this sheet and then select Excel's Name Manager on the Formulas ribbon. In the "Refers to" box, enter **Euro-Model!RiskfreeRate.** (See Figure 29.7.) This creates a "sheet-level" name. You can then proceed similarly to create the name **AmerModel!RiskfreeRate** for cell B9 of the AmerModel worksheet. If you later refer to Range("RiskfreeRate") in VBA code, it will refer to cell B9 of the *active* sheet.

The AmerModel sheet sets up a **binomial tree** for calculating the price of an American call or put. A finished version of this sheet appears in Figure 29.8 for a call option with duration 6 days. The binomial tree calculations are performed in the two triangular ranges, which in general have as many rows and columns as the duration plus one. Without going into the technical details, I will simply state that the option price is always in the upper-left corner of the bottom triangle—in this

Figure 29.8 Finished AmerModel Sheet

	A	B	C	D	E	F	G	H
1	Binomial tree model for pricing American calls, puts							
2								
3	Input data							
4	Type of option (1 for call, 2 for put)	1						
5	Stock price	$60.00						
6	Exercise price	$60.00						
7	Today's date	07-Nov-08						
8	Exercise date	17-Nov-08						
9	Riskfree interest rate	8%						
10	StDev of annual return	30%						
11								
12	Duration (trading days)	6						
13								
14	Parameters for binomial tree							
15	Up factor	1.019						
16	Down factor	0.982						
17	Probability of up	0.504						
18	Probability of down	0.496						
19								
20	Future prices		0	1	2	3	4	5	6
21		0	$60.00	61.126762	62.274684	63.44416	64.6356	65.84942	67.08603
22		1		58.8940079	60	61.12676	62.27468	63.44416	64.6356
23		2			57.808403	58.89401	60	61.12676	62.27468
24		3				56.74281	57.8084	58.89401	60
25		4					55.69686	56.74281	57.8084
26		5						54.67019	55.69686
27		6							53.66244
28									
29	Option values		0	1	2	3	4	5	6
30		0	1.10167896	1.68300012	2.4813738	3.499522	4.672516	5.867879	7.08603
31		1		0.51256507	0.8740295	1.449919	2.311596	3.462622	4.635604
32		2			0.1461483	0.290286	0.576577	1.145221	2.274684
33		3				9.07E-16	1.8E-15	3.58E-15	7.11E-15
34		4					0	0	0
35		5						0	0
36		6							0

case, about $1.11.[1] These triangular ranges must be calculated at run time. The only template that can be created at design time appears in Figure 29.9.

Finally, the AmerPutReport sheet, shown earlier in Figure 29.5, must be filled in almost entirely at run time. The only template that can be set up at design time contains labels, as shown in Figure 29.10.

---

[1] A good explanation of binomial trees and how they can be implemented in Excel appears in Chapter 56 of Winston, W., *Financial Models Using Simulation and Optimization*, Palisade Corporation, 1998.

Figure 29.9 Template for AmerModel Sheet

	A	B	C
1	**Binomial tree model for pricing American calls, puts**		
2			
3	**Input data**		
4	Type of option (1 for call, 2 for put)	1	
5	Stock price	$60.00	
6	Exercise price	$60.00	
7	Today's date	07-Nov-08	
8	Exercise date	17-Nov-08	
9	Riskfree interest rate	8%	
10	StDev of annual return	30%	
11			
12	Duration (trading days)	6	
13			
14	**Parameters for binomial tree**		
15	Up factor	1.019	
16	Down factor	0.982	
17	Probability of up	0.504	
18	Probability of down	0.496	
19			
20	Future prices		

Figure 29.10 Template for AmerPutReport Sheet

	A	B	C	D	E	F	G
1	**Option price and early exercise boundary for the American put option**						
2							
3	Price of option			View Explanation Sheet			
4							
5	Early exercise boundary: exercise only if stock price on this day is below the value in column B.						
6	Trading date	Boundary price					

29.5 Getting Started with the VBA

The application includes one user form named frmInputs and a module. The Solver add-in is never used, so no reference to it is necessary. (The Goal Seek tool *is* used, but no reference is necessary for it.) Once these items are added, the Project Explorer window will appear as in Figure 29.11.

Figure 29.11 Project Explorer Window

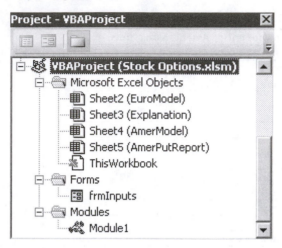

Workbook_Open Code

To guarantee that the Explanation sheet appears when the file is opened, the following code is placed in the ThisWorkbook code window. It also uses a For Each loop to hide all sheets except the Explanation sheet.

```
Private Sub Workbook_Open
    Dim ws As Worksheet
    Worksheets("Explanation").Activate
    Range("F4").Select
    For Each ws In ActiveWorkbook.Worksheets
        If ws.Name <> "Explanation" Then ws.Visible = False
    Next
End Sub
```

29.6 The User Form and Its Event Handlers

The design for frmInputs, shown in Figure 29.12, contains the usual OK and Cancel buttons, an explanation label, four text boxes and associated labels, a calendar and an associated label, and a frame that contains four option buttons. The text boxes are named txtCurrentPrice, txtExercisePrice, txtRiskfreeRate, and txtVolatility. The option buttons are named optEuroCall, optEuroPut, optAmer-Call, and optAmerPut.

A Note on the Calendar control. For the exercise price, I have used a calendar control instead of the text box used in previous editions. This is a very handy control for obtaining a date. It requires almost no work on the programmer's part, and it is very easy for the user. To find a calendar control, right-click on

Figure 29.12 frmInputs Design

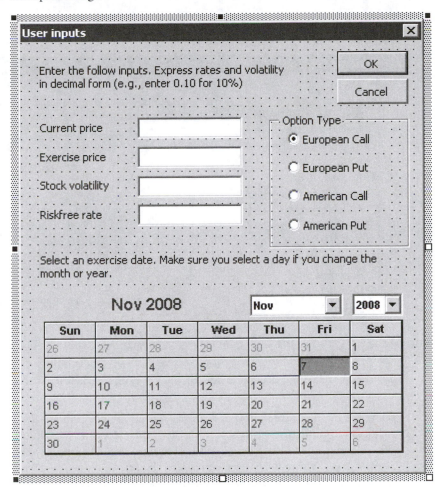

Figure 29.13 Additional Controls

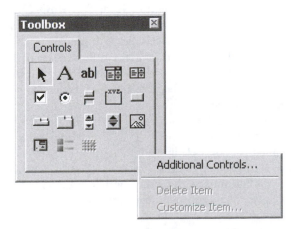

Figure 29.14 Adding the Calendar Control

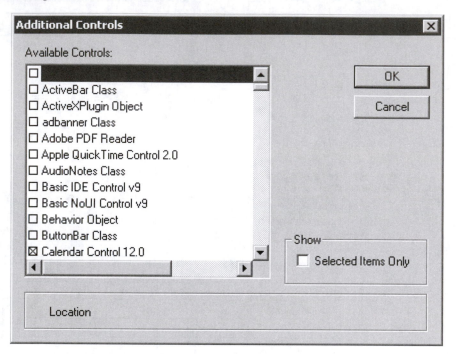

some blank gray area of the Control Toolbox (see Figure 29.13) and select Additional Controls. Then select the Calendar control (see Figure 29.14), and the calendar control will be added to the Toolbox. Among other properties, the control has a **Value** property that returns the selected date (as a Date type). It also has **Year, Month**, and **Day** properties that return these values for the selected date. (Month returns 1 to 12.) The only annoying feature of this control is that if the user changes the month or year, no day is selected, which leads to unexpected behavior. This is the reason for the prompt in Figure 29.12.

Most of the event handler code is straightforward. The **btnOK_Click** sub does a fair amount of error checking and finally captures the user's choices in a number of public variables for later use. The **btnCancel_Click** sub unloads the form and terminates the program. However, there is one twist in the rest of the event code. I want the four text boxes and the calendar to be filled with the inputs from the EuroModel sheet if either of the first two option buttons is checked, and I want them to be filled with the inputs from the AmerModel sheet if either of the bottom two option buttons is checked. Therefore, I write a "utility" sub called FillInputs that takes an argument country, which will be "Euro" or "Amer." The **Userform_Initialize** checks the European Call option button by default and then calls FillInputs with argument "Euro." But this is not all. I also add event handlers for the Click event of each option button. Each of these calls FillInputs with the appropriate argument. This way, the text boxes and the calendar are filled with data from the appropriate sheet regardless of which option button is checked.

frmInputs Event Handlers

```vba
Private Sub btnCancel_Click
    Unload Me
    End
End Sub

Private Sub btnOK_Click
    ' Perform error checking for user inputs.
    Dim ctl As Control
    For Each ctl In Me.Controls
        ' Make sure the non-date boxes have positive numeric values.
        If ctl.Name = "txtCurrentPrice" Or ctl.Name = "txtExercisePrice" Or _
            ctl.Name = "txtRiskfreeRate" Or ctl.Name = "txtVolatility" Then
            If ctl.Value = "" Or Not IsNumeric(ctl) Then
                MsgBox "Enter a positive value in this box.", _
                    vbInformation, "Invalid entry"
                ctl.SetFocus
                Exit Sub
            End If
            If ctl.Value <= 0 Then
                MsgBox "Enter a positive value in this box.", _
                    vbInformation, "Invalid entry"
                ctl.SetFocus
                Exit Sub
            End If
        End If
    Next

    ' Capture the dates. Note that the current date is entered in the
    ' EuroModel and AmerModel sheets as today's date (or the next Monday
    ' if today is a weekend day.)
    currentDate = Worksheets("EuroModel").Range("B7").Value
    exerciseDate = calExerciseDate.Value

    ' Make sure the exercise date is after the current date.
    If currentDate >= exerciseDate Then
        MsgBox "The exercise date must be after the next trading day (" _
            & Format(currentDate, "mm/dd/yyyy") & ").", _
            vbInformation, "Invalid dates"
        calExerciseDate.SetFocus
        Exit Sub
    End If

    ' Capture the other inputs.
    currentPrice = txtCurrentPrice.Text
    exercisePrice = txtExercisePrice.Text
    riskfreeRate = txtRiskfreeRate.Text
    volatility = txtVolatility.Text
    Select Case True
        Case optEuroCall.Value
            optionType = 1
        Case optEuroPut.Value
            optionType = 2
        Case optAmerCall.Value
            optionType = 3
        Case optAmerPut.Value
            optionType = 4
    End Select
```

```
        Unload Me
End Sub

Private Sub FillInputs(country As String)
    With Worksheets(country & "Model")
        txtCurrentPrice.Text = Format(.Range("CurrentPrice").Value, "0.00")
        txtExercisePrice.Text = Format(.Range("ExercisePrice").Value, "0.00")
        calExerciseDate.Value = .Range("ExerciseDate").Value
        txtRiskfreeRate.Text = Format(.Range("RiskfreeRate").Value, "0.000")
        txtVolatility.Text = Format(.Range("Volatility").Value, "0.000")
    End With
End Sub

Private Sub optAmerCall_Click
    Call FillInputs("Amer")
End Sub

Private Sub optAmerPut_Click
    Call FillInputs("Amer")
End Sub

Private Sub optEuroCall_Click
    Call FillInputs("Euro")
End Sub

Private Sub optEuroPut_Click
    Call FillInputs("Euro")
End Sub

Private Sub UserForm_Initialize
    ' Initialize by checking the European call option and entering the values
    ' for the other parameters from the EuroModel sheet.
    optEuroCall.Value = True
    Call FillInputs("Euro")
End Sub
```

29.7 The VBA Code in the Module

The module consists of a **Main** sub that "shows" frmInputs and then calls the appropriate sub, EuroModel or AmerModel. The **EuroModel** sub is simple because the EuroModel sheet is already set up at design time. However, the **AmerModel** sub is considerably more complex. It has to create all of the formulas for the binomial tree method. In addition, it needs to calculate the early exercise boundary for an American put option. The details in the code are not spelled out here. They won't make much sense unless you thoroughly understand binomial trees and how they can be used to calculate the option price and the early exercise boundary.[2] I will simply present the code and let the comments speak for themselves.

---

[2]However, a great exercise is to read the Winston chapter referenced earlier and then see how the code in this application implements his method.

Option Statements and Public Variables

```
Option Explicit
Option Base 1

' Definitions of public variables:
'    optionType: 1 (European call), 2 (European put),
'        3 (American call), or 4 (American put)
'    optionName: "call" or "put"
'    currentPrice: current stock price
'    exercisePrice: exercise price of option
'    currentDate: current date (when option is purchased)
'    exerciseDate: exercise date of option
'    riskfreeRate: riskfree rate (annual)
'    volatility: volatility of stock
'    duration: duration of option (in trading days)
'    cutoff: an array showing the early exercise boundary for
'        an American put
'    optionPrice: price of the option
'    wantExtra: vbYes or vbNo, indicates whether the user wants to
'        calculate the early exercise boundary for an American put

Public optionType As Integer, optionName As String
Public currentPrice As Single, exercisePrice As Single
Public currentDate As Date, exerciseDate As Date
Public riskfreeRate As Single, volatility As Single
Public duration As Integer
Public optionPrice As Single
Public cutoff As Variant, wantExtra As Integer
```

Main Code

```
Sub Main
    ' This sub runs when the user clicks on the button on the Explanation sheet.

    ' Get the user inputs.
    frmInputs.Show

    ' Check whether user wants the early exercise boundary (only for an American put).
    wantExtra = vbNo
    If optionType = 4 Then
        wantExtra = MsgBox("Do you want to calculate the early exercise boundary? " _
            & "(If you click on No, you will get only the price of the option.)", _
            vbYesNo, "Extra info")
    End If

    ' Define option name, depending on whether the user wants to analyze a call or a put.
    If optionType = 1 Or optionType = 3 Then
        optionName = "call"
    Else
        optionName = "put"
    End If

    ' Do the appropriate analysis, either for a European or an American option.
    If optionType <= 2 Then
```

```
        Call EuroModel
    Else
        Call AmerModel
    End If
End Sub
```

EuroModel Code

The **EuroModel** sub activates the EuroModel sheet, calls the **EnterInputs** sub to enter the user's inputs in the appropriate cells, hides the EuroModel sheet, and displays a message for the option price.

```
Sub EuroModel
    ' This sub shows the EuroModel sheet, enters the user inputs in input cells,
    ' and displays the price of the option. The formulas for calculating the Black-Scholes
    ' price are already in the sheet.
    Application.ScreenUpdating = False

    ' Unhide and activate the EuroModel sheet.
    With Worksheets("EuroModel")
        .Visible = True
        .Activate
    End With

    ' Enter the inputs for the European model.
    Call EnterInputs
    optionPrice = Range("B18").Value

    ' Hide the EuroModel sheet and activate the Explanation sheet.
    Worksheets("EuroModel").Visible = False
    Worksheets("Explanation").Activate
    Range("F4").Select
    Application.ScreenUpdating = True

    ' Display the results.
    MsgBox "The price of this European " & optionName & " is " _
        & Format(optionPrice, "$0.00"), vbInformation, optionName & " price"
End Sub
```

EnterInputs Code

The **EnterInputs** sub takes the user's inputs and enters them in the input cells of the currently active model sheet. Because the input cells have the same range names in both the EuroModel and the AmerModel sheets, this same code can be called from both the EuroModel and AmerModel subs. This means that it has to be written only *once*. Note that if the duration of the option is extremely long, the range for the binomial tree (for an American option) could extend beyond the right edge of the worksheet. (Of course, this is much less likely in Excel 2007, which has *many* more columns.) A check is made for this by using **ActiveSheet.Columns.Count**. This returns the number of columns in a worksheet.

```
Sub EnterInputs
    ' This sub enters the user's inputs into the appropriate sheet (EuroModel or AmerModel).
    ' Note that this same sub is called for both the European and the American models.

    If optionType <= 2 Then
        Range("EuroOptType") = optionType
    Else
        Range("AmerOptType") = optionType - 2
    End If
    Range("CurrentPrice").Value = currentPrice
    Range("ExercisePrice").Value = exercisePrice
    Range("ExerciseDate").Value = exerciseDate
    Range("RiskfreeRate").Value = riskfreeRate
    Range("Volatility").Value = volatility
    duration = Range("Duration").Value

    ' Check whether the duration would take the American model beyond the limits of a
    ' typical worksheet. If it does, quit.
    If optionType >= 3 And duration > ActiveSheet.Columns.Count - 2 Then
        MsgBox "Excel cannot accommodate " & duration & " trading days. Its " _
            & "maximum is " & ActiveSheet.Columns.Count - 2 & ". " _
            & "Try again with less days till the exercise date.", _
            vbInformation, "Too many trading days"
        Worksheets("Explanation").Activate
        End
    End If

    ' Redim cutoff array in case the user wants the early exercise boundary for an American put.
    If optionType = 4 And wantExtra = vbYes Then
        ReDim cutoff(duration)
    End If
End Sub
```

AmerModel Code

The **AmerModel** sub implements the American option pricing. It unhides and activates the AmerModel sheet, runs the same **EnterInputs** sub as above, and then calls the **DevelopAmerModel** sub to do most of the work. If the option is an American put and the user wants the early exercise boundary, this sub also calls the **CreateAmerReport** sub to report this information.

```
Sub AmerModel
    ' This sub creates the binomial tree model for an American option.
    Application.ScreenUpdating = False

    ' Unhide and activate the AmerModel sheet.
    With Worksheets("AmerModel")
        .Visible = True
        .Activate
    End With

    ' Enter the user inputs.
    Call EnterInputs

    ' Develop the model
    Call DevelopAmerModel
```

```
' Display the option price unless it is a put option and the user wants the early
' exercise boundary. In this case, create a report.
If optionType = 3 Or wantExtra = vbNo Then
    ' Hide the AmerModel sheet, activate the Explanation sheet, and display a
    ' message about the option's price.
    Worksheets("AmerModel").Visible = False
    Worksheets("Explanation").Activate
    Range("F4").Select
    Application.ScreenUpdating = True
    MsgBox "The price of this American " & optionName & " is " _
        & Format(optionPrice, "$0.00"), vbInformation, optionName & " price"

Else
    ' This is an American put and the user wants the early exercise boundary,
    ' so it must be created.
    Worksheets("AmerModel").Visible = False
    With Worksheets("AmerPutReport")
        .Visible = True
        .Activate
    End With
    Call CreateAmerReport
End If

Application.ScreenUpdating = True
End Sub
```

DevelopAmerModel Code

The **DevelopAmerModel** sub acts as its own control center, calling a number of subs (**ErasePrevious**, **CalcFuturePrices**, **CalcValues**, and, in the case of an early exercise boundary, **EraseRowCol** and **RunGoalSeek**) to set up the AmerModel sheet and, if appropriate, calculate the early exercise boundary.

A Note on Status Bar Messages. The calculations for the early exercise boundary can take a while, so it is useful to indicate the progress to the user in the status bar at the bottom of the screen. Two properties of the **Application** object are useful here. The **DisplayStatusBar** property is Boolean; it is True if the status bar is visible, and it is False otherwise. The **StatusBar** property returns the message in the status bar. However, this property can also be set to False, which deletes the current message from the status bar.

To illustrate these properties, the next two lines capture whether the status bar was visible (in the Boolean variable oldStatusBar) and then ensure that it *is* visible.

```
oldStatusBar = Application.DisplayStatusBar
Application.DisplayStatusBar = True
```

The next line displays a progress indicator on the status bar that keeps changing as the program proceeds through a For loop.

```
Application.StatusBar = "Running Goal Seek on trading day " & duration - i + 1 & " of " & duration
```

Finally, the first of the next two lines removes the message, and the second restores the status bar to its original state (visible or not visible).

```
Application.StatusBar = False
Application.DisplayStatusBar = oldStatusBar
```

This technique can be very useful if your program takes a long time to run. Users will at least know that something is happening! Try running the program for an American put option with a duration of several months, and you will see what I mean.

Here is the **DevelopAmerModel** sub in its entirety.

```
Sub DevelopAmerModel
    ' This sub develops the binomial tree model for an American option.
    Dim i As Integer
    Dim oldStatusBar As Boolean

    ' Clear any previous model.
    Call ErasePrevious
    ' Calculate the possible future stock prices in a triangular range.
    Call CalcFuturePrices
    ' Calculate the expected cash flows from the option by following an optimal strategy.
    Call CalcValues

    ' Calculate the early exercise boundary if the user requests it.
    If optionType = 4 And wantExtra = vbYes Then

        ' The StatusBar statements allow the user to track the progress of the calculations.
        oldStatusBar = Application.DisplayStatusBar
        Application.DisplayStatusBar = True

        ' The following loop solves a series of Goal Seek problems. Each finds the early
        ' exercise cutoff price (exercise only if current price is below this price) for a
        ' particular trading day. In this loop, i represents the row and column of the binomial
        ' tree "values" area that will be erased.  This corresponds to trading day duration-i+1.
        Range("A20").Offset(duration + 2, 0).Value = "Goal Seek set cell:"
        For i = duration To 2 Step -1
            Application.StatusBar = "Running Goal Seek on trading " _
                & "day " & duration - i + 1 & " of " & duration
            Call EraseRowCol(i)
            Call RunGoalSeek
            cutoff(duration - i + 1) = Range("B21").Value
        Next

        ' Delete the message from the status bar and restore it to its original state.
        Application.StatusBar = False
        Application.DisplayStatusBar = oldStatusBar

        ' The cutoff on the last day requires no calculation; it is the exercise price.
        cutoff(duration) = exercisePrice
    End If
End Sub
```

ErasePrevious Code

The **ErasePrevious** sub clears the contents of the triangular ranges in the AmerModel sheet from a previous run, if any.

```
Sub ErasePrevious
    ' This sub clears the calculations from any previous model in the AmerModel sheet.
    With Range("A20")
        Range(.Offset(0, 0), _
            .End(xlToRight).End(xlDown).End(xlDown).End(xlDown)) _
            .ClearContents
    End With
End Sub
```

CalcFuturePrices Code

The binomial tree method is based on an approximation where the stock price can go up or down on any particular day. The **CalcFuturePrices** sub calculates all possible future prices in the first triangular array in the AmerModel sheet. (Each column corresponds to a particular day in the future.)

```
Sub CalcFuturePrices
    ' This sub sets up the possible future stock prices for the binomial tree method in
    ' a triangular region, starting in cell B21.
    Dim j As Integer

    With Range("A20")
        .Value = "Future prices"

        ' Enter headings in top row, left column.
        For j = 0 To duration
            .Offset(j + 1, 0).Value = j
            .Offset(0, j + 1).Value = j
        Next

        ' Get started by entering the current price in the top left cell of the triangular region.
        .Offset(1, 1).Value = Range("CurrentPrice").Value

        ' Each entry in the top row is just UpFactor times the previous entry.
        Range(.Offset(1, 2), .Offset(1, duration + 1)) _
            .FormulaR1C1 = "=UpFactor*RC[-1]"

        ' Each entry in other rows is (DownFactor/UpFactor) times the entry right above it.
        Range(.Offset(2, 1), .Offset(duration + 1, duration + 1)) _
            .FormulaR1C1 = "=If(RC1<=R20C,(DownFactor/UpFactor)*R[-1]C,"""")"
    End With
End Sub
```

CalcValues Code

The key to the binomial tree method is that at the beginning of each day, the decision on whether to exercise or not is based on the maximum of two quantities:

the value from exercising now and the expected value from waiting a day and then deciding whether to exercise. This permits a simple recursion that is implemented in the **CalcValues** sub. The FormulaR1C1 line in this sub enters the *same* formula (using relative addressing) in the entire second triangular range of the AmerModel sheet.

A Note on Double Quotes Embedded in Strings. Suppose you want to use VBA to enter a formula such as **=IF(A5<=10,15,"NA")** in cell B5. This formula uses a pair of double quotes to enter a string in the cell B5 if the condition is false. It is tempting to write the following line of code:

```
Range("B5").Formula = "=If(A5<=10,15,"NA")"
```

This line enters the formula literally between the two outer double quotes. However, it will not work correctly! The problem is that VBA will read the formula up through "=If(A5<=10,15," and think it is finished because it has run into a second double quote. You need to indicate that the *inner* two double quotes should be treated as literals, not as double quotes enclosing the string that the formula consists of.

In general, if you want a double quote in a string to be treated as a literal and not as one of the double quotes enclosing the string, you need to precede it with *another* double quote. The following line does the job:

```
Range("B5").Formula = "=If(A5<=10,15,""NA"")"
```

The formula toward the bottom of the following sub illustrates how this technique is used. In fact, it can be used for any strings, not just formulas. For example, the following line illustrates how to handle double quotes around the word *strange* in a message box.

```
MsgBox "The results from this run were somewhat ""strange""."
```

Again, any two double quotes in a row inside a string are interpreted as one *literal* double quote.

Here is the **CalcValues** sub in its entirety.

```
Sub CalcValues
    ' This sub implements the binomial tree method in another triangular region, right
    ' below the previous one. Each formula says that the price of the option at any point
    ' of the time is the maximum of two quantities: the cash flow from exercising now and
    ' the expected value from waiting a day and then deciding.
    Dim j As Integer

    With Range("A20").Offset(duration + 3, 0)

    ' Enter headings.
```

```
            .Value = "Option values"
            For j = 0 To duration
                .Offset(j + 1, 0).Value = j
                .Offset(0, j + 1).Value = j
            Next

            ' Enter the ending value of the option in the last column.
            If optionType = 3 Then ' call option
                Range(.Offset(1, duration + 1), .Offset(duration + 1, duration + 1)).FormulaR1C1 = _
                    "=Max(R[-" & duration + 3 & "]C-ExercisePrice,0)"
            Else 'put option
                Range(.Offset(1, duration + 1), .Offset(duration + 1, duration + 1)).FormulaR1C1 = _
                    "=Max(ExercisePrice-R[-" & duration + 3 & "]C,0)"
            End If

            ' Enter the appropriate formula in the rest of the cells of the triangular region.
            If optionType = 3 Then ' call option
                Range(.Offset(1, 1), .Offset(duration, duration)).FormulaR1C1 = _
                    "=If(RC1<=R20C,(PrUp*RC[1]+PrDown*R[1]C[1])/(1+RiskfreeRate/260),"""")"

            Else ' put option
                Range(.Offset(1, 1), .Offset(duration, duration)).FormulaR1C1 = _
                    "=If(RC1<=R20C,Max(ExercisePrice-R[-" & duration + 3 & "]C," _
                    & "(PrUp*RC[1]+PrDown*R[1]C[1])/(1+RiskfreeRate/260)),"""")"
            End If

            ' The option price is the top left entry of the region.
            optionPrice = .Offset(1, 1).Value
        End With
End Sub
```

EraseRowCol and RunGoalSeek Code

The calculation of the early exercise boundary (as explained in the Winston chapter referenced earlier) can be accomplished by a suitable modification of the second triangular range of the AmerModel sheet and a call to Excel's Goal Seek tool. (Goal Seek is used in general to solve one equation in one unknown.) The following two subs implement this method.

```
sub EraseRowCol(i As Integer)
    ' A quick way to get the early exercise boundary is to delete the bottom and
    ' leftmost row and column of the triangular "values" region and then run Goal Seek.
    ' This sub deletes row i and column i of the region.
    With Range("A20").Offset(duration + 3, 0)
        Range(.Offset(i + 1, 1), .Offset(i + 1, i + 1)).ClearContents
        Range(.Offset(1, i + 1), .Offset(i + 1, i + 1)).ClearContents
    End With
End Sub
```

A Note on Using Goal Seek in VBA. Goal Seek is an Excel tool (found under the What-If Analysis dropdown on the Data ribbon) for solving one equation in one unknown. It requires you to specify three things: (1) a cell containing a formula that you want to force to some value, (2) the value you want to force it to, and (3) a "changing cell" that can be varied to force the formula to the required value. It is easy to invoke Goal Seek from VBA, using the **GoalSeek** method of a Range object. The following line illustrates how it is done.

```
Range("B20").GoalSeek 0, Range("B21")
```

This line will force the value in cell B20 to 0, using cell B21 as the changing cell. As this example shows, the GoalSeek method takes two arguments: the value to be forced to and the changing cell. It is used to calculate the early exercise boundary in the following **RunGoalSeek** sub.

```
sub RunGoalSeek
    ' This sub runs Goal Seek. (It would also be possible to run Solver, but Goal Seek
    ' is easier.) The changing cell is B21, which contains a trial value for the price
    ' of the stock. Initialize it to a value that is certainly too high: the exercise price.

    With Range("B21")
        .Value = exercisePrice
        .NumberFormat = "General"
    End With

    ' In between the two triangular regions (in column B), enter a formula: the difference
    ' between the cash flow from exercising now and the optimal cash flow. Then run Goal Seek,
    ' trying to drive the value from this formula to 0.
    With Range("A20").Offset(duration + 2, 1)
        .Formula = "=ExercisePrice-B21-" & .Offset(2, 0).Address
        .NumberFormat = "General"
        .GoalSeek 0, Range("B21")
    End With
End Sub
```

CreateAmerReport Code

Finally, the **CreateAmerReport** sub fills in the AmerPutReport sheet with the information (calculated earlier and stored in the cutoff array) about the early exercise boundary. The most interesting part of this sub is the handling of dates. Note how the report in Figure 29.5 skips dates corresponding to weekend days (nontrading days). This is implemented in the sub with an If construct and Excel's WEEKDAY function. Again, this function returns 7 for a Saturday and 1 for a Sunday. Note that the thisDate variable needs to be declared as a Date variable to make this work properly.

```
Sub CreateAmerReport
    ' This sub creates a report of the option price and the early exercise boundary, but
    ' only for an American put and only when the user requests the early exercise boundary.
    Dim i As Integer
    Dim thisDate As Date

    ' Record the option price.
    Range("B3").Value = optionPrice

    ' Record the early exercise prices, starting in cell B7. Note that thisDate captures
    ' the actual date, but it excludes weekends.
```

```
    With  Range("A6")
        Range(.Offset(1,  0),  .Offset(1,  1).End(xlDown)).ClearContents
        thisDate  =  currentDate
        For  i  =  1  To  duration
            thisDate  =  thisDate  +  1

                ' If thisDate is a Saturday, make it the next Monday.
                If  Application.Weekday(thisDate)  =  7  Then
                    thisDate  =  thisDate  +  2

                ' If thisDate is a Sunday, make it the next Monday.
                ElseIf  Application.Weekday(thisDate)  =  1  Then
                    thisDate  =  thisDate  +  1
                End  If
                .Offset(i,  0).Value  =  thisDate
                .Offset(i,  1).Value  =  cutoff(i)
        Next
    End  With

    Range("A2").Select
End  Sub
```

ViewExplanation Code

This sub is used for navigational purposes (from the button on the AmerPutReport sheet).

```
sub  ViewExplanation
    Worksheets("AmerPutReport").Visible  =  False
    Worksheets("Explanation").Activate
    Range("F4").Select
End  Sub
```

TradeDays Function

Two inputs to the option-pricing model are the current date and exercise date. The pricing models actually require the **duration** of the option, defined as the number of trading days until the exercise date. To calculate the duration, I created a function specifically for this purpose, with the code listed below. It again uses Excel's WEEKDAY function to skip weekends. It can then be used in an Excel formula in the usual way. For example, the formula in cell B12 of the EuroModel sheet (see Figure 29.6) is

```
=TradeDays(CurrentDate,ExerciseDate)
```

This is a perfect example of *creating* a function to perform a particular task when Excel doesn't have a built-in function to perform it. If you want to use this function in your own workbooks, you should insert a module in your workbook and copy the following code to it.

```
Function TradeDays(firstDate As Date, lastDate As Date) As Integer
    ' This function returns the number of trading days between two dates. It excludes
    ' weekends only, although with extra logic, it could be changed to exclude other days
    ' (such as Christmas). Note how it uses Excel's Weekday function, which returns 1 for
    ' Sundays, 7 for Saturdays.

    Dim nDays As Integer
    Dim i As Integer
    Dim currentDay As Integer

    ' Start with the number of days from FirstDate to LastDate
    nDays = lastDate - firstDate
    TradeDays = nDays

    ' Now subtract a day for every weekend day.
    For i = 1 To nDays
        currentDay = Application.WorksheetFunction.Weekday(firstDate + i)
        If currentDay = 1 Or currentDay = 7 Then
            TradeDays = TradeDays - 1
        End If
    Next
End Function
```

29.8 Summary

This application doesn't require a lot of inputs, and it doesn't produce a lot of outputs, but it does perform a number of rather complex calculations in the background to produce some very useful results. Considering that the options business in the financial community is a billion-dollar business annually, an application such as this one can be extremely valuable to financial analysts and investors.

EXERCISES

1. Develop a message box statement that displays the following message, exactly as it's written here: When you want a literal double quote, ", in a string, you should precede it by another double quote, as in "".
2. Consider the following formula that you want to enter, via VBA, in cell C3: **=If (A3="West","Los Angeles",If(A3="East","New York",""))**. Write a VBA statement to set the Formula property of cell C3 correctly.
3. The file **IRR.xlsx** contains data on an investment that requires an initial cost at the beginning of year 1 and then receives cash inflows at the ends of years 1 through 10. The net present value (NPV) of this investment is calculated in cell B11 for the discount rate in cell B3. The **internal rate of return** (IRR) of the investment is defined as the discount rate that makes the NPV equal to 0. Write a VBA sub, using

the GoalSeek method, to calculate the IRR and display it in a message box, formatted as a percentage with two decimals. (*Note*: Excel has a built-in IRR function. See if you can use it to get the same result that your VBA sub obtains.)

4. The file **Certainty Equivalent.xlsx** contains the probability distribution of the monetary outcome for a given investment. Assume that the decision maker is risk averse and has an exponential utility function with the risk tolerance parameter R given in cell B3. Then the **utility** of any monetary outcome x is $e^{-x/R}$, the **expected utility** of an investment is the "sumproduct" of probabilities and utilities of monetary outcomes, and the **certainty equivalent** of the investment is the dollar amount such that its utility is equal to the expected utility of the investment. In words, the certainty equivalent is the monetary value such that the investor is indifferent between (1) getting this monetary value for sure and (2) getting into the risky investment. Write a sub that calculates the expected utility of the investment described from row 7 down and uses the GoalSeek method to calculate the certainty equivalent. Display both of these outputs in a message box. Write the sub so that it will work for *any* probability distribution listed from row 7 down and any risk tolerance given in cell B3.

5. Change the TradeDays function so that it also excludes the *fixed* dates January 1, December 25, and July 4. (In addition, you can exclude any other fixed dates you want to exclude. However, it would be much more difficult to exclude a "floating" holiday such as Thanksgiving, so don't worry about these.) Then change the CreateAmerReport sub so that it also excludes these fixed dates.

6. The preceding exercise claimed that it would be difficult to exclude "floating" holidays like Thanksgiving (the fourth Thursday in November). Is this true? Write a function subroutine called Thanksgiving that takes one argument called Year. (For example, this argument will have values like 2009.) It then returns the date that Thanksgiving falls on. Then redo the previous exercise, excluding Thanksgiving as well as the other fixed dates.

7. The file **City Sales.xlsx** contains sales of 100 products for five cities in California (each on a different sheet) for each day over a two-year period. Write a sub that fills a two-dimensional array maxSale, where maxSale(i,j) is the maximum sale, over all days, for product j in city i. This will take a while to run, so display a message such as "Analyzing product 17 in San Diego" that shows the current city and product being analyzed. Make sure the message disappears when all cities and products have been analyzed.

An Application for Finding Betas of Stocks

30

30.1 Introduction

The **beta** of a stock is a measure of how the stock's price changes as a market index changes.[1] It is actually the coefficient of the market return when the returns of the stock are regressed on the market returns. If the beta of a stock is greater than 1, then the stock is relatively volatile; if the market changes by a certain percentage, the stock's price tends to change by a *larger* percentage. The opposite is true when the beta of a stock is less than 1. This application calculates the beta for any company given historical price data on the company's monthly stock prices and a market index. It uses one of four possible criteria to find the best-fitting regression equation.

The application also illustrates another way of getting data from an application—from another Excel file that is not currently open.

New Learning Objectives: VBA

- To illustrate how to capture data from one workbook for use in a VBA application in another workbook.
- To illustrate two features of list boxes: the use of two columns and the **RowSource** property for populating a list box.

New Learning Objectives: Non-VBA

- To learn how nonlinear optimization can be used to estimate the beta of a stock, using any of four possible optimization criteria.

30.2 Functionality of the Application

The application, stored in the file **Stock Beta.xlsm**, gets the required stock return data from another file, **Stock Data.xlsx**. The application is written so that these two files must be in the *same* folder. The **Stock Data.xlsx** file contains monthly stock price data for many large U.S. companies from 1992 until the end

---

[1]More details on estimation of stock betas can be found in Chapter 7 of *Practical Management Science.*

of 2007.[2] It also contains monthly data on an S&P 500 market index during this same period. The user can choose any of these companies, a period of time containing at least 36 months (such as January 2000 to December 2004), and one of four criteria to minimize: sum of squared errors, weighted sum of squared errors, sum of absolute errors, or maximum absolute error. (I chose the 36-month limit somewhat arbitrarily.) The application then uses the company's returns and the market returns for this period, and it estimates the stock's beta using the specified criterion. It does this by estimating a regression equation of the form $Y = a + bX$, where Y is the stock return, X is the market return, and b estimates the stock's beta. It is also possible to view a time series plot of the stock's returns, with the predictions of its returns from the regression equation superimposed on the plot.

Each stock in the **Stock Data.xlsx** file has its own worksheet. The user can add more sheets for other stocks, and the application will automatically recognize them. If the user wants to run the application with more recent data (for 2008 and 2009, say) on the included companies or any other companies, only a few changes in the VBA code are necessary. As it stands, however, it expects monthly data from January 1992 through December 2007, but these can be changed easily in the code.

30.3 Running the Application

When the **Stock Beta.xlsm** file is opened, the Explanation sheet in Figure 30.1 appears. After clicking on the button in this sheet, the user sees the dialog box in Figure 30.2. As it is filled out here, it will find the beta for IBM, based on the returns from January 2003 to December 2007, using the weighted sum of squared errors criterion with a weighting constant of 0.98. Note that I have chosen to use calendar controls instead of the text boxes that were used in the previous edition. These are much nicer for the user. Because the data are monthly, it doesn't matter which *day* of the month the user chooses in either of the calendars. However, a day *does* need to be chosen or completely wrong dates will be returned.

At this point, the data from the IBM and S&P500 sheets in the **Stock Data.xlsx** file are copied to the Model sheet in the **Stock Beta.xlsm** file. Then a Solver model is set up and optimized according to the specified criterion. The resulting beta is displayed in the message box in Figure 30.3, and the full details (with a number of hidden rows) appear in the Model sheet in Figure 30.4.

When the left button on the Model sheet is clicked, the chart in Figure 30.5 is displayed. It shows the stock's returns with the predictions from the best-fitting regression equation superimposed.

---

[2]I purposely did not include 2008 data because of the wild stock market in the latter half of the year. Also, if you compare older prices (2002, say) from the second edition to those listed here, you will see slight differences. I got this data from the same Yahoo! site in each edition, but for reasons unknown to me (or my finance colleagues), the historical data on Yahoo! sometimes changes!

Figure 30.1 Explanation Sheet

Application for Estimating Stock Betas

> Run the application

This application uses monthly stock return data for many of the largest companies in the U.S. to find their "betas". The stock return data are in a separate file called Stock Data.xlsx, and this file should be in the same directory as the current workbook. The "beta" of the stock can be estimated for any of the companies in the Stock Data file, and it can be based on any period from January 1992 to December 2007. There are four possible optimization criteria: (1) sum of squared errors, (2) weighted sum of squared errors, (3) sum of absolute errors, and (4) minimax (minimize the maximum absolute error). Solver performs the appropriate optimization, based on the criterion specified.

The Stock Data file is set up so that each company has its own data sheet, with monthly closing prices from December 1991 to December 2007, and corresponding returns from January 1992 to December 2007. Similar sheets for other companies can be added by the user. Any additional sheet should be named with the company's ticker symbol, and the name of the company should be entered in cell E1 of its sheet. There is also market data for the same time period in the S&P500 sheet of the Stock Data file.

30.4 Setting Up the Excel Sheets

The **Stock Beta.xlsm** file contains an Explanation sheet, a Model sheet, and a chart sheet named TSChart. The **Stock Data.xlsx** file contains an S&P500 sheet and a separate sheet for each company. These individual company sheets are named by the company's ticker symbol (for example, EK for Eastman Kodak, JNJ for Johnson & Johnson, and so on). A typical company sheet is structured as in Figure 30.6. It contains dates (in reverse chronological order) in column A, monthly closing prices in column B, corresponding returns in column C, and the company's name in cell E1. (Note that many rows are not shown in the figure.) The user can add sheets for additional companies in the **Stock Data.xlsx** file, but they should all be structured in this way. The S&P500 sheet is structured similarly, as shown in Figure 30.7. Note that the closing prices extend back to December 1991, whereas the returns extend back only to January 1992. This is because each return, being a percentage change, requires the *previous* closing price.

The Model sheet in the **Stock Beta.xlsm** file can be set up at design time as a template, with the labels and range names shown in Figure 30.8. The body of it must be filled in at run time. The TSChart chart sheet can be created with Excel's chart tools at design time, using any trial data. It is then linked to the actual data on the Model sheet at run time.

Figure 30.2 Inputs Dialog Box

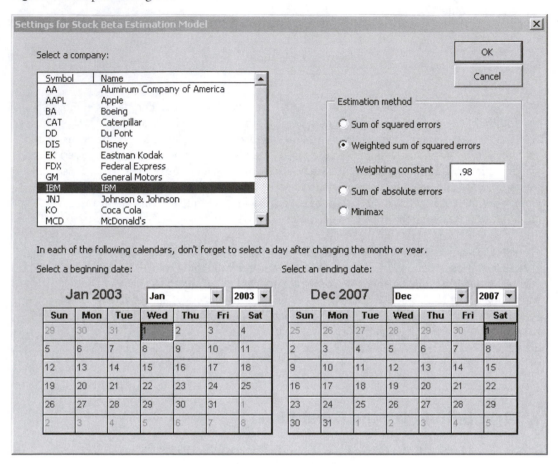

Figure 30.3 Beta for IBM

Figure 30.4 Completed Model Sheet for IBM

	A	B	C	D	E	F	G	H	I	J	K	L
1	Estimation model for IBM: period from 01/2003 to 12/2007, weighted sum of squared errors estimation method											
2												
3	Parameters											
4	Alpha	-0.0008		View Time Series Chart			View Explanation Sheet					
5	Beta	1.2183										
6												
7	Weighting constant	0.98										
8												
9	Optimization model											
10	Date	Mkt return	Stock return	Predicted	Error	SqError	AbsError	Weight		Target for optimization		
11	Dec-07	-0.00863	0.02771	-0.0113	0.0390	0.00152	0.0390	1.0000		WSSE	0.0601585	
12	Nov-07	-0.04404	-0.09095	-0.0545	-0.0365	0.00133	0.0365	0.9800				
13	Oct-07	0.01482	-0.01431	0.0172	-0.0316	0.00100	0.0316	0.9604				
14	Sep-07	0.03579	0.00948	0.0428	-0.0333	0.00111	0.0333	0.9412				
66	May-03	0.05090	0.03897	0.0612	-0.0222	0.00049	0.0222	0.3292				
67	Apr-03	0.08104	0.08246	0.0979	-0.0155	0.00024	0.0155	0.3226				
68	Mar-03	0.00836	0.00614	0.0094	-0.0032	0.00001	0.0032	0.3161				
69	Feb-03	-0.01700	-0.00123	-0.0215	0.0203	0.00041	0.0203	0.3098				
70	Jan-03	-0.02741	0.00894	-0.0342	0.0431	0.0019	0.0431	0.3036				

Figure 30.5 Time Series Plot of Returns and Predictions

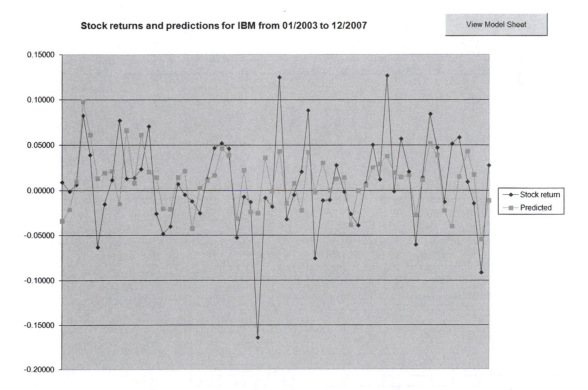

Stock returns and predictions for IBM from 01/2003 to 12/2007

Figure 30.6 Typical Company Sheet

	A	B	C	D	E
1	Monthly closing prices and returns for:				IBM
2					
3	Date	Close	Return		
4	Dec-07	106.83	0.02771		
5	Nov-07	103.95	-0.09095		
6	Oct-07	114.35	-0.01431		
7	Sep-07	116.01	0.00948		
8	Aug-07	114.92	0.05839		
9	Jul-07	108.58	0.05132		

Figure 30.7 S&P500 Sheet

	A	B	C	D	E	F	G	H	I	J	K
1	Monthly closing prices and returns				Market index (S&P 500)			Lookup ^GSPC for ticker symbol			
2											
3	Date	Close	Return								
4	Dec-07	1468.36	-0.00863								
5	Nov-07	1481.14	-0.04404								
6	Oct-07	1549.38	0.01482								
7	Sep-07	1526.75	0.03579								
8	Aug-07	1473.99	0.01286								
9	Jul-07	1455.27	-0.03198								

Figure 30.8 Template for Model Sheet

	A	B	C	D	E	F	G	H	I	J	K	L
1	Estimation model for											
2												
3	Parameters											
4	Alpha			View Time Series Chart			View Explanation Sheet					
5	Beta											
6												
7	Weighting constant											
8												
9	Optimization model											
10	Date	Mkt return	Stock return	Predicted	Error	SqError	AbsError	Weight		Target for optimization		
11												
12												
13										Range names used:		
14										Alpha	=Model!$B$4	
15										AlphaBeta	=Model!$B$4:$B$5	
16										Beta	=Model!$B$5	
17										Target	=Model!$K$11	
18										Weight	=Model!$B$7	

Figure 30.9 Project Explorer Window

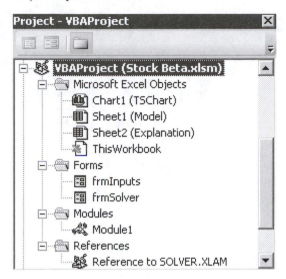

30.5 Getting Started with the VBA

The **Stock Beta.xlsm** file includes a single user form named frmInputs, a module, and a reference to Solver.[3] Once these items are added, the Project Explorer window will appear as in Figure 30.9.

Workbook_Open Code

To guarantee that the Explanation sheet appears when the file is opened, the following code is placed in the ThisWorkbook code window. As usual, it hides all sheets except the Explanation sheet.

```
Private Sub Workbook_Open()
    Worksheets("Explanation").Activate
    Range("E4").Select
    Worksheets("Model").Visible = False
    Charts("TSChart").Visible = False
    frmSolver.Show
End Sub
```

---

[3]It also contains the usual frmSolver that displays a message about possible Solver problems when the workbook is opened.

Figure 30.10 frmInputs Design

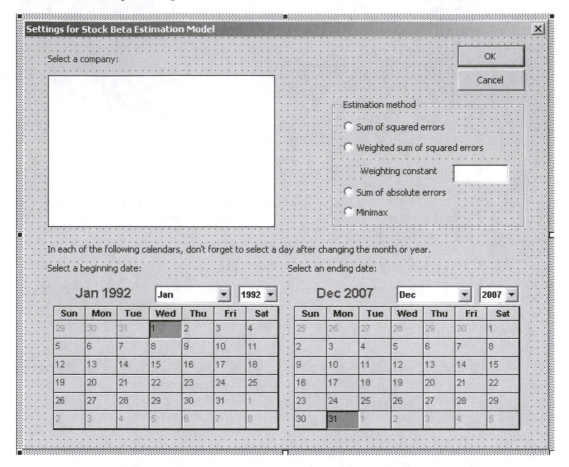

30.6 The User Form and Its Event Handlers

The design of frmInputs appears in Figure 30.10. It contains the usual OK and Cancel buttons, several labels, a text box, a frame for grouping, four option buttons, a list box, and two calendar controls. (See the previous chapter for information about the very useful calendar control.) The text is named txtWeight, the option buttons are named optSSE, optWSSE, optSAE, and optMinimax, the list box is named lbCompanies, and the calendars are named calBeginning and calEnding.

The text boxes and option buttons are standard. However, the list box presents two new features. Specifically, its **ColumnCount** property is set to 2 at design time. (See Figure 30.11.) This indicates that the list will contain two columns, one for the ticker symbols and one for the company names. The **BoundColumn** property of the list box then specifies which column the **Value** property refers to. For example, if you want to get an item from the list in the first column, you set the BoundColumn

Figure 30.11 Properties of List Box

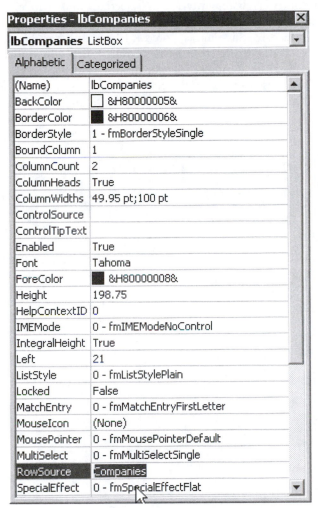

property to 1 before accessing the Value property. Finally, the **RowSource** property is set to the worksheet range named Companies at design time (using the Properties window). Then the list box is automatically populated with the list in this range.

Event Handlers for frmInputs

The **UserForm_Initialize** event selects the first company in the list box, it sets the calendars to the earliest and latest dates in the data set, it checks the SSE option, and it clears the weight box and disables it. The **btnOK_Click** does a considerable amount of error checking before finally capturing the user's inputs in a number of public variables. There is also an event handler for each option button's **Click** event. This enables or disables the weight box, depending on which button has been checked. It makes no sense for the user to enter a value for the weight unless the weighted sum of squares criterion is selected. The **btnCancel_Click** sub unloads the dialog box and terminates the program. It also closes the **Stock Data.xlsx** file (which by this time is stored in the public variable dataFile). Note the use of VBA's **DateDiff** function in the btnOK_Click sub. It takes three arguments: a time period (for example, "m" for month) and two dates, and it returns the number of time periods between these two dates. For example, it returns 3 if the time period is a month and the dates are March 2003 and June 2003.

```vba
Private Sub UserForm_Initialize()
    ' Note that the list box is populated by setting its ColumnCount property
    ' to 2 and its RowSource property to Companies. These are both set at
    ' design time in the Properties window. The Companies range (in the Model
    ' sheet) is populated, right before this user form is displayed, with the
    ' CreateCompanyList sub in the Module1 sheet.
    lbCompanies.ListIndex = 0
    With calBeginning
        .Day = 1: .Month = 1: .Year = 1992
    End With
    With calEnding
        .Day = 31: .Month = 12: .Year = 2007
    End With
    optSSE.Value = True
    With txtWeight
        .Text = ""
        .Enabled = False
    End With
End Sub

Private Sub btnCancel_Click()
    Unload Me
    dataFile.Close
    End
End Sub

Private Sub btnOK_Click()
    Dim ctl As Control

    ' Get the ticker symbol and company name from the user's selection.
    ' The BoundColumn of a list box indicates which column the Value
    ' property refers to.
    With lbCompanies
        .BoundColumn = 1
        ticker = .Value
        .BoundColumn = 2
        company = .Value
    End With

    ' Capture the dates in public variables.
    firstMonth = calBeginning.Month
    lastMonth = calEnding.Month
    firstYear = calBeginning.Year
    lastYear = calEnding.Year

    ' Build the Date variables. Because we're using monthly
    ' data, we can assume the day of the month is 1, regardless
    ' of what the user selects.
```

```vba
firstDate = DateSerial(firstYear, firstMonth, 1)
lastDate = DateSerial(lastYear, lastMonth, 1)

' Make sure the dates are allowable.
If firstDate < earliestDate Then
    MsgBox "The beginning date cannot be before " & _
        Format(earliestDate, "mm/dd/yyyy") & ". Choose again.", _
        vbExclamation, "Invalid date"
    calBeginning.SetFocus
    Exit Sub
ElseIf lastDate > latestDate Then
    MsgBox "The ending date cannot be after " & _
        Format(latestDate, "mm/dd/yyyy") & ". Choose again.", _
        vbExclamation, "Invalid date"
    calEnding.SetFocus
    Exit Sub
End If

' Use the VBA DateDiff function to get number of months between two dates.
' The first argument "m" means month, the second and third arguments are the
' first and last dates for the difference. Note that a literal month is again
' enclosed in pound signs.
nMonths = DateDiff("m", firstDate, lastDate) + 1
' Check that the last date is at least 3 years after the first date.
If nMonths < 36 Then
    MsgBox "Choose dates so that you have at least " _
        & "36 months of data", vbExclamation, "Invalid dates"
    calBeginning.SetFocus
    Exit Sub
End If

' Capture the method to use for optimization.
Select Case True
    Case optSSE.Value
        method = "SSE"

    Case optWSSE.Value
        method = "WSSE"
        ' Check that the weight box is not blank and is numeric.
        If Not IsNumeric(txtWeight) Or txtWeight.Text = "" Then
            MsgBox "Enter a numerical weight between 0 and 1.", _
                vbInformation, "Invalid weight"
            txtWeight.SetFocus
            Exit Sub
        Else
            ' Capture the weight in a public variable.
            weight = txtWeight.Text
            ' Check that the weight is between 0 and 1.
            If weight < 0 Or weight > 1 Then
                MsgBox "Enter a weight between 0 and 1.", vbInformation, _
                    "Invalid weight"
                txtWeight.SetFocus
                Exit Sub
            End If
        End If
```

```
        Case optSAE.Value
            method = "SAE"
        Case optMinimax.Value
            method = "Minimax"
    End Select

    Unload Me
End Sub
```

Event Handlers for Option Buttons

We usually write event handlers only for the Initialize event of a user form and the Click event of OK and Cancel buttons. However, remember that event handlers can be written for numerous events for *any* of the controls on a user form. The following subs illustrate how this works for the Click events of option buttons. Specifically, these subs enable or disable txtWeight, depending on which optimization method has been chosen. This text box should be enabled when the user clicks on the WSSE option, and it should be disabled when the user clicks on any of the other option buttons. (To see the effect, run the application and click on the various option buttons.)

```
' The following subs enable or disable the txtWeight box,
' depending on which optimization method has been chosen.
Private Sub optSSE_Click()
    txtWeight.Enabled = False
End Sub

Private Sub optWSSE_Click()
    With txtWeight
        .Enabled = True
        .SetFocus
    End With
End Sub

Private Sub optSAE_Click()
    txtWeight.Enabled = False
End Sub

Private Sub optMinimax_Click()
    txtWeight.Enabled = False
End Sub
```

30.7 The VBA Code in the Module

The **MainStockBeta** sub is attached to the button on the Explanation sheet. It first creates a list of companies by opening the **StockData.xlsx** file and looping through its sheets. Then it "shows" frmInputs to get the user's inputs. Next, it sets up a model and optimizes it, and it updates the chart. It also takes care of closing the **StockData.xlsx** file when it is no longer needed.

The public variables and the main sub are listed below.

Option Statement and Public Variables

```
Option Explicit

' Definition of public variables
'     ticker - ticker ticker of selected company
'     company - name of selected company
'     method - optimization method used
'     weight - weighting constant (for weighted least squares only)
'     firstMonth - first month (1-12) of selected time period
'     lastMonth - last month of selected time period
'     firstYear - first year of selected time period
'     lastYear - last year of selected time period
'     firstDate - first date of selected time period
'     lastDate - last date of selected time period
'     nMonths - number of months in selected time period
'     firstDateRow - first row of data for estimation period (remember
'         that data are listed in reverse chronological order)
'     dataFile - a workbook object variable for the Stock Data file

Public ticker As String, company As String
Public method As String, weight As Single
Public firstMonth As Integer, lastMonth As Integer
Public firstYear As Integer, lastYear As Integer
Public firstDate As Date, lastDate As Date
Public nMonths As Integer, firstDateRow As Integer
Public dataFile As Workbook

Public Const earliestDate = #1/1/1992#, latestDate = #12/31/2007#
```

MainStockBeta Code

```
Sub MainStockBeta()
    ' This sub runs when the user clicks on the button in the Explanation sheet.

    ' Create a list of companies in the Companies range.
    Call CreateCompanyList

    ' Get user choices.
    frmInputs.Show

    firstDateRow = DateDiff("m", lastDate, latestDate) + 1

    Application.ScreenUpdating = False

    ' Comment out the next line and run the program. You'll probably be
    ' asked about saving information on the clipboard – annoying, so
    ' I added the following line.
    Application.DisplayAlerts = True

    ' Set up the model in the Model sheet, use the Solver to optimize,
    ' and update the time series chart.
    Call SetupModel
    Call RunSolver
    Call UpdateChart
```

```
    Application.ScreenUpdating = True

    ' Display the beta in a message box.
    ' (Details are displayed to the user in the Model sheet.)
    MsgBox "The beta for " & company & " for this period is " _
        & Format(Range("Beta"), "0.000") & ". The rest of this sheet " _
        & "shows the model for estimating this beta.", vbInformation, "Beta"
End Sub
```

CreateCompanyList Code

The **CreateCompanyList** sub opens the **Stock Data.xlsx** workbook and loops through all of its sheets (other than the S&P500 sheet) to see which companies are included. As it does this, it creates a list in columns AA and AB of the Model sheet and names the corresponding range Companies. (See Figure 30.12.) This range is the source for the list box in frmInputs because its **RowSource** property is set to Companies at design time. (See Figure 30.11.) Note the error-handling code. If the **Stock Data.xlsx** file cannot be found, control passes to the MissingFile label. At that point, an error message is displayed, and the program

Figure 30.12 Companies List in Model Sheet

	AA	AB	AC	AD
1	Symbol	Name		
2	AA	Aluminum Company of America		
3	AAPL	Apple		
4	BA	Boeing		
5	CAT	Caterpillar		
6	DD	DuPont		
7	DIS	Disney		
8	EK	Eastman Kodak		
9	FDX	Federal Express		
10	GM	General Motors		
11	IBM	IBM		
12	JNJ	Johnson & Johnson		
13	KO	Coca Cola		
14	MCD	McDonald's		
15	MO	Philip Morris		
16	MRK	Merck		
17	MSFT	Microsoft		
18	T	AT&T		
19	WMT	Wal-Mart		

ends. However, if there is no error—the file exists—an **Exit Sub** statement ensures that the lines following the label are *not* executed.

```vba
Sub CreateCompanyList()
    ' This sub creates a list of companies in the Companies range
    ' (in columns AA, AB of the Model sheet) for populating the list box
    ' in the user form.
    Dim ws As Worksheet
    Dim i As Integer

    ' Clear old list.
    Range("Companies").ClearContents

    ' Open the Stock Data file. If it is not in the same folder as the
    ' Stock Beta file, an error occurs, and the program ends. Otherwise, make
    ' Stock Beta the active workbook. Remember that ThisWorkbook refers to
    ' the file that contains the code, i.e., this one.
    On Error GoTo MissingFile
    Set dataFile = Workbooks.Open(ThisWorkbook.Path & "\Stock Data.xlsx")
    ThisWorkbook.Activate

    ' Go through all worksheets in the Stock Data file. If the name is not S&P500,
    ' add to the list. The sheet name is the ticker symbol, and its cell E1 should
    ' contain the company name. Note that the RowSource property of the list box in
    ' frmInputs is set to Companies. So as soon as the Companies range is populated,
    ' the list box is populated also.
    i = 0
    With Worksheets("Model").Range("AA1")
        For Each ws In dataFile.Worksheets
            If ws.Name <> "S&P500" Then
                i = i + 1
                .Offset(i, 0).Value = ws.Name
                .Offset(i, 1).Value = ws.Range("E1").Value
            End If
        Next
        Range(.Offset(1, 0), .Offset(i, 1)).Name = "Companies"

    ' Sort the list on the ticker symbol.
        .Sort Key1:=.Cells(1, 1), Header:=xlYes
    End With
    Exit Sub

MissingFile:
    MsgBox "There is no Stock Data.xlsx file in the same folder as this " _
        & "workbook, so the application cannot continue.", _
        vbExclamation, "Missing file"
    End
End Sub
```

SetupModel Code

The **SetupModel** sub activates the Model sheet and then calls two subs, **CopyData** and **EnterFormulas**, to set up the model for estimating the beta of the stock.

```
Sub SetupModel()
    ' This sub sets up the optimization model.
        ' Unhide and activate the Model sheet.
    With Worksheets("Model")
        .Visible = True
        .Activate
    End With

    ' Set up the model.
    Call CopyData
    Call EnterFormulas

    Range("A2").Select
End Sub
```

CopyData Code

At this point, the **Stock Data.xlsx** file is still open, so the **CopyData** sub copies the data on dates and monthly returns from the selected company sheet and the S&P500 sheet to the Model sheet. It uses the **PasteSpecial** method to paste the monthly return *formulas* as values.

```
Sub CopyData()
    ' This sub copies the data from the S&P500 sheet and the sheet for the selected
    ' company to the Model sheet.

    ' First, clear any previous results from the Model sheet.
    With Range("A10")
        Range(.Offset(1, 0), .End(xlDown).End(xlToRight)).ClearContents
    End With

    ' Copy the dates and returns from the S&P500 sheet of the Stock Data file to
    ' columns A and B of the Model sheet. Because the Returns columns of the
    ' stock sheets contain formulas, they are pasted special as values in the
    ' Model sheet.
    With dataFile.Worksheets("S&P500").Range("A3")
        Range(.Offset(firstDateRow, 0), .Offset(firstDateRow + nMonths - 1, 0)).Copy _
            Destination:=Range("A11")
        Range(.Offset(firstDateRow, 2), .Offset(firstDateRow + nMonths - 1, 2)).Copy
        Range("B11").PasteSpecial xlPasteValues
    End With

    ' Similarly, copy the returns from the selected company to column C of the
    ' Model sheet.
    With dataFile.Worksheets(ticker).Range("A3")
        Range(.Offset(firstDateRow, 2), .Offset(firstDateRow + nMonths - 1, 2)).Copy
        Range("C11").PasteSpecial xlPasteValues
    End With

    ' Close the Stock Data file.
    dataFile.Close
End Sub
```

EnterFormulas Code

The **EnterFormulas** sub is somewhat long, but it is straightforward. It enters the formulas for the optimization model, including the predicted returns, the errors, the squared errors, the absolute errors, the weights for the weighted sum of squares method, and the appropriate objective for the criterion selected. The Case construct is used here to perform different tasks depending on the value of method.

```vba
Sub EnterFormulas()
    ' This sub enters all the required formulas in the Model sheet.
    Dim methodName As String
    ' First, enter an appropriate label in cell A1.
    Select Case method
        Case "SSE": methodName = "sum of squared errors"
        Case "WSSE": methodName = "weighted sum of squared errors"
        Case "SAE": methodName = "sum of absolute errors"
        Case "Minimax": methodName = "minimax"
    End Select
    Range("A1") = "Estimation model for " & company & ": period from " _
        & Format(firstDate, "mm/yyyy") & " to " & Format(lastDate, "mm/yyyy") _
        & ", " & methodName & " estimation method"

    ' Enter the weight in the Weight cell (if weighted least squares is selected).
    If method = "WSSE" Then
        Range("Weight").Value = weight
    Else
        Range("Weight").Value = "NA"
    End If

    ' Enter the predictions, errors, squared errors, and absolute errors with
    ' the appropriate formulas in columns D-G.
    With Range("D10")
        Range(.Offset(1, 0), .Offset(nMonths, 0)).FormulaR1C1 = "=Alpha+Beta*RC[-2]"
        Range(.Offset(1, 1), .Offset(nMonths, 1)).FormulaR1C1 = "=RC[-2]-RC[-1]"
        Range(.Offset(1, 2), .Offset(nMonths, 2)).FormulaR1C1 = "=RC[-1]^2"
        Range(.Offset(1, 3), .Offset(nMonths, 3)).FormulaR1C1 = "=Abs(RC[-2])"
        If method = "WSSE" Then
            .Offset(0, 4).Value = "Weight"
            .Offset(1, 4).Value = 1
            Range(.Offset(2, 4), .Offset(nMonths, 4)).FormulaR1C1 = "=Weight*R[-1]C"
        Else
            .Offset(0, 4).Value = ""
        End If
    End With

    ' Name the appropriate range and then enter a formula for the appropriate objective
    ' in the Target cell.
    Select Case method
        Case "SSE"
            With Range("F10")
                Range(.Offset(1, 0), .Offset(nMonths, 0)).Name = "SqErrs"
            End With
            With Range("Target")
                .Offset(0, -1).Value = method
                .Formula = "=Sum(SqErrs)"
            End With
        Case "WSSE"
            With Range("F10")
```

```
                    Range(.Offset(1, 0), .Offset(nMonths, 0)).Name = "SqErrs"
            End With
            With Range("H10")
                    Range(.Offset(1, 0), .Offset(nMonths, 0)).Name = "Weights"
            End With
            With Range("Target")
                .Offset(0, -1).Value = method
                .Formula = "=Sumproduct(Weights,SqErrs)"
            End With
        Case "SAE"
            With Range("G10")
                    Range(.Offset(1, 0), .Offset(nMonths, 0)).Name = "AbsErrs"
            End With
            With Range("Target")
                .Offset(0, -1).Value = method
                .Formula = "=Sum(AbsErrs)"
            End With
        Case "Minimax"
            With Range("G10")
                    Range(.Offset(1, 0), .Offset(nMonths, 0)).Name = "AbsErrs"
            End With
            With Range("Target")
                .Offset(0, -1).Value = method
                .Formula = "=Max(AbsErrs)"
            End With
    End Select
End Sub
```

RunSolver Code

The **RunSolver** sub is particularly simple because Solver can be set up completely at design time and the *size* of the model never changes. Note that the Solver setup minimizes the Target cell, has the AlphaBeta range as changing cells, and has *no* constraints. (With no constraints, there is no need to check for feasibility—there is bound to be a feasible solution.)

```
Sub RunSolver()
    ' Run Solver, which is developed once and for all at design time.
    SolverSolve UserFinish:=True
End Sub
```

UpdateChart Code

The time series chart is created at design time, so all the **UpdateChart** sub has to do is link the chart to the correct data and modify its title appropriately.

```
Sub UpdateChart()
    ' This sub updates the existing chart with the results of the optimization.
    Dim sourceData As Range, sourceDates As Range

    ' Set range variables for the dates and data ranges for the chart.
    With Range("A10")
```

```vba
        Set sourceDates = Range(.Offset(1, 0), .Offset(nMonths, 0))
        Set sourceData = Range(.Offset(0, 2), .Offset(nMonths, 3))
    End With

    ' Update the chart, including its title.
    With Charts("TSChart")
        .SetSourceData sourceData
        .SeriesCollection(1).XValues = sourceDates
        .ChartTitle.Text = "Stock returns and predictions for " & company _
            & " from " & Format(firstDate, "mm/yyyy") & " to " _
            & Format(lastDate, "mm/yyyy")
    End With
End Sub
```

Navigational Subs

The remaining subs are for navigational purposes.

```vba
Sub ViewExplanation()
    With Worksheets("Explanation")
        .Visible = True
        .Activate
    End With
    Range("E4").Select
End Sub

Sub ViewModel()
    With Worksheets("Model")
        .Visible = True
        .Activate
    End With
    Range("A2").Select
End Sub

Sub ViewChart()
    With Charts("TSChart")
        .Visible = True
        .Activate
        .Deselect
    End With
End Sub
```

30.8 Summary

This application illustrates another way to obtain data for a VBA application: from another Excel file. If the data are already stored in another Excel file, there is no point in appending all of the data to the file that contains the application. Instead, the data file can be opened (and later closed) programmatically, and the necessary data can be copied to the application file. This application also illustrates four common and useful estimation methods that can be used not only for estimating stock betas but for many other estimation problems.

EXERCISES

1. The file **Sales Offices.xlsx** contains data on a company's sales offices. Each row lists the location of the office (country, state or province, if any, and city) and the sales for the current year. Open another file, and insert a user form and a module in this new file. The user form should contain the usual OK and Cancel buttons and a list box (with an appropriate label above the list box for explanation). The list box should contain three columns: one for country, one for state/province, and one for city. The user should be allowed to choose exactly one item from the list. There should then be a sub in the module that shows the user form, and then displays a message for the selected location, such as "The yearly sales for the office in the city of Vancouver in the province of British Columbia in Canada has yearly sales of $987,000." Note that the part about the state/province will be absent for the offices not in the United States or Canada. This sub will also have to open the **Sales Office.xlsx** file (and close it at the end) with VBA code.

2. Repeat the previous exercise, but now allow the user to select any number of locations from the list. Then, inside a loop, the sub should display the same type of message for each location selected.

3. Change the application in this chapter and the data file as follows. For the data file, go to a suitable source (probably the Web), find monthly closing prices for the companies in the file for months after this application was written (from January 2008 on), and add them to the tops of the sheets in the **Stock Data.xlsx** file. You will also have to find the corresponding market index data. It has ticker symbol ^GSPC. Feel free to add sheets for other companies as well, if you like. Then make any necessary updates to the **Stock Beta.xlsm** file, including the code, to make it work with the expanded data set.

4. Suppose the **Stock Data.xlsx** file has stock price data for different months for different companies. For example, it might have data going back to 1992 for one company and data going back to only 1995 for another company. Rewrite the code in the **Stock Beta.xlsm** file to ensure that it uses only the data available. Should the dialog box in Figure 30.2 be redesigned? Should its event handlers be changed? These are design issues you can decide. In any case, you can assume that there are plenty of data for the S&P500 market index—it goes back at least as far as any of the companies—and that the most *recent* closing price date is the same for all companies.

5. The current **Stock Data.xlsx** sheets all have stock *returns* calculated in column C. Suppose these are *not* yet calculated—each column C is blank. For example, this might be the case if you downloaded the closing prices from some source, and this source gave only the prices, not the returns. Change the VBA code as necessary so that it calculates the required returns on the fly.

6. Suppose the stock price data are in some file (in the same format as given here) in some folder, but the file name is not necessarily **Stock Data.xlsx** and the folder is not necessarily the same as the folder where the **Stock Beta.xlsm** file resides. Therefore, you need to give the user a way to locate the data file. You could do this with an input box (and risk having the user spell something wrong), but Excel provides an easier way with the **FileDialog** object as illustrated in Chapter 13 (or

the **GetOpenFilename** method of the **Application** object if you have Excel 2000 or an earlier version). Use either of these to change the application so that it prompts the user for the name and location of the data file. Actually, you should probably precede the above line with a MsgBox statement so that the user knows she is being asked to select the file with the data. Then try the modified application with your own Excel file, stored in a *different* folder from the folder containing the Excel application.

31 A Portfolio Optimization Application

31.1 Introduction

This application is probably the most ambitious application in the book, and it might also be the most exciting one. There is a Yahoo Web site that contains historical monthly stock price data for many companies during any time period. The application retrieves this stock price data into an Excel file, calculates the summary measures (means, standard deviations, and correlations) for the corresponding stock returns, sets up a portfolio optimization model to minimize the portfolio risk (variance) for a given minimum required mean return, and solves this model for several minimum required mean returns to find the efficient frontier, which is shown in tabular and graphical form. The user can select any group of stocks and any time period. All of this is done in real time, so an active Web connection is required.

There is a price to pay for anything this powerful—the VBA code is lengthy and sometimes rather difficult. But if you have the perseverance to work through it, you are well on your way to becoming a real—and valuable—programmer.

Unfortunately, this application relies on a data source that we as programmers cannot control: the Web. The Yahoo site changes unpredictably from time to time, so there is no guarantee that the code presented here will always work. I have literally seen it work in the morning and then not in the afternoon. If I could fix this once and for all, I would; it has been a source of frustration for years. However, to avoid crashes, the current application, as opposed to those in previous editions, performs an error check. If the Web query fails, then rather than present an obscure error message, the application continues with some fixed stock price data that I downloaded at the time I was writing this edition. (This fixed data is stored in a hidden sheet called StockPricesFixed. You can substitute your own data for mine if you like.) Admittedly, the rest of the output will not be for the stocks or dates you requested, but it's better than a crash!

New Learning Objectives: VBA

- To learn how to run Web queries with VBA code.

New Learning Objectives: Non-VBA

- To gain some experience with portfolio optimization and efficient frontiers.
- To learn what Web queries are, and how to run them through the Excel interface.

31.2 Functionality of the Application

The application is stored in the **Stock Query.xlsm** file. At run time, this file contains no data except a list of companies and their stock symbols in the Stocks sheet.[1] The user can add to this list if desired. The application allows the user to select any stocks from the current list and a time period, such as from January 1997 to December 2004. It then performs a **Web query**, which opens Yahoo Web pages for the selected stocks and time period, and imports the monthly stock price data back into the **Stock Query.xlsm** file. From that point, the Web part of the application is finished, and the necessary calculations leading to the efficient frontier are performed.

31.3 Running the Application

The first step is to make sure an Internet connection is available. The user does *not* have to go to the Yahoo Web site. Next, when the **Stock Query.xlsm** file is opened, the Explanation sheet in Figure 31.1 appears. When the user clicks on the button on this sheet, the dialog box in Figure 31.2 is displayed, where the user

Figure 31.1 Explanation Sheet

Creating Optimal Portfolios Based on Data from the Web

Run the application

The purpose of this application is to get stock prices from the Web for any period of time and any chosen stocks. It brings the Web data into a temporary sheet, then it transfers all of the closing stock prices to the ClosingPrices sheet, and then it calculates the stock returns on the Returns sheet. Next, it creates summary data (means, standard deviations, and correlations) for the stock returns on the SummaryMeasures sheet. Finally, it sets up a portfolio selection optimization model on the Model sheet and runs Solver several times to obtain the efficient frontier. The results appear in tabular and graphical form in the EfficientFrontier sheet.

You must enter choices for the starting and ending time periods of interest, as well as a time interval (monthly, weekly, or daily). You must also select the stocks for which you want data. The Stocks sheet has a list of stocks you can choose from. Before running the application, you can add stocks to this list if you like. But see the note on the Stocks sheet about possible problems.

Due to the peculiarities of the Yahoo site that this application queries, the application fails to work sometimes. I am convinced that it has to do with browser settings or the Yahoo site, but I'm not sure which settings guarantee success (or failure). Rather than having the application fail with an obscure error message, I changed the application so that if the Web query fails, the *rest* of the application starts with *fixed* stock price data I downloaded when I created this application. (This fixed data is on the hidden StockPricesFixed sheet.) Of course, unless you replace this fixed data with new data, the application will give the same results every time you run it, but this is better than nothing!

---

[1]The file might also contain some leftover data from a previous run, but these data are eventually deleted. Additionally, it includes the hidden StockPricesFixes sheet discussed in the introduction.

Figure 31.2 Stock Selection Dialog Box

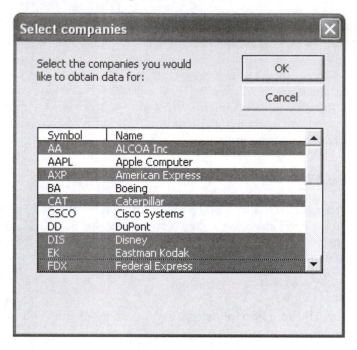

can select any number of stocks from the list. (A portfolio will eventually be formed from the stocks selected.) Then the dialog box in Figure 31.3 appears, where the user can select a time period.

After these selections, there is no further user involvement. From here, the application does its work in steps. First, it retrieves the data from the Web. A new Query worksheet for each selected stock is created, and the Web data are imported into it. A sample appears in Figure 31.4. The only data on this page that are used in the application are the adjusted closing prices (adjusted for dividends and stock splits) in the last column H. The next section discusses Web queries in some detail.

The data from this Query sheet are transferred to the ClosingPrices sheet, and then the Query sheet is deleted. This is done for each selected stock. Next, the monthly *returns* (percentage changes in the adjusted closing prices) are calculated for all stocks on the Returns sheet. Both the closing prices and returns are listed in *increasing* chronological order. (Note that the order is reversed in Figure 31.4. This is how it comes back from the Web.) Portions of the ClosingPrices and Returns sheets appear in Figures 31.5 and 31.6. (These and later outputs are based on the data in ClosingPricesFixed sheet.) Note that the first month, Dec-96, is missing in the Returns sheet. This is because no percentage change can be calculated for Dec-96 if the stock price for Nov-96 is not requested.

The next step is to calculate summary measures (means, standard deviations, and correlations) for these historical returns. This is done in the

Figure 31.3 Dates Selection Dialog Box

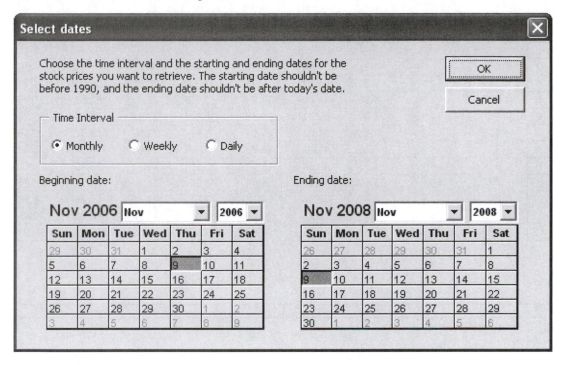

Figure 31.4 Data from Typical Web Query

Date	Open	High	Low	Close	Avg Vol	Adj Close*
8-Nov	19.78	21.04	18	18.86	109,129,100	18.86
8-Oct	24	25.75	17.27	19.51	164,650,600	19.51
18-Sep-08	$ 0.31 Dividend					
8-Sep	28.54	29.28	22.16	25.5	105,769,100	25.5
8-Aug	28.43	30.39	27.76	28.1	43,604,700	27.73
8-Jul	26.42	29.89	25.6	28.29	69,943,000	27.92
19-Jun-08	$ 0.31 Dividend					
8-Jun	30.75	31.14	26.15	26.69	75,216,900	26.34
8-May	32.8	33.62	30.21	30.72	52,851,400	29.98
8-Apr	37.36	38.52	31.55	32.7	64,485,500	31.91
8-Mar	33.34	37.74	31.65	37.01	59,927,700	36.12
21-Feb-08	$ 0.31 Dividend					
8-Feb	35.59	36.3	33.09	33.14	44,926,300	32.34
8-Jan	37.1	37.45	32.92	35.36	55,123,800	34.2

Figure 31.5 ClosingPrices Sheet

	A	B	C	D	E	F	G	H	I
1	Monthly closing prices from 12/1996 until 12/2007								
2									
3	Date	AA	AAPL	BA	CAT	DD	DIS	EK	FDX
4	1	12.66	5.22	44.17	14.21	33.21	20.99	56.03	21.73
5	2	13.7	4.16	44.42	14.74	38.68	21.97	60.57	25.03
6	3	14.19	4.06	42.31	14.85	38.04	22.38	62.97	25.15
7	4	13.55	4.56	41.01	15.23	37.6	21.97	53.32	25.46
8	5	13.97	4.25	41.01	16.98	37.64	24.69	58.32	26.37
9	6	14.72	4.16	43.94	18.62	38.75	24.72	58.45	25.58
10	7	15.07	3.56	44.25	20.48	44.87	24.24	54.14	28.27
11	8	17.69	4.38	48.94	21.46	47.85	24.45	47.26	31.53
12	9	16.49	5.44	45.56	22.25	44.67	23.24	46.41	32.45
13	10	16.44	5.42	45.51	20.67	44.13	24.39	46.11	39.07

Figure 31.6 Returns Sheet

	A	B	C	D	E	F	G	H	I
1	Corresponding returns								
2									
3	Time period	AA	AAPL	BA	CAT	DD	DIS	EK	FDX
4	2	0.082	-0.203	0.006	0.037	0.165	0.047	0.081	0.152
5	3	0.036	-0.024	-0.048	0.007	-0.017	0.019	0.040	0.005
6	4	-0.045	0.123	-0.031	0.026	-0.012	-0.018	-0.153	0.012
7	5	0.031	-0.068	0.000	0.115	0.001	0.124	0.094	0.036
8	6	0.054	-0.021	0.071	0.097	0.029	0.001	0.002	-0.030
9	7	0.024	-0.144	0.007	0.100	0.158	-0.019	-0.074	0.105
10	8	0.174	0.230	0.106	0.048	0.066	0.009	-0.127	0.115
11	9	-0.068	0.242	-0.069	0.037	-0.066	-0.049	-0.018	0.029
12	10	-0.003	-0.004	-0.001	-0.071	-0.012	0.049	-0.006	0.204

SummaryMeasures sheet, with the results shown in Figure 31.7. These summary measures are used as the input data for a portfolio optimization model, which is created in the Model sheet, as shown in Figure 31.8 (with several rows and columns hidden). This optimization model finds the optimal weights (fractions of each dollar invested in the various stocks) that minimize the variance of the portfolio (in cell B31) subject to achieving a minimum required mean return (in cell D28).

Finally, the application solves this model for 11 equally spaced values of the minimum required mean return in cell D28. These values vary from the minimum return to the maximum return in row 5. This sweeps out the efficient frontier, which is reported in the EfficientFrontier sheet in Figures 31.9 and 31.10. Note that this worksheet also shows the optimal weights for the various

Figure 31.7 SummaryMeasures Sheet

	A	B	C	D	E	F	G	H	I
1	**Summary measures for stock returns**								
2									
3	**Stocks**	AA	AAPL	BA	CAT	DD	DIS	EK	FDX
4	**Means**	0.0128	0.0403	0.0088	0.0158	0.0044	0.0064	-0.0029	0.0141
5	**Stdevs**	0.1024	0.1534	0.0855	0.0862	0.0708	0.0793	0.0923	0.0846
6									
7	**Correlations**	AA	AAPL	BA	CAT	DD	DIS	EK	FDX
8	AA	1.000	0.359	0.364	0.614	0.541	0.329	0.485	0.241
9	AAPL	0.359	1.000	0.014	0.132	0.047	0.162	0.274	0.226
10	BA	0.364	0.014	1.000	0.418	0.364	0.383	0.175	0.259
11	CAT	0.614	0.132	0.418	1.000	0.542	0.313	0.364	0.242
12	DD	0.541	0.047	0.364	0.542	1.000	0.285	0.366	0.250
13	DIS	0.329	0.162	0.383	0.313	0.285	1.000	0.348	0.284
14	EK	0.485	0.274	0.175	0.364	0.366	0.348	1.000	0.168
15	FDX	0.241	0.226	0.259	0.242	0.250	0.284	0.168	1.000

Figure 31.8 Model Sheet

	A	B	C	D	E	F	G	H	I	R	S	T
1	Portfolio selection model											
2												
3	Stock	AA	AAPL	BA	CAT	DD	DIS	EK	FDX	T	WMT	Sum
4	Weights	0	1	0	0	0	0	0	0	0	0	1
5	Means	0.012809	0.040252	0.008789	0.015758	0.004415	0.006425	-0.00293	0.014147	0.009861	0.014247	
6												
7	Covariances	AA	AAPL	BA	CAT	DD	DIS	EK	FDX	T	WMT	
8	AA	0.010415	0.005599	0.003163	0.005374	0.003889	0.002652	0.004546	0.002069	0.002225	0.001687	
9	AAPL	0.005599	0.023355	0.000187	0.001727	0.00051	0.001957	0.003844	0.002917	-0.00058	0.000404	
10	BA	0.003163	0.000187	0.00725	0.003057	0.002187	0.002577	0.00137	0.00186	0.001382	0.000425	
11	CAT	0.005374	0.001727	0.003057	0.007366	0.003276	0.002119	0.002872	0.001749	0.001838	0.001373	
12	DD	0.003889	0.00051	0.002187	0.003276	0.004968	0.001585	0.002372	0.001484	0.001289	0.001533	
13	DIS	0.002652	0.001957	0.002577	0.002119	0.001585	0.006236	0.002524	0.001889	0.001135	0.000724	
14	EK	0.004546	0.003844	0.00137	0.002872	0.002372	0.002524	0.008452	0.001304	0.001572	0.000142	
15	FDX	0.002069	0.002917	0.00186	0.001749	0.001484	0.001889	0.001304	0.007104	0.001894	0.002171	
24	T	0.002225	-0.00058	0.001382	0.001838	0.001289	0.001135	0.001572	0.001894	0.006674	0.001355	
25	WMT	0.001687	0.000404	0.0004	0.001373	0.001533	0.000724	0.000142	0.002171	0.001355	0.005353	
26												
27	Constraint on mean return											
28		0.040252	>=	0.040252								
29												
30	Portfolio variance											
31		0.023355										
32												
33	Portfolio standard deviation											
34		0.152822										

Figure 31.9 EfficientFrontier Data

	A	B	C	D	E	F	G	H	I	J	K	L	M	N	U	V
1	Efficient frontier															
2					Weights for these optimal portfolios											
3		PortStdev	ReqdReturn		AA	AAPL	BA	CAT	DD	DIS	EK	FDX	IBM	JNJ	T	WMT
4		0.0386	-0.0029		0.0000	0.0498	0.0474	0.0000	0.0827	0.0789	0.0147	0.0601	0.0000	0.2318	0.0455	0.1527
5		0.0386	0.0014		0.0000	0.0498	0.0474	0.0000	0.0827	0.0789	0.0147	0.0601	0.0000	0.2318	0.0455	0.1527
6		0.0386	0.0057		0.0000	0.0498	0.0474	0.0000	0.0827	0.0789	0.0147	0.0601	0.0000	0.2318	0.0455	0.1527
7		0.0386	0.0100		0.0000	0.0498	0.0474	0.0000	0.0827	0.0789	0.0147	0.0601	0.0000	0.2318	0.0455	0.1527
8		0.0393	0.0143		0.0000	0.0854	0.0562	0.0274	0.0294	0.0602	0.0000	0.0665	0.0000	0.2330	0.0344	0.1811
9		0.0458	0.0187		0.0000	0.1932	0.0037	0.0875	0.0000	0.0000	0.0000	0.0519	0.0000	0.1633	0.0000	0.2177
10		0.0606	0.0230		0.0000	0.3368	0.0000	0.0922	0.0000	0.0000	0.0000	0.0000	0.0000	0.0376	0.0000	0.2438
11		0.0803	0.0273		0.0000	0.4897	0.0000	0.0690	0.0000	0.0000	0.0000	0.0000	0.0000	0.0000	0.0000	0.2065
12		0.1030	0.0316		0.0000	0.6596	0.0000	0.0261	0.0000	0.0000	0.0000	0.0000	0.0000	0.0000	0.0000	0.1200
13		0.1273	0.0359		0.0000	0.8288	0.0000	0.0000	0.0000	0.0000	0.0000	0.0000	0.0000	0.0000	0.0000	0.0237
14		0.1528	0.0403		0.0000	1.0000	0.0000	0.0000	0.0000	0.0000	0.0000	0.0000	0.0000	0.0000	0.0000	0.0000

Figure 31.10 Efficient Frontier Chart

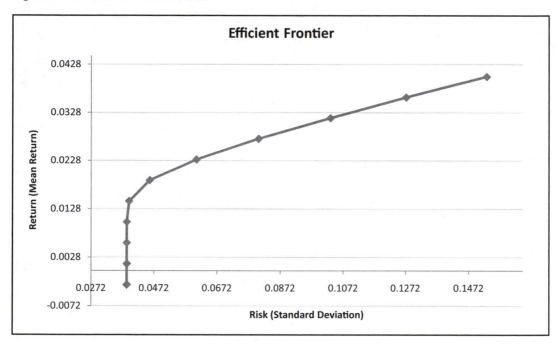

portfolios. For example, Disney is in the optimal portfolio when a small mean return is required, but it is evidently too safe when a larger mean return is required. In contrast, Apple Computer gets almost all of the weight when a larger mean return is required. It evidently has higher return—and higher risk.

All of this occurs behind the scenes, and fairly quickly, when the user clicks on the OK button in Figure 31.3. The connection to the Yahoo site is made, the data are returned, the calculations are performed, and, like magic, the user sees the efficient frontier chart. (Again, remember that even if the Web query fails, the user will see all of these reports for the data in the StockPricesFixed sheet.)

31.4 Web Queries in Excel

To understand this application, you must first understand a bit about Web queries. The application uses VBA to perform a Web query, but a Web query can be performed through the Excel interface, without any VBA. To do this, open a blank sheet in Excel and click on the **From Web** button on the **Data** ribbon. This brings up the dialog box in Figure 31.11, although the top box will depend on the home page for your browser. The essence of the procedure is that when you type a URL in the top box, the *tables* from the corresponding Web site are designated with yellow arrows. When you click on any of them, it turns green. Then, when you click on Import, all the tables with green buttons are imported into Excel.

Sometimes the Web site, like the Yahoo site for this application, asks for parameters—the dates and the stock symbol, as in Figure 31.12. When you click on Go in Figure 31.12, you get the requested data on a page with URL http://finance.yahoo.com/q/hp?s=AA&a=10&b=8&c=2006&d=10&e=8&f=2008&g=m&y=0.

You have probably seen URLs like this, where there is a question mark followed by several "key-value" pairs, such as c=2006, separated by &s. The part following

Figure 31.11 Web Query Dialog Box.

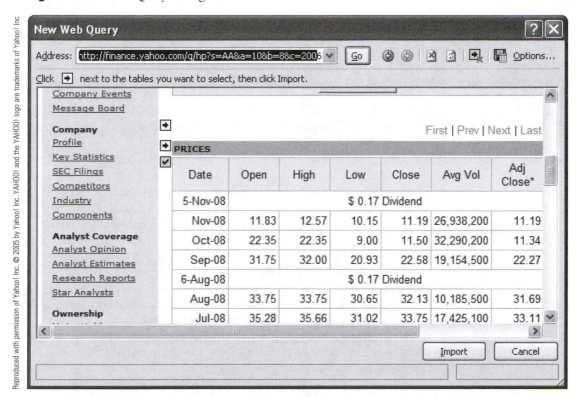

Figure 31.12 Web Site Request for Stock Prices

the question mark is called a **query string.** It indicates the information the user wants. This one has nine keys, named s, a, b, c, d, e, f, g, and y. The first indicates the stock symbol, the next three indicate the initial date requested (month, day, year), where for some reason the months are indexed 0 through 11. The next three indicate the ending date requested. The part g=m indicates that you want monthly data. Finally, y=0 has something to do with how many rows are returned per page.

This is simply the way the Yahoo site works, but you have to understand its query string to understand the code in the application. The code essentially fills in the pieces of the query string, depending on the user's choices from the user forms in Figures 31.2 and 31.3. Specifically, you will see the following code later on:

```
connectString = "URL;http://finance.yahoo.com/q/hp?" _
    & "s=" & tickerSymbol(iStock) _
    & "&a=" & Month(startDate) - 1 _
    & "&b=" & Day(startDate) & "&c=" & Year(startDate) _
    & "&d=" & Month(endDate) - 1 & "&e=" & Day(endDate) _
    & "&f=" & Year(endDate) & "&g=" & timeInterval
```

This line essentially "builds" the URL required to access the stock data for a particular set of dates and a particular ticker symbol. (The part containing the "y" element isn't shown here, but it is in the application.) This **connection string** is the key to the whole process. It specifies where the data are located on the Web and which data you want from that site. Except for the fact that this string starts with **URL;**, it is just like the URL in the dialog box in Figure 31.11.

This brief introduction gives you a taste of Web queries—how they can be performed through the Excel interface and what you need to perform them with VBA. This whole topic is still fairly new, and more user-friendly tools for extracting data from the Web into Excel will probably be developed. Right now, you typically must do some detective work on each Web site you want to query and then hope for the best. This stock application is not as "bulletproof" as the other applications discussed in this book. There is no guarantee that the Web sites will remain as they are, and there is no guarantee that they will return clean data or any data at all.

For these reasons, you might encounter problems when you run this application with new stocks or different time periods. In fact, you might experience problems I never even anticipated. Unfortunately, these are the perils of working with the Web.

31.5 Setting Up the Excel Sheets

The **Stock Query.xlsm** file contains the following sheets at design time: the Explanation, Stocks, ClosingPrices, Returns, SummaryMeasures, Model, EfficientFrontier, and ClosingPricesFixed worksheets. There is very little that can be done at design time to set up these sheets. The only steps possible are to list the stocks in the Stocks sheet, as shown in Figure 31.13, and to develop a scatter chart in the EfficientFrontier sheet using any trial data. The chart will then be populated with the actual data at run time.

31.6 Getting Started with the VBA

The application requires two user forms, named frmStocks and frmDates, a module, and a reference to Solver.[2] Once these items are added, the Project Explorer window will appear as in Figure 31.14

Figure 31.13 Stocks Sheet

	A	B	C	D	E	F	G	H	I	J	K
1	Stock symbols and names to choose from										
2											
3	Symbol	Name									
4	AA	ALCOA Inc									
5	AAPL	Apple Computer									
6	AXP	American Express									
7	BA	Boeing									
8	CAT	Caterpillar									
9	CSCO	Cisco Systems									
10	DD	DuPont									
11	DIS	Disney									
12	EK	Eastman Kodak									
13	FDX	Federal Express									
14	GE	General Electric									
15	GM	General Motors									
16	GT	Goodyear Tire & Rubber									
17	HP	Hewlett Packard									
18	IBM	International Business Machines									
19	IP	International Paper									

You can add any other stocks to this list (or delete any). If you want to add any, enter the stock symbol in column A, the name in column B. However, I suggest you first visit the Web with a URL something like the following:

http://finance.yahoo.com/q/hp?s=IBM&a=0&b=1&c=1992&d=3&e=1&f=2008&g=m

This gets monthly prices for IBM from January 1992 through April 2008. In general, you can replace the s parameter by the stock's ticker symbol, the a and d by the months (starting at 0) you want, the b and e parameters by the days you want, the c and f parameters by the years you want, and the g parameter by d, w, or m (daily, weekly, or monthly). If any prices are missing, then adding this stock to your portfolio could cause the application to fail.

If you add any stocks to the list, make sure the name of the range that includes the ticker symbols and the company names (columns A, B, starting in row 4) is still **Stocks**. This range name is used to populate the list of stocks when you run the query.

---

[2]It also contains the usual frmSolver that displays a message about possible Solver problems when the workbook is opened.

Figure 31.14 Project Explorer Window

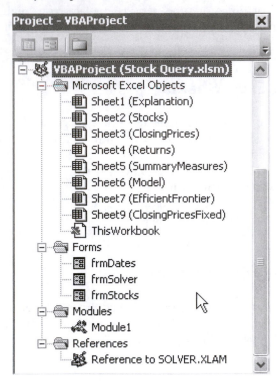

Workbook_Open Code

To guarantee that the Explanation sheet appears when the file is opened, the following code is placed in the ThisWorkbook code window. For a change, it doesn't bother to hide any sheets.

```
Private Sub Workbook_Open()
    Worksheets("Explanation").Activate
    Range("F4").Select
    frmSolver.Show
End Sub
```

31.7   The User Forms and Their Event Handlers

frmStocks

The design for frmStocks appears in Figure 31.15. It contains the usual OK and Cancel buttons, an explanation label, and a list box named lbCompanies. At

Figure 31.15 frmStocks Design

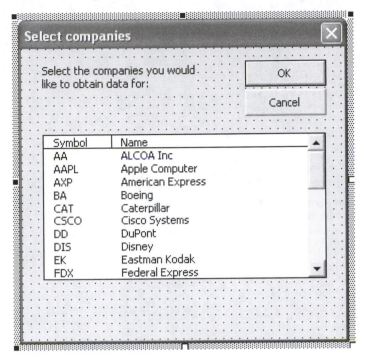

design time, you should change three of the list box's properties: change the **MultiSelect** property to option 2 (so that multiple companies can be selected), change the **ColumnCount** property to 2, and change the **RowSource** property to Stocks. This is the range name in the Stocks sheet where the list of companies and ticker symbols are located. (See Figure 31.13.)

Event Handlers for frmStocks

The event handlers for this form are fairly straightforward. The **UserForm_ Initialize** sub selects the first company in the list by default. Then the **btnOK_ Click** sub uses the **Selected** array property of the list box to capture the names and ticker symbols of the selected stocks in the public arrays stockName and ticker. The **btnCancel_Click** sub unloads the dialog box and terminates the program.

A Note on Multicolumn List Boxes. Like the user form from the previous chapter, this list box has two columns. You could use a combination of the **BoundColumn** and **Value** properties to retrieve values from the two columns. (See the previous chapter for details.) Alternatively, you can use the **List** property like a two-dimensional array, which is done here. The first index indicates how far down the list you are (starting with index 0 for the first item in the list), and the second index is 0 for the first column and 1 for the second column. With list boxes, there always seems to be more than one way to accomplish the same thing.

```
Private Sub btnCancel_Click()
    Unload Me
    End
End Sub

Private Sub btnOK_Click()
    Dim i As Integer

    ' Capture the number of stocks selected, their symbols, and their names.
    nStocks = 0
    For i = 0 To lbCompanies.ListCount - 1
        If lbCompanies.Selected(i) Then
            nStocks = nStocks + 1
            If nStocks = 1 Then
                ReDim tickerSymbol(nStocks)
                ReDim stockName(nStocks)
            Else
                ReDim Preserve tickerSymbol(nStocks)
                ReDim Preserve stockName(nStocks)
            End If
            tickerSymbol(nStocks) = lbCompanies.List(i, 0)
            stockName(nStocks) = lbCompanies.List(i, 1)
        End If
    Next

    Unload Me
End Sub

Private Sub UserForm_Initialize()
    lbCompanies.Selected(0) = True
End Sub
```

frmDates

This form, with design shown in Figure 31.16, contains OK and Cancel buttons, some labels, three option buttons, and two calendar controls. The option buttons are named optMonth, optWeek, and optDay, and the calendars are named calStartDate and calEndDate.

Event Handlers for frmDates

The event handlers for this form, listed below, contain no new ideas. Other than some obvious checks on dates, it makes no other error checks. If the user requests dates for which the Web site has no data, the program will not work correctly.

```
Private Sub btnCancel_Click()
    Unload Me
    End
End Sub

Private Sub btnOK_Click()
    ' Capture the dates.
    startDate = calStartDate.Value
    endDate = calEndDate.Value
    ' Make sure the beginning date isn't after the ending date.
```

Figure 31.16 frmDates Design

```
    If startDate >= endDate Then
        MsgBox "The starting date should be before the ending date.", _
            vbInformation, "Invalid dates"
        calStartDate.SetFocus
        Exit Sub
    ElseIf startDate < DateSerial(1990, 1, 1) Then
        MsgBox "The starting date shouldn't be before 1990.", vbInformation, "Start date too early"
        calStartDate.SetFocus
        Exit Sub
    ElseIf endDate > Date Then
        MsgBox "The ending date shouldn't be after today's date.", vbInformation, "End date too late"
        calEndDate.SetFocus
        Exit Sub
    End If

    Select Case True
        Case optMonth: timeInterval = "m"
        Case optWeek: timeInterval = "w"
        Case optDay: timeInterval = "d"
    End Select

    Unload Me
End Sub

Private Sub UserForm_Initialize()
    calStartDate.Value = DateSerial(Year(Date) - 2, Month(Date), Day(Date))
    calEndDate.Value = Date
    optMonth.Value = True
End Sub
```

31.8 The VBA Code in the Module

The module must accomplish a long list of tasks. It starts with the **MainStock-Query** sub, which is attached to the button on the Explanation sheet. This sub "shows" the two user forms and then calls a number of other subs to accomplish the various tasks. The public variables and the code for the MainStockQuery sub are listed below.

Option Statements and Public Variables

```
Option Explicit
Option Base 1

' Definitions of public variables:
'   nStocks: number of stocks chosen by user
'   tickerSymbol(): array of ticker symbols of stocks chosen by user
'   stockName(): array of company names for stocks chosen by user
'   startDate: starting date for data (user input)
'   endDate: ending date for data (user input)

Public nStocks As Integer
Public tickerSymbol() As String
Public stockName() As String
Public startDate As Date
Public endDate As Date
Public timeInterval As String
Public nWebQueries As Integer
Public minReturn As Single
Public maxReturn As Single
```

MainStockQuery Code

```
Sub MainStockQuery()
    Dim iStock As Integer
    Dim oldStatusBar As Boolean
    Dim successful As Boolean
    Dim ws As Worksheet

    ' Name the range with the ticker symbols and company names.
    With Worksheets("Stocks").Range("A3")
        Range(.Offset(1, 0), .Offset(1, 1).End(xlDown)).Name = "Stocks"
    End With

    ' Get the user's choices of stocks and dates.
    frmStocks.Show
    frmDates.Show

    ' Yahoo evidently returns 67 months or weeks per screen, but only 66 days.
    ' I figured this out with a lot of trial and error. Unfortunately, there is
    ' no guarantee that it won't change.
    Select Case timeInterval
        Case "m"
```

```vba
        If DateDiff("m", startDate, endDate) + 1 Mod 67 = 0 Then
            nWebQueries = (DateDiff("m", startDate, endDate) + 1) / 67
        Else
            nWebQueries = Int((DateDiff("m", startDate, endDate) + 1) / 67) + 1
        End If
    Case "w"
        If DateDiff("w", startDate, endDate) + 1 Mod 67 = 0 Then
            nWebQueries = (DateDiff("w", startDate, endDate) + 1) / 67
        Else
            nWebQueries = Int((DateDiff("w", startDate, endDate) + 1) / 67) + 1
        End If
    Case "d"
        If (DateDiff("w", startDate, endDate) + 1) * 5 Mod 66 = 0 Then
            nWebQueries = (DateDiff("w", startDate, endDate) + 1) * 5 / 66
        Else
            nWebQueries = Int((DateDiff("w", startDate, endDate) + 1) * 5 / 66) + 1
        End If
End Select

Application.ScreenUpdating = False

Call ClearOldData

oldStatusBar = Application.DisplayStatusBar
Application.DisplayStatusBar = True

' For each requested stock, add a new sheet and run a Web query. Show the
' progress in the status bar.
For iStock = 1 To nStocks
    Application.StatusBar = "Running web query for " & tickerSymbol(iStock)
    Call RunQuery(iStock, successful)
    If Not successful Then
        MsgBox "The Web query didn't succeed, so the rest of the application " _
            & "will proceed with the fixed stock price data on the (hidden) " _
            & "ClosingPricesFixed sheet.", vbInformation, "Web query failed"
        Exit For
    End If
Next
Application.StatusBar = False
Application.DisplayStatusBar = oldStatusBar

' Add stock labels and sort appropriately.
If successful Then
    Call FinishConsolidate
Else
    ' Work with data on (hidden) ClosingPricesFixed sheet.
    Set ws = Worksheets("ClosingPrices")
    With ws
        .Activate
        .UsedRange.ClearContents
        Worksheets("ClosingPricesFixed").UsedRange.Copy _
            Destination:=.Range("A1")
        With .Range("A3")
            nStocks = Range(.Offset(0, 1), .End(xlToRight)).Columns.Count
            ReDim tickerSymbol(nStocks)
            For iStock = 1 To nStocks
                tickerSymbol(iStock) = .Offset(0, iStock).Value
            Next
        End With
    End With
End If
```

```
' Calculate returns.
Call Returns

' Calculate summary measures on the SummaryMeasures sheet.
Call SummaryMeasures

' Create the portfolio optimization model and optimize.
Call CreateModel
Call RunSolver

' Create the chart of the efficient frontier and update its chart.
Call EfficientFrontier
Call UpdateChart
Application.ScreenUpdating = True
End Sub
```

ClearOldData Code

The **ClearOldData** sub clears all previous data from ClosingPrices sheet and adds some labels for the new data.

```
Sub ClearOldData()
    ' Clear contents from the ClosingPrices sheet.
    With Worksheets("ClosingPrices").Range("A3")
        Range(.Offset(0, 0), .End(xlDown).End(xlToRight)).ClearContents
        Select Case timeInterval
            Case "m": .Value = "Month"
            Case "w": .Value = "Week"
            Case "d": .Value = "Day"
        End Select
    End With
End Sub
```

RunQuery Code

The **RunQuery** sub is the crucial sub. It creates a **connection string** (stored in the connectString variable), which is essentially the URL for the Web site, as discussed in Section 31.4. It then adds a **QueryTable** object to the active sheet, with the output range starting in cell A1, with the following line. (By this time, qryTable has been declared as a QueryTable object.)

```
Set qryTable = ActiveSheet.QueryTables.Add(Connection:=connectString, _
        Destination:=Range("A1"))
```

This is followed by various properties of the QueryTable object. As the comment indicates, I discovered this code by creating the Web query through the Excel menu interface with the macro recorder on. I do not claim to understand all of the fine details, but they are all explained in the Object Browser.

```
Sub RunQuery(iStock As Integer, successful As Boolean)
    ' This sets up a new Web query and runs it, placing the Web
    ' data into the active sheet.
    Dim connectString As String
    Dim qryTable As QueryTable
    Dim rowOffset As Integer
    Dim iQuery As Integer
    Dim foundNothing As Boolean

    rowOffset = 1
    foundNothing = False
    For iQuery = 1 To nWebQueries
        Worksheets.Add
        ActiveSheet.Name = "Query"
        ' The next line builds a long string that is essentially the URL
        ' (preceded by URL;). It is used to define the query. Note how it
        ' inserts the user's inputs into the string. The "keys", such as a, b,
        ' and so on) store the user's inputs (dates and ticker symbol). (For some
        ' unknown reason, Yahoo's month code is 0-based. E.g., 2 is for March.
        connectString = "URL;http://finance.yahoo.com/q/hp?" _
            & "s=" & tickerSymbol(iStock) _
            & "&a=" & Month(startDate) - 1 _
            & "&b=" & Day(startDate) & "&c=" & Year(startDate) _
            & "&d=" & Month(endDate) - 1 & "&e=" & Day(endDate) _
            & "&f=" & Year(endDate) & "&g=" & timeInterval
    If timeInterval = "m" Or timeInterval = "w" Then
        connectString = connectString & "&y=" & (iQuery - 1) * 67
    Else
        connectString = connectString & "&y=" & (iQuery - 1) * 66
    End If

        ' The next few lines create a QueryTable object with appropriate properties.
        ' I got this code by recording, then deleting parts that appeared unnecessary.
        Set qryTable = ActiveSheet.QueryTables.Add(Connection:=connectString, _
                Destination:=Range("A1"))
        On Error Resume Next
        With qryTable
            .Name = "StockPrices_" & iStock & "_" & iQuery
            .SaveData = True
            .AdjustColumnWidth = True
            .WebSelectionType = xlAllTables
            .WebFormatting = xlWebFormattingAll
            .WebPreFormattedTextToColumns = False
            .WebConsecutiveDelimitersAsOne = True
            .WebSingleBlockTextImport = False
            .WebDisableDateRecognition = False
            .Refresh BackgroundQuery:=False
        End With

        If Err.Number = 0 Then
            successful = True
            Call TransferPrices(iStock, rowOffset, foundNothing)
        Else
            successful = False
        End If
        If foundNothing Then successful = False

        ' In any case, delete the Query sheet.
        Application.DisplayAlerts = False
```

```
        Worksheets("Query").Delete
        Application.DisplayAlerts = True
    Next
End Sub
```

TransferPrices Code

The rest of the subs handle the details—and there are a lot of details. The comments provide most of the explanation you should need. In fact, in complex programs such as this one, extensive and well-written comments are crucial.

The **TransferPrices** sub must copy the data below the "Adj Close" label in the Query sheet (see Figure 31.4) to the appropriate column in the ClosingPrices sheet. Then it must transform the closing prices to returns (percentage changes) on the Returns sheet. There are two problems that it encounters, both caused by the format of the imported Web data (over which we have no control). First, it is possible that some stocks will return no data. Second, there are several blank cells in the data below the "Adj Close" label because of dividends and stock splits. The VBA code must be written to skip over these blanks.

```
Sub TransferPrices(iStock As Integer, rowOffset As Integer, foundNothing As Boolean)
    ' This sub transfers the closing prices from the Query sheet to the
    ' ClosingPrices sheet. It puts the resulting prices in the correct format.
    Dim counter As Integer
    Dim adjCloseCell As Range
    Dim closeRange As Range

    ' Activate the ClosingPrices sheet.
    Worksheets("ClosingPrices").Activate

    counter = 1

    ' Try to find the label "Adj Close" in this stock's sheet. This Find method
    ' returns a range object, which is set to adjCloseCell. If the Web query
    ' couldn't find any data for this stock (for whatever reason), this find
    ' will be unsuccessful and adjCloseCell will be set to Nothing.
    Set adjCloseCell = Worksheets("Query").Cells.Find(What:="Adj Close")
    If adjCloseCell Is Nothing Then
        foundNothing = True
        Exit Sub
    End If
    Set closeRange = Worksheets("Query").Range(adjCloseCell.Address)

    ' Loop through the rows until encountering a blank cell.
    Do Until Left(closeRange.Offset(counter, -6).Value, 1) = ""
        ' rowOffset is how far down the ClosingPrices sheet (below A3) we are.
        ' counter is how far down the Query sheet we are.
        If closeRange.Offset(counter, 0).Value <> "" Then
            ' Enter date indexes in column A of the ClosingPrices sheet.
            If iStock = 1 Then _
                Range("A3").Offset(rowOffset, 0).Value = rowOffset

            ' Transfer the closing price to the appropriate row and column of the
            ' ClosingPrices sheet.
            Range("A3").Offset(rowOffset, iStock).Value _
```

```
             = closeRange.Offset(counter, 0).Value

          ' Update rowOffset after every transfer.
          rowOffset = rowOffset + 1
        End If

        ' Update counter whether or not a blank was found in the
        ' Adj Close column.
        counter = counter + 1
    Loop
End Sub
```

FinishClosingPrices Code

The **FinishClosingPrices** sub adds some labels and sorts the closing prices in increasing chronological order.

```
Sub FinishClosingPrices()
    ' This sub finishes setting up the ClosingPrices sheet.
    Dim i As Integer, j As Integer
    Dim nPrices As Integer
    Dim sortRange As Range

    ' Enter tickerSymbol symbols as headings in the ClosingPrices sheet.
    For i = 1 To nStocks
        Range("A3").Offset(0, i).Value = tickerSymbol(i)
    Next

    ' Sort the data from earliest to latest (the Web query brings them in
    ' in the opposite order).
    Range("A3").Sort Key1:=Range("A:A"), Order1:=xlDescending, Header:=xlYes

    ' Put the date indexes back into increasing order.
    Set sortRange = Range(Range("A3"), Range("A3").End(xlDown))
    sortRange.Sort Key1:=Range("A:A"), Order1:=xlAscending, Header:=xlYes

    Select Case timeInterval
        Case "m"
            Range("A1") = "Monthly closing prices from " _
                & Format(startDate, "mm/dd/yyyy") & " to " & Format(endDate, "mm/dd/yyyy")
        Case "w"
            Range("A1") = "Weekly closing prices from " _
                & Format(startDate, "mm/dd/yyyy") & " to " & Format(endDate, "mm/dd/yyyy")
        Case "d"
            Range("A1") = "Daily closing prices from " _
                & Format(startDate, "mm/dd/yyyy") & " to " & Format(endDate, "mm/dd/yyyy")
    End Select
End Sub
```

Returns Code

The **Returns** sub creates the stock returns (percentage changes) on the Returns sheet.

```
Sub Returns()
    Dim pricesSheet As Worksheet
    Dim returnsSheet As Worksheet
    Dim rowOffset As Integer
    Dim iStock As Integer

    Set pricesSheet = Worksheets("ClosingPrices")
    Set returnsSheet = Worksheets("Returns")

    With returnsSheet
        .Cells.ClearContents
        .Range("A1").Value = "Corresponding returns"
        .Range("A3").Value = "Time period"
        For iStock = 1 To nStocks
            .Range("A3").Offset(0, iStock).Value = tickerSymbol(iStock)
        Next
    End With

    With pricesSheet.Range("A3")
        rowOffset = 1
        Do
            If .Offset(rowOffset + 1, 0).Value <> "" Then
                returnsSheet.Range("A3").Offset(rowOffset, 0).Value = rowOffset + 1
            End If
            For iStock = 1 To nStocks
                If .Offset(rowOffset, iStock).Value <> "" _
                        And .Offset(rowOffset + 1, iStock).Value <> "" Then
                    returnsSheet.Range("A3").Offset(rowOffset, iStock).Value = _
                        .Offset(rowOffset + 1, iStock).Value _
                            / .Offset(rowOffset, iStock).Value - 1
                End If
            Next
            rowOffset = rowOffset + 1
        Loop Until .Offset(rowOffset, 0).Value = ""
    End With

    With returnsSheet.Range("A3")
        For iStock = 1 To nStocks
            With .Offset(0, iStock)
                Range(.Offset(1, 0), .Offset(rowOffset - 2, 0)).Name = _
                    tickerSymbol(iStock)
            End With
        Next
    End With
End Sub
```

SummaryMeasures Code

The **SummaryMeasures** sub uses Excel's Average, Stdev, and Correl functions to summarize the stock return data in the SummaryMeasures sheet.

```
Sub SummaryMeasures()
    Dim summarySheet As Worksheet
    Dim i As Integer
    Dim j As Integer
```

```
            Set summarySheet = Worksheets("SummaryMeasures")

    ' Enter formulas for averages and standard deviations (using Excel functions).
    With summarySheet
        .Cells.ClearContents
        .Range("A1").Value = "Summary measures for stock returns"
        .Range("A3").Value = "Stocks"
        .Range("A4").Value = "Means"
        .Range("A5").Value = "Stdevs"
        .Range("A7").Value = "Correlations"
        For i = 1 To nStocks
            .Range("A3").Offset(0, i).Value = tickerSymbol(i)
            .Range("A4").Offset(0, i).Formula = "=Average(" & tickerSymbol(i) & ")"
            .Range("A5").Offset(0, i).Formula = "=Stdev(" & tickerSymbol(i) & ")"
        Next

        ' Create a table of correlations (using Excel's Correl function).
        With .Range("A7")
            For i = 1 To nStocks
                .Offset(i, 0).Value = tickerSymbol(i)
                .Offset(0, i).Value = tickerSymbol(i)
            Next
            For i = 1 To nStocks
                For j = 1 To nStocks
                    .Offset(i, j).Formula = _
                        "=Correl(" & tickerSymbol(i) & "," & tickerSymbol(j) & ")"
                Next
            Next
        End With
    End With
End Sub
```

CreateModel Code

The **CreateModel** sub uses the summary measures from the previous sub as inputs to a portfolio optimization model (See Figure 31.8).

```
Sub CreateModel()
    ' This sub creates the portfolio optimization model in the Model sheet.
    Dim modelSheet As Worksheet
    Dim i As Integer
    Dim j As Integer

    Set modelSheet = Worksheets("Model")

    With modelSheet
        .Activate
        .Cells.ClearContents

        ' Enter title and headings.
        .Range("A1").Value = "Portfolio selection model (solution shown is when " _
            & "required return is halfway between minimum and maximum of stock returns)"
        With .Range("A3")
            .Value = "Stock"
            .Offset(1, 0).Value = "Weights"
            .Offset(2, 0).Value = "Means"
            For i = 1 To nStocks
```

```
                    .Offset(0, i).Value = tickerSymbol(i)

                ' Enter initial equal weights for the portfolio (Solver will find the optimal)
                ' weights and formulas for the average returns.
                .Offset(1, i).Value = 1 / nStocks
                .Offset(2, i).Formula = "=Average(" & tickerSymbol(i) & ")"
        Next
    End With

    ' Name some ranges.
    With .Range("A4")
        Range(.Offset(0, 1), .Offset(0, 1).End(xlToRight)).Name = "Weights"
        Range(.Offset(1, 1), .Offset(1, 1).End(xlToRight)).Name = "Means"
    End With

    ' Find the smallest and largest of the average returns, which will be used
    ' to create the efficient frontier.
    minReturn = Application.WorksheetFunction.Min(Range("Means"))
    maxReturn = Application.WorksheetFunction.Max(Range("Means"))

    ' Calculate the sum of weights (which will be constrained to be 1).
    With .Range("A3").Offset(0, nStocks + 1)
        .Value = "Sum"
        .Offset(1, 0).Name = "SumWeights"
        .Offset(1, 0).Formula = "=Sum(Weights)"
    End With

    ' Calculate table of covariances (using Excel's Covar function).
    With .Range("A7")
        .Value = "Covariances"
        For i = 1 To nStocks
            .Offset(i, 0).Value = tickerSymbol(i)
            .Offset(0, i).Value = tickerSymbol(i)
        Next
        For i = 1 To nStocks
            For j = 1 To nStocks
                .Offset(i, j).Formula = _
                    "=Covar(" & tickerSymbol(i) & "," & tickerSymbol(j) & ")"
            Next
        Next
        Range(.Offset(1, 1), .Offset(nStocks, nStocks)).Name = "Covar"
    End With

    ' Form lower bound constraint on mean portfolio return, using an intial lower
    ' bound halfway between the smallest and largest mean returns. (This lower bound
    ' will be varied through the whole range when finding the efficient frontier.)
    With .Range("A7").Offset(nStocks + 2, 0)
        .Value = "Constraint on mean return"
        .Offset(1, 1).Formula = "=Sumproduct(Weights,Means)"
        .Offset(1, 2).Value = ">="
        .Offset(1, 3).Value = (minReturn + maxReturn) / 2
        .Offset(1, 1).Name = "MeanReturn"
        .Offset(1, 3).Name = "RequiredReturn"

        ' Calculate the variance of the portfolio (using Excel's MMult and
        ' Transpose matrix functions.) Note that it uses the FormulaArray property.
        ' This is analogous to pressing Ctrl-Shift-Enter in Excel.
        .Offset(3, 0).Value = "Portfolio variance"
        With .Offset(4, 1)
            .FormulaArray = "=MMult(Weights,MMult(Covar,Transpose(Weights)))"
            .Name = "PortfolioVariance"
```

```
            End With
            ' Calculate the standard deviation of the portfolio.
            .Offset(6, 0).Value = "Portfolio standard deviation"
            With .Offset(7, 1)
                .Formula = "=Sqrt(PortfolioVariance)"
                .Name = "PortfolioStdev"
            End With
        End With

        ' Adjust width of column A.
        .Columns("A:A").ColumnWidth = 11
    End With
End Sub
```

RunSolver Code

The **RunSolver** sub is straightforward. It sets up the Solver and then runs it.

```
Sub RunSolver()
    ' Set up and run Solver.
    SolverReset
    SolverOk SetCell:=Range("PortfolioVariance"), MaxMinVal:=2, _
        ByChange:=Range("Weights")
    SolverAdd CellRef:=Range("SumWeights"), Relation:=2, FormulaText:=1
    SolverAdd CellRef:=Range("MeanReturn"), Relation:=3, _
        FormulaText:="RequiredReturn"
    SolverOptions AssumeNonNeg:=True
    SolverSolve UserFinish:=True
End Sub
```

EfficientFrontier Code

The **EfficientFrontier** sub runs Solver several times and records the results in the EfficientFrontier sheet. Each run uses a different minimum required mean portfolio return. Finally, it calls the UpdateChart sub to update the efficient frontier chart.

```
Sub EfficientFrontier()
    ' For each of 11 equally spaced values of the required mean portfolio return, run
    ' Solver and record the results on the EfficientFrontier sheet.
    ' Note the Model sheet is still the active sheet.
    ' The sheet with the Solver model must be active to run Solver.
    Dim EFSheet As Worksheet
    Dim iStock As Integer
    Dim iRun As Integer

    Set EFSheet = Worksheets("EfficientFrontier")

    With EFSheet
        .Cells.ClearContents
        .Range("A1").Value = "Efficient frontier"
        .Range("B3").Value = "PortStdev"
        .Range("C3").Value = "ReqdReturn"
```

```
            .Range("E2").Value = "Weights for these optimal portfolios"
        With .Range("D3")
            For iStock = 1 To nStocks
                .Offset(0, iStock).Value = tickerSymbol(iStock)
            Next
        End With
    End With

    ' Portfolio standard deviations and means are recorded in columns B and C.
    ' The corresponding portfolio weights are recorded from column E over.
    ' First, enter headings.
    With EFSheet.Range("E3")
        For iStock = 1 To nStocks
            .Offset(0, iStock - 1).Value = tickerSymbol(iStock)
        Next
    End With

    ' Run the Solver 11 times and record the results.
    For iRun = 0 To 10
        Range("RequiredReturn") = minReturn + iRun * (maxReturn - minReturn) / 10
        SolverSolve UserFinish:=True
        With EFSheet.Range("B4")
            .Offset(iRun, 0).Value = Range("PortfolioStdev").Value
            .Offset(iRun, 1).Value = Range("RequiredReturn").Value
        End With
        With EFSheet.Range("E4")
            For iStock = 1 To nStocks
                .Offset(iRun, iStock - 1).Value _
                    = Range("Weights").Cells(iStock).Value
            Next
        End With
    Next

    EFSheet.Activate
    Call UpdateChart
End Sub
```

UpdateChart Code

The efficient frontier chart already exists as a scatter chart (of the type with the dots connected). The **UpdateChart** sub populates it with the newly calculated data in the EfficientFrontier sheet. The sub also ensures that the graph fills the sheet by adjusting its axis scales appropriately.

```
Sub UpdateChart()
    ' This sub updates the efficient frontier chart.
    Dim sourceRange As Range
    Dim minX As Single, maxX As Single
    Dim minY As Single, maxY As Single
    Dim xLength As Single, yLength As Single

    ' Set minX, minY, etc. is for scaling the axes nicely.
    With ActiveSheet
        Set sourceRange = .Range("B4:C14")
        minX = .Range("B4")
        maxX = .Range("B14")
```

```
            minY = .Range("C4")
            maxY = .Range("C14")
            xLength = maxX - minX
            yLength = maxY - minY
    End With

    ' Update the chart settings to update the chart.
    With ActiveSheet.ChartObjects(1).Chart
        .SetSourceData sourceRange
        With .Axes(xlCategory)
            .MinimumScale = minX - 0.1 * xLength
            .MaximumScale = maxX + 0.1 * xLength
        End With
        With .Axes(xlValue)
            .MinimumScale = minY - 0.1 * yLength
            .MaximumScale = maxY + 0.1 * yLength
        End With
    End With

    Range("A2").Select
End Sub
```

31.9 Summary

This application has been developed to impress—and to be useful to financial analysts and investors. To achieve anything this ambitious, a lot of code must be written, and it is not always straightforward. However, I hope you agree that it is well worth the effort. You should pay particular attention to the RunQuery sub, where the data from the Web site is retrieved. In fact, I suspect that many of you will be anxious to make appropriate modifications to this code to obtain data from other Web sites. The ability to get access to the mounds of data available on the Web and then analyze the data with Excel's many tools is indeed a powerful combination. But remember that you are at the mercy of the Web developers. If they change their site, they can easily break your code!

EXERCISES

1. Note that all summary measures are entered as *formulas* in the SummaryMeasures sub. There is no real need to do it this way. Change this sub so that all summary measures are entered as *values*.
2. The TransferPrices sub uses the **Find** method to find a cell with some specified value. There is also a **FindNext** method. (Each is a method of the **Range** object.) These can be used in VBA similar to the way they are used in the usual Excel interface to find a piece of information (or the next such piece of information). The file **Piano Orders.xlsx** contains a list of orders for Steinway pianos. It lists the date of the order and the state where the order was made. Write a sub that searches through the list of states to find each occurrence of California and

colors the background of each such cell yellow. (*Hint:* Look up the Find and FindNext methods of the Range object in the Object Browser.)

3. Find a Web site that contains at least one table of data and allows the user to make a choice, such as I did in this application when I got to choose the period of time and the ticker symbol. Then write a sub that retrieves the data specified by a user's choices. These choices can be obtained from an input box or a user form, whichever is more natural for the context. (For example, in this application I got the user's choices from the dialog boxes in Figure 31.2 and Figure 31.3.)

4. Sometimes you get lucky with Web sites. I was looking for annual salary data for baseball players, and I found data for all players by year and team at the USA Today site. Specifically, a URL such as http://content.usatoday.com/sports/baseball/salaries/teamdetail.aspx?team=3&year=2009 lists all of the salaries for team 3 (Boston Red Sox) in 2009. To get data for any other team or any other year, just replace the team index (1 to 30) and year at the end of the URL with the ones you want. (You will have to experiment with the team indexes; they are not according to alphabetical order.) Now try the following: (1) Run a Web query manually from one of these URLs. (2) Run it again with the recorder on. (3) Learning from the recorded code, write a VBA program that finds the salary data for all teams in a given year such as 2009 and lists it on a worksheet. The format should be as indicated in the file **Baseball Salaries.xlsx**.

5. Repeat exercise 4 for football salaries. There are 32 teams, and the typical URL is http://content.usatoday.com/sports/football/nfl/salaries/teamdetail.aspx?team=10&year=2008.

6. Repeat exercise 4 for basketball salaries. There are 30 teams, and the typical URL is http://content.usatoday.com/sports/basketball/nba/salaries/teamdetail.aspx?team=2&year=2008-09. (Be careful. The Seattle SuperSonics were replaced by the Oklahoma City Thunder in the 2008-09 season. To avoid other team changes, don't go back before the 2004-2005 season.)

A Data Envelopment Analysis Application

32

32.1 Introduction

Data Envelopment Analysis (DEA) is a method for comparing the relative efficiency of organizational units such as banks, hospitals, and schools, where efficiency relates to the ability to transform inputs into outputs. For example, DEA could analyze several branch banks, where the inputs for each branch might be labor hours, square feet of space, and supplies used, and the outputs might be the numbers of loan applications, deposits processed, and checks processed during some time period. DEA could then use these data in several linear programming models, one for each branch, to see whether each branch can attach unit costs to its inputs and unit prices to its outputs to make itself appear efficient. By definition, a branch is "efficient" if the total value of its outputs is equal to the total value of its inputs. It is inefficient if the total value of its outputs is *less* than the total value of its inputs.

This application takes data from a text (.txt) file, sets up a Solver model, runs it for each of the organizational units, and reports the results. Among other things, this application illustrates how to import data from a text file into an Excel application.

New Learning Objectives: VBA

- To learn how the data from a comma-delimited text file can be imported into an Excel application (although this material was covered briefly in Chapter 13).
- To see how a comma-delimited string can be parsed by using appropriate loops and string functions.

New Learning Objectives: Non-VBA

- To learn how the DEA procedure can compare various organizational units for efficiency.

32.2 Functionality of the Application

The data for the application are in a file called **DEA.txt**. This is a simple text file that can be created with the Windows NotePad. It lists the names of the inputs and outputs, the names of the organizational units, and the inputs used and outputs produced by each unit. The application imports these data into the **DEA.xlsm** application file, where they are used as input data for a linear programming model. This model is solved for each organizational unit to see whether the unit is efficient. The results are then reported in a Report sheet.

As the application is currently written, the **DEA.txt** and **DEA.xlsm** files should be stored in the same folder. The current **DEA.txt** file contains data on four organizational units (departments in a university), each with three inputs and two outputs. However, these data can be replaced with any data, with any numbers of organizational units, inputs, and outputs, and the application will respond appropriately. The format for the data in the **DEA.txt** file is discussed below.

32.3   Running the Application

When the **DEA.xlsm** file is opened, the Explanation sheet in Figure 32.1 appears. When the button on this sheet is clicked, the application then opens the **DEA.txt** file, reads the data and stores it in arrays, sets up a linear programming model in a (hidden) Model sheet, solves it once for each organizational unit, and reports the results in the Report sheet shown in Figure 32.2.

There are three sections in this report. The one on the left indicates whether the units are efficient by reporting the maximum total output value

Figure 32.1   Explanation Sheet

A Data Envelopment Analysis (DEA) Application

> Run the application

This application automates DEA to see which of several organization units are efficient in their use of inputs to produce outputs. The user enters the number of organization units, the number of inputs, and the number of outputs, where it is assumed that all units have the same list of inputs and outputs. Then the application gets the actual data from a text (.txt) file named DEA.txt. This file contains the names for the units, inputs, and outputs, as well as the amounts of the inputs used by each unit and the amounts of the outputs produced by each unit. It then sets up a DEA linear programming model and runs Solver, once for each unit, to see which of the units is efficient. This is determined by maximizing the value for the unit's outputs, subject to constraining the value of its inputs to be 1. If this maximum output value is 1, the unit is efficient. Otherwise, it is inefficient. A list of the units and whether they are efficient or inefficient, as well as other pertinent infomation, is shown on the Report sheet.

The DEA.txt file currently contains data for four units, each of which uses three inputs and produces two outputs. However, users can substitute their own data in this file (any number of units, inputs, and outputs), and the application will accept them.

Figure 32.2 Report Sheet

Summary of analysis

[View Explanation Sheet]

Efficiency of units

Unit	LP maximum output	Efficient?
Business	1.000	Yes
Education	1.000	Yes
Arts & Sciences	1.000	Yes
HPER	0.848	No

Given data from text file

Unit	Inputs used			Outputs produced	
	Faculty	Support Staff	Supply Budget	Credit Hours	Research Pubs
Business	150.00	70.00	5.00	15.00	225.00
Education	60.00	20.00	3.00	5.40	70.00
Arts & Sciences	800.00	140.00	20.00	56.00	1300.00
HPER	30.00	15.00	1.00	2.10	40.00

Values from LP model

Unit	Total costs of inputs used			Total values of outputs produced	
	Faculty	Support Staff	Supply Budget	Credit Hours	Research Pubs
Business	0.597	0.403	0.000	0.875	0.125
Education	0.674	0.326	0.000	0.890	0.110
Arts & Sciences	0.798	0.202	0.000	0.819	0.181
HPER	1.000	0.000	0.000	0.152	0.696

from the linear programming model for each unit. Because the total input values are scaled to be 1, a unit is efficient only if its total output value is 1. For these data, all units are efficient except HPER. The section on the top right reports the original data. It shows the quantities of inputs used and outputs produced for each unit.

Finally, the section on the bottom right indicates input costs and output values from the linear programming model, where input costs are scaled so that they sum to 1 for each unit. For example, Education (internally) assigns *unit* costs to its inputs so that the total values of its faculty and support staff used are 0.674 and 0.326, respectively. It attaches zero value to its supply budget input. Similarly, it attaches *unit* prices to its outputs so that the total values of its credit hours and research pubs produced are 0.890 and 0.110, respectively. With these unit costs and unit prices, Education's total output value is equal to its total input value (both equal 1), which means that it is an efficient unit.

This report is based on the linear programming model shown in Figure 32.3. The version shown here is for checking the efficiency of unit 4 (HPER). For later reference, the following range names are created at run time for the Model sheet. Of course, the actual ranges would change if there were different numbers of organizational units, inputs, or outputs.

Range	Name
B6:D9	InputsUsed
G6:H9	OutputsProduced
B11:D11	InputCosts
G11:H11	OutputPrices
B15:B18	InputValues
D15:D18	OutputValues
B21	SelInputValue
B24	SelOutputValue

Figure 32.3 Completed Model Sheet

	A	B	C	D	E	F	G	H
1	DEA model							
2								
3	Selected unit	4						
4								
5	Inputs used	Faculty	Support Staff	Supply Budget		Outputs used	Credit Hours	Research Pubs
6	Business	150	70	5		Business	15	225
7	Education	60	20	3		Education	5.4	70
8	Arts & Sciences	800	140	20		Arts & Sciences	56	1300
9	HPER	30	15	1		HPER	2.1	40
10								
11	Unit costs	0.033	0	0		Unit prices	0.0725	0.0174
12								
13	Constraints that input costs must cover output values							
14	Unit index		Input costs		Output values			
15	1		5	>=	5			
16	2		2	>=	1.609			
17	3		26.667	>=	26.667			
18	4		1	>=	0.848			
19								
20	Constraint that selected unit's input cost must equal a nominal value of 1							
21	Selected unit's input cost	1	=		1			
22								
23	Maximize selected unit's output value (to see if it is 1, hence efficient)							
24	Selected unit's output value	0.848						

The VBA code sets up this model at run time. It then substitutes the index for each organizational unit (1–4 in this example) in cell B3. The formulas in cells B21 and B24 are linked to this value through VLOOKUP functions so that they update automatically. Then Solver is run for each index in cell B3.

32.4 Setting Up the Excel Sheets and the Text File

The **DEA.xlsm** file contains three worksheets named Explanation, Model, and Report. However, there are no templates for the Model and Report sheets. At design time, they are blank. The reason is that if the numbers of organizational units, inputs, or outputs change due to new data in the **DEA. txt** file, the Model and Report setups will change dramatically. Therefore, it is easier to start with a clean slate and then fill these sheets completely—values, formulas, headings, and formatting—through VBA code at run time.

The **DEA.txt** file should be structured as a comma-delimited file, as shown in Figure 32.4. The first row should contain the names of the inputs, separated by commas. The second row should contain the names of the outputs, separated by commas. There should then be three lines for each organizational unit. The first should contain the unit's name, and the second and third should contain its inputs used and outputs produced, respectively,

Figure 32.4 Structure of DEA.txt File

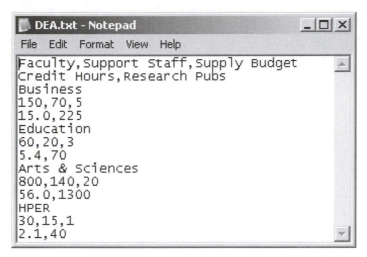

with input values separated by commas and output values separated by commas. There should *not* be any spaces following the commas. If the data are not structured in this way, the application will either crash (with a "nice" error message) or yield misleading results.

32.5 Getting Started with the VBA

The application contains a single user form named frmInputs, a module, and a reference to Solver. Once these items are added, the Project Explorer window will appear as in Figure 32.5.[1]

Workbook_Open Code

To guarantee that the Explanation sheet appears when the file is opened, the following code is placed in the ThisWorkbook code window. This sub also hides the Model and Report sheets.

```
Private Sub Workbook_Open()
    Worksheets("Explanation").Activate
    Range("F5").Select
    Worksheets("Report").Visible = False
    Worksheets("Model").Visible = False
    frmSolver.Show
End Sub
```

---

[1]It also contains the usual frmSolver that displays a message about possible Solver problems when the workbook is opened.

Figure 32.5 Project Explorer Window

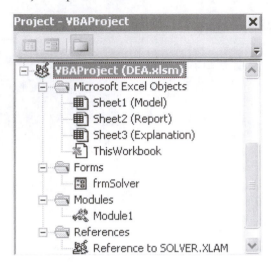

32.6   Getting Data from a Text File

Perhaps the most interesting part of this application, at least from a VBA standpoint, is the way the data are obtained from the **DEA.txt** file. To open the text file, the following line is required:[2]

```
Open ThisWorkbook.Path & "\DEA.txt" For Input As #1
```

The "*#1*" essentially means that this is the *first* text file opened. (If another were opened in the same session, it would be opened as #2, and so on.) Eventually, the file should be closed with the line

```
Close #1
```

To read a single line from the text file, the following code is required, where dataLine is a string variable:

```
Line Input #1, dataLine
```

Each time this line of code is executed, the next entire line of data is stored as a string in the dataLine variable. Typically, there are several pieces of data in a line of text, separated by commas. The individual pieces must then be **parsed**. Because

---

[2]Although the steps for importing text data into Excel were discussed briefly in Chapter 13, they are repeated here for convenience.

this parsing operation is required several times, the program contains a **ParseLine** sub that is called whenever it is needed. The ParseLine sub takes three arguments: the dataLine string, the expected number of pieces of data, and an array (I've named it returnArray) to be filled with the individual pieces of data. It then passes the filled returnArray array *back* to a **GetData** sub, where its contents are put into public array variables, such as inputName. The details appear in the next section.

Summarizing, the steps required to import data from a text file are: (1) open the file, (2) read an entire line, (3) parse the line into its separate pieces of data, repeat steps (2) and (3) for each line in the text file, and (4) close the file.

32.7   The VBA Code in the Module

Almost everything is done at run time with the code in the module. The button on the Explanation sheet is attached to the **MainDEA** sub. This sub first captures the data from the **DEA.txt** file in public array variables. Next, it sets up the linear programming model and solves it for each organizational unit. Finally, it creates the report. The public variables and the MainDEA sub are listed below.

Option Statements and Public Variables

```
Option Explicit
Option Base 1

' Definitions of public variables:
'   nUnits: number of organization units
'   unitName(): array of names of units
'   nInputs: number of inputs for each unit
'   inputName(): array of names of inputs
'   inputUsed(): two-dimensional array of inputs used by units (first
'       dimension is the unit, second is the input)
'   nOutputs: number of outputs for each unit
'   outputName(): array of names of outputs
'   outputProduced(): two-dimensional array of outputs produced by units (first
'       dimension is the unit, second is the output)
'   totalInputCost(): two-dimensional array (first subscript is unit,
'       second is input) - e.g., TotalInputCost(1,3) is the unit cost
'       of input 3 multiplied by the amount of input 3 used by unit 1
'   totalOutputValue(): same as TotalInputCost array, except for outputs.
'   effIndex(): an array of maximum outputs from LP model, one for each unit

Public nUnits As Integer, unitName() As String
Public nInputs As Integer, inputName() As String, inputUsed() As Single
Public nOutputs As Integer, outputName() As String, outputProduced() As Single
Public totalInputCost() As Single, totalOutputValue() As Single
Public efficiencyIndex() As Single
```

MainDEA Code

```
Sub Main()
    ' This sub runs when the user clicks on the button in the Explanation sheet.
    Application.ScreenUpdating = False
```

```
' Get data from the DEA.txt file
Call GetData
' Create the model in the Model sheet.
Call CreateModel
' Set up and run the Solver several times, once for each unit.
Call RunSolver
' Fill in the Report sheet.
Call CreateReport
Application.ScreenUpdating = True
End Sub
```

GetData Code

The **GetData** sub is responsible for importing the data from the text file into Excel. First, an attempt is made to open the text file. If there is an error (no such file exists, at least not in the same folder as the application file), an error message is displayed and the program ends. Otherwise, the file is read line by line. If there is ever an error of any type (probably because the text file isn't structured properly), control passes to the BadData label, a message is displayed, and the program ends. Note how the **On Error** statements discussed in Chapter 12 are used here to trap for these errors.

Pay particular attention to the **ParseLine** calls. (The code for the ParseLine sub is listed below.) For example, after the first line of the text file (the one with the names of the inputs) is stored in the dataLine string, the following line is called:

```
Call ParseLine(dataLine, nInputs, returnArray)
```

The second argument indicates the number of separate pieces of data that are expected in the dataLine string. This string is then parsed, and its pieces are placed in the returnArray array (this is done in the ParseLine sub) so that the array is available for the GetData sub.

```
Sub GetData()
    ' Read the data from the DEA.txt file and store it in arrays.

    Dim i As Integer, j As Integer
    Dim dataLine As String
    Dim returnArray() As String
    Dim nInputsRead As Integer, nOutputsRead As Integer

    ' Try to open the DEA.txt file, but check for an error in case it doesn't exist.
    On Error Resume Next
    Open ThisWorkbook.Path & "\DEA.txt" For Input As #1

    ' Quit if there is no DEA.txt file in the directory of this workbook.
    If Err.Number <> 0 Then
        MsgBox "There is no DEA.txt file in the same directory as " _
            & "this workbook, so the application cannot continue.", _
                vbInformation, "Missing file"
        End
```

```
End If

' Quit if anything goes wrong reading the file.
On Error GoTo BadData

' The first line contains the names of the inputs.
Line Input #1, dataLine
Call ParseLine(dataLine, nInputs, returnArray)

' Transfer the contents of the returnArray array to the inputName array.
ReDim inputName(nInputs)
For i = 1 To nInputs
    inputName(i) = returnArray(i)
Next

' Do it again, reading the second line for the output names.
Line Input #1, dataLine
Call ParseLine(dataLine, nOutputs, returnArray)
ReDim outputName(nOutputs)
For i = 1 To nOutputs
    outputName(i) = returnArray(i)
Next

' Now go through each organizational unit.
nUnits = 0
Do While Not EOF(1)

    ' Add another unit and redimension arrays appropriately. Note that
    ' only the second dimension of a two-dimensional array can be
    ' redimensioned dynamically with a Redim statement using Preserve.
    nUnits = nUnits + 1
    ReDim Preserve unitName(nUnits)
    ReDim Preserve inputUsed(nInputs, nUnits)
    ReDim Preserve outputProduced(nOutputs, nUnits)

    ' The unit's name is in the first line - no parsing required.
    Line Input #1, dataLine
    unitName(nUnits) = dataLine

    ' The unit's inputs used are in the second line.
    Line Input #1, dataLine
    Call ParseLine(dataLine, nInputsRead, returnArray)

    ' Quit if the number of data items in this line is not the same
    ' as the number of inputs (which is known by now).
    If nInputsRead <> nInputs Then
        GoTo BadData
    End If

    ' Store the input data in this line for later use.
    For j = 1 To nInputs
        inputUsed(j, nUnits) = returnArray(j)
    Next

    ' Do the same for the unit's outputs produced, which are in the next line.
    Line Input #1, dataLine
    Call ParseLine(dataLine, nOutputsRead, returnArray)

    If nOutputsRead <> nOutputs Then
        GoTo BadData
    End If
```

```
        For j = 1 To nOutputs
            outputProduced(j, nUnits) = returnArray(j)
        Next
    Loop

    ' Close the data file.
    Close #1

    ' Now that we know the numbers of units, inputs and outputs,
    ' redimension other arrays.
    ReDim efficiencyIndex(nUnits)
    ReDim totalInputCost(nInputs, nUnits)
    ReDim totalOutputValue(nOutputs, nUnits)

    Exit Sub

BadData:
    MsgBox "The data file is not set up properly, so the application " _
        & "cannot continue.", vbInformation, "Invalid data"
    End
End Sub
```

ParseLine Code

To parse a string dataLine into its individual pieces of data, the **ParseLine** sub uses a For loop to go through the string one character at a time (from left to right), using the **Mid** function. Specifically, Mid(dataLine, i, 1) returns the character in position i of the string dataLine. As it reads these characters, it builds a currentText string. As it progresses, it checks whether each character is a comma or the last character in the dataLine string. In either case, it captures the characters stored in the currentText string as the next element of the returnArray array and resets currentText to the empty string. If it ever fills the array with the expected number of elements *before* parsing the entire dataLine string, it exits prematurely. (This could be the case if a text line contained more data than is required.)

It is very instructive to step through this sub one line at a time (with the F8 key) and keep a watch on the dataLine and currentText strings in the **Watch** window. This allows you to see exactly how the strings are parsed.

```
Sub ParseLine(dataLine As String, nValues As Integer, returnArray() As String)
    ' This sub parses a line of data from the text file into individual pieces of data.
    ' It returns an array of the pieces of data and number of pieces (in nValues).

    Dim i As Integer
    Dim char As String
    Dim counter As Integer ' counts the pieces of data in the line
    Dim currentText As String ' text since last comma

    ' Counter counts the number of pieces of data in the line.
    counter = 1
    ReDim returnArray(counter)
    ' currentText is any piece of data in the line, where the pieces
```

```
' are separated by commas.
currentText = ""

' Go through the string a character at a time.
For i = 1 To Len(dataLine)

    ' Get the character in position i.
    char = Mid(dataLine, i, 1)

    ' Check if the character is a comma or the last character in the string.
    If char = "," Then
        returnArray(counter) = currentText

        ' Get ready for the next piece of data.
        currentText = ""
        counter = counter + 1
        ReDim Preserve returnArray(counter)

    ElseIf i = Len(dataLine) Then
        ' Capture this last piece of data and return the number of pieces.
        currentText = currentText & Mid(dataLine, i, 1)
        returnArray(counter) = currentText
        nValues = counter

    Else
        ' Add this character to the currentText string.
        currentText = currentText & Mid(dataLine, i, 1)
    End If
Next i

End Sub
```

CreateModel Code

The **CreateModel** sub clears the Model sheet completely by using the ClearContents method of the UsedRange. (Recall from Chapter 6 that the **UsedRange** of a worksheet is basically the area of the worksheet that contains any data.) Then it calls two subs, **EnterInputsOutputs** and **CalcFormulas**, to develop the linear programming model.

```
Sub CreateModel()
    ' This sub creates the LP model and reports the results.

    ' First, unhide and activate the Model sheet and clear all contents.
    With Worksheets("Model")
        .Visible = True
        .Activate
        .UsedRange.ClearContents
    End With

    ' Enter labels. (Cell B3 will contain the index of the unit currently being
    ' analyzed for efficiency.)
    Range("A1").Value = "DEA model"
    Range("A3").Value = "Selected unit"
```

```
' Enter the user data.
Call EnterInputsOutputs

' Calculate all required formulas for the model.
Call CalcFormulas
End Sub
```

EnterInputsOutputs Code

The **EnterInputsOutputs** sub enters the data from the text file, which are by now stored in arrays (from the GetData sub), into the Model sheet. It also enters descriptive headings. Keep in mind that the Model sheet is practically blank when this sub and the next sub are called, so they have a considerable amount of work to do. Refer to Figure 32.3 and the list of range names right above it as you read this code.

```
Sub EnterInputsOutputs()
    ' This sub enters the inputs for the DEA model.
    Dim i As Integer, j As Integer

    ' Enter labels and data.
    With Range("A5")
        .Value = "Inputs used"
        For j = 1 To nInputs
            .Offset(0, j).Value = inputName(j)
        Next
        For i = 1 To nUnits
            .Offset(i, 0).Value = unitName(i)
            For j = 1 To nInputs
                .Offset(i, j).Value = inputUsed(j, i)
            Next
        Next

        ' Name the range of input amounts.
        ' It will be used for formulas in the Model sheet.
        Range(.Offset(1, 1), .Offset(nUnits, nInputs)).Name = "InputsUsed"

        ' Enter 0's as initial values for the input cost changing cells.
        With .Offset(nUnits + 2, 0)
            .Value = "Unit costs"
            For j = 1 To nInputs
                .Offset(0, j).Value = 0
            Next

            ' Name the range of the changing cells for inputs.
            Range(.Offset(0, 1), .Offset(0, nInputs)).Name = "InputCosts"
        End With
    End With

    ' Do the same for the outputs.
    With Range("A5").Offset(0, nInputs + 2)
        .Value = "Outputs used"
        For j = 1 To nOutputs
            .Offset(0, j).Value = outputName(j)
```

```
            Next
            For i = 1 To nUnits
                .Offset(i, 0).Value = unitName(i)
                For j = 1 To nOutputs
                    .Offset(i, j).Value = outputProduced(j, i)
                Next
            Next
            Range(.Offset(1, 1), .Offset(nUnits, nOutputs)).Name = "OutputsProduced"
            With .Offset(nUnits + 2, 0)
                .Value = "Unit prices"
                For j = 1 To nOutputs
                    .Offset(0, j).Value = 0
                Next
                Range(.Offset(0, 1), .Offset(0, nOutputs)).Name = "OutputPrices"
            End With
        End With
    End With
End Sub
```

CalcFormulas Code

The **CalcFormulas** sub continues the model development by entering all required formulas and naming various ranges. Again, refer to Figure 32.3 and the list of range names right above it as you read this code.

```
Sub CalcFormulas()
    ' This sub calculates formulas for the Model, starting just below the changing
    ' cells from the previous sub.

    Dim i As Integer
    With Range("A5").Offset(nUnits + 4, 0)

        ' Set up constraints that input costs incurred must be greater than
        ' or equal to output values achieved.
        .Value = "Constraints that input costs must cover output values"
        .Offset(1, 0).Value = "Unit index"
        .Offset(1, 1).Value = "Input costs"
        .Offset(1, 3).Value = "Output values"

        ' There is a constraint for each unit.
        For i = 1 To nUnits

            ' Labels in column A (1, 2, etc.) are needed for later on, to
            ' enable use of VLookup function.
            .Offset(1 + i, 0).Value = i

            ' The input cost incurred for any unit is the sumproduct of the changing
            ' cell range (UnitCosts) and the appropriate input data row. The same goes
            ' for output value. Note how the appropriate row is specified.
            .Offset(1 + i, 1).Formula = _
                "=Sumproduct(InputCosts," & Range("InputsUsed").Rows(i).Address & ")"
            .Offset(1 + i, 2).Value = ">="
            .Offset(1 + i, 3).Formula = _
                "=Sumproduct(OutputPrices," _
                & Range("OutputsProduced").Rows(i).Address & ")"
        Next
```

```
            ' Name appropriate ranges. LTable is for later on with the VLookup function.
            Range(.Offset(2, 1), .Offset(nUnits + 1, 1)).Name = "InputValues"
            Range(.Offset(2, 3), .Offset(nUnits + 1, 3)).Name = "OutputValues"
            Range(.Offset(2, 0), .Offset(nUnits + 1, 3)).Name = "LTable"
    End With

    ' Set up constraint that the selected unit's total input cost is 1.
    With Range("A5").Offset(2 * nUnits + 7, 0)
        .Value = "Constraint that selected unit's input cost must " _
            & "equal a nominal value of 1"
        .Offset(1, 0).Value = "Selected unit's input cost"

        ' Get the selected unit's total input cost with a VLookup.
        With .Offset(1, 1)
            .Formula = "=VLookup(B3,LTable,2)"
            .Name = "SelInputValue"
        End With
        .Offset(1, 2).Value = "="
        .Offset(1, 3).Value = 1
        .Offset(3, 0).Value = "Maximize selected unit's output value " _
            & "(to see if it is 1, hence efficient)"
        .Offset(4, 0).Value = "Selected unit's output value"

        ' Get the selected unit's total output value with a VLookup.
        ' It is the target cell for maximization.
        With .Offset(4, 1)
            .Formula = "=VLookup(B3,LTable,4)"
            .Name = "SelOutputValue"
        End With
    End With
End Sub
```

RunSolver Code

The **RunSolver** sub uses a For loop to go through each organizational unit and solve the appropriate model. (The particular unit being analyzed depends on the index placed in cell B3.) It then captures the Solver results in the arrays efficiencyIndex, totalInputCost, and totalOuputValue for later use in the report.

```
Sub RunSolver()
    ' This sub sets up and runs Solver once for each unit, first placing
    ' its index (1, 2, etc.) in cell B3.
    Dim i As Integer, j As Integer

    For i = 1 To nUnits
        Range("B3").Value = i
        SolverReset
        SolverOk SetCell:=Range("SelOutputValue"), MaxMinVal:=1, _
            ByChange:=Union(Range("InputCosts"), Range("OutputPrices"))
        SolverAdd CellRef:=Range("InputValues"), Relation:=3, FormulaText:="OutputValues"
        SolverAdd CellRef:=Range("SelInputValue"), Relation:=2, FormulaText:=1
        SolverOptions AssumeLinear:=True, AssumeNonNeg:=True
        SolverSolve UserFinish:=True
        ' Capture the quantities for the report in the totalInputCost,
```

```
        ' totalOutputValue, and effIndex arrays.
        For j = 1 To nInputs
            totalInputCost(j, i) = Range("InputCosts").Cells(j).Value * inputUsed(j, i)
        Next
        For j = 1 To nOutputs
            totalOutputValue(j, i) = Range("OutputPrices").Cells(j).Value * outputProduced(j, i)
        Next
        efficiencyIndex(i) = Range("SelOutputValue").Value
    Next

    ' Hide the Model sheet.
    Worksheets("Model").Visible = False
End Sub
```

CreateReport Code

To create the report, the current Report sheet is cleared completely. (Again, it is easier to start from scratch than to try to salvage anything from a previous report.) This provides a fresh start, but it means that all of the data transfers *and* all desired formatting must be done at run time through VBA code. There is nothing difficult about it, but there are a lot of steps. In the spirit of modularizing, the **CreateReport** sub does a few tasks and then calls three subs, **FirstSection**, **SecondSection**, and **ThirdSection**, to do the majority of the work.

```
Sub CreateReport()
    ' This sub creates a report of the Solver results.
    Dim i As Integer, j As Integer

    ' It's easier to start with a brand new Report sheet, so
    ' everything is cleared from the old one.
    With Worksheets("Report")
        .Cells.Clear
        .Visible = True
        .Activate
    End With

    ' Shrink column width of column A and format the title in cell B2.
    Columns("A:A").ColumnWidth = 3
    With Range("B1")
        .Value = "Summary of analysis"
        .RowHeight = 40
        .VerticalAlignment = xlCenter
        .Font.Bold = True
        .Font.Size = 16
    End With

    ' Build the rest of the report in three sections with the following three subs.
    Call FirstSection
    Call SecondSection
    Call ThirdSection

    Range("A1").Select
End Sub
```

FirstSection, SecondSection, ThirdSection Code

Referring to the report in Figure 32.2 , the first section is the section on the left, the second section is the top-right section, and the third section is the bottom-right section. Each of the following subs adds headings and data and then formats its section appropriately. (Interestingly, Excel 2007 no longer shows an AutoFormat method for a Range in the Object Browser, but the old AutoFormat method still works.)

```vba
Sub FirstSection()
    ' This sub enters the efficiencies for the units.
    Dim i As Integer

    ' Enter headings.
    With Range("B3")
        .Value = "Efficiency of units"
        .Font.Bold = True
        .Font.Size = 12
    End With
    With Range("B4")
        .Value = "Unit"
        .Offset(0, 1).Value = "LP maximum output"
        .Offset(0, 2).Value = "Efficient?"
        For i = 1 To nUnits
            .Offset(i, 0).Value = unitName(i)

            ' Enter target values from the optimization.
            .Offset(i, 1) = efficiencyIndex(i)

            ' Enter Yes or No depending on whether the target = 1 or < 1.
            If efficiencyIndex(i) < 1 Then
                .Offset(i, 2).Value = "No"
            Else
                .Offset(i, 2).Value = "Yes"
            End If
        Next

        ' Format appropriately.
        Range(.Offset(1, 1), .Offset(nUnits, 1)).NumberFormat = "0.000"
        Range(.Offset(0, 0), .Offset(nUnits, 2)).AutoFormat xlRangeAutoFormatClassic3
        .HorizontalAlignment = xlLeft
        Range(.Offset(1, 2), .Offset(nUnits, 2)).HorizontalAlignment = xlRight
    End With
End Sub
```

```vba
Sub SecondSection()
    ' This sub enters the given data from the DEA.txt file.
    Dim i As Integer, j As Integer

    ' Enter headings.
    With Range("F2")
        .Value = "Given data from text file"
        .Font.Bold = True
        .Font.Size = 12
```

```
        End With
        With Range("F4")

            ' Enter more headings.
            .Value = "Unit"
            With .Offset(-1, 1)
                .Value = "Inputs used"
                .Font.Bold = True
            End With
            With .Offset(-1, nInputs + 1)
                .Value = "Outputs produced"
                .Font.Bold = True
            End With
            For i = 1 To nUnits
                .Offset(i, 0).Value = unitName(i)
            Next
            For j = 1 To nInputs
                .Offset(0, j).Value = inputName(j)
            Next
            For j = 1 To nOutputs
                .Offset(0, nInputs + j).Value = outputName(j)
            Next

            ' Enter the inputs used and outputs produced.
            For i = 1 To nUnits
                For j = 1 To nInputs
                    .Offset(i, j).Value = inputUsed(j, i)
                Next
                For j = 1 To nOutputs
                    .Offset(i, nInputs + j).Value = outputProduced(j, i)
                Next
            Next

            ' Format appropriately.
            Range(.Offset(1, 1), .Offset(nUnits, nInputs + nOutputs)) _
                .NumberFormat = "0.00"
            Range(.Offset(0, 0), .Offset(nUnits, nInputs + nOutputs)) _
                .AutoFormat xlRangeAutoFormatClassic3
            .HorizontalAlignment = xlLeft
        End With
End Sub
```

```
Sub ThirdSection()
    ' This sub is almost the same as the previous sub, but now the data are
    ' total costs of inputs used and total values of outputs produced, as
    ' calculated from the LP model.
    Dim i As Integer, j As Integer

    With Range("F4").Offset(nUnits + 2, 0)
        .Value = "Values from LP model"
        .Font.Bold = True
        .Font.Size = 12
    End With

    With Range("F4").Offset(nUnits + 4, 0)
        .Value = "Unit"
        With .Offset(-1, 1)
```

```
                    .Value = "Total costs of inputs used"
                    .Font.Bold = True
            End With
            With .Offset(-1, nInputs + 1)
                    .Value = "Total values of outputs produced"
                    .Font.Bold = True
            End With
            For i = 1 To nUnits
                    .Offset(i, 0).Value = unitName(i)
            Next
            For j = 1 To nInputs
                    .Offset(0, j).Value = inputName(j)
            Next
            For j = 1 To nOutputs
                    .Offset(0, nInputs + j).Value = outputName(j)
            Next

            ' Enter the data from the LP runs. (These were calculated in the RunSolver sub.)
            For i = 1 To nUnits
                For j = 1 To nInputs
                        .Offset(i, j).Value = totalInputCost(j, i)
                Next
                For j = 1 To nOutputs
                        .Offset(i, nInputs + j).Value = totalOutputValue(j, i)
                Next
            Next
            Range(.Offset(1, 1), .Offset(nUnits, nInputs + nOutputs)) _
                    .NumberFormat = "0.000"
            Range(.Offset(0, 0), .Offset(nUnits, nInputs + nOutputs)) _
                    .AutoFormat xlRangeAutoFormatClassic3
            .HorizontalAlignment = xlLeft
        End With
End Sub
```

ViewExplanation Code

The **ViewExplanation** sub lets the user navigate back to the Explanation sheet. It also hides the Report sheet.

```
Sub ViewExplanation()
    Worksheets("Report").Visible = False
    Worksheets("Explanation").Activate
    Range("F5").Select
End Sub
```

32.8 Summary

This application has illustrated a very useful method, DEA, for comparing organizational units for relative efficiency. This method has been used in a number of real applications in various industries. (See the references in Chapter 4 of *Practical*

Management Science.) In addition, this chapter has illustrated a method for importing data from a comma-delimited text file into Excel. This involves parsing data into its individual pieces, a technique that is very useful in its own right in a number of contexts.

EXERCISES

1. If you ever try to open a text (.txt) file in Excel, you'll see that it takes you through a wizard. One of the steps asks for the character delimiter. One choice is the comma (the one used here), and another is the tab character. Rewrite the ParseLine sub so that the separating character is the tab rather than the comma. Then get into Notepad, open the **DEA.txt** file, replace each comma by a tab (highlight the comma and press the Tab key), and rerun the application with your new ParseLine sub. You should get the same results as before. (*Hint:* Open the VBA library in the Object Browser and look under Constants to find the tab character.)

2. Rewrite the ParseLine sub so that it is slightly more general. It should receive an extra argument called separator, declared as String type. The separator is any single character that separates the pieces of the long string being parsed. In the application, the separator was the comma, but it might be another character in other applications.

3. Suppose a line from a text file uses a *single* comma to separate pieces of data, but it uses two *consecutive* commas to indicate a comma is part of a piece a data. For example the line 23,290,21,,200 has three pieces of data: 23, 290, and 21,200. Rewrite the ParseLine sub to parse a typical line with this comma convention.

4. I claimed that this application works with any data, provided that the text file is structured properly. Try it out. Open the **DEA.txt** file in Notepad and change its data in some way. (For example, try adding another academic department and/or adding an input or an output.) Then rerun the application to see if it still works properly. It should!

5. Repeat the previous exercise, but now create a *new* text file called **MyData.txt** (stored in the same folder as the Excel application), structured exactly as **DEA.txt**, and add some data to it. Then rerun the application to see if it still works properly. (Note that you will have to change the VBA code slightly, so that it references the correct name of your new text file.)

6. The previous exercise indicates a "fix" that no business would ever tolerate—they would never be willing to get into the VBA code to change a file name reference. A much better alternative is to change the VBA code in the first place so that it asks the user for the location and name of the database file. You could do this with an input box (and risk having the user spell something wrong), but Excel provides an easier way with the **FileDialog** object as illustrated in Chapter 13 (or the **GetOpenFilename** method of the **Application** object if you have Excel 2000 or an earlier version). Use either of these to change the application so that it prompts the user for the name and location of the data

file. Actually, you should probably precede the above line with a MsgBox statement so that the user knows he's being asked to select the file with the data. Then try the modified application with your own text file, stored in a folder *different* from the folder containing the Excel application.

7. Put the ideas from Exercises 2 and 6 together to make the application fairly general. First, create a user form that allows the user to choose the separator character from a list of option buttons. (Make the choices reasonable, such as comma, tab, and semicolon.) Then pass the user's choice to the revised ParseLine sub discussed in Exercise 2 as the separator argument. Second, let the user select the text file with the data, as discussed in Exercise 6. Now the application should work with any text file with any separator in your list.

An AHP Application for Choosing a Job

33

33.1 Introduction

This application implements the analytical hierarchy process (AHP) in the context of choosing a job. AHP is useful in many multiobjective decision problems.[1] You list a number of criteria and a number of possible decisions that meet the criteria to various degrees. In this case, the criteria are salary, nearness to family, benefits, and possibly others, and the decisions are your available job offers. The first step in AHP is to compare the criteria—which are the most important to you? This is discovered through a series of pairwise comparisons. The jobs are then compared to each other on each criterion, again by making a series of pairwise comparisons. The final result is a score for each job, and the job with the highest score is identified as your preferred job.

New Learning Objectives: VBA

- To learn how online help can be provided on a worksheet by taking advantage of a worksheet's BeforeDoubleClick event.
- To learn several new controls for user forms: scrollbars, combo boxes, and command buttons other than the usual OK/Cancel combination.

New Learning Objectives: Non-VBA

- To learn the basic elements of AHP.

33.2 Functionality of the Application

The application first asks the user to specify the criteria that are relevant for making the job decision. Several criteria, such as salary, location, and benefits, are already in the list of possibilities, but the user can add other criteria to the list if desired. Next, the user is asked to list the available job offers. The user is asked to make a series of pairwise comparisons, first between pairs of criteria

---

[1] A good reference on AHP can be found in Chapter 9 of *Practical Management Science*.

and then between pairs of jobs on each criterion. After all pairwise comparisons have been made, the application performs the necessary calculations for AHP and reports the results on a Report sheet, highlighting the job with the highest score. The scores for the various jobs can also be viewed graphically. Finally, to check whether the user was internally consistent when making the pairwise comparisons (because it is easy to be inconsistent), consistency indexes are reported.

After a given AHP analysis, the user can run another analysis with the *same* criteria and jobs (by making new pairwise comparisons). Alternatively, the user can run another analysis with entirely new inputs.

33.3 Running the Application

The application is stored in the file **AHP.xlsm**. When this file is opened, the Explanation sheet in Figure 33.1 appears. Because AHP is probably not well known to most users, the application provides some help in a text box. This text box is currently hidden, but it can be displayed by double-clicking anywhere in row 1 of the Explanation sheet. The help text box then appears, as in Figure 33.2. It can be hidden by again double-clicking in row 1. The way this online help is accomplished with VBA is explained later in the chapter.

Clicking on the button in Figure 33.1 produces the dialog box in Figure 33.3. It has a combo box with a dropdown list of criteria the user can choose from. Alternatively, the user can type a *new* criterion in the box. After a criterion is

Figure 33.1 Explanation Sheet

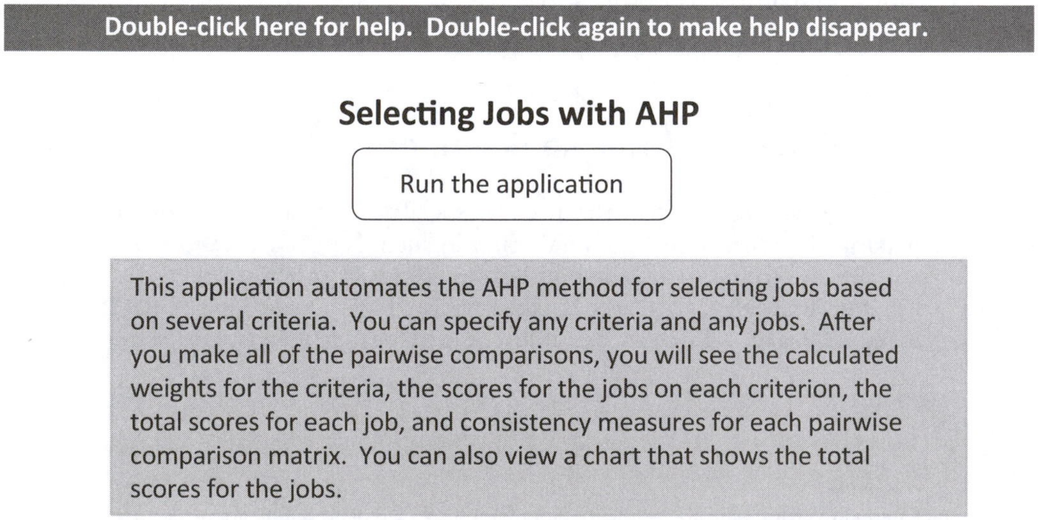

> Double-click here for help. Double-click again to make help disappear.

Selecting Jobs with AHP

> Run the application

This application automates the AHP method for selecting jobs based on several criteria. You can specify any criteria and any jobs. After you make all of the pairwise comparisons, you will see the calculated weights for the criteria, the scores for the jobs on each criterion, the total scores for each job, and consistency measures for each pairwise comparison matrix. You can also view a chart that shows the total scores for the jobs.

Figure 33.2   Help for AHP

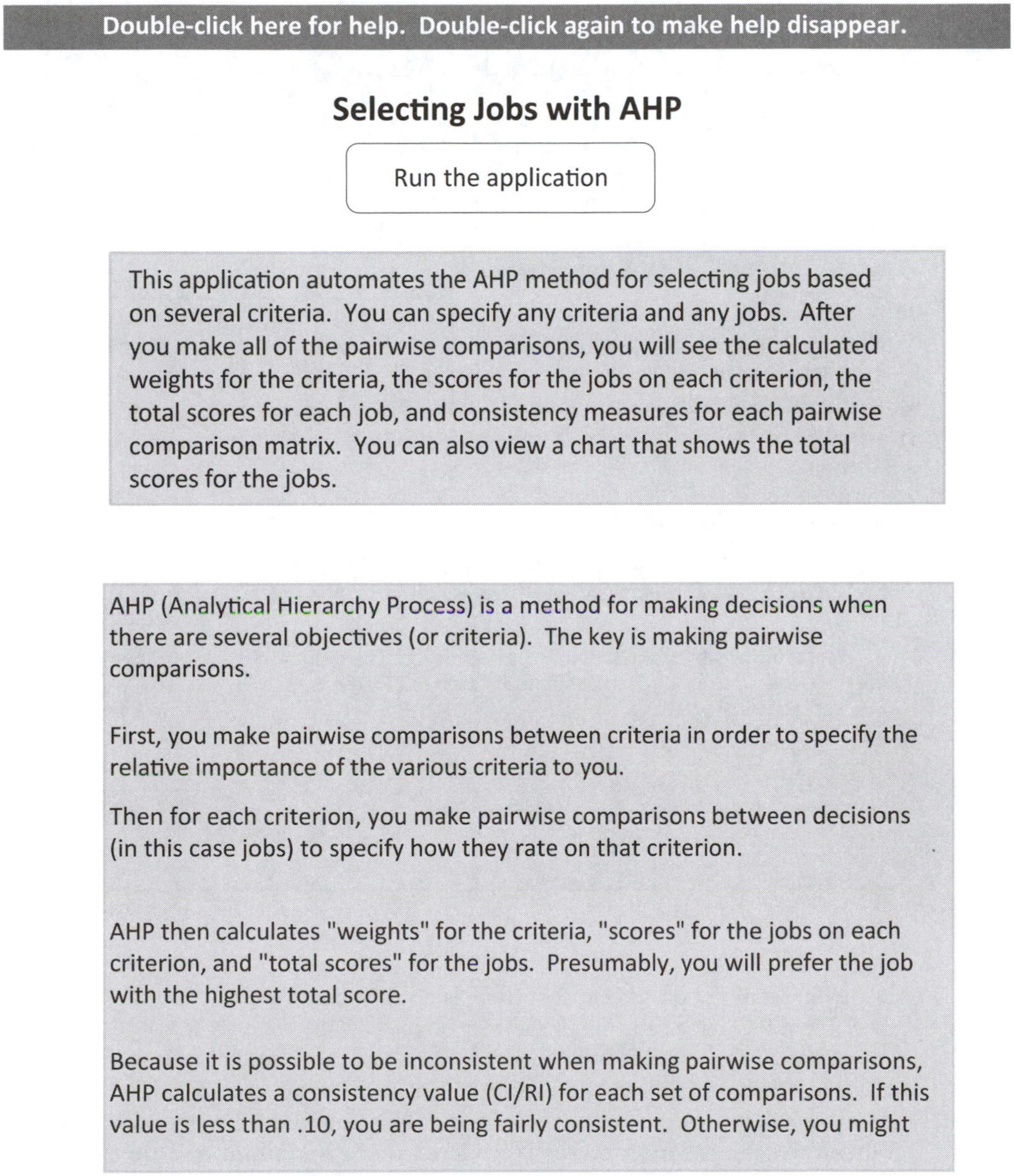

Double-click here for help. Double-click again to make help disappear.

Selecting Jobs with AHP

> Run the application

This application automates the AHP method for selecting jobs based on several criteria. You can specify any criteria and any jobs. After you make all of the pairwise comparisons, you will see the calculated weights for the criteria, the scores for the jobs on each criterion, the total scores for each job, and consistency measures for each pairwise comparison matrix. You can also view a chart that shows the total scores for the jobs.

AHP (Analytical Hierarchy Process) is a method for making decisions when there are several objectives (or criteria). The key is making pairwise comparisons.

First, you make pairwise comparisons between criteria in order to specify the relative importance of the various criteria to you.

Then for each criterion, you make pairwise comparisons between decisions (in this case jobs) to specify how they rate on that criterion.

AHP then calculates "weights" for the criteria, "scores" for the jobs on each criterion, and "total scores" for the jobs. Presumably, you will prefer the job with the highest total score.

Because it is possible to be inconsistent when making pairwise comparisons, AHP calculates a consistency value (CI/RI) for each set of comparisons. If this value is less than .10, you are being fairly consistent. Otherwise, you might

---

entered in the box, the user should click on the Add button to add the criterion to the list that will be used in making the decision.

When all desired criteria have been added, the user should click the No More button. The dialog box shown in Figure 33.4 appears. It has the same functionality

Figure 33.3 Dialog Box for Choosing Criteria

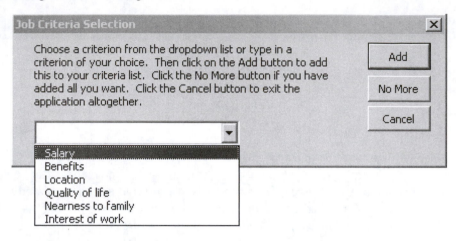

Figure 33.4 Dialog Box for Choosing Jobs

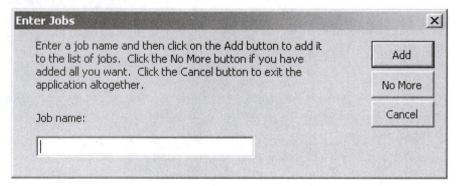

as the first dialog box, except that there is no dropdown list; the user must enter all available jobs, one at a time, in the text box.

After all criteria and jobs have been entered, several dialog boxes similar to the one shown in Figure 33.5 appear. Each asks the user to make a pairwise comparison between two of the criteria. This can be done by clicking on the button for the criterion that is considered more important and then using the scrollbar to indicate how much more important it is. (The scrollbar goes in discrete one-unit steps, from 1 to 9. The labels below the scrollbar attach meanings to the numbers.) Note that there can be quite a few pairwise comparisons to make. For example, if there are four criteria, then there are six such pairwise comparisons (the number of ways two things can be chosen from four things). The counter on the dialog box reminds the user how many more pairwise comparisons remain.

Figure 33.5 Pairwise Comparison Dialog Box for Criteria

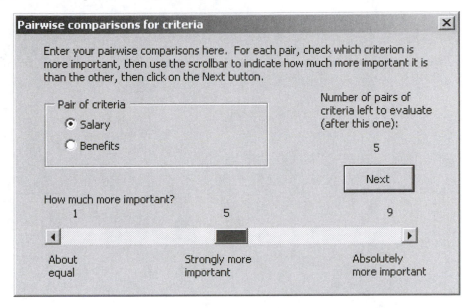

The application then presents a series of dialog boxes similar to those in Figures 33.6 and 33.7, where the user must make pairwise comparisons between pairs of jobs on the various criteria. Again, if there are quite a few criteria and jobs, the number of required pairwise comparisons will be large.

Figure 33.6 Pairwise Comparison Between Jobs on Salary Criterion

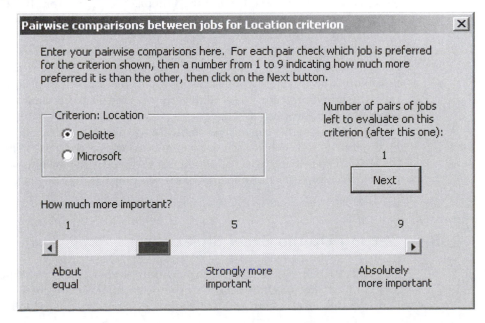

Figure 33.7 Pairwise Comparison Between Jobs on Quality of Life Criterion

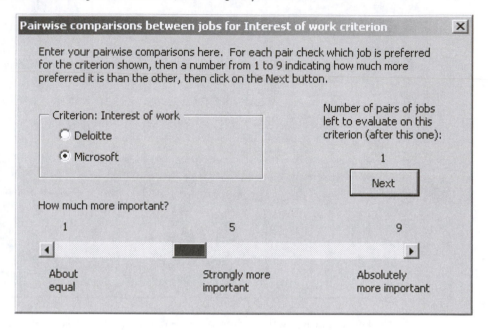

When all pairwise comparisons have been made, the application does the AHP calculations and reports the results in a Report sheet, as shown in Figure 33.8. This report lists the weights for the criteria, the scores for the jobs on each criterion, and the total scores for the jobs. The job with the highest total score is boldfaced. (In this example, Microsoft is the winner.) The bottom of the report lists consistency indexes. If the user has to make many pairwise comparisons, there is a good chance of being inconsistent. This bottom section alerts the user to this possibility. Specifically, if it reports inadequate consistency (as this example does), the user should probably go through the process again and attempt to make more consistent comparisons.

By clicking on the top button on the Report sheet, the user can view the chart in Figure 33.9, which indicates the total scores for the jobs. The other two buttons on the Report sheet allow the user to repeat the analysis with the same criteria and jobs (by making new pairwise comparisons) or with entirely new inputs.

33.4 Setting Up the Excel Sheets

The **AHP.xlsm** file contains Explanation and Report worksheets and a ScoresChart sheet. (Unlike most of the other applications in the book, there is no Model sheet where most of the calculations take place. All calculations

Figure 33.8 Report Sheet

Results from AHP

View chart of job scores

Repeat with new pairwise comparisons

Repeat entire analysis

Weights for Criteria

Salary	Benefits	Location	Interest of work
0.375	0.075	0.157	0.394

Scores for jobs on various criteria

	Salary	Benefits	Location	Interest of work
Deloitte	0.3	0.328	0.581	0.201
MMM	0.415	0.261	0.309	0.118
Microsoft	0.285	0.411	0.11	0.681

Overall job scores (best score highlighted)

Deloitte	MMM	**Microsoft**
0.307	0.27	**0.423**

Relative Consistency Indexes

Pairwise comparisons among criteria

	0.025	(adequate consistency)

Pairwise comparisons among jobs on various criteria

On Salary	1.427	(consistency not adequate)
On Benefits	0.046	(adequate consistency)
On Location	0.003	(adequate consistency)
On Interest of work	0.021	(adequate consistency)

in this application are done directly in memory with VBA—that is, they are *not* performed through spreadsheet formulas.) The Report sheet, shown earlier in Figure 33.8, must be completed almost entirely at run time. The only template that can be developed at run time appears in Figure 33.10. However, the chart can be developed with the Excel's chart tools at design time, using any set of trial inputs, and then it can be tied to the actual job scores at run time.

33.5 Getting Started with the VBA

The application contains four user forms named frmCriteria, frmJobs, frmPairwiseCriteria, and frmPairwiseJobs, and a single module. Once these are inserted, the Project Explorer window will appear as in Figure 33.11.

Figure 33.9 Chart of Total Job Scores

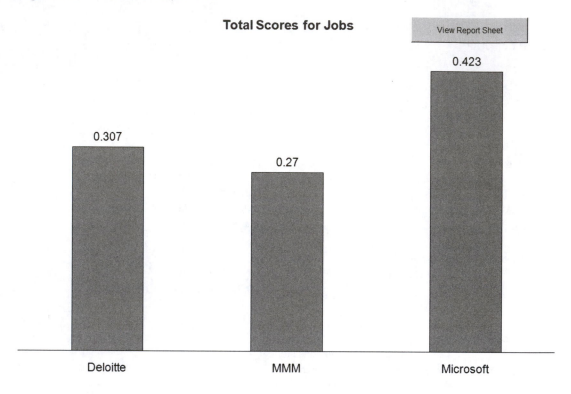

Figure 33.10 Template for Report Sheet

	A	B	C	D	E	F	G	H	I
1			**Results from AHP**						
2									
3			Weights for Criteria						
4									
5									
6									
7			Scores for jobs on various criteria						

In the header area (rows 1–2): View chart of job scores · Repeat with new pairwise comparisons · Repeat entire analysis

Workbook_Open Code

To guarantee that the Explanation sheet appears when the file is opened, the following code is placed in the ThisWorkbook code window. This code also hides the Report and ScoresChart sheets.

Figure 33.11 Project Explorer Window

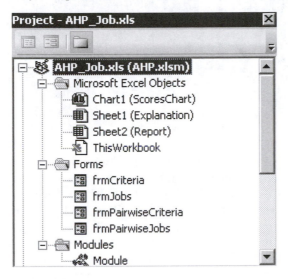

```
Private Sub Workbook_Open()
    Worksheets("Explanation").Activate
    Range("F5").Select
    Worksheets("Report").Visible = False
    Charts("ScoresChart").Visible = False
End Sub
```

Worksheet_BeforeDoubleClick Event Handler

The Workbook_Open sub has been used repeatedly in previous applications. It responds to the Open event of the Workbook object. When the workbook opens, this code runs. There are many other events that objects can respond to. In each case, it is possible to write an event handler for the event. This can come in very handy. As an example, remember how the user can double-click in row 1 of the Explanation sheet to display or hide a help text box? This is accomplished by the following event handler for the worksheet's **BeforeDoubleClick** event. The built-in sub for this event comes with an argument called **Target**. This argument is the cell that is double-clicked. Therefore, an If statement checks whether Target.Row equals 1. If it does, this means that the user double-clicked somewhere in row 1. In this case, the Visible property of the HelpBox (the name of the text box that contains the help) is toggled from True to False or vice versa. Note that the text box is named HelpBox at *design* time. A text box can be named exactly like a range—just select it and then type a name in the name box area in Excel.

```
Private Sub Worksheet_BeforeDoubleClick(ByVal Target As Range, Cancel As Boolean)
    ' This sub runs when the user double-clicks anywhere in the
    ' Explanation sheet.  It toggles a pre-formed text box between
    ' visible and not visible.
    Dim helpBox As Shape
    If Target.Row = 1 Then
        Set helpBox = Worksheets("Explanation").Shapes("HelpBox")
        helpBox.Visible = Not helpBox.Visible
        Range("F5").Select
    End If
End Sub
```

This code should be stored in the code window for the Explanation sheet. To get to it, double-click on the Explanation sheet item in the Project Explorer window of the VBE. (See Figure 13.11.) Then in the code window, select Worksheet in the left dropdown list and double-click on the BeforeDoubleClick item in the right dropdown list. (See Figure 33.12.) This inserts a "stub" for the event handler, as in the following two lines. You can then enter the code you need in the middle. Note that the Target and Cancel arguments are built in—you have no choice whether to include them in the first line. However, only the Target argument is used in our code; the Cancel argument is ignored.

```
Private Sub Worksheet_BeforeDoubleClick(ByVal Target As Range, Cancel As Boolean)

End Sub
```

How can you learn about events like this? Probably the best way is to use the Object Browser in the VBE. Figure 33.13 shows where I discovered that a

Figure 33.12 Inserting a Sub for BeforeDoubleClick Event

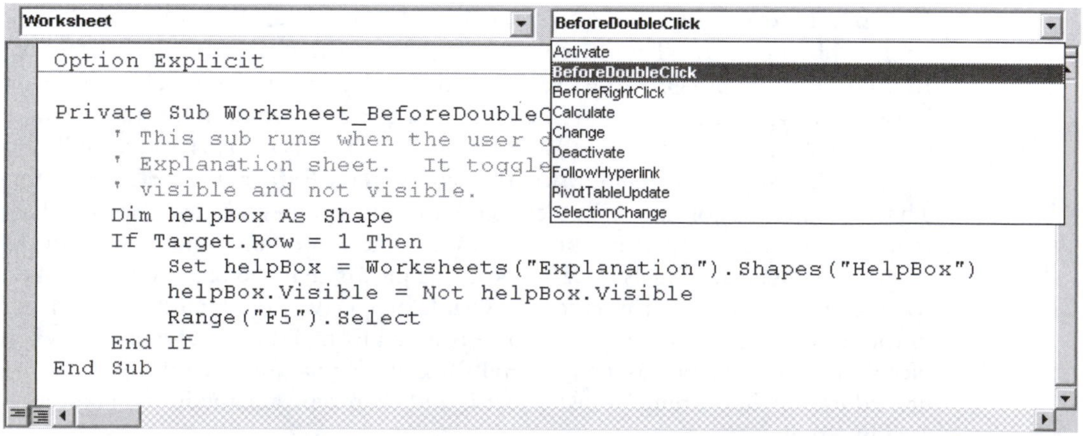

Figure 33.13 Object Browser for BeforeDoubleClick Worksheet Event

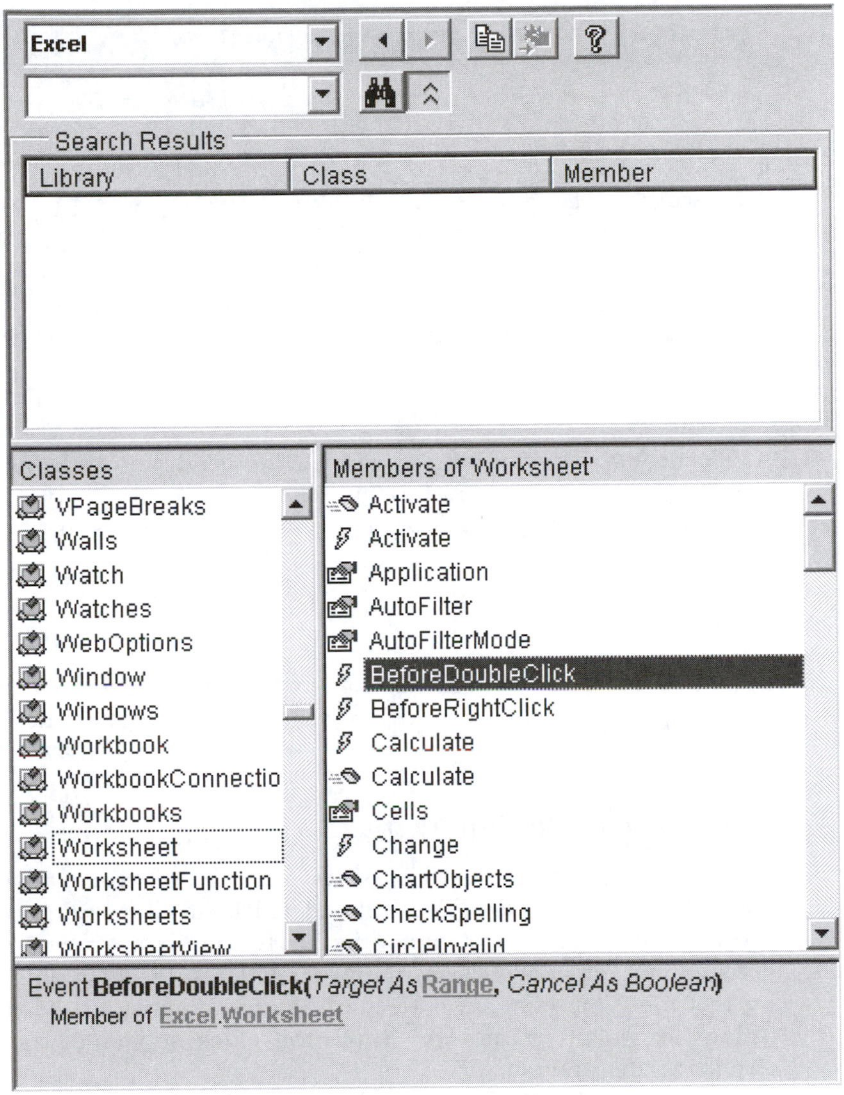

Worksheet has a BeforeDoubleClick event. The online help then describes the details, such as what the Target and Cancel arguments mean.

33.6 The User Forms and Their Event Handlers

The user forms include some features not seen in previous chapters: frmCriteria has a combo box control, frmPairwiseCriteria and frmPairwiseJobs each have a

Figure 33.14 frmCriteria Design

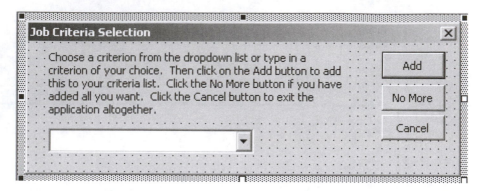

scrollbar control, and the buttons on frmCriteria and frmJobs are not the standard OK/Cancel pair. However, this just illustrates the flexibility of the controls available in the Control Toolbox. You can choose the ones that are most appropriate for your application.

frmCriteria

This form has three buttons named btnAdd, btnNoMore, and btnCancel, an explanation label, and a combo box named cboCriteria. Its design appears in Figure 33.14.

Event Handlers for frmCriteria

The **UserForm_Initialize** sub creates an array of criteria that is used to populate the combo box. The **btnAdd_Click** sub does some error checking and then adds the newly chosen criterion to the list of criteria in the publicly declared criterion array. The **btnNoMore_Click** sub simply unloads the form. By this time, the user has entered all desired criteria, so she just wants the dialog box to disappear. The **btnCancel_Click** sub unloads the form and terminates the program.

Note that a **ComboBox** control is essentially a blend of a list box and a text box. Specifically, its **List** property can be set equal to an array to populate the list, and its **Value** property returns the item in the box.

```
Private Sub btnAdd_Click()
    Dim newItem As String, isNew As Boolean

    Dim i As Integer
    ' Check that a criterion has been entered and that it is not a criterion
    ' that was already entered. (If it is, set isNew to False.)
    With cboCriteria
        If .Value = "" Then
```

```
                        MsgBox "Please make a selection", vbExclamation, "No selection"
                        .SetFocus
                        Exit Sub
                Else
                        newItem = .Value
                        isNew = True
                        If nCriteria > 0 Then

                                ' This loop goes through criteria already entered to check
                                ' whether the current criterion is new.
                                For i = 1 To nCriteria
                                        If newItem = criterion(i) Then
                                                MsgBox "You already chose this item.", _
                                                        vbExclamation, "Duplicate"
                                                isNew = False
                                                Exit For
                                        End If
                                Next
                        End If

                        ' Update the number of criteria only if isNew is True.
                        If isNew Then
                                nCriteria = nCriteria + 1
                                If nCriteria = 1 Then
                                        ReDim criterion(nCriteria)
                                Else
                                        ReDim Preserve criterion(nCriteria)
                                End If
                                criterion(nCriteria) = newItem
                        End If

                        ' Get ready for the next criterion.
                        .Text = ""
                        .SetFocus
                End If
        End With
End Sub

Private Sub btnCancel_Click()
        Unload Me
        End
End Sub

Private Sub btnNoMore_Click()
        Unload Me
End Sub

Private Sub UserForm_Initialize()
        ' Define an array of items that make up the "default" list in the combo box.
        ' The user can add a different item at run time if desired.
        Dim criteriaArray As Variant
        criteriaArray = Array("Salary", "Benefits", "Location", "Quality of life", _
                "Nearness to family", "Interest of work")

        ' Fill the combo box, but don't select any items by default.
        With cboCriteria
                .List = criteriaArray
                .Value = ""
        End With
End Sub
```

frmJobs

This form, shown earlier in Figure 33.4, is analogous to frmCriteria, so its design and event handlers are not repeated here. The only difference is that it contains a text box for capturing the job name, not a combo box.

frmPairwiseCriteria

The design for this form appears in Figure 33.15. It has ten labels, a command button named btnNext, a frame that contains two option buttons named optChoice1 and optChoice2, and a scrollbar named scbCompareValue. Note that the numbers and descriptions above and below the scrollbar are all *labels*, as is the highlighted number in the figure. This latter label is named lblNLeft. A **ScrollBar** control has several properties, **Min**, **Max**, **LargeChange**, and **SmallChange**, that can be set at design time. For this application, the Small-Change and LargeChange properties can be left at their default values of 1, but the Min and Max properties should be changed to 1 and 9. (You can probably guess what these properties are all about. See online help on the ScrollBar control for more details.)

Event Handlers for frmPairwiseCriteria

The **UserForm_Initialize** sub uses three public variables, criterion1, criterion2, and nPairsLeft, which have been declared publicly in the module, to initialize

Figure 33.15 frmPairwiseCriteria Design

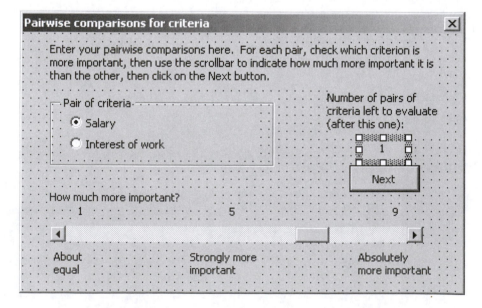

the user form. The first two of these are used as captions for the option buttons, and the third (an integer) is used as the caption for the lblNLeft label. By default, the scrollbar is put at its leftmost position, and the first option button is checked. The **btnNext_Click** sub then captures the option that has been checked and the value of the scrollbar in the public variables choseFirst and pairwiseValue. Note that the **Value** property of a **ScrollBar** control is its default property. It is an integer between the scrollbar's Min and Max, determined by the position of the "slider" on the scrollbar.

```
Private Sub btnNext_Click()
    ' Capture which of the two options is favored (choseFirst) and by how
    ' much (pairwiseValue).
    choseFirst = optChoice1.Value
    pairwiseValue = scbCompareValue.Value
    Unload Me
End Sub

Private Sub UserForm_Initialize()
    ' Set up the dialog box. It uses the public variables criterion1,
    ' criterion2, and nPairsLeft, defined in the module.
    With optChoice1
        .Value = True
        .Caption = criterion1
    End With
    optChoice2.Caption = criterion2
    scbCompareValue.Value = 1
    lblNLeft.Caption = nPairsLeft
End Sub
```

frmPairwiseJobs

This form, shown earlier in Figure 33.6 and 33.7, is very similar to frmPairwise-Criteria, so its design and event handlers are not repeated here.

33.7 The VBA Code in the Module

The bulk of the work is performed in the module. When the user clicks on the button in the Explanation sheet, the **Main** sub runs. It "shows" frmCriteria and frmJobs to get the lists of criteria and jobs, redimensions a number of arrays, and then calls the DoCalculations sub to perform the AHP. For a change, I will not list all of the VBA code here. Unless you understand the calculations that go into the AHP methodology, this code won't make much sense. Besides, from a VBA viewpoint, there is nothing new. If you do happen to be familiar with the AHP methodology and want to see how it is implemented with VBA, the code is available in the **AHP.xlsm** file.

33.8 Summary

This chapter has presented an application that should be useful for many readers of this book—students who are looking for a job. It is easy to use, and it is realistic. The VBA details are somewhat complex, and they will be mysterious to readers who are not familiar with the inner workings of AHP. However, this is part of the beauty of VBA applications. They can be used by people who are not familiar with what is happening "under the hood."

EXERCISES

1. Open a new workbook and draw an oval on it, positioned and captioned approximately as in Figure 33.16. (This was on the Drawing toolbar in Excel 2003 and earlier; it is on the Shapes dropdown on the Insert ribbon in Excel 2007.) Then insert a text box, positioned approximately as in the figure, and type some text into it. (Make up anything.) Now write code so that when the user clicks on the oval the text box appears (if it was invisible) or disappears (if it was visible). (*Hint*: Once you create the oval, right-click on it. You'll see that you can attach a macro to it. This macro, placed in a *module*, is where you'll store your code. This isn't exactly the behavior I expected when I wrote this exercise. The resulting macro isn't really an event handler, because you can

Figure 33.16 Online Help

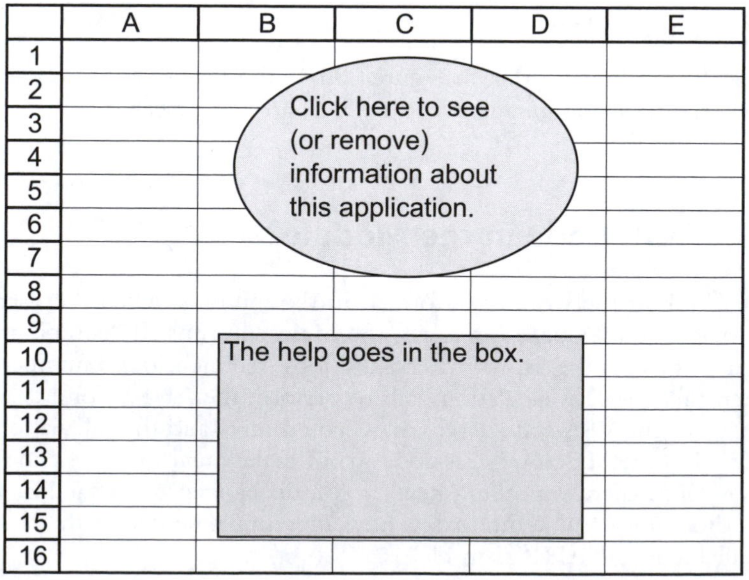

Figure 33.17 Spinner Button and Text Box

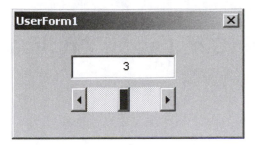

name it anything. However, it does illustrate how you can attach a macro to a shape object in Excel.)

2. The scrollbars used for the pairwise comparison are just one possibility. Another possibility is to use a spinner button and an accompanying text box, as illustrated in Figure 33.17. Change the application so that it uses this approach instead of scrollbars. Make sure the resulting frmPairwiseCriteria and frmPairwiseJobs are laid out nicely and are meaningful for the user. (Look up help for spinner controls in the MSForms library in the Object Browser.)

3. Most people who use the AHP method suggest a 1 to 9 scale for making the pairwise comparisons, and this is what was implemented here. Change the application so that the scale is from 1 to 5. Now the index 5 means what the old index 9 meant. There are simply fewer choices for the user. From a user's standpoint, which of these two scales would you rather use?

4. Change the application so that it pertains to deciding where to go on vacation. Change the automatic entries in frmCriteria's combo box to ones that might be used in this type of decision. Also, replace the text box in frmJobs by a combo box. Place two automatic entries in this combo box: Wife's parents and Husband's parents. (You can assume that these are *always* possible vacation spots, even if they aren't necessarily the preferred ones!)

5. If you open the **AHP.xlsm** file and look at the code in the module, you will see that the CreateReport sub is too long for the taste of many programmers. Rewrite it so that it calls several smaller subs that perform the individual tasks. You can choose the number of smaller subs, but they should make logical sense.

34

A Poker Simulation Application

34.1 Introduction

This final application is a bit less serious than the other applications in the book, but it should be interesting to poker players, and it contains some interesting VBA code.[1] In case you are not a poker player, a player is dealt 5 cards from a 52-card deck. There are several types of hands the player can be dealt, as described in the following list:

- **a pair**: two of some denomination and three of other distinct denominations
- **two pairs**: two of one denomination, two of another denomination, and another card
- **three of a kind**: three of one denomination and two of other distinct denominations
- **a straight**: five denominations in progression, such as 4, 5, 6, 7, 8
- **a flush**: five cards of the same suit, such as five hearts
- **a full house**: three of one denomination and two of another denomination
- **four of a kind**: four of one denomination and another card
- **straight flush**: a straight, all of the same suit
- **a bust**: none of the above

Except for a bust, the hands in this list are shown in increasing value, so that, for example, three of a kind beats two pairs. They all beat a bust.

The application simulates 100,000 5-card hands, all from a "well-shuffled" 52-card deck, and counts the number of each type of hand in the above list. It should be interesting to see whether the probabilities of being dealt the hands go in the opposite order of their values. For example, is a hand with two pairs more likely than three of a kind? The simulation will help answer this question.

New Learning Objectives: VBA

- To illustrate how VBA can perform a simulation completely with code—no spreadsheet model.
- To illustrate how rather complex logic can be accomplished with the use of appropriate If constructs, loops, and arrays.

---

[1]Since I wrote this application for the first edition, poker has become extremely popular. It seems to be on ESPN or ESPN2 every time I turn on the TV.

New Learning Objectives: Non-VBA

- To show how simulation can be used to see how a game like poker works and whether its rules are reasonable. (Do the values of the hands go along with their likelihoods?)

34.2 Functionality of the Application

The only purpose of this application is to repeatedly simulate 5-card hands from a 52-card deck, tally the numbers of hands of each type, and display the relative frequencies in a worksheet.

34.3 Running the Application

The application is stored in the file **Poker.xlsm**. This file contains a single sheet named Report, shown in Figure 34.1, which the user sees upon opening the file.

Each time the user clicks on the button, 100,000 *new* 5-card hands are simulated, all from a fresh 52-card deck, and the results are displayed in the sheet, as shown in Figure 34.2.

Figure 34.1 Report Sheet before Running the Simulation

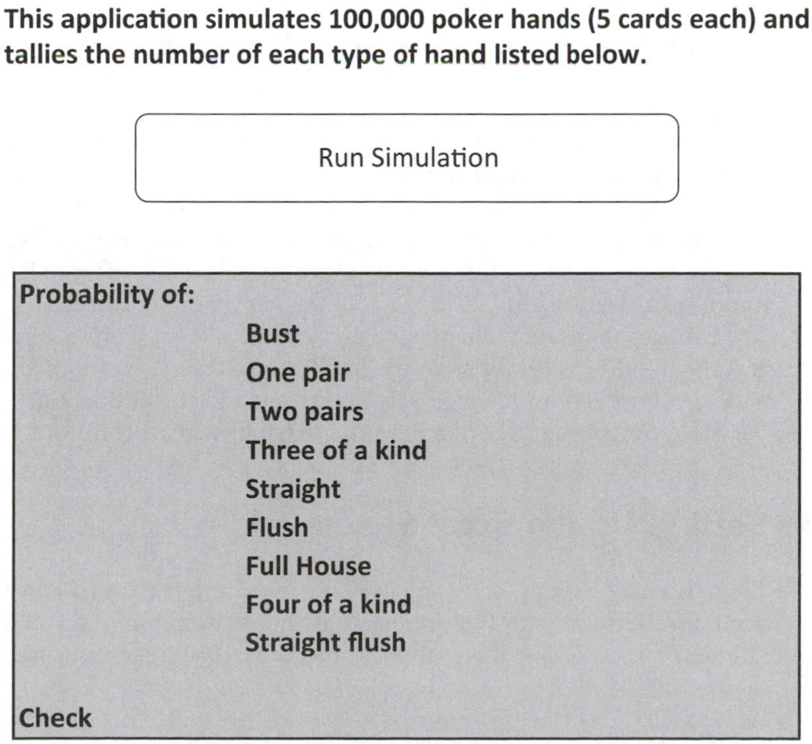

This application simulates 100,000 poker hands (5 cards each) and tallies the number of each type of hand listed below.

Run Simulation

Probability of:

Bust
One pair
Two pairs
Three of a kind
Straight
Flush
Full House
Four of a kind
Straight flush

Check

Figure 34.2 Results from a Simulation Run

This application simulates 100,000 poker hands (5 cards each) and
tallies the number of each type of hand listed below.

Run Simulation

Probability of:	
Bust	50.26%
One pair	42.18%
Two pairs	4.67%
Three of a kind	2.16%
Straight	0.35%
Flush	0.20%
Full House	0.14%
Four of a kind	0.03%
Straight flush	0.00%
Check	100.00%

I say that 100,000 *new* hands are simulated because each run uses a new set of random numbers for the simulation. Therefore, the results will be slightly different each time the application is run. Figure 34.3 shows results from a different set of 100,000 hands. They are very similar to the results in Figure 34.2, but they are not exactly the same. Of course, this is the nature of simulation. You will undoubtedly get slightly different results each time you run it.

Each of these runs illustrates what can be shown from a formal probability argument—the probabilities of the hands go in reverse order of the values of the hands. A bust is most likely, a pair is next most likely, and so on.[2] And if you are counting on getting four of a kind or a straight flush, dream on!

34.4 Setting Up the Excel Sheets

There is really nothing to set up at design time other than to enter labels and do some formatting in the Report sheet, as shown in Figure 34.1. There is nothing "hidden" here. Other than labels, the sheet is blank, waiting for the simulated

---

[2]Again, because of the nature of simulation, it is *possible* that you will get results where, for example, there are more flushes than straights, but this is due to what statisticians call sampling error.

Figure 34.3 Results from Another Simulation Run

This application simulates 100,000 poker hands (5 cards each) and tallies the number of each type of hand listed below.

Run Simulation

Probability of:	
Bust	50.01%
One pair	42.28%
Two pairs	4.88%
Three of a kind	2.13%
Straight	0.36%
Flush	0.18%
Full House	0.14%
Four of a kind	0.02%
Straight flush	0.00%
Check	100.00%

results. Furthermore, the simulation occurs completely in VBA code. There is no worksheet where calculations are performed.

34.5 Getting Started with the VBA

The application requires only a module—no user forms or references. After the module is added, the Project Explorer window will appear as in Figure 34.4.

Figure 34.4 Project Explorer Window

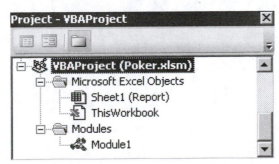

Workbook_Open Code

The following code is placed in the ThisWorkbook code window. It clears results from any previous simulation run.

```
Private Sub Workbook_Open()
    Range("D10:D20").ClearContents
    Range("C6").Select
End Sub
```

34.6   The VBA Code in the Module

To this point, it might sound like this application is a fun little exercise for card players. However, the VBA code is far from trivial. It requires some careful logic, and it makes heavy use of arrays. It is an interesting illustration of how humans can easily perceive patterns that computers can discover only with tricky programming. For example, a poker player can look at his hand, without even rearranging the cards, and immediately see that he has a pair, a straight, or whatever. As the code will show, however, it takes a considerable amount of code to recognize these patterns.

The module-level variables are listed first. Note that they are declared with the keyword Dim, not with Public. This is perfectly acceptable. The Public keyword makes variables known to other *modules*, including event code modules, but there is only a single module in this application. Still, these module-level variables need to be declared at the top of the module, outside of the subs, so that all of the subs in the module can recognize them.

Option Statements and Module-Level Variables

```
Option Explicit
Option Base 1

' Definitions of module-level variables and constant:
'   nBusts - number of the 100,000 hands that results in a bust (with similar
'       definitions for nPairs, n2Pairs, etc.
'   denom() - array that indicates which denomination (1 to 13) each card
'       in the deck is
'   card() - array that indicates the cards in the hand - e.g., if card(3) = 37,
'       this means the third card dealt is the 37th card in the deck
'   nReps - number of simulated hands, in this case 100,000

Dim nBusts As Long, nPairs As Long, n2Pairs As Long, n3ofKinds As Long, _
    nFullHouses As Integer, n4ofKinds As Integer, nStraights As Integer, _
    nFlushes As Integer, nStraightFlushes As Integer
Dim denom(52) As Integer
Dim card(5) As Integer

Const nReps = 100000
```

Main Code

The **Main** sub runs when the user clicks on the button on the Report sheet. It first calls the **InitStats** sub to set all counters to 0. Next, it calls the **SetupDeck** sub to "define" the cards in the deck. Then it uses a For loop to run the 100,000 replications of the simulation. In each replication it calls the **Deal** sub to deal the cards and the **Evaluate** sub to check what type of hand is obtained. Finally, it calls the **Report** sub to put the results in the Report sheet. VBA's Randomize function is placed near the top of the Main sub to ensure that a new set of random numbers is used each time the simulation is run.

```
Sub Main()
    Dim iRep As Long ' replication index
    Randomize

    ' Set counters to 0.
    Call InitializeStats

    ' "Name" the cards in the deck.
    Call SetupDeck

    ' Deal out nReps poker hands and evaluate each one.
    For iRep = 1 To nReps
        Call Deal
        Call EvaluateHand
    Next

    ' Report the summary stats from the nReps hands.
    Call Report

    Range("C6").Select
End Sub
```

InitStats Code

The **InitStats** sets all counters (the number of busts, the number of pairs, and so on) to 0.

```
Sub InitStats()
    ' This sub sets all statistical counters to 0.
    nBusts = 0
    nPairs = 0
    n2Pairs = 0
    n3ofKinds = 0
    nStraights = 0
    nFlushes = 0
    nFullHouses = 0
    n4ofKinds = 0
    nStraightFlushes = 0
End Sub
```

SetupDeck Code

The **SetupDeck** sub "defines" the deck by filling the denom array. It does this with two nested For loops. If you follow the logic closely, you will see that denom(1) through denom(4) are set to 1 (corresponding to the Aces), denom(5) through denom(8) are set to 2 (corresponding to the 2s), and so on. You can think of denomination 11 as the Jacks, denomination 12 as the Queens, and denomination 13 as the Kings. Also, there are no explicit hearts, diamonds, clubs, and spades, but you can think of cards 1, 5, 9, and so on as the hearts; cards 2, 6, 10, and so on as the diamonds; cards 3, 7, 11, and so on as the clubs; and cards 4, 8, 12, and so on as the spades.

```
Sub SetupDeck()
    Dim iDenom As Integer ' denomination index
    Dim iSuit As Integer ' suit index
    ' Give the first 4 cards denomination 1 (aces),
    ' the next 4 denomination 2 (deuces), and so on
    For iDenom = 1 To 13
        For iSuit = 1 To 4
            denom(4 * (iDenom - 1) + iSuit) = iDenom
        Next
    Next
End Sub
```

Deal Code

The **Deal** sub randomly chooses five cards from the 52-card deck. It is the only sub where any simulation takes place; that is, it is the only code that uses random numbers. It uses VBA's **Rnd** function (which is essentially equivalent to Excel's **Rand** function) to simulate a single random number uniformly distributed between 0 and 1. The following line generates a uniformly distributed *integer* from 1 to 52:

```
cardIndex = Int(Rnd * 52) + 1
```

Note how this works. The quantity Rnd*52 is a uniformly distributed *decimal* number between 0 and 52. Then VBA's **Int** function chops off the decimal, leaving an integer from 0 to 51. Finally, 1 is added to obtain an integer from 1 to 52.

The Boolean isUsed array keeps track of which of the 52 cards in the deck have *already* been dealt in the current hand. Essentially, random integers are generated until five *distinct* integers have been obtained. When an integer is generated that is distinct from the previous integers, its isUsed value is set to True, so that it cannot be used again (in this hand). By the end of this sub, the indexes of the five cards dealt are stored in the card array. For example, if card(4) = 47, this means that the fourth card in the hand is the 47th card in the deck (the Queen of clubs).

```
Sub Deal()
    Dim i As Integer ' index of cards in deck
    Dim j As Integer ' index of cards in hand
    Dim cardIndex As Integer
    Dim used(52) As Boolean
    Dim newCard As Boolean

    ' Initially, no cards have been dealt.
    For i = 1 To 52
        used(i) = False
    Next

    ' For each of 5 cards, keep generating until a new card is dealt.
    For j = 1 To 5
        newCard = False
        Do
            cardIndex = Int(Rnd * 52) + 1
            If Not used(cardIndex) Then
                newCard = True
                used(cardIndex) = True
            End If
        Loop Until newCard = True

        ' Records the card number this card in this hand.
        card(j) = cardIndex
    Next
End Sub
```

Evaluate Code

The most difficult part of the program is the **Evaluate** sub. By this time, the card array has been generated. It might show that the hand contains the cards 2, 7, 19, 28, and 47. What kind of a hand is this? Is it a bust, a pair, or what? The Evaluate sub goes through the necessary logic to check all possibilities.

The first check is for a straight. It finds the denominations of the five cards and stores them in the cardDenom array. For example, the denomination of the first card is denom(card(1)), which is stored in cardDenom(1). These denominations might be out of order, such as 5, 3, 7, 6, 4, so it uses two nested For loops to sort them in increasing order. It then checks whether the sorted denominations form a progression, such as 3, 4, 5, 6, 7. (If this sounds overly complex, just try doing it any other way.)

The second check is for a flush. For example, the hand with cards 3, 15, 23, 39, 51 is a flush. This is because cards 3, 7, 11, 15, 19, 23, 27, 31, 35, 39, 43, 47, and 51 are the 13 cards of a certain suit (clubs, say). An easy way to check whether *any* five cards are of the same suit is to divide each of them by 4 and see whether the remainders are all equal. (This is the case for 3, 15, 23, 39, and 51. Each has remainder 3.) This can be done with VBA's **Mod** operator. For example, **51 Mod 4** is the remainder when 51 is divided by 4.

If the hand is a straight or a flush (or both), then no further checks are necessary. Otherwise, checks for a pair, two of a kind, and the rest are necessary. All of these involve the numbers of like denominations in a hand. For example, a hand with two pairs contains two of some denomination, two of another, and one of another. The groups array is used to collect this information. A full house has groups(3) = 1 and groups(2) = 1, which says that it has one group of size 3 and one group of size 2. Similarly, a bust has groups(1) = 5, three of a kind has groups(3) = 1 and groups(1) = 2, and so on. So by filling the groups array and checking its contents, the program can discover which type of hand has been dealt.

```
Sub EvaluateHand()
    Dim i As Integer, j As Integer
    Dim count(13) As Integer, groups(4) As Integer
    Dim hasStraight As Boolean, hasFlush As Boolean
    Dim cardDenom(5) As Integer, temp As Integer

    ' First, check for a straight.
    hasStraight = False
    For i = 1 To 5
        cardDenom(i) = denom(card(i))
    Next

    ' Sort the denominations in increasing order.
    For i = 1 To 4
        For j = i + 1 To 5
            If cardDenom(j) < cardDenom(i) Then
                temp = cardDenom(j)
                cardDenom(j) = cardDenom(i)
                cardDenom(i) = temp
            End If
        Next
    Next

    ' Check if they are in a progression, like 4, 5, 6, 7, 8.
    ' If you consider Aces as denomination 13, then this code
    ' counts only "Ace high" straights.
    If cardDenom(2) = cardDenom(1) + 1 And _
        cardDenom(3) = cardDenom(2) + 1 And _
        cardDenom(4) = cardDenom(3) + 1 And _
        cardDenom(5) = cardDenom(4) + 1 Then
        hasStraight = True
        nStraight = nStraight + 1
    End If

    ' Next, check for a flush.
    hasFlush = False
    If card(1) Mod 4 = card(2) Mod 4 And card(2) Mod 4 = card(3) Mod 4 _
            And card(3) Mod 4 = card(4) Mod 4 And _
            card(4) Mod 4 = card(5) Mod 4 Then
        hasFlush = True
        nFlush = nFlush + 1
    End If

    ' Next, check for a straight flush.
    If hasStraight And hasFlush Then
        nStraightFlush = nStraightFlush + 1
        ' Don't count this a straight or a flush
        nStraight = nStraight - 1
        nFlush = nFlush - 1
    End If
```

```
' There's no need to check the rest if the hand is a straight
' or a flush (or both).
If hasStraight Or hasFlush Then Exit Sub

' Otherwise, check all the other possibilities.
' count(i) is the number of cards of denomination i in the hand.
For i = 1 To 13
    count(i) = 0
Next
For i = 1 To 5
    count(denom(card(i))) = count(denom(card(i))) + 1
Next

' groups(i) will be the number of "groups" of size i.
' For example, if groups(2) = 1, then there is one group of
' size 2, that is, one pair (of some demonimation).
For i = 1 To 4
    groups(i) = 0
Next
For i = 1 To 13
    If count(i) > 0 Then groups(count(i)) = groups(count(i)) + 1
Next

' Now go through all of the possibilities.
If groups(1) = 5 Then
    nBust = nBust + 1
Elseif groups(1) = 3 And groups(2) = 1 Then
    nPair = nPair + 1
Elseif groups(1) = 1 And groups(2) = 2 Then
    n2Pair = n2Pair + 1
Elseif groups(1) = 2 And groups(3) = 1 Then
    n3ofKind = n3ofKind + 1
Elseif groups(2) = 1 And groups(3) = 1 Then
    nFullHouse = nFullHouse + 1
Else
    n4ofKind = n4ofKind + 1
End If
End Sub
```

Report Code

The **Report** sub lists the results in the Report sheet. Note that it reports the *relative* frequencies, such as the number of busts divided by the total number of replications. The formula in cell D20 is not really necessary, but it provides a comforting check that the relative frequencies sum to 1, as they should. If a number other than 1 appeared in cell D20, this would indicate a bug in the program.

```
Sub Report()
    Range("D10").Value = nBust / nReps
    Range("D11").Value = nPair / nReps
    Range("D12").Value = n2Pair / nReps
    Range("D13").Value = n3ofKind / nReps
    Range("D14").Value = nStraight / nReps
    Range("D15").Value = nFlush / nReps
```

```
     Range("D16").Value = nFullHouse / nReps
     Range("D17").Value = n4ofKind / nReps
     Range("D18").Value = nStraightFlush / nReps

     ' Check that they sum to 1.
     Range("D20").Formula = "=Sum(D10:D18)"
End Sub
```

34.7 Summary

The application in this chapter is not earthshaking, except perhaps to avid poker players, but it does illustrate an interesting and certainly nontrivial use of logic, loops, and arrays. In addition, the results of the simulation agree with our intuition about the game of poker itself. They show that as hands become more valuable, they become less likely. And if you always thought you were unlucky because you got a lot of busts, you now realize that this happens about 50% of the time.

EXERCISES

1. Change the application so that it contains a chart sheet displaying the frequencies of the various types of hands, as in Figure 34.5. Put a button on the Report sheet to navigate to this chart sheet. (Do you need to write any code to update the chart after each run?)

2. There are many versions of poker. Change the application so that it works for a version where the player is dealt six cards and then gets to discard any one of them. Assume that the player will discard the card that makes the remaining hand as valuable as possible. (*Hint:* Probably the simplest approach is to run the Evaluate sub on each of the possible five-card hands with one of the six cards omitted and take the best.)

3. A more realistic version of the previous exercise is where the player is dealt five cards. He can discard as many as four of these and request replacements from the remaining deck. The problem with simulating this version is that you have to know the player's strategy—depending on what he is dealt and what he will discard. Simulate the following strategy. (*Hint:* Run the Evaluate sub on the original hand to see what he should discard. Then run it again on the final hand.)
    *   If dealt a bust, discard all but a single card. (Normally, a player would keep the highest card, but it doesn't make any difference here.)
    *   If dealt a pair, keep the pair and discard the other three cards.
    *   If dealt two pairs, keep the pairs and discard the other card.
    *   If dealt three of a kind, keep these three and discard the other two cards.
    *   If dealt any other type of hand, keep it and discard nothing.

4. (More difficult) In the preceding exercise, the player never tries to "fill in" partial straights or flushes. For example, if he has a 4, 5, 6, 7, and 10, he doesn't discard

Figure 34.5 Chart Sheet for Exercise 1

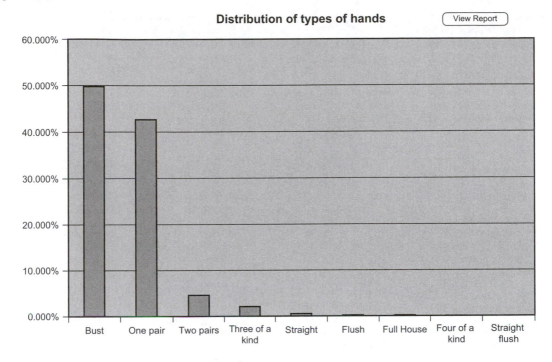

the 10, hoping to fill the straight with a 3 or an 8. Similarly, if he has four hearts and a spade, he doesn't discard the spade, hoping to fill the flush with another heart. Simulate such a strategy. Specifically, assume he first checks for a bust. If he has a bust, then he checks whether he has a partial straight that could be completed on *either* end. (This means, for example, 4, 5, 6, 7, but not 1, 2, 3, 4. Trying to complete this latter straight is too risky because only a 5 will do it.) If he has such a partial "inside" straight, he discards the other card. Otherwise, still assuming he has a bust, he checks whether he has four cards of one suit. If so, he discards the other card. Otherwise, he discards any four cards from the bust. The rest of his strategy is the same as the last four bulleted points in the previous exercise. In other words, he tries to complete a straight or a flush only when he has a bust. Based on your simulation results, is this strategy better or worse than the strategy in the previous exercise?

5. In the game of bridge, each of four players is dealt 13 cards from a 52-card deck. Concentrate for now on a particular player. Develop a simulation similar to the poker simulation that finds the distribution of the number of aces the player is dealt. (*Note:* Since you are concentrating on one player only, you need to simulate 13 cards only; you can ignore what the other three players get.)

6. Continuing the previous exercise, again concentrate on a single player and simulate the distribution of the maximum number of any suit the player is dealt. For example, if the hand has 5 hearts, 3 diamonds, 3 clubs, and 2 spades, this maximum number is 5. How likely is it that a player will get at least 11 cards of some suit?

Index